ANNUAL EDITIONS

Race and Ethnic Relations 11/12

Eighteenth Edition

EDITOR

John A. Kromkowski
Catholic University of America

John A. Kromkowski is president of The National Center for Urban Ethnic Affairs (NCUEA) and Associate Professor in the Department of Politics at the Catholic University of America (CUA) in Washington, D.C. NCUEA is a nonprofit research, technical assistance, advocacy and educational institute focused on ethnic relations, urban affairs and neighborhood revitalization. Along with overseeing NCUEA sponsored programs and projects, Kromkowski is the editor of scores of books and director of Washington internships. He is the Associate Director of the CUA Center for the Study of Culture and Values and a Fellow of the CUA Institute for Policy Research and Catholic Studies (IPRCS). He serves on the Executive Committee of Council for Research in Values and Philosophy (CRVP), an international forum, convener of scholarly seminars and publisher of a multivolume series titled *Cultural Heritage and Contemporary Change.* Kromkowski has served on national boards of the PIAST Institute, the Ancestry Question Working Group, The Geno Baroni Institute, One America Foundation, Campaign for Human Development, U.S. Department of Education Ethnic Heritage Studies Program, White House Fellows Program, National Neighborhood Coalition, and American Revolution Bicentennial Administration (ARBA).

McGraw Hill — Connect Learn Succeed™

The McGraw·Hill Companies

 Connect
Learn
Succeed™

ANNUAL EDITIONS: RACE AND ETHNIC RELATIONS, EIGHTEENTH EDITION

Annual Editions is published by the **Contemporary Learning Series** group within the
McGraw-Hill Higher Education division.

1 2 3 4 5 6 7 8 9 0 QDB/QDB 1 0 9 8 7 6 5 4 3 2 1

ISBN 978-0-07-805089-3
MHID 0-07-805089-8
ISSN 1075-5195 (print)
ISSN 2159-0794 (online)

Managing Editor: *Larry Loeppke*
Developmental Editor: *David Welsh*
Permissions Coordinator: *DeAnna Dausener*
Marketing Specialist: *Alice Link*
Senior Project Manager: *Joyce Watters*
Design Coordinator: *Margarite Reynolds*
Buyer: *Susan K. Culbertson*
Cover Designer: *Kristine Jubeck*

Compositor: Laserwords Private Limited
Cover Image: The McGraw-Hill Companies, Inc./Andrew Resek, photographer (inset);
Larry Brownstein/Getty Images (background)

Editors/Academic Advisory Board

Members of the Academic Advisory Board are instrumental in the final selection of articles for each edition of ANNUAL EDITIONS. Their review of articles for content, level, and appropriateness provides critical direction to the editors and staff. We think that you will find their careful consideration well reflected in this volume.

ANNUAL EDITIONS: Race and Ethnic Relations 11/12
18th Edition

EDITOR

John A. Kromkowski
Catholic University of America

ACADEMIC ADVISORY BOARD MEMBERS

Preface

In publishing ANNUAL EDITIONS we recognize the enormous role played by the magazines, newspapers, and journals of the public press in providing current, first-rate educational information in a broad spectrum of interest areas. Many of these articles are appropriate for students, researchers, and professionals seeking accurate, current material to help bridge the gap between principles and theories and the real world. These articles, however, become more useful for study when those of lasting value are carefully collected, organized, indexed, and reproduced in a low-cost format, which provides easy and permanent access when the material is needed. That is the role played by ANNUAL EDITIONS.

This collection is a contemporary guide to understanding growing public attention to race and ethnicity. Race and ethnicity are manifested as aspects of urbanization and central city isolation. Widespread immigration and plight of refugees, the expansion and contraction of the workforce, globalization of a market economy, violence, and war are other aspects of race and ethnic relations in America and the world. We are increasingly aware of the ways that group and personal identity are interwoven and expressed in culture, as well as the economy, polities, and the sociality and religiosity of the human condition. Vivid samples of the widespread public discourse about cultural diversity and ethnic pluralism were selected and arranged to illustrate the American experiences and the governance of race and ethnic relations. Today, consciousness of the pluralism expressed in ethnic, racial, and cultural diversity is neither a neglected dimension of public discourse nor a variable not included in serious analytics of both the social sciences and humanities. Race and ethnicity are important, meaningful and significant dimensions of history, politics, and social order in America and throughout the world.

In Unit 1 the experiences of diversity, expressed in race and ethnicity, are presented as aspects of personal and group identity that are significantly, if not essentially, shaped by social, economic, and cultural forces and practices. Nearly all contemporary theories of history, politics and society are attentive to race and ethnicity. The grounding of such theories in local experiences of persons engaged in political and economic and community processes of change reveal the interactive and indeterminate character of the human condition. Agents of change employ creativity, imagination, and the evocation of religion into the arena and dynamics processes of ethnic and racial relations. Unit 1 provides case studies that are illustrative of the articulation of ethnicity-specific and particular intersection of groups at the micro-level.

Unit 2 presents the foundational legal construction of diversity. This unit illustrates how the most basic legal principles of a society are especially significant for the delineation of ethnic groups. The demography of American diversity is broached in Unit 3. From its very beginning, the experiences of diversity in America have been embedded into our history as a colonial and immigrant receiving country and by racial exclusion, by conquest and domination. And yet political action for new forms of governance and enactment of the legal remedies to overcome past practices and to chart a new horizon for race and ethnic relations are essential features of modernity as well as post-modernity. Expression of such openness emerged as full-force in the revival of large scale immigration in 1965, and in the enforcement of the civil liberties and civil rights that implemented the promise liberty and justice for all. Today we are entering another threshold of governance as we address impacts of globalization, attacks to our homeland and military action related to our ascendancy as the world-scale superpower.

Other units of this collection frame has new discussions of race and ethnic relations that include the uniquely American revival of cultural form by indigenous groups found in Unit 4. Profiles of the two largest ethnic populations, their experiences, the mobility strategies of the descendants from slavery, and extension of the country in lands that was previously related to the Spanish empire in America are treated in the articles found in Unit 5 on Hispanic/Latino Americans and in Unit 6 on African Americans. Unit 7 explores various dimensions of the Asian American experience. Unit 8 extends the discussion of ethnic identity for Americans of European and Mediterranean background. Unit 9, titled "Horizons in Pluralism" articulates a set of issues related to the persistence of the ethnic factor and its impact on personal and regional aspects of American unity and diversity. Unit 10 presents the ethnic factor and international challenges.

A new perspective on race and ethnic relations grounded in aspirations to overcome insularity, isolation, and dichotomous mentalities derived from the rural foundations has emerged over the last three generations. Its thrust is to re-apply the moral imagination articulated in human rights and cultural rights movements. Its origins are rooted in the American promise of liberty and justice and the re-articulation of these promises in law and governance within the American tradition. By necessity this tradition is rooted in the experiences of pluralism discovered by immigrants and others as they moved beyond the cultural icons, dichotomous logic, and divisive social practices. Clearly, we have not entirely overcome xenophobia, racialism, and color consciousness and their institutional remnants. Nonetheless, a re-interpretive project of education and research has fostered recognition and celebration of a more complex matrix of ethnicities. Moreover, the appreciation of various ethnic cultures and the legal defense of such claims to identity constitute a new from of balanced citizenships and cultural democracy in American and perhaps in other countries as well.

In addition to the annotated table of contents, this edition of *Annual Editions: Race and Ethnic Relations* contains a list of Internet References that can be used to further explore articles and a Topic Guide to reference articles by subjects. New to this edition are Critical Thinking study questions after each article. These questions will greatly aid students in better understanding the content of this book. Readers may have input for the next edition of *Annual Editions: Race and Ethnic Relations* by completing and returning the prepaid article rating form in the back of the book.

Thank you,

John A. Kromkowski
Editor

Contents

Preface   iv

Correlation Guide   xi

Topic Guide   xii

Internet References   xvi

UNIT 1
The Experiences of Racial and Ethnic Identity, Communities, and Diversity in America

Unit Overview   xviii

1. **Chicago and the Irish,** Tom Deignan, *Irish America,* August/September, 2008

   Deignan's profile of the Irish in Chicago, and the compilation of personal expressions of ethnic identity reveal the dual characteristics nature of affinities to places and culture that shapes the personality of the members of an ethnic group.   2

2. **Cajun Country Still Sizzles: But, Podna, You'd Better Partake in the Traditions Soon,** Josh Noel, *The Baltimore Sun,* March 28, 2010

   Josh Noel's photo essay and narrative projects an inviting vista of Cajun ethnic tradition in Louisiana, and promotes tourism and travel into this accessible world of food, fun, and festival.   5

3. **Farmer Fills Hala Niche While Feeding His Soul,** Tara Bahrampour, *The Washington Post,* April 13, 2010

   Tara Bahrampour's profile of the Hossian family and their adaptation to the market for meat in accord with Islamic Law reveals personal and group transitions that emerge when ethno-religious communities reach certain levels of size and the sustainability of new cultures and new entrepreneurs.   7

4. **In Brooklyn, an Evolving Ethnicity,** Delizia Flaccavento, *Ambassador, National Italian American Foundation,* Summer 2006

   This profile of the streets of Bensonhurst recounts the efforts taken by the Federation of Italian American Organizations toward the recultivation of neighborhood-based ethnicity that flourished in this original ethnic enclave.   9

5. **In Armenian Enclave, Turkish Deal Arouses Suspicion: Ethnic Leaders in Glendale, Calif., See Detente Announcement as a Ploy on Day Commemorating 1915 Killings,** Nicholas Casey, *The Wall Street Journal,* April 25–26, 2009

   This report by Nicholas Casey on activities of the most robust Armenian settlements in America and the dismay of Armenian Americans to the announcement–a thaw in relations between Turkey and Armenia–reveals a few dimensions of ethnic conflict related to oppositional identity, the politics of memory, and historical victimization.   11

6. **The Hotel Africa,** G. Pascal Zachary, *The Wilson Quarterly,* Summer 2006

   This account of the growing number of African immigrants, and their ongoing relationship with their countries and regions of origin provides a window to new dimensions of American pluralism.   13

UNIT 2
The Legal Construction of Diversity and Disparity

Unit Overview   18

7. **Racial Restrictions in the Law of Citizenship,** Ian F. Haney López, *White By Law: The Legal Construction of Race,* New York University Press, 1996

   This article traces the legal history of naturalization in the development of the definitions and legal norms that affected American citizenship.   21

The concepts in bold italics are developed in the article. For further expansion, please refer to the Topic Guide.

8. **Dred Scott v. Sandford,** Supreme Court of the United States, 1856

This case is concerned with the claim by Dred Scott, a slave, who was taken by his master to live in a free state, and then claimed to have lost his status as a slave. The Court ruled that the U.S. Constitution did not protect him, nor other African Americans, whether they were considered free or held as slaves.   **26**

9. **"There's No One as Irish as Barack O'Bama": The Policy and Politics of American Multiracialism,** Jennifer Hochschild and Vesia Mae Weaver, *Perspectives on Politics: The American Political Science Association,* September 2010

This scholarly article addresses a variety of implications and impacts on racial and ethnic understandings and loyalties that flow from the data collection for the 2000 Census which allowed individuals to choose more than one race.   **30**

10. **Brown et al. v. Board of Education of Topeka et al.** from *U.S. Reports,* 1954

In this case the Court overturned **Plessy v. Ferguson,** and ended **dejure** segregation of public schools. The Court ruled that "separate but equal has no place in public education for separate education and facilities are inherently unequal."   **49**

11. **'Bakke' Set a New Path to Diversity for Colleges,** Peter Schmidt, *The Chronicle of Higher Education,* June 20, 2008

In Bakke a splintered Court ruled to uphold a lower court order that addressed the question of special admission to medical school guaranteed the rights of certain ethnic minorities over the claim to rights of better-qualified non-minority applicants.   **52**

12. **Shaare Tefila Congregation v. Cobb** and **Saint Francis College v. Al-Khazraji,** from *U.S. Reports,* 1987

The Supreme Court reviewed the legislative intent of Congress, and discovered that the civil rights law of 1866 should be applied to discrimination based on race and ethnicity and thus, extend prohibitions against state and private discrimination based on group distinctions to all ethno-religious groups.   **55**

13. **Historical Discrimination in the Immigration Laws,** from *The Tarnished Golden Door,* September 1980

This article summarizes the history of immigration laws and their effects on immigrants groups: the Nativist movement of the 1830s, The Chinese Exclusion Acts of the 1880s, the quota system of the 1920s, and the McCarran-Walter Act of 1952.   **59**

14. **The Diversity Visa Lottery—A Cycle of Unintended Consequences in United States Immigration Policy,** Anna O. Law, *Journal of American Ethnic History,* Summer 2002

Anna Law's account of the **immigration reforms** dating from 1965, and the current public practice of awarding visas by country lottery reveals the curious logic and trajectory of cultural, economic, and democratic assumptions.   **64**

UNIT 3
The Demography of Ethnicity

Unit Overview   **76**

15. **Ancestry 2000: Census 2000 Brief,** Angela Brittingham and G. Patricia de la Cruz, *U.S. Department of Commerce, Economics and Statistics Administration, U.S. Census Bureau,* June 2004

This report, with its tables and figures, presents troves of data regarding ethnic populations, the persistence of ancestral affinities, and self-identification and regional clustering of cultures in the United States.   **79**

16. **The American Community Survey: The New Dimensions of Race and Ethnicity in America,** John David Kromkowski, *Building Blocks: Occasional Papers NCUEA,* September 15, 2010

This article about the new research possibilities derived from **The American Community Survey** and illustrative tables guide the reader from history into a stunning new age of information and statistical tests regarding race and ethnicity in America.   **87**

17. **Nation's Linguistic Diversity: Population Speaking a Language Other than English at Home Increases by 140 Percent in Past Three Decades,** *U.S. Department of Commerce, Economics and Statistics Administration, US Census Bureau,* April 27, 2010

This compilation of data based on the American Community Survey and the other Census collections from 1980–2007 details aggregate and state level information about the increases and declines of the 303 languages, other than English, that are spoken in homes throughout America.   **95**

The concepts in bold italics are developed in the article. For further expansion, please refer to the Topic Guide.

18. **A Profile of Today's Italian Americans: A Report Based on the Year 2000 Census Compiled by the Sons of Italy,** *The Order Sons of Italy in America,* 2000
This report presents data regarding Italian Americans. It describes the municipal, state, and regional status of the Italian American population in the United States. **106**

19. **Polonia in Numbers: How Many of Us Are out There?,** *Good News,* The American Institute of Polish Culture/The Piast Institute, 2006/2007
This report about Polish Americans presents data gathered from the U.S. Census and self-identification of respondents. These tables reveal municipal and state clustering of Polish Americans in the United States. **112**

20. **Irish-American Heritage Month (March) and Saint. Patrick's Day (March 17): 2010,** *U.S. Department of Commerce, Economics and Statistics Administration, U.S. Census Bureau,* February 22, 2010
This report, with its tables of data about Irish Americans, locates and quantifies the persistence and extent of Irish ethnicity, and its regional clusters in America. **117**

21. **Still Unmelted after All These Years,** John David Kromkowski, *Occasional Papers Series, NCUEA,* June 20, 2008
This article systematically measures American ethnic diversity, quantifies, and compares levels of ethnic variety at the state level, and presents graphic evidence of profound ethnic clustering. **119**

UNIT 4
Indigenous Ethnic Groups

Unit Overview **124**

22. **Who Is a Native American?,** Peter Ortiz, *DiversityInc,* December 2004/January 2005
Peter Ortiz's answer to this question surely includes ethnic tradition, but also move well beyond such matters to the wider range of concerns related to participation in America. **126**

23. **Tribal Philanthropy Thrives,** Daniel Gibson, *Native Peoples: Arts and Lifeways,* August 2008
Daniel Gibson's report on the social value of sharing, and profiles of Native American associations and their contributions and self-help efforts adds a new dimension to mainstream knowledge of Native Americans, beyond their activities in gaming. **131**

24. **American Indian and Alaska Native Heritage Month: November 2008,** U.S. Department of Commerce, Economics and Statistics Administration, U.S. Census Bureau, November 2007
This report on Native American populations provides a quantitative profile of data regarding ethnic populations and thus a fuller understanding of the persistence of ancestral affinities and self-identification as well as the clustering of indigenous cultures in the United States. **133**

UNIT 5
African Americans

Unit Overview **136**

25. **Black (African–American) History Month: February 2010,** U.S. Department of Commerce, Economics and Statistics Administration, U.S. Census Bureau, December 2009
This report on African Americans presents a trove of tables and a compilation of social and economic indicators, regional data, and profiles of the African American population. **139**

26. **Transcript of Obama's Speech,** Barack Obama, *Transcript of Philadelphia Speech,* March 18, 2008
This speech by Barack Obama presented in a symbolically important city, Philadelphia, at a moment of intense passion provoked by video and live engagement of Rev. Jeremiah Wright seemed to be a defining moment for the campaign and perhaps for the discussion of race in America. **143**

27. **Redefining Black Women in America,** Krissah Thompson, *The Washington Post,* March 13, 2010
Krissah Thompson's report on images of black women articulated at a two-day summit of successful black women convened to address the obstacles and possibilities beyond demeaning stereotypes. **148**

The concepts in bold italics are developed in the article. For further expansion, please refer to the Topic Guide.

UNIT 6
Hispanic/Latino/a Americans

Unit Overview　　　　　　　　　　　　　　　　　　　　**150**

28. **Who's Hispanic?,** Jeffrey Passel and Paul Taylor, *Pew Hispanic Center,*
May, 28, 2009
Jeffrey Passel and Paul Taylor provide a guide as they answer a few questions posed by the fluid
process of developing a language of ethnicity and identity driven by data categories devised by the
US Census and the Hispanic leaders.　　　　　　　　　　　　　　　**152**

29. **Race and Hispanic Origin of the Foreign-Born Population in the United States:
2007,** Elizabeth M. Grieco, *American Community Survey Reports,* January 2010
This report describes the race and Hispanic-origin composition of foreign-born population in the
United States and compares it to that of the total and native-born population.　　**155**

30. **Latino Agricultural Workers and Their Young Families: Advancing Theoretical
and Empirically Based Conceptualizations,** Sandra Barrueco and Robert O'Brien,
Occasional Paper, *Research funded by The U.S. Department of Health and Human
Services,* July 2010
This pioneering report on the state of millions of Latino children provides a comprehensive review of
findings and an analytical framework of the complex constellation of facets that must be addressed
by public policies and practices related to the well-being children and families in the agricultural
workforce.　　　　　　　　　　　　　　　　　　　　　**168**

UNIT 7
Asian Americans

Unit Overview　　　　　　　　　　　　　　　　　　　　**176**

31. **Asian/Pacific American Heritage Month: May 2010,** *U.S. Department of Commerce,
American Community Survey, Census Bureau News,* May 2010
This report on the variety of ethnic groups that constitute the Asian/Pacific American Population
and a reference guide to web-based information of these population presents a trove of information and
a profile constructed from social and economic indicators, compiled by the U.S. Census Bureau, and
mandated by Congress in 1978 when Asian/Pacific American Week was established.　　**178**

32. **To Be Asian in America,** Angela Johnson Meadows, *DiversityInc,* April 2005
The profiles of persons from Asian ethnicities arrayed in this collage of interviews by Angela Johnson
Meadows present an interesting and representative set of events and experiences.　　**183**

UNIT 8
European and Mediterranean Ethnics

Unit Overview　　　　　　　　　　　　　　　　　　　　**188**

33. **Migrations to the Thirteen British North American Colonies, 1770–1775: New
Estimates,** Aaron Fogelman, *Journal of Interdisciplinary History,* Spring 1992
In this article, Aaron Fogelman documents the foundational ethnic texture of colonial America and
establishes the baselines from which our analysis of understanding of drama of ethnic variety must
begin.　　　　　　　　　　　　　　　　　　　　　　　**191**

34. **Fecund Newcomers or Dying Ethnics? Demographic Approaches to the History of
Polish and Italian Immigrants and Their Children in the United States, 1880–1980,**
John Radzilowski, *Journal of American Ethnic History,* Fall 2007
In this article John Radzilowski provides demographic lenses and a fresh view of the historical development of two large ethnic groups in America which challenges the foundation of approaches and
models that have shaped both scholarship and popular perceptions of these groups as well as advocacy research of assimilation theory, "the new ethnicity", and the "whiteness" paradigm.　**201**

The concepts in bold italics are developed in the article. For further expansion, please refer to the Topic Guide.

35. **Ethnics No More or Ethnogenesis: From Syrian to Arab American,** Philip Kayak and Kristine Ajrouch, *Occasional Papers, National Center for Urban Ethnic Affairs,* June 2010

This article by Philip Kayal and Kristine Ajrouch not only reviews previous research but also provides a pioneering detailed exploration into the social process of ethnic group formation and change in America.   **209**

36. **Neither Natural Allies Nor Irreconcilable Foes: Alliance Building Efforts between African Americans and Immigrants,** Yusuf Sarfati and Cheryl McLaughlin, *Kirwan Institute Update,* Spring 2008

The authors review strategies for intergroup relations, and also pose a larger question about culture and the common good.   **220**

UNIT 9
Horizons in Pluralism

Unit Overview   **222**

37. **Bigots I Have Loved,** Mark Phillips, *Notre Dame Magazine,* Winter 2009–2010

These personal accounts or meditations on experiences invite the readers into the contours of meaning that are embedded in cultures, and the process of unpacking racism and prejudice.   **225**

38. **From Every End of This Earth,** Steven V. Roberts, *HarperCollins,* 2009

The framework provided in the ***Introduction and Afterword,*** to Steven V. Roberts' lively and penetrating profiles of lives of immigrants, was designed to provide a deeper understanding of personal sagas always missed in the immigration policy debate.   **229**

UNIT 10
International Aspects of Ethnic Relations

Unit Overview   **236**

39. **The Ultimate Crime: Katyn and the Invention of Genocide,** John Connelly, *Commonweal,* August 2010

In this article, written shortly after the tragic events that occurred as Russia and Poland moved toward reconciliation, John Connelly traces the history of events that have become a evil icon of modern statecraft, and its murderous strategy of national annihilation called genocide.   **238**

40. **Never Underestimate the Power of Ethnicity in Iraq,** Amy Chua and Jed Rubenfeld, *The Washington Post,* January 4, 2004

This account on ethnicity in Iraq, written by Chua and Rubenfeld, explores essential issues about the foundations of social order in Iraq, and the realities addressed suggest implications that extend to the very core of our democratic assumptions.   **242**

41. **Burqa Is Banned in France,** David Gauthier-Villars and Charles Forelle, *The Wall Street Journal,* September 15, 2010

This account of issues in France and other European countries regarding religion, personal freedom, human rights, and growing suspicion and anger in the face of diversity and change highlight the intersection of law, ethnicity and religion, and the central value and implementation questions of contemporary pluralism and claims of universal human rights.   **244**

Test-Your-Knowledge Form   **246**
Article Rating Form   **247**

The concepts in bold italics are developed in the article. For further expansion, please refer to the Topic Guide.

Correlation Guide

The *Annual Editions* series provides students with convenient, inexpensive access to current, carefully selected articles from the public press. **Annual Editions: Race and Ethnic Relations, 18/e** is an easy-to-use reader that presents articles on important topics such as *demography, immigration, local experiences,* and many more. For more information on *Annual Editions* and other *McGraw-Hill Contemporary Learning Series* titles, visit www.mhhe.com/cls.

This convenient guide matches the units in **Annual Editions: Race and Ethnic Relations, 18/e** with the corresponding chapters in two of our best-selling McGraw-Hill Sociology textbooks by Aguirre/Turner and Kottak/Kozaitis.

Annual Editions: Race and Ethnic Relations, 18/e	American Ethnicity, 7/e by Aguirre/Turner	On Being Different, 4/e by Kottak/Kozaitis
Unit 1: The Experiences of Racial and Ethnic Identity, Communities, and Diversity in America	**Chapter 4:** White Ethnic Americans **Chapter 5:** African Americans **Chapter 6:** Native Americans **Chapter 7:** Latinos **Chapter 8:** Asian and Pacific Island Americans **Chapter 9:** Arab Americans	**Chapter 4:** The Multicultural Society **Chapter 14:** Places and Spaces
Unit 2: The Legal Construction of Diversity and Disparity	**Chapter 1:** Ethnicity and Ethnic Relations	
Unit 3: The Demography of Ethnicity	**Chapter 1:** Ethnicity and Ethnic Relations **Chapter 2:** Explaining Ethnic Relations	**Chapter 13:** Class **Chapter 14:** Places and Spaces
Unit 4: Indigenous Ethnic Groups	**Chapter 6:** Native Americans	**Chapter 3:** Globalization and Identity
Unit 5: African Americans	**Chapter 5:** African Americans	**Chapter 5:** Ethnicity **Chapter 8:** Race: Its Social Construction **Chapter 15:** Linguistic Diversity
Unit 6: Hispanic/Latina/o Americans	**Chapter 7:** Latinos	**Chapter 5:** Ethnicity
Unit 7: Asian Americans	**Chapter 8:** Asian and Pacific Island Americans	**Chapter 5:** Ethnicity
Unit 8: European and Mediterranean Ethnics	**Chapter 4:** White Ethnic Americans **Chapter 9:** Arab Americans	**Chapter 5:** Ethnicity
Unit 9: Horizons in Pluralism		**Chapter 4:** The Multicultural Society
Unit 10: International Aspects of Ethnic Relations	**Chapter 1:** Ethnicity and Ethnic Relations **Chapter 2:** Explaining Ethnic Relations	**Chapter 4:** The Multicultural Society **Chapter 17:** Conclusion

Topic Guide

This topic guide suggests how the selections in this book relate to the subjects covered in your course. You may want to use the topics listed on these pages to search the Web more easily.

On the following pages a number of websites have been gathered specifically for this book. They are arranged to reflect the units of this Annual Editions reader. You can link to these sites by going to www.mhhe.com/cls

All the articles that relate to each topic are listed below the bold-faced term.

African American

7. Racial Restrictions in the Law of Citizenship
8. *Dred Scott v. Sandford*
9. "There's No One as Irish as Barack O'Bama": The Policy and Politics of American Multiracialism
10. *Brown et al. Board of Education of Topeka et al.*
11. 'Bakke' Set a New Path to Diversity for Colleges
12. *Shaare Tefila Congregation v. Cobb* and *Saint Francis College v. Al-Khazraji*
15. Ancestry 2000: Census 2000 Brief
16. The American Community Survey: The New Dimensions of Race and Ethnicity in America
21. Still Unmelted after All These Years
25. Black (African–American) History Month: February 2010
26. Transcript of Obama's Speech
27. Redefining Black Women in America

Arab Americans

3. Farmer Fills Hala Niche While Feeding His Soul
12. *Shaare Tefila Congregation v. Cobb* and *Saint Francis College v. Al-Khazraji*
15. Ancestry 2000: Census 2000 Brief
16. The American Community Survey: The New Dimensions of Race and Ethnicity in America
17. Nation's Linguistic Diversity: Population Speaking a Language Other than English at Home Increases by 140 Percent in Past Three Decades
21. Still Unmelted after All These Years
35. Ethnics No More or Ethnogenesis: From Syrian to Arab American

Census

9. "There's No One as Irish as Barack O'Bama": The Policy and Politics of American Multiracialism
15. Ancestry 2000: Census 2000 Brief
16. The American Community Survey: The New Dimensions of Race and Ethnicity in America
17. Nation's Linguistic Diversity: Population Speaking a Language Other than English at Home Increases by 140 Percent in Past Three Decades
18. A Profile of Today's Italian Americans: A Report Based on the Year 2000 Census Compiled by the Sons of Italy
19. Polonia in Numbers: How Many of Us Are out There?
20. Irish-American Heritage Month (March) and Saint Patrick's Day (March 17): 2010
21. Still Unmelted after All These Years
25. Black (African–American) History Month: February 2010
29. Race and Hispanic Origin of the Foreign-Born Population in the United States: 2007
31. Asian/Pacific American Heritage Month: May 2010

Civil rights

7. Racial Restrictions in the Law of Citizenship
8. *Dred Scott v. Sandford*
10. *Brown et al. Board of Education of Topeka et al.*
11. 'Bakke' Set a New Path to Diversity for Colleges
12. *Shaare Tefila Congregation v. Cobb* and *Saint Francis College v. Al-Khazraji*
26. Transcript of Obama's Speech
41. Burqa Is Banned in France

Communities

1. Chicago and the Irish
2. Cajun Country Still Sizzles: But, Podna, You'd Better Partake in the Traditions Soon
3. Farmer Fills Hala Niche While Feeding His Soul
5. In Armenian Enclave, Turkish Deal Arouses Suspicion: Ethnic Leaders in Glendale, Calif., See Detente Announcement as a Ploy on Day Commemorating 1915 Killings
18. A Profile of Today's Italian Americans: A Report Based on the Year 2000 Census Compiled by the Sons of Italy
19. Polonia in Numbers: How Many of Us Are out There?
20. Irish-American Heritage Month (March) and Saint Patrick's Day (March 17): 2010
21. Still Unmelted after All These Years
22. Who Is a Native American?
25. Black (African–American) History Month: February 2010
26. Transcript of Obama's Speech
28. Who's Hispanic?
30. Latino Agricultural Workers and Their Young Families: Advancing Theoretical and Empirically Based Conceptualizations
31. Asian/Pacific American Heritage Month: May 2010
35. Ethnics No More or Ethnogenesis: From Syrian to Arab American
38. From Every End of This Earth

Cultural formation

2. Cajun Country Still Sizzles: But, Podna, You'd Better Partake in the Traditions Soon
3. Farmer Fills Hala Niche While Feeding His Soul
7. Racial Restrictions in the Law of Citizenship
9. "There's No One as Irish as Barack O'Bama": The Policy and Politics of American Multiracialism
17. Nation's Linguistic Diversity: Population Speaking a Language Other than English at Home Increases by 140 Percent in Past Three Decades
18. A Profile of Today's Italian Americans: A Report Based on the Year 2000 Census Compiled by the Sons of Italy
19. Polonia in Numbers: How Many of Us Are out There?
20. Irish-American Heritage Month (March) and Saint Patrick's Day (March 17): 2010
22. Who Is a Native American?
25. Black (African–American) History Month: February 2010
26. Transcript of Obama's Speech
35. Ethnics No More or Ethnogenesis: From Syrian to Arab American
38. From Every End of This Earth

Culture

1. Chicago and the Irish
2. Cajun Country Still Sizzles: But, Podna, You'd Better Partake in the Traditions Soon
3. Farmer Fills Hala Niche While Feeding His Soul
5. In Armenian Enclave, Turkish Deal Arouses Suspicion: Ethnic Leaders in Glendale, Calif., See Detente Announcement as a Ploy on Day Commemorating 1915 Killings
17. Nation's Linguistic Diversity: Population Speaking a Language Other than English at Home Increases by 140 Percent in Past Three Decades
18. A Profile of Today's Italian Americans: A Report Based on the Year 2000 Census Compiled by the Sons of Italy

19. Polonia in Numbers: How Many of Us Are out There?
20. Irish-American Heritage Month (March) and Saint Patrick's Day (March 17): 2010
21. Still Unmelted after All These Years
22. Who Is a Native American?
25. Black (African–American) History Month: February 2010
32. To Be Asian in America
33. Migrations to the Thirteen British North American Colonies, 1770–1775: New Estimates
35. Ethnics No More or Ethnogenesis: From Syrian to Arab American
41. Burqa Is Banned in France

Discrimination

5. In Armenian Enclave, Turkish Deal Arouses Suspicion: Ethnic Leaders in Glendale, Calif., See Detente Announcement as a Ploy on Day Commemorating 1915 Killings
7. Racial Restrictions in the Law of Citizenship
8. *Dred Scott v. Sandford*
10. *Brown et al. Board of Education of Topeka et al.*
11. 'Bakke' Set a New Path to Diversity for Colleges
12. *Shaare Tefila Congregation v. Cobb* and *Saint Francis College v. Al-Khazraji*
13. Historical Discrimination in the Immigration Laws
14. The Diversity Visa Lottery—A Cycle of Unintended Consequences in United States Immigration Policy
26. Transcript of Obama's Speech
37. Bigots I Have Loved
41. Burqa Is Banned in France

Economy

3. Farmer Fills Hala Niche While Feeding His Soul
13. Historical Discrimination in the Immigration Laws
14. The Diversity Visa Lottery—A Cycle of Unintended Consequences in United States Immigration Policy
17. Nation's Linguistic Diversity: Population Speaking a Language Other than English at Home Increases by 140 Percent in Past Three Decades
22. Who Is a Native American?
30. Latino Agricultural Workers and Their Young Families: Advancing Theoretical and Empirically Based Conceptualizations
38. From Every End of This Earth

Education

10. *Brown et al. Board of Education of Topeka et al.*
11. 'Bakke' Set a New Path to Diversity for Colleges
17. Nation's Linguistic Diversity: Population Speaking a Language Other than English at Home Increases by 140 Percent in Past Three Decades
30. Latino Agricultural Workers and Their Young Families: Advancing Theoretical and Empirically Based Conceptualizations
37. Bigots I Have Loved

Families

14. The Diversity Visa Lottery—A Cycle of Unintended Consequences in United States Immigration Policy
30. Latino Agricultural Workers and Their Young Families: Advancing Theoretical and Empirically Based Conceptualizations
37. Bigots I Have Loved
38. From Every End of This Earth

Government

7. Racial Restrictions in the Law of Citizenship
8. *Dred Scott v. Sandford*
9. "There's No One as Irish as Barack O'Bama": The Policy and Politics of American Multiracialism
10. *Brown et al. Board of Education of Topeka et al.*
11. 'Bakke' Set a New Path to Diversity for Colleges
12. *Shaare Tefila Congregation v. Cobb* and *Saint Francis College v. Al-Khazraji*
13. Historical Discrimination in the Immigration Laws
14. The Diversity Visa Lottery—A Cycle of Unintended Consequences in United States Immigration Policy

15. Ancestry 2000: Census 2000 Brief
16. The American Community Survey: The New Dimensions of Race and Ethnicity in America
26. Transcript of Obama's Speech
41. Burqa Is Banned in France

History

2. Cajun Country Still Sizzles: But, Podna, You'd Better Partake in the Traditions Soon
5. In Armenian Enclave, Turkish Deal Arouses Suspicion: Ethnic Leaders in Glendale, Calif., See Detente Announcement as a Ploy on Day Commemorating 1915 Killings
7. Racial Restrictions in the Law of Citizenship
8. *Dred Scott v. Sandford*
22. Who is a Native American?
25. Black (African–American) History Month: February 2010
26. Transcript of Obama's Speech
31. Asian/Pacific American Heritage Month: May 2010
33. Migrations to the Thirteen British North American Colonies, 1770–1775: New Estimates
34. Fecund Newcomers or Dying Ethnics? Demographic Approaches to the history of Polish and Italian Immigrants and Their Children in the United States, 1880–1980
35. Ethnics No More or Ethnogenesis: From Syrian to Arab American

Identity

1. Chicago and the Irish
2. Cajun Country Still Sizzles: But, Podna, You'd Better Partake in the Traditions Soon
3. Farmer Fills Hala Niche While Feeding His Soul
5. In Armenian Enclave, Turkish Deal Arouses Suspicion: Ethnic Leaders in Glendale, Calif., See Detente Announcement as a Ploy on Day Commemorating 1915 Killings
9. "There's No One as Irish as Barack O'Bama": The Policy and Politics of American Multiracialism
10. *Brown et al. Board of Education of Topeka et al.*
11. 'Bakke' Set a New Path to Diversity for Colleges
12. *Shaare Tefila Congregation v. Cobb* and *Saint Francis College v. Al-Khazraji*
17. Nation's Linguistic Diversity: Population Speaking a Language Other than English at Home Increases by 140 Percent in Past Three Decades
18. A Profile of Today's Italian Americans: A Report Based on the Year 2000 Census Compiled by the Sons of Italy
19. Polonia in Numbers: How Many of Us Are out There?
20. Irish-American Heritage Month (March) and Saint Patrick's Day (March 17): 2010
21. Still Unmelted after All These Years
22. Who Is a Native American?
25. Black (African–American) History Month: February 2010
26. Transcript of Obama's Speech
27. Redefining Black Women in America
28. Who's Hispanic?
31. Asian/Pacific American Heritage Month: May 2010
32. To Be Asian in America
35. Ethnics No More or Ethnogenesis: From Syrian to Arab American
37. Bigots I Have Loved
40. Never Underestimate the Power of Ethnicity in Iraq

Immigration

3. Farmer Fills Hala Niche While Feeding His Soul
4. In Brooklyn, an Evolving Ethnicity
13. Historical Discrimination in the Immigration Laws
14. The Diversity Visa Lottery—A Cycle of Unintended Consequences in United States Immigration Policy
17. Nation's Linguistic Diversity: Population Speaking a Language Other than English at Home Increases by 140 Percent in Past Three Decades
28. Who's Hispanic?
34. Fecund Newcomers or Dying Ethnics? Demographic Approaches to the history of Polish and Italian Immigrants and Their Children in the United States, 1880–1980
35. Ethnics No More or Ethnogenesis: From Syrian to Arab American
38. From Every End of This Earth

Irish Americans

1. Chicago and the Irish
15. Ancestry 2000: Census 200 Brief
16. The American Community Survey: The New Dimensions of Race and Ethnicity in America
20. Irish-American Heritage Month (March) and Saint Patrick's Day (March 17): 2010
21. Still Unmelted after All These Years
29. Race and Hispanic Origin of the Foreign-Born Population in the United States: 2007
31. Asian/Pacific American Heritage Month, May 2010.
37. Bigots I Have Loved

Islam

3. Farmer Fills Hala Niche While Feeding His Soul
12. *Shaare Tefila Congregation v. Cobb* and *Saint Francis College v. Al-Khazraji*
35. Ethnics No More or Ethnogenesis: From Syrian to Arab American
40. Never Underestimate the Power of Ethnicity in Iraq
41. Burqa Is Banned in France

Italian Americans

15. Ancestry 2000: Census 2000 Brief
19. Polonia in Numbers: How Many of Us Are out There?
17. Nation's Linguistic Diversity: Population Speaking a Language Other than English at Home Increases by 140 Percent in Past Three Decades
18. A Profile of Today's Italian Americans: A Report Based on the Year 2000 Census Compiled by the Sons of Italy
22. Who Is a Native American?
34. Fecund Newcomers or Dying Ethnics? Demographic Approaches to the history of Polish and Italian Immigrants and Their Children in the United States, 1880–1980

Languages

2. Cajun Country Still Sizzles: But, Podna, You'd Better Partake in the Traditions Soon
17. Nation's Linguistic Diversity: Population Speaking a Language Other than English at Home Increases by 140 Percent in Past Three Decades
22. Who Is a Native American?
26. Transcript of Obama's Speech
38. From Every End of This Earth

Migration

13. Historical Discrimination in the Immigration Laws
14. The Diversity Visa Lottery—A Cycle of Unintended Consequences in United States Immigration Policy
21. Still Unmelted after All These Years
30. Latino Agricultural Workers and Their Young Families: Advancing Theoretical and Empirically Based Conceptualizations
38. From Every End of This Earth

Polish Americans

15. Ancestry 2000: Census 2000 Brief
16. The American Community Survey: The New Dimensions of Race and Ethnicity in America
17. Nation's Linguistic Diversity: Population Speaking a Language Other than English at Home Increases by 140 Percent in Past Three Decades
19. Polonia in Numbers: How Many of Us Are out There?
22. Who Is a Native American?
34. Fecund Newcomers or Dying Ethnics? Demographic Approaches to the history of Polish and Italian Immigrants and Their Children in the United States, 1880–1980
39. The Ultimate Crime: Katyn and the Invention of Genocide

Politics

5. In Armenian Enclave, Turkish Deal Arouses Suspicion: Ethnic Leaders in Glendale, Calif., See Detente Announcement as a Ploy on Day Commemorating 1915 Killings
7. Racial Restrictions in the Law of Citizenship
8. *Dred Scott v. Sandford*
9. "There's No One as Irish as Barack O'Bama": The Policy and Politics of American Multiracialism
13. Historical Discrimination in the Immigration Laws
14. The Diversity Visa Lottery—A Cycle of Unintended Consequences in United States Immigration Policy
26. Transcript of Obama's Speech
39. The Ultimate Crime: Katyn and the Invention of Genocide

Prejudice

5. In Armenian Enclave, Turkish Deal Arouses Suspicion: Ethnic Leaders in Glendale, Calif., See Detente Announcement as a Ploy on Day Commemorating 1915 Killings
8. *Dred Scott v. Sandford*
10. *Brown et al. Board of Education of Topeka et al.*
11. 'Bakke' Set a New Path to Diversity for Colleges
12. *Shaare Tefila Congregation v. Cobb* and *Saint Francis College v. Al-Khazraji*
25. Black (African–American) History Month: February 2010
26. Transcript of Obama's Speech
27. Redefining Black Women in America
37. Bigots I Have Loved
41. Burqa Is Banned in France

Public policy

3. Farmer Fills Hala Niche While Feeding His Soul
5. In Armenian Enclave, Turkish Deal Arouses Suspicion: Ethnic Leaders in Glendale, Calif., See Detente Announcement as a Ploy on Day Commemorating 1915 Killings
7. Racial Restrictions in the Law of Citizenship
8. *Dred Scott v. Sandford*
9. "There's No One as Irish as Barack O'Bama": The Policy and Politics of American Multiracialism
10. *Brown et al. Board of Education of Topeka et al.*
11. 'Bakke' Set a New Path to Diversity for Colleges
12. *Shaare Tefila Congregation v. Cobb* and *Saint Francis College v. Al-Khazraji*
13. Historical Discrimination in the Immigration Laws
14. The Diversity Visa Lottery—A Cycle of Unintended Consequences in United States Immigration Policy
15. Ancestry 2000: Census 2000 Brief
16. The American Community Survey: The New Dimensions of Race and Ethnicity in America
17. Nation's Linguistic Diversity: Population Speaking a Language Other than English at Home Increases by 140 Percent in Past Three Decades
22. Who Is a Native American?
25. Black (African–American) History Month: February 2010
26. Transcript of Obama's Speech
27. Redefining Black Women in America
30. Latino Agricultural Workers and Their Young Families: Advancing Theoretical and Empirically Based Conceptualizations
39. The Ultimate Crime: Katyn and the Invention of Genocide
41. Burqa Is Banned in France

Refugees

13. Historical Discrimination in the Immigration Laws
14. The Diversity Visa Lottery—A Cycle of Unintended Consequences in United States Immigration Policy

Religion

3. Farmer Fills Hala Niche While Feeding His Soul
12. *Shaare Tefila Congregation v. Cobb* and *Saint Francis College v. Al-Khazraji*
39. The Ultimate Crime: Katyn and the Invention of Genocide
40. Never Underestimate the Power of Ethnicity in Iraq
41. Burqa Is Banned in France

Schools

10. *Brown et al. Board of Education of Topeka et al.*
11. 'Bakke' Set a New Path to Diversity for Colleges
12. *Shaare Tefila Congregation v. Cobb* and *Saint Francis College v. Al-Khazraji*

17. Nation's Linguistic Diversity: Population Speaking a Language Other than English at Home Increases by 140 Percent in Past Three Decades
25. Black (African–American) History Month: February 2010
30. Latino Agricultural Workers and Their Young Families: Advancing Theoretical and Empirically Based Conceptualizations
41. Burqa Is Banned in France

Violence

5. In Armenian Enclave, Turkish Deal Arouses Suspicion: Ethnic Leaders in Glendale, Calif., See Detente Announcement as a Ploy on Day Commemorating 1915 Killings
39. The Ultimate Crime: Katyn and the Invention of Genocide
40. Never Underestimate the Power of Ethnicity in Iraq

Internet References

The following Internet sites have been selected to support the articles found in this reader. These sites were available at the time of publication. However, because websites often change their structure and content, the information listed may no longer be available. We invite you to visit www.mhhe.com/cls for easy access to these sites.

Annual Editions: Race and Ethnic Relations 18/e

General Sources

Library of Congress
www.loc.gov

Examine this extensive Web site to learn about resource tools, library services/resources, exhibitions, and databases in many different fields related to race and ethnicity.

Social Science Information Gateway
http://sosig.esrc.bris.ac.uk

Access an online catalog of thousands of Internet resources relevant to social science education and research at this site. Every resource is selected and described by a librarian or subject specialist.

Sociosite
www.sociosite.net

Open this enormous site of the University of Amsterdam's Sociology Department to gain insights into a number of social issues. A six-column alphabetical list provides links to activism, affirmative action, discrimination, poverty, race and ethnic relations, urbanization, women's issues, and much more.

UNIT 1: The Experiences of Racial and Ethnic Identity, Communities, and Diversity in America

American Civil Liberties Union (ACLU)
www.aclu.org

This site contains links to the ACLU's archives of information about civil rights in the United States and around the world, now and historically. Consult the index to find discussions of such topics as racial equality and immigrants' rights.

Human Rights Web
www.hrweb.org

The history of the human-rights movement, text on seminal figures, landmark legal and political documents, and ideas on how individuals can get involved in helping to protect the rights of all peoples around the world can be found at this valuable site. Links to related sites can also be accessed here.

Supreme Court/Legal Information Institute
http://supct.law.cornell.edu/supct/index.html

Open this site for current and historical information about the Supreme Court. The archive contains many opinions issued since May 1990 as well as a collection of nearly 600 landmark decisions of the Court.

UNIT 2: The Legal Construction of Diversity and Disparity

U.S. Supreme Court Reports
http://bulk.resource.org/courts.gov/c/US

U.S. Census Bureau
www.census.gov

Here is a link to the U.S. Census Bureau, which provides useful demographic research and statistics.

UNIT 3: The Demography of Diversity

U. S. Census Bureau
www.census.gov

The U.S. Census Bureau contains a wealth of information on topics such as populations and their breakdowns according to race, ethnicity, work status, etc.

Diversity.com
www.diversity.com

This site is an excellent source for recruiting job seekers from diverse ethnic cultures, life styles, life stages, creative persuasions, abilities, religious affiliations and gender. Diversity .com provides best-in-class recruitment advertising and diversity branding.

U. S. Bureau of Citizenship and Immigration Services
www.USCIS.gov/portal/site/uscis

Visit the home page of the USCIS to learn U.S. policy vis-à-vis immigrants, laws and regulations, and statistics.

UNIT 4: Indigenous Ethnic Groups

American Indian Science and Engineering Society (AISES)
www.aises.org

This AISES "Multicultural Educational Reform Programs" site provides a framework for learning about science, mathematics, and technology. There are useful links to programs for Native American education.

UNIT 5: African Americans

National Association for the Advancement of Colored People (NAACP)
www.naacp.org

Open this home page to explore the NAACP's stances regarding many topics in race and ethnic relations. Many links to other organizations and resources are provided.

Internet References

AIDs and Black New Yorkers
www.villagevoice.com/issues/0024/wright.php

This article, which is one of six, gives some understanding on the still growing death toll on the black community due to AIDs.

UNIT 6: Hispanic/Latina/o Americans

Latino American Network Information Center (LANIC)
http://lanic.utexas.edu

The purpose of this site is to offer Latinos sources of information on everything of importance. The site links to housing, employment, ethnicity, income, and political issues. It also offers the latest news of interest to Latinos and Hispanics.

National Council of La Raza (NCLR)
www.nclr.org

Explore NCLR's home page for links to health and education issues in the Hispanic community. Many other economic, political, and social concerns are also covered at this site.

UNIT 7: Asian Americans

Asian American Studies Center
www.aasc.ucla.edu/default.asp

Asian American for Equality
www.aafe.org

Asian-Nation
www.asian-nation.org/index.shtml

UNIT 8: European and Mediterranean Ethnics

Africa News Online
www.africanews.org

Open this site for *Africa News* on the Web. This source provides extensive, up-to-date information on all of Africa, with reports from Africa's newspapers and other sources.

Cultural Survival
www.culturalsurvival.org

This nonprofit organization works to defend and protect the human rights and cultural autonomy of indigenous peoples and oppressed ethnic minorities around the world. Learn about policies intended to avoid genocide and ethnic conflict.

The North-South Institute
www.nsi-ins.ca/ensi/index.html

Searching this site of the North-South Institute—which works to strengthen international development cooperation and enhance social equity—will help you find information on a variety of issues related to international race and ethnicity.

Order Sons of Italy in America
www.osia.org

This site encourages the study of Italian language and culture in American schools and universities.

The National Italian American Foundation
www.niaf.org

This is the website of The National Italian American Foundation. They are know as advocates in helping young Italian Americans with their educations and careers as well as strengthening cultural and economic ties between Italy and the U.S.

The Chicago Jewish News Online
www.chicagojewishnews.org

This site is an up-to-date news watch of what is happening in the Jewish community.

Polish American Congress
www.polamcon.org

At this site you can discover the current issues and recent events in the Polish community.

Polish American Journal
www.polamjournal.com

This is the site of the Polish American Journal, a monthly newspaper dedicated to the promotion and preservation of Polish American culture.

UNIT 9: Horizons in Pluralism

CNN Election Headquarters
www.cnn.com/ELECTION/2008

Visit CNN's site for election coverage and results for the 2008 presidential and other races.

President-Elect Obama's website
http://change.gov

This site was set up to inform citizens of Barak Obama's agenda, his transition team, and other information.

UNIT 10: International Aspects of Ethnic Relations

Yale University Guide to American Ethnic Studies
www.library.yale.edu/rsc/ethnic/internet.html

This site, provided by Yale University, contains a list of resources regarding ethnic identity research and links to organizations that deal with ethnic identity.

American Indian Ritual Object Repatriation Foundation
www.repatriationfoundation.org

Visit this home page of the American Indian Ritual Object Repatriation Foundation, which aims to assist in the appropriate return of sacred ceremonial material.

Center for Research in Ethnic Relations
www.warwick.ac.uk/fac/soc/CRER_RC

This eclectic site provides links to a wealth of resources on the Internet related to race and ethnic relations.

The International Center for Migration, Ethnicity, and Citizenship
www.newschool.edu/icmec

The Center is engaged in scholarly research and public policy analysis bearing on international migration, refugees, and the incorporation of newcomers in host countries.

UNIT 1

The Experiences of Race and Ethnic Identity, Communities, and Diversity in America

Unit Selections

1. **Chicago and the Irish,** Tom Deignan
2. **Cajun Country Still Sizzles: But, Podna, You'd Better Partake in the Traditions Soon,** Josh Noel
3. **Farmer Fills Hala Niche While Feeding His Soul,** Tara Bahrampour
4. **In Brooklyn, an Evolving Ethnicity,** Delizia Flaccavento
5. **In Armenian Enclave, Turkish Deal Arouses Suspicion: Ethnic Leaders in Glendale, Calif., See Detente Announcement as a Ploy on Day Commemorating 1915 Killings,** Nicholas Casey
6. **The Hotel Africa,** G. Pascal Zachary

Learning Objectives

- In what respect does location define race and ethnic relations?
- Does the rise of ethnic marketing foster the assimilation of new immigrants?
- What opinions do you have about churches comprised of populations that are predominately one ethnic group?
- Comment on the following observation: Sunday morning is the most racially segregated time in America.
- Are relations between new immigrants and America to which they are attracted significantly different from region to region? City to city? Group to group?
- Does the economic climate of a particular time significantly influence group relations? What additional variables are important for inter-group relations?
- Explore the racial and ethnic diversity of neighborhoods, towns, and counties that are within your experience and compare them to state and national data. Use the U.S. Census ancestry data.
- Why do some persons feel threatened by public emphasis on ethnicity and race?
- Have local newspapers presented race and ethnic groups and new immigrant groups as sources of conflict?

Student Website
www.mhhe.com/cls

Internet References

American Civil Liberties Union (ACLU)
www.aclu.org
Human Rights Web
www.hrweb.org
Supreme Court/Legal Information Institute
http://supct.law.cornell.edu/supct/index.html

Ethnic and racial identities are social constructions of culture. They are derived from and cultivated in local communities. Thus localism is a feature of race and ethnic relations experienced in specific communities, and the bonds of shared values and traditions that are formative of personal consciousness and group identity. Articles in this unit present a sample of case studies. This sampling, like the many thousands of weekly profiles of ethnics, immigrants, and enclave populations that appear in your local papers and magazines, provide access to distinctive locations and their particular qualities. In composite, they are the pieces of pluralism within our social fabric, our consciousness of human variety, and values rooted in rural and various national traditions that are part of the American reality. The challenges and opportunities of contemporary race and ethnic relations in America are shaped within the framework of social, political, economic, and cultural institutions. Contemporary trends, and currents of opinion and attitude, are influenced by significant events, communications as well as imaginative portrayals at times called literary ethnicity. Such social processes are woven into a porous configuration of local, regional, and national relationships. Viewed from this perspective, a significant facet of what constitutes the American reality is derived from its fundamentally localized demography. To adopt this perspective requires attention to the variety of populations, their settlement patterns, and the movement and succession of groups and cultures from the old neighborhoods to new neighborhoods. This social and analytical approach invites the observer to examine the American reality as a dynamic process involving the shifting and clustering of racial and ethnic groups and their renegotiation of relationships in new places, in new ways, and with new opportunities and challenges that are endemic to American pluralism.

These articles recount experiences of ethnic populations in specific situations and places. They portray unresolved dilemmas related to American pluralism. Ethnic clustering was driven in part by the creative destructiveness of economic growth and the bonds of group affinity their choices, opportunities, and challenges experienced in both turbulent group relations and the hopeful processes of recovering viable urban communities. The pivotal significance of terrorism on immigration is particularly salient for the entire country. Yet the process of forging new relations among communities reveals the development of new strategies and the formation of shared values derived from various traditions, and articulated as each group negotiates the pathway from immigrant to ethnic American. Thus, "becoming American" occurs in the ongoing process of addressing challenges and opportunities. This shift in consciousness regarding race and ethnic relations as well as the technological capacity, information and data explosion, produces new models and explanations of society and culture, and further increases awareness of ethnicity and race.

Modern ethnicities and races are not simply primordial givens. On the contrary, they are dynamic and changing cultural forms. They are fashioned from relationships among persons and in the constitutions of groups, and they are significantly, if not essentially, shaped by the willful orchestration of leaders intent on explanations and action within social, economic, and cultural institutions.

The focus of these articles addresses the particularities of places and rivets our attention on the importance of local knowledge, the qualities of enclave cultures, and the attendant challenges. These articles are foundational for our ability to focus on larger scale dimensions of race and ethnic relations, especially regional forces that shaped cultural patterns. The particular social history of a region clearly shapes its self-articulation. The articles of this unit express the ongoing presence of the past, and reveal its impact on the present state of race relations.

© Ryan McVay/Getty Images

A new overarching synthesis founded in the appreciation of American ethnic and religious pluralism must stand the test of social and political realism, and its pressure for a mono-culturalism, color consciousness, and anti-immigrant xenophobia. Divisive strategies of ethnic group relations exist. Today the global challenge is to fashion an even wider and more inclusive ethno-religious synthesis and the reaffirmation and the refashioning of ethnic and racial relationships in support of peaceful resolution of differences, and participation in a form of citizenship driven by strategies of convergence and inclusion. Muslims in America and all others must address and explore the development of a pluralistic form of Islam and a new politics of values, and the attendant search for deeper convergence among people and traditions. Such a search for order waits for creative leaders who can cast new forms of social imaginations and renewed processes that differentiate religious, ethnic, and cultural modes of conveying meaning to persons and toward their collective legacies as groups. Such an effort requires the confirmation of the integrity of American political institutions and processes, and its attendant conferral of legitimacy to the political sphere as a parallel from of socioeconomic order within which cultural, ethnic, and religious and economic relationships may flourish.

Chicago and the Irish

Tom Deignan

Before he was the trailblazing Democratic nominee for president, Barack Obama was an ambitious young politician who learned a valuable lesson thanks to the Chicago Irish.

The year was 1999. Obama, a state senator, announced he was going to challenge Congressman Bobby L. Rush, a legend in the working-class African-American wards of Chicago's South Side. Decades earlier, the South Side was heavily Irish. It was the world that James T. Farrell recreated in his famous Studs Lonigan trilogy of novels from the 1930s.

In fact, for all the changes in Chicago, the same rules have always applied when it comes to politics: you have to pay your dues before you challenge a veteran.

Meanwhile, though it's true that the district that Obama hoped to win was 65 percent black, it also had "several relatively affluent Irish-American neighborhoods," as *The New York Times* noted recently.

Obama (himself Irish on his mother's side) was ultimately trounced in the South Side race, and learned that when it came to Windy City politics, he still had some dues to pay.

Obama's loss illustrates key facts about the Chicago Irish experience. First, the Irish have been playing a crucial political role in Chicago for over 150 years. Furthermore, the Irish have always had to build coalitions among other racial, ethnic and religious groups. Often, they did so successfully, though other times, the result was tension and violence.

Either way, from Studs Lonigan, Michael Flatley and Mrs. O'Leary's infamous cow to Comiskey Park and O'Hare International Airport, the Irish have left a deep impression upon Chicago.

"City on the Prairie"

Unlike Boston, New York or Philadelphia, Chicago was not settled until the 1800s. So the Chicago Irish did not face the worst kind of anti-Catholic, anti-Irish bigotry from established, native-born elites. This also allowed early Irish immigrants to, in a sense, get in on the ground floor of Chicago.

"For the Irish, Chicago's emergence as the nascent city on the prairie was timely," writes John Gerard McLaughlin in his book *Irish Chicago*. "The construction of the Illinois and Michigan Canal, which would connect the Great Lakes to the Mississippi River, began in 1836, drawing Irish laborers. . . . The completion of the canal in 1848 coincided with the mass emigration from Ireland caused by the Great Famine."

Kerry native Dr. William Bradford was among the earliest boosters of Chicago and the opportunities presented by the canal's construction. Bradford, a physician, was also one of Chicago's earliest successful real estate speculators.

Canal work brought hordes of additional laborers—as well as class tension and cries for unionization. It also meant that when the Great Hunger struck Ireland, some Chicago laborers were able to send money, food and other materials back to Ireland.

"Depraved, Debased, Worthless"

Although Chicago was spared the anti-Irish violence of other large American cities, there was no lack of rabid anti-Irish sentiment. The *Chicago Tribune*, edited by Joseph Medill (a descendant of Scotch-Irish Presbyterians), regularly dismissed the Irish as lazy and shiftless.

"Who does not know that the most depraved, debased, worthless and irredeemable drunkards and sots which curse the community are Irish Catholics?" the *Tribune* sneered. This came even as Irish laborers worked feverishly to complete Chicago's stately St. Patrick's church at Adams and Desplaines Streets in the mid-1850s.

Besides Dr. Bradford, another example of Chicago's Irish rising class was Cork native James Lane. In this city which would lead the nation in meat production, Lane is said to have opened Chicago's first meat market in 1836. He marched in the city's first St. Patrick's Day parade in 1843—and was still doing so five decades later, in the 1890s.

Meanwhile, decades before Jane Addams and Hull House became synonymous with Chicago charity, Carlow native Agatha O'Brien and nuns from the Mercy Sisters worked in hospitals, schools and asylums caring for victims of cholera and other diseases.

By the 1870s, the Irish-born population of Chicago was approaching 70,000—over 25 percent of the people. Then came a calamity which transformed the city forever.

The Great Fire

According to legend, the Great Chicago Fire was started by Mrs. O'Leary's cow. The immigrant family was ultimately exonerated, but the O'Learys were subjected to awful harassment. The fire scorched large swaths of Chicago, including a dressmaking business owned by Cork native and future labor leader Mary Harris "Mother" Jones, who entered the labor movement soon after the fire. The newly rebuilt city saw further upward mobility for the Irish.

A priest at St. John's parish on the South Side, Father Woldron, watched "in sorrow as hundreds of beloved families surrendered their humble homes and moved."

By the 1880s, 30 percent of Chicago's police force and other civil service jobs were held by Irish Americans. Many of Chicago's Irish Americans now earned enough money to move to neighborhoods such as Englewood, where (much to the dismay of local Protestants) they laid foundations for working- or middle-class parishes such as St. Bernard's.

Politics, Labor and Religion

The Irish, as they did in many other cities, proved adept at politics, as well as parish life.

Again, Chicago is unique in that, while the Irish were the largest immigrant minority group in other large cities, they were just one of many in Chicago. Germans, Poles, Jews and other Eastern Europeans flocked to Chicago in large numbers.

"Second generation Chicago Irishmen assumed the role of buffers between the strange speaking newcomers and the native, older residents," Paul M. Green has written.

Affairs in Ireland were also profoundly important to the Chicago Irish. The revolutionary group Clan na Gael had a strong presence in the city, where support was strong for controversial measures such as the London bombing campaign of the 1880s, meant to draw attention to the cause of freedom for Ireland. This became a tougher stance to defend, however, in the wake of the infamous Haymarket Square bombing of 1886, when Irish nationalists in Chicago struggled to draw distinctions between anti-British nationalism and homegrown American anarchism.

Meanwhile, Irish pride in Chicago was not merely confined to the continued struggle against the British.

According to Ellen Skerrit: "Since the 1890s, the city's Irish have played a leading role in the cultural revival of traditional music and dance."

Cork native Francis O'Neill, a police chief, was one of the driving forces behind reviving traditional Irish music in the Chicago area.

Meanwhile, as Charles Fanning has noted, Chicago writer Finley Peter Dunne created one of the great voices in American letters at the turn of the century: Mr. Dooley, the saloon keeper/philosopher with the exaggerated brogue who was beloved by millions in nationwide newspapers and books.

Finally, early 1900s labor leaders included Margaret Haley, president of the Chicago Teachers Federation, and John Fitzpatrick, leader of Chicago's Federation of Labor.

Gangsters and "Studs"

There was also a dark side to Chicago Irish life, painted most memorably in the 1930s Studs Lonigan trilogy of novels by James T. Farrell. Particularly disturbing is the racism, violence and narrow-mindedness we see among Studs, his family and friends. It should be added, however, that Farrell also wrote another series of novels about a youth named Danny O'Neill, who escaped Chicago and chased his dreams. Chicago groups such as the Catholic Interracial Council also showed that some Chicago Irish were promoters of racial justice.

Meanwhile, by the 1920s, though many Chicago Irish moved into the American mainstream, another group chose a very different path. This was evident on the morning of February 14, 1929—Valentine's Day—when two men dressed as police officers ushered six gangsters into a garage on Chicago's North Side. A hail of bullets followed.

The famous massacre had been ordered by Al Capone. He was gunning for Bugs Moran, but the Irish crime boss had escaped. The St. Valentine's Day massacre was the culmination of Irish-Italian turf wars which dominated the 1920s. Prohibition, and competition over the sale of illegal booze, led to these gang wars, and Chicago was the center of Irish organized crime. (Jimmy Cagney's electrifying film *The Public Enemy*, from 1931, was set in the Windy City.)

Deanie O'Banion was the era's most prominent Irish gangster. He grew up in a notorious neighborhood known as Little Hell. Even when he became a full-time murderer, O'Banion sported a rosary in his pocket and a carnation in his jacket. In fact, O'Banion so loved flowers that he opened a flower shop on North State Street, which was where he was killed in 1924, after he had swindled members of Capone's crew.

The Daley Dynasty

All in all, Chicago has had a dozen Irish mayors. Early city leaders include John Comiskey (father of White Sox baseball owner Charles Comiskey), John Coughlin, "Foxy" Ed Cullerton and Johnny Powers. Later, in 1979, Irish-American Jane Byrne was the first woman to serve as Chicago mayor.

The most powerful Irish-American mayor ever was Richard J. Daley, who ran Chicago for over 20 years, beginning with his 1955 election. Daley was a humble, devout Catholic who raised his family not far from the South Side Irish enclave where he grew up. As a multi-ethnic town, Chicago required a mayor who knew how to reward all ethnic groups, a task which Daley mastered.

Daley became such a key figure in the Democratic Party that he was known as a "president-maker," whose support was needed to nominate any White House candidate.

Daley's image was tarnished by the violent events of the 1968 Chicago Democratic convention. But in the mayoral election of 1971, Daley received nearly 60 percent of the vote. He died while in office in 1976. Fittingly, his son, Richard M. Daley, was later elected Chicago mayor in 1989.

The New Chicago Irish

By the 1980s, many Chicago Irish had been in the city three or four generations. But a whole new wave of immigrants then arrived, escaping an Ireland which was still struggling economically.

These immigrants breathed new life into Chicago's Irish-American life and culture. A daughter of immigrants, Liz Carroll is a Chicago native who is one of today's top Irish fiddlers. Then, of course, there is *Riverdance* star Michael Flatley. A native of the South Side, Flatley reinvented Irish dance and brought it to the international masses.

Dance is not something we would expect to arise from the streets once stalked by Studs Lonigan and his band of roughs. But history shows us that, when it comes to the Chicago Irish, there is one thing you should expect: the unexpected.

Critical Thinking

1. In what respects are Irish Americans in Chicago different from Irish Americans in Boston and New York?

2. What are the major elements of the ethnic narrative presented in this article?

3. From among the five or six central features of this narrative which are the most revealing, and which utterly essential to our understanding of this ethnic group?

From *Tom Deignan/Irish America,* August/September 2008. Copyright © 2008 by Irish America. Reprinted by permission.

Cajun Country Still Sizzles
But, Podna, You'd Better Partake in the Traditions Soon

JOSH NOEL

Houma, La.—You could come all this way to watch alligators eat raw chicken thrown from a tour boat and say you've had an authentic Cajun experience. But ask a good 'ol Cajun how to find the real thing, and the answer isn't quite so tidy.

"Go up and down the bayou and see the shrimp boats," said Werlien Prosperie, a lively, compact 74-year-old who owns Jolly Inn, the lone Cajun dance hall in an area once teeming with Cajun dance halls. "See how people make a living. We still live off the land here."

Traditionally, to be Cajun has meant being different: different language, different food, even a wariness of "Americans"—the sometimes pejorative term for those outside their cultural borders. But the differences are shrinking. Prosperie's born-on-a-houseboat-in-the-bayou upbringing is mostly gone. The last generation that grew up speaking French in the home is in its 50s and 60s. And the region's gentle country sensibility—punctuated by dance hall joy and Mardi Gras celebration—has been diluted by the uniformity wrought by television and the Internet.

The losses are part of the reason that Prosperie opened Jolly Inn 12 years ago. His wood-walled dance hall is no down and dirty Texas honky-tonk; it's a clean, well-lit, family-friendly place to put on your best jeans and let a fiddle-accordion-washboard band propel you all night from the Cajun waltz to the Cajun shuffle.

"The younger children knew nothing of this, and the middle-aged people weren't enthusiastic," Prosperie said. "It's a beautiful culture, and I wanted to restore it."

After an evening of bottled beer and rusty moves, I took Prosperie's advice and sought out what I could of the old Cajun life. No offense to the relatively landlocked prairie Cajuns north of Lafayette, but it brought me more than anything else to water: kayaking with alligators in Lake Fausse Pointe State Park, sleeping on a houseboat in Henderson, eating seafood at least twice a day and, yes, taking swamp tours.

There are the large swamp tours, such as Ron "Black" Guidry's in the soupy waters west of Houma. For his 30-plus passengers, Guidry puts on a show: He talks French, guarantees a gator sighting (thank you, raw chicken) and strums Hank Williams' "Jambalaya (On the Bayou)" on his battered acoustic guitar.

"If someone wants the true Cajun experience, you have to go to the most out-of-the-way places you can find," Guidry said (it seems there are about eight last names down here, and Guidry is one of them). "I used to play music in those places. Man, they're all gone."

Then there is Norbert LeBlanc (another of those eight last names), who wears a bushy white beard and takes just seven people at a time into the cypress-thick swamps near Breaux Bridge. For 40 years, LeBlanc trapped gators in these swamps, a brutal process involving meat, a hook and a pistol. He laments that none of his kids speaks French or has mastered the family tree's peach-tinged moonshine that his uncle taught him to make.

"Most of the kids are too busy with computers to watch a flame burn for 12 or 14 hours," LeBlanc said.

Moonshine is illegal, so I don't want to say that LeBlanc serves samples to his guests, but if you get thirsty on the water, let's just say you'll be set. And happy. You also won't have a problem getting close to gators, because LeBlanc knows where to look.

"That one there is a finger alligator," LeBlanc said, pointing at a 2-footer sunning itself on a log. "They only take one finger at a time!"

In Point-Aux-Chenes, I met David Nehlig, 55, and his son, Alvin, 35, who fished in a marsh that seemed like the end of the earth. David, a retired crabber, had just lassoed a red fish the length of his arm, which he proudly led me to his truck to show off while a cigarette hung from his lips.

"If someone gets stressed out, they just come out here and catch a fish or two," he said. "There's a lot of work going on down here but a lot of pleasure too. It's all good, man."

Finally I took my own shot at the life. In the map-speck town of Chauvin, I went to Sportsman's Paradise to hit the water with Cuda Scheer, a boyish 33, who got his first boat at 8 and started running charters after graduating high school. Beneath a high, bright sun, we visited the grassy marshes just north of the Gulf. I hooked my first fish—a 28-inch red drum—within two minutes. The next one, a black drum, found me 30 seconds later.

Six fish later we were back at the dock, Scheer slicing, dicing and spraying the cleaned fish. He kept half the fish for his family, and the kitchen grilled and fried the other half for me.

I asked Scheer if he often ate dinner that had been swimming a few hours earlier.

"Oh, yeah," he said. "We never freeze fish. Living here, what's the point?"

We said our goodbyes, and I drove around a bit more, winding up on Louisiana Highway 55, another two-lane highway that ends at the bottom of the state. As the sun got low and orange, I passed a man and woman lying on a porch while smoking cigarettes and watching dusk approach. A positively idyllic scene. At the dead end half a mile on, I turned around and came across that same couple. This time they were engaged in an act of, well, let's call it physical admiration. Right there on their festive Cajun porch.

Laissez les bon temps rouler. Right?

Critical Thinking

1. What does the term "Cajun" mean?
2. Would you refer to the Cajun experience as a lifestyle or a culture? Why?

From *Baltimore Sun*, March 28, 2010. Copyright © 2010 by PARS International Corp.. Reprinted by permission.

Farmer Fills Halal Niche While Feeding His Soul

Immigrant finds demand high for goats he raises according to Islamic law.

TARA BAHRAMPOUR

Mukit Hossain drove up to a large Centreville home one day last week, rummaged in his Jeep Cherokee and pulled out two plastic bags. Looking harried after spending two hours on Interstate 95, he hurried up the driveway and called out to the couple waiting inside.

On the granite island in their kitchen, he spread out packages wrapped in white paper and labeled "Hams," "Neck" and "Ribs." The lady of the house, Seema Khan, handed him a glass of water. "So, now, did you slaughter the goat by yourself?" she asked.

"Yes, I did," Hossain said proudly.

It was his first delivery in Northern Virginia, made just a couple of weeks after he had e-mailed fliers to area Muslims informing them that he was selling naturally raised, humanely slaughtered, home-delivered goat meat that was halal, or in accordance with Islamic law.

What the e-mail recipients didn't know was that Hossain was doing all the raising, slaughtering and delivering himself.

Like many of Hossain's customers, the Khans had known him as a civic activist and telecommunications executive. Hossain, 49, who emigrated from Bangladesh in the 1970s, was living in the Cascades section of Loudoun County when he became concerned that his work on behalf of day laborers was affecting his business relationships and that his daughters were becoming more interested in designer labels than core values. By 2008, he was wondering about the path his life had taken.

"I thought, 'There's got to be something better I can do rather than run this corporate rat race.'"

—Mukit Hossain, a civic activist and former telecommunications executive who raises halal goats.

"I thought, 'There's got to be something better I can do rather than run this corporate rat race,'" said Hossain, a compact and energetic man. "We were thinking about doing something with the land, and it occurred to me that there are close to 300,000 Muslims in Northern Virginia. The majority eat halal," he said, and to the best of his knowledge, no organic halal goat meat was being produced in Virginia.

Abdullah Wasay, who manages Madina, a Middle Eastern market in Herndon, said the demand for halal goat meat is high, especially among Indian and Pakistani customers or those seeking especially lean meat.

"Ten or 12 years ago, there were only a few customers for goat, but now lots of customers are buying goat," Wasay said. The store went from selling about 10 goats a week a decade ago to 50 now, Wasay said, although it has become harder to find high-quality meat as farms have been sold to local developers.

Although lamb is heavily consumed by Middle Easterners, Hossain said, "if you're looking at Africa or anywhere east of Pakistan, goat is very popular."

Still, when Hossain sold his four-bedroom house and moved his family to a 15-acre farm near Fredericksburg in late 2008, some people in Bangladesh questioned his sanity. He had never lived in a rural area, and goat farming was not how most would-be immigrants envisioned life in the United States.

"Some folks think I have completely lost it," he said. "A friend said, 'Why would you get a degree from Duke if you were going to become a farmer?'" Even his wife, Sabrina, an accounting student raised in Kuwait and Canada, wondered whether it was a good idea. (There was some precedent for Hossain's decision: His grandfather, a prominent lawyer in Bangladesh, had at the height of his career given it all up to become a farmer. Everyone thought he had lost it, too.)

But as Hossain stood outside his barn last week, sucking on a Peterson bent pipe, he radiated contentedness. "This is the most peaceful job I have ever done," he said as he watched two workers, including a Congolese refugee, build fences for his 67 goats and the additional 150 on their way from another farm.

Most of the herd had been sired by Darth Vader, an imposing black Spanish billy goat with a crown of curled horns, and Señor, a sturdy-looking brown and white Boer goat. Hossain's daughters, Maya, 10, and Hana, 8, have named many of the animals, although he tries to keep them away from the ones destined for slaughter.

As the fencing went up, Maya and Hana arrived home from school and pulled on cowboy boots. They collected eggs from the chickens in the barn and peeked in on a newborn goat with its mother.

The girls have changed since moving, their father said. "In the Cascades, when they were with their friends, they were talking about boyfriends and Gucci and the Gap and the latest brands," he said. "Now it's, 'My friend Brianna's horse just had a baby,' or 'So-and-so is in 4-H, and she's taking her pigs and chickens to a fair.'"

But farm life is not always easy. A day earlier, several goats had escaped from their corral and eaten poisonous holly. Two died; Hossain saved the rest by feeding them Pepto Bismol to soothe their stomachs and coffee to make them vomit.

"One thing about being a farmer is, you have to become a vet; you have to become an animal psychologist," he said. You also have to become an economist and a marketer. You have to wake before sunrise (which Hossain said he does anyway for the Muslim dawn prayer), and, in his case, you have to understand what it is to produce an Islamically pure product.

"I wanted to create halal in every sense of the word, from the time it's born," he said, standing on a grassy field as a half-grown goat nuzzled his leg. He laughed and shook it off. "One of the things people don't realize about halal is it's not just the way they are slaughtered. It's the way they are raised. If all that is not done as humanely as possible, what is the concept, really?"

Allowing an animal to become stressed or confining it in tight spaces goes against the spirit of halal, Hossain said. So does squeezing too much profit from the customer. "If the concept of halal is something that's beneficial, trying to sell halal at an exorbitant price goes against that."

Hossain said he has seen organic non-halal goat meat for $12 to $14 a pound; he sells his meat for $3.75 to $4.75 a pound, about the same as commercially produced nonorganic halal goat meat. "Philosophically speaking, the whole concept is, as social beings we have some responsibility—it's not just cutthroat I'll-make-as-much-as-I can."

Layered Responsibilities

Hossain learned halal slaughter from an imam. "The knife has to be extremely sharp so you don't put the animal under undue duress," he said, explaining that when slitting the animals'

throats he tries to cut the jugular vein and the nerve that goes to the spine in one smooth motion. The technique can also enhance flavor; some aficionados say they can taste the difference in an animal that was not afraid before it died.

One of the most important requirements, Hossain said, is to invoke the name of God before and during the act.

In 2006, he worked with area Jewish leaders to push legislation in the Virginia General Assembly that makes it a crime to call a product halal or kosher when it's not.

Still, even humane killing is killing.

"It's not pleasant," he said. "There is a psychological and emotional toll in every slaughter, and I have taken the responsibility to do this. It's a responsibility to the animal and also a responsibility to the consumer. I'm telling them that 'I'm giving you halal' and I need to ensure that it is halal. . . . If I leave this part to somebody else, I don't know exactly what the process is going to be. It's one part that I really, really want to do myself."

That might work as long as he has only a handful of goats to slaughter each week, butchering them to each customer's specifications. But during his first week in business, a wholesaler asked whether Hossain could provide him with 800 goats a month, much more than the 200 a month he had aimed to sell.

"I think there is a tremendous amount of pent-up demand," he said. If the demand becomes too overwhelming, Hossain said, he might talk to an imam about getting help. He plans to hire a delivery driver to relieve him of some of the commuting.

With an initial investment of $200,000, the farm has not broken even, but Hossain said he is optimistic. In addition to Northern Virginia, he has tapped into Richmond's Muslim community and refugees from goat-eating African countries.

"The refugee community loves goats," said Munira Marlowe, who runs Imani, a center for refugees in Spotsylvania. "And it's very popular in Latin American countries."

The farm, which Hossain named Netoppew after a Powhatan word for "friends," has also given his family less tangible benefits.

"I think that here, there's not as much sense of keeping up with the Joneses," Sabrina Hossain said. "I think this is the healthiest decision we've made."

Critical Thinking

1. Do you think Mr. Hossain's achievement can be replicated in other parts of the United States without many obstacles?

From *The Washington Post*, April 13, 2010, p. B4. Copyright © 2010 by Washington Post Writers Group. Reprinted by permission via PARS International Corp.

At a Crossroad

In Brooklyn, an Evolving Ethnicity

The Italian immigrants who came to Brooklyn, New York, in the mid-twentieth century are gradually aging and moving away. The Federation of Italian American Organizations in Brooklyn is hoping to cultivate their cultural identity with new Italian language programs and community centers.

DELIZIA FLACCAVENTO

The streets of Bensonhurst, a Brooklyn neighborhood in New York City, are dotted with pasticcerie, paesani clubs, pizzeria, barber shops and tailors—examples of how Italian immigrants overcame homesickness by incorporating the food and habits of the old country into their new neighborhood's daily rhythms.

But, as the last wave of these immigrants from the 1950s, 1960s, and 1970s ages, these last bastions of their culture are disappearing. Faced with watching their heritage fade away, some Brooklyn residents are using language, athletic, and social programs as modern methods of preserving their heritage and attracting young Italian Americans back to the neighborhoods their parents left.

"First-generation Italian Americans struggled and they succeeded in order to survive. That time is gone," says Brooklyn resident G. Jack Spatola, chairman of the Federation of Italian-American Organizations in Brooklyn, which represents 44 local associations. "A new generation has been brought up, an American generation that is proud of its Italian heritage but wants more than a few tables and decks of cards to be motivated to come together and share their common roots."

The Neighborhood

Things have changed considerably since the days when 18th Avenue between 65th and 75th Streets was an Italian "enclave" where newcomers could speak Italian to shop and socialize. Today, more recent Chinese and Russian immigrants are buying the businesses and houses that once belonged to Italians.

In the early 1980s, there were more than 600,000 Italian Americans in Brooklyn, according to research by sociologist Jerome Krase, a professor at Brooklyn College of the City University of New York. Less than 200,000 remain, according to the 2000 U.S. Census. Rising real estate costs coupled

with the desire for better schools and a less urban lifestyle have led second-generation Italian Americans to relocate to Staten Island, New Jersey and Long Island, New York.

As has already happened on Mulberry Street in Manhattan, this part of New York City is losing much of its Italian cultural identity. Although Brooklyn still has a number of pasticcerie where one can smell and taste centuries of culinary tradition, the neighborhood is changing. In the streets, the sight of elderly men wearing tailored topcoats, cuffed trousers, and coppolas—traditional Sicilian floppy berets with short visors—reinforces the awareness that a way of life is fading away.

"People in a sense, they're nostalgic," said Brooklyn resident Jim Grundy, an employee of the Federation. "They see the change and they wish it could always stay the same, but it never is that way of course."

On 18th Avenue, 86th Street and in downtown Brooklyn near the port, there are many clubs of paesani—immigrants born in the same city, town, or village—such as the Society of the Citizens of Pozzallo, and the Sciacca, Vizzini, Militello and Palermo. Membership in these clubs is dwindling.

Emanuele Tumino, a retired carpenter who has lived in Brooklyn for nearly 45 years, spends his days talking of the old days, drinking coffee and playing cards at the Societá Figli di Ragusa on 18th Avenue, a social club for immigrants born in the Sicilian town of Ragusa. "In those times, there was nothing in Italy, otherwise would we ever have come to America?" he said in January, explaining both the impetus that drove him to the United States and his longing for the old country's way of life.

"The immigrants, mostly from the South and from Sicily, were poor and unskilled and had a real need for the assistance and the comfort of the paesani societies, which also helped them maintain a feeling of closeness to home," explained Bay Ridge resident Frank Susino.

But despite their once-vital role, many of these social clubs are losing membership, acknowledged Salvatore Fronterré, director of the Patronato Ital-Uil, a Brooklyn office funded by the Italian government that helps first-generation Italian Americans with bureaucratic problems and pensions. "Many clubs are closing down and nothing can really be done to stop history from taking its course," he said.

Saint Dominic's Roman Catholic Church on 20th Avenue in Bensonhurst is one of the very few churches still offering daily masses in Italian. Although Sunday services are full, Father Ellis Tommaseo predicts that won't last much longer. "I came to the U.S. less than one year ago; people were so happy and excited to hear that a priest would be assigned here from Italy," he said in January. "I found a very warm environment, but we are already fewer than we were when I got here. In less than 15 years, there will be nobody left."

Creating a Change

Father Tommaseo strongly believes that language is the key to preserving cultural heritage and, outside the church, has joined the Federation of Italian-American Organizations of Brooklyn language program. He teaches today's Italian to adults who know only old dialects and children who want to connect with their heritage.

Similarly, Federation members are working to attract young Italian Americans now scattered across New York City back to traditionally Italian communities.

"The community is concerned because the young people are not staying," said Grundy. "They're moving out to the suburbs and things like that."

Spatola says the disappearance of Brooklyn's Italian soul can be avoided only if the Italians remaining in the area unite to invest in leisure and cultural centers. Therefore, paesani social clubs could be replaced by Italian-American community centers offering athletic and leisure facilities, language and cooking classes, libraries, art galleries and movie screening spaces.

In May, the Federation was in the final negotiations to purchase a property in Bensonhurst for the area's first such Italian-American community center. An estimated $6 million is needed to build the center, much of which could come from the New York City government, said Grundy, the Federation's project coordinator.

The Federation plans to open a two-story structure and gradually add two more stories, creating a full-fledged community center with gymnasium, swimming pool, community meeting center and classrooms, Grundy said. Eventually, the center would house all of the disparate youth outreach, language, and soccer programs now offered by the Federation all over Brooklyn.

Such programs can also provide support to the children of Italian immigrants. Born in Brooklyn to Sicilian parents, Salvina Barresi, 23, often feels trapped between the American drive to do what is best for the individual and the Italian pressure to do what is best for the family. She still cannot answer whether she is Italian, American, or both. "During my last trip to Italy, I was Sicilian in Rome, American in Sicily and Sicilian again in New York," she said.

Salvina's mother, Giovanna, said she considers herself an Italian living in America. Many immigrants feel similarly, but in at least one borough, some are carving out a place where their children can have the best of both worlds.

Critical Thinking

1. Explain the reasons why second-generation Italian Americans are moving away from Brooklyn.
2. What is a "paesani society" and what role do they play for the average immigrant?

From *Ambassador*, vol. 18, no. 2, Summer 2006, pp. 11–13. Copyright © 2006 by National Italian American Foundation. Reprinted by permission.

In Armenian Enclave, Turkish Deal Arouses Suspicion

Ethnic Leaders in Glendale, Calif., See Detente Announcement as a Ploy on Day Commemorating 1915 Killings

Nicholas Casey

Glendale, Calif.—Turkey and Armenia may be about to embark on a historic diplomatic thaw, but in the large community of Armenian expatriates here, distrust remains high.

"There's been a lot of disappointment," said Andrew Kzirian, executive director of the Armenian National Committee's Western region, speaking from his office here.

The two nations' announcement on Thursday that they agreed on a framework for restoring relations came just ahead of the annual April 24 commemoration of the 1915 killing of Armenians at the hand of the Ottoman Turks, an event many refer to as a genocide. On Friday, hundreds gathered for a religious gathering at a park in nearby Montebello, a prelude to larger protests planned for the evening in Los Angeles.

Mr. Kzirian sees the latest development not so much as a detente between the countries, but as another public-relations effort by the Turks to deflect attention from the killings. "Any politico would see that [the statement] was directly designed to push back recognition of the Armenian genocide," he said.

This Los Angeles suburb is home to one of America's most robust Armenian diaspora communities, with 80,000 to 100,000 ethnic Armenians making up about a third of the population. Community leaders estimate 500,000 ethnic Armenians dwell in California, many of them and their forbears drawn here by the dry landscape's likeness to the Middle East.

Many residents are descendants of expatriates who fled the Ottoman Empire after the 1915 killing and deportation of some 1.5 million ethnic Armenians. The massacre—and Turkey's insistence that it was a consequence of World War I rather than a deliberate policy—offer a common reference point for a heterogeneous community of Armenians who trace their roots from Lebanon to the former Soviet Union. On Friday, some stores closed here for the annual memorial of the killings.

Many residents of the area—including Rep. Adam Schiff, their voice in Congress—are pushing in Washington for the adoption of a nonbinding resolution, introduced in 2007, that characterizes the event as genocide. Glendale is also watching Yerevan, the Armenian capital, as it negotiates with Turkey to reopen its borders with the country. That could bring added wealth to Armenia, where many send remittances to family members.

At the Armenian cafe Urartu off Broadway, Appo Jabarian scans his email inbox for news of what he dubs the recent "secret agreement." The 51-year-old managing editor of U.S.A. Armenian Life Magazine said he has been placing calls to journalists abroad to learn more about developments between Turkey and Armenia.

For Mr. Jabarian, who said more than 84 members of his family were lost in the slaughter, "Turkey is always trying to shortchange the Armenians." He is currently mulling the angle of an editorial for next week's magazine that will address the agreement.

For Vache Thomassian, 24, the timing of Turkey's announcement, falling a day before the commemoration, is "some sort of ploy." The chairman of the Armenian Youth Federation's Western region said the Turkish government has no sincere intention of reconciling with his people, and is simply "trying to take our attention from the April 24 commemoration."

On Friday, Mr. Thomassian prepared for a protest at the Turkish consulate in Los Angeles that day, an event he said was attended by some 10,000 people last year. Mr. Thomassian, who believes two of his great-grandparents were killed by the Turks, said the Ankara government is involved in an effort to "reverse history" by denying the crimes ever occurred. Still, he said, he counts many Turkish people among his friends and spent a recent summer at the Armenian town of Gyumri, near the Turkish border.

Critical Thinking

1. Explain why many American Armenians are pushing for official U.S. recognition of the 1915 killing of Armenians at the hands of Ottoman Turks?
2. Do you believe official recognition of the 1915 killings will go far in healing the wounds that have festered over the last 85 years?

From *The Wall Street Journal*, April 25–26, 2009. Copyright © 2009 by Dow Jones & Company, Inc. Reprinted by permission via Rightslink.

The Hotel Africa

A growing number of Africans are arriving in the United States in search of a better life. But even as these immigrants learn to negotiate a complex new culture, they cannot forget the beloved and blighted lands that sent them forth, yet call them back.

G. PASCAL ZACHARY

I dread phone calls from Africa.

A sister is having a baby, her fifth, and wants us to send cash before the birth. An aunt calls on Christmas Day, hoping to tap our holiday spirit. Can't we pay for human traffickers to sneak her into the United States? The price is "only" $5,000, which strikes me as suspiciously low. My father-in-law rings just long enough to ask for a return call. Another aunt calls to announce that, tired of waiting for us to send money, she's changed her name from Patience to Joy. She really has. Then there is the distant relative phoning for the first time, asking us to pay his rent, his children's school fees, anything.

These people telephone because my wife, Chizo, is an African living in America. To be precise, Chizo is a Nigerian living in northern California. The telephoners are Nigerians too. They don't know California from the Carolinas, but they are poor, needy, and, by comparison with Chizo, in dire straits. They want her help, and usually help means sending cash. Chizo is a hair braider, working long hours for low pay and earning nothing when there are no heads to braid. Her mother and father live in Nigeria's second-largest city, where they can afford to rent only a small, windowless room with no running water, bathroom, or kitchen. Chizo regularly sends money to her parents, her six siblings, and her favorite aunts. She also supports a daughter in Togo, whom we are preparing to bring to America.

No matter how much money Chizo sends, her African relatives are never satisfied, and she feels that her obligations to them remain unmet. She is haunted by Africa, haunted by requests for money and her great distance from the motherland. From all of 8,000 miles away, she misses Africa, and the ache in her heart is not diminished by her support of family members.

When Chizo came to California three years ago, she joined an estimated one million African immigrants living in the United States, many of whom have come in recent years because of changes in U.S. immigration laws. Before 1980, African immigrants overwhelmingly moved to Europe, in part because its former colonial powers left more doors open. That year,

Congress made it easier to enter the United States as a refugee, and in 1990 it created visa "lotteries" for high school graduates from nations historically underrepresented in the United States, such as Ghana and Nigeria. "This lottery," notes Salih Omar Eissa, a child of Sudanese parents who has studied immigration law, "quickly became the primary method by which Africans immigrated" to the United States.

As a result of these changes, the African-born population has boomed. More than half of the sub-Saharan, or black, Africans living in the United States today have arrived since 1990. Hailing from Nigeria, my wife is part of the largest single African contingent. More immigrants—an estimated 150,000—have come to the United States from Nigeria than from any other sub-Saharan country. Newcomers from Ghana rank second, Ethiopians third, Liberians fourth, Somalis and Kenyans fifth and sixth. Though these numbers reflect both legal and illegal immigration, they seem to undercount Africans in the United States. No matter what the actual number is, Africans are a tiny part, a mere 2.8 percent, of the foreign-born population legally in the United States, according to the U.S. Census Bureau.

Yet the significance of these new African immigrants eclipses their relatively small number, for it highlights the enormous changes in American society over the past 40 years while reminding us that for centuries Africans came to this country in chains. "More Africans Enter U.S. Than in Days of Slavery," *The New York Times* headlined a front-page article last year. Because of the central role of slavery in American history and the still-vexing problem of black-white relations, African immigrants are worth watching.

To be sure, generalizing about Africans is tricky. Africa south of the Sahara is highly diverse. The term "African" is a construction open to gross misunderstanding. (George W. Bush, during his first presidential campaign, compared Africa to Mexico, as if both were countries.) Travel within sub-Saharan Africa is frequently difficult, and people from different parts of the region often do not display any immediate solidarity, racial or otherwise. I was reminded of Africa's great diversity when I attended a private party recently at an Oakland nightclub, not far from where Chizo and I live. The guests were mainly from Cameroon and spoke French. In the same club, in the next room, a group of Ethiopians were also partying. The two groups ate different foods, listened to different music, dressed differently, danced differently—and carried on separately. No wonder. Paris and Moscow are much closer to each other than Lagos and Addis Ababa.

Years abroad haven't diminished Ike Nwadeyi's sense of identity. "You can't put a Nigerian in your pocket," he says.

Despite such differences and a tendency to stick close to their own, African immigrants in the United States have much in common. They tend to be highly educated and to come from relatively privileged backgrounds. More than four in 10 hold university degrees; an astonishing 98 percent reportedly have completed high school. One-third of African women and 38 percent of African men hold professional and managerial jobs. Because of their education and because Africans generally live in the largest American cities, where wages tend to be highest, both sexes earn about 20 percent more than the median pay of all American workers. African immigrants are younger than other immigrants. Only 2.6 percent are over 65, the lowest percentage of any immigrant group; more than 70 percent are between 25 and 54.

I talk with Africans regularly in my frequent visits to Africa and in the United States, and so I meet them in Africa dreaming about coming to America and meet them in America dreaming of returning to or saving their motherland. The principal challenge for recently arrived Africans in America is not succeeding in the United States—they are—but realizing their desire to maintain a dynamic relationship with Africa. Their attachment to the motherland arises at least partly from a belief that the enormous outflow of talent from Africa, however understandable given the hardships of life there, poses a great developmental handicap. "Africans are doing incredible things in the U.S.," says Derrick Ashong, a Ghanaian-born Harvard graduate who lives in New York City and is building an African media company. "Would our countries be underdeveloped if our energies were applied back home?" So long as Africa suffers under the burden of poverty and inequity, war and disease, Ashong's question is both a challenge and a reproach to Africans in America.

Ike Nwadeyi is a stickler for manners. He wants his daughter to greet him each day with the words, "Good morning, sir." When she lived in America with him, she told him, "Hi, Daddy." He angrily replied, "You don't tell me, 'Hi, Daddy.'"

This breakfast banter explains why Nwadeyi's seven-year-old daughter is growing up in Nigeria while he works in Washington,

D.C., and obtains his American citizenship. "America will spoil my daughter," he insists. "Children have no manners here. By growing up in Nigeria, she'll know what I mean by respect."

Nwadeyi's daughter lives with his wife, a geologist working for Chevron in oil-rich Nigeria. Her job is too well paying and too interesting for her to abandon. So she stays in Nigeria, while Nwadeyi lives in the United States and drives a taxi. "There's no enjoyment in this country," he says. "Nothing. This country has no life." But working in America affords him the chance to visit Nigeria for long stretches when he wishes. His presence in the United States and his American citizenship give his family an insurance policy against the instability that always threatens Nigeria, but he is typical of the many Africans who leave their young children behind in Africa so they can be raised properly.

Before Nwadeyi came to the United States, he lived in Thessalonica, where he studied business at a Greek university. His many years in Europe and the United States, however, have not diminished his sense of identity. "You can't hide a Nigerian," he says. "We are loud. It is natural. You can't put a Nigerian in your pocket."

Nwadeyi's straddle of two worlds is typical of recent African immigrants. "Africans represent a new type of immigrant," writes Sylviane A. Diouf, a scholar of African migration who is a researcher at the Schomburg Center for Research in Black Culture in New York City. "They are transnationals, people who choose to maintain their separateness in the host country and retain tight links to their community of origin." Drawing strength from migration, Diouf observes, "they generally view their American experience as transitory, the most effective way to construct a better future at home for themselves and their relatives."

Of course, Diouf's description of Africans might be applied to many immigrant groups. Filipinos, Koreans, Central Americans, Mexicans, Russians, Chinese, and Indians maintain strong ties to their countries of origin. What sets Africans apart is the undeniable marginalization of their homeland. Sub-Saharan Africa is the only major region of the world that has grown poorer over the past several decades and that has seen a dramatic decline in the job market for highly skilled workers. The development arcs of Mexico, China, India, South Korea, and most other countries exporting people to the United States are traveling in the opposite direction. These countries are increasingly sophisticated, wealthy, and accommodative of the needs of talented people. Indeed, in some parts of India and China and elsewhere, job opportunities are now far better than in the United States.

Only in black Africa, among the world's regions, have conditions deteriorated, and not just for the elite. Because of the plights of their home countries, Africans are forced to create a distinctive relationship with both America and Africa. In short, no other immigrant group carries anything like the baggage that Africans carry—a homeland that is a source of embarrassment but also offers an unparalleled opportunity to give back.

Africans feel that the quickest route to becoming "superempowered" individuals capable of giving back to the motherland is success in the United States. The pull of their homeland paradoxically drives them to greater heights in America. "They are fast learning how to live the American dream," wrote Joseph Takougang, a professor of African history at the University of Cincinnati, in a recent survey. "They are becoming involved in their communities, starting small businesses, and participating in local politics."

As people of African origin have gained visibility in America in recent years, their sometimes-troubled relations with African Americans have belied Americans' monolithic views of race. Many white Americans as well as African Americans have assumed that African immigrants are natural allies of African Americans, and are surprised when tensions surface.

One figure who has put the spotlight on Africa is Illinois senator Barack Obama, son of a Kenyan. In his 2004 senatorial campaign, he had to establish his "blackness" in the eyes of the African-American electorate because he had been raised by a white mother. Even his Africanness was considered attenuated. In his memoir, *Dreams From My Father: A Story of Race and Inheritance (1995),* Obama symbolically reclaims his Africanness by traveling to Kenya. None of these gymnastics in the establishment of identity makes sense in an African context. In the United States, Obama's carefully constructed identity is critical to his public career.

The friction between African immigrants and African Americans is perhaps starkest in applications of affirmative action policies. Often, hiring preferences work to the advantage of people who have just arrived in the United States. Because many African immigrants are highly educated, they can compete for jobs that might otherwise to go to African Americans. Tensions between the two groups are exacerbated by African insensitivity. "Too many Africans are dismissive of African Americans in a general way," says Victor Mallet, a Ghanaian who works with black small-business owners in Philadelphia. He notes that Africans fear being lumped together with African Americans as second-class citizens. They also harbor some of the same stereotypes of African Americans held by many whites.

To be sure, Africans in America experience racism and outrages, such as the death of Amadou Diallo, an unarmed New York street vendor from Guinea who was shot by police in 1999. Events such as the Diallo killing promote a common understanding of what it means to be black in America by reminding Africans that black people still face sometimes-fatal racial prejudice. Mallet, who grew up in Africa with a white mother and a black father, feels obliged to sympathetically hear out African-American objections to mainstream American society. "More Africans need to look past the appealing notion that America is a meritocracy and that there is equal opportunity for all," says Mallet, who first came to the United States to attend the Massachusetts Institute of Technology in the 1990s. "While Africans are right not to hide behind the excuse of racial bias, they also must comprehend the history of African-American exclusion—and how racial awareness continues to distort American life today."

The core division between Africans and African Americans is rooted in radically different notions of identity, and is therefore unlikely to vanish anytime soon. For Africans, ethnic identification—what was once known as tribe—trumps race. When my wife first came to California, she did not view black people as natural allies, but sought help from West Africans, people reared close to her home turf. She visited braiding shops, looking for casual work and new friends, and joined a shop managed by two Cameroonian women and staffed by braiders from Senegal and Gabon. The braiders became Chizo's best friends and the shop a virtual Africa that helped ease her transition to a new and alien country.

My wife is the only Nigerian in the braiding shop, but she found many nearby, even members of her own ethnic group, the Igbo. A local grocery story, run by an Igbo man, sells her favorite foods from home: *gari* (cassava), dried fish, fresh yams, plantains, and an exotic spice called *ugba*. A community of Igbo Catholics holds a monthly Mass in her native language. In our living room, she hangs a Nigerian flag (and the flags of the United States and Ghana, where she and I first met).

Too great an attachment to one's community of origin can encourage provincial thinking, of course. Chizo's own fellow Igbos are quite clannish, and of the scores I have met in America, not one is married to a non-Igbo, and certainly not a white American. To the Igbos I meet, my wife is somewhat suspect. They question why she would marry, not outside her race, but outside her ethnic group. Possessing pride born partly from their communal suffering during the Biafran war, Igbos have the kind of ethnic solidarity found in Armenian, Jewish, and Kosovar communities.

Africans have no monopoly on ethnic narcissism. More striking, actually, is their openness to wide currents and their willingness to draw on materials not indigenous to Africa. A young African writer, Taiye Tuakli-Wosornu, a Yale graduate living in New York, has coined the term "Afropolitan" to highlight the benefits of blending a cosmopolitan outlook with continuing participation in one's African community. "Perhaps what most typifies the Afropolitan consciousness is this . . . effort to understand what is ailing Africa alongside the desire to honor what is uniquely wonderful," Tuakli-Wosornu writes.

Economic, social, and technological forces are driving Africans in America toward playing a larger role in their home countries.

The Afropolitans must succeed in America, but in a manner that pushes them toward Africa, not away from it. The emergence of a new generation of African writers, who succeed first in the United States and then gain an audience in Africa, illustrates this pattern. In his short-story collection *The Prophet of Zongo Street* (2005), Mohammed Naseehu Ali, who lives in Brooklyn and has spent 17 years in the United States since arriving at the age of 18 to attend university, rescues the rich folk stories of his Hausa forebears in Ghana and Nigeria. Ensconced in America, by day he works at the database company Lexis-Nexis, and at night he emerges in Brooklyn as a troubadour of the wisdom of his ancestors. "I have great hope for Africa," he says.

Like a number of African writers, Ali published first in the United States and is preoccupied with the African experience, home and away. Uzodinma Iweala, who last year published a celebrated short novel, *Beasts of No Nation,* also draws on African sources in his tale about child soldiers. Shuttling between D.C. and Lagos, he is now building a literary reputation in Nigeria on the strength of his American success. "You can't ever escape being a Nigerian," he told an interviewer in the United States recently, adding:

> If you try to say, 'No, I am not Nigerian,' people say, 'What are you talking about? I know where your father is from. I know the village. There is no way that you can tell me you are not Nigerian.' In fact, if you don't come back and maintain the ties, people start asking questions. It's not as if when you leave you are looked down upon for leaving your country. Most Nigerians that you speak to here expect to return to Nigeria at some point in time—whether or not that will actually happen is not important. It's the mentality.

In the past, many new immigrants to America said they would maintain tight links to their countries of origin, but over time they—and their children and grandchildren—have not. Fidelity to Africa, so intensely felt by most immigrants, may also fade over time. "Are they [African immigrants] going to melt into the African-American population?" historian Eric Foner asked in an article in *The New York Times* last year. "Most likely yes."

The opposite could well happen. Economic, social, and technological forces are driving Africans in America toward playing a larger role in their home countries in the years ahead. The spread of cell phones in Africa and the rise of Internet telephony in the United States make calling back to Africa—once an expensive and tedious task often requiring many connection attempts—inexpensive and easy. Flights to all parts of sub-Saharan Africa, while not cheap, are more frequent than ever. And private companies operating in Africa are beginning to see the pool of skilled Africans working in the United States as a source of managerial and professional talent. Though Africa's brain drain continues, a small but significant number of people are returning to the continent to take jobs or start businesses.

Demographic forces are at play too. As the first big wave of African immigrants from the 1980s approaches retirement, some look homeward. No statistics are kept on Africans who move back for good. But some members of all immigrant groups do return home and always have, even before the days of easy travel, telephone calls, and money transfers. Roughly half of all Italian immigrants to the United States before World War I returned home permanently. Today, because documentation is essential for crossing borders, legal immigrants must first acquire a green card and then, usually, a U.S. passport. Once in possession of papers, an African who leaves the United States invariably will come back to it, if only to work. As they age, some Africans are retiring to their home countries, funding an African lifestyle with American dollars. So many Ghanaians are repatriating, for instance, that a Texas homebuilder has an operation in Ghana that has constructed hundreds of houses for returnees.

Africans commonly travel back and forth, motivated as much by opportunity and nostalgia as by a kind of survivor's guilt. My wife often expresses nagging doubts about the fairness of living affluently in America while her family lives in deprivation back home. "Why did I escape the poverty of Africa," she asks. "What kind of God chooses paradise for me and misery for my loved ones?"

The cries of Africans left behind are difficult to drown out, and they shape the aspirations of Africans in America. Consider the choices made by my friend Guy Kamgaing, an engineer from Cameroon who arrived in the United States to attend graduate school 11 years ago. Now 35, he has built a successful career in Los Angeles in the burgeoning field of mobile telephony. He holds a green card, is married (to another Cameroonian, an accountant), and has two children. He is living, in short, the American dream, and the corruption and difficulty of doing business in Cameroon make him reluctant to return full time. Yet Kamgaing maintains a big African dream. He is renovating a hotel in the Cameroon port city of Douala that his father, now 72 and still living in the city, built and ran through good times and bad. The 160-room hotel is a relic—sprawling, decrepit, a nuisance, and, until recently, shuttered.

One morning, I met Kamgaing on the roof of the hotel. He has opened a café there, and the waiter served us café au lait and croissants. I could see for miles: the Atlantic Ocean, the forests ringing the city, the crowded streets. It was the rainy season, the air was heavy, and I could feel the two of us moving back in time, to 40 years ago, soon after independence, when Cameroon was wealthy thanks to abundant timber, oil, and agricultural production; it was home to tens of thousands of French people; and the future looked bright. The hotel, called the Beausejour Mirabel, is a means by which Kamgaing can honor his father and revive his country.

The task is difficult. He has renovated the lobby and is repairing rooms floor by floor. Soon he will reopen the long-empty pool on the roof. He knows that the project is a drain, robbing him of capital he might invest in his American life, but he finds it irresistible. "Sometimes when I think about this hotel, it brings tears to my eyes," he says. "I am resurrecting my father's pride and joy." The hotel even boasts wireless Internet access, which not even its poshest competitors in Douala offer. Kamgaing wants to establish a mid-priced hotel, but the odds are against him because the city's few foreign visitors usually want luxury, not nostalgia and value.

The cries of Africans left behind are difficult to drown out, and they shape the aspirations of Africans in America.

Back in northern California recently, Kamgaing visited my house for dinner. While he spooned up my wife's goat meat and pepper soup, he admitted that perhaps he has gone slightly mad in reviving the old hotel. But he's proving that he hasn't forsaken the land of his birth.

My wife has yet to find her Hotel Africa. I was reminded of the delicacy of her search one night not long ago, when she and I dined with a Jewish friend and his father, approaching 85, who was visiting from Long Island. As a child living near the home of Anne Frank in Amsterdam, the father had been snatched by the Nazis and sent to a death camp. Chizo told him that his ordeal and that of the Jewish people in Europe reminded her of the suffering of her own people, the Igbo, who tried to secede from Nigeria some 35 years ago and form their own nation, Biafra. Her older brother and sister, then infants, died during the war that followed—along with a million other Nigerians. "Every people suffer," she said. The old survivor smiled.

The persistence of suffering in Africa may bind African immigrants to their homeland in unexpected ways. Perhaps Africans will never forget, and will be defined by memory, just as Jews have been.

Critical Thinking

1. Why do many African immigrants in the United States feel guilty about their homeland?

2. Can you explain why there is a tenseness between native-born African Americans and their African immigrant counterparts?

G. Pascal Zachary, a former foreign correspondent for *The Wall Street Journal,* often writes on African affairs. His books include *The Diversity Advantage: Multicultural Identity in the New World Economy* (2003), and he is currently working on a memoir of his marriage to an African.

Reprinted with permission from *The Wilson Quarterly,* Summer 2006, pp. 48–55. Copyright © 2006 by G. Pascal Zachary. Reprinted by permission.

UNIT 2

The Legal Construction of Diversity and Disparity

Unit Selections

7. **Racial Restrictions in the Law of Citizenship,** Ian F. Haney López
8. **Dred Scott v. Sandford,** *Supreme Court of the United States,* 1856
9. **"There's No One as Irish as Barack O'Bama": The Policy and Politics of American Multiracialism,** Jennifer Hochschild and Vesia Mae Weaver
10. **Brown et al. v. Board of Education of Topeka et al.,** from *U.S. Reports,* 1954
11. **'Bakke' Set a New Path to Diversity for Colleges,** Peter Schmidt
12. **Shaare Tefila Congregation v. Cobb** and **Saint Francis College v. Al-Khazraji,** from U.S Reports 1987
13. **Historical Discrimination in Immigration Laws,** from *The Tarnished Golden Door,* September, 1980
14. **The Diversity Visa Lottery—A Cycle of Unintended Consequences in United States Immigration Policy,** Anna O. Law

Learning Objectives

- What signs have you seen of an increase in racist, anti-Semitic, anti-immigrant, and anti-minority group acts that recent studies apparently confirm? Does anti-Catholicism still exist?

- What explains the fact that large population studies confirm that in the areas of ethnic, racial, and religious differences, Americans are more tolerant than ever?

- Why do teenagers commit 80 percent of all bias-related acts?

- What problems does conflict in ethnic and race relations pose for corporate and governmental institutions?

- What media images of race and ethnicity are dominant?

Student Website
www.mhhe.com/cls

Internet References

U.S. Census Bureau
www.census.gov
U.S. Supreme Court Reports
http://bulk.resource.org/courts.gov/c/US/

The increase in racial violence and hatred on campuses across the country is manifested in acts ranging from hateful speech to physical violence. Strategies for dealing with this problem on a campus include increased awareness through mandatory ethnic studies, the empowerment of targets of violence, and fostering social and cultural interaction in festivals, folk-arts fairs, and literary and political forums. Systematic knowledge about ethnic groups has not been a central scholarly concern. In fact, mainstream literary, humanistic, and historical disciplines have only recently begun to displace sociological attention to the pathologies of urban ethnicity as the primary contact, and source of information and interpretation of ethnic traditions. The historic role that voluntary groups have played in the reduction of bias and bigotry also needs to be revalued and revitalized. Voluntary associations can take part in a host of state and local initiatives to improve inter-group relations. Schools and parents can help children understand commonalities and differences among and within ethnic traditions and groups. The incorporation of everyday experiences of families and a formal pedagogy rooted in accurate and locally relevant resources are essential building blocks for understanding diversity.

The embedded interpretive categories and models which frame the discussion and analysis of race and ethnic relations and the enormity of the educational effort that is required as we attempt to move beyond the ethnocentrism and racism which bred hatred and destructive relationships between persons and communities is revealed in a variety of ways. Philosophic reflection on the epistemological issues associated with explaining human variety is rarely invited. However, it is precisely at this intersection of social philosophy and science that the crucial breakthroughs in understanding are likely to appear. The continual mismeasures of intelligence and misreading of meaning indicate the long-term need for critical reformulation of the very idea of race.

The Supreme Court's attempt to redress the complex relationship between our constitutional system and the diverse society it governs is mediated by a political leadership that has not persistently sought equal justice under the law for all persons.

Beginning with the earliest legislation, from the very outset, America put racial restriction on citizenship. Our efforts regarding immigration from the founding fathers to the most recent searchers for reform statutes at both the state and national levels reveal other dimensions of an ambiguous legacy related to diversity and the dynamics of economic growth. Our legal framework mirrors political forces and social attitudes that drive the definition of citizenship and strain the bonds of ethnic identity and participation of ethnic groups in America.

The legacies of African slavery, racial segregation, and ethnic discrimination established by the Constitution and subsequent Court doctrines are traced in the following summaries of U.S. Supreme Court opinions. In *Dred Scott v. Sandford* (1856), the Supreme Court addressed the constitutional status of an African held in bondage who had been moved to a state that prohibited slavery. U.S. Supreme Court chief justice Roger B. Taney attempted to resolve the increasingly divisive issue of slavery by declaring that the Negro African race whether free or

© Scott T. Baxter/Getty Images

slave was not intended to be included under the word citizens in the Constitution, and can therefore claim none of the rights and privileges that instrument provides for and secures to citizens of the United States.

In *Plessy v. Ferguson* (1896), the Supreme Court upheld the constitutionality of "Jim Crow" laws that segregated public facilities on the basis of an individual's racial ancestry. The Court reasoned that this "separate but equal" segregation did not violate any rights guaranteed by the U.S. Constitution, nor did it stamp the colored race with a badge of inferiority. Instead, the Court argued that if "this be so, it is not by reason of anything found in the act but solely because the colored race chooses to put that construction upon it." In contrast, Justice John M. Harlans vigorous dissent from the Court's Plessy opinion contends that "our Constitution is colorblind, and neither knows nor tolerates classes among citizens." The history of the Court's attention to citizenship provides a view of a culturally embedded character of color consciousness and the strict textual dependence of the justices who interpreted the Constitution. Another perspective, however, emerges from the congressional debate that occurred when a civil rights law ensuring equal protection and voting rights was passed shortly after the Civil War. That legislative history is cited extensively in Shaare Tefila/Al-khazraji (1987). The expansive view of protection for all ethnic groups cited in these decisions and the origin of these views in congressional intention voiced by elected legislators were indications of the Court's new directions. The Court's dependence on statutes rather than on the exercise of constitutional authority as the judiciary, and thus as a policy maker and initiator, appeared to be waning. Moreover, the Court, under the influence of a colorblind doctrine, seemed ready to challenge policies that significantly rely on race and ethnicity, thus changing the landscape as well as the discussion of race and ethnicity, inviting all of us to reexamine both the intentions and outcomes of all legislation in this field. This was not always the case.

In *Brown et al. v. Board of Education of Topeka et al.* (1954), the Supreme Court began the ambitious project of dismantling state-supported racial segregation. In Brown a unanimous Court overturned *Plessy v. Ferguson,* arguing that in the field of public education the doctrine of separate but equal has no place, because separate educational facilities are inherently unequal. However, this era of civil rights consensus embodied in the landmark actions of the Supreme Court has been challenged by contemporary plaintiffs who have turned to the Court for clarification regarding specific cases related to the significance of race and ethnic criteria in public affairs. Moreover, the lack of popular support for the implementation of policies and the judicial leadership of those policies is a political and electoral constraint. Popular concern was played out in referenda suggesting that the country may well face tension and acrimony between the will of the people in particular states and the rule and supremacy of national law. The mediation between law and popular expression, the political nexus of state and federal legitimacy, will no doubt be challenged by these contentions, and require national and community-based leadership prepared to clarify the purposes and goals of a multi-ethnic civil society. Revisiting the legislative history of the civil rights era can shed new light on our national public understanding of the thrust of that period. By reviewing the congressional deliberation in support of the Civil Rights Act and its goal of equal protection and equality before the law, and then juxtaposing the contemporary legal arguments and current politics of equal protection, the reader will discover a complex set of considerations. A careful analysis of the moral foundations of our legal system and its expectations and attention to the practical consequence of defining and achieving an epoch of equality and the limits of legal remedies, will emerge from these reconsiderations, and the attendant search for new remedies and assurance of fairness and nonexclusionary practices.

Racial Restrictions in the Law of Citizenship

Ian F. Haney López

The racial composition of the U.S. citizenry reflects in part the accident of world migration patterns. More than this, however, it reflects the conscious design of U.S. immigration and naturalization laws.

Federal law restricted immigration to this country on the basis of race for nearly one hundred years, roughly from the Chinese exclusion laws of the 1880s until the end of the national origin quotas in 1965.[1] The history of this discrimination can briefly be traced. Nativist sentiment against Irish and German Catholics on the East Coast and against Chinese and Mexicans on the West Coast, which had been doused by the Civil War, reignited during the economic slump of the 1870s. Though most of the nativist efforts failed to gain congressional sanction, Congress in 1882 passed the Chinese Exclusion Act, which suspended the immigration of Chinese laborers for ten years.[2] The Act was expanded to exclude all Chinese in 1884, and was eventually implemented indefinitely.[3] In 1917, Congress created "an Asiatic barred zone," excluding all persons from Asia.[4] During this same period, the Senate passed a bill to exclude "all members of the African or black race." This effort was defeated in the House only after intensive lobbying by the NAACP.[5] Efforts to exclude the supposedly racially undesirable southern and eastern Europeans were more successful. In 1921, Congress established a temporary quota system designed "to confine immigration as much as possible to western and northern European stock," making this bar permanent three years later in the National Origin Act of 1924.[6] With the onset of the Depression, attention shifted to Mexican immigrants. Although no law explicitly targeted this group, federal immigration officials began a series of round-ups and mass deportations of people of Mexican descent under the general rubric of a "repatriation campaign." Approximately 500,000 people were forcibly returned to Mexico during the Depression, more than half of them U.S. citizens.[7] This pattern was repeated in the 1950s, when Attorney General Herbert Brownell launched a program to expel Mexicans. This effort, dubbed "Operation Wetback," indiscriminately deported more than one million citizens and noncitizens in 1954 alone.[8]

Racial restrictions on immigration were not significantly dismantled until 1965, when Congress in a major overhaul of immigration law abolished both the national origin system and the Asiatic Barred Zone.[9] Even so, purposeful racial discrimination in immigration law by Congress remains constitutionally permissible, since the case that upheld the Chinese Exclusion Act to this day remains good law.[10] Moreover, arguably racial discrimination in immigration law continues. For example, Congress has enacted special provisions to encourage Irish immigration, while refusing to ameliorate the backlog of would-be immigrants from the Philippines, India, South Korea, China, and Hong Kong, backlogs created in part through a century of racial exclusion.[11] The history of racial discrimination in U.S. immigration law is a long and continuing one.

As discriminatory as the laws of immigration have been, the laws of citizenship betray an even more dismal record of racial exclusion. From this country's inception, the laws regulating who was or could become a citizen were tainted by racial prejudice. Birthright citizenship, the automatic acquisition of citizenship by virtue of birth, was tied to race until 1940. Naturalized citizenship, the acquisition of citizenship by any means other than through birth, was conditioned on race until 1952. Like immigration laws, the laws of birthright citizenship and naturalization shaped the racial character of the United States.

Birthright Citizenship

Most persons acquire citizenship by birth rather than through naturalization. During the 1990s, for example, naturalization will account for only 7.5 percent of the increase in the U.S. citizen population.[12] At the time of the prerequisite cases, the proportion of persons gaining citizenship through naturalization was probably somewhat higher, given the higher ratio of immigrants to total population, but still far smaller than the number of people gaining citizenship by birth. In order to situate the prerequisite laws, therefore, it is useful first to review the history of racial discrimination in the laws of birthright citizenship.

The U.S. Constitution as ratified did not define the citizenry, probably because it was assumed that the English common law rule of *jus soli* would continue.[13] Under *jus soli*, citizenship accrues to "all" born within a nation's jurisdiction. Despite the seeming breadth of this doctrine, the word "all" is qualified because for the first one hundred years and more of this country's history it did not fully encompass racial minorities. This is the import of the *Dred Scott* decision.[14] Scott, an enslaved man, sought to use the federal courts to sue for his freedom.

However, access to the courts was predicated on citizenship. Dismissing his claim, the United States Supreme Court in the person of Chief Justice Roger Taney declared in 1857 that Scott and all other Blacks, free and enslaved, were not and could never be citizens because they were "a subordinate and inferior class of beings." The decision protected the slave-holding South and infuriated much of the North, further dividing a country already fractured around the issues of slavery and the power of the national government. *Dred Scott* was invalidated after the Civil War by the Civil Rights Act of 1866, which declared that "All persons born . . . in the United States and not subject to any foreign power, excluding Indians not taxed, are declared to be citizens of the United States."[15] *Jus soli* subsequently became part of the organic law of the land in the form of the Fourteenth Amendment: "All persons born or naturalized in the United States, and subject to the jurisdiction thereof, are citizens of the United States and of the state wherein they reside."[16]

Despite the broad language of the Fourteenth Amendment— though in keeping with the words of the 1866 act—some racial minorities remained outside the bounds of *jus soli* even after its constitutional enactment. In particular, questions persisted about the citizenship status of children born in the United States to noncitizen parents, and about the status of Native Americans. The Supreme Court did not decide the status of the former until 1898, when it ruled in *U.S. v. Wong Kim Ark* that native-born children of aliens, even those permanently barred by race from acquiring citizenship, were birthright citizens of the United States.[17] On the citizenship of the latter, the Supreme Court answered negatively in 1884, holding in *Elk v. Wilkins* that Native Americans owed allegiance to their tribe and so did not acquire citizenship upon birth.[18] Congress responded by granting Native Americans citizenship in piecemeal fashion, often tribe by tribe. Not until 1924 did Congress pass an act conferring citizenship on all Native Americans in the United States.[19] Even then, however, questions arose regarding the citizenship of those born in the United States after the effective date of the 1924 act. These questions were finally resolved, and *jus soli* fully applied, under the Nationality Act of 1940, which specifically bestowed citizenship on all those born in the United States "to a member of an Indian, Eskimo, Aleutian, or other aboriginal tribe."[20] Thus, the basic law of citizenship, that a person born here is a citizen here, did not include all racial minorities until 1940.

Unfortunately, the impulse to restrict birthright citizenship by race is far from dead in this country. Apparently, California Governor Pete Wilson and many others seek a return to the times when citizenship depended on racial proxies such as immigrant status. Wilson has called for a federal constitutional amendment that would prevent the American-born children of undocumented persons from receiving birthright citizenship.[21] His call has not been ignored: thirteen members of Congress recently sponsored a constitutional amendment that would repeal the existing Citizenship Clause of the Fourteenth Amendment and replace it with a provision that "All persons born in the United States . . . of mothers who are citizens or legal residents of the United States . . . are citizens of the United States."[22] Apparently, such a change is supported by 49 percent of Americans.[23] In addition to explicitly

discriminating against fathers by eliminating their right to confer citizenship through parentage, this proposal implicitly discriminates along racial lines. The effort to deny citizenship to children born here to undocumented immigrants seems to be motivated not by an abstract concern over the political status of the parents, but by racial animosity against Asians and Latinos, those commonly seen as comprising the vast bulk of undocumented migrants. Bill Ong Hing writes, "The discussion of who is and who is not American, who can and cannot become American, goes beyond the technicalities of citizenship and residency requirements; it strikes at the very heart of our nation's long and troubled legacy of race relations.[24] As this troubled legacy reveals, the triumph over racial discrimination in the laws of citizenship and alienage came slowly and only recently. In the campaign for the "control of our borders," we are once again debating the citizenship of the native-born and the merits of *Dred Scott*.[25]

Naturalization

Although the Constitution did not originally define the citizenry, it explicitly gave Congress the authority to establish the criteria for granting citizenship after birth. Article I grants Congress the power "To establish a uniform Rule of Naturalization."[26] From the start, Congress exercised this power in a manner that burdened naturalization laws with racial restrictions that tracked those in the law of birthright citizenship. In 1790, only a few months after ratification of the Constitution, Congress limited naturalization to "any alien, being a free white person who shall have resided within the limits and under the jurisdiction of the United States for a term of two years."[27] This clause mirrored not only the de facto laws of birthright citizenship, but also the racially restrictive naturalization laws of several states. At least three states had previously limited citizenship to "white persons": Virginia in 1779, South Carolina in 1784, and Georgia in 1785.[28] Though there would be many subsequent changes in the requirements for federal naturalization, racial identity endured as a bedrock requirement for the next 162 years. In every naturalization act from 1790 until 1952, Congress included the "white person" prerequisite.[29]

The history of racial prerequisites to naturalization can be divided into two periods of approximately eighty years each. The first period extended from 1790 to 1870, when only Whites were able to naturalize. In the wake of the Civil War, the "white person" restriction on naturalization came under serious attack as part of the effort to expunge *Dred Scott*. Some congressmen, Charles Sumner chief among them, argued that racial barriers to naturalization should be struck altogether. However, racial prejudice against Native Americans and Asians forestalled the complete elimination of the racial prerequisites. During congressional debates, one senator argued against conferring "the rank, privileges, and immunities of citizenship upon the cruel savages who destroyed [Minnesota's] peaceful settlements and massacred the people with circumstances of atrocity too horrible to relate."[30] Another senator wondered "whether this door [of citizenship] shall now be thrown open to the Asiatic population," warning that to do so would spell for the Pacific coast "an end to republican government there, because it is very well ascertained that those people have no appreciation of that form of government; it seems to be obnoxious to their very nature; they seem to be incapable either of understanding or carrying it out."[31] Sentiments such as these ensured that even after the Civil War, bars against Native American and Asian naturalization would continue.[32] Congress opted to maintain the "white person" prerequisite, but to extend the right to naturalize to "persons of African nativity, or African descent."[33] After 1870, Blacks as well as Whites could naturalize, but not others.

During the second period, from 1870 until the last of the prerequisite laws were abolished in 1952, the White-Black dichotomy in American race relations dominated naturalization law. During this period, Whites and Blacks were eligible for citizenship, but others, particularly those from Asia, were not. Indeed, increasing antipathy toward Asians on the West Coast resulted in an explicit disqualification of Chinese persons from naturalization in 1882.[34] The prohibition of Chinese naturalization, the only U.S. law ever to exclude by name a particular nationality from citizenship, was coupled with the ban on Chinese immigration discussed previously. The Supreme Court readily upheld the bar, writing that "Chinese persons not born in this country have never been recognized as citizens of the United States, nor authorized to become such under the naturalization laws."[35] While Blacks were permitted to naturalize beginning in 1870, the Chinese and most "other non-Whites" would have to wait until the 1940s for the right to naturalize.[36]

World War II forced a domestic reconsideration of the racism integral to U.S. naturalization law. In 1935, Hitler's Germany limited citizenship to members of the Aryan race, making Germany the only country other than the United States with a racial restriction on naturalization.[37] The fact of this bad company was not lost on those administering our naturalization laws. "When Earl G. Harrison in 1944 resigned as United States Commissioner of Immigration and Naturalization, he said that the only country in the world, outside the United States, that observes racial discrimination in matters relating to naturalization was Nazi Germany, 'and we all agree that this is not very desirable company.'"[38] Furthermore, the United States was open to charges of hypocrisy for banning from naturalization the nationals of many of its Asian allies. During the war, the United States seemed through some of its laws and social practices to embrace the same racism it was fighting. Both fronts of the war exposed profound inconsistencies between U.S. naturalization law and broader social ideals. These considerations, among others, led Congress to begin a process of piecemeal reform in the laws governing citizenship.

In 1940, Congress opened naturalization to "descendants of races indigenous to the Western Hemisphere."[39] Apparently, this "additional limitation was designed 'to more fully cement' the ties of Pan-Americanism" at a time of impending crisis.[40] In 1943, Congress replaced the prohibition on the naturalization of Chinese persons with a provision explicitly granting them this boon.[41] In 1946, it opened up naturalization to persons from the Philippines and India as well.[42] Thus, at the end of the war, our naturalization law looked like this:

The right to become a naturalized citizen under the provisions of this Act shall extend only to—

1. white persons, persons of African nativity or descent, and persons of races indigenous to the continents of North or South America or adjacent islands and Filipino persons or persons of Filipino descent;
2. persons who possess, either singly or in combination, a preponderance of blood of one or more of the classes specified in clause (1);
3. Chinese persons or persons of Chinese descent; and persons of races indigenous to India; and
4. persons who possess, either singly or in combination, a preponderance of blood of one or more of the classes specified in clause (3) or, either singly or in combination, as much as one-half blood of those classes and some additional blood of one of the classes specified in clause (1).[43]

This incremental retreat from a "Whites only" conception of citizenship made the arbitrariness of U.S. naturalization law increasingly obvious. For example, under the above statute, the right to acquire citizenship depended for some on blood-quantum distinctions based on descent from peoples indigenous to islands adjacent to the Americas. In 1952, Congress moved towards wholesale reform, overhauling the naturalization statute to read simply that "[t]he right of a person to become a naturalized citizen of the United States shall not be denied or abridged because of race or sex or because such person is married."[44] Thus, in 1952, racial bars on naturalization came to an official end.[45]

Notice the mention of gender in the statutory language ending racial restrictions in naturalization. The issue of women and citizenship can only be touched on here, but deserves significant study in its own right.[46] As the language of the 1952 Act implies, eligibility for naturalization once depended on a woman's marital status. Congress in 1855 declared that a foreign woman automatically acquired citizenship upon marriage to a U.S. citizen, or upon the naturalization of her alien husband.[47] This provision built upon the supposition that a woman's social and political status flowed from her husband. As an 1895 treatise on naturalization put it, "A woman partakes of her husband's nationality; her nationality is merged in that of her husband; her political status follows that of her husband."[48] A wife's acquisition of citizenship, however, remained subject to her individual qualification for naturalization—that is, on whether she was a "white person."[49] Thus, the Supreme Court held in 1868 that only "white women" could gain citizenship by marrying a citizen.[50] Racial restrictions further complicated matters for noncitizen women in that naturalization was denied to those married to a man racially ineligible for citizenship, irrespective of the woman's own qualifications, racial or otherwise.[51] The automatic naturalization of a woman upon her marriage to a citizen or upon the naturalization of her husband ended in 1922.[52]

The citizenship of American-born women was also affected by the interplay of gender and racial restrictions. Even though under English common law a woman's nationality was unaffected by marriage, many courts in this country stripped women who married noncitizens of their U.S. citizenship.[53] Congress

23

recognized and mandated this practice in 1907, legislating that an American woman's marriage to an alien terminated her citizenship.[54] Under considerable pressure, Congress partially repealed this act in 1922.[55] However, the 1922 act continued to require the expatriation of any woman who married a foreigner racially barred from citizenship, flatly declaring that "any woman citizen who marries an alien ineligible to citizenship shall cease to be a citizen."[56] Until Congress repealed this provision in 1931,[57] marriage to a non-White alien by an American woman was akin to treason against this country: either of these acts justified the stripping of citizenship from someone American by birth. Indeed, a woman's marriage to a non-White foreigner was perhaps a worse crime, for while a traitor lost his citizenship only after trial, the woman lost hers automatically.[58] The laws governing the racial composition of this country's citizenry came inseverably bound up with and exacerbated by sexism. It is in this context of combined racial and gender prejudice that we should understand the absence of any women among the petitioners named in the prerequisite cases: it is not that women were unaffected by the racial bars, but that they were doubly bound by them, restricted both as individuals, and as less than individuals (that is, as wives).

Notes

1. U.S. COMMISSION ON CIVIL RIGHTS, THE TARNISHED GOLDEN DOOR: CIVIL RIGHTS ISSUES IN IMMIGRATION 1–12 (1990).

2. Chinese Exclusion Act, ch. 126, 22 Stat. 58 (1882). *See generally* Harold Hongju Koh, *Bitter Fruit of the Asian Immigration Cases,* 6 CONSTITUTION 69 (1994). For a sobering account of the many lynchings of Chinese in the western United States during this period, *see* John R. Wunder, *Anti-Chinese Violence in the American West, 1850–1910,* LAW FOR THE ELEPHANT, LAW FOR THE BEAVER: ESSAYS IN THE LEGAL HISTORY OF THE NORTH AMERICAN WEST 212 (John McLaren, Hamar Foster, and Chet Orloff eds., 1992). Charles McClain, Jr., discusses the historical origins of anti-Chinese prejudice and the legal responses undertaken by that community on the West Coast. Charles McClain, Jr., *The Chinese Struggle for Civil Rights in Nineteenth Century America: The First Phase, 1850–1870,* 72 CAL. L. REV. 529 (1984). For a discussion of contemporary racial violence against Asian Americans, *see* Note, *Racial Violence against Asian Americans,* 106 HARV. L. REV. 1926 (1993); Robert Chang, *Toward an Asian American Legal Scholarship: Critical Race Theory, Post-Structuralism, and Narrative Space,* 81 CAL. L. REV. 1241, 1251–58 (1993).

3. Act of July 9, 1884, ch. 220, 23 Stat. 115; Act of May 5, 1892, ch. 60, 27 Stat. 25; Act of April 29, 1902, ch. 641, 32 Stat. 176; Act of April 27, 1904, ch. 1630, 33 Stat. 428.

4. Act of Feb. 5, 1917, ch. 29, 39 Stat. 874.

5. U.S. COMMISSION ON CIVIL RIGHTS, *supra,* at 9.

6. *Id. See* Act of May 19, 1921, ch. 8, 42 Stat. 5; Act of May 26, 1924, ch. 190, 43 Stat. 153.

7. U.S. COMMISSION ON CIVIL RIGHTS, *supra,* at 10.

8. *Id.* at 11. *See generally* JUAN RAMON GARCIA, OPERATION WETBACK: THE MASS DEPORTATION OF MEXICAN UNDOCUMENTED WORKERS IN 1954 (1980).

9. Act of Oct. 2, 1965, 79 Stat. 911.

10. Chae Chan Ping v. United States, 130 U.S. 581 (1889). The Court reasoned in part that if "the government of the United States, through its legislative department, considers the presence of foreigners of a different race in this country, who will not assimilate with us, to be dangerous to its peace and security, their exclusion is not to be stayed." For a critique of this deplorable result, *see* Louis Henkin, *The Constitution and United States Sovereignty: A Century of Chinese Exclusion and Its Progeny,* 100 HARV. L. REV. 853 (1987).

11. For efforts to encourage Irish immigration, *see, e.g., Immigration Act of 1990, § 131, 104 Stat. 4978 (codified as amended at 8 U.S.C. § 1153 (c) [1994]).* Bill Ong Hing argues that Congress continues to discriminate against Asians. *"Through an examination of past exclusion laws, previous legislation, and the specific provisions of the Immigration Act of 1990, the conclusion can be drawn that Congress never intended to make up for nearly 80 years of Asian exclusion, and that a conscious hostility towards persons of Asian descent continues to pervade Congressional circles."* Bill Ong Hing, Asian Americans and Present U.S. Immigration Policies: A Legacy of Asian Exclusion, *ASIAN AMERICANS AND THE SUPREME COURT: A DOCUMENTARY HISTORY 1106, 1107 (Hyung-Chan Kim ed., 1992).*

12. Louis DeSipio and Harry Pachon, Making Americans: Administrative Discretion and Americanization, *12 CHICANO-LATINO L. REV. 52, 53 (1992).*

13. CHARLES GORDON AND STANLEY MAILMAN, IMMIGRATION LAW AND PROCEDURE § 92.03[1][b] (rev. ed. 1992).

14. Dred Scott v. Sandford, 60 U.S. (19 How.) 393 (1857). For an insightful discussion of the role of *Dred Scott* in the development of American citizenship, see JAMES KETTNER, *THE DEVELOPMENT OF AMERICAN CITIZENSHIP, 1608–1870, at 300–333 (1978); see also KENNETH L. KARST, BELONGING TO AMERICA: EQUAL CITIZENSHIP AND THE CONSTITUTION 43–61 (1989).*

15. Civil Rights Act of 1866, ch. 31, 14 Stat. 27.

16. U.S. Const. amend. XIV.

17. 169 U.S. 649 (1898).

18. 112 U.S. 94 (1884).

19. Act of June 2, 1924, ch. 233, 43 Stat. 253.

20. Nationality Act of 1940, § 201(b), 54 Stat. 1138. See generally *GORDON AND MAILMAN, supra, at § 92.03[3][e].*

21. Pete Wilson, Crack Down on Illegals, *USA TODAY, Aug. 20, 1993, at 12A.*

22. H. R. J. Res. 129, 103d Cong., 1st Sess. (1993). An earlier, scholarly call to revamp the Fourteenth Amendment can be found in PETER SCHUCK and ROGER SMITH, CITIZENSHIP WITHOUT CONSENT: ILLEGAL ALIENS IN THE AMERICAN POLITY (1985).

23. Koh, *supra,* at 69–70.

24. Bill Ong Hing, Beyond the Rhetoric of Assimilation and Cultural Pluralism: Addressing the Tension of Separatism and Conflict in an Immigration-Driven Multiracial Society, *81 CAL. L. REV. 863, 866 (1993).*

25. Gerald Neuman warns against amending the Citizenship Clause. Gerald Neuman, Back to *Dred Scott? 24 SAN DIEGO L. REV. 485, 500 (1987).* See also *Note,* The Birthright

Citizenship Amendment: A Threat to Equality, *107 HARV. L. REV. 1026 (1994)*.

26. U.S. Const. art. I, sec. 8, cl. 4.

27. Act of March 26, 1790, ch. 3, 1 Stat. 103.

28. KETTNER, *supra, at 215–16*.

29. One exception exists. In revisions undertaken in 1870, the "white person" limitation was omitted. However, this omission is regarded as accidental, and the prerequisite was reinserted in 1875 by "an act to correct errors and to supply omissions in the Revised Statutes of the United States." Act of Feb. 18, 1875, ch. 80, 18 Stat. 318. See *In re Ah Yup, 1 F.Cas. 223 (C.C.D.Cal. 1878) ("Upon revision of the statutes, the revisors, probably inadvertently, as Congress did not contemplate a change of the laws in force, omitted the words 'white persons.'")*.

30. Statement of Senator Hendricks, 59 CONG. GLOBE, 42nd Cong., 1st Sess. 2939 (1866). See also *John Guendelsberger, Access to Citizenship for Children Born Within the State to Foreign Parents, 40 AM. J. COMP. L. 379, 407–9 (1992)*.

31. Statement of Senator Cowan, 57 CONG. GLOBE, 42nd Cong., 1st Sess. 499 (1866). For a discussion of the role of anti-Asian prejudice in the laws governing naturalization, see generally *Elizabeth Hull*, Naturalization and Denaturalization, *ASIAN AMERICANS AND THE SUPREME COURT: A DOCUMENTARY HISTORY 403 (Hyung-Chan Kim ed., 1992)*.

32. The Senate rejected an amendment that would have allowed Chinese persons to naturalize. The proposed amendment read: "That the naturalization laws are hereby extended to aliens of African nativity, and to persons of African descent, and to persons born in the Chinese empire." BILL ONG HING, MAKING AND REMAKING ASIAN AMERICA THROUGH IMMIGRATION POLICY, 1850–1990, at 239 n.34 (1993).

33. Act of July 14, 1870, ch. 255, § 7, 16 Stat. 254.

34. Chinese Exclusion Act, ch. 126, § 14, 22 Stat. 58 (1882).

35. Fong Yue Ting v. United States, 149 U.S. 698, 716 (1893).

36. Neil Gotanda contends that separate racial ideologies function with respect to "other non-Whites," meaning non-Black racial minorities such as Asians, Native Americans, and Latinos. Neil Gotanda, "Other Non-Whites" in American Legal History: A Review of *Justice at War, 85 COLUM. L. REV. 1186 (1985). Gotanda explicitly identifies the operation of this separate ideology in the Supreme Court's jurisprudence regarding Asians and citizenship. Neil Gotanda, Asian American Rights and the "Miss Saigon Syndrome," ASIAN AMERICANS AND THE SUPREME COURT: A DOCUMENTARY HISTORY 1087, 1096–97 (Hyung-Chan Kim ed., 1992)*.

37. Charles Gordon, The Racial Barrier to American Citizenship, *93 U. PA. L. REV. 237, 252 (1945)*.

38. MILTON KONVITZ, THE ALIEN AND THE ASIATIC IN AMERICAN LAW 80–81 (1946) (citation omitted).

39. Act of Oct. 14, 1940, ch. 876, § 303, 54 Stat. 1140.

40. Note, The Nationality Act of 1940, *54 HARV. L. REV. 860, 865 n.40 (1941)*.

41. Act of Dec. 17, 1943, ch. 344, 3, 57 Stat. 600.

42. Act of July 2, 1946, ch. 534, 60 Stat. 416.

43. Id.

44. Immigration and Nationality Act of 1952, ch. 2, § 311, 66 Stat. 239 (codified as amended at 8 U.S.C. 1422 [1988]).

45. Arguably, the continued substantial exclusion of Asians from immigration not remedied until 1965, rendered their eligibility for naturalization relatively meaningless. "[T]he national quota system for admitting immigrants which was built into the 1952 Act gave the grant of eligibility a hollow ring." Chin Kim and Bok Lim Kim, Asian Immigrants in American Law: A Look at the Past and the Challenge Which Remains, *26 AM. U. L. REV. 373, 390 (1977)*.

46. *See generally Ursula Vogel, Is Citizenship Gender-Specific? THE FRONTIERS OF CITIZENSHIP 58 (Ursula Vogel and Michael Moran eds., 1991)*.

47. Act of Feb. 10, 1855, ch. 71, § 2, 10 Stat. 604. Because gender-based laws in the area of citizenship were motivated by the idea that a woman's citizenship should follow that of her husband, no naturalization law has explicitly targeted unmarried women. GORDON AND MAILMAN, *supra, at § 95.03[6] ("An unmarried woman has never been statutorily barred from naturalization.")*.

48. PRENTISS WEBSTER, LAW OF NATURALIZATION IN THE UNITED STATES OF AMERICA AND OTHER COUNTRIES 80 (1895).

49. Act of Feb. 10, 1855, ch. 71, § 2, 10 Stat. 604.

50. Kelly v. Owen, 74 U.S. 496, 498 (1868).

51. GORDON AND MAILMAN, *supra at § 95.03[6]*.

52. Act of Sept. 22, 1922, ch. 411, § 2, 42 Stat. 1021.

53. GORDON AND MAILMAN, *supra at § 100.03[4][m]*.

54. Act of March 2, 1907, ch. 2534, § 3, 34 Stat. 1228. This act was upheld in MacKenzie v. Hare, 239 U.S. 299 (1915) (expatriating a U.S.-born woman upon her marriage to a British citizen).

55. Act of Sept. 22, 1922, ch. 411, § 3, 42 Stat. 1021.

56. *Id.* The Act also stated that "[n]o woman whose husband is not eligible to citizenship shall be naturalized during the continuance of the marriage."

57. Act of March 3, 1931, ch. 442, § 4(a), 46 Stat. 1511.

58. The loss of birthright citizenship was particularly harsh for those women whose race made them unable to regain citizenship through naturalization, especially after 1924, when the immigration laws of this country barred entry to any alien ineligible to citizenship. Immigration Act of 1924, ch. 190, § 13(c), 43 Stat. 162. *See, e.g.,* Ex parte (Ng) Fung Sing, 6 F.2d 670 (W. D. Wash. 1925). In that case, a U.S. birthright citizen of Chinese descent was expatriated because of her marriage to a Chinese citizen, and was subsequently refused admittance to the United States as an alien ineligible to citizenship.

Critical Thinking

1. Explain the relationship between the U.S. Congress and racial prejudice and citizenship.

2. What does this article about American history have meaning for current events and contemporary society?

3. In what ways has birthright citizenship and naturalization intersected with race and gender in the development of the American Constitution?

Dred Scott v. Sandford

December term 1856.

Mr. Chief Justice Taney delivered the opinion of the court.

This case has been twice argued. After the argument at the last term, differences of opinion were found to exist among the members of the court; and as the questions in controversy are of the highest importance, and the court was at that time much pressed by the ordinary business of the term, it was deemed advisable to continue the case, and direct a re-argument on some of the points, in order that we might have an opportunity of giving to the whole subject a more deliberate consideration. It has accordingly been again argued by counsel, and considered by the court; and I now proceed to deliver its opinion.

There are two leading questions presented by the record:

1. Had the Circuit Court of the United States jurisdiction to hear and determine the case between these parties? And
2. If it had jurisdiction, is the judgment it has given erroneous or not?

The plaintiff in error, who was also the plaintiff in the court below, was, with his wife and children, held as slaves by the defendant, in the State of Missouri; and he brought this action in the Circuit Court of the United States for that district, to assert the title of himself and his family to freedom.

The declaration is in the form usually adopted in that State to try questions of this description, and contains the averment necessary to give the court jurisdiction; that he and the defendant are citizens of different States; that is, that he is a citizen of Missouri, and the defendant a citizen of New York.

The defendant pleaded in abatement to the jurisdiction of the court, that the plaintiff was not a citizen of the State of Missouri, as alleged in his declaration, being a negro of African descent, whose ancestors were of pure African blood, and who were brought into this country and sold as slaves.

To this plea the plaintiff demurred, and the defendant joined in demurrer. The court overruled the plea, and gave judgment that the defendant should answer over. And he thereupon put in sundry pleas in bar, upon which issues were joined; and at the trial the verdict and judgment were in his favor. Whereupon the plaintiff brought this writ of error.

Before we speak of the pleas in bar, it will be proper to dispose of the questions which have arisen on the plea in abatement.

That plea denies the right of the plaintiff to sue in a court of the United States, for the reasons therein stated.

If the question raised by it is legally before us, and the court should be of opinion that the facts stated in it disqualify the plaintiff from becoming a citizen, in the sense in which that word is used in the Constitution of the United States, then the judgment of the Circuit Court is erroneous, and must be reversed.

It is suggested, however, that this plea is not before us; and that as the judgment in the court below on this plea was in favor of the plaintiff, he does not seek to reverse it, or bring it before the court for revision by his writ of error; and also that the defendant waived this defence by pleading over, and thereby admitted the jurisdiction of the court.

But, in making this objection, we think the peculiar and limited jurisdiction of courts of the United States has not been adverted to. This peculiar and limited jurisdiction has made it necessary, in these courts, to adopt different rules and principles of pleading, so far as jurisdiction is concerned, from those which regulate courts of common law in England, and in the different States of the Union which have adopted the common-law rules.

In these last-mentioned courts, where their character and rank are analogous to that of a Circuit Court of the United States; in other words, where they are what the law terms courts of general jurisdiction; they are presumed to have jurisdiction, unless the contrary appears. No averment in the pleadings of the plaintiff is necessary, in order to give jurisdiction. If the defendant objects to it, he must plead it specially, and unless the fact on which he relies is found to be true by a jury, or admitted to be true by the plaintiff, the jurisdiction cannot be disputed in an appellate court.

Now, it is not necessary to inquire whether in courts of that description a party who pleads over in bar, when a plea to the jurisdiction has been ruled against him, does or does not waive his plea; nor whether upon a judgment in his favor on the pleas in bar, and a writ of error brought by the plaintiff, the question upon the plea in abatement would be open for revision in the appellate court. Cases that may have been decided in such courts, or rules that may have been laid down by common-law pleaders, can have no influence in the decision in this court. Because, under the Constitution and laws of the United States, the rules which govern the pleadings in its courts, in questions of jurisdiction, stand on different principles and are regulated by different laws.

This difference arises, as we have said, from the peculiar character of the Government of the United States. For although it is sovereign and supreme in its appropriate sphere of action, yet it does not possess all the powers which usually belong to the sovereignty of a nation. Certain specified powers, enumerated in the Constitution, have been conferred upon it; and neither the legislative, executive, nor judicial departments of the Government can lawfully exercise any authority beyond the limits marked out by the Constitution. And in regulating the judicial department, the cases in which the courts of the United States shall have jurisdiction are particularly and specifically enumerated and defined; and they are not authorized to take cognizance of any case which does not come within the description therein specified. Hence, when a plaintiff sues in a court of the United States, it is necessary that he should show, in his pleading, that the suit he brings is within the jurisdiction of the court, and that he is entitled to sue there. And if he omits to do this, and should, by any oversight of the Circuit Court, obtain a judgment in his favor, the judgment would be reversed in the appellate court for want of jurisdiction in the court below. The jurisdiction would not be presumed, as in the case of a common-law English or State court, unless the contrary appeared. But the record, when it comes before the appellate court, must show, affirmatively, that the inferior court had authority under the Constitution, to hear and determine the case. And if the plaintiff claims a right to sue in a Circuit Court of the United States, under that provision of the Constitution which gives jurisdiction in controversies between citizens of different States, he must distinctly aver in his pleading that they are citizens of different States; and he cannot maintain his suit without showing that fact in the pleadings.

This point was decided in the case of *Bingham v. Cabot,* (in 3 Dall., 382,) and ever since adhered to by the court. And in *Jackson v. Ashton,* (8 Pet., 148,) it was held that the objection to which it was open could not be waived by the opposite party because consent of parties could not give jurisdiction.

It is needless to accumulate cases on this subject. Those already referred to, and the cases of *Capron v. Van Noorden,* (in 2 Cr., 126) and *Montalet v. Murray,* (4 Cr., 46,) are sufficient to show the rule of which we have spoken. The case of *Capron v. Van Noorden* strikingly illustrates the difference between a common-law court and a court of the United States.

If, however, the fact of citizenship is averred in the declaration, and the defendant does not deny it, and put it in issue by plea in abatement, he cannot offer evidence at the trial to disprove it, and consequently cannot avail himself of the objection in the appellate court, unless the defect should be apparent in some other part of the record. For if there is no plea in abatement, and the want of jurisdiction does not appear in any other part of the transcript brought up by the writ of error, the undisputed averment of citizenship in the declaration must be taken in this court to be true. In this case, the citizenship is averred, but it is denied by the defendant in the manner required by the rules of pleading, and the fact upon which the denial is based is admitted by the demurrer. And, if the plea and demurrer, and judgment of the court below upon it, are before us upon this record, the question to be decided is, whether the facts stated in the plea are sufficient to show that the plaintiff is not entitled to sue as a citizen in a court of the United States. . . .

We think they are before us. The plea in abatement and the judgment of the court upon it, are a part of the judicial proceedings in the Circuit Court, and are there recorded as such; and a writ of error always brings up to the superior court the whole record of the proceedings in the court below. And in the case of the *United States v. Smith,* (11 Wheat., 172) this court said, that the case being brought up by writ of error, the whole record was under the consideration of this court. And this being the case in the present instance, the plea in abatement is necessarily under consideration; and it becomes, therefore, our duty to decide whether the facts stated in the plea are or are not sufficient to show that the plaintiff is not entitled to sue as a citizen in a court of the United States.

This is certainly a very serious question, and one that now for the first time has been brought for decision before this court. But it is brought here by those who have a right to bring it, and it is our duty to meet it and decide it.

The question is simply this: Can a negro, whose ancestors were imported into this country, and sold as slaves, become a member of the political community formed and brought into existence by the Constitution of the United States, and as such become entitled to all the rights, and privileges, and immunities, guarantied by that instrument to the citizen? One of which rights is the privilege of suing in a court of the United States in the cases specified in the Constitution.

It will be observed, that the plea applies to that class of persons only whose ancestors were negroes of the African race, and imported into this country, and sold and held as slaves. The only matter in issue before the court, therefore, is, whether the descendants of such slaves, when they shall be emancipated, or who are born of parents who had become free before their birth, are citizens of a State, in the sense in which the word citizen is used in the Constitution of the United States. And this being the only matter in dispute on the pleadings, the court must be understood as speaking in this opinion of that class only, that is, of those persons who are the descendants of Africans who were imported into this country, and sold as slaves.

The situation of this population was altogether unlike that of the Indian race. The latter, it is true, formed no part of the colonial communities, and never amalgamated with them in social connections or in government. But although they were uncivilized, they were yet a free and independent people, associated together in nations or tribes, and governed by their own laws. Many of these political communities were situated in territories to which the white race claimed the ultimate right of dominion. But that claim was acknowledged to be subject to the right of the Indians to occupy it as long as they thought proper, and neither the English nor colonial Governments claimed or exercised any dominion over the tribe or nation by whom it was occupied, nor claimed the right to the possession of the territory, until the tribe or nation consented to cede it. These Indian Governments were regarded and treated as foreign Governments, as must so as if an ocean had separated the red man from the white; and their freedom has constantly been acknowledged, from the time of the first emigration to the English colonies to the present day, by the different Governments which succeeded each other. Treaties have been negotiated with them, and their alliance sought for in war; and the people who compose these Indian political communities have always been treated as foreigners not living under our Government. It is true that the course of events has brought the Indian tribes within the limits of the United States under subjection to the white race; and it has been found necessary, for their sake as well as our own, to regard them as in a state of pupilage, and to legislate to a certain extent over them and the territory they occupy. But they may, without doubt, like the subjects of any other foreign Government, be naturalized by the authority of Congress, and become citizens of a State, and of the United States; and if an individual should leave his nation or tribe, and take up his abode among the white population, he would be entitled to all the rights and privileges which would belong to an emigrant from any other foreign people.

We proceed to examine the case as presented by the pleadings.

The words "people of the United States" and "citizens" are synonymous terms, and mean the same thing. They both describe the political body who, according to our republican institutions, form the sovereignty and who hold the power and conduct the Government through their representatives. They are what we familiarly call the "sovereign people," and every citizen is one of this people, and a constituent member of this sovereignty. The question before us is, whether the class of persons described in the plea in abatement compose a portion of this people, and are constituent members of this sovereignty? We think they are not, and that they are not included, and were not intended to be included, under the word "citizens" in the Constitution, and can therefore claim none of the rights and privileges which that instrument provides for and secures to citizens of the United States. On the contrary, they were at that time considered as a subordinate and inferior class of beings, who had been subjugated by the dominant race, and, whether emancipated or not, yet remained subject to their authority, and had no rights or privileges but such as those who held the power and the Government might choose to grant them.

It is not the province of the court to decide upon the justice or injustice, the policy or impolicy, of these laws. The decision of that question belonged to the political or law-making power; to those who formed the sovereignty and framed the Constitution. The duty of the court is, to interpret the instrument they have framed, with the best lights we can obtain on the subject, and to administer it as we find it, according to its true intent and meaning when it was adopted.

In discussing this question, we must not confound the rights of citizenship which a State may confer within its own limits, and the rights of citizenship as a member of the Union. It does not by any means follow, because he has all the rights and privileges of a citizen of a State, that he must be a citizen of the United States. He may have all of the rights and privileges of the citizen of a State, and yet not be entitled to the rights and privileges of a citizen in any other State. For, previous to the adoption of the Constitution of the United States, every State had the undoubted right to confer on whomsoever it pleased the character of citizen, and to endow him with all its rights. But this character of course was confined to the boundaries of the State, and gave him no rights or privileges in other States beyond those secured to him by the laws of nations and the comity of States. Nor have the several States surrendered the power of conferring

these rights and privileges by adopting the Constitution of the United States. Each State may still confer them upon an alien, or any one it thinks proper, or upon any class or description of persons; yet he would not be a citizen in the sense in which that word is used in the Constitution of the United States, nor entitled to sue as such in one of its courts, nor to the privileges and immunities of a citizen in the other States. The rights which he would acquire would be restricted to the State which gave them. The Constitution has conferred on Congress the right to establish a uniform rule of naturalization, and this right is evidently exclusive, and has always been held by this court to be so. Consequently, no State, since the adoption of the Constitution, can by naturalizing an alien invest him with the rights and privileges secured to a citizen of a State under the Federal Government, although, so far as the State alone was concerned, he would undoubtedly be entitled to the rights of a citizen, and clothed with all the rights and immunities which the Constitution and laws of the State attached to that character.

It is very clear, therefore, that no State can, by any act or law of its own, passed since the adoption of the Constitution, introduce a new member into the political community created by the Constitution of the United States. It cannot make him a member of this community by making him a member of its own. And for the same reason it cannot introduce any person, or description of persons, who were not intended to be embraced in this new political family which the Constitution brought into existence, but were intended to be excluded from it.

The question then arises, whether the provisions of the Constitution, in relation to the personal rights and privileges to which the citizen of a State should be entitled, embraced the negro African race, at that time in this country or who might afterwards be imported, who had then or should afterwards be made free in any State; and to put it in the power of a single State to make him a citizen of the United States, and endue him with the full rights of citizenship in every other State without their consent? Does the Constitution of the United States act upon him whenever he shall be made free under the laws of a State, and raised there to the rank of a citizen, and immediately clothe him with all the privileges of a citizen in every other State, and in its own courts?

The courts think the affirmative of these propositions cannot be maintained. And if it cannot, the plaintiff in error could not be a citizen of the State of Missouri, within the meaning of the Constitution of the United States, and, consequently, was not entitled to sue in its courts.

It is true, every person, and every class and description of persons, who were at the time of the adoption of the Constitution recognised as citizens in the several States, became also citizens of this new political body; but none other; it was formed by them, and for them and their posterity, but for no one else. And the personal rights and privileges guaranteed to citizens of this new sovereignty were intended to embrace those only who were then members of the several State communities, or who should afterwards by birthright or otherwise become members, according to the provisions of the Constitution and the principles on which it was founded. It was the union of those who were at that time members of distinct and separate political communities into one political family, whose power, for certain specified purposes, was to extend over the whole territory of the United States. And it gave to each citizen rights and privileges outside of his State which he did not before possess, and placed him in every other State upon a perfect equality with its own citizens as to rights of person and rights of property; it made him a citizen of the United States.

It becomes necessary, therefore, to determine who were citizens of the several States when the Constitution was adopted. And in order to do this, we must recur to the Governments and institutions of the thirteen colonies, when they separated from Great Britain and formed new sovereignties, and took their places in the family of independent nations. We must inquire who, at that time, were recognised as the people or citizens of a State, whose rights and liberties had been outraged by the English Government; and who declared their independence, and assumed the powers of Government to defend their rights by force of arms.

In the opinion of the court, the legislation and histories of the times, and the language used in the Declaration of Independence, show, that neither the class of persons who had been imported as slaves, nor their descendants, whether they had become free or not, were then acknowledged as a part of the people, nor intended to be included in the general words used in that memorable instrument. . . .

Critical Thinking

1. What are the questions at issue in *Dred Scott v. Sandford?*

2. Explain in what ways does the Court view "the Indian race," "Negroes of African blood," and "people of the United States?"

Supreme Court of the United States, 1856.

"There's No One as Irish as Barack O'Bama": The Policy and Politics of American Multiracialism

For the first time in American history, the 2000 United States census allowed individuals to choose more than one race. That new policy sets up our exploration of whether and how multiracialism is entering Americans' understanding and practice of race. By analyzing briefly earlier cases of racial construction, we uncover three factors important to understanding if and how intensely a feedback effect for racial classification will be generated. Using this framework, we find that multiracialism has been institutionalized in the federal government, and is moving toward institutionalization in the private sector and other governmental units. In addition, the small proportion of Americans who now define themselves as multiracial is growing absolutely and relatively, and evidence suggests a continued rise. Increasing multiracial identification is made more likely by racial mixture's growing prominence in American society—demographically, culturally, economically, and psychologically. However, the politics side of the feedback loop is complicated by the fact that identification is not identity. Traditional racial or ethnic loyalties and understandings remain strong, including among potential multiracial identifiers. Therefore, if mixed-race identification is to evolve into a multiracial identity, it may not be at the expense of existing group consciousness. Instead, we expect mixed-race identity to be contextual, fluid, and additive, so that it can be layered onto rather than substituted for traditional monoracial commitments. If the multiracial movement successfully challenges the longstanding understanding and practice of "one drop of blood" racial groups, it has the potential to change much of the politics and policy of American race relations.

JENNIFER HOCHSCHILD AND VESLA MAE WEAVER

O'Leary, O'Riley, O'Hare, and O'Hara
There's no one as Irish as Barack O'Bama.
His mam's daddy's grandaddy was one
Fulmuth Kearney
He's as Irish as any from the lakes of Killarney
His mam's from a long line of great Irish mamas;
There's no one as Irish as Barack O'Bama.

> —Hardy Drew and the Nancy Boys

It is possible that, by 2050, today's racial and ethnic categories will no longer be in use.

> —Migration News[1]

The Hart-Cellar Immigration Act of 1965 that removed immigration restrictions based on national origin and the 1967 Supreme Court decision in *Loving v. Virginia* that struck down laws forbidding interracial marriage jointly facilitated powerful demographic changes in the United States. Immigration rose, to over a million people a year in some years. Interracial and interethnic

marriages occurred much more often than before; the number and proportion of mixed-race children grew; and multiple ways of recognizing group mixture arose in the society, culture, and economy. These changes were politicized in the 1990s by advocacy groups seeking official recognition of mixed-race ancestry and identity, and at the same time federal agencies studied new classification systems for counting and analyzing the rapidly changing American population. By 2000, eight states and the federal government recognized self-identified racial mixture for the first time in American history, and almost seven million respondents chose more than one race in the 2000 census (823 chose all six possibilities).[2] Multiracial advocacy organizations celebrated the beginning of a new era.

Recognition of multiracialism received its biggest subsequent boost, of course, in the person of Barack Obama. His White American mother was descended from a wigmaker who left Moneygall, Ireland, in 1850—thereby making possible the song, "There's no one as Irish as Barack O'Bama," which has been downloaded from YouTube by millions around the world. The irony of the song, as any sentient person knows, is that Obama's father was a Black Kenyan and Obama grew up as almost but not quite African American.

Article 9. "There's No One as Irish as Barack O'Bama": The Policy and Politics of American Multiracialism

Is Obama the wave of the future? As the song puts it, is it the case that "From Fenian to Kenyan, it's the American way?" More soberly, how does multiracialism relate to the United States' commonly-accepted sharp distinctions among a few races and ethnicities? Various answers are possible. At one extreme, multiracialism will dissolve extant groups into one grand cosmopolitan melange, as in the O'Bama song or José Vasconcelos' concept of the "cosmic race."[3] Alternatively, multiracial advocates and their famous representative are an anomaly in the deeply entrenched, and sometimes cherished, American racial classification system. After all, only a few percent of Americans call themselves multiracial regardless of their ancestry; Obama may be as unusual in his identity as he is in his political skills. Or, multiracialism will contribute to changing, but not dissolving, the ways in which Americans understand, identify with, and practice race. In that view, people will come to understand the concept of race differently, so that they can layer a multiracial identity into a racial identity, rather than thinking of racial identity as fixed, knowable, and singular.

We analyze the development of multiracialism in the United States and its relationship to the recent history and current politics of the American racial order. *Migration News'* startling prediction in the second epigraph suggests what is at stake: increasing recognition of mixture and more people identifying as mixed could together signal as well as promote a major change in how Americans understand, identify with, and practice race and ethnicity.[4] For most of the twentieth century, Americans' racial understandings and practices rested on assumptions that racial groups are mutually distinct, that there are only a few races, and that a person is a member of and identifies with only one race. Political and policy disputes revolved around the appropriate relationship among the few exhaustive and mutually exclusive races, focusing especially on the degree to which racial hierarchy could be justified or how it should be dismantled.

But multiracialism challenges that set of assumptions. Viewed optimistically, it could provide a bridge between previously isolated categories. If "we" and "they" are linked in our own bodies or those of our children or friends, it might be harder (though not impossible, as we know from the antebellum South or the history of most Latin American nations) for one group to separate from and dominate the other. As Herbert Gans puts it, "Most likely, . . . the larger the number of multiracials and of multiracial variations, the more difficult it will be for non-Blacks to define and enforce racial boundaries, or to figure out which of the many darker-skinned varieties of multiracials had Black ancestors. In that case, an eventual end of racial discrimination is possible."[5] Such, at any rate, is the hope of advocates of multiracial recognition and identity as well as of optimistic interpreters of Barack Obama's presidential victory.

Looked at pessimistically, an increase in multiracial recognition and identity may dangerously challenge group loyalties that remain essential in a polity where races and ethnicities are still arrayed hierarchically. Multiracialism may even reinforce hierarchy by permitting some non-Anglos to distance themselves from disfavored minority groups—"a whole host of light-skinned black Americans running for the door the minute they have another choice," in the words of Arthur Fletcher, then chair of the U.S. Civil Rights Commission.[6] If multiracials have higher socioeconomic status than do monoracial non-Whites, as some evidence suggests, they may be preferred in arenas such as affirmative action or electoral politics, thus deepening non-Anglo subordination.

Looked at skeptically, multiracial self-description may remain rare and multiracial identity thin despite official recognition. In that case, the policy of permitting people to select more than one racial designation is best understood as a minor accommodation of a small fraction of the population and a statistical headache for data analysts. It will matter little, politically or theoretically, and the extant American racial and ethnic order will remain largely intact.

It is too early in the history of multiracial classification and identification to tell whether a strong identity will develop and what impact such an identity might have on the American racial order. As we will show, however, potent forces in the polity and society are encouraging Americans to relax the assumptions about race that predominated over the past few generations. The speculation by *Migration News* seems right; the alternative of reverting to a few discrete nominal categories is becoming more and more unlikely for Americans in the twenty-first century.

We propose to gain leverage on the recent development and possible futures of multiracial identity by bringing together two disparate topics—the trajectories of racial classification schemes in the United States and the scholarly literature on policy-politics feedback. That is, we will briefly show how racial mixture has been discursively, legally, and politically constituted in the United States since the Civil War, and how interactions among policy, politics, institutions, and social dynamics reinforced or undermined those racial constructions. We argue that three factors—demographic change and societal dynamics, formal institutionalization, and the balance between political support and opposition—shape whether feedback processes occur such that a change in classification becomes entrenched over time, or whether the policy fails to generate feedbacks so that a change in classificatory policy does not last. We then use this framework to analyze the many facets of contemporary multiracial identity and identification.

The analysis yields fascinating puzzles, which will keep questions about racial construction and the blurring of categorical boundaries vibrant for years to come. We find that mixed-race categories are being widely institutionalized, that multiracial *self-identification* is growing and is likely to continue to do so, but that multiracial *identity* either is weak or is not generating the kind of race-based political organization and mobilization that Americans have become familiar with. The policy, institutions, and social context all point toward a new set of political configurations revolving around mixture—but the politics are not moving in that direction, at least not yet or not in the ways that we expect them to.

Why not? One possibility is simply that multiracial identity is and will remain too weak or diffuse to compete against established monoracial identities. But another possibility is that multiracialism cannot be understood as adding another group to the American racial order, like Hispanics were added after 1970. Instead, multiracial identity may contradict our usual understanding of racial identity as singular; multiracials might be a group without group boundaries, united mainly by the sense of *not* being racially unitary. Their identity may be fluid and additive rather than zero-sum and exclusive.[7] Indeed, as we show later, multiracials' beliefs and attitudes are generally located in the middle of the traditional racial divide. Thus the growth of multiracial self-definition could lead to a softening of racial opinion polarization, or at least create an important middle group that could be a constituency for compromise on racially divisive issues.

The study of multiracialism provides a new angle of vision into a wide array of questions about a racial order. One could compare Americans' treatment of racial mixture with that of other nations.[8] One could use the framing of a policy-politics feedback loop to evaluate why broad racial orders persist, evolve, or disappear.[9] One could compare biracialism to other forms of intersectionality

31

in order to probe ways in which race is, and is not, "like" gender, class, or sexuality.[10] One could weigh the normative value of intense solidarity within a monoracial group against the value of celebrating mixture, hybridity, and impurity.[11] All of those topics, and more, could be illuminated by studying American multiracialism—but we save them for another day. If we can explicate what is happening in this arena, why, how it relates to earlier ventures in the same direction, and why it matters for the future of American racial dynamics, that will more than suffice for one article.

American Adventures in Racial Construction

By now a voluminous literature has developed on racial construction in the United States over the past 400 years.[12] Here we focus on only a small part of it, the creation of racial categories through deliberate governmental policy choices. Classification rules can be an important element of a policy-politics feedback loop since they "play an active role in constructing and positioning . . . groups, defining their boundaries and infusing them with political meaning." Sarah Igo's observation about opinion surveys holds also for official data collection: "a society [is] changed by the very tools employed to represent it. . . . The public is simultaneously object, participant, and audience." Even more than a survey, an official census can foster a new politics because "censuses created serial, aggregable, counterposed majorities and minorities, which, starting as formal entities, were positioned in due course to assume political reality"—including to try to change the classification system itself.[13]

As we noted earlier, some official attempts at racial construction endure for decades, while others quickly disappear. Some have a deep impact on group formation and practice, while others remain "merely" classificatory. By looking at two pairings of racial constructions that did, and did not, take hold and deepen over the twentieth century, we can see what factors generate a self-reinforcing policy feedback loop in the arena of a racial order. That will set the stage for looking more closely at the contemporary phenomenon of multiracialism.

The Mexican Race and Hispanic Ethnicity

In 1930, the U.S. census bureau added "Mexican" to the "Color or Race" inquiry, instructing its enumerators that "practically all Mexican laborers are of a racial mixture difficult to classify, though usually well recognized in the localities where they are found. In order to obtain separate figures for this racial group, it has been decided that all persons born in Mexico, or having parents born in Mexico, who are definitely not white, Negro, Indian, Chinese, or Japanese, should be returned as Mexican." When the census was taken, the Mexican government, members of Congress with Mexican American constituents, and advocacy groups vehemently protested on the grounds that all Mexicans were White.[14] To our knowledge, no one supported this change in the classification system—especially the potential constituency group that would lose its tenuous hold on White status in an intensely hierarchical racial order. The census bureau retreated, with the director noting wryly that "the classification by race or color of . . . populations is not only very difficult, but is a very delicate matter to the United States Government," and decreeing that henceforth "Mexicans are Whites and must be classified as 'White'. This order does not admit of any further discussion, and must be followed to the letter."[15]

There the matter rested for three decades; Mexicans were officially White. In 1970, however, the Nixon administration instructed the census bureau to enumerate some Hispanics, as part of the Republican Party's effort to woo a growing group of relatively unattached voters.[16] The "procedural flow chart" for 1970s enumerators unintentionally demonstrated just how complicated it was to define and find Hispanics: Nevertheless, the category persisted, and remains the lone ethnicity that the authoritative Office of Management and Budget (OMB) permits.[17]

Three factors—demographic change, the balance between political support and opposition, and the degree of institutional support for the new designation—explain both the rise and fall of "the Mexican race" and the rise and persistence of Hispanic ethnicity in federal classification systems. In a 1928 appropriations hearing, a member of Congress asked the census director "what you did with those Mexicans who came over in swarms?" The response was the Mexican race on the subsequent census. After 1930, protest overrode Congressional pressure and in any case, many Mexicans were repatriated in the 1930s—so the political and demographic balances shifted in the opposite direction, and the Mexican race disappeared. Since there had been no institutional structure built around the addition of a new racial category on the 1930 census, the new category could be abolished as readily as it was created.

By 1970, the number of Mexicans "coming over" was again rising. But this time the party in power chose to woo rather than (only) subject them to surveillance. And as a consequence of inclusion in civil rights, affirmative action, and voting rights laws and regulations after decades of de facto segregation and subordination, Hispanics could see benefits to a separate designation that outweighed the costs of losing putative Whiteness.[18] Some potential supporters of the new policy also appreciated the social and cultural value of a non-White identity. Finally, unlike the 1930s, after 1970, Hispanic members of Congress, energetic advocacy groups, census advisory committees, and experts who wanted to keep track of the rising Latino immigration combined to keep Hispanic on the census, despite occasional and rather half-hearted opposition.[19]

Over time, this separate ethnic designation has solidified in everything from classification systems to policy networks, electoral campaigns and candidacies, individuals' identities, and popular culture; it is hard to imagine that the steps down this path will ever reverse or change direction. In short, the feedback loop between the invention of Hispanic ethnicity on the census and the politics of Hispanicity began with the impetus of demographic change and grew through institutionalization and the creation of a robust, committed constituency.

Mulattoes and the One-Drop-of-Blood Rule

Starting in 1850, for eighty years the federal government enumerated mulattoes, and occasionally quadroons and octoroons. The rules for defining these groups varied over the years and were never very precise; one typical census instruction to enumerators read

Be particularly careful to distinguish between blacks, mulattoes, quadroons, and octoroons. The word "black" should be used to describe those persons who have three-fourths or more black blood; "mulatto," those persons who have from three-eighths to five-eighths black blood; "quadroon," those persons who have one-fourth black blood; and "octoroon," those persons who have one-eighth or any trace of black blood.[20]

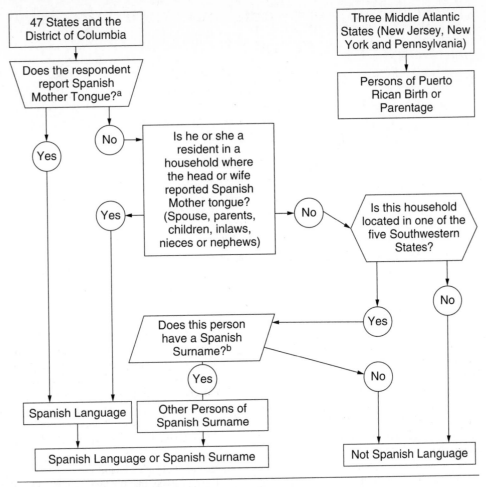

Figure 1   Tabulation plan for Spanish heritage definition, 1970 Census

[a] Spanish Mother Tongue: all persons who reported that Spanish was spoken in the home when they were a child.

[b] Spanish Surname: coded only for Arizona, California, Colorado, New Mexico and Texas by matching surnames recorded in the questionnaire with those included in a list of over 8,000 Spanish surnames.

Source: Hernandez et al. 1973 (675).

The reasons for enumeration remained as murky and inconsistent as the designations of individuals were.[21] Nevertheless, government officials clearly perceived and attempted to quantify racial mixture.[22] "Mulatto" lasted on the census through 1920 (except in 1900), after which it disappeared from political, legal, and mainstream media usage.

At the same time that mulattos were being enumerated and their socioeconomic characteristics carefully tabulated, states were developing laws aimed at sharpening and heightening the division between racial groups. Legislators knew that they were constructing racial boundaries; as one careful analyst pointed out in 1910, "it is this gradual sloping off from one race into another which has made it necessary for the law to set artificial lines."[23] It turned out to be frustratingly difficult to do so. For several decades, southern states passed an array of laws broadening the definition of who counted as Negro, adding new groups to the list of people prohibited from marrying or bequeathing property to one another, and deepening penalties for violation of the new laws.[24] The changes mandated by these sequential laws were not always linear, some were contested, and the timing was inconsistent across states. The 1910 reference book required eight closely-reasoned pages to explain "What is a Negro?", culminating in a diagram, reproduced in Figure 2, that was

optimistically described as "probably clarify[ing] these definitions." (The book then required another two pages to explain the diagram.)

By the mid-1920s, however, states had mostly completed writing laws which subsumed everyone with mixed Black and White ancestry under the category of Negro.[25] They became known as "one drop of blood laws" because they broadened the definition of a Negro to include anyone with one Black ancestor from five generations earlier. The one-drop rule became the reigning understanding of Blackness in the United States for the rest of the twentieth century, locked firmly into place in legal and policy arrangements as well as in social and cultural interactions, individual identities, and political practice. It achieved an almost taken-for-granted quality in Americans' racial practice.

The decline of "mulatto" and the solidification of sharp boundaries between Black and White were not inevitable. Public discourse and public policies had recognized racial mixture for the prior three centuries of American history, and most other countries with both Blacks and Whites continue to officially recognize racial mixture. So why did the one-drop rule attain hegemony in the American racial order? Unlike the case of the Mexican race and Hispanics, demographic change and a shifting political balance between support for and opposition to an innovation do not explain the rise and decline of mulatto and the rise and persistence of the official effort

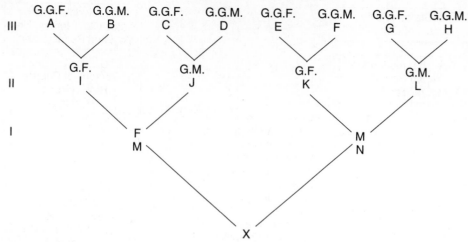

Figure 2   Explaining boundaries between Negroes and Whites, 1910
Source: Stephenson 1910 (18)

to maintain White purity. The explanation lies in other mechanisms that foster a policy feedback loop—social norms and practices, and institutionalization—as well as in a distinct and unusual form of politics that consisted of incontestable power rather than a changing balance between supporters and opponents.

African Americans were individually and collectively ambivalent about the category of mulatto. Some were proud to claim mixed heritage and some were ashamed of it; some thought that racial boundary blurring would help the Black race overcome hierarchy and oppression while others thought that any move toward boundary blurring would undermine essential group solidarity.[26] But in terms of policy development and implementation, it did not matter what Blacks thought or wanted; they had no power in the first few decades of the twentieth century to influence any policy decisions. Whites controlled all the policy levers.

Since Whites controlled all policy choices in the racial arena, one must look to their preferences to explain the shift from mulatto to one-drop rules. Mulatto first appeared on the census through an unlikely alliance of northern liberals seeking information about slaves to show that they were people and southern supporters of the theory of polygenesis seeking information about slaves to prove their claim of separate species. It remained on the census through the early twentieth century because a few well-placed White politicians and scholars sought to determine if people with "mixed blood" were indeed physically degenerate and incapable of reproduction. Once census data proved that belief wrong, interest in enumerating and evaluating racially mixed people (Indian/White combinations as well as Black/White combinations) waned.

Conversely, demand for one-drop-of-blood rules grew as southern states broadened and deepened Jim Crow segregation policies in the early 1900s. The logic is simple; one cannot segregate Blacks from Whites, never mind humiliate and endanger them, if the two groups cannot be sharply differentiated. As Whites' preferences for racially segregated hierarchy was institutionalized, other policies and politics followed—creating a tight and robust feedback loop. Southern Black men were disfranchised, so with rare exceptions, White candidates could compete on the grounds of being more enthusiastic about segregation than their rival. The southern economy depended on a poor, immobile, and powerless workforce; mainstream southern media and culture offered virtually no alternative visions. To summarize a long and complex dynamic, one-drop

laws directly enabled institutions such as separate schools, hospitals, courts, and transportation systems, and indirectly fostered others that engaged in social interactions, market processes, and electoral politics—all of which depended on and reinforced the bright line between Black and White. Until the powerful disruptions of World War II, the Cold War, Black and White resistance, and mass media portrayals of White violence undermined Jim Crow segregation, the feedback loop was robust. Even with the successes of the civil rights era, it took another generation for the separate institutions to (partially) unwind and for the classification system underlying Jim Crow segregation to be challenged.

Thus, in a way that the long-standing classification of racial mixture never did, one-drop rules united compatible social norms, an all-powerful constituency with no serious opposition, and society-wide institutionalization into a tight cluster. This feedback loop was reinforced by Blacks' eventual enthusiastic incorporation of one-drop racial identification as a way to maintain group solidarity and fight racial inequality. That point, of course, leads directly to the politics of multiracialism.

Other systems for classifying people with complex ancestry—enumerating Whites' "mixed parentage" and mother tongues, Indians' fractions of black and white blood, the Asian nationality of "Hindoo"—came and went during the decades between the Civil War and the Depression. We note them here to remind readers of just how fluid the system of racial categorization has been at some points in American history. But changes in these classificatory policies can be explained by the same factors we used to explain changes in classification of Hispanics and blacks, so we need not detail them here. Demographic change and societal norms and practices, institutionalization, and the political balance between support and opposition for a given policy together provide the mechanisms for understanding the trajectory of a policy-politics feedback loop, at least in the arena of racial construction.

Recognizing Self-Identified Racial Mixture

By the last half of the twentieth century, Americans had largely forgotten most of this history of robust racial construction and deconstruction. At least since the 1930s, European immigrants of mixed parentage and many mother tongues have been consolidated into Whites; mulattoes, quadroons, octoroons, griffes, and Melungeons had all become Black; half-breeds were Indians; and Hindoos were no more. Hispanics remained ambiguously an ethnicity or a race, but were commonly understood to be not White. The American racial order revolved around an apparently stable, small set of exhaustive and mutually exclusive races; policies were designed and implemented with this set of groups in mind, as were the politics of racial contestation and identity. Americans' disputes about race focused on how hierarchical the racial order should be, not who was in what race or what a race consisted of.

This stable feedback loop started to change in the 1980s, when supporters of the concept of multiracial identity sought governmental recognition of self-defined racial mixture. Many activists identified with one race, but had spouses of a different race and racially mixed children; a few were themselves racially mixed and committed to multiracialism as a stand-alone identity.[27] After congressional hearings in 1993 and 1997, reports from the National Academy of Sciences and other experts on the United States' demographic change, survey experiments on the likelihood of multiracial identification, analyses by a federal interagency review committee and by the census bureau itself, and adoption of "select one or more" by several states,[28] the federal government acted.

In 1997, OMB issued the first executive branch ruling on racial data classification since 1977. These *Revisions to the Standards for the Classification of Federal Data on Race and Ethnicity* changed the definitions of some monoracial categories, distinguished another, and mandated that "when self-identification is used, a method for reporting more than one race should be adopted." While focusing on the 2000 census, the *Revisions* also stated that "other Federal programs should adopt the standards as soon as possible, but not later than January 1, 2003, for use in household surveys, administrative forms and records, and other data collections."[29]

Census 2000 duly included the instruction, "Mark one or more races to indicate what this person considers himself/herself to be"[30] in question 8, "What is Person 1's race?" With that, according to then-census director Kenneth Prewitt, "We turned a corner about how we think about race in this country."[31]

Institutional Expansion of the New Policy

"This will make our whole education system look different, and nobody will know whether we are going forward or backward."

—Gary Orfield

"The [traditional] racial categories have lost their meaning."

—Superintendent Jack Dale of Fairfax County Public Schools[32]

Whether one laments the change, like Orfield, or endorses it as timely and appropriate, like Superintendent Dale, the policy of permitting the report of multiple races has been institutionalized. It first moved deeply into the federal government, and is now moving broadly into American society. Thus one mechanism for a policy-politics feedback loop—and one that is necessary, if not sufficient—is in place.

Government Agencies

In 2001, in accord with OMB's mandate in the *Revisions to the Standards* and with its routine oversight of proposed federal systems for collecting new data, the Department of Justice began to "include counts of persons who have identified themselves as members of more than one racial category." The Department of Commerce also brought its surveys into compliance, as did the Department of Agriculture and the Federal Reserve Board in 2002. The Department of Health and Human Services followed suit the next year, and the Department of Defense also declared itself compliant with the new OMB rules.[33]

Momentum picked up as the decade advanced. In 2005, the Centers for Disease Control and Prevention and Department of Labor required, and the Food and Drug Administration recommended, that funded research include "Multiracial." The Equal Employment Opportunity Commission (EEOC) published a new standard for employers' reports requiring "two or more races" in order to "accommodate . . . the government-wide *Revisions* [of 1997]." The National Science Foundation now asks applicants to "select one or more." Most important was the 2007 "Final Guidance on Maintaining, Collecting, and Reporting Racial and Ethnic Data to the U.S. Department of Education." By 2010–11, all educational institutions must collect information on "whether the respondent is from one or more races" and report the number choosing "two or more races."[34] In short, the new federal classification policy of permitting more than one racial self-definition has grown strong roots; the undramatic but powerful means was OMB's standard authority to review and approve agencies' proposals for new data collection.

At levels or agencies of government not subject to OMB directives, the pattern of policy change remains mixed. The National Mail Voter Registration Form, valid in almost all states, includes "Multiracial" but tells users to follow their state's instructions for identifying race or ethnicity. As of 2008, only North Carolina specified "two or more races," although seven others permit more than one choice, sometimes on the federal form only and sometimes on both state and federal forms.

Most states have been slow to change their classification systems. Even in California, where a quarter of the United States' mixed-race population lives, legislators have proposed to no avail the "Ethnic Heritage Respect and Recognition Act," which would require the use of "mark one or more" in state data collection. An expert explained why it has not passed:

The bill would force changes in the way state agencies count and store data—thereby costing money—and it's often very hard to clear bills from the appropriations committees if they have more than insignificant costs. That said, getting out of the appropriations committees is not impossible if there's enough political support. . . . There was very little official opposition to the bill . . . but a certain degree of indifference.[35]

Concern about costs and legislators' need to set priorities are standard features of political calculation; absent a powerful push, the status quo is not changed. OMB provided that push at the federal level, but there is no equivalent agency at the state level. It seems plausible, however, that states will eventually follow the path of the federal government as their own demographics change and as they find it increasingly costly and inefficient to be at odds with federal classification systems.

Private Organizations

Until recently, most private actors also lacked a mandate or incentive to change their practices in this arena, and few did so. But that situation is changing. To comply with the 2007 Department of Education ruling, all educational institutions from prekindergarten through universities will soon permit students to choose more than one race.[36] High school students taking ACT's Scholastic Test now have the option of "multiracial," and the College Board is experimenting with two SAT formats, both telling the user to "check one or more of the following options that you identify with." As of 2009, the Common Application form used by about 350 American colleges and universities instructs students to "select one or more of the following ethnicities," with five specified groups (as in the census, Hispanic identification is asked separately). In short, institutionalization has moved from federal agencies to organizations with direct mandates to comply with or indirect links to the new classification policy.

Some private enterprises are also responding to the new federal policy. In fall 2009, we examined the application form for entry-level white collar jobs at *Fortune Magazine*'s hundred largest corporations. Fifty permitted applicants to specify two or more races, twenty permitted only one racial response, nineteen did not ask for racial and ethnic data, and we were unable to obtain the relevant information for the final thirteen. As in the educational arena, newly implemented changes in federal agencies' reporting requirements may be inducing at least large employers to make the same change; the Chamber of Commerce endorsed EEOC's 2003 proposal to require reporting the number of employees identifying with two or more races.[37]

In another arena, an increasing number of public opinion surveys or polls have started to permit multiple racial identifications. They include the American National Election Studies, the *Washington Post* (on some occasions), the National Longitudinal Survey of Adolescent Health, *Newsweek* surveys in 1995 and 2009, the National Longitudinal Survey of Freshmen (NLSF), the Children of Immigrants Longitudinal Study (CILS), the National Youth Risk Behavior Survey, the Panel Survey of Income Dynamics, the Current Population Survey, the General Social Survey—and perhaps others. In a recent survey, the American Political Science Association asked respondents, "What is your race or ethnic origin? *Check all that apply*" (emphasis original). The Implicit Association Test, downloaded by over three and a half million users, also allows a multiracial designation. If more survey organizations follow these leads, a classification system that includes the option of choosing more than one race may become an analytic, and then empirical, commonplace.

A key component of a policy-politics feedback loop—institutionalization—is established in the federal government, and growing in organizations that deal with federal agencies and among researchers. As more public and private actors change their procedures for enumerating race, the cost of retaining earlier classification systems grows and the benefits of following the new policy increase. By following the trajectory of one-drop rules and becoming embedded in laws and their public manifestations, multiracialism could supersede that long-standing classification system.

Social Context and Underlying Trends

As we saw with one-drop laws and the category of Hispanic, a feedback loop is much more likely to take hold if it accords, respectively, with broad societal trends or major demographic shifts. No political scientist accepts the cliché that demography is destiny, and almost none believe any longer that political disputes merely manifest structural economic conflict. Nevertheless, all would agree that one is more likely to reach a destination by flowing with a tide than fighting against it. The direction of the tide in this case is clear; the United States is becoming more multiracial in a variety of ways.

Demographic trajectories. To begin with, literal multiracialism is increasing. Intermarriage is rising sharply; by 2004, almost a fifth of marriages by Black men under age 30 and a tenth of marriages by young Black women were to non-Black spouses. About 20 percent of young Asian Americans, both men and women, married outside their race, as did fully two-thirds of young American Indians. In none of these cases is marriage to Hispanics counted as interracial; if it did, the proportions would be higher.[38]

Trajectory may matter more than absolute numbers in determining a social trend. There is no ambiguity here, with the possible exception of Asian American intermarriage, as Figure 3 shows.

As the scale on the Y axes shows, the absolute level of Asian intermarriage remains the highest even though it has declined in recent decades, probably due to the rise in the number of Asian immigrants.[39] The main point of Figure 3, however, is the clear inflection point in the 1970s, followed by a steep upward slope in intermarriage for two of the three groups. Continued increasing rates of intermarriage seem likely, and a reversal of the trend unlikely, especially since multiracials themselves tend to marry Whites. Furthermore, unlike several decades ago, in all three racial groups the better-educated are now more likely to intermarry.[40]

Interracial relationships are now the norm for young adults in some places; two-thirds of young Californians have dated someone of another race and almost nine out of ten profess willingness to marry across racial lines.[41] Less than a fifth of adult children of immigrants in New York City think endogamous marriages are important. Between 30 and 56 percent (depending on the interviewees' nationality) of those married or cohabiting have partners outside their group. In this young, urban sample, even three in ten native-born Whites and Blacks have partners outside their own race. "Feelings about intergroup dating sharply differentiated second generation youth from their immigrant parents," but even parents seem to be coming around.[42] Older adults are themselves moving outside their own group: 27 percent of adult Hispanics, 30 percent of Asians, and 35 percent of African Americans have dated across racial lines.[43]

An unsurprising consequence of rising intermarriage is the increasing number and proportion of demographically mixed-race children. Among children below age 18 in married-couple families, fewer than one percent had parents of different races in 1970, compared with 6.7 percent in 2000. Furthermore, since interracial unions are about twice as common among unmarried partners as among spouses, the number of mixed-race children born outside married-couple families is rising even more rapidly. As of 1997, 14 percent of births in California were multiracial or multiethnic,[44] and the proportion is surely higher by now. Almost half of the 6.7 million people identified with more than one race in census 2000 were under age 18.

Since families are not comprised only of parents and children, a single intermarriage or interracial child can have an impact well beyond

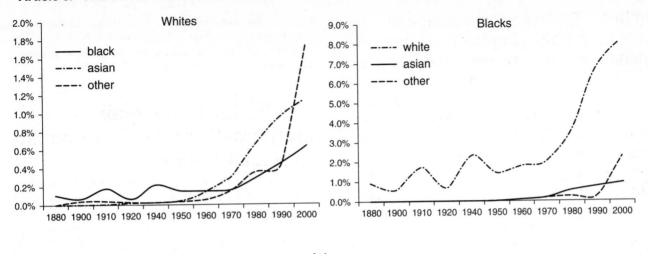

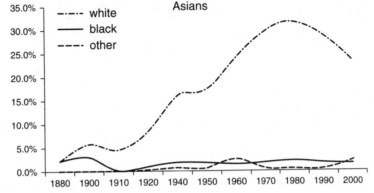

Figure 3   Interracial marriage rates, 1880–2000

Source: Adapted from Fryer 2007

the nuclear family. The number of White and Black Americans with a family member or close kin of a different race is increasing exponentially. The proportions among Asian Americans and American Indians are approaching 100 percent. Table 1 shows the pattern.

The calculations in Table 1 exclude marriages or offspring involving Latinos, or individuals who have multiracial ancestry but consider themselves to be members of one racial group. Even so, in 2000, "the fraction of Whites with kinship networks that cross either racial or Hispanic ethnic lines is nearing one-half," using the less conservative estimate of 14.4 marriages over three generations.[45] By some reasonable measures, then, half of Americans have a family member of a different racial group from their own.

Normative support for multiracialism. As literal interracialism increases, so does normative acceptance. Until a few decades ago, some Whites described racially mixed individuals as an detestable corruption of the natural order: half-breeds, "a scourge to both races," and so on.[46] That abhorrence did not, of course, stop (often forced) interracial intercourse; as journalists for the Black press repeatedly observed, "it was the Southern white man who tipped the scales of social intimacy so far until it is now at times, in certain sections, hard to tell where the white race starts and the colored race begins."[47] But Whites' predominant ideological stance was clear.

As we noted earlier, they were backed by the law and an elaborate system of social practices and institutions. Gunnar Myrdal noted bemusedly that "sex becomes . . . the principle around which the whole structure of segregation of the Negroes—down to disfranchisement and denial of equal opportunities on the labor market—is

organized."[48] The Supreme Court ignored interracial marriage in the years after *Brown v. Board of Education* on the grounds that, as Justice Harlan is reported to have said, "One bombshell at a time is enough." (Thurgood Marshall apparently concurred.) Only 4 percent of American adults approved of interracial marriage in a 1958 Gallup poll.[49] That is not an ambiguous norm or practice.

Forty years later, the norm was equally unambiguous—but reversed. In 2007, the analogous Gallup question found 77 percent approval, including 75 percent of Whites, 85 percent of Blacks, and 87 percent of Hispanics. Fully 86 percent of Whites under age 50 concurred. More liberals than conservatives approved, but almost as many Republicans as Democrats. Almost a decade earlier, more than three-fifths of respondents had endorsed interracial marriages "because they help break down racial barriers." Similar proportions found it "good for the country for more Americans to think of themselves as multiracial." Most interesting, perhaps, is that respondents dramatically exaggerated the proportion of American multiracial identifiers. Thirteen percent guessed that at least seven in ten define themselves as multiracial, and almost 80 percent guessed that a fifth of Americans do so.[50] They were wrong, but seemed undisturbed by their overestimates.

Cultural trends. It is hard to canvass cultural trends systematically, but a good indicator is the fact that actors with economic incentives find multiracialism to be worth their attention. Book publishers provide one example. After eliminating books that did not refer to individuals, we identified twenty-six in the decade of the 1990s on Amazon.com that included "multiracial," "biracial," "mixed-race,"

Table 1 Estimated percentage of Americans belonging to mixed-race kinship networks, by race and decade

	White	Black	Asian American	American Indian
1960	1.9	9.2	81.1	89.6
1970	3.6	10.9	87.5	99.0
1980	9.8	21.9	91.5	99.9
1990	9.0	28.3	79.5	99.8
2000	22.4	49.8	83.9	100

Note: Results are based on kinship network size of 10 marriages over three generations. With a less conservative estimate of 14.4 marriages over three generations, 30.5 percent of Whites, 62.9 percent of Blacks, and 92.8 percent of Asian Americans had kin of a different race in 2000.
Source: Joshua Goldstein, communication with the authors, January 29, 2009. See also Goldstein 1999.

"mulatto," or "racial mixture" in the titles. In the 2000s so far, there are more than sixty such books. Mass-audience magazines provide additional evidence. The cover of *Parade* magazine shows a group of smiling, adorable children under the headline of "The Changing Faces of America;" the *New York Times* "Style" section showcases "Generation E.A.: Ethnically Ambiguous;" and *Newsweek* portrays yet another set of adorable children in a cover story on "The New Face of Race." More systematically, for the 1990s, LexisNexis identified 1,890 usages in magazines of the same five keywords as for the Amazon.com search, and 2,826 so far in the 2000s (as of June 12, 2009). The industry trade press showed the same pattern, more dramatically: 284 LexisNexis usages of the five keywords in the 1990s, and 1,032 so far in the 2000s.

Food packagers targeting a mass market also reveal the cultural diffusion of multiracialism:

> To see the new face of the United States, . . . look at a box of Betty Crocker-brand food products. Betty's portrait is now in its eighth incarnation since the first composite painting debuted in 1936 with pale skin and blue eyes. Her new look is brown-eyed and dark-haired. She has a duskier complexion . . . , with features representing an amalgam of White, Hispanic, Indian, African and Asian ancestry. A computer created this new Betty in the mid-1990s by blending photos of 75 diverse women.[51]

Finally, market research firms, by definition, aspire to the closest connection with emerging cultural trends. One example suffices here: a claim to "anticipate the enormous demographic shift already underway in the U.S." In this "new . . . market, it is essential to get beyond ethnic segmentation and understand that it is the very intermingling of cultures and ethnicities that defines the . . . sensibility." Its peroration asks a home question: "Will you [our clients] be ready for this new, multi-colored, multi-cultural, multi-ethnic, and multi-lingual general market?"[52]

In short, even before Obama's presidential candidacy, multiracialism had arrived on the American public scene—demographically, normatively, behaviorally, culturally, and economically. To the degree that a feedback effect is reinforced or even permitted by the fact that it accords with societal trends, the new racial classification policy has received an unambiguous

boost. In that sense only, contemporary multiracialism is analogous to the old one-drop-of-blood laws and the 1970 invention of Hispanic—and not analogous to the categories of mulatto or the Mexican race.

The Political Balance: Identification with and Hostility to Racial Mixture

The theory of a policy-politics feedback loop holds that a new policy creates a political constituency or fact on the ground, which then enables the policy to become sufficiently embedded that it survives its original context. That is, the newly institutionalized policy needs supporters with incentives to maintain and deepen it, or it must become so much a part of citizens' daily lives that rescinding it becomes politically unthinkable.[53] To continue with our examples, the category of Hispanic developed a strong constituency, and the southern one-drop rules became an unexamined part of everyday life; both have survived.

Conversely, for the feedback loop to take hold, political opposition to the new policy must be weak enough that it can be consistently overcome, or it must be of the sort that actually galvanizes constituents into stronger support of rather than undermining their commitments to the new policy. The Mexican race ran into strong opposition and had almost no constituency; it disappeared at once. The mulatto category eventually lost its white constituency and succumbed to political opponents seeking racial purity; it too was removed from the official classification system.

In the case of the new policy of recognizing racial mixture, overtly political constituent development remains uncertain, while the entry of multiracialism into citizens' daily lives might be occurring, albeit slowly. Overt political opposition has diminished and is likely to remain weak. But group loyalties persist; they could either sap the strength of multiracial identity or change the way in which large numbers of Americans understand and practice racial politics. The political arena, in short, remains complicated and volatile.

Multiracial Self-definition

Most Americans do not see themselves as multiracial, at least as evidenced in classification systems. Analyses of the 2000 census and subsequent American Community Surveys (ACS) led sociologist Reynolds Farley to conclude in 2004 that "identifying with multiple races [was] a social movement that succeeded but failed. . . . I doubt . . . that 'multiracial' will be commonly used as if it were a race, either when people identify themselves or when agencies and courts wrestle with equal opportunities for all races."[54] Farley's conclusion, however, may have been premature. Figure 4 updates and extends his findings, using two sets of census calculations and another large, repeated survey.

One must be cautious about these data for several reasons.[55] Nevertheless, these series provide the best available evidence, and they all show the same basic facts: identification with two or more races is low, and has been rising since 2005.

Disaggregating these data provides reasons to expect mixed-race identification to continue to rise. The category of Black plus another race is the most politically and emotionally fraught. Yet the proportion of people choosing Black plus another race rose from 4.8 percent in 2000 to 6.5 percent in the 2008 ACS. The proportion of American Indians plus another race similarly rose, from 39.9 to

48.5 percent. And the proportion choosing "some other race" (SOR) plus a named race declined dramatically, from 17.1 to 8.3 percent, suggesting that multiracialism is less frequently a stand-in for White Hispanics than it was a few years ago.[56]

Another reason to anticipate a rise in mixed-race identification is that people under age 18 disproportionately call themselves (or are labeled by their parents as) multiracial. Barely two percent of adults identified with more than one race in the 2000 census, compared with twice as many of those under 18. In the 2008 ACS, the ratio was three to one. Put another way, a quarter of the American population was under age 18 in 2008, whereas almost half of the two-or-more-races population was.[57] As Figure 4 shows, the National Health Interview Survey (NHIS) shows the same relative youthful overrepresentation. If these young people retain mixed-race identity in adulthood and pass it on to their children, and given that future birth cohorts will have more mixed-race children since interracial marriage is rising, the proportion of self-defined multiracials will likely increase.

The proportion of self-identified multiracials is sometimes much higher in recent smaller surveys. In order to investigate a more "fluid portrait of ethno-racial self-identification," Taeku Lee asked respondents in a 2003 California survey to allocate ten points among racial or ethnic groups to indicate their own group heritage. Just over a quarter gave at least one point to more than one group. As Lee points out, "this is several magnitudes of order greater than the proportion of multi-racial identifiers we find using categorical measures." In 2009, *Newsweek* found that 16 percent of its respondents considered themselves to "be of mixed race." Eleven percent have a mixed-race child; a quarter have a close family member with a spouse or partner of a different race; and very large majorities know someone of mixed race or an interracial couple.[58]

Mixed-race identification might also rise because the United States' future high-status adults have a relatively high propensity to define themselves in terms of more than one race. Fully 17 percent of participants in a survey of first-year students at selective colleges and universities who were identified by their institution as Black reported being of mixed race. Comparable figures for Latinos were 28.2 percent, for Asians 7.4 percent, and for Whites 1.7 percent. In 2007, 8.3 percent of the roughly 48,000 students in 31 highly selective private American colleges and universities (in some cases the same schools) identified with more than one race.[59]

Scholars at UCLA have surveyed hundreds of thousands of full-time, first-year students attending American colleges and universities for decades, and have permitted them to choose more than one race since 1971. Figure 5 shows the pattern for all students, based on the weighted sample and including Hispanic as a "race" analogous to Black, White, Asian, and American Indian. By 2007, over 8 percent of students entering American colleges identified with more than one of these groups; the rise since 1990 has been uneven but unmistakable, and no evidence points to reversal.

Multiracial self-identification might also increase due to the fact that the proportion of Americans who are Hispanic is rising, and Hispanics have a long cultural tradition of defining themselves as multiracial. Probably few Latinos are conversant with José Vasconcelos's vision of *la raza cósmica,* but many might recognize themselves in his description of a group with mingled White, Black, and American Indian ancestry. In the 2001 Children of Immigrants Longitudinal Study, for example, which involves a sample of young adults in two highly diverse American cities, 11 percent defined themselves as multiracial.[60]

Finally, more people may define themselves in terms of more than one race for the simple reason that the possibility is becoming more available. As people moving into adulthood are routinely offered the option of choosing multiple races or "multiracial" when they register for school, apply to college, get a driver's license, apply for a job, join the military, fill out federal forms, answer surveys, or go to a doctor, it could become simply an uncomplicatedly appropriate option to an increasing number of Americans. After all, young adults see highly visible figures from Barack Obama through Tiger Woods and Halle Berry identify as multiracial; these young adults are embedded in increasingly diversified kinship networks; they are becoming more likely to come across interracial couples and their children; and they are encountering ever more attention to multiracialism from commercial enterprises. For all of these reasons, defining oneself in terms of multiple races is likely to spread through the American population, slowly perhaps, but steadily.

Even if that expectation is met, the conditions for a robust policy-politics feedback loop are not yet satisfied. For a new classification system to really take hold and help to shape the policy, it needs a politically strong constituency that moves beyond simple acceptance of a new set of boxes to check. Identification, that is, must become identity of some sort.

Resistance to Multiracial Identity

Much research has examined whether immigrants and their descendents from Latin America or Asia come to identify as Hispanics or Asian Americans instead of continuing to understand themselves and practice politics with reference to their nationality of origin.[61] That is, are they developing a racial identity analogous to that of African Americans? Perhaps, and that is precisely what opponents feared when the issue of multiracialism reached the political agenda in the 1990s. Some opponents were vehement, such as Representative Eleanor Holmes Norton (D-DC):

At one point, blacks thought they might mitigate the effects of being black by claiming something else in their heritage. "Oh, I am black, but I am also American Indian. . . ." Oh, it was so pitiful. About the only thing that American racism did for us is saying, "No, you are one or the other. . . ." So I sit here as a light skin black woman and I sit here to tell you that I am black. That people who are my color in this country will always be treated as black. . . . We who are black have got to say, "Look, we are people of color, and we are readily identified. Any discrimination against one of us is discrimination against another."

Others were cool and legalistic, as was Harold McDougall of the NAACP:

Overcoming the long history of discrimination in employment, lending, housing, and education requires that demographic data be kept on racial and ethnic groups who have historically been the targets of discrimination by members of the European-American majority group. . . . Thus the creation of a multiracial classification might disaggregate the apparent numbers of members of discrete minority groups, diluting benefits to which they are entitled as a protective class under civil rights laws and under the Constitution itself. In our quest for self-identification, we must take care not to recreate, reinforce or even expand the caste system we are all trying so hard to overcome.[62]

Only one of the thirty-nine members of the Congressional Black Caucus supported recognition of racial mixture in the late 1990s.

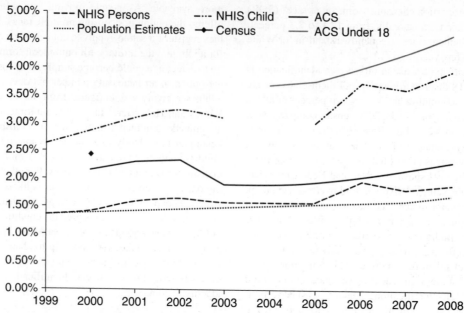

Figure 4 Identification with racial mixture in key surveys

Note: Starting in 2004, the ACS sample includes about 3 million households annually. NHIS samples range from a) for persons, 100,760 in 2001 to 74,236 in 2008; b) for a separate adult sample, 33,326 in 2001 to 21,781 in 2008, and c) for a separate child sample, 13,579 in 2001 to 8,815 in 2008.

Sources: 1) U.S. Census 2000, at factfinder.census.gov/servlet/AdvSearchByKeywordServlet?_lang=en; American Community Survey, at: www.census.gov/acs/www/index.html; Population Estimates at U. S. Bureau of the Census 2009, various codebooks for NHIS, 1999–2008. In the NHIS and ACS, those under 18 are a subset of the broader sample.

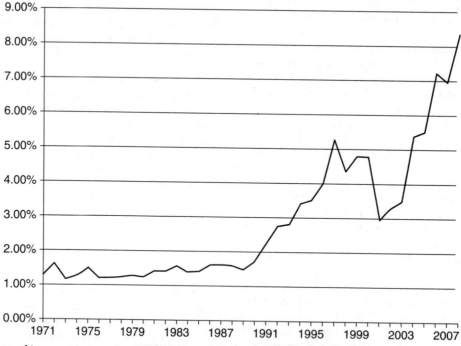

Figure 5 Percentage of two or more races, HERI College Freshmen Survey, 1971–2008

Source: analysis for the authors by HERI staff. CIRP Freshman Survey, Higher Education Research Institute at UCLA, 1971 to 2008. Data include only full-time students at 4-year institutions, and institutions with at least a 60 percent participation rate. Sample sizes range from 142,000 to 286,000, in hundreds of institutions chosen by a careful stratification system.

We coded the testimony at the 1993 and 1997 Congressional hearings on proposed changes in the federal system of racial classification, and found at least fifteen distinct arguments among the fifty-eight speakers. Opponents most commonly concurred with Rep. Norton, that multiracialism was merely a way to escape identification with a disfavored race or ethnicity. Their second most common claim echoed Mr. McDougall's, that the change would undermine enforcement of civil rights or voting rights laws. Supporters frequently contradicted the latter view, arguing that the new classification system would enhance civil rights or voting rights enforcement. But many endorsed a version of the former claim, that the new classification system would enable people to choose a new identity; that was their goal.[63]

Surely few Americans of any race attended to Congressional hearings or OMB decisions about the forthcoming census. But the issue moved into the public arena. During the month of census enumeration, *Ebony Magazine,* with a circulation of about 1.5 million, urged readers to "actively take part in the 2000 Census," on grounds articulated by "the highest-ranking Black at the Census:" it is "a matter of pride. There's the whole issue of respect. When you have the numbers, people listen." *Ebony* went on, however, to describe

> one concern African-American leaders continue to have with the census form . . . , the question of race. William Spriggs, director of research and public policy for the National Urban League, says that the question is worded in a way that would force many Blacks to check several boxes, which would lead to a Black person being counted as 'other' instead of African-American. One rule of thumb, Spriggs says: "If you get treated like you're Black, then check Black."[64]

Few Blacks did, in fact, choose more than one race.

After 2000, racial advocacy groups were less vocal, though not silent, on the issue of multiracial classification. In 2005 the Mexican American Legal Defense Fund (MALDEF) and the Reverend Jesse Jackson protested the EEOC's plan to add a category of "two or more races" to employers' reporting forms. Speaking as groups "concerned about the advancement of people of color," they formally expressed their concern that "the category of 'Two or more races' would not be meaningful for affirmative action purposes under OFCCP's [Office of Federal Contract Compliance Programs] authority." Two years later, the Department of Education reported similarly: "Some commentators suggested that reporting two or more races will have a detrimental impact on compliance with, and enforcement of, civil rights laws; ignores OMB guidance for aggregation and allocation of multiple race responses for purposes of civil rights reporting; and limits public access to important information by civil rights advocates, parents, and others."[65] Sprinkled through the *Federal Register* are similar expressions of continuing concern and monitoring.

Overt opposition to recognition of or identification with more than one race has declined further since Barack Obama's candidacy and electoral victory. Some continue to worry that parents who define their children as mixed race "set up their kids for a life of minefields and rejections. It's (unintentionally) cruel, selfish and shortsighted to produce multiracial children in a predominantly racist society."[66] But most explicit rejection of multiracialism has dissipated.

Multiracial Advocacy: Despite the decline in overt opposition, as identities are usually defined, multiracial identity remains weak. For example, multiracial groups are less involved in advocacy than they were a decade ago, and are waning. Kim Williams located about sixty local and national groups in the 1990s that publicly promoted multiracialism.[67] Using the *Encyclopedia of Associations,* internet searches, and listings on other group websites, we found 109 named groups in 2008. That looks like evidence of increasing robustness, but it is not. Only twenty-one had an active website, some of which had not been updated for at least a year. Over half had no publicly listed e-mail address or telephone number. Only ten of the 109 groups featured any political activism such as discussions of policy issues or efforts to educate legislators about multiracial rights; the most common specified goal was to "organize social gatherings where members can relax, share our experiences, and learn from

the experiences of others," in the words of Montclair, New Jersey's Getting Interracial Families Together. To our knowledge, multiracial groups have not sought further changes in the federal statistical system or testified in hearings on the 2010 census.

Thus unlike in the case of social security and AARP,[68] or the case of Hispanics and MALDEF or La Raza, for example, consolidation of multiracial identifiers into a powerful constituent group that politicians cannot afford to ignore or flout is not occurring.

Multiracial Identity

More analytically, multiracialism functions politically neither like interests represented by lobbies nor like race with its array of supportive organizations. On interests: People who gain materially from a new policy have an incentive to find each other and form an organized constituency to support consolidation—that is, to create a vigorous policy-politics feedback loop. But identifying as multiracial provides no material policy gains; no policies designed to compensate disadvantaged minorities for past injustices, such as affirmative action, majority-minority electoral districting, or small business set-asides, include people of more than one race as a designated category. Nor do universities or corporations seeking diversity include "multiracial" as a component of their desired membership.

On race: In the decades after Americans decided to treat race as a few exclusive, exhaustive groups, a powerful set of norms, emotions, and cognitive maps developed. As scholars and activists have consistently noted, many non-Whites now have a strong group consciousness, group loyalty, and perception of linked fate. These values are often associated with distinctive political and policy views.[69] Thus, if framed in opposition to monoracial loyalty, multiracial identity is unlikely to grow much even among those who define themselves in terms of more than one race. A classification or interpretive policy is simply too weak to develop a politics on its own; at least in the foreseeable future, we do not expect to see a strong form of multiracial identity in which people think of themselves as multiracial rather than some other race, experience life in arenas such as work, school, or politics distinctively, feel a special attachment to other multiracials, and unite in the political or public arena. People with Black and White ancestry, for example, seldom feel part of the same group as people with Asian and Hispanic ancestry.

But multiracial identity need not be perceived or felt as a new racial group identity analogous to being Black, White, or Asian in order to affect the American racial order. It can be understood as an addition rather than an alternative, a contextual choice rather than a fixed characteristic, a way of remaining connected to two (or more) poles rather than choosing one instead of the other. That, at any rate, is what prominent proponents of multiracialism appear to believe.

In 2005, then-Senator Barack Obama emphasized the link between racial identity and multiracial identity: "I don't think you can consider the issue of mixed race outside of the issue of race. I think it's important to try to avoid that sense of exclusivity. . . . Don't ever think of yourself as so unique that you divorce yourself from your communities."[70] A decade earlier, Maria Root's widely-disseminated "Bill of Rights for People of Mixed Heritage" emphasized context and fluidity: mixed-race people have the rights "not to be responsible for people's discomfort with my physical or ethnic ambiguity," "to identify myself differently in different situations," "to change my identity over my lifetime—and more than once," and "to have loyalties and identification with more than one group of people."[71] These claims have a very different tone from assertions of linked fate, racial solidarity, or group interests.

Little direct evidence exists on whether this distinctive understanding of multiracial identity, and therefore of race as a whole, is growing. But indicators are suggestive. To begin with, many Americans, presumably including people with a strong racial identity, endorse recognition of multiple ancestries; as early as 1995, 49 percent of Black and 36 percent of White survey respondents agreed that "the US Census should add a 'multiracial' category to population surveys so some people aren't forced to deny part of a family member's heritage by having to choose a single racial category."[72] In addition, at least some multiracial groups explicitly resist conventional understandings of races as exhaustive and exclusive. Three groups representing mixed-race people recently objected to a "multiracial" item on the University of California system's application form, on the grounds that a single category would limit "their choice to a generic multiracial/multiethnic category [that] ignores this diversity and severely limits the ability of UC to gain a clear and detailed picture of its student population." They wanted the form to allow multiple choices so that students' racial identities would be noted along with their mixed-race identification. The MAVIN Foundation sounds the same note in its mission statement; it is

> committed to creating a society that recognizes the complexity of race, racism and identity. We support the right to self-identify, and think it's important for mixed heritage and transracially adopted people to strengthen their involvement in existing ethnic and affinity communities. Although we reject exclusive and outdated notions of race, we see our work as part of a larger movement to end discrimination and inequality on individual and systemic levels.[73]

A spokesperson for MALDEF had made the same point many years earlier; he was "hard pressed to find a situation where understanding diversity better, understanding complexity better, is a hindrance."[74]

It is not surprising, therefore, that psychologists find self-defined multiracials to be more likely than others to see race as a social construction and as a fluid concept.[75] Multiracials have unusually diverse friendship networks, and are more comfortable in interracial relationships.[76] As early as 1995, they endorsed interracial dating more than did Blacks and Whites, and they were less likely than Blacks to agree that Blacks should be seen as a single racial group.[77] In the CILS survey, young adult multiracials are more likely to marry other multiracials than are monoracial respondents—but they are also more likely to marry Blacks, Asians, and people from "Other" races than are respondents not in those groups.[78] In all of these ways, they are signaling that multiracial identity blurs, but need not dissolve, traditional racial commitments.

Possibilities for a fluid and additive multiracial identity are bolstered by the fact that monoracial group identities may be weakening. In the 1995 poll in which many Americans endorsed a multiracial category, a third of Blacks and almost three-fifths of Whites agreed that "Black Americans today have such differing mixtures of African and European ancestry that it no longer makes much sense to think of them as Black and members of a single racial group." In 2007, 37 percent of Blacks agreed that "Blacks today can no longer be thought of as a single race because the Black community is so diverse."[79]

Finally, the scant survey data available supports the metaphor of this population as a bridge between more polarized groups. For example, in a 1995 survey, a twelve-point gap separated monoracial Blacks and Whites when asked if racial relations were poor in the United States; mixed-race respondents were right between, not as likely to see poor race relations as Blacks but not as optimistic as

Whites.[80] In a smaller 2001 survey, when asked if "too little attention is paid to race and racial issues" and if there are "still major problems facing minorities in this country," multiracials again fell between the racial poles, more likely than Whites but less likely than Blacks to agree with both claims.[81] The national survey by the Higher Education Research Institute at UCLA asked first-year college students how important "helping to promote racial understanding" was to them. As is typically the case, Whites were less committed to this goal than were Blacks, with 29 percent of the former and over 60 percent of the latter agreeing that promoting racial understanding was "essential" or "very important" to them. In contrast, the two largest sets of multiracial respondents—White/Hispanic and White/Asian—fell in between, with 36 and 39 percent agreement, respectively.[82] In the *National Longitudinal Survey of Freshmen*, people who described themselves as Black plus some other race or Hispanic plus some other race were less likely than monoracial Blacks or Hispanics to express a sense of racial linked fate, more likely to see a promising racial future with less discrimination, and less likely to agree that one should vote for a co-racial candidate, shop at co-racially owned stores, have friends primarily in one's own group, and so on.[83] Consistently across these surveys, multiracials' support for affirmative action measures, racial redistricting, or government intervention to ensure equality falls between that of Blacks and Whites. So do their perceptions of racial tension and disenfranchisement.[84] If the results of these initial surveys hold up over time and in the political arena, people who describe themselves as multiracial, even if they do not develop a strong group-based identity, may come to occupy a middle ground between traditional racial poles. Like President Obama, they may take as one of their missions to be an interlocutor and compromising voice when still heated debates over race flare up. Whether they (or he) can succeed, of course, remains an open question.

Development of a strong, shared multiracial identity would be the final phase of an emergent policy-politics feedback loop. But even if it develops, arguably this identity will not be the same kind of sentiment as a strong Black, Asian, White, or Hispanic identity. Ironically, in this way if no other, the closest analogy for contemporary multiracials may be turn-of-the-century mulattoes or Whites distinguished by mother tongue or mixed parentage; none of these groups abjured a monoracial identity but all added something to it that distinguished them in meaningful ways from people with a single ancestry and moved them closer to another group. Analysts and activists should remain open to the possibility that the "mutts," as Barack Obama referred to people like himself, believe and behave differently than the purebreds, without being any less members of the same species.

The Possible Futures of American Multiracialism

"The significance of race as we know it in today's legal and governmental categories will be obsolete in less than 20 years. The rise of mixed-race voters will dilute the racial identity politics that have become prevalent in past elections."

—William Frey[85]

After, though not before, the 1920s, Americans settled on an understanding of race that revolved around a few exhaustive and mutually exclusive groups with bright lines between them. Although it was historically unprecedented and very unusual in comparison with other countries, this understanding still sets the stage for Americans' political disputes around race. The evolving multiracial movement challenges this understanding of race—not by proposing an addition to the small set of recognized races but by undermining the sharp distinctions implied by one-drop rules and one-choice classification systems. If supporters of multiracialism succeed in their challenge, what is now a small, anomalous annoyance to statisticians and advocacy groups could change much of the politics and policy of American race relations.

History teaches us to refrain from any strong prediction; too many racial classifications, even some that lasted almost a century, have come and gone. "Mark one or more" could go the way of mulatto, the Mexican race, half-breeds, mother tongue, Hindoos, mixed parentage, and other efforts to classify and make sense of the United States' wonderfully complex mix of people. Nevertheless, although some aspects of multiracialism are spreading faster than others, we are reasonably confident that enough feedbacks have taken hold to reinforce the trajectory of self-defined mixture. As public and private actors move to a "mark one or more" classification system, as racial mixture increases demographically and multiracial identification grows socially, and as opposition to the new formulation wanes, returning to the twentieth-century racial order becomes increasingly unlikely.

To what end? Permitting people to connect with more than one race seems like a small move, but it may set a new path for racial development in the United States. Perhaps most importantly and not coincidentally, multiracial identification can reinforce a significant cohort change. Evidence shows consistently that many members of the generation coming of age during the Obama era see racial difference as less important, or differently important, than their elders do. Young adults do not share a collective racial memory that revolves around civil rights battles, the urgent need for group solidarity, and the sharp antagonisms that result from losing dominance. Instead, young adults' most vivid racial memory may be the election and power of a biracial president who received more support from all groups than did his recent Democratic predecessors. The United States is certainly not post-racial after November 2008, but it is arguably more multiracial—and if the new collective racial memory persists and deepens among young adults, a perception of identity as additive rather than substitutive may well produce feedbacks of its own.

There will be costs to such a future. Desperately poor people of color may be left without the language of group solidarity and pride that has for decades provided a partial weapon against and insight into their situation. Claims of race-based discrimination and profiling could be met with even more skepticism than they meet with now, and may be harder to prove in court. Racially-inflected inequality may persist and be harder to pinpoint and rectify. For worse as well as for better, however, Americans appear to be moving away from the last century's racial order. Who will benefit, and who will pay the price, remains to be seen—perhaps by our children.

Notes

1. www.youtube.com/watch?v=EADUQWKoVek; *Migration News* 2004.

2. U. S. Bureau of the Census 2001.

3. Vasconcelos 1979.

4. A few words on terminology: we use mixed race, multiracial(ism), biracial, and racial mixture interchangeably. We specify at appropriate locations whether Hispanics or Latinos are a "race" for purposes of the analysis. Except where specified, we do not treat people of mixed nationalities (Japanese-Korean; Swedish-Armenian) as multiracial.

   By "recognition," we mean that an external actor or agency (e.g. employer, census) permits individuals to describe themselves as multiracial or to choose more than one race. "Self-definition" or "identification" means that an individual chooses his or her own racial label. By "identity," we mean that the person sees his or her racial self-definition to be an important constitutive part of who he or she really is, with political, emotional, behavioral, or cultural implications.

   We define a society's racial order as the widely understood and accepted system of beliefs, laws, and practices that organize relationships among groups defined as races or ethnicities; see Powell 2009.

5. Gans 2007 (271–72).

6. Quoted in K. Williams 2006 (42).

7. For a similar argument see Rockquemore et al. 2009.

8. Sidanius et al. 2001, Telles 2004, Morning 2008.

9. Marx 1998, King and Smith 2005, Sawyer 2005, R. Smith 2007 and the books therein.

10. Hancock 2007.

11. Shelby 2005, Joseph 2007, Hollinger 2006, Rodriguez 2007, Valle and Torres 2000.

12. A very small sample includes Jacobson 1998, Roediger 2005, Hattam 2007, Hochschild and Powell 2008, Novkov 2008, Gross 2008, and Pascoe 2009.

13. Quotations in this paragraph are from, in order, Mettler and Soss 2004 (61), Igo 2007 (4), and Anderson 2002 (38). See also Foucault 1979 and Scott 1998.

14. Siegel and Passel 1979.

15. Quoted in Schor 2005 (99–100).

16. Skerry 2000, Skrentny 2002.

17. Office of Management and Budget 1977, Office of Management and Budget 1997.

18. Montejano 1987, Skrentny 2002, Haney-López 2003.

19. Hispanic remains an ethnicity rather than becoming a race on the census because tests have shown that more people define themselves as Hispanic or Latino when it remains a separate question, prior to the race question, than when it is added to the list of federally-approved races on official data collection forms.

20. U. S. Bureau of the Census 2002 (27). No instruction explained how to determine fractions of black blood.

21. Nobles 2000, Hochschild and Powell 2008.

22. The census office understood that these boundaries among groups were hopelessly blurred. As the 1895 *Report on Population* put it,

    The persons of negro descent are further classified under the law, as follows: negroes, 6,337,980; mulattoes, 956,989; quadroons, 105,135, and octoroons, 69,936. These figures are of little value. Indeed, as an indication of the extent to which the races have mingled, they are misleading; U. S. Census Office 1895 (xciii).

23. Stephenson 1910 (14).

24. Murray 1997, Hollinger 2003, D. Williams 2006, Novkov 2008.

25. We base this claim on our analysis of Murray 1997. Before 1920, most state laws defined as Negro all people with one Black grandparent (that is, having one-quarter Negro "blood"). After 1920, most state laws about marriage, segregation, and property ownership broadened the definition of Black to include people with "any appreciable amount of Negro blood" or as having one-eighth or one-sixteenth Black ancestry. Some variation persisted across states; as David Hollinger notes, "hypodescent . . . was not universally applied in all states even after 1924. Louisiana law, for example, was always more responsive to degrees of African descent than the laws of most other states." He provides a citation to Zackondik 2001 (in Hollinger 2003, n. 29).

26. Hochschild, Powell, and Weaver 2008.

27. For this history, see Jones 2000, DaCosta 2004, K. Williams 2006.

28. NAS reports included Edmonston and Schultze 1995 and Edmonston, Goldstein, and Lott 1996. Experts included J. Smith and Edmonston 1997; Hirschman, Kasinitz, and DeWind 1999; and Goldstein and Morning 2000. Wallman 1998 gives the government analysis, and K. Williams 2006 analyses state activity.

29. Office of Management and Budget 1997.

30. Some multiracial proponents were disappointed that OMB gave respondents the option to choose one or more races, rather than establishing a stand-alone category of "multiracial." In the eyes of its proponents, "multiracial" would have signaled a distinct group identity, whereas "mark one or more" permits individual or governmental analysts to reallocate mixed-race individuals back into their specific races.

31. Prewitt 2001 (40). Prewitt implemented the decision, but did not hold the position of census director when OMB issued its 1997 *Revisions*.

32. Both comments are quoted in Chandler and Glod 2009.

33. *Federal Register* 2001.

34. U. S. Equal Employment Opportunity Commission 2005 (71295); U. S. Department of Education 2007; ibid., (59267). *Education Week* described this "Guidance" as "holding firm in the face of objections" http://edweek.org/ew/articles/2007/10/23/09raceregs_web.h27.html? (accessed 2/17/08). Hinting at some, the Association for Institutional Research noted that the new standards "may require institutions to make considerable investments of both time and money," ranging from computer programming to analyses of any statistically-induced rise in Latino and decline in African American enrollment; Broh and Minicucci 2008. AIR also observed, more favorably, that "the new federal rules . . . will increase what many institutions know about the diversity of their community by capturing information on the increasing number of people who identify with more than one race" http://www.airweb.org/page.asp?page=1393 (accessed 2/17/08).

35. Communication with authors, January 2008.

36. Broh and Minicucci 2008.

37. U. S. Equal Employment Opportunity Commission 2005 (71296).

38. On intermarriage, see Farley 2007; Qian and Lichter 2007.

    An analysis of pooled 1997–2001 data from the National Health Interview Survey (NHIS) does include Hispanics as a "racial" group. It finds that among married women, 97 percent of Whites, 96 percent of Blacks, 74 percent of Asians, 46 percent of American Indians, and 82 percent of Hispanics are in homogamous marriages. Among married men, the percentages are respectively 97, 87, 88, 41, and 83. Thus Hispanics' intermarriage rate is roughly comparable to that of Asian Americans; Bratter and Eschbach 2006.

39. The decline in Asian intermarriage does not hold for native-born persons (http://economics.harvard.edu/faculty/fryer/files/interracial_marriage_onlineappendix_figs.pdf, fig. 1). These data exclude Hispanics, but a separate analysis found that about 14 percent of married Hispanics have non-Hispanic spouses. Intermarriage is much higher among native-borns than among immigrants; Lee and Edmonston 2006. These estimates are conservative, since the data do not take into account the third generation "loss" of Hispanics into White-only identity, or the higher intermarriage rate of "some other race" identifiers, who are disproportionately Hispanic.

40. Fryer Jr. 2007.

41. New American Media 2007a.

42. Kasinitz et al. 2008.

43. New American Media 2007b. The survey excluded Whites.

44. On children, see Farley 2007. On unmarried partners, see Simmons and O'Connell 2003. On California, see Tafoya 2000.

45. Goldstein communication with the authors, January 29, 2009.

46. Hochschild, Powell, and Weaver 2008.

47. *Chicago Defender,* Jan. 22, 1949 (7).

48. Myrdal 1944.

49. Gallup 2007.

50. The Gallup Poll in Gallup 2007. Endorsement of intermarriage in Pew Research Center for the People and the Press 1999. Exaggeration in Gallup/CNN/*U.S.A. Today* 2001.

51. Stanfield 1999.

52. Waterston 2004, emphasis original.

53. Wilson 1989, Shklar 1991, Mettler 2002, Schuck 2009.

54. Farley 2004 (123, 147).

55. Direct comparisons between census 2000 and later ACS's are inappropriate because imputation rules for allocating respondents into racial categories differ across years. In addition, the sampling frame and procedures for the ACS have only recently been stabilized, and some demographers doubt the comparability to the census of even recent data. The census bureau's Annual Population Estimates differ from the ACS because of different imputation rules as well as different strategies for calculating groups' sizes. The Estimates take into account births, deaths, and net migration, but not self-reports in the years after the census; they therefore do not incorporate any changes in people's propensity to identify with multiple races, as the ACS can do. Finally, the NHIS differs from both census bureau measures, presumably because of sampling strategies, question wording and placement, and other house effects.

    For the 2000 census itself, it may be appropriate to drop respondents who chose Some Other Race (SOR) plus one of the standard races from the category of multiracial, on the grounds that many chose White and wrote in Hispanic or an equivalent term—that is, they are White Hispanics rather than being of mixed race as that term is commonly used. Deleting SORs from the 2000 census leaves a self-identified multiracial population for that year of 1.4 percent.

56. The proportions choosing another race + either Asian, White, Native Hawaiian or Other Pacific Islander (NHOPI), or Hispanic all remained stable or declined slightly from census 2000 to the 2007 ACS.

57. http://factfinder.census.gov: table S0201.

58. Lee 2004 (15); *Newsweek* 2009.

59. For first year students, see Massey et al. 2003; for selective colleges, see Broh and Minicucci 2008 (16).

60. Authors' analysis of Portes and Rumbaut 1991–2006.

61. Espiritu 1992, Haney-López 2003, Lien et al. 2004, Aoki and Takeda 2009, Garcia Bedolla 2009.

62. Norton 1997 (260), McDougall 1997 (308).

63. Hochschild and Burch 2007.

64. "Why the Census Is Important to You" 2000.

65. U. S. Equal Employment Opportunity Commission 2005 (71296), Department of Education 2007 (59271).

66. St. James 2007.

67. K. Williams 2006.

68. Campbell 2003.

69. Dawson 1994, Chong and Rogers 2004, Hutchings et al. 2005, Lien et al. 2003.

70. www.mavinfoundation.org/index.html

71. www.drmariaroot.com/doc/BillOfRights.pdf

72. Authors' analysis of *Survey by Newsweek and Princeton Survey Research Associates* 1995. Since usually more than half of African Americans express a sense of linked fate and racial consciousness when asked, at least some of the Black endorsers of multiracialism in the *Newsweek* survey are presumably also strongly racially identified.

73. Mavin Foundation 2006.

74. UC groups are in Andrews and Chun 2007, (89); MAVIN mission statement is at http://mavinfoundation.org/about/mission.html; MALDEF is quoted in K. Williams 2006 (42).

75. Shih et al. 2007, Bonam & Shih 2009.

76. Quillian and Redd 2009, Shih et al. 2007.

77. Authors' analysis of *Newsweek* 1995.

78. Authors' analysis of Portes and Rumbaut 1991–2006.

79. Authors' analysis of *Newsweek* 1995, Pew Research Center for the People and the Press 2007.

80. *Newsweek* 1995.

81. *Washington Post* et al. 2001. See also Matsuoka 2008.

82. Those who identified as Black plus some other race, however, held views on this question similar to the views of Black monoracials. Analysis for the authors by HERI staff of Cooperative Institutional Research Program (various).

83. Authors analysis of Massey and Charles 2006.

84. The only exceptions to multiracials' intermediate position come in measures that revolve around mixture, such as support for

interracial dating, and counting multiracials on the Census. Not surprisingly, more multiracials supported these measures than did their monoracial peers.

85. Quoted in Yen 2009.

References

Anderson, Benedict. 2002. *The Spectre of Comparison.* London: Verso

Andrews, Matthew and Jeffrey Chun. 2007. "(Mis) Educating about 'Mixed Race': Discourse on Multiraciality and the Prospects of Higher Education Policy." *Asian American Policy Review* 16(1): 87–94.

Aoki, Andrew and Okiyoshi Takeda. 2009. *Asian American Politics.* Cambridge, UK: Polity Press.

Bonam, Courtney M. and Margaret Shih. 2009. "Exploring Multiracial Individuals' Comfort with Intimate Interracial Relationships." *Journal of Social Issues* 65(1): 87–103.

Bratter, Jenifer and Karl Eschbach. 2006. "'What about the Couple?' Interracial Marriage and Psychological Distress." *Social Science Research* 35(4): 1025–47.

Broh, C. Anthony and Stephen Minicucci. 2008. "Racial Identity and Government Classification: A Better Solution." Presented at the Association for Institutional Research, Seattle, WA, May 28.

Campbell, Andrea. 2003. *How Policies Make Citizens: Senior Political Activism and the American Welfare State.* Princeton, NJ: Princeton University Press.

Chandler, Michael and Maria Glod. 2009. "Multiracial Pupils to Be Counted in a New Way." *Washington Post,* March 23, A1.

Chong, Dennis and Reuel Rogers. 2004. "Reviving Group Consciousness." In *The Politics of Democratic Inclusion,* ed. Christina Wolbrecht and Rodney Hero. Philadelphia, PA: Temple University Press.

Cooperative Institutional Research Program. (various). *Freshman Survey.* UCLA, Graduate School of Education and Information Services, Higher Education Research Institute, Los Angeles, CA.

DaCosta, Kimberly. 2004. "All in the Family: The Familial Roots of Racial Division." In *The Politics of Multiracialism,* ed. Heather Dalmadge. Albany, NY: State University of New York Press.

Dawson, Michael. 1994. *Behind the Mule: Race and Class in African-American Politics.* Princeton, NJ: Princeton University Press.

Edmonston, Barry, Joshua Goldstein, and Juanita Lott. 1996. *Spotlight on Heterogeneity: The Federal Standards for Racial and Ethnic Classification.* Washington, DC: National Academy Press.

Edmonston, Barry and Charles Schultze. 1995. *Modernizing the U.S. Census.* Washington, DC: National Academy Press.

Espiritu, Yen Le. 1992. *Asian American Panethnicity: Bridging Institutions and Identities.* Philadelphia: Temple University Press.

Farley, Reynolds. 2004. "Identifying with Multiple Races: A Social Movement that Succeeded but Failed?" In *The Changing Terrain of Race and Ethnicity, ed.* Maria Krysan and Amanda Lewis. New York: Russell Sage Foundation.

————. 2007. "The Declining Multiple Race Population of the United States: The American Community Survey, 2000 to 2005." Presented at the Population Association of America conference, New York, NY, March 29–31.

Fields, A N. 1949. "Readers May Judge For Selves Of Social, Political Changes" *The Chicago Defender* (Jan 22): 7.

Foucault, Michel. 1979. *Discipline and Punish.* New York: Vintage Books.

Fryer, Roland, Jr. 2007. "Guess Who's Been Coming to Dinner? Trends in Interracial Marriage over the 20th Century." *Journal of Economic Perspectives* 21(2): 71–90.

Gallup. 2007. Most Americans Approve of Interracial Marriages. Gallup Organization. (http://gallup.com/poll/28417/Most-Americans-Approve-Interracial-Marriages.aspx).

Gallup/CNN/*U.S.A. Today.* 2001. *Poll—March Wave 1.* March 9–11.

Gans, Herbert. 2007. "The Possibility of a New Racial Hierarchy in the Twenty-First-Century United States." In *The Inequality Reader: Contemporary and Foundational Readings in Race, Class, and Gender,* eds. David Grusky and Szonja Szelényi. Boulder CO: Westview Press.

Garcia Bedolla, Lisa. 2009. *Latino Politics.* Cambridge, UK: Polity Press.

Goldstein, Joshua. 1999. "Kinship Networks That Cross Racial Lines: The Exception or the Rule?" *Demography* 36(3): 399–407.

Goldstein, Joshua and Ann Morning. 2000. "The Multiple-Race Population of the United States: Issues and Estimates." *Proceedings of the National Academy of Sciences* 97(11): 6230–35.

Gross, Ariela. 2008. *What Blood Won't Tell: A History of Race on Trial in America.* Cambridge, MA: Harvard University Press.

Hancock, Ange-Marie. 2007. "When Multiplication Doesn't Equal Quick Addition: Examining Intersectionality as a Research Paradigm." *Perspectives on Politics* 5(1): 63–80.

Haney-López, Ian. 2003. *Racism on Trial: The Chicano Fight for Justice.* Cambridge, MA: Belknap Press of Harvard University Press.

Hattam, Victoria. 2007. *Ethnic Shadows: Jews, Latinos, and Race Politics in the United States.* Chicago, IL: University of Chicago Press.

Hernandez, Jose', Leo Estrada, and David Alvirez. 1973. "Census Data and the Problem of Conceptually Defining the Mexican American Population." *Social Science Quarterly* 53(4): 671–87.

Hirschman, Charles, Philip Kasinitz, and Josh DeWind, eds. 1999. *The Handbook of International Migration: The American Experience.* New York: Russell Sage Foundation.

Hochschild, Jennifer and Traci Burch. 2007. "Contingent Public Policies and Racial Hierarchy: Lessons from Immigration and Census Policies." In *Political Contingency: Studying the Unexpected, the Accidental, and the Unforeseen,* eds. Ian Shapiro and Sonu Bedi. New York: New York University Press.

Hochschild, Jennifer and Brenna Marea Powell. 2008. "Racial Reorganization and the United States Census 1850–1930: Mulattoes, Half-Breeds, Mixed Parentage, Hindoos, and the Mexican Race." *Studies in American Political Development* 22(1): 59–96.

Hochschild, Jennifer, Brenna Marea Powell, and Vesla Weaver. 2008. "Political Discourse on Racial Mixture: American Newspapers, 1865 to 1970." Presented at the Policy History Conference, St. Louis, MO, May 29–31.

Hollinger, David. 2003. "Amalgamation and Hypodescent: The Question of Ethnoracial Mixture in the History of the United States." *American Historical Review* 108(5): 1363–90.

———. 2006. *Postethnic America: Beyond Multiculturalism.* New York: Basic Books.

Hutchings, Vincent, Cara Wong, Ronald Brown, James Jackson, and Nakesha Faison. 2005. "The National Ethnic Politics Study (NEPS): Ethnic Pluralism & Politics in the 21st Century." Presented at the American Association of Public Opinion Research conference, Miami Beach, FL, May 12.

Igo, Sarah. 2007. *The Averaged American: Surveys, Citizens, and the Making of a Mass Public.* Cambridge, MA: Harvard University Press.

Jacobson, Matthew. 1998. *Whiteness of a Different Color: European Immigrants and the Alchemy of Race.* Cambridge, MA: Harvard University Press.

Jones, Trina. 2000. "Shades of Brown: The Law of Skin Color." *Duke Law Journal* 49: 1487–557.

Joseph, Peniel. 2007. *Waiting 'Til the Midnight Hour: A Narrative History of Black Power in America.* New York: Holt.

Kasinitz, Philip, John Mollenkopf, Mary Waters, and Jennifer Holdaway. 2008. *Inheriting the City: The Children of Immigrants Come of Age.* New York and Cambridge: Russell Sage Foundation and Harvard University Press.

King, Desmond and Rogers Smith. 2005. "Racial Orders in American Political Development." *American Political Science Review* 99(1): 75–92.

Lee, Sharon and Barry Edmonston. 2006. "Hispanic Intermarriage, Identification, and U.S. Latino Population Change." *Social Science Quarterly* 87(5): 1263–79.

Lee, Taeku. 2004. "Social Construction, Self-Identification, and the Survey Measurement of 'Race'." Presented at the American Political Science Association Annual Convention, Chicago IL.

Lien, Pei-te, M. Margaret Conway, and Janelle Wong. 2003. "The Contours and Sources of Ethnic Identity Choices among Asian Americans." *Social Science Quarterly* 84(2): 461–81.

———. 2004. *The Politics of Asian Americans: Diversity and Community.* New York: Routledge.

Marx, Anthony. 1998. *Making Race and Nation: A Comparison of South Africa, the United States, and Brazil.* New York: Cambridge University Press.

Massey, Douglas and Camille Charles. 2006. *National Longitudinal Survey of Freshmen.* Princeton University, Office of Population Research. October 20, 2006 (http://nlsf.princeton.edu/index.htm).

Massey, Douglas, Camille Charles, Garvey Lundy, and Mary Fischer. 2003. *The Source of the River: The Social Origins of Freshmen at America's Selective Colleges and Universities.* Princeton, NJ: Princeton University Press.

Matsuoka, Natalie. 2008. "Political Attitudes and Ideologies of Multiracial Americans." *Political Research Quarterly* 61(2): 253–67.

Mavin Foundation. 2006. Mission Statement. (www.mavinfoundation.org/about/mission.html), accessed March 8, 2010.

McDougall, Harold. 1997. *Statement at Hearings on "Federal Measures of Race and Ethnicity and the Implications for the 2000 Census".* Washington DC: U.S. Government Printing Office. 301–16.

Mettler, Suzanne. 2002. "Bringing the State Back in to Civic Engagement: Policy Feedback Effects of the G.I. Bill for World War II Veterans." *American Political Science Review* 96(2): 351–65

Mettler, Suzanne and Joe Soss. 2004. "The Consequences of Public Policy for Democratic Citizenship: Bridging Policy Studies and Mass Politics." *Perspectives on Politics* 2(1): 55–74.

Migration News. 2004. Census, Welfare, California, New York City. University of California, Davis. (http://migration.ucdavis.edu/mn/more.php?id=2994_0_2_0).

Montejano, David. 1987. *Anglos and Mexicans in the Making of Texas, 1836–1986.* Austin: University of Texas Press.

Morning, Ann. 2008. "Ethnic Classification in Global Perspective: A Cross-National Survey of the 2000 Census Round." *Population Research and Policy Review* 27(2): 239–272.

Murray, Pauli. 1997 [1950]. *States' Laws on Race and Color.* Athens: University of Georgia Press.

Myrdal, Gunnar. 1944. *An American Dilemma.* New York: Harper & Brothers.

New American Media. 2007a. California Dreamers: A Public Opinion Portrait of the Most Diverse Generation the Nation Has Known. (http://news.newamericamedia.org/news/view_custom.html?custom_page_id=340).

———. 2007b. "Deep Divisions, Shared Destiny." (http://news.newamericamedia.org/news/view_article.html?article_id=28501933d0e5c5344b21f9640dc13754).

Nobles, Melissa. 2000. *Shades of Citizenship: Race and the Census in Modern Politics.* Stanford, CA: Stanford University Press.

Norton, Eleanor Holmes. 1997. *Statement at Hearings on "Federal Measures of Race and Ethnicity and the Implications for the 2000 Census".* Washington, DC: U.S. Government Printing Office. 259–61.

Novkov, Julie. 2008. *Racial Union: Law, Intimacy, and the White State in Alabama, 1865–1954.* Ann Arbor: University of Michigan Press.

Office of Management and Budget. 1977. *Statistical Policy Directive Number 15: Race and Ethnic Standards for Federal Statistics and Administrative Reporting.* Washington DC: U.S. Government Printing Office.

———. 1997. *Revisions to the Standards for the Classification of Federal Data on Race and Ethnicity.* Washington DC: Executive Office of the President, OMB Office of Information and Regulatory Affairs. (http://whitehouse.gov/omb/fedreg/1997standards.html).

Pascoe, Peggy. 2009. *What Comes Naturally: Miscegenation Law and the Making of Race in America.* Oxford; New York: Oxford University Press.

Pew Research Center for the People and the Press. 1999. *Millenium Survey.* April 6–May 6.

———. 2007. "Racial Attitudes in America." Pew Research Center. (http://pewsocialtrends.org/assets/pdf/Race.pdf).

Portes, Alejandro and Rubén Rumbaut. 1991–2006. *Children of Immigrants Longitudinal Study (CILS) [Computer file].* ICPSR20520-v1. Ann Arbor, MI: Interuniversity Consortium for Political and Social Research [distributor].

Powell, Brenna. 2009. *Grey Area: Defining Race and the Struggle for Equality in Brazil.* Cambridge, MA: Harvard University, Government and Social Policy Program.

Prewitt, Kenneth. 2001. "Census 2000 and the Fuzzy Boundary Separating Politics and Science." *Bulletin of the American Academy of Arts and Sciences* 54(4): 32–40.

Qian, Zhenchao and Daniel Lichter. 2007. "Social Boundaries and Marital Assimilation: Interpreting Trends in Racial and Ethnic Intermarriage." *American Sociological Review* 72(1): 68–94.

Quillian, Lincoln and Rozlyn Redd. 2009. "The Friendship Networks of Multiracial Adolescents." *Social Science Research* 38(2): 279–95.

Rockquemore, Kerry, David Brunsma, and Daniel Delgado. 2009. "Racing to Theory or Retheorizing Race? Understanding the Struggle to Build a Multiracial Identity Theory." *Journal of Social Issues* 65(1): 13–34.

Rodriguez, Gregory. 2007. *Mongrels, Bastards, Orphans, and Vagabonds: Mexican Immigration and the Future of Race in America.* New York: Pantheon Books.

Roediger, David. 2005. *Working Toward Whiteness.* New York: Basic Books.

Sawyer, Mark. 2005. *Racial Politics in Post-Revolutionary Cuba.* New York: Cambridge University Press.

Schor, Paul. 2005. "Mobilising for Pure Prestige? Challenging Federal Census Ethnic Categories in the USA (1850–1940)." *International Social Science Journal* 57(183): 89–101.

Schuck, Peter. 2009. "Immigrants' Incorporation in the United States after 9/11: Two Steps Forward, One Step Back." In *Bringing Outsiders In: TransAtlantic Perspectives on Immigrant Political Incorporation, ed.* Jennifer Hochschild and John Mollenkopf. Ithaca, NY: Cornell University Press.

Scott, James. 1998. *Seeing Like a State: How Certain Schemes to Improve the Human Condition Have Failed.* New Haven, CT: Yale University Press.

Shelby, Tommie. 2005. *We Who Are Dark: The Philosophical Foundations of Black Solidarity.* Cambridge, MA: Harvard University Press.

Shih, Margaret, Courtney Bonam, Diana Sanchez, and Courtney Peck. 2007. "The Social Construction of Race: Biracial Identity and Vulnerability to Stereotypes." *Cultural Diversity and Ethnic Minority Psychology* 13(2): 125–33.

Shklar, Judith. 1991. *American Citizenship.* Cambridge, MA: Harvard University Press.

Sidanius, Jim, Yesilernis Peña, and Mark Sawyer. 2001. "Inclusionary Discrimination: Pigmentocracy and Patriotism in the Dominican Republic." *Political Psychology* 22(4): 827–51.

Siegel, Jacob, and Jeffrey Passel. 1979. *Coverage of the Hispanic Population of the United States in the 1970 Census: A Methodological Analysis.* Washington, DC: U. S. Bureau of the Census.

Simmons, Tavia and Martin O'Connell. 2003. *Married-Couple and Unmarried-Partner Households: 2000.* Washington, DC: U.S. Bureau of the Census.

Skerry, Peter. 2000. *Counting on the Census? Race, Group Identity, and the Evasion of Politics.* Washington, DC: Brookings Institution Press.

Skrentny, John David. 2002. *The Minority Rights Revolution.* Cambridge, MA: Belknap Press of Harvard University Press.

Smith, James and Barry Edmonston, ed. 1997. *The New Americans: Economic, Demographic, and Fiscal Effects of Immigration.* Washington, DC: National Academy Press.

Smith, Rogers. 2007. "Studies in American Racial Development: An Interim Report." *Perspectives on Politics* 5(2): 325–33.

St. James, Phillip. 2007. "Letter to the Editor" *Ebony.* 62: 31.

Stanfield, Rochelle. 1999. "The Blending of the United States." U.S. Department of State, International Information Programs. (http://usinfo.state.gov/journals/itsv/0699/ijse/stanfld.htm).

Stephenson, Gilbert. 1910. *Race Distinctions in American Law.* New York and London: D. Appleton and Company.

Survey by Newsweek and Princeton Survey Research Associates International, January 14–January 15, 2009. Retrieved June 15, 2009 from the iPOLL Databank, The Roper Center for Public Opinion Research, University of Connecticut. (www.ropercenter.uconn.edu/ipoll.html).

Survey by Newsweek and Princeton Survey Research Associates, February 1–February 3, 1995. Retrieved June 15, 2009 from the iPOLL Databank, The Roper Center for Public Opinion Research, University of Connecticut. (http://www.ropercenter.uconn.edu/ipoll.html).

Tafoya, Sonya. 2000. "Check One or More . . . Mixed Race and Ethnicity in California." Public Policy Institute of California. (http://ppic.org/content/pubs/cacounts/CC_100STCC.pdf).

Telles, Edward. 2004. *Race in Another America: The Significance of Skin Color in Brazil.* Princeton, NJ: Princeton University Press.

U. S. Bureau of the Census. 2001. *The Two or More Races Population: 2000.* Washington, DC: U.S. Department of Commerce.

———. 2002. *Measuring America: The Decennial Censuses From 1790 to 2000.* Washington, DC: U.S. Department of Commerce.

———. 2009 *Annual Estimates of the Resident Population by Sex, Race, and Hispanic Origin for the United States: April 1, 2000 to July 1, 2008.* Washington, DC: U.S. Census Bureau.

U. S. Census Office. 1895. *Report on Population of the United States at the Eleventh Census: 1890.* Washington, DC: Government Printing Office.

U. S. Department of Education. 2007. "Final Guidance on Maintaining, Collecting, and Reporting Racial and Ethnic Data to the U. S. Department of Education." *Federal Register.* 72(202): 59266–79.

U.S. Department of Justice. 2001. "Guidance Concerning Redistricting and Retrogression under Section 5 of the Voting Rights Act, 42 U.S.C. 1973c." *Federal Register* 66(12): 5412–5414.

U.S. Equal Employment Opportunity Commission. 2005. "Agency Information Collection Activities: Notice of Submission for OMB Review, Final Comment Request." *Federal Register* 70(227): 71294–303.

Valle, Victor and Rodolfo Torres. 2000. *Latino Metropolis.* Minneapolis: University of Minnesota Press.

Vasconcelos, José. 1979 [1925]. *The Cosmic Race: A Bilingual Edition.* Baltimore, MD: Johns Hopkins University Press.

Wallman, Katherine. 1998. "Data on Race and Ethnicity: Revising the Federal Standard." *American Statistician* 52(1): 31–33.

Washington Post, Kaiser Family Foundation, and Harvard University School of Public Health. 2001. *Race and Ethnicity in 2001: Attitudes, Perceptions, and Experiences.* Menlo Park, CA: Kaiser Family Foundation.

Waterston, Adriana. 2004. *The Dawning of Multicultural America.* Larchmont, NY: Horowitz Associates Inc. Market Research & Consulting. (www.horowitzassociates.com/dawning.pdf).

"Why the Census is Important to You." 2000. *Ebony.* April, 31ff.

Williams, Diana. 2006. *Family Drama: The Political Economy of Interracial Inheritance in Nineteenth Century Louisiana.* Cambridge, MA: Harvard University, Program in the History of American Civilization. (www.dianairenewilliams.com).

Williams, Kim. 2006. *Mark One or More: Civil Rights in Multiracial America.* Ann Arbor, MI: University of Michigan Press.

Wilson, James Q. 1989. *Bureaucracy: What Government Agencies Do and Why They Do It.* New York: Basic Books.

Yen, Hope. 2009. *Multiracial Americans Become Fastest Growing US Group.* June 4, 2009 (www.huffingtonpost.com/2009/05/29/).

Zackondik, Teresa. 2001. "Fixing the Color Line: The Mulatto, Southern Courts, and Racial Identity." *American Quarterly* 53: 420–51.

Critical Thinking

1. What race or ethnicity do you most identify with? Why?
2. What is multiracial identity and explain why those who believe themselves to be multiracial tend to have a wider base of friends and acquaintances?

JENNIFER HOCHSCHILD is Henry LaBarre Professor of Government and Professor of African and African American Studies at Harvard University (Hochschild@gov.harvard.edu). **VESLA M. WEAVER** is Assistant Professor of Politics at the University of Virginia and a Faculty Associate at the Miller Center of Public Affairs (vmweaver@virginia.edu). They wish to thank Andrew Benitez, Richard Coffin, Tiffany Jones, Daniel Koh, Jay Lundy, and Brenna Powell for their excellent research assistance. Thanks also to Traci Burch, our co-author in the larger project of which this article is a part, for managing the coding of Congressional hearings and general all-round contributions to developing this argument. Audiences and seminar participants at City University of London, Harvard University, Princeton University, University of California at Berkeley, and University of Manchester made contributions that deepened and clarified our analyses. Finally, we are grateful to C. Anthony Broh, Suzann Evinger, Reynolds Farley, Michael Fortner, Jacob Hacker, David Hollinger, Jeffrey Isaac, Kenneth Prewitt, Lydia Saad, KatherineWallman, Kim Williams, and several anonymous reviewers for very helpful comments on earlier drafts or in response to queries.

Brown et al. v. Board of Education of Topeka et al.

347 U.S. 483 (1954).

Mr. Chief Justice Warren delivered the opinion of the Court:

These cases come to us from the States of Kansas, South Carolina, Virginia, and Delaware. They are premised on different facts and different local conditions, but a common legal question justifies their consideration together in this consolidated opinion.[1]

In each of the cases, minors of the Negro race, through their legal representatives, seek the aid of the courts in obtaining admission to the public schools of their community on a non-segregated basis. In each instance, they had been denied admission to schools attended by white children under laws requiring or permitting segregation according to race. This segregation was alleged to deprive the plaintiffs of the equal protection of the laws under the Fourteenth Amendment. In each of the cases other than the Delaware case, a three-judge federal district court denied relief to the plaintiffs on the so-called "separate but equal" doctrine announced by this Court in *Plessy v. Ferguson,* 163 U.S. 537. Under that doctrine, equality of treatment is accorded when the races are provided substantially equal facilities, even though these facilities be separate. In the Delaware case, the Supreme Court of Delaware adhered to that doctrine, but ordered that the plaintiffs be admitted to the white schools because of their superiority to the Negro schools.

The plaintiffs contend that segregated public schools are not "equal" and cannot be made "equal," and that hence they are deprived of the equal protection of the laws. Because of the obvious importance of the question presented, the Court took jurisdiction.[2] Argument was heard in the 1952 Term, and reargument was heard this Term on certain questions propounded by the Court.[3]

Reargument was largely devoted to the circumstances surrounding the adoption of the Fourteenth Amendment in 1868. It covered exhaustively consideration of the Amendment in Congress, ratification by the states, then existing practices in racial segregation, and the views of proponents and opponents of the Amendment. This discussion and our own investigation convince us that, although these sources cast some light, it is not enough to resolve the problem with which we are faced. At best, they are inconclusive. The most avid proponents of the post–War Amendments undoubtedly intended them to remove all legal distinctions among "all persons born or naturalized in the United States." Their opponents, just as certainly, were antagonistic to both the letter and the spirit of the Amendments and wished them to have the most limited effect. What others in Congress and the state legislatures had in mind cannot be determined with any degree of certainty.

An additional reason for the inconclusive nature of the Amendment's history, with respect to segregated schools, is the status of public education at that time.[4] In the South, the movement toward free common schools, supported by general taxation, had not yet taken hold. Education of white children was largely in the hands of private groups. Education of Negroes was almost nonexistent, and practically all of the race were illiterate. In fact, any education of Negroes was forbidden by law in some states. Today, in contrast, many Negroes have achieved outstanding success in the arts and sciences as well as in the business and professional world. It is true that public school education at the time of the Amendment had advanced further in the North, but the effect of the Amendment on northern States was generally ignored in the congressional debates. Even in the North, the conditions of public education did not approximate those existing today. The curriculum was usually rudimentary; ungraded schools were common in rural areas; the school term was but three months a year in many states; and compulsory school attendance was virtually unknown. As a consequence, it is not surprising that there should be so little in the history of the Fourteenth Amendment relating to its intended effect on public education.

In the first cases in this Court construing the Fourteenth Amendment, decided shortly after its adoption, the Court interpreted it as proscribing all state-imposed discriminations against the Negro race.[5] The doctrine of "separate but equal" did not make its appearance in this Court until 1896 in the case of *Plessy v. Ferguson, supra,* involving not education but transportation.[6] American courts have since labored with the doctrine for over half a century. In this Court, there have been six cases involving the "separate but equal" doctrine in the field of public education.[7] In *Cumming v. County Board of Education,* 175 U.S. 528, and *Gong Lum v. Rice,* 275 U.S. 78, the validity of the doctrine itself was not challenged.[8] In more recent cases, all on the graduate school level, inequality was found in that specific benefits enjoyed by white students were denied to

Negro students of the same educational qualifications. *Missouri ex rel. Gaines v. Canada,* 305 U.S. 337; *Sipuel v. Oklahoma,* 332 U.S. 631; *Sweatt v. Painter,* 339 U.S. 629; *McLaurin v. Oklahoma State Regents,* 339 U.S. 637. In none of these cases was it necessary to reexamine the doctrine to grant relief to the Negro plaintiff. And in *Sweatt v. Painter, supra,* the Court expressly reserved decision on the question whether *Plessy v. Ferguson* should be held inapplicable to public education.

In the instant cases, that question is directly presented. Here, unlike *Sweatt v. Painter,* there are findings below that the Negro and white schools involved have been equalized, or are being equalized, with respect to buildings, curricula, qualifications and salaries of teachers, and other "tangible" factors.[9] Our decision, therefore, cannot turn on merely a comparison of these tangible factors in the Negro and white schools involved in each of the cases. We must look instead to the effect of segregation itself on public education.

In approaching this problem, we cannot turn the clock back to 1868 when the Amendment was adopted, or even to 1896 when *Plessy v. Ferguson* was written. We must consider public education in the light of its full development and its present place in American life throughout the Nation. Only in this way can it be determined if segregation in public schools deprives these plaintiffs of the equal protection of the laws.

Today, education is perhaps the most important function of state and local governments. Compulsory school attendance laws and the great expenditures for education both demonstrate our recognition of the importance of education to our democratic society. It is required in the performance of our most basic public responsibilities, even service in the armed forces. It is the very foundation of good citizenship. Today it is a principal instrument in awakening the child to cultural values, in preparing him for later professional training, and in helping him to adjust normally to his environment. In these days, it is doubtful that any child may reasonably be expected to succeed in life if he is denied the opportunity of an education. Such an opportunity, where the state has undertaken to provide it, is a right which must be made available to all on equal terms.

We come then to the question presented: Does segregation of children in public schools solely on the basis of race, even though the physical facilities and other "tangible" factors may be equal, deprive the children of the minority group of equal educational opportunities? We believe that it does.

In *Sweatt v. Painter, supra,* in finding that a segregated law school for Negroes could not provide them equal educational opportunities, this Court relied in large part on "those qualities which are incapable of objective measurement but which make for greatness in a law school." In *McLaurin v. Oklahoma State Regents, supra,* the Court, in requiring that a Negro admitted to a white graduate school be treated like all other students, again resorted to intangible considerations: ". . . his ability to study, to engage in discussions and exchange views with other students, and, in general, to learn his profession." Such considerations apply with added force to children in grade and high schools. To separate them from others of similar age and qualifications solely because of their race generates a feeling of inferiority as to their status in the community that may affect their hearts and minds in a way unlikely ever to be undone. The effect of this separation on their educational opportunities was well stated by a finding in the Kansas case by a court which nevertheless felt compelled to rule against the Negro plaintiffs:

"Segregation of white and colored children in public schools has a detrimental effect upon the colored children. The impact is greater when it has the sanction of the law; for the policy of separating the races is usually interpreted as denoting the inferiority of the negro group. A sense of inferiority affects the motivation of a child to learn. Segregation with the sanction of law, therefore, has a tendency to [retard] the educational and mental development of negro children and to deprive them of some of the benefits they would receive in a racial[ly] integrated school system."[10]

Whatever may have been the extent of psychological knowledge at the time of *Plessy v. Ferguson,* this finding is amply supported by modern authority.[11] Any language in *Plessy v. Ferguson* contrary to this finding is rejected.

We conclude that in the field of public education the doctrine of "separate but equal" has no place. Separate educational facilities are inherently unequal. Therefore, we hold that the plaintiffs and others similarly situated for whom the actions have been brought are, by reason of the segregation complained of, deprived of the equal protection of the laws guaranteed by the Fourteenth Amendment. This disposition makes unnecessary any discussion whether such segregation also violates the Due Process Clause of the Fourteenth Amendment.[12]

Because these are class actions, because of the wide applicability of this decision, and because of the great variety of local conditions, the formulation of decrees in these cases presents problems of considerable complexity. On reargument, the consideration of appropriate relief was necessarily subordinated to the primary question—the constitutionality of segregation in public education. We have now announced that such segregation is a denial of the equal protection of the laws. In order that we may have the full assistance of the parties in formulating decrees, the cases will be restored to the docket, and the parties are requested to present further argument on Questions 4 and 5 previously propounded by the Court for the reargument this Term.[13] The Attorney General of the United States is again invited to participate. The Attorneys General of the states requiring or permitting segregation in public education will also be permitted to appear as *amici curiae* upon request to do so by September 15, 1954, and submission of briefs by October 1, 1954.[14]

It is so ordered.

Notes

1. In the Kansas case, *Brown v. Board of Education,* the plaintiffs are Negro children of elementary school age residing in Topeka. They brought this action in the United States District Court for the District of Kansas to enjoin enforcement of a Kansas statute which permits, but does not require, cities of more than 15,000 population to maintain separate school facilities for Negro and white students. Kan. Gen. Stat. §72–1724 (1949). Pursuant to that authority, the Topeka Board of Education elected to establish segregated elementary schools. Other public schools in the community, however, are operated on a nonsegregated basis.

In the South Carolina case, *Briggs v. Elliott,* the plaintiffs are Negro children of both elementary and high school age residing in Clarendon County. They brought this action in the United States District Court for the Eastern District of South Carolina to enjoin enforcement of provisions in the state constitution and statutory code which require the segregation of Negroes and whites in public schools. . . .

In the Virginia case, *Davis v. County School Board,* the plaintiffs are Negro children of high school age residing in Prince Edward County. They brought this action in the United States District Court for the Eastern District of Virginia to enjoin enforcement of provisions in the state constitution and statutory code which require the segregation of Negroes and whites in public schools. . . .

In the Delaware case, *Gebhart v. Belton,* the plaintiffs are Negro children of both elementary and high school age residing in New Castle county. They brought this action in the Delaware Court of Chancery to enjoin enforcement of provisions in the state constitution and statutory code which require the segregation of Negroes and whites in public schools. . . .

2. technical footnote deleted.

3. technical footnote deleted.

4. technical footnote deleted.

5. technical footnote deleted.

6. technical footnote deleted.

7. technical footnote deleted.

8. technical footnote deleted.

9. technical footnote deleted.

10. technical footnote deleted.

11. K. B. Clark, Effect of Prejudice and Discrimination on Personality Development (Midcentury White House Conference on Children and Youth, 1950); Witmer and Kotinsky, Personality in the Making (1952), c. VI; Deutscher and Chein, The Psychological Effects of Enforced Segregation: A Survey of Social Science Opinion, 26 *J. Psychol.* 259 (1948); Chein, What Are the Psychological Effects of Segregation Under Conditions of Equal Facilities?, 3 *Int. J. Opinion and Attitude Res.* 229 (1949); Brameld, Educational Costs, in Discrimination and National Welfare (MacIver, ed., 1949), 44–48; Frazier, The Negro in the United States (1949), 674–681. And see generally Myrdal, An American Dilemma (1944).

12. technical footnote deleted.

13. technical footnote deleted.

14. technical footnote deleted.

Critical Thinking

1. In retrospect, does ending racial segregation in schools without ending segregation in housing seem to be the fundamental constraint on the success desired and the type of fairness and equal protection sought by the Supreme Court in this case?

2. What are *de jure* and *de facto* forms or types of racial segregation?

Supreme Court of the United States, 1954.

'Bakke' Set a New Path to Diversity for Colleges

30 years after the ruling, academe still grapples with race in admissions.

PETER SCHMIDT

Thirty years ago, Justice Lewis F. Powell Jr. sent the nation's selective colleges down a path where few had ventured before.

In the U.S. Supreme Court's landmark ruling in *Regents of the University of California v. Bakke,* he wrote that colleges were legally justified in giving some modest consideration to their applicants' race, so long as they were motivated by a desire to attain the educational benefits of diversity.

Before *Bakke,* selective colleges regarded race-conscious admissions policies mainly as a way to remedy past societal discrimination against black, Hispanic, and Native American applicants. The *Bakke* ruling declared that justification off limits, replacing a rationale grounded in history with one grounded in educational theory.

The approaching 30th anniversary of that Supreme Court decision, announced on June 23, 1978, finds many in higher education wondering where Justice Powell's guidance has gotten them—and what, exactly, lies ahead.

His rationale for race-conscious policies may have ensured their long-term survival in the courts, by linking them to a common educational concern that is unlikely to go away anytime soon. But the decision also limited the reach of such policies, forcing colleges to consider race only as a "plus factor." They had to abandon quests for enrollments that reflected society's racial composition in favor of having enough minority students to ensure a variety of perspectives.

The Supreme Court upheld Justice Powell's reasoning in 2003, in a case involving a challenge to the race-conscious admissions policies of the University of Michigan's law school. But the argument that such policies have educational benefits has not protected them from political challenges. Michigan's residents subsequently voted to ban the use of affirmative action by public colleges and other state and local agencies. Similar measures were adopted by California and Washington State in the 1990s and are seen as likely to pass in Arizona, Colorado, and Nebraska if critics of affirmative action succeed in getting them on the ballot this fall.

Some advocates for minority students express frustration that the educational-diversity rationale has led colleges to seek out all different types of students rather than focusing on trying to increase their black, Hispanic, and Native American enrollments. At the end of the day, the advocates argue, pursuing diversity for educational purposes is not the same thing as pursuing racial equality and social justice—and is not nearly enough.

"There are some of us who still believe there is a strong remedial justification for affirmative action," says William L. Taylor, chairman of the Citizens' Commission on Civil Rights, a Washington-based group that monitors the federal government's compliance with civil-rights laws. Mr. Taylor, a leading civil-rights lawyer since 1954, says he holds the view that Justice Harry A. Blackmun expressed in a dissenting opinion in *Bakke,* that "in order to get beyond racism, we must first take account of race."

The Missing Motive

In *Bakke,* the court affirmed a lower court's decision that Allan P. Bakke had to be admitted to a University of California medical school because it had discriminated against him because he was white.

But the path that Justice Powell chose for colleges in his *Bakke* opinion was so new that the Supreme Court's eight other justices had not seen it at all. They were evenly divided over the only two options they thought they had: Letting colleges continue to use affirmative action to remedy societal discrimination, or telling colleges that they could not use such preferences at all.

Certainly the court and the nation's colleges had considered the idea that diversity might have educational benefits. In the Supreme Court's pivotal 1950 *Sweatt v. Painter ruling,* calling for the desegregation of the University of Texas law school, the majority opinion talked of "the interplay of ideas and the exchange of views" found in classrooms with students from different backgrounds.

But when selective colleges adopted race-conscious admissions policies in the late 1960s, their leaders said little about educational benefits. Instead they argued that such policies were needed for two other reasons: to remedy societal discrimination and to send a clear signal—during a time of devastating urban riots—that the "establishment" many black Americans were fighting was in fact open to them.

In the *Bakke* case, the University of California said little about the educational benefits of diversity in opposing the lawsuit that Mr. Bakke had filed after twice being rejected by the medical school on its Davis campus. Its lawyers argued that such policies provided minority students with educational opportunities that societal discrimination might otherwise deny them.

The ruling that was being appealed by the university—a California Supreme Court decision striking down the medical school's admissions policy—held that the educational benefits of diversity were irrelevant.

The argument that campus diversity has educational benefits was introduced into the case through friend-of-the-court briefs.

Columbia, Harvard, and Stanford Universities and the University of Pennsylvania joined in arguing that diversity "makes the university a better learning environment," and that many faculty members reported "that the insights provided by the participation of minority students enrich the curriculum, broaden the teachers' scholarly interests, and protect them from insensitivity to minority perspectives."

Early Obstacles

The educational-diversity rationale offered in *Bakke* may have been untried, but the social-justice rationale already was showing signs of serious wear.

Within just a few years of adopting race-conscious admissions, selective colleges began scaling back their efforts to enroll black students from poor urban settings, concluding that many were too academically unprepared.

At the same time, many began expanding the scope of their affirmative-action programs to include Native Americans as well as Hispanic people—some of whom were Cuban immigrants or otherwise came from backgrounds that made it difficult for them to argue their families had historically experienced oppression on U.S. soil.

By the mid-70s, the fledgling neoconservative movement had developed a critique of race-conscious admissions steeped in the civil-rights movement's own rhetoric, stressing individual rights and colorblindness.

The legal threats to race-conscious policies were real enough by 1977 to prompt the Carnegie Council on Policy Studies in Higher Education to urge colleges to consider minority students' experiences, rather than simply their race or heritage, in the admissions process, because not all "have special characteristics that we believe warrant consideration."

One thing selective colleges showed little interest in doing was acknowledging any past discrimination on their own part. The Davis medical school was exceptional in how divorced it was from American higher education's history of discrimination. The school opened in 1966 and reserved seats for minority

applicants almost from the start. Minority groups had urged the University of California not to appeal the case to the Supreme Court, because they thought the policy would be hard to justify.

When the Supreme Court finally ruled in the *Bakke* case, its nine members were so divided they issued six different opinions, with Justice Powell in the tie-breaker role. He sided with the four justices who said the university's use of quotas amounted to illegal discrimination. And he joined the same four in rejecting the use of social policies to remedy societal discrimination, saying the government should not be in the business of trying to sort out which segments of society owed what to whom.

Justice Powell was reluctant, however, to cause upheaval in higher education, and therefore he refused to go along with the four conservatives in holding that colleges should give up all consideration of applicants' race for purposes other than court-ordered desegregation. Unwilling to embrace the liberal faction's views on the need to remedy societal discrimination, he instead put forward an educational rationale for considering race as a "plus factor" in admissions. His opinion spoke approvingly of the policy that Harvard described in its friend-of-the-court brief.

Birth of a Buzzword

Because no other justices signed on to Justice Powell's opinion stating an educational rationale for race-conscious admissions, legal scholars and federal judges would later argue that his view on the matter did not represent the holding of the court. That debate was largely laid to rest in 2003, however, when a five-member Supreme Court majority embraced Justice Powell's thinking in upholding the University of Michigan law school's admissions policies in *Grutter v. Bollinger.*

Certainly the confusion over how to interpret the *Bakke* decision did not deter higher education—or, for that matter, the business sector and much of the rest of society—from adopting the term "diversity" as both a buzzword and goal. Academics used it in calling for the college curriculum to accommodate movements such as Afrocentrism, feminism, and multiculturalism. Businesses went from talking about the need to have more black and Hispanic employees to saying they needed to employ a wide spectrum of people to reflect the diversity of society and position themselves to compete globally.

John A. Payton, president of the NAACP Legal Defense and Educational Fund, credits the *Bakke* decision with creating an environment in which colleges proudly list their minority enrollments on their Web sites as a measure of their quality. "They actually compete on that basis," he says. "And that has resulted in higher education being pretty diverse, and that has been to the benefit of higher education and the whole country."

So broad was the imprint left by Justice Powell's reasoning in *Bakke* that Justice John Paul Stevens would later remark, in a speech delivered three months after the *Grutter* decision, that he had argued to his fellow justices that rejecting the diversity rationale would cause a "sea change" in American society.

Truth be told, however, many college administrators still describe race- and ethnicity-conscious admissions policies as tools for improving black and Hispanic access to their institutions.

Relatively few colleges have done any research showing that their policies produce favorable educational outcomes.

Arthur L. Coleman, a veteran higher-education lawyer now at Education-Counsel, a for-profit law and policy center, says many people "still don't get" that "we are looking at issues of diversity in a fundamentally educationally oriented way." In advising colleges, he says, he does not use the term "affirmative action," and he warns that focusing on enrollment numbers or talking about promoting social justice is "at core a mistake."

Roger B. Clegg, president of the Center for Equal Opportunity and a leading opponent of race-conscious admissions policies, says he hears talk of remedying past discrimination pop up in the statements of judges and lawyers who know that such justifications fall outside *Bakke*.

He cites Justice Sandra Day O'Connor's statement in the Supreme Court's *Grutter* decision that colleges will not need race-conscious admissions policies in 25 years, or the Democratic presidential candidate Barack Obama's belief that his daughters should not be given extra consideration in admissions because of the privileges they had growing up.

Better Law than Politics?

Some higher-education leaders believe that the Supreme Court's *Grutter* decision broadened the legal rationale for race-conscious admissions. In writing for the five-member *Grutter* majority, Justice O'Connor said colleges must ensure that the path to positions of leadership is "visibly open to talented and qualified individuals of every race and ethnicity."

William G. Bowen, a former president of Princeton University and co-author of several books on with college admissions, says Justice O'Connor's opinion made clear that the government's interest in allowing such policies "is not just about better learning environments on campuses."

Mr. Coleman says he believes the *Grutter* majority established a "strong foundation for arguing" such a rationale, even though it is unclear whether the courts will go along. But Sheldon E. Steinbach, a lawyer at the Dow Lohnes law firm, in Washington, and a former general counsel at the American Council on Education, says a college that expands its race-conscious admissions policies on the basis of such an interpretation of the law places itself at "more than reasonable" legal risk.

Also open to debate is the question of whether Justice Powell's rationale for race-conscious admissions policies has left them more, or less, vulnerable to political challenge.

Some leading opponents of affirmative-action preferences argue that the public is unswayed by assertions that such policies have educational benefits. "People are losing jobs, and their kids are not getting into colleges, and they want to know why," says Terence J. Pell, president of the Center for Individual Rights, a Washington-based group that has provided legal assistance to plaintiffs in several major challenges to race-conscious admissions. "Someone needs to explain this with a political rationale and not a legal rationale that barely makes sense in the political sphere."

But Mr. Payton, of the NAACP Legal Defense and Educational Fund, says the political campaigns against such policies have succeeded mainly by convincing large numbers of people—wrongly, he believes—that there is no longer any need to remedy past racial discrimination.

Mr. Coleman says having an educational rationale for such policies has helped rally higher education and business leaders around them, and has enabled defenders of such policies to argue that "it is not about us versus them. It is about benefits to all students."

Critical Thinking

1. What signs of affirmative action do you see at your university?

2. Is diversity a value or social fact and the reality of multi-ethnic, large countries?

Shaare Tefila Congregation v. Cobb and *Saint Francis College v. Al-Khazraji*

Shaare Tefila Congregation v. Cobb

Cite as 107 S.Ct. 2019 (1987).

Justice White delivered the opinion of the Court.

On November 2, 1982, the outside walls of the synagogue of the Shaare Tefila Congregation in Silver Spring, Maryland, were sprayed with red and black paint and with large anti-Semitic slogans, phrases and symbols. A few months later, the Congregation and Federal District Court, alleging that defendants' desecration of the synagogue had violated 42 U.S.C. § § 1981, 1982, 1985(3) and the Maryland common law of trespass, nuisance, and intentional infliction of emotional distress. On defendants' motion under Fed. Rule Civ.Proc. 12(b)(1) and (6), the District Court dismissed all the claims. The Court of Appeals affirmed in all respects. 785 F.2d 523 (CA4 1986). Petitioners petitioned for writ of certiorari. We granted the petition, 479 U.S. _____, 107 S.Ct. 62, 93 L.Ed.2d 21 (1986), and we now reverse the judgment of the Court of Appeals.

[1] Section 1982 guarantees all citizens of the United States, "the same right . . . as is enjoyed by white citizens . . . to inherit, purchase, lease, sell, hold, and convey real and personal property." The section forbids both official and private racially discriminatory interference with property rights, *Jones v. Alfred H. Mayer Co.,* 392 U.S. 409, 88 S.Ct. 2186, 20 L.Ed.2d 1189 (1968). Petitioners' allegation was that they were deprived of the right to hold property in violation of § 1982 because the defendants were motivated by racial prejudice. They unsuccessfully argued in the District Court and Court of Appeals that Jews are not a racially distinct group, but that defendants' conduct is actionable because they viewed Jews as racially distinct and were motivated by racial prejudice. The Court of Appeals held that § 1982 was not "intended to apply to situations in which a plaintiff is not a member of a racially distinct group but is merely *perceived* to be so by defendants." 785 F.2d, at 526 (emphasis in original). The Court of Appeals believed that "[b]ecause discrimination against Jews is not racial discrimination," *id.,* at 527, the District Court was correct in dismissing the § 1982 claim.

[2] We agree with the Court of Appeals that a charge of racial discrimination within the meaning of § 1982 cannot be made out by alleging only that the defendants were motivated by racial animus; it is necessary as well to allege that defendants' animus was directed towards the kind of group that Congress intended to protect when it passed the statute. To hold otherwise would unacceptably extend the reach of the statute.

[3–5] We agree with petitioners, however, that the Court of Appeals erred in holding that Jews cannot state a § 1982 claim against other white defendants. That view rested on the notion that because Jews today are not thought to be members of a separate race, they cannot make out a claim of racial discrimination within the meaning of § 1982. That construction of the section we have today rejected in *Saint Francis College v. Al-Khazraji,* _____ U.S., at _____, 107 S.Ct., at _____. Our opinion in that case observed that definitions of race when § 1982 was passed were not the same as they are today and concluded that the section was "intended to protect from discrimination identifiable classes of persons who are subjected to intentional discrimination solely because of their ancestry or ethnic characteristics." At _____, 107 S.Ct., at 2028. As *St. Francis* makes clear, the question before us is not whether Jews are considered to be a separate race by today's standards, but whether, at the time § 1982 was adopted, Jews constituted a group of people that Congress intended to protect. It is evident from the legislative history of the section reviewed in *Saint Francis College,* a review that we need not repeat here, that Jews and Arabs were among the peoples then considered to be distinct races and hence within the protection of the statute. Jews are not foreclosed from stating a cause of action against other members of what today is considered to be part of the Caucasian race.

The judgment of the Court of Appeals is therefore reversed and the case is remanded for further proceedings consistent with this opinion.

Saint Francis College v. Al-Khazraji

Cite as 107 S.Ct. 2022 (1987).

Justice White delivered the opinion of the Court.

Respondent, a citizen of the United States born in Iraq, was an associate professor at St. Francis College, one of the petitioners here. In January 1978, he applied for tenure; the Board of Trustees denied his request on February 23, 1978. He accepted a 1-year, nonrenewable contract and sought administrative reconsideration of the tenure decision, which was denied on February 6, 1979. He worked his last day at the college on May 26, 1979. In June 1979, he filed complaints with the Pennsylvania Human Relations Commission and the Equal Employment Opportunities Commission. The State agency dismissed his claim and the EEOC issued a right to sue letter on August 6, 1980.

On October 30, 1980, respondent filed a *pro se* complaint in the District Court alleging a violation of Title VII of the Civil Rights Act of 1964 and claiming discrimination based on national origin, religion, and/or race. Amended complaints were filed, adding claims under 42 U.S.C. §§ 1981, 1983, 1985(3), 1986, and state law. The District Court dismissed the 1986, 1985(3) and Title VII claims as untimely but held that the §§ 1981 and 1983 claims were not barred by the Pennsylvania 6-year statute of limitations. The court at that time also ruled that because the complaint alleged denial of tenure because respondent was of the Arabian race, an action under § 1981 could be maintained. Defendants' motion for summary judgment came up before a different judge, who construed the pleadings as asserting only discrimination on the basis of national origin and religion, which § 1981 did not cover. Even if racial discrimination was deemed to have been alleged, the District Court ruled that § 1981 does not reach claims of discrimination based on Arabian ancestry.[1]

The Court of Appeals rejected petitioners' claim that the § 1981 claim had not been timely filed. Under the Court of Appeals' holding in *Goodman v. Lukens Steel Co.,* 777 F.2d 113 (CA 2 1985), that the Pennsylvania 2-year statute of limitations governed § 1981 cases, respondent's suit would have been barred. The Court of Appeals, however, relying on *Chevron Oil Co. v. Huson,* 404 U.S. 97, 92 S.Ct. 349, 30 L.Ed.2d 296 (1971), held that *Goodman* should not be retroactively applied and that this suit was timely under its pre-*Goodman* cases which had borrowed the State's 6-year statute.

Reaching the merits, the Court of Appeals held that respondent had alleged discrimination based on race and that although under current racial classifications Arabs are Caucasians, respondent could maintain his § 1981 claim.[2] Congress, when it passed what is now § 1981, had not limited its protections to those who today would be considered members of a race different from the race of the defendant. Rather, the legislative history of the section indicated that Congress intended to forbid "at the least, membership in a group that is ethnically and physiognomically distinctive." 784 F.2d 505, 517 (CA 3 1986). Section 1981, "at a minimum," reaches "discrimination directed against an individual because he or she is genetically part of an ethnically and physiognomically distinctive sub-grouping of *homo sapiens.*" *Ibid.* Because respondent had not had full discovery and the record was not sufficient to determine whether he had been subjected to the sort of prejudice § 1981 would redress, respondent was to be given the opportunity to prove his case.[3]

We granted certiorari. 479 U.S. _____, 107 S.Ct. 62, 93 L.Ed.2d 21 (1986), limited to the statute of limitations issue and the question whether a person of Arabian ancestry was protected from racial discrimination under § 1981, and now affirm the judgment of the Court of Appeals.

I

[1] We agree with the Court of Appeals that respondent's claim was not time barred. *Wilson v. Garcia,* 471 U.S. 261, 105 S.Ct. 1938, 85 L.Ed.2d 254 (1985), required that in selecting the applicable state statute of limitations in § 1983 cases, the lower federal courts should choose the state statute applicable to other personal injury torts. Thereafter, the Third Circuit in *Goodman* held that *Wilson* applies to § 1981 cases as well and that the Pennsylvania 2-year statute should apply. The Court of Appeals in this case, however, held that when respondent filed his suit, which was prior to *Wilson v. Garcia,* it was clearly established in the Third Circuit that a § 1981 plaintiff had six years to bring an action and that *Goodman* should not be applied retroactively to bar respondent's suit.

Insofar as what the prevailing law was in the Third Circuit, we have no reason to disagree with the Court of Appeals. Under controlling precedent in that Circuit, respondent had six years to file his suit, and it was filed well within that time. See 784 F.2d, at 512–513. We also assume but do not decide that *Wilson v. Garcia* controls the selection of the applicable state statute of limitations in § 1981 cases. The Court of Appeals, however, correctly held that its decision in *Goodman* should not be retroactively applied to bar respondent's action in this case. The usual rule is that federal cases should be decided in accordance with the law existing at the time of decision. *Gulf Offshore Co. v. Mobil Oil Corp.,* 453 U.S. 473, 486, n. 16, 101 S.Ct. 2870, 2879, n. 16, 69 L.Ed.2d 784 (1981); *Thorpe v. Durham Housing Authority,* 393 U.S. 268, 281, 89 S.Ct. 518, 526, 21 L.Ed.2d 474 (1969); *United States v. Schooner Peggy,* 1 Cranch 103, 110, 2 L.Ed. 49 (1801). But *Chevron Oil Co. v. Huson, supra,* counsels against retroactive application of statute of limitations decision in certain circumstances. There, the Court held that its decision specifying the applicable state statute of limitations should be applied only prospectively because it overruled clearly established circuit precedent on which the complaining party was entitled to rely, because retroactive application would be inconsistent with the purpose of the underlying substantive statute, and because such application would be manifestly inequitable.

The Court of Appeals found these same factors were present in this case and foreclosed retroactive applications of its decision in *Goodman*. We perceive no good reason for not applying *Chevron* where *Wilson* has required a Court of Appeals to overrule its prior cases. Nor has petitioner persuaded us that there was any error in the application of *Chevron* in the circumstances existing in this case.

II

Section 1981 provides:

"All persons within the jurisdiction of the United States shall have the same right in every State and Territory to make and enforce contracts, to sue, be parties, give evidence, and to the full and equal benefit of all laws and proceedings for the security of persons and property as is enjoyed by white citizens, and shall be subject to like punishment, pains, penalties, taxes, licenses, and exactions of every kind, and to no other."

[2] Although § 1981 does not itself use the word "race," the Court has construed the section to forbid all "racial" discrimination in the making of private as well as public contracts. *Runyon v. McCrary*, 427, U.S. 160, 168, 174–175, 96 S.Ct. 2586, 2593, 2596–2597, 49 L.Ed.2d 415 (1976). The petitioner college, although a private institution, was therefore subject to this statutory command. There is no disagreement among the parties on these propositions. The issue is whether respondent has alleged *racial* discrimination within the meaning of § 1981.

[3] Petitioners contend that respondent is a Caucasian and cannot allege the kind of discrimination § 1981 forbids. Concededly, *McDonald v. Sante Fe Trail Transportation Co.*, 427 U.S. 273, 96 S.Ct. 2574, 49 L.Ed.2d 493 (1976), held that white persons could maintain a § 1981 suit; but that suit involved alleged discrimination against a white person in favor of a black, and petitioner submits that the section does not encompass claims of discrimination by one Caucasian against another. We are quite sure that the Court of Appeals properly rejected this position.

Petitioner's submission rests on the assumption that all those who might be deemed Caucasians today were thought to be of the same race when § 1981 became law in the 19th century; and it may be that a variety of ethnic groups, including Arabs, are now considered to be within the Caucasian race.[4] The understanding of "race" in the 19th century, however, was different. Plainly, all those who might be deemed Caucasian today were not thought to be of the same race at the time § 1981 became law.

In the middle years of the 19th century, dictionaries commonly referred to race as a "continued series of descendants from a parent who is called the *stock*," N. Webster, An American Dictionary of the English Language 666 (New York 1830) (emphasis in original), "[t]he lineage of a family," N. Webster, 2 A Dictionary of the English Language 411 (New Haven 1841), or "descendants of a common ancestor," J. Donald, Chambers's Etymological Dictionary of the English Language 415 (London 1871). The 1887 edition of Webster's expanded the definition somewhat: "The descendants of a common ancestor; a family, tribe, people or nation, believed or presumed to belong to the

same stock." N. Webster, Dictionary of the English Language (W. Wheeler ed. 1887). It was not until the 20th century that dictionaries began referring to the Caucasian, Mongolian and Negro races, 8 The Century Dictionary and Cyclopedia 4926 (1911), or to race as involving divisions of mankind based upon different physical characteristics. Webster's Collegiate Dictionary 794 (1916). Even so, modern dictionaries still include among the definitions of race as being "a family, tribe, people, or nation belonging to the same stock." Webster's Third New International Dictionary Mass.1870 (1971); Webster's Ninth New Collegiate Dictionary 969 (Springfield, Mass. 1986).

Encyclopedias of the 19th century also described race in terms of ethnic groups, which is a narrower concept of race than petitioners urge. Encyclopedia Americana in 1858, for example, referred in 1854 to various races such as Finns, vol. 5, p. 123, gypsies, 6 *id.*, at 123, Basques, 1 *id.*, at 602, and Hebrews, 6 *id.*, at 209. The 1863 version of the New American Cyclopaedia divided the Arabs into a number of subsidiary races, vol. 1, p. 739; represented the Hebrews as of the Semitic race, 9 *id.*, at 27, and identified numerous other groups as constituting races, including Swedes, 15 *id.*, at 216, Norwegians, 12 *id.*, at 410, Germans, 8 *id.*, at 200, Greeks, *id.*, at 438, Finns, 7 *id.*, at 513, Italians, 9 *id.*, at 644–645 (referring to mixture of different races), Spanish, 14 *id.*, at 804, Mongolians, 11 *id.*, at 651, Russians, 14 *id.*, at 226, and the like. The ninth edition of the Encyclopedia Britannica also referred to Arabs, vol. 2, p. 245 (1878), Jews, 13 *id.*, at 685 (1881), and other ethnic groups such as Germans, 10 *id.*, at 473 (1879), Hungarians, 12 *id.*, at 365 (1880), and Greeks, 11 *id.*, at 83 (1880), as separate races.

These dictionary and encyclopedic sources are somewhat diverse, but it is clear that they do not support the claim that for the purposes of § 1981, Arabs, Englishmen, Germans and certain other ethnic groups are to be considered a single race. We would expect the legislative history of § 1981, which the Court held in *Runyon v. McCrary* had its source in the Civil Rights Act of 1866, 14 Stat. 27, as well as the Voting Rights Act of 1870, 16 Stat. 140, 144, to reflect this common understanding, which it surely does. The debates are replete with references to the Scandinavian races, Cong.Globe, 39th Cong., 1st Sess., 499 (1866) (remarks of Sen. Cowan), as well as the Chinese, *id.*, at 523 (remarks of Sen. Davis), Latin, *id.*, at 238 (remarks of Rep. Kasson during debate of home rule for the District of Columbia), Spanish, *id.*, at 251 (remarks of Sen. Davis during debate of District of Columbia suffrage) and Anglo-Saxon races, *id.*, at 542 (remarks of Rep. Dawson). Jews, *ibid.*, Mexicans, see *ibid.*, (remarks of Rep. Dawson), blacks, *passim,* and Mongolians, *id.*, at 498 (remarks of Sen. Cowan), were similarly categorized. Gypsies were referred to as a race. *Ibid.*, (remarks of Sen. Cowan). Likewise, the Germans:

"Who will say that Ohio can pass a law enacting that no man of the German race . . . shall ever own any property in Ohio, or shall ever make a contract in Ohio, or ever inherit property in Ohio, or ever come into Ohio to live, or even to work? If Ohio may pass such a law, and exclude a German citizen . . . because he is of the German nationality or race, then may every other State do so." *Id.*, at 1294 (Remarks of Sen. Shellabarger).

There was a reference to the Caucasian race, but it appears to have been referring to people of European ancestry. *Id.,* at 523 (remarks of Sen. Davis).

The history of the 1870 Act reflects similar understanding of what groups Congress intended to protect from intentional discrimination. It is clear, for example, that the civil rights sections of the 1870 Act provided protection for immigrant groups such as the Chinese. This view was expressed in the Senate. Cong.Globe, 41st Cong., 2d Sess., 1536, 3658, 3808 (1870). In the House, Representative Bingham described § 16 of the Act, part of the authority for § 1981, as declaring "that the States shall not hereafter discriminate against the immigrant from China and in favor of the immigrant from Prussia, nor against the immigrant from France and in favor of the immigrant from Ireland." *Id.,* at 3871.

[4–6] Based on the history of § 1981, we have little trouble in concluding that Congress intended to protect from discrimination identifiable classes of persons who are subjected to intentional discrimination solely because of their ancestry or ethnic characteristics. Such discrimination is racial discrimination that Congress intended § 1981 to forbid, whether or not it would be classified as racial in terms of modern scientific theory.[5] The Court of Appeals was thus quite right in holding that § 1981, "at a minimum," reaches discrimination against an individual "because he or she is genetically part of an ethnically and physiognomically distinctive sub-grouping of *homo sapiens.*" It is clear from our holding, however, that a distinctive physiognomy is not essential to qualify for § 1981 protection. If respondent on remand can prove that he was subjected to intentional discrimination based on the fact that he was born an Arab, rather than solely on the place or nation of his origin, or his religion, he will have made out a case under § 1981.

The Judgment of the court of Appeals is accordingly affirmed.

Supreme Court of the United States, 1980.

Notes

1. technical footnote deleted.
2. technical footnote deleted.
3. technical footnote deleted.
4. There is a common popular understanding that there are three major human races—Caucasoid, Mongoloid, and Negroid. Many modern biologists and anthropologists, however, criticize racial classifications as arbitrary and of little use in understanding the variability of human beings. It is said that genetically homogeneous populations do not exist and traits are not discontinuous between populations; therefore, a population can only be described in terms of relative frequencies of various traits. Clear-cut categories do not exist. The particular traits which have generally been chosen to characterize races have been criticized as having little biological significance. It has been found that differences between individuals of the same race are often greater than the differences between the "average" individuals of different races. These observations and others have led some, but not all, scientists to conclude that racial classifications are for the most part sociopolitical, rather than biological, in nature.
5. technical footnote deleted.

Critical Thinking

1. What did Congress intend when it passed the Civil Rights Act of 1866?
2. Do these cases mean that the law protects every ethnic group?
3. Where did the notion that some ethnic groups are minority groups come from?

Historical Discrimination in the Immigration Laws

The Early Years

During the formative years of this country's growth, immigration was encouraged with little restraint. Any restrictions on immigration in the 1700s were the result of selection standards established by each colonial settlement. The only Federal regulation of immigration in this period lasted only 2 years and came from the Alien Act of 1798, which gave the President the authority to expel aliens who posed a threat to national security.[1]

Immigrants from northern and western Europe began to trickle into the country as a result of the faltering economic conditions within their own countries. In Germany, unfavorable economic prospects in industry and trade, combined with political unrest, drove many of its nationals to seek opportunities to ply their trades here.[2] In Ireland, the problems of the economy, compounded by several successive potato crop failures in the 1840s, sent thousands of Irish to seaports where ships bound for the United States were docked.[3] For other European nationals, the emigration from their native countries received impetus not only from adverse economic conditions at home but also from favorable stories of free land and good wages in America.[4]

The Nativist Movements

As a result of the large numbers of Catholics who emigrated from Europe, a nativist movement began in the 1830s.[5] It advocated immigration restriction to prevent further arrivals of Catholics into this country. Anti-Catholicism was a very popular theme, and many Catholics and Catholic institutions suffered violent attacks from nativist sympathizers. The movement, however, did not gain great political strength and its goal of curbing immigration did not materialize.

Immigrants in the mid-19th century did not come only from northern and western Europe. In China, political unrest and the decline in agricultural productivity spawned the immigration of Chinese to American shores.[6] The numbers of Chinese immigrants steadily increased after the so-called Opium War, due not only to the Chinese economy, but also to the widespread stories of available employment, good wages, and the discovery of gold at Sutter's Mill, which filtered in through arrivals from the Western nations.[7]

The nativist movement of the 1830s resurfaced in the late 1840s and developed into a political party, the Know-Nothing Party.[8] Its western adherents added an anti-Chinese theme to the eastern anti-Catholic sentiment.[9] But once again, the nativist movement, while acquiring local political strength, failed in its attempts to enact legislation curbing immigration. On the local level, however, the cry of "America for Americans" often led to discriminatory State statutes that penalized certain racially identifiable groups.[10] As an example, California adopted licensing statutes for foreign miners and fishermen, which were almost exclusively enforced against Chinese.[11]

In the mid-1850s, the Know-Nothing Party lost steam as a result of a division over the question of slavery, the most important issue of that time.[12] The nativist movement and antiforeign sentiment receded because of the slavery issue and the Civil War. It maintained this secondary role until the Panic of 1873 struck.

Chinese Exclusion

The depression economy of the 1870s was blamed on aliens who were accused of driving wages to a substandard level as well as taking away jobs that "belonged" to white Americans. While the economic charges were not totally without basis, reality shows that most aliens did not compete with white labor for "desirable" white jobs. Instead, aliens usually were relegated to the most menial employment.[13]

The primary target was the Chinese, whose high racial visibility, coupled with cultural dissimilarity and lack of political power, made them more than an adequate scapegoat for the economic problems of the 1870s.[14] Newspapers adopted the exhortations of labor leaders, blaming the Chinese for the economic plight of the working class. Workers released their frustrations and anger on the Chinese, particularly in the West.[15] Finally, politicians succumbed to the growing cry for exclusion of Chinese.

Congress responded by passing the Chinese Exclusion Act of 1882.[16] That act suspended immigration of Chinese laborers for 10 years, except for those who were in the country on November 17, 1880. Those who were not lawfully entitled to reside in the United States were subject to deportation. Chinese immigrants were also prohibited from obtaining United States citizenship after the effective date of the act.

The 1882 act was amended in 1884 to cover all subjects of China and Chinese who resided in any other foreign country.[17] Then in 1888, another act was enacted that extended the

suspension of immigration for all Chinese except Chinese officials, merchants, students, teachers, and travelers for pleasure.[18]
Supplemental legislation to that act also prohibited Chinese
laborers from reentering the country, as provided for in the
1882 act, unless they reentered prior to the effective date of the
legislation.[19]

Senator Matthew C. Butler of South Carolina summed up the
congressional efforts to exclude Chinese by stating:

> [I]t seems to me that this whole Chinese business has
> been a matter of political advantage, and we have not been
> governed by that deliberation which it would seem to me
> the gravity of the question requires. In other words, there is
> a very important Presidential election pending. One House
> of Congress passes an act driving these poor devils into
> the Pacific Ocean, and the other House comes up and says,
> "Yes, we will drive them further into the Pacific Ocean, not-
> withstanding the treaties between the two governments."[20]

Nevertheless, the Chinese exclusion law was extended in 1892[21]
and 1902,[22] and in 1904 it was extended indefinitely.[23]

Although challenged by American residents of Chinese
ancestry, the provisions of these exclusion acts were usually
upheld by judicial decisions. For example, the 1892 act[24] mandated that Chinese laborers obtain certificates of residency
within 1 year after the passage of the act or face deportation.
In order to obtain the certificate, the testimony of one credible
white witness was required to establish that the Chinese laborer
was an American resident prior to the passage of the act. That
requirement was upheld by the United States Supreme Court in
Fong Yue Ting v. United States.[25]

Literacy Tests and the Asiatic Barred Zone

The racial nature of immigration laws clearly manifested itself
in further restrictions on prospective immigrants who were
either from Asian countries or of Asian descent. In addition to
extending the statutory life of the Chinese exclusion law, the
1902 act also applied that law to American territorial possessions, thereby prohibiting not only the immigration of noncitizen Chinese laborers from "such island territory to the mainland
territory," but also "from one portion of the island territory of
the United States to another portion of said island territory."[26]
Soon after, Japanese were restricted from free immigration to
the United States by the "Gentleman's Agreement" negotiated
between the respective governments in 1907.[27] Additional evidence would be provided by the prohibition of immigration
from countries in the Asia-Pacific Triangle as established by
the Immigration Act of 1917.[28]

During this period, congressional attempts were also made
to prevent blacks from immigrating to this country. In 1915 an
amendment to exclude "all members of the African or black
race" from admission to the United States was introduced in the
Senate during its deliberations on a proposed immigration bill.[29]
The Senate approved the amendment on a 29 to 25 vote,[30] but
it was later defeated in the House by a 253 to 74 vote,[31] after
intensive lobbying by the NAACP.[32]

In 1917 Congress codified existing immigration laws in the
Immigration Act of that year.[33] That act retained all the prior
grounds for inadmissibility and added illiterates to the list of
those ineligible to immigrate, as a response to the influx of
immigrants from southern and eastern Europe. Because of a
fear that American standards would be lowered by these new
immigrants who were believed to be racially "unassimilable"
and illiterate, any alien who was over 16 and could not read
was excluded. The other important feature of this statute was
the creation of the Asia-Pacific Triangle, an Asiatic barred
zone, designed to exclude Asians completely from immigration to the United States. The only exemptions from this zone
were from an area that included Persia and parts of Afghanistan
and Russia.

The 1917 immigration law reflected the movement of American immigration policy toward the curbing of free immigration.
Free immigration, particularly from nations that were culturally
dissimilar to the northern and western European background of
most Americans, was popularly believed to be the root of both
the economic problems and the social problems confronting this
country.

The National Origins Quota System

Four years later, Congress created a temporary quota law that
limited the number of aliens of any nationality who could immigrate to 3 percent of the United States residents of that nationality living in the country in 1910.[34] The total annual immigration
allowable in any one year was set at 350,000. Western Hemisphere aliens were exempt from the quota if their country of
origin was an independent nation and the alien had resided there
at least 1 year.

The clear intent of the 1921 quota law was to confine immigration as much as possible to western and northern European
stock. As the minority report noted:

> The obvious purpose of this discrimination is the adoption
> of an unfounded anthropological theory that the nations
> which are favored are the progeny of fictitious and hitherto
> unsuspected Nordic ancestors, while those discriminated
> against are not classified as belonging to that mythical
> ancestral stock. No scientific evidence worthy of consider-
> ation was introduced to substantiate this pseudoscientific
> proposition. It is pure fiction and the creation of a journal-
> istic imagination. . . .

> The majority report insinuates that some of those who
> have come from foreign countries are non-assimilable
> or slow of assimilation. No facts are offered in support
> of such a statement. The preponderance of testimony
> adduced before the committee is to the contrary.[35]

Notwithstanding these objections, Congress made the temporary quota a permanent one with the enactment of the 1924
National Origins Act.[36] A ceiling of 150,000 immigrants per
year was imposed. Quotas for each nationality group were
2 percent of the total members of that nationality residing in the

United States according to the 1890 census.[37] Again, Western Hemisphere aliens were exempt from the quotas (thus, classified as "nonquota" immigrants). Any prospective immigrant was required to obtain a sponsor in this country and to obtain a visa from an American consulate office abroad. Entering the country without a visa and in violation of the law subjected the entrant to deportation without regard to the time of entry (no statute of limitation). Another provision, prohibiting the immigration of aliens ineligible for citizenship, completely closed the door on Japanese immigration, since the Supreme Court had ruled that Japanese were ineligible to become naturalized citizens.[38] Prior to the 1924 act, Japanese immigration had been subjected to "voluntary" restraint by the Gentleman's Agreement negotiated between the Japanese Government and President Theodore Roosevelt.

In addition to its expressed discriminatory provisions, the 1924 law was also criticized as discriminatory against blacks in general and against black West Indians in particular.[39]

The Mexican "Repatriation" Campaign

Although Mexican Americans have a long history of residence within present United States territory,[40] Mexican immigration to this country is of relatively recent vintage.[41] Mexican citizens began immigrating to this country in significant numbers after 1909 because of economic conditions as well as the violence and political upheaval of the Mexican Revolution.[42] These refugees were welcomed by Americans, for they helped to alleviate the labor shortage caused by the First World War.[43] The spirit of acceptance lasted only a short time, however.

Spurred by the economic distress of the Great Depression, Federal immigration officials expelled hundreds of thousands of persons of Mexican descent from this country through increased Border Patrol raids and other immigration law enforcement techniques.[44] To mollify public objection to the mass expulsions, this program was called the "repatriation" campaign. Approximately 500,000 persons were "repatriated" to Mexico, with more than half of them being United States citizens.[45]

Erosion of Certain Discriminatory Barriers

Prior to the next recodification of the immigration laws, there were several congressional enactments that cut away at the discriminatory barriers established by the national origins system. In 1943 the Chinese Exclusion Act was repealed, allowing a quota of 105 Chinese to immigrate annually to this country and declaring Chinese eligible for naturalization.[46] The War Brides Act of 1945[47] permitted the immigration of 118,000 spouses and children of military servicemen. In 1946 Congress enacted legislation granting eligibility for naturalization to Pilipinos[48] and to races indigenous to India.[49] A Presidential proclamation in that same year increased the Pilipino quota from 50 to 100.[50] In 1948 the Displaced Persons Act provided for the entry of approximately 400,000 refugees from Germany, Italy, and

Austria (an additional 214,000 refugees were later admitted to the United States).[51]

The McCarran-Walter Act of 1952

The McCarran-Walter Act of 1952,[52] the basic law in effect today, codified the immigration laws under a single statute. It established three principles for immigration policy:

1. the reunification of families,
2. the protection of the domestic labor force, and
3. the immigration of persons with needed skills.

However, it retained the concept of the national origins system, as well as unrestricted immigration from the Western Hemisphere. An important provision of the statute removed the bar to immigration and citizenship for races that had been denied those privileges prior to that time. Asian countries, nevertheless, were still discriminated against, for prospective immigrants whose ancestry was one-half of any Far Eastern race were chargeable to minimal quotas for that nation, regardless of the birthplace of the immigrant.

"Operation Wetback"

Soon after the repatriation campaigns of the 1930s, the United States entered the Second World War. Mobilization for the war effort produced a labor shortage that resulted in a shift in American attitudes toward immigration from Mexico. Once again Mexican nationals were welcomed with open arms. However, this "open arms" policy was just as short lived as before.

In the 1950s many Americans were alarmed by the number of immigrants from Mexico. As a result, then United States Attorney General Herbert Brownell, Jr., launched "Operation Wetback," to expel Mexicans from this country. Among those caught up in the expulsion campaign were American citizens of Mexican descent who were forced to leave the country of their birth. To ensure the effectiveness of the expulsion process, many of those apprehended were denied a hearing to assert their constitutional rights and to present evidence that would have prevented their deportation. More than 1 million persons of Mexican descent were expelled from this country in 1954 at the height of "Operation Wetback."[53]

The 1965 Amendments

The national origins immigration quota system generated opposition from the time of its inception, condemned for its attempts to maintain the existing racial composition of the United States. Finally, in 1965, amendments to the McCarran-Walter Act abolished the national origins system as well as the Asiatic barred zone.[54] Nevertheless, numerical restrictions were still imposed to limit annual immigration. The Eastern Hemisphere was subject to an overall limitation of 170,000 and a limit of 20,000 per country. Further, colonial territories were limited to 1 percent of the total available to the mother country (later raised to 3 percent or 600 immigrants in the 1976 amendments). The Western Hemisphere, for the first time, was subject to an overall limitation of 120,000 annually, although no individual per country limits were imposed. In place of the national origins system, Congress created a seven category preference system giving immigration priority to relatives of United States residents and immigrants with needed talents or skills.[55] The 20,000 limitation per country and the colonial limitations, as well as the preference for relatives of Americans preferred under the former selections process, have been referred to by critics as "the last vestiges of the national origins system" because they perpetuate the racial discrimination produced by the national origins system.

Restricting Mexican Immigration

After 1965 the economic conditions in the United States changed. With the economic crunch felt by many Americans, the cry for more restrictive immigration laws resurfaced. The difference from the 19th century situation is that the brunt of the attacks is now focused on Mexicans, not Chinese. High "guesstimates" of the number of undocumented Mexican aliens entering the United States, many of which originated from Immigration and Naturalization Service sources, have been the subject of press coverage.[56]

As a partial response to the demand for "stemming the tide" of Mexican immigration, Congress amended the Immigration and Nationality Act in 1976,[57] imposing the seven category preference system and the 20,000 numerical limitation per country on Western Hemisphere nations. Legal immigration from Mexico, which had been more than 40,000[58] people per year, with a waiting list 2 years long, was thus cut by over 50 percent.

Recent Revisions of the Immigrant Quota System

Although the annual per-country limitations have remained intact, Congress did amend the Immigration and Nationality Act in 1978 to eliminate the hemispheric quotas of 170,000 for Eastern Hemisphere countries and 120,000 for Western Hemisphere countries. Those hemispheric ceilings were replaced with an overall annual worldwide ceiling of 290,000.[59]

In 1980 the immigrant quota system was further revised by the enactment of the Refugee Act. In addition to broadening the definition of refugee, that statute eliminated the seventh preference visa category by establishing a separate worldwide ceiling for refugee admissions to this country. It also reduced the annual worldwide ceiling for the remaining six preference categories to 270,000 visas, and it increased the number of visas allocated to the second preference to 26 percent.[60]

Notes

1. Ch. 58, 1 Stat. 570 (1798).
2. Carl Wittke, *We Who Built America* (rev. 1964), p. 67.
3. Ibid., pp. 129–33.
4. Ibid., pp. 101–10.
5. Ibid., pp. 491–97.
6. Li Chien-nung, *The Political History of China, 1840–1928* (1956), pp. 48–49; Stanford Lyman, *Chinese Americans* (1974), pp. 4–5.
7. Mary Roberts Coolidge, *Chinese Immigration* (1909), pp. 16–17.
8. Wittke, *We Who Built America*, pp. 497–510.
9. Coolidge, *Chinese Immigration*, p. 58.
10. Ibid., pp. 69–82. Some municipalities also adopted ordinances that discriminated against Chinese. As an example, a San Francisco municipal ordinance, subsequently held unconstitutional in Yick Wo v. Hopkins, 118 U.S. 356 (1886), was enacted regulating the operation of public laundries but in practice was enforced almost exclusively against Chinese.
11. Ibid., pp. 33–38, 69–74.
12. Wittke, *We Who Built America*, pp. 509–10.
13. As one author noted, "[b]efore the late 1870s the Chinese engaged only in such work as white laborers refused to perform. Thus the Chinese not only were noninjurious competitors but in effect were benefactors to the white laborer." S.W. Kung, *Chinese in American Life: Some Aspects of Their History, Status, Problems, and Contributions* (1962), p. 68.
14. Carey McWilliams, *Brothers Under the Skin* (rev. 1951), pp. 101–03.
15. Coolidge, *Chinese Immigration*, p. 188.
16. Ch. 126, 22 Stat. 58 (1882).
17. Ch. 220, 23 Stat. 115 (1884).
18. Ch. 1015, 25 Stat. 476 (1888).
19. Ch. 1064, 25 Stat. 504 (1888).
20. 19 Cong. Rec. 8218 (1888).
21. Ch. 60, 27 Stat. 25 (1892).
22. Ch. 641, 32 Stat. 176 (1902).
23. Ch. 1630, 33 Stat. 428. (1904).
24. Ch. 60, 27 Stat. 25 (1892).
25. 149 U.S. 698 (1893).
26. Ch. 641, 32 Stat. 176 (1902).
27. The Gentleman's Agreement of 1907, U.S. Department of State, *Papers Relating to the Foreign Relations of the United States 1924* (1939), vol. 2, p. 339.
28. Ch. 29, 39 Stat. 874 (1917).
29. 52 Cong. Rec. 805 (1914).
30. *Id.* at 807.
31. *Id.* at 1138–39.
32. See *Crisis,* vol. 9 (February 1915), p. 190.
33. Ch. 29, 39 Stat. 874 (1917).
34. Ch. 8, 42 Stat. 5 (1921).
35. As reprinted in the legislative history of the INA [1952] U.S. Code Cong. and Ad. News 1653, 1668.
36. Ch. 190, 43 Stat. 153 (1924).
37. That act provided, however, that:

    The annual quota of any nationality for the fiscal year beginning July 1, 1927, and for each fiscal year thereafter, shall be a number which bears the same ratio to 150,000 as the number of inhabitants in continental United States in 1920 having that national origin (ascertained as hereinafter provided in this section) bears to the number of inhabitants in continental United States in 1920, but the minimum quota of any nationality shall be 100.

Ch. 190, 43 Stat. 153, 159, § 11(b).

38. Early congressional enactments restricted eligibility for naturalization to free white persons (ch. 3, 1 Stat. 103 (1790)) and to persons of African nativity or descent (Rev. Stat. §2169 (1875)). But when Congress passed the Naturalization Act of June 29, 1906 (ch. 3592, 34 Stat. 596), persons of Japanese ancestry began submitting petitions to become naturalized citizens under the procedures established by that act. The Supreme Court, however, held that the 1906 act was limited by the prior congressional enactments and thus Japanese were ineligible for naturalization. Ozawa v. United States, 260 U.S. 178 (1922).

39. "West Indian Immigration and the American Negro," *Opportunity,* October 1924, pp. 298–99.

40. Under the Treaty of Guadalupe Hidalgo, many Mexican citizens became United States citizens after the annexation of territory by the United States following the Mexican War. Leo Grebler, Joan W. Moore, and Ralph C. Guzman, *The Mexican American People* (1970), pp. 40–41. The Treaty of Guadalupe Hidalgo is reprinted in Wayne Moquin, *A Documentary History of the Mexican Americans* (1971), p. 183.

41. Grebler, Moore, and Guzman, *The Mexican Americans People,* pp. 62–63.

42. Ibid.

43. Ibid., p. 64.

44. Ibid., pp. 523–26.

45. Moquin, *A Documentary History of the Mexican Americans,* p. 294.

46. Ch. 344, 57 Stat. 600 (1943).

47. Ch. 591, 59 Stat. 659 (1945).

48. 60 Stat. 1353.

49. Ch. 534, 60 Stat. 416 (1946).

50. Presidential Proclamation No. 2696, [1946] U.S. Code Cong. and Ad. News 1732.

51. Ch. 647, 62 Stat. 1009 (1948).

52. Ch. 477, 66 Stat. 163 (1952).

53. Grebler, Moore, and Guzman, *The Mexican American People,* pp. 521–22. Mark A. Chamberlin *et al.,* eds., "Our Badge of Infamy: A Petition to the United Nations on the Treatment of the Mexican Immigrant," in *The Mexican American and the Law* (1974 ed.), pp. 31–34.

54. Pub. L. No. 89–236, 79 Stat. 911 (1965).

55. The 1965 amendments to the Immigration and Nationality Act provided the following seven category preference system:

First preference: unmarried sons and daughters of U.S. citizens. (20 percent)

Second preference: spouses and unmarried sons and daughters of lawful resident aliens. (20 percent plus any visas not required for first preference)

Third preference: members of the professions and scientists and artists of exceptional ability and their spouses and children. (10 percent)

Fourth preference: married sons and daughters of U.S. citizens and their spouses and children. (10 percent plus any visas not required for first three preferences)

Fifth preference: brothers and sisters of U.S. citizens and their spouses and children. (24 percent plus any visas not required for first four preferences)

Sixth preference: skilled and unskilled workers in occupations for which labor is in short supply in this country, and their spouses and children. (10 percent)

Seventh preference: refugees. (6 percent)

Spouses and minor children of American citizens are exempt from the preference system.

56. "6–8 million," *New West Magazine,* May 23, 1977; "4–12 million," *Los Angeles Times,* Aug. 7, 1977.

57. Pub. L. No. 94–571, 90 Stat. 2703 (1976).

58. In 1976 there were 57,863 immigrants from Mexico; in 1975, 62,205. U.S., Immigration and Naturalization Service, *Annual Report 1976,* p. 89.

59. Pub. L. No. 95–412, 92 Stat. 907 (1978).

60. Refugee Act of 1980, Pub. L. No. 96–212 (to be codified in scattered sections of 8 U.S.C.). The Refugee Act also increased the allocation of refugee visas to 50,000 annually for the first three fiscal years under the statute and provided that the number of refugee admissions in the following years would be determined by the President after consultation with Congress.

Critical Thinking

1. From among the various historical actions taken to regulate immigration, select three that are particularly hard to understand?

2. What is "Operation Wetback?"

3. What is the National Origins Quota System?

From *The Tarnished Golden Door,* September 1980.

The Diversity Visa Lottery—
A Cycle of Unintended Consequences
in United States Immigration Policy

ANNA O. LAW

E ach year since 1988, the federal government of the United States runs an unusual lottery—not a lottery that awards cash, but one that awards 50,000 visas to nationals of a special list of designated countries that are deemed "underrepresented" in the current legal immigration system. The lucky winners of the visa lottery are granted a visa to enter the United States, lawful permanent residence status (the coveted green card), and the recipients eventually qualify for naturalization. Many immigration analysts and others in the public may have heard by now of this small and obscure provision.[1] What is not known is the true origin of the provision including the impetus for its creation, and how far the program has strayed from its originally intended purpose. How did such a bizarre program that contradicts the philosophy of American immigration admissions become a temporary, and then later a permanent part of the Immigration and Nationality Act?

This article argues that the factors that created the push for the diversity lottery in existence today had its roots in the changed immigration patterns wrought by the Immigration Act of 1965. The diversity lottery idea actually dates much further back in time than the late 1980s when the program first met with legislative success. This article further argues that the chain of unanticipated consequences emanating from the 1965 Act led to the creation of the diversity lottery, a policy which itself, spawned further unintended consequences in the shifting group of beneficiaries. Using Congressional hearing reports, other government documents, and personal interviews with actors who took part in creating and implementing the diversity lottery, this article traces the creation and evolution of the lottery and the role of several key Congressmen who sought to create a policy to benefit their ethnic constituents in the time honored practice of pork barrel politics.

Impact of the 1965 Act

To truly understand the reason for the existence of the diversity lottery today, one must understand the impetus for the policy that dates back to the passage of the Immigration Act of 1965 because today's lottery is actually a direct response to these changes.[2] The present lottery system is also a cobbling together of different concepts and strategies devised by many different Congressmen over the years who were responding to the changed immigration patterns.

The Immigration Act of 1965 was viewed as a watershed act and one of the most liberal and expansive reforms to the American system because of its abolition of race, ethnicity and national origin from the immigration selection process.[3] The 1965 Act revamped the entire immigration selection system by replacing national origin considerations with a seven-category preference system. This preference system prioritized immigrant admissions based primarily on close family relationships to a United States citizen or a lawful permanent resident (a green-card holder), and secondarily on considerations for employment skills. The 1965 Act completely abolished race, ethnicity and national origin as criteria for immigrant admissions and replaced it with the neutral preference system and a 20,000 per country limit within the Eastern Hemisphere, which also had an overall hemisphere limit of 170,000. Originally, the 1965 Act did not place per country limits on the Western Hemisphere, although the region was capped at 170,000. In 1978, Congress passed a law without controversy that brought the Western Hemisphere countries under a worldwide cap and imposed a 20,000 per country limit on all countries worldwide. With this change, the reforms begun in 1965 were finally complete.[4]

As will become clear, the call for the creation of the diversity lottery arose from a group of politically well-situated Irish and Italian-American Members of Congress who sought to benefit their ethnic constituents by rigging the immigration system in favor of these ethnic groups. To comprehend why these two particular groups led the charge, one needs to understand some of the unforeseen circumstances that resulted from the overhaul of the immigration system in 1965 and their connection to the movement to create the diversity lottery in the late 1980s.

Unanticipated Results of the 1965 Act and Early Remedies

One major unforeseen, and certainly unintended, result of the 1965 Act was that it precipitated a huge shift in the ethnic and racial composition of the immigrant flow. Architects of the 1965 Act expected Europeans to be the main beneficiaries of the new preference system since it was expected that the groups who were already in the United States in large numbers would be the ones to petition for their relatives and not the small numbers of racial minorities like the Asians and Africans, for example. In a Department of Justice form letter sent to members of the public who wrote to the Johnson Administration regarding the 1965 Act and also in an informal briefing book sent out to Congressional staff, the Administration addressed the racists' and xenophobes' charge that "the bill would let in hordes of Africans and Asiatics"

> The bill would not let in hordes from anywhere at all. Persons from Africa and Asia would continue to be in effect, quota immigrants, as they were under present law, but would be treated like everyone else ... but immigrants will have to compete and to qualify to get in, and immigration will not be predominantly from Asia and Africa ... The simple fact is that nations differ greatly in the number of their people who have occupational attainment, or the family ties in the United States, to obtain a preference ... Indeed very few people from certain areas could even pay the cost of tickets to come here.[5]

The statement shows that the Administration and authors of the 1965 Act did not anticipate the shift in the national origin composition of immigrants that happened after the 1965 reforms.[6] Whereas the previous immigrant flow was largely from Northern and Western Europe, the 1965 Act led to a modest increase in Eastern and Southern immigration, but an explosion in immigration from Asia and Latin America. By 1975, immigrants from Asia and Latin America accounted for about two-thirds of the immigration to the United States.[7]

Lottery supporters have often cited the empirically observable shift as justification for their approach to distributing immigration visas, the logic being that older immigrant groups like the Italians and Irish were being shut out of the system due to the shift toward Asian and Latino admissions that was facilitated by the 1965 changes. While Asian and Latino immigration rose, immigration from Ireland went on a steep decline after 1965, and Italy developed large waiting lists in family preference categories. The *INS Statistical Yearbook* reports that while immigration from Ireland was an average of 4,836 per year in the decade 1951–1960, and 8,597 per year in 1961–1970, the numbers decreased precipitously in 1971–1980 to 1,149 per year. By 1985, on the eve of the debate over the first version of the lottery provision legal immigration from Ireland numbered 1,397.[8]

However, to focus on the observable increase in numbers of legal immigrants from Asia and Latin America, and the decline of Irish immigrants and the growing demand for Italian immigration, is to focus on the symptoms of the phenomena and not the root causes. Two particular provisions in the 1965 Act directly caused the drop in Irish and Italian immigration as well as backlogs[9] under the fifth family preference (brothers and sisters of United States citizens): the labor certification requirement and the lack of a preference system governing Western Hemisphere immigration after the 1965 changes. In finding solutions to these problems that plagued Irish and Italian immigration in the late 1960s, several enterprising Congressmen devised initial approaches to benefiting their ethnic constituents that lay the groundwork for what is the diversity lottery today.

The Irish and Labor Certification

The connection between the labor certification requirement which was created by the 1965 Act and the rise of the diversity visa movement is a little known fact.[10] Prior to the labor certification requirement created by the 1965 Act, the labor certification was a negative requirement; an alien was ineligible for immigration only if the Secretary of Labor determined that qualified United States workers were available for the job or the alien's employment would adversely affect American workers in the same line of employment. Under this system, it was rare for the Secretary of Labor to take this type of action and the labor certification "requirement" was not really any kind of screen on immigration at all. After the passage of the 1965 Act that amended section 212(a)(14) of the Immigration and Nationality Act, the labor certification requirement (which was a last minute addition to the Act) became an affirmative requirement. An alien could immigrate only if he/she obtained, *prior to the issuance of their visa,* the Secretary of Labor's pre-clearance that they would not adversely affect the job market for United States workers.[11]

The pre-1965 system also had a loose version of the preference system in place before and after 1965. Under this system, there was a "non-preference" category of immigrants to which no percentage was assigned, but who would receive all the unused numbers of the preference categories. For countries with high immigration in comparison to their quota, the non-preference route was foreclosed. For instance, Italy with its pre-1965 annual quota of 5,600 always had more demand for immigration than supply of visas so there were no non-preference numbers left. The case in Ireland however was very different. It was a high quota country with a demand for immigration that was below the supply of visas. Most Irish immigrants utilized this non-preference category to get to the United States. The procedure for non-preference immigrants to get a visa was fairly simple and "pretty much any Irish man or woman who wanted to immigrate could just pick up and do so, with relative ease."[12]

In fact, for most of the Irish, the non-preference route to immigration was the only route available to them. The majority of the Irish who wanted to immigrate had only distant relatives in the United States (cousins, aunts, uncles) and none close enough to petition for them.[13] Those who had no relatives to petition for them could theoretically obtain a visa by qualifying through one of the employment preferences, but few of the Irish possessed the skills and education to qualify via an employment preference. The last nail in the coffin was that now the new "affirmative" labor certification requirement was in place and the requirement applied fully to non-preference immigrants. The labor certification requirement devastated Irish non-preference immigration. With no close relatives to petition for them, unskilled, semi-skilled, and even some skilled workers had great difficulty qualifying under the employment preferences.[14]

The Department of Labor pre-clearance requirement prevented many Irish intending immigrants from coming to the United States, which led to a drastic decline in admission numbers from 1968 forward. From 1971 forward, Ireland ranked among the highest of the countries that did not use up their annual quotas and among the countries that had a huge gap in the number of immigrants the country was actually sending and the number of visas allotted annually to that country. In his testimony before the House Immigration Subcommittee in 1973, John P. Collins, on behalf of the American Irish National Immigration Committee,[15] testified to that effect when he noted that individuals who were seeking to escape the civil unrest in Ireland were prevented from doing so by the immigration laws:

> These individuals, not yet large in number, have aunts, uncles and cousins in the United States. Lacking sisters and brothers who are U.S. citizens, they cannot qualify for fifth preference visas. Nor can they meet the requirement of the other family related preferences. The stringent application of labor clearance makes it impossible for them to qualify for a nonpreference, third preference, or sixth preference visa. Their only hope is to seek asylum here and obtain status as a refugee.[16]

Collins' also offered anecdotes and documents from the INS in his testimony indicating that the Irish attempts at applying for political asylum were by and large being rejected. One of the letters to his client from the INS that Collins quoted noted that the Irishman was ineligible for asylum because he was not coming from a Communist country. Collins' testimony fits the pattern of United States asylum policy before the 1980 reforms in which asylum policy was an extension of United States cold war foreign policy, where almost any and all applicants for asylum from Communist countries were successful and few nationals from non-Communist countries were successful.

The labor pre-clearance policy created by the 1965 Act prevented many Irish from immigrating through the formerly heavily utilized non-preference category, effectively cutting off the most popular way of legally immigrating to the United States. In an earlier appearance before Congress, Collins also confirmed the direct effect of the labor certification requirement on Irish immigration, "there is no doubt that section 212(a)(14) of the Act has caused a decrease in Irish immigration to the United States, as many Irish visa applicants are unskilled or semi-skilled workers, they are unable to qualify."[17]

As a byproduct of their inability to qualify for family, employment, or non-preference immigration, a large number of Irish entered the United States under temporary, nonimmigrant visas and overstayed their visas with the implicit consent of the United States consulate. In his 17 June 1973 testimony before the House Subcommittee on Immigration, Collins was asked what he thought about the large number of Irish "tourists" who were coming to the states. The questioning went as follows:

> Mr. Cline. We understand, Mr. Collins that there are approximately 20,000 visitor visas issued in the Republic of Ireland each year. I wonder whether there is intent to immigrate rather than a temporary visit, if they know they could apply somehow for 234(h) and stay deportation. If so, would many people from the six counties come to Southern Ireland and attempt to obtain visitor visas?
>
> Mr. Collins. That is possible. The fact that there are 20,000 visitors coming to this country from Ireland, I think is one of the problems inherent in the present law. I think, we would be kidding ourselves and this committee be kidding itself, if it believed that all these 20,000 coming here from Ireland were just coming here, in fact, just as visitors.[18]

Collins and the members of Congress were aware of the growing illegal Irish population in the United States and seemed to look the other way. Another source also confirmed that the United States consulate in Ireland was "issuing nonimmigrant visas left and right."[19] The American consulate personnel appeared complicit in creating an undocumented Irish population in the United States. The growth and presence of this illegal Irish population would eventually be another source of pressure for the creation of the diversity lottery.

The Italians and the Fifth Preference Backlog

Italian migration patterns under the changes created by the 1965 Act were quite different from the Irish. The problem plaguing Italian immigration was oversubscribed categories that led to backlogs, especially in the fifth preference (brothers and sisters of United States citizens).[20] Prior to 1965, Italy had an annual quota of 5,600, which was heavily oversubscribed.[21] When the 1965 Act was passed, the people on the waiting list simply got transferred over to the new waiting list. The new system prescribed by the 1965 Act did not actually take full effect until 1968. In the interim, there was a transitional system where the old quotas remained, but unused quota numbers were assigned to a pool that would go toward clearing backlogs. There was "an expectation" that the Italian backlog numbers would go down during the transition period. However, this did not happen and by 1 July 1968, there were still about 100,000 Italians on the fifth preference waiting list.[22]

By 1970, there was a call to "do something for the Italians," the rationale being that the system was not working as intended to reduce backlogs, and that Italian families should not be kept apart. Rev. Joseph Cogo, representing the American Committee on Italian Migration, appeared as a witness to testify about the fifth preference backlog and other immigration issues relating to the Italians. In 1973, he appeared before the House Subcommittee on Immigration to testify in favor of the preference system (like the one already in place in the Eastern hemisphere) being imposed on the Western Hemisphere. While endorsing many of the changes created by the 1965 Act, Cogo explained why he supported a preference system for the Western Hemisphere.

> We fully support the establishment of a preference system for natives of the Western Hemisphere. The present 18-month backlogs experienced by qualified applicants from the Western Hemisphere are deplorable. Moreover, to treat all applicants subject to the numerical limitation identically without regard to closeness of family ties or job skills inflicts great hardship upon applicants.[23]

Cogo was referring to Italy's backlogs in the fifth preference that existed from 1970 to a portion of 1973 and voicing his support for a preference system that would at least prioritize the clearing of the backlog. Without a preference system, all intending immigrants were granted visa priority dates according to a first come first serve basis, not based on the closeness of ties to relatives in the United States.

Although the rhetoric emphasized the urgent need to "do something for the Italians," the fact was that many Italians eventually lost interest in immigrating to the United States by the early 1970s. The Department of State (DOS) visa office tried to show the distinction between people on the backlog waiting list and those whose turn had been reached but not yet issued a visa. From the visa office's point of view, the application was valid indefinitely, or for as long as the relationship between the United States petitioner and Italian beneficiary existed. The DOS had no idea why people were not responding when they got the call that their priorities date had been reached. Some could have moved without a forwarding address, others could have died, but whatever the case, many of the eligible immigrants who were contacted by the DOS were not responding.[24] One might suspect this drop in interest was due to the improving economic conditions in Italy (and in Europe more generally) and the fact that Italy was an original member of the European Community (later the European Union), thus making it easier for their nationals to travel to other parts of Europe rather than come to the United States.

In any event, the demand for Italian visas dropped considerably and at a 1976 hearing, Congressman Joshua Eilberg (D-PA) expressed gratification that the backlog in the fifth preference for Italy was no longer a problem. He asked Reverend Cogo to explain the reason for the clearance of the backlog. Cogo responded:

> In my opinion, the primary reason for the tremendous fallout under fifth preference is the fact that the American citizen is more anxious to give his counterpart Italian brother or sister a chance to migrate here than the Italian is actually to come. . . . Another great factor for the fallout is the present uncertain situation of the American economy and the poverty of job opportunities.[25]

Cogo too realized that the demand for immigration from Italy was decreasing. While he was a frequent witness at Congressional hearings on immigration to press the Italian cause (appearing nine times before Congress between 1970 and 1989) the reality was that by 1970 many of the Italians had lost interest in coming. Yet, the *idea* of continuing to admit Italian immigrants

had taken on a life of its own. When the DOS visa office tried to explain that their letters offering American visas were not being answered, their efforts to explain "fell on deaf ears, and, in fact, simply infuriated many people, both because the explanation was complicated" and because it was a politically unpopular idea that the Italians simply had no interest in coming.[26] So the efforts to "do something for the Italians" continued.

Joining Forces and the Rhetoric of "Reform"

The Irish had the labor certification problem and the Italians, for a while, had the backlog problem. They decided to join forces to increase their political strength and because the two groups' goals were very similar—to amend the Immigration and Nationality Act specifically to benefit nationals from Italy and Ireland. The two groups also faced the same political and public relations problems of justifying the rigging of the system to benefit certain countries, which in fact constituted a return to the national origins principle that the 1965 Act had both wiped out and renounced.

At this point, several policy entrepreneurs[27] stepped in to champion the causes of the Irish and Italians. One of the first was William "Frits" Ryan (D-NY), a member of the House immigration subcommittee, who repeatedly attempted from 1968 to 1973 to introduce bills to benefit the Irish, but without success. H.R. 165 introduced in 1969 is an example of one of Ryan's bills. This bill attempted to place a floor on the level of immigration for each country in the Eastern Hemisphere of which Ireland was a part. The floor would be computed as 75 percent of the average annual number of immigrant visas made available to each country during the 10-year period preceding the 1965 Act. If a country after 1965 did not use up its annual allotment, the difference between that number and the floor would result in extra visas outside of the numerical limit of 20,000 per country and would be exempted from the labor certification requirement.[28] In so doing, Ryan was attempting to address the low usage of Irish visa numbers and deal directly with the source of the problem by eliminating the labor certification requirement that was preventing the majority of the Irish from immigrating.

While Ryan was trying to help the Irish, Peter Rodino (D-NJ) tried to pass bills to benefit the Italians and Irish, first in 1968, again in 1969 and several times after that. Examples of his attempts were H.R. 10618 and H.R. 2118, both introduced in 1968. This bill would be a three-year temporary measure, not a permanent measure like the one Ryan was suggesting. The approach Rodino took was to authorize the utilization of available but unused visa numbers for a three-year period beginning in 1968. These additional visas would also be exempt from the labor certification requirement. H.R. 10618 though intended to aid the Irish and Italians, was neutral in language, and it sought to confer benefits on any other "disadvantaged countries" who did not use up their annual allotment of visas in 1968. These extra visas would be issued on a first come first serve basis, not by country. Rodino argued that without this legislation, the unused numbers would simply be lost.[29] The Irish interest groups however, favored Ryan's bill citing the temporary nature of Rodino's bill as insufficient to alleviate the Irish problem in the long run.

In the late 1960s and through the 1970s, Ryan, Rodino and Emmanuel Celler (D-NY)[30] wrote bills to benefit the Irish and Italians. These seasoned politicians realized that to argue for additional visas for a group of what could be generally characterized as unskilled, not well educated workers, and with no close family ties to those in the United States, but who wished to immigrate, was not a politically savvy or viable move. Instead they adopted two rhetorical strategies to champion their cause. One was to introduce the concept of "new seed immigrants," an idea that was largely Celler's invention.[31] "New seed immigrants" or "independent immigrants" were young, single immigrants who would be allowed to immigrate under a "new seed" visa category and who would be exempt from labor certification. Using the concept was a clever way to distract from the fact that these immigrants had neither close family ties to the United States nor qualifying job skills, and otherwise did not qualify for immigration. Celler and others argued that a number of seed immigrants should be admitted each year because there was something valuable in someone who simply wanted to come to the United States not because of family relations or work skills, but because of their pioneering spirit and immigrant work ethic.

A related rhetorical strategy was to wax nostalgic about the great contributions to this country by the earliest immigrant groups. For example, in one of his appearances before Congress, Collins catalogued the Irish and their historical contributions in the American Revolution, the Civil War, and of Andrew Jackson, the first American President of partial Irish extraction. Collins added:

> If the handiwork of the Irish were painted green, the average American city would be splashed in all sides with emerald hues. . . . It is safe to say that all the Irish have done for America has never been fully told . . . but despite these facts we now find that the restrictive new immigration law has drastically reduced the issuance of immigration visas to Ireland.[32]

Similarly, Edward J. Sussman, National Secretary of the Steuben Society of America[33] stated:

> We cannot conceive that Congress or the people want a law which would all but "dry up" immigration from all of northern Europe. It is inequitable and unjust to those components of the American people who contributed most generously to the founding and building of the nation.[34]

The rhetoric of "seed immigrants" fused with the "we built this country" rhetoric became the verbal strategy of the Irish and Italian pro-immigration forces.

The champions of the diversity lottery also used a third rhetorical strategy, one of a claim of discrimination against these two groups. This strategy was to present the observable decline in Irish and Italian immigration as *prima facie* evidence that the post-1965 system constituted discrimination (intentional or not) against these two groups, even if the 20,000 per country

limit was designed to guard against national origin discrimination. Some of this language of discrimination rose to the level of hyperbole, comparing the present immigration laws to the Chinese Exclusion Acts. Philip O'Rourke, Chairman of the California branch of the American Irish Immigration Committee asserted, "Having corrected such past inequities as the 'Chinese Exclusion Act,' it surely was not the intent of Congress that there be an 'Irish Exclusion Act' contained in the present law."[35] What the language of "new seed," "we built this country" and "discrimination" had in common was simply that the rhetoric was a calculated way to gain support for what was purely pork barrel politics and to mask the reality of a return to a national origins based system which privileged some countries over others in the immigration system.

The rhetorical efforts and other political maneuvering by the pro-Irish and Italian immigration congressmen culminated in a House bill that was passed on 17 March 1973, not coincidentally, on St. Patrick's Day. The bill contained specific provisions to benefit the Irish and Italians. The plan was to take a historical average of the number of visas that adversely affected countries that had been issued prior to 1965, and then to restore those visa numbers to make up for the drop off in numbers in the post-1965 period.[36] However, the bill got no further than the House. Sen. James Eastland (D-MS), then chair of the Senate Judiciary committee, a staunch foe of increased immigration and a supporter of national origins quotas, was not about to let another immigration bill remain active in wake of the results of the 1965 Act. Between 1966 and 1976, Eastland did not hold a single hearing on any immigration bill and any bill that was sent to his committee got bottled up there and died.[37]

The 1980s and the Immigration Reform and Control Act of 1986 (IRCA)

The issue lay untouched for many years after Ryan's death in 1976 and was not taken up again until the mid 1980s. No bills came to the floor in the 1980s to address the Italian and Irish question because the nation's attention had by then turned to the question of illegal immigration.[38] There was no movement on the Irish/Italian immigration until the swirl of politics involving the passage of IRCA in 1986.

By the mid 1980s, the Italians had thoroughly lost interest in immigrating but the Irish had not due in large part to the sizeable illegal population in the United States seeking legal status and the worsening economic conditions in Ireland. Representative Brian J. Donnelly (D-MA) and others stepped in and took over Frits Ryan's role as champion of Irish immigration. These new advocates of Irish and Italian immigration adopted such concepts as "new seed immigration," "adversely affected countries," and "discrimination" from the late 1960s and 1970s and worked them into their bills. Donnelly's program called NP-5, sought to amend section 314 of the Immigration and Nationality Act.[39] The Donnelly amendment provided 10,000 visas for nationals of "adversely affected countries." Edward Kennedy (D-MA) filed companion legislation in the Senate.

Donnelly and Kennedy's efforts also received an important and timely boost from then Speaker of the House, Tip O'Neal. As Speaker, he had great influence over the House Rules Committee that determines which bills would be allowed to the floor for debate. When Rodino, chair of the Judiciary Committee, went to see O'Neal about scheduling IRCA for floor debate, O'Neal told Rodino that the before the bill came out of committee there had better be something in the bill for the Irish or the bill would never see floor action.[40] Rodino agreed and allowed the Donnelly/Kennedy amendment to remain, O'Neal waived the necessary points of order, and the Donnelly/Kennedy provision became part of the law when IRCA eventually passed. From a timely *quid pro quo* was born the first incarnation of the diversity visa lottery.

Donnelly's NP-5 program benefited persons from "adversely affected countries." A list of "adversely affected countries" would be generated with such a country defined as any country that did not use more than 25 percent of its 20,000 annual allotment of visas. The Department of State was charged with compiling the statistics to determine which countries were the top thirty-six "adversely affected countries." After crunching the numbers, these countries were designated as "adversely affected": Albania, Algeria, Argentina, Austria, Belgium, Bermuda, Canada, Czechoslovakia, Denmark, Estonia, Finland, France, The Federal Republic of Germany, the German Democratic Republic, Great Britain and Northern Ireland, Guadeloupe, Hungary, Iceland, Indonesia, Ireland, Italy, Japan, Latvia, Liechtenstein, Lithuania, Luxembourg, Monaco, the Netherlands, New Caledonia, Norway, Poland, San Marino, Sweden, Switzerland, and Tunisia.[41] Nationals of these predominantly European and African countries would be allowed to submit their names and the first 10,000 applicants who were drawn based on their applications' arrival time in the mail would obtain immigration visas.

The Department of State received a whopping 1.4 million applications for the NP-5 program during a seven-day registration period in January 1987! The NP-5 results showed that, the countries that benefited the most from the program and the respective number of lottery winners were: Ireland (3,112), Canada (2,078), and Great Britain (1,181).[42] The high success rate of the Irish was due to their well-planned and coordinated efforts that involved that country chartering planes and literally depositing the applications in post office boxes on Capitol Hill.[43]

Donnelly, like previous proponents before him argued that there was a great need for such a program because certain countries, especially Ireland, were being "shut out" under the current admission system. Donnelly gave three reasons for introducing the visa lottery. First he noted, "our Nation must reintroduce into the immigrant stream those countries that have been determined to be adversely affected by the reform act of 1965 and face the same barriers with the passage of the 1986 reform bill." Second, he added that the NP-5 program held out the possibility of legal immigration for those who would normally come illegally (or who were presently illegally residing in the United States). Third, Donnelly noted that NP-5 would allow for natives of the adversely affected thirty-six countries to compete in a more "equitable" manner with other nationalities.

Donnelly agreed that the goal of the 1965 Act was admirable in ending discrimination against immigrants based on national origins and added that it was "a principle I would not wish to change." However, Donnelly asserted that "the southern and eastern Europeans who are expected to benefit from the 1965 law are now effectively excluded from the immigrant pool on an equal basis with residents of northern and western Europe."[44] In his rhetoric, Donnelly simply drew from and adopted the ideas of Ryan, Celler and Cogo that had been floating around for a while and until then, had not met with legislative success.

After the NP-5 program and during the debate leading up to the Immigration Act of 1990 (IMMACT '90) Donnelly was counseled to add the diversity concept as a political tactic to gain the support of Asian and Latino ethnic groups and employers who were all lobbying for different provisions to be included in IMMACT '90.[45] These groups were not at all fooled by the politically correct language, as evident in their testimonies before Congress.[46] Of course the politics surrounding the entire diversity lottery itself, going back to its origins in the late 1960s, cast serious doubt on the sincerity and commitment of the provisions supporters of true diversity. Perhaps by utilizing the term "diversity" Donnelly and his supporters hoped to tap into the popularity and influence of the multicultural movement that was in vogue in the 1980s. But the use of the terms "diversity," "independent immigrant" and "new seed immigrant" to describe the NP-5 and its progeny, glossed over the real return to national origin considerations represented in these programs.

The Immigration Act of 1990 (Immact '90)

After major legislation concerning illegal immigration was enacted in the Immigration Reform and Control Act of 1986, Congress turned its attention to legal immigration. Legal or permanent immigration became an issue for two reasons. First, there was concern over the imbalance between the overwhelming majorities of immigrants admitted on family reunification track as opposed to the number of "independent immigrants." The diversity lottery in the 1990s was partially a response to the claim that Asians and Latinos have a "lock" on the family-based preferences. Others have raised the accusation that the diversity lottery actually had more sinister intentions to carefully calibrate the lottery to minimize Mexican and Asian migration while maximizing the migration of European and African immigrants.[47] I found no evidence that this was the case, although the strange classification of Mexico as a country in South/Central America rather than North America was curious.

Second, there was concern over the backlogs under the family-based immigration petition preference system, specifically the second preference (spouses, and minor children of permanent residents; and also unmarried sons and daughters of lawful permanent residents); and the fifth preference (brothers and sisters of United States citizens). This time, the backlogs were hurting Asian and Latino families and intending immigrants.

Reflecting these concerns, the primary focus on IMMACT '90 was the numerical limits and preference systems that regulate the current permanent legal immigration admission system.

IMMACT '90 established a three track preference system for the admission of immigrants: family-sponsored, employment-sponsored, and an independent track. Highlights of IMMACT '90 included an increase in the worldwide cap, an increase in employment-based visas from 54,000 to 140,000, and a *permanent* provision for the diversity lottery.[48]

Many different interest groups in addition to the Irish and Italians organized to affect the outcome of IMMACT '90, including Asians and Latinos. While Asian and Latino interests found the diversity lottery idea repugnant because of its clear return to national origin considerations, potentially the most damaging proposals in IMMACT '90 from these groups' point of view were proposals to cut back on numbers on the second preferences (spouses, children and unmarried sons and daughters of lawful permanent residents) and to eliminate altogether the fifth preference (brothers and sisters of United States citizens). These were and continue to be the admissions preferences most heavily used by Asians and Latinos. The rationale for cutting back on these two categories was to minimize "chain migration." In particular, some Congressmen argued that brothers and sisters and adult children were not nuclear family members and that the system should not allow an immigrant to bring "extended" family members.[49]

It is necessary to understand how important the family preference issues were to Asian and Latino interests and how much they had at stake because the battles over these provisions eventually eclipsed their efforts to defeat the diversity provision, thus allowing the lottery to eventually pass. Asian and Latino interests were victorious in preventing the constriction of the family preferences and the second and fifth preferences remained intact. However, despite their opposition (and others) to the diversity lottery, the provision became a part of IMMACT '90.

Legislative History of the "Diversity Lottery" in Immact '90

The diversity lottery that is in existence today was a relatively obscure provision buried in a huge omnibus immigration bill. The diversity lottery, being neither a family nor employment-based policy, was classified under the independent immigration track. It is precisely because the lottery was neither family nor employment based that made the provision extremely controversial. The fact that such a provision was even under consideration at all was highly unusual given the primary goals of American immigration to reunify families and secondarily to address employment needs of the country. Even during the era of national origins and Chinese exclusion, American immigration policy had always operated on the understanding that this nation purposefully and deliberately selects immigrants based on their family ties to those already in the country and based on the jobs skills they will contribute. But the lottery approach to immigration admissions dispenses with the affirmative selection of immigrants by introducing a random selection process.

In effect, there were two diversity programs. One program was a transitional program that ran in fiscal years 1991 to 1994. This transitional program provided for 40,000 visas for each fiscal year. At this point, the program was changed from a first come first serve basis to a true lottery where applications received would be assigned a number and a computer would randomly draw numbers from the total applications received. As testament to the influence of the bill's architects, during the transitional programs, *40 percent (18,000) of the 40,000 visas for each fiscal year 1992 through 1994 would be reserved for Ireland.* Beginning in fiscal year 1995, 50,000 visas would be allotted each year for the diversity lottery with the top ten countries that have contributed the most immigrants to the United States (after the 1965 reforms), excluded from eligibility. These ineligible countries are China, Taiwan, Colombia, Dominican Republic, India, Jamaica, Korea, Mexico, Philippines, Great Britain, Guyana, and Haiti. The only requirements of lottery applicants was that they have either a high school education or at least two years of work experience in an occupation which requires two years of training or experience. Applicants would be selected randomly by computer and would have to re-register each year if not selected.[50]

In the debate leading up to the passage of IMMACT '90 in 1987, Congressman Donnelly again introduced legislation that sought to make the visa lottery a permanent part of the immigration system since the NP-5 program was to expire after the 1988 fiscal year. Donnelly further justified the need for the permanent lottery system citing the tremendous response to the NP-5 program, especially from natives of "older sources of immigration" such as Canada, Ireland, Italy, and other nations in Europe. In a 1987 Congressional hearing before the subcommittee on Immigration, Donnelly stated:

> The cumulative effect of the policy for the last twenty years has been to discriminate against any of the peoples who have traditionally made up our immigrant stock . . . Today we have an opportunity to correct these imbalances in immigration and open our doors once again to legal immigration slammed shut on those nations that enjoy long historic and family ties with our country.[51]

In the question and answer period following Donnelly's testimony, Chairman Romano Mazzolli (D-NY) probed Donnelly on his motivation for introducing the lottery and asked whether there were many illegals on the Eastern seaboard. Donnelly admitted that the program was intended as a backdoor amnesty program for the Irish when he answered:

> [B]ecause we were unable to extend the amnesty program, they would still have an undocumented illegal status like any other—most especially I think you are indicating the young Irish undocumented workers . . . of which I have in my constituency alone over 10,000.[52]

Even if his illegal constituents could not vote, Donnelly as an elected official was in the position to help them in a direct way through creative law making.

On the Senate side, the main supporters of the lottery approach to visa allocation were Senators Edward Kennedy (D-MA) and Daniel P. Moynihan (D-NY); and Senator Alfonse D'Amato (R-NY), all with considerable seniority and influence. In addition, Senator Kennedy was a member of the Judiciary Subcommittee on Immigration, Refugees, and International

Affairs. Senator Kennedy introduced companion legislation to the House bill to redress the "unforeseen problems" posed by the 1965 Act that inadvertently restricted immigration from "old seed sources of our heritage."[53] Meanwhile, Senator Moynihan argued, "fairness is at issue" and added "we need to help the descendants of our forefathers, to open the doors to opportunity for them also."[54] Senator D'Amato, another supporter of the lottery, charged that the current visa system dominated by Asian and Latin American countries "is an injustice which I believe we should work to correct . . . it is simply not fair to penalize so many countries, and it is not in our self-interest."[55] Again, the same mantras of discrimination, new seed immigration, and nostalgia for the past permeated their rhetoric, divorced from the reality of the pork barrel politics that was going on.

While Donnelly took the initiative in creating the NP-5 program, the move to make it a permanent part of the immigration system required the lottery provision to be passed as part of an overall immigration act. Enter Congressman Bruce Morrison (D-CT) who was then the first term chairman of the Judiciary's Subcommittee on Immigration, Refugees and International Law. Morrison has been credited as the author and "prime architect" of IMMACT '90. Although he worked closely with Senators Edward Kennedy and Alan Simpson (R-WY) Morrison reportedly "galled some of his colleagues by his single-handed steering of the legislation." Morrison saw to it that when his bill was being scaled back that the lottery provision remained intact. Opponents of the measure dubbed the lottery provision the "Irish Amnesty Provision."[56]

But this time, the pro-Irish lobby met not opposition in the form of a James Eastland, but in other ethnic interests. Asians and Latinos, through their interest group representatives, vigorously protested against the lottery system arguing that it would represent a backsliding in immigration policy and a reintroduction of discriminatory national origins considerations into immigrant admissions policy. In a statement before the Senate Judiciary Committee, a representative of the Mexican American Legal Defense [and Education] Fund (MALDEF) said:

> If Congress lends its imprimatur to the legislation, it will signal a major reversal of policy in which national origins will once again play a role in determining which persons can be admitted into the United States.[57]

Many other groups joined MALDEF and individuals in their protest against the lottery provision or any point system that would award extra points for English language ability, and award extra points to nationals from "adversely affected countries." *La Raza,* the Asian American Legal Defense Fund, Organization of Chinese Americans, and Japanese American Citizens League were other ethnic lobbies that protested against both the lottery system and a point system that would favor Europeans.

The Asian and Latino interests were not the only groups that objected to the diversity lottery. Other non-Latino and non-Asian groups and individuals found the diversity lottery equally objectionable on principle, even if they did not have a personal stake in the matter. Also posing objections to the lottery were the American Immigration Lawyers Association,

Doris Meissner (of the Carnegie Endowment for International Peace and former INS Commissioner) and Lawrence Fuchs of Brandeis University, a well-known scholar of American immigration. Fuchs asserted that the visa lottery made no sense because it was based on the idea that "nations and countries immigrated, rather than individuals." Reminding the committee of the progress made in the abolition of national origins by the 1965 Act he said, "we should seek them as immigrants because they are desirable for their attributes as persons, and not because of their national origins backgrounds."[58] Fuchs underscored a fact that the lottery proponents were trying to conceal, that "the Filipino, Mexican, or Chinese who lacked employment skills or close relatives were in the same predicament as the Irish and Italian"—any bias in the system was not nation specific but specific to the individual circumstances of the intending immigrant.[59] Like many other observers, Fuchs realized that the lottery was an attempt to legalize the illegal Irish population since many of the illegal Irish had missed the eligibility cutoff date for the 1986 amnesty program, a second chance amnesty and a throwback to national origins based immigration.[60]

Despite objections from many sectors, the diversity lottery passed and remains a part of today's immigration system. Several factors contributed to the lottery's legislative success. The first, was the leadership of Morrison who was in a key position of power as the Immigration Subcommittee Chair, and the tireless efforts of Donnelly and the support of other senior members of Congress. The second, was the neutralizing of the opposition in Asian and Latino interests who had their hands full fighting the cutbacks on family preferences. Despite attempts to cut back on the second and fifth preferences, those preferences remained untouched in IMMACT '90. The Asian and Latino communities considered this development a huge victory for them since they had all along viewed the preservation of these preferences as their first priority in the IMMACT '90 debate. When these provisions of the law remained untouched or when their "piece of the pie" was given back they were willing to stomach the passage of the diversity lottery. Finally, the relatively small number of visas (44,000 for the first three years, and 50,000 thereafter) as well as the temporary nature of the pro-Irish bias made the lottery more palatable.

Post Immact '90—Variation on a Theme of Unintended Consequences

After the passage of IMMACT '90, interest in the diversity lottery issue seemed to fade from the political radar screen.[61] There were no further hearings on the subject after 1990 and there were no serious efforts to remove the provision from the immigration law. By 1996, the attention of the policy and immigrant communities had again shifted to much larger issues such as the preservation of alien welfare rights and the fate of criminal aliens as Congress debated and eventually passed the [Illegal] Immigration Reform and Immigrant Responsibility Act (IIRIRA), Anti-Terrorism and Death [Effective] Penalty Act (AEDPA), and sweeping welfare reform legislation in the Personal Responsibility and Work Opportunity Reconciliation

Act (PRWORA). Later, in 2001, the Bush Administration's discussion of the possibility of another amnesty or "regularization" for approximately 3 million illegal immigrants from Mexico (and potentially other groups) took center stage. The amnesty proposal was in turn eclipsed by the terrorist attacks on 11 September 2001. These two events relegated the comparatively insignificant 50,000 diversity visas to the back burner for policymakers.

Eventually, the Irish also lost interest in the visa lottery that was created for them. The economic situation in Ireland greatly improved by 1995. The *Financial Times* reported, "Ireland's crippling unemployment problem eased sharply in 1994–95 as the economy created 49,000 new jobs, the biggest annual increase since 1972." The same article also noted that the improved economy in Ireland had slowed the flow of emigration, "The recent economic recovery has also stemmed the flow of net migration, which reached a peak of 43,900 in 1989."[62] Also, because Ireland was admitted to the European Union in 1973, their nationals, like the Italians are now able to travel and work in other parts of Europe which may in turn have further cut down on Irish emigration to the U.S. After the improved economy beginning in 1995, the Irish abandonment of the diversity lottery was clear and the stark statistics tell the story. As late as 1994, the last year of the diversity lottery transition program, a total of 16,344 Irish immigrated via the diversity lottery. But by 1996, the number dropped to 963, by 1997 it was 359 and by 1998 the number was 318![63]

Perhaps one of the strangest footnotes to the diversity lottery odyssey is that the lottery unintentionally came to benefit many more nationalities than its original target beneficiaries. The neutral mathematical formula devised by the Department of State to determine which were the adversely affected countries produced a list that in addition to Italy and Ireland included many African and European countries, and a few Asian countries. Although the largest beneficiaries were the Irish in the NP-5 program and transitional programs, the most recent Immigration and Naturalization statistics from 1996 through 1998 show that the latest beneficiaries of the lottery have been largely the nationals of other European and African nations. More specifically, in fiscal year 1996 nationals from Nigeria, Ghana, Bangladesh, Ethiopia, and Poland were the most successful in the lottery. In fiscal year 1997, the top diversity visa receiving countries were Albania, Poland, Bangladesh, Ethiopia and Nigeria. And in fiscal year 1998 (the most recent and complete set of INS statistics available) the top diversity visa receiving countries were: Albania, Nigeria, Bulgaria, Bangladesh, and Romania.[64] Although the official numbers are not yet available for the 1999 and 2000 lotteries, *This Day,* a Nigerian newspaper in Lagos, reported that Nigerian nationals received approximately 6,000 visas in the fiscal year 2000 visa lottery, a number up from the approximately 4,000 figure in 1999.[65] These numbers place Nigeria as first or second among diversity visa receiving countries in 1999 and 2000. A program that was created by and intended for the Irish and Italians and then abandoned by those two groups has become a permanent part of the immigration system benefitting entirely different groups of individuals.[66]

Conclusion

The story of policy making in general, and American immigration policy in particular, is often marked by unintended consequences that flow from previously implemented policies. The diversity lottery is an example of the efforts of a group of policy entrepreneurs who had the will and the way to mitigate the unintended effects of the 1965 Act that had foreclosed using national origins as a selection criterion. The end result of their efforts led to even more unpredictable outcomes. The unanticipated consequences emanating from the Immigration Act of 1965 begot the diversity lottery which in turn, went on autopilot, and begot an unanticipated group of beneficiaries. Perhaps the biggest irony of the diversity visa lottery is that the lottery, conceived for less than principled purposes, is in fact producing a stream of immigrants from countries that are very different than the ones that currently dominate the immigration system.

Notes

I wish to thank Sandy Levinson, Cara Wong, Lawrence Fuchs, Gary Freeman, and the anonymous reviewer(s) who read earlier drafts of the essay and provided helpful suggestions. I am also indebted to Cornelius "Dick" Scully, Arthur "Skip" Endres, Brett Endres, and Edward Skerrett for providing me with information crucial to the essay.

1. See for example Stephen Legomsky, *Immigration and Refugee Law and Policy,* 2nd ed. (New York, 1997), pp. 204–211, Walter Jacob, "Note: Diversity Visas: Muddled Thinking and Pork Barrel Politics," *Georgetown Immigration Law Journal* (June 1992) and numerous articles in the print media and ethnic media. Jacob attributes the origin of the diversity lottery idea to the recommendations of the Select Commission on Immigration and Refugee Policy that existed in the mid-1980s.

2. I am very grateful to Cornelius "Dick" Scully for pointing out to me that the roots of the lottery go much further back than the late 1980s.

3. David Reimers, *Still the Golden Door—The Third World Comes to America.* (New York, 1985), pp. 80–81.

4. David Reimers, "An Unintended Reform: The 1965 Immigration Act and Third World Immigration to the United States," *Journal of American Ethnic History,* 3 (Fall 1983): 80, 87, 89.

5. Letter in Q & A form from Norbert A. Schlei, Assistant Attorney General, Office of Legal Counsel to "Fellow Citizens" in response to the public writing in about the immigration act. Also published in the *Congressional Record* of the 89th Congress, 28 April 1965. "Legislative Background Immigration Law 1965" Box 1. Folder "Road to Final Passage" Lyndon Baines Johnson Presidential Library, Austin, Texas.

6. See also Reimers, "An Unintended Reform." Reimers lays out in detail how the unintended shift in the ethnicity in immigrants came about.

7. U.S. Immigration and Naturalization Service, *Statistical Yearbook of the Immigration and Naturalization Services, 1994* (Washington, D.C., 1996), p. 12.

8. U.S. Immigration and Naturalization Service, *Statistical Yearbook of the Immigration and Naturalization Service, 1994* (Washington, D.C., 1996), pp. 27–28.

9. Due to the implementation of the 20,000 per country limit for immigrant admissions, some countries had developed large backlogs in certain family petition categories because there are more people who wish to immigrate per year than there are available visa numbers. For example, U.S. citizens petitioning for their unmarried brothers and sisters in the Philippines or China must wait 18–20 years before their brothers and sisters will have a current visa priority date that would allow them to enter the United States and obtain permanent residence (get a greencard). Some argued that these lengthy backlogs undermine the credibility of the system.

10. Dick Scully explained in detail what this connection was. Cornelius "Dick" Scully, telephone conversation with author, 28 June 2001.

11. Cornelius "Dick" Scully, telephone conversation with the author, 28 June 2001 and email communication to the author, 26 July 2001. Mr. Scully (now retired) was a career civil servant at the Department of State between 1968 and 1997. He was for many years, the Director of the Office of Legislation, Regulations and Advisory Assistance, which was the technical section of the visa office at State. While at his position, Mr. Scully was responsible for writing all the regulatory orders to implement all the various lotteries, including the current one. Given the many years he was at the Department of State's visa section, Mr. Scully is truly the institutional memory of the place.

12. Additionally, the process for immigrating under the non-preference quota was quick. One simply wrote a letter to the consular officer stating their desire to immigrate; the officer would send them a biographical information form to fill out. Upon receipt of the form the officer would check whether there were actual numbers available for the non-preference applicant. If there were, which was always the case in Ireland, the applicant was sent information to prepare for a visa interview. If the interview went smoothly, the visa would be issued on the spot and the applicant could travel to the US. (Scully, email communication to author 26 July 01.)

13. Under U.S. immigration law, only close relatives such as spouses, sons and daughters, and brothers/sisters have petitioning rights—not more distant relatives like cousins, aunts, uncles or grandparents.

14. David Reimers "An Unintended Reform," pp. 73–74 and Scully, telephone interview with author 28 June 2001.

15. This umbrella organization was composed of members of all the major Irish American organizations in the U.S. including the Ancient Order of Hibernians, the Knights of Equity, and the Gaelic Athletic Association.

16. Testimony of John P. Collins, House Subcommittee on Immigration, *Western Hemisphere Immigration Hearing on H.R. 981*, 93rd cong., 1st session, 1973, p. 324.

17. Testimony of John P. Collins. Subcommittee No. I of the Committee on the Judiciary, House of Representatives, *The Effect of the Act of October 5, 1965, on Immigration From Ireland and Northern Europe*, 91st cong., 1st session, 1969, p. 15.

18. Testimony of John P. Collins, House Subcommittee on Immigration, *Western Hemisphere Immigration Hearings on H.R. 981*, 93rd cong., 1st sess., 1973, p. 323.

19. Arthur "Skip" Endres, phone interview with author, 11 July 2001. Mr. Endres was Chief Counsel to Congressman Peter Rodino (D-NJ) when Rodino was first Chair of the House Immigration Subcommittee and then Chair of the full Judiciary Committee. Rodino and his staff played active leadership roles in the passage of the 1986 Immigration Reform and Control Act and the Immigration Act of 1990.

20. Backlogs result when more persons than 20,000 wish to immigrate each year to a particular country. If the 20,000 slots are already used up that year, the persons must wait on a wait list until the year a slot opens up for them.

21. Dick Scully reports that at one point, there were well over 100,000 registrants on the Italian waiting list for brothers and sisters of U.S. citizens. (Scully, email communication to author 26 July 2001.)

22. Scully, email communication to author, 26 July 2001.

23. Testimony of Rev. Joseph A. Cogo, *Western Hemisphere Immigration*, 1975, p. 313. Reimers notes the Italians were also in favor of the 20,000 per country limit even though it meant an increase in backlogs because the general feeling at the time was that no country should dominate the immigration system and a set per country limit would be the fairest way to ensure that goal. (Reimers, "An Unintended Reform," p. 74.)

24. Scully, email communication to author, 26 July 2001. Scully adds that in the late 1960s the U.S. government took the extraordinary step of instructing the Italian postal service to find the persons whom the visa approval letters had been sent to and get them into the immigration process.

25. Testimony of Rev. Joseph A. Cogo, House Immigration Subcommittee Hearing on H.R. 981, *Western Hemisphere Immigration*, 1973, p. 320.

26. Scully, email communication to author, 26 July 2001.

27. In the political science literature, policy entrepreneurs are described as "advocates who are willing to invest their resources—time, energy, reputation, and money—to promote a position in return for anticipated future gain in the form of material, purposive or solidary benefits." Kingdon further articulates three common qualities of such entrepreneurs. They have some claim to a hearing as a representative of a group or an "authoritative decision-making position; they are known for their political connections and negotiating skills, and they are persistent and tenacious." John Kingdon, *Agendas, Alternatives, and Public Policies*, (New York, 1995), pp. 179–181. One will see that Kingdon's description of policy entrepreneurs quite aptly describes the Members of Congress who negotiated previous and present versions of the diversity lottery.

28. Opening statement of Michael Feighan, Hearings of the U.S. House, Committee on the Judiciary, Subcommittee No. 1, *The Effect of the Act of October 3, 1965 on the Immigration from Ireland and Northern Europe*, 91st cong., 1st sess., 1969, pp. 2–3.

29. Opening remarks of Peter Rodino. *The Effect of the Act of October 3, 1965 on the Immigration from Ireland and Northern Europe*, 1969, pp. 4–5, 8–9.

30. Celler, and later Rodino, served first as chair of the House Immigration Subcommittee then the House Judiciary committee.

31. Endres, telephone interview with author, 11 July 2001.

32. Testimony of John P. Collins, Hearings of the U.S. House Committee on the Judiciary, Subcommittee, *The Effect of the Act of October 3, 1965 on the Immigration from Ireland and Northern Europe*, 1969, pp. 11–12.

33. The society is a national organization of American citizens wholly or in part of Germanic origin and who have been actively interested in U.S. immigration issues.

34. Testimony of Edward J. Sussman, U.S. House, Committee on the Judiciary, Subcommittee on Immigration, *The Effect of the Act of October 3, 1965 on the Immigration from Ireland and Northern Europe.* 1969, pp. 26–27.

35. Statement of Philip O'Rourke, U.S. House, Committee on the Judiciary, Subcommittee No. 1, *The Effect of the Act of October 3, 1965 on the Immigration from Ireland and Northern Europe,* 1969, p. 30.

36. Endres, phone interview with author, 11 July 2001.

37. Scully, email communication to author, 26 July 2001. Scully speculated that Eastland bottled up all immigration legislation because he felt he would lose control of an immigration bill if it went to the floor.

38. Endres, telephone interview with author, 11 July 2001.

39. House Report 100-1038, *Immigration Amendments of 1988,* Document submitted by Peter Rodino to accompany H.R. 5115.

40. Endres, telephone interview with author, 11 July 2001. Mr. Endres, as chief counsel of the Judiciary, was present at the meeting between O'Neal and Rodino when this deal transpired.

41. 52 *Federal Register* 1,449 (1987).

42. U.S. Senate, Committee on the Judiciary, *Diversity Lottery Program, 1987: Hearings on S. 161,* 101st cong., 1st sess., 1987, p. 4.

43. Endres, telephone interview with author, 11 July 2001. It was clear that the Irish government took a very active interest in this lottery given the depressing economic situation in that country. Endres reports that during the events leading up to the passage of IRCA, he asked Donnelly whether the Irish are interested in the provision and why Rodino had not heard from the Irish consulate. Rodino received a call the following day from the Irish Prime Minister.

44. Testimony of Brian J. Donnelly, U.S. House, Subcommittee on Immigration, Refugees, and International Law, 100th cong., 2nd sess., 1988, p. 7.

45. Walter Jacob, "Note: Diversity Visas," p. 313. Jacob writes that Harris Miller, the chief lobbyist for the Irish Immigration Reform Movement told him that the diversity language was used to gain support from the other interest groups.

46. See the statements of objection to the diversity provision in the testimonies from representatives from the Organization of Chinese Americans, La Raza, Mexican American Legal Defense Fund, and the Japanese American Citizens League among others in U.S. Senate, Subcommittee on Immigration, *Hearings on S 161—the Diversity Lottery Program,* 101st cong., 1st sess., 1987.

47. Scully pointed out that no Administration had ever treated Mexico as anything but a North American country. (Scully, telephone interview with author 28 June 2001) The gerrymandering of Mexico into South/Central America seems to lend credence to the charge that the current lottery is a reaction against Latino migration. With Mexico in another hemisphere, the only three countries left in the Northern Hemisphere are the U.S., Canada and the Bahamas. Under the present diversity lottery rules, each hemisphere has a cap and each country has a cap. Moving Mexico to another hemisphere would free up more visas for the remaining countries in North America.

48. Joyce Vialet and Larry Eig, *Immigration Act of 1990* (P.L. 101-649) Congressional Research Service report to Congress, 1990 (no. 90–601), pp. 1–2.

49. Asian and Latino interests strenuously fought the proposals that would cut back on family preferences. Both these groups criticized the proposal's definition of "nuclear family" as Eurocentric and culturally insensitive. Asian interest groups also argued that it was too soon to cut back on these preferences especially when their communities had just recently begun to enjoy the benefits of the liberalized immigration laws provided by the 1965 Act after they had been discriminated for so long under the Asia-Pacific Triangle system.

50. U.S. Department of State, *Visa Bulletin Number* 2a Volume VII, p. 3.

51. Statement of Brian Donnelly, U.S. House, Subcommittee on Immigration, *Hearings on S. 161, Diversity Lottery Program,* 101st cong., 1st sess., 1987, p. 52.

52. Statement of Brian Donnelly, U.S. House, Subcommittee on Immigration, Refugees, and International Law of the Committee on the Judiciary House of Rep., 100th cong., 2nd sess., 1988, p. 11. The Immigration Reform and Control Act (IRCA) in 1986 granted amnesty to illegal aliens who were residing in the country but most of the illegal Irish missed the cut-off date for eligibility because the economic problems in Ireland that precipitated a large number of illegals coming to the U.S. occurred *after* the amnesty cut-off date. Since IRCA was intended as a one-time only amnesty opportunity that could not be repeated, the diversity lottery was designed as a "back door amnesty" for the Irish illegals.

53. Statement of Edward Kennedy, U.S. House, Subcommittee on Immigration, Refugees, and International Law of the Committee on the Judiciary, 100th cong., 2nd sess., 1988, p. 2.

54. Statement of Patrick Moynihan, U.S. House, Subcommittee on Immigration, Refugees, and International Law of the Committee on the Judiciary, 100th cong., 2nd sess., 1988, pp. 37, 40.

55. Statement of Alfonse D'Amato, U.S. House, Subcommittee on Immigration, Refugees, and International Law of the Committee on the Judiciary. 100th cong., 2nd sess., 1988, p. 41.

56. Dick Kirschten, "Opening the Door," *National Journal* (1990): 2003.

57. Statement of MALDEF. U.S. House, Subcommittee on Immigration, Refugees, and International Law of the Committee on the Judiciary, 100th cong., 2nd sess., 1988, p. 519.

58. Testimony of Lawrence Fuchs, U.S. House, Subcommittee on Immigration, Refugees, and International Law of the Committee on the Judiciary, 100th cong., 2nd sess., 1988, p. 180.

59. I have elsewhere written about Fuchs' objection to the provision and the logic inconsistencies of the lottery defenders' arguments. Anna O. Law, "Race, Ethnicity and National Origins in Public Policy—When Should it Matter?" *Georgetown Immigration Law Journal* (1986) vol. 10: 71, 75.

60. Lawrence Fuchs, telephone interview with the author, 13 March 1998. Fuchs added that there was no illusion on the part of the sponsors of the bill that the lottery provision could be justified on principle. All the rhetoric about diversity was "just window dressing."

61. Scully's view was that by the time IMMACT '90 passed, the interest groups and the policy community were more generally worn out over the battle and gave up on attacking the lottery. He notes that even the Federation for American Immigration Reform, a restrictionist group, has stopped attacking the diversity lottery (email communication with author 19 July 2001). Between 1996 and the present, the *New York Times* ran fewer than a dozen stories on the diversity lottery. Most of these stories were about the effects of the lottery on individuals' lives or on neighborhoods and communities. However, I suspect the lottery received far more coverage in the ethnic media,

especially in countries that were meeting with high rates of success with the lottery.

62. John Murray Brown, "Irish economic recovery brings biggest rise in jobs since 1972," *Financial Times* (London, 25 October 1995).

63. U.S. Immigration and Naturalization Service, *Statistical Yearbook of the Immigration and Naturalization Service, 1994* (Washington, D.C.,) (1994, p. 44, 1996, p. 46, 1997, p. 44, 1998, p. 32) INS Statistical Yearbooks for 1999–2000 are not yet available.

64. U.S. Immigration and Naturalization Service, *Statistical Yearbook of the Immigration and Naturalization Service, 1994* (Washington, D.C.,) (1996, pp. 46–47, 1997, p. 44–45 1998, 32–33) INS Statistical Yearbooks for 1999–2000 are not yet available.

65. Chidi Uzor, "US Embassy Issues 3000 Diversity Visas to Nigerians," *This Day,* (Lagos, Nigeria) 5 April 2001.

66. It is unclear whether there is a constituency supporting the diversity lottery today and who that constituency may be because there has been no serious policy discussion about the lottery since 1990. However, one might suspect that new interest groups (other than the Irish and Italian ones) would emerge to defend the lottery if the provision was under attack.

Critical Thinking

1. What are main features of the Immigration Reform Act of 1965?

2. What is the Visa Lottery?

3. When people speak today of Immigration Reform what features of the current law and policy are most passionately discussed? Is the most significant aspect of this discussion related to elections and political parties or to some other civic culture concern?

ANNA O. LAW is a PhD candidate in the Department of Government at the University of Texas at Austin (Austin, TX 78712). She is currently completing her dissertation on the effects of institutional norms (such as legal principles, cognitive structures, and institutional arrangements) on the judicial behavior of Supreme Court and Federal Circuit court judges in immigration cases. Her research interests include United States immigration law and policy, constitutional law, American political development, and the effects of race and ethnicity in American politics. Prior to returning to graduate school, she was an analyst at the United States Commission on Immigration Reform.

From *Journal of American Ethnic History,* Summer 2002, pp. 3–28. Copyright © 2002 by The Immigration and Ethnic History Society. Reprinted by permission.

UNIT 3

The Demography of Diversity

Unit Selections

15. **Ancestry 2000: Census 2000 Brief,** Angela Brittingham and G. Patricia de la Cruz
16. **The American Community Survey: The New Dimensions of Race and Ethnicity in America,** John David Kromkowski,
17. **Nation's Linguistic Diversity: Population Speaking a Language Other than English at Home Increases by 140 Percent in Past Three Decades,** *U.S. Department of Commerce, Economics and Statistics Administration, US Census Bureau,* April 27, 2010
18. **A Profile of Today's Italian Americans: A Report Based on the Year 2000 Census Compiled by the Sons of Italy,** *The Order Sons of Italy in America,* 2000
19. **Polonia in Numbers: How Many of Us Are out There?,** *Good News,*
20. **Irish American Heritage Month (March) and Saint Patrick's Day (March 17): 2010,** *U.S. Department of Commerce, Economics and Statistics Administration, U.S. Census Bureau,* February 22, 2010
21. **Still Unmelted after All These Years,** John David Kromkowski

Learning Objectives

- Given the newly authorized tabulation of multiple race and ethnic identifications, can you calculate the number of combinations and permutations of race and ethnic identity?

- In what senses are these combinations of self-identification reflective of American attitudes toward self-identification?

- Should the U.S. Census collect data of religious affiliation?

- What does hyper-pluralism do to the notion of group solidarity and the mobilization of group goals and objectives related to affinity groups and identity politics as it has been known and practiced?

- Are ethnic interest groups really representative of their constituencies? What does representation mean?

- In what does membership in a group differ from member in a private association?

- When representation is defined in terms of spatial, i.e., geography/territory such as city council, a state assembly, or a congressional district, the respective boundaries of such areas can be drawn to concentrate members of a group into an electoral power.

- In light of the nature of geographic boundaries, what positive and negative impacts are associated with the concentration of ethnic groups into nearly homogenous enclaves?

- Does public attention to race and ethnicity reinforce mentalities that are deeply formative of race and ethnic identities and relationships among persons and organizations?

- Do such mentalities foster negative stereotypes and positive prototypes of race and ethnicites?

- In what respect does the attention to the history of slavery and immigration shape contemporary consciousness, attitudes toward self and others?

Student Website

www.mhhe.com/cls

Internet References

U.S. Census Bureau
www.census.gov

Diversity.com
www.diversity.com

U.S. Bureau of Citizenship and Immigration Services
www.USCIS.gov/portal/site/uscis

The history of immigration and ethnic group diversity is embedded in the demography of America. The material in this unit reveals the ongoing process of peopling America. The persistence of ethnic identification and the arrival of new immigrants are measured in these data. The specific dynamics of group isolation and integration point to the complexity generated by public policy, most importantly the designations available for racial and ethnic identity offered for the first time in the 2000 U.S. Census. The plentitude of resources and the social imagination of community leaders as well as specific characteristics of race and ethnic populations, their size, scale, and scope, and the range of governmental policies determine race and ethnic relations. American demography is a neglected dimension of race and ethnic relations. These aspects are broached in the articles selected for this unit.

Complex features of the American reality become more knowledgeable because of the attention to American demography:

- The variety and specificity of populations,

- The particular scale and region of demographic patterns of settlement, and

- The re-investigation of historically embedded characteristics of dominant cultures and their interaction with minority groups.

The particular demography of a region clearly shapes its self-articulation, but demography alone cannot express the ongoing presence of the past and reveal its impact on current approaches to race relations. These aspects will be revisited in other units. Interestingly, the South has by far the largest population of African Americans. In the 1990 Census, the South and West were the only regions of the United States that had a measurable white population. The South has by far the largest percentage and absolute number of persons claiming the United States as their ancestry. Moreover, unlike other regions with large immigrant populations and descendants of nineteenth-century immigrants, over 15 percent of the population of the South provided no answer to the ancestry question on the 1990 Census.

The American experience from 1870 to 1924 addressed the influence of these groups and in so doing shifted American consciousness of itself. Even 100 years later, America's public mind continues to identify and divide its history as an immigrant-receiving country into two periods: The Old Immigration, meaning Northern Europeans, and the New Immigration, meaning Others—the Mediterranean and eastern European as well as Asian and Hispanic populations. One marker of this division can be found in the Report of the Dillingham Commission (1910), a congressional and presidential blue ribbon panel that warned America that the eastern European and Mediterranean character was less capable of Americanization than the Nordics and Teutonics who had peopled America.

The considerable fluidity of the immigrant experiences, as well as the complex processes of cultural identity and political use of cultural symbols, such as race and ethnicity, the search for more analytical rigor in this field is far from complete. Some guide to discernable and measurable features of ethnic

© scenicireland.com/Christopher Hill Photographic/Alamy

phenomena and characteristics that are attributes of ethnicity was developed in a fine collection of materials on this topic, The Harvard Encyclopedia of American Ethnic Groups which lists the following markers of ethnic groups: common geographic origin, migratory status, language/dialect, religious faith(s), ties that transcend kinship, neighborhood, and community boundaries, shared traditions values, and symbols, literature, folklore, music, food preferences, settlement and employment patterns, special interests in regard to politics in the homeland and in the United States, institutions that specifically serve and maintain the group, and internal sense of distinctiveness and an external perception of distinctiveness. With the addition of a demographic data base developed by the U.S. Census, a much more rigorous set of analytics can be applied to anthropological and humanistic approaches to ethnic groups.

The material in this unit reveals the ongoing process of peopling America and the remarkably "lumpy" distribution of geographic patterns in various states and regions. The persistence of ethnic identification and the arrival of new immigrants are measured in these data and can now be accessed and systematically analyzed. . The specific dynamics of group isolation and integration point to the complexity generated by public policy, most importantly the designations available for racial and ethnic identity offered for the first time in the 2000 U.S. Census. The plentitude of resources and the social imagination of community leaders as well as specific characteristics of race and ethnic populations, their size, scale, and scope, and the range of governmental policies determine race and ethnic relations.

As a guide for your own study, the U.S. Commission on Civil Rights has noted the following issues for both recent arrivals and Americans by birth:

$ Employment: The areas of occupation selected by or imposed upon various ethnic populations trace ethnic group mobility strategies and ethnic succession in the workplace, especially in manufacturing, hospitals, restaurants, and maintenance and custodial positions. Some ethnic populations appear to have greater numbers of highly educated persons in professional or semiprofessional positions.

$ Institutional and societal barriers: The job preferences and discrimination against the ethnic enclaves and persons in small communities that are isolated from mainstream English-speaking society suggest the value of second-language competencies. Mutual accommodation is required to minimize the effect of inadequate language skills and training and difficulties in obtaining licenses, memberships, and certification.

$ Exploitation of workers: The most common form is the payment of wages below minimum standards. Alien workers have been stereotyped as a drain on public services. Such scape-goating is insupportable.

$ Taking jobs from Americans: Fact or fiction?: The stunning fact is that immigrants are a source of increased productivity and a significant, if not utterly necessary, addition to the workforce as well as to the consumer power that drives the American economy.

Ancestry 2000
Census 2000 Brief

ANGELA BRITTINGHAM AND G. PATRICIA DE LA CRUZ

ncestry is a broad concept that can mean different things to different people; it can be described alternately as where their ancestors are from, where they or their parents originated, or simply how they see themselves ethnically. Some people may have one distinct ancestry, while others are descendants of several ancestry groups, and still others may know only that their ancestors were from a particular region of the world or may not know their ethnic origins at all. The Census Bureau defines ancestry as a person's ethnic origin, heritage, descent, or "roots," which may reflect their place of birth, place of birth of parents or ancestors, and ethnic identities that have evolved within the United States.

This report is part of a series that presents population and housing data collected by Census 2000, where 80 percent of respondents to the long form specified at least one ancestry. (About one-sixth of households received the long form.) It presents data on the most frequently reported ancestries and describes population distributions for the United States, including regions, states, counties, and selected cities.[1] The listed ancestries were reported by at least 100,000 people, and the numbers cited in this report represent the number of people who reported each ancestry either as their first or second response.

The question on ancestry first appeared on the census questionnaire in 1980, replacing a question on where a person's parents were born. The question on parental birthplace provided foreign-origin data only for people with one or both parents born outside the United States. The current ancestry question allows everyone to give one or two attributions of their "ancestry or ethnic origin" (Figure 1), and in doing so, enables people to identify an ethnic background, such as German, Lebanese, Nigerian, or Portuguese, which was not otherwise identified in the race or Hispanic-origin questions.

The ancestries in this report also include the groups covered in the questions on race and Hispanic origin, such as African American, Mexican, American Indian, and Chinese. For these groups, the results from the ancestry question and the race and Hispanic-origin questions differ, but the latter are the official sources of data for race and Hispanic groups. In some cases, the totals reported on the ancestry question are lower than the numbers from the race or Hispanic-origin question. For

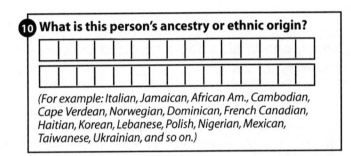

10 What is this person's ancestry or ethnic origin?

(For example: Italian, Jamaican, African Am., Cambodian, Cape Verdean, Norwegian, Dominican, French Canadian, Haitian, Korean, Lebanese, Polish, Nigerian, Mexican, Taiwanese, Ukrainian, and so on.)

Figure 1 Reproduction of the Question on Ancestry from Census 2000.

Source: U.S. Census Bureau, Census 2000 questionnaire.

instance, nearly 12 million fewer people specified "African American" as their ancestry than gave that response to the race question. One reason for this large difference is that some people who reported Black or African American on the race question reported their ancestry more specifically, such as Jamaican, Haitian, or Nigerian, and thus were not counted in the African American ancestry category. Similarly, more than 2 million fewer people reported Mexican ancestry than gave that answer to the Hispanic-origin question.[2] In other cases, the ancestry question produced higher numbers, such as for Dominicans, whose estimated totals from the ancestry question were over 100,000 higher than from the Hispanic-origin question, where many Dominicans may have reported a general term (like Hispanic) or checked "other" without writing in a detailed response.[3]

More than four out of five people specified at least one ancestry.

In 2000, 58 percent of the population specified only one ancestry, 22 percent provided two ancestries, and 1 percent reported an unclassifiable ancestry such as "mixture" or "adopted." Another 19 percent did not report any ancestry at all, a substantial increase from 1990, when 10 percent of the population left the ancestry question blank (Table 1).

Table 1   Ancestry Reporting: 1990 and 2000

Ancestry	1990[1] Number	Percent	2000 Number	Percent	Change, 1990 to 2000 Numerical	Percent
Total population	248,709,873	100.0	281,421,906	100.0	32,712,033	13.2
Ancestry specified	222,608,257	89.5	225,310,411	80.1	2,702,154	1.2
Single ancestry	148,836,950	59.8	163,315,936	58.0	14,478,986	9.7
Multiple ancestry	73,771,307	29.7	61,994,475	22.0	−11,776,832	−16.0
Ancestry not specified	26,101,616	10.5	56,111,495	19.9	30,009,879	115.0
Unclassified	2,180,245	0.9	2,437,929	0.9	257,684	11.8
Not reported	23,921,371	9.6	53,673,566	19.1	29,752,195	124.4

(Data based on sample. For information on confidentiality protection, sampling error, nonsampling error, and definitions, see www.census.gov/prod/cen2000/doc/sf3.pdf)

[1]1990 estimates in this table differ slightly from 1990 Summary Tape File 3 in order to make them fully consistent with data from Census 2000.

Source: U.S. Census Bureau, Census 2000 Summary File 3 and 1990 special tabulation.

Nearly one of six people reported their ancestry as German.

In 2000, 42.8 million people (15 percent of the population) considered themselves to be of German (or part-German) ancestry, the most frequent response to the census question (Figure 2).[4] Other ancestries with over 15 million people in 2000 included Irish (30.5 million, or 11 percent), African American (24.9 million, or 9 percent), English (24.5 million, or 9 percent), American (20.2 million, or 7 percent), Mexican (18.4 million, or 7 percent), and Italian (15.6 million, or 6 percent).

Other ancestries with 4 million or more people included Polish, French, American Indian, Scottish, Dutch, Norwegian, Scotch-Irish, and Swedish.

In total, 7 ancestries were reported by more than 15 million people in 2000, 37 ancestries were reported by more than 1 million people, and 92 ancestries were reported by more than 100,000 people (Table 2).

The largest European ancestries have decreased in population, while African American, Hispanic, and Asian ancestries have increased.

The highest growth rates between 1990 and 2000 occurred in groups identified by a general heritage rather than a particular country of ancestry. For example, the number of people who reported Latin American, African, or European all more than quadrupled (Latin American increased from 44,000 in 1990 to 250,000 in 2000, African grew from 246,000 to 1.2 million, and European rose from 467,000 to 2.0 million). Other general heritage groups that at least doubled in size included Western European, Northern European, Asian, Hispanic, and White.

The three largest ancestries in 1990 were German, Irish, and English. In 2000, these groups were still the largest European ancestries, but each had decreased in size by at least 8 million and by more than 20 percent (Table 2). As a proportion of the

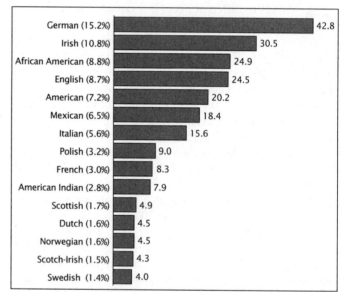

Figure 2   Fifteen Largest Ancestries: 2000. (In millions. Percent of total population in parentheses. Data based on sample. For information on confidentiality protection, sampling error, nonsampling error, and definitions, see www.census.gov/prod/cen2000/doc/sf3.pdf).

Source: U.S. Census Bureau, Census 2000 special tabulation.

population, German decreased from 23 percent in 1990 to 15 percent in 2000, while Irish and English decreased from 16 percent to 11 percent, and from 13 percent to 9 percent, respectively. Several other large European ancestries also decreased over the decade, including Polish, French, Scottish, Dutch, and Swedish.

The number of people who reported African American ancestry increased by nearly 1.2 million, or 4.9 percent, between 1990 and 2000, making this group the third largest ancestry. However, the proportion of African Americans decreased slightly over the decade, from 9.5 percent to 8.8 percent.

The population of many ancestries, such as Mexican, Chinese, Filipino, and Asian Indian, increased during the decade, reflecting sizable immigration, especially from Latin America and Asia. Several small ancestry populations, including Brazilian, Pakistani, Albanian, Honduran, and Trinidadian and Tobagonian, at least doubled.

Table 2 Ancestries with 100,000 or More People in 2000: 1990 and 2000

Ancestry	1990		2000		Change, 1990 to 2000	
	Number	Percent of total population	Number	Percent of total population	Numerical	Percent
Total population	248,709,873	100.0	281,421,906	100.0	32,712,033	13.2
African*	245,845	0.1	1,183,316	0.4	937,471	381.3
African American*[1,2]	23,750,256	9.5	24,903,412	8.8	1,153,156	4.9
Albanian	47,710	–	113,661	–	65,951	138.2
American*	12,395,999	5.0	20,188,305	7.2	7,792,306	62.9
American Indian*	8,689,344	3.5	7,876,568	2.8	−812,776	−9.4
Arab*	127,364	0.1	205,822	0.1	78,458	61.6
Armenian	308,096	0.1	385,488	0.1	77,392	25.1
Asian*	107,172	–	238,960	0.1	131,788	123.0
Asian Indian	569,338	0.2	1,546,703	0.5	977,365	171.7
Austrian	864,783	0.3	730,336	0.3	−134,447	−15.5
Belgian	380,403	0.2	348,531	0.1	−31,872	−8.4
Brazilian	65,875	–	181,076	0.1	115,201	174.9
British	1,119,140	0.4	1,085,718	0.4	−33,422	−3.0
Cambodian[2]	134,955	0.1	197,093	0.1	62,138	46.0
Canadian	549,990	0.2	638,548	0.2	88,558	16.1
Chinese	1,505,229	0.6	2,271,562	0.8	766,333	50.9
Colombian	351,717	0.1	583,986	0.2	232,269	66.0
Croatian[1]	544,270	0.2	374,241	0.1	−170,029	−31.2
Cuban	859,739	0.3	1,097,594	0.4	237,855	27.7
Czech	1,296,369	0.5	1,258,452	0.4	−37,917	22.9
Czechoslovakian	315,285	0.1	441,403	0.2	126,118	40.0
Danish	1,634,648	0.7	1,430,897	0.5	−203,751	−12.5
Dominican[1,2]	505,690	0.2	908,531	0.3	402,841	79.7
Dutch	6,226,339	2.5	4,541,770	1.6	−1,684,569	−27.1
Ecuadorian[1]	197,374	0.1	322,965	0.1	125,591	63.6
Egyptian	78,574	–	142,832	0.1	64,258	81.8
English	32,651,788	13.1	24,509,692	8.7	−8,142,096	−24.9
European*	466,718	0.2	1,968,696	0.7	1,501,978	321.8
Filipino	1,450,512	0.6	2,116,478	0.8	665,966	45.9
Finnish	658,854	0.3	623,559	0.2	−35,295	−5.4
French	10,320,656	4.1	8,309,666	3.0	−2,010,990	−19.5
French Canadian[1,2]	2,167,127	0.9	2,349,684	0.8	182,557	8.4
German[1]	57,947,171	23.3	42,841,569	15.2	−15,105,602	−26.1
Greek	1,110,292	0.4	1,153,295	0.4	43,003	3.9
Guatemalan	241,559	0.1	463,502	0.2	221,943	91.9
Guyanese	81,665	–	162,425	0.1	80,760	98.9
Haitian[1,2]	289,521	0.1	548,199	0.2	258,678	89.3
Hawaiian	256,081	0.1	334,858	0.1	78,777	30.8
Hispanic*	1,113,259	0.4	2,451,109	0.9	1,337,850	120.2
Hmong	84,823	–	140,528	–	55,705	65.7
Honduran	116,635	–	266,848	0.1	150,213	128.8
Hungarian	1,582,302	0.6	1,398,702	0.5	−183,600	−11.6
Iranian	235,521	0.1	338,266	0.1	102,745	43.6
Irish[1]	38,735,539	15.6	30,524,799	10.8	−8,210,740	−21.2
Israeli	81,677	–	106,839	–	25,162	30.8
Italian[1,2]	14,664,189	5.9	15,638,348	5.6	974,159	6.6
Jamaican[1,2]	435,024	0.2	736,513	0.3	301,489	69.3
Japanese	1,004,622	0.4	1,103,325	0.4	98,703	9.8
Korean[1,2]	836,987	0.3	1,190,353	0.4	353,366	42.2
Laotian	146,947	0.1	179,866	0.1	32,919	22.4
Latin American*	43,521	–	250.052	0.1	206,531	474.6
Lebanese[1,2]	394,180	0.2	440,279	0.2	46,099	11.7
Lithuanian	811,865	0.3	659,992	0.2	−151,873	−18.7

(See footnotes on next page)

(continued)

Table 2 Ancestries with 100,000 or More People in 2000: 1990 and 2000 (continued)

Ancestry	1990 Number	1990 Percent of total population	2000 Number	2000 Percent of total population	Change, 1990 to 2000 Numerical	Change, 1990 to 2000 Percent
Mexican[1,2]	11,580,038	4.7	18,382,291	6.5	6,802,253	58.7
Nicaraguan	177,077	0.1	230,358	0.1	53,281	30.1
Nigerian[1,2]	91,499	–	164,691	0.1	73,192	80.0
Northern European*	65,993	–	163,657	0.1	97,664	148.0
Norwegian[2]	3,869,395	1.6	4,477,725	1.6	608,330	15.7
Pakistani	99,974	–	253,193	0.1	153,219	153.3
Panamanian	88,649	–	119,497	–	30,848	34.8
Pennsylvania German	305,841	0.1	255,807	0.1	−50,034	−16.4
Peruvian	161,866	0.1	292,991	0.1	131,125	81.0
Polish[1,2]	9,366,051	3.8	8,977,235	3.2	−388,816	−4.2
Portuguese	1,148,857	0.5	1,173,691	0.4	24,834	2.2
Puerto Rican	1,955,323	0.8	2,652,598	0.9	697,275	35.7
Romanian	365,531	0.1	367,278	0.1	1,747	(NS)
Russian	2,951,373	1.2	2,652,214	0.9	−299,159	−10.1
Salvadoran	499,153	0.2	802,743	0.3	303,590	60.8
Scandinavian	678,880	0.3	425,099	0.2	−253,781	−37.4
Scotch-Irish	5,617,773	2.3	4,319,232	1.5	−1,298,541	−23.1
Scottish	5,393,581	2.2	4,890,581	1.7	−503,000	−9.3
Serbian	116,795	–	140,337	–	23,5422	0.2
Slavic	76,923	–	127,136	–	50,213	65.3
Slovak[1]	1,882,897	0.8	797,764	0.3	−1,085,133	−57.6
Slovene	124,437	0.1	176,691	0.1	52,254	42.0
Spaniard	360,858	0.1	299,948	0.1	−60,910	−16.9
Spanish	2,024,004	0.8	2,187,144	0.8	163,140	8.1
Swedish	4,680,863	1.9	3,998,310	1.4	−682,553	−14.6
Swiss	1,045,492	0.4	911,502	0.3	−133,990	−12.8
Syrian	129,606	0.1	142,897	0.1	13,291	10.3
Taiwanese[1,2]	192,973	0.1	293,568	0.1	100,595	52.1
Thai[1]	112,11	–	146,577	0.1	34,460	30.7
Trinidadian and Tobagonian	76,270	–	164,738	0.1	88,468	116.0
Turkish	83,850	–	117,575	–	33,725	40.2
Ukrainian[1,2]	740,723	0.3	892,922	0.3	152,199	20.5
United States*	643,561	0.3	404,328	0.1	−239,233	−37.2
Vietnamese	535,825	0.2	1,029,420	0.4	493,595	92.1
Welsh	2,033,893	0.8	1,753,794	0.6	−280,099	−13.8
West Indian*	159,167	0.1	147,222	0.1	−11,945	−7.5
Western European*	42,409	–	125,300	–	82,891	195.5
White*	1,799,711	0.7	3,834,122	1.4	2,034,411	113.0
Yugoslavian	257,986	0.1	328,547	0.1	70,561	27.4
Other ancestries	3,989,728	1.6	4,380,380	1.6	390,652	9.8

(Data based on sample. For information on confidentiality protection, sampling error, nonsampling error, and definitions, see www.census.gov/prod/cen2000/doc/sf3.pdf)
– Rounds to 0.0.

*General response which may encompass several ancestries not listed separately (i.e., African American includes Black and Negro). NS Not statistically different from zero at the 90-percent confidence level.
[1]Included in the list of examples on the census questionnaire in 1990.
[2]Included in the list of examples on the census questionnaire in 2000.

Notes: Because of sampling error, the estimates in this table may not be significantly different from one another or from other ancestries not listed in this table. People who reported two ancestries were included once in each category. The estimates in this table differ slightly in some cases from the estimates in other data products due to the collapsing schemes used. For example, here German does not include Bavarian. Some groups correspond to groups identified separately in the race and Hispanic-origin questions. The race item provides the primary source of data for White, Black, American Indian, Alaska Native, Asian groups, Native Hawaiian, and Pacific Islander groups. The Hispanic-origin question is the primary identifier for Mexican, Puerto Rican, Cuban, and other Hispanic groups.
Source: U.S. Census Bureau, 1990 Census and Census 2000 special tabulations.

Seven percent of the U.S. population reported their ancestry as American.

The number who reported American and no other ancestry increased from 12.4 million in 1990 to 20.2 million in 2000, the largest numerical growth of any group during the 1990s.[5] This figure represents an increase of 63 percent, as the proportion rose from 5.0 percent to 7.2 percent of the population.

The Geographic Distribution of Ancestries

In each of the four regions, a different ancestry was reported as the largest.

Among the four regions, the largest ancestries in 2000 were Irish in the Northeast (16 percent), African American in the South (14 percent), German in the Midwest (27 percent), and Mexican in the West (16 percent, see Table 3).[6]

At the state level, 8 different ancestries were each the largest reported in 1 or more states. German led in 23 states, including every state in the Midwest, the majority of states in the West, and 1 state in the South. In 3 of those states, German was reported by more than 40 percent of the population: North Dakota (44 percent), Wisconsin (43 percent), and South Dakota (41 percent).

The other leading ancestries at the state level were African American in 7 contiguous states from Louisiana to Maryland and in the District of Columbia (also notably high at 43 percent); American in Arkansas, Tennessee, Kentucky, and West Virginia; Italian in Connecticut, New Jersey, New York, and Rhode Island; Mexican in 4 states from California to Texas; English in Maine, Utah and Vermont; Irish in Delaware, Massachusetts and New Hampshire; and Japanese in Hawaii.

Many other ancestries were not the largest ancestry in any state but represented more than 10 percent of a state's population, including American Indian in Oklahoma (12 percent) and Alaska (11 percent); Filipino (18 percent) and Hawaiian (16 percent) in Hawaii; French in Maine (14 percent), Vermont (15 percent), and Rhode Island (11 percent); French Canadian in New Hampshire (10 percent); and Norwegian in North Dakota (30 percent), Minnesota (17 percent), South Dakota (15 percent), and Montana (11 percent, see Table 3).

Other ancestries not noted above were among the 5 largest in a state but represented less than 10 percent of the state's population. Examples include Chinese in Hawaii (8.3 percent), Czech in Nebraska (4.9 percent), Danish in Utah (6.5 percent), Eskimo in Alaska (6.1 percent), Polish in Michigan (8.6 percent), Portuguese in Rhode Island (8.7 percent), Spanish in New Mexico (9.3 percent), and Swedish in Minnesota (9.9 percent).

Twenty-four different ancestries were the largest in at least one county in the United States.

German was the leading ancestry reported in many counties across the northern half of the United States, from Pennsylvania to Washington, as well as some counties in the southern half. Mexican was the leading ancestry along the southwestern border of the United States, and American and African American were the most commonly reported ancestries in many southern counties, from Virginia to eastern Texas.

Several ancestries that did not predominate in any state were the most common within one or more counties. Examples include Aleut and Eskimo in some counties of Alaska; American Indian in counties in Alaska, Arizona, California, Montana, Nebraska, Nevada, New Mexico, North Carolina, Oklahoma, Oregon, South Dakota, Washington, and Wisconsin; Finnish in several counties in the Upper Peninsula of Michigan; French in counties in Connecticut, New York, Maine, New Hampshire, Vermont, and Louisiana; French Canadian in counties in Maine; Dutch in several counties in Michigan and Iowa; Norwegian in counties in Iowa, Minnesota, Montana, North Dakota, and Wisconsin; Polish in one county in Pennsylvania; and Portuguese in one county each in Massachusetts and Rhode Island.

African American and Mexican were the most commonly reported ancestries in the ten largest cities in the United States.

In 2000, African American was the most frequently reported ancestry in New York City, Chicago, Philadelphia, and Detroit (Table 4).[7] Mexican was the leading ancestry in Los Angeles, Houston, Phoenix, San Diego, Dallas, and San Antonio.

Additional Findings
What Combinations Were the Most Common among Respondents Who Reported Two Ancestries?

The most common ancestry combinations in 2000 were German and Irish (2.7 percent of the population), German and English (1.7 percent), and Irish and English (1.4 percent).

What Other Ancestries Were Reported?

Overall, about 500 different ancestries were reported during Census 2000. The category "Other ancestries" in Table 2 consists of all ancestries with fewer than 100,000 people (such as Venezuelan, Samoan, or Latvian) as well as all religious identifications (which are not tabulated).[8]

Table 3 Largest Ancestries for the United States, Regions, States, and for Puerto Rico: 2000

Ancestry	Total population	Ancestry	Percent	Ancestry	Percent	Ancestry	Percent	Ancestry	Percent	Ancestry	Percent
United States	281,421,906	German	15.2	Irish	10.8	African Am.	8.8	English	8.7	American	7.2
Region											
Northeast	53,594,378	Irish	15.8	Italian	14.1	German	13.6	English	8.3	African Am.	6.5
Midwest	64,392,776	German	26.6	Irish	11.8	English	8.4	African Am.	7.8	American	6.5
South	100,236,820	African Am.	14.0	American	11.2	German	10.0	Irish	8.8	English	8.4
West	63,197,932	Mexican	16.0	German	13.3	English	9.9	Irish	9.0	American	4.1
State											
Alabama	4,447,100	African Am.	19.9	American	16.8	English	7.8	Irish	7.7	German	5.7
Alaska	626,932	German	16.6	Irish	10.8	Am. Indian	10.5	English	9.6	Eskimo	6.1
Arizona	5,130,632	Mexican	18.0	German	15.6	English	10.4	Irish	10.2	Am. Indian	6.1
Arkansas	2,673,400	American	15.7	African Am.	11.9	Irish	9.5	German	9.3	English	7.9
California	33,871,648	Mexican	22.2	German	9.8	Irish	7.7	English	7.4	African Am.	5.1
Colorado	4,301,261	German	22.0	Irish	12.2	English	12.0	Mexican	9.0	American	5.0
Connecticut.....	3,405,565	Italian	18.6	Irish	16.6	English	10.3	German	9.8	Polish	8.3
Delaware	783,600	Irish	16.6	German	14.3	African Am.	14.0	English	12.1	Italian	9.3
District of Columbia	572,059	African Am.	43.4	Irish	4.9	German	4.8	English	4.4	Salvadoran	2.3
Florida	15,982,378	German	11.8	Irish	10.3	English	9.2	African Am.	8.6	American	7.8
Georgia	8,186,453	African Am.	21.6	American	13.3	English	8.1	Irish	7.8	German	7.0
Hawaii	1,211,537	Japanese	20.7	Filipino	17.7	Hawaiian	16.3	Chinese	8.3	German	5.8
Idaho	1,293,953	German	18.8	English	18.1	Irish	10.0	American	8.1	Mexican	5.5
Illinois	12,419,293	German	19.6	Irish	12.2	African Am.	11.5	Mexican	8.2	Polish	7.5
Indiana	6,080,485	German	22.6	American	11.8	Irish	10.8	English	8.9	African Am.	6.5
Iowa	2,926,324	German	35.7	Irish	13.5	English	9.5	American	6.6	Norwegian	5.7
Kansas	2,688,418	German	25.8	Irish	11.5	English	10.8	American	8.7	Mexican	4.7
Kentucky.	4,041,769	American	20.7	German	12.7	Irish	10.5	English	9.7	African Am.	5.7
Louisiana	4,468,976	African Am.	25.5	French	12.2	American	10.0	German	7.0	Irish	7.0
Maine	1,274,923	English	21.5	Irish	15.1	French	14.2	American	9.3	Fr. Canadian	8.6
Maryland.......	5,296,486	African Am.	20.5	German	15.7	Irish	11.7	English	9.0	American	5.6
Massachusetts ..	6,349,097	Irish	22.5	Italian	13.5	English	11.4	French	8.0	German	5.9
Michigan	9,938,444	German	20.4	African Am.	11.0	Irish	10.7	English	9.9	Polish	8.6
Minnesota......	4,919,479	German	36.7	Norwegian	17.3	Irish	11.2	Swedish	9.9	English	6.3
Mississippi	2,844,658	African Am.	28.3	American	14.0	Irish	6.9	English	6.1	German	4.5
Missouri	5,595,211	German	23.5	Irish	12.7	American	10.4	English	9.5	African Am.	8.8
Montana	902,195	German	27.0	Irish	14.8	English	12.6	Norwegian	10.6	Am. Indian	7.4
Nebraska	1,711,263	German	38.6	Irish	13.4	English	9.6	Swedish	4.9	Czech	4.9
Nevada........	1,998,257	German	14.1	Mexican	12.7	Irish	11.0	English	10.1	Italian	6.6
New Hampshire .	1,235,786	Irish	19.4	English	18.0	French	14.6	Fr. Canadian	10.3	German	8.6
New Jersey.....	8,414,350	Italian	17.8	Irish	15.9	German	12.6	African Am.	8.8	Polish	6.9
New Mexico	1,819,046	Mexican	16.3	Am. Indian	10.3	German	9.8	Hispanic	9.4	Spanish	9.3
New York	18,976,457	Italian	14.4	Irish	12.9	German	11.2	African Am.	7.7	English	6.0
North Carolina ..	8,049,313	African Am.	16.6	American	13.7	English	9.5	German	9.5	Irish	7.4
North Dakota ...	642,200	German	43.9	Norwegian	30.1	Irish	7.7	Am. Indian	5.1	Swedish	5.0
Ohio	11,353,140	German	25.2	Irish	12.7	English	9.2	African Am.	9.1	American	8.5
Oklahoma	3,450,654	American	12.6	Am. Indian	12.1	German	11.2	Irish	10.3	English	8.4
Oregon	3,421,399	German	20.5	English	13.2	Irish	11.9	American	6.2	Mexican	5.5
Pennsylvania ...	12,281,054	German	25.4	Irish	16.1	Italian	11.5	English	7.9	African Am.	7.4
Rhode Island ...	1,048,319	Italian	19.0	Irish	18.4	English	12.0	French	10.9	Portuguese	8.7
South Carolina ..	4,012,012	African Am.	22.8	American	13.7	German	8.4	English	8.2	Irish	7.9
South Dakota ...	754,844	German	40.7	Norwegian	15.3	Irish	10.4	Am. Indian	8.2	English	7.1
Tennessee	5,689,283	American	17.3	African Am.	13.0	Irish	9.3	English	9.1	German	8.3
Texas	20,851,820	Mexican	22.6	German	9.9	African Am.	8.7	Irish	7.2	American	7.2
Utah	2,233,169	English	29.0	German	11.5	American	6.6	Danish	6.5	Irish	5.9
Vermont	608,827	English	18.4	Irish	16.4	French	14.5	German	9.1	Fr. Canadian	8.8
Virginia	7,078,515	African Am.	14.9	German	11.7	American	11.2	English	11.1	Irish	9.8
Washington	5,894,121	German	18.7	English	12.0	Irish	11.4	Norwegian	6.2	American	5.2
West Virginia ...	1,808,344	American	18.7	German	14.0	Irish	11.0	English	9.7	Am. Indian	4.4
Wisconsin	5,363,675	German	42.6	Irish	10.9	Polish	9.3	Norwegian	8.5	English	6.5
Wyoming	493,782	German	25.9	English	15.9	Irish	13.3	American	6.4	Am. Indian	4.7
Puerto Rico	3,808,610	Puerto Rican	69.0	American	2.5	Spaniard	2.1	Dominican	1.7	Hispanic	0.8

(Data based on sample. For information on confidentiality protection, sampling error, nonsampling error, and definitions, see *www.census.gov/prod/cen2000/doc/sf3.pdf*)

Notes: Because of sampling error, the estimates in this table may not be significantly different from one another or from other ancestries not listed in this table.

People who reported two ancestries were included once in each category. Some groups correspond to groups identified separately in the race and Hispanic-origin questions. The race item provides the primary source of data for White, Black, American Indian, Alaska Native, Asian groups, Native Hawaiian, and Pacific Islander groups. The Hispanic-origin question is the primary identifier for Mexican, Puerto Rican, Cuban, and other Hispanic groups.

About Census 2000
Why Census 2000 Asked about Ancestry

Information about ancestry is required to enforce provisions under the Civil Rights Act that prohibit discrimination based upon race, sex, religion, and national origin. More generally, these data are needed to measure the social and economic characteristics of ethnic groups and to tailor services to accommodate cultural differences.

Data about ancestry assist states and local agencies on aging to develop health care and other services tailored to address the language and cultural diversity of various groups.

Under the Public Health Service Act, ancestry is one of the factors used to identify segments of the population who may not be receiving medical services.

Accuracy of the Estimates

The data contained in this report are based on the sample of households who responded to the Census 2000 long form. Nationally, approximately 1 out of every 6 housing units was included in this sample. As a result, the sample estimates may differ somewhat from the 100-percent figures that would have been obtained if all housing units, people within those housing units, and people living in group quarters had been enumerated using the same questionnaires, instructions, enumerators, and so forth. The sample estimates also differ from the values that would have been obtained from different samples of housing units, people within those housing units, and people living in group quarters. The deviation of a sample estimate from the average of all possible samples is called the sampling error.

In addition to the variability that arises from the sampling procedures, both sample data and 100-percent data are subject to nonsampling error. Nonsampling error may be introduced during any of the various complex operations used to collect and process data. Such errors may include: not enumerating every household or every person in the population, failing to obtain all required information from the respondents, obtaining incorrect or inconsistent information, and recording information incorrectly.

In addition, errors can occur during the field review of the enumerators' work, during clerical handling of the census questionnaires, or during the electronic processing of the questionnaires.

Nonsampling error may affect the data in two ways: (1) errors that are introduced randomly will increase the variability of the data and, therefore, should be reflected in the standard errors; and (2) errors that tend to be consistent in one direction will bias both sample and 100-percent data in that direction. For example, if respondents consistently tend to underreport their incomes, then the resulting estimates of households or families by income category will tend to be understated for the higher income categories and overstated for the lower income categories. Such biases are not reflected in the standard errors.

While it is impossible to completely eliminate error from an operation as large and complex as the decennial census, the Census Bureau attempts to control the sources of such error

Table 4 Largest Ancestry for the Ten Cities with the Highest Population: 2000

City	Total population	Largest ancestry			
		Ancestry	Number of people	Percent of population	90-percent confidence interval
New York, NY	8,008,278	African American	922,116	11.5	11.4–11.6
Los Angeles, CA	3,694,834	Mexican	983,157	26.6	26.5–26.8
Chicago, IL	2,895,964	African American	804,053	27.8	27.6–27.9
Houston, TX	1,954,848	Mexican	467,213	23.9	23.7–24.1
Philadelphia, PA	1,517,550	African American	493,177	32.5	32.3–32.8
Phoenix, AZ	1,320,994	Mexican	320,092	24.2	24.0–24.5
San Diego, CA	1,223,341	Mexican	237,867	19.9	19.2–19.7
Dallas, TX	1,188,204	Mexican	306,072	25.8	25.5–26.0
San Antonio, TX	1,144,554	Mexican	472,324	41.3	41.0–41.6
Detroit, MI	951,270	African American	599,667	63.0	62.7–63.4

(Data based on sample. For information on confidentiality protection, sampling error, nonsampling error, and definitions, see *www.census.gov/prod/cen2000/doc/sf3.pdf*)

Notes: Because of sampling error, the estimates in this table may not be significantly different from one another or from other ancestries not listed in this table. People who reported two ancestries were included once in each category. Some groups correspond to groups identified separately in the race and Hispanic-origin questions. The race item provides the primary source of data for White, Black, American Indian, Alaska Native, Asian groups, Native Hawaiian, and Pacific Islander groups. The Hispanic-origin question is the primary identifier for Mexican, Puerto Rican, Cuban, and other Hispanic groups.

Source: U.S. Census Bureau, Census 2000 special tabulation.

during the data collection and processing operations. The primary sources of error and the programs instituted to control error in Census 2000 are described in detail in *Summary File 3 Technical Documentation* under Chapter 8, "Accuracy of the Data," located at www.census.gov/prod /cen2000/doc/sf3.pdf.

All statements in this Census 2000 Brief have undergone statistical testing and all comparisons are significant at the 90-percent confidence level, unless otherwise noted. The estimates in tables, maps, and other figures may vary from actual values due to sampling and nonsampling errors. As a result, estimates in one category may not be significantly different from estimates assigned to a different category. Further information on the accuracy of the data is located at www.census.gov/prod/cen2000/doc/sf3.pdf. For further information on the computation and use of standard errors, contact the Decennial Statistical Studies Division at 301-763-4242.

For More Information

The Census 2000 Summary File 3 data are available from the American Factfinder on the Internet (factfinder.census.gov). They were released on a state-by-state basis during 2002. For information on confidentiality protection, nonsampling error, sampling error, and definitions, also see www.census.gov /prod/cen2000/doc/sf3.pdf or contact the Customer Services Center at 301-763-INFO (4636).

Information on population and housing topics is presented in the Census 2000 Brief series, located on the Census Bureau's Web site at www.census.gov/population/www/cen2000/briefs. html. This series presents information on race, Hispanic origin, age, sex, household type, housing tenure, and social, economic, and housing characteristics, such as ancestry, income, and housing costs.

For additional information on ancestry, including reports and survey data, visit the Census Bureau's Web site on at www.census.gov /population/www/ancestry.html. To find information about the availability of data products, including reports, CD-ROMs, and DVDs, call the Customer Services Center at 301-763-INFO (4636), or e-mail webmaster@census.gov.

Notes

1. The text of this report discusses data for the United States, including the 50 states and the District of Columbia. Data for the Commonwealth of Puerto Rico are shown in Table 3.

2. The estimates in this report are based on responses from a sample of the population. As with all surveys, estimates may vary from the actual values because of sampling variation or other factors. All statements made in this report have undergone statistical testing and are significant at the 90-percent confidence level unless otherwise noted.

3. For more information about race and Hispanic groups, see Census 2000 Briefs on Hispanic, American Indian and Alaska Native, Asian, Black, Native Hawaiian and Pacific Islander, White, and Two or More Races populations, available on the Census Bureau Web site at www.census.gov/prod/cen2000/index.html.

4. The estimates in Figure 2 and Table 2 in some cases differ slightly from the estimates in other data products due to the collapsing schemes used. For example, here German does not include Bavarian.

5. American was considered a valid ancestry response when it was the only ancestry provided by a respondent.

6. The Northeast region includes the states of Connecticut, Maine, Massachusetts, New Hampshire, New Jersey, New York, Pennsylvania, Rhode Island, and Vermont. The Midwest region includes the states of Illinois, Indiana, Iowa, Kansas, Michigan, Minnesota, Missouri, Nebraska, North Dakota, Ohio, South Dakota, and Wisconsin. The South region includes the states of Alabama, Arkansas, Delaware, Florida, Georgia, Kentucky, Louisiana, Maryland, Mississippi, North Carolina, Oklahoma, South Carolina, Tennessee, Texas, Virginia, West Virginia, and the District of Columbia, a state equivalent. The West region includes the states of Alaska, Arizona, California, Colorado, Hawaii, Idaho, Montana, Nevada, New Mexico, Oregon, Utah, Washington, and Wyoming.

7. Census 2000 showed 245 places in the United States with 100,000 or more population. They included 238 incorporated places (including 4 city-county consolidations) and 7 census designated places that were not legally incorporated. For a list of places by state, see www.census.gov/population/www/cen2000/phc-t6.html.

8. Smaller groups are listed at www.census.gov/population/www/ancestry.html.

Critical Thinking

1. Does the Ancestry Question used on the US Census since 1980 seem like a good way to collect information?

2. Prior to reviewing these data, did you have any idea about the population size of various ethnic groups?

3. From among the tabulations by State which data clusters were surprising? Why?

From U.S. Census Bureau, June 2004, pp. 1–10.

The American Community Survey: The New Dimensions of Race and Ethnicity in America

JOHN DAVID KROMKOWSKI

Since 1980, most ethnic and ancestry information was collected by the US Census Bureau from the 'Long Form' of the Decennial Enumeration of the Population of the The United States. The record of data collection regarding race, ethnic, and color (bracketing the distinction between native or foreign-born) can be viewed in Table 1, *Comparison of US census classifications of race and color, 1890–1990.*

Demographers and other data users have long viewed the collection interval of ten years between censuses as a severe constraint to understanding change in modern America. In 1995, the US Census Bureau began to address such limitations and to devise new approaches to generating national data that would more rapidly update information requirements of our contemporary society and economy and to measure the accelerating rates of social change and mobility. The mission, goal and objective was to institute a new data collection process for obtaining demographic, housing, social, and economic information previously obtained from the 'Long Form' of the Decennial Census. Congress authorized the American Community Survey (ACS) and testing of the American Community Survey began in 1996. The ACS program began producing test data in 2000. In addition to the data base derived decennial censuses, the American Community Survey introduced an ongoing data collection process and the production of accurate and statistically sound surveys. The U.S. Census Bureau sends questionnaires to approximately 250,000 addresses monthly (or 3 million per year). The Bureau regularly gathers information previously contained only in the Long Form of the decennial census. This effort is the largest data collection project, except for the decennial census that the Census Bureau administers.

Recently, the data produced by ACS has become available online via the Census Bureau web site. (See http://census.gov/acs/www/) The array of information available is stunning in its scope. A researcher can download data for over 7000 geographic units and over 175 ethnicities and develop crosstabs and do statistical tests for a variety of general, social,

economic and housing variables related to specific ethnicities. For any selected population group, data is available for hundreds of variables that are grouped under the following thirty-two major headings: total number of races reported, sex and age, relationship, households by type, marital status, school enrollment, educational attainment, fertility, responsibility for grandchildren under 18 years, veteran status, disability status, residence 1 year ago, place of birth, citizenship status and year of entry, world region of birth of foreign born, language spoken at home and ability to speak english, employment status, commuting to work, occupation, industry class of worker, income in the past 12 months, poverty rates for families and people for whom poverty status is determined, housing tenure, units in structure, year structure built, vehicles available, house heating fuel, selected housing characteristics, selected monthly owner costs as a percentage of household income in the past 12 months, owner characteristics, gross rent as a percentage of household income in the past 12 months, and gross rent.

By 2002, the data collected by the sampling was encompassing enough to make national estimates. Because it includes the Ancestry Question, the Hispanic Origin Question as well as the "race" question, it is an increasingly important tool for a demographic understanding of race and ethnicity in America. The available data also provides sufficient information to obtain standard errors. As a result, doing statistical tests to determine significance is not difficult. The determination of statistical significance takes into account the difference between the two estimates as well as the standard errors of both estimates.

In broadest outline, what the data reveal is that America is diverse and that statistically meaningful distinction continue to exist and to evolve in what can be characterized as remarkable "lumpy" society and a geographically clustering of ethnicities which can not be described by concepts such as integration and segregation. To understand population clustering of this sort and at this magnitude demands more detailed analysis of ethnic

Table 1   Comparison of US census classifications of race or colour, 1890–1990[a]

1890	1900	1910	1920	1930	1940	1950	1960	1970[g]	1980[h]	1990[i]
White	White	White	White	White	White[e]	White[e]	White[f]	White	White	White
Black	Black	Black	Black	Negro	Indian	Negro	Negro	Negro or Black	Black or Negro	Black or Negro
Mulatto	Chinese	Mulatto	Mulatto	Mexican	Chinese	American Indian	American Indian	Indian (Amer.)	Japanese	Indian (Amer.)
Quadroon	Japanese	Chinese	Chinese	Indian[d]	Japanese	Japanese	Japanese	Japanese	Chinese	Eskimo
Octoroon	Indian[b]	Japanese	Japanese	Chinese	Filipino	Chinese	Chinese	Chinese	Filipino	Aleut
Chinese		Indian[b]	Indian[b]	Japanese	Hindu	Filipino	Filipino	Filipino	Korean	Asian or Pacific Islander (API)
Japanese		Other[c]	Other	Filipino	Korean	Other	Hawaiian	Hawaiian	Vietnamese	Chinese
Indian[b]				Hindu	Other		Part Hawaiian	Korean	Indian (Amer.)	Filipino
				Korean			Aleut	Other	Asian Indian	Hawaiian
				Other			Eskimo		Hawaiian	Korean
							Other, etc.[f]		Guamanian	Vietnamese
									Samoan	Japanese
									Eskimo	Asian Indian
									Aleut	Samoan
									Other	Guamanian
										Other

Notes:

[a]The racial classifications are from the question on race or colour in each decennial population schedule. The source for Table 1 is US Bureau of the Census (1989).

[b]Separate enumerations of the Indian population on reservations were carried out in these years, in addition to the enumeration of Indians who lived among the 'general' population. The proportion of 'Indian blood' (whether 'full' or 'mixed blood') and type of mixture (with white or black) were also noted on the separate Indian schedules.

[c]The category, 'other,' included groups that varied in number and characteristics over time. The Census Bureau routinely instructed enumerators to assign these responses to one of the given classifications but sometimes retained a classification for 'other' (for example), Asian Indians in 1960.

[d]Beginning in 1930, there were no more separate schedules for enumerating Indians who live on reservations. Instead, a supplement was attached to the general population schedule in order to collect additional information on Indians who live on reservations.

[e]Mexicans were included in the white category, beginning in 1940.

[f]Enumerators were instructed to classify (by observation) Puerto Ricans, Mexicans, and other persons of Latin descent as 'white' when they were definitely not Negro, Indian, or some other race. Southern European and Near Eastern people were also to be considered 'white,' but Asian Indians were to be classified as 'other'.

[g]Respondents self-identified themselves on the race question but enumerators were instructed to change responses such as 'Chicano', 'La Raza', 'Mexican American', 'Moslem' or 'Brown' to 'White' and 'Brown (Negro)' to 'Negro' or 'Black'.

[h]In 1980, the lead-in to the question on race dropped any mention of race, Instead, the question read: 'Is this person—?'

[i]In 1990, the question on race read: 'What is—'s race?'

Source: "Racial Classifications in the US Census: 1890–1990," Sharon M. Lee, *Ethnic and Racial Studies*, January 1993, p. 78.

and race patterns along with other economic and social indicators. The interesting question include: Why do such distinctions and differences remain and in what respect are they salient explanations for other questions posed by the social sciences as well as humanistic reflections on culture and identity? What are the boundaries of community? What are the intersection of the personal and social identity? Are ethnic and racial variables or epiphenomena? The accessibility of this throve of information provide ample opportunity for investigation by social scientists as well as a compelling backdrop for an argument that simplistic black/white racial demography is past its usefulness because there is a much more complicated and more nuance to the story of American pluralism that is yet to be discovered, explained and pondered.

The following four tables provide a rudimentary profile of ethnic and race in America. The appended, **Instructions for Applying Statistical Testing to ACS 2007 Data** will guide the reader to applying statistical tests to such data sets. This is an invitation to investigate a new, rich and online accessible data source of the U.S. Census. Such enquiries will extend the explorations of social and economic indicators regarding race and ethnicity and deepen your grasp of race and ethnic relations and the various local, regional and national configurations of pluralism in America.

2008 American Community Survey

	People			Gender		
	Est. Pop 2008	Percent		Male	Female	
Nation	**304,059,728**	**100.0%**	French except Basque	45.7%	54.3%	Y
White*	234,238,744	77.0%	Japanese*	45.7%	54.3%	Y
German	50,271,790	16.5%	Filipino*	45.8%	54.2%	Y
Black/African American*	40,211,186	13.2%	Dominican**	46.0%	54.0%	Y
Irish	36,278,332	11.9%	Korean*	46.5%	53.5%	Y
Mexican**	30,738,559	10.1%	Swedish	47.1%	52.9%	Y
English	27,516,394	9.0%	Cherokee*	47.7%	52.3%	
American	17,927,125	5.9%	Chinese*	47.7%	52.3%	Y
Italian	17,748,513	5.8%	Black/African Amer*	47.8%	52.2%	Y
Polish	9,887,099	3.3%	Danish	47.8%	52.2%	
French except Basque	9,446,760	3.1%	English	47.8%	52.2%	Y
Scottish	5,827,046	1.9%	Irish	47.8%	52.2%	Y
Dutch	4,928,607	1.6%	Hungarian	48.0%	52.0%	
Norwegian	4,643,339	1.5%	Dutch	48.4%	51.6%	Y
Swedish	4,390,058	1.4%	Russian	48.5%	51.5%	
Puerto Rican**	4,216,533	1.4%	French Canadian	48.6%	51.4%	
Chinese*	3,622,496	1.2%	American	48.7%	51.3%	Y
Scotch-Irish	3,538,444	1.2%	Polish	48.7%	51.3%	Y
Russian	3,129,738	1.0%	Czech	48.8%	51.2%	
Filipino*	3,088,000	1.0%	Norwegian	48.8%	51.2%	
European	3,006,134	1.0%	Portuguese	48.8%	51.2%	
Asian Indian*	2,725,594	0.9%	Scotch-Irish	48.9%	51.1%	
French Canadian	2,079,170	0.7%	**Nation**	**49.3%**	**50.7%**	
Vietnamese*	1,728,532	0.6%	White*	49.4%	50.6%	
Cuban**	1,617,010	0.5%	German	49.5%	50.5%	
Korean*	1,609,980	0.5%	British	49.7%	50.3%	
Czech	1,593,535	0.5%	Italian	49.7%	50.3%	
Hungarian	1,538,824	0.5%	Vietnamese*	49.9%	50.1%	
Danish	1,458,787	0.5%	Puerto Rican**	50.0%	50.0%	
Portuguese	1,419,428	0.5%	Cuban**	50.2%	49.8%	
Greek	1,350,600	0.4%	Greek	50.3%	49.7%	
Dominican**	1,327,685	0.4%	European	50.8%	49.2%	Y
Japanese*	1,298,890	0.4%	Mexican**	52.4%	47.6%	Y
British	1,113,762	0.4%	Scottish	52.7%	47.3%	Y
Cherokee*	1,047,083	0.3%	Asian Indian*	53.1%	46.9%	Y
	Est. Pop 2008	**Percent**		**Male**	**Female**	

*From Race Question, totals include multiple responses

**From Hispanic Origin Question

Remaining ethnicities from Ancestry Question

"Y" denotes meaningful deviation from national response (beyond 3 standard deviations)

Source: 2008 American Community Survey (ACS), US Census

2008 American Community Survey

	1 Race		2 Races	Race Responses	3 Races		4+ Races	
American	99.3%	Y	0.7%	Y	0.0%	Y	0.0%	
Russian	99.0%	Y	1.0%	Y	0.1%	Y	0.0%	
Polish	98.9%	Y	1.1%	Y	0.0%	Y	0.0%	
Czech	98.9%	Y	1.0%	Y	0.1%		0.0%	
Danish	98.8%	Y	1.1%	Y	0.1%		0.0%	
English	98.7%	Y	1.3%	Y	0.1%	Y	0.0%	
Swedish	98.7%	Y	1.2%	Y	0.0%	Y	0.0%	
Norwegian	98.6%	Y	1.3%	Y	0.1%	Y	0.0%	
Hungarian	98.6%	Y	1.3%	Y	0.0%	Y	0.0%	
German	98.5%	Y	1.5%	Y	0.1%	Y	0.0%	
British	98.5%	Y	1.5%	Y	0.0%	Y	0.0%	
Italian	98.4%	Y	1.5%	Y	0.1%	Y	0.0%	
Scotch-Irish	98.4%	Y	1.5%	Y	0.1%	Y	0.0%	
Greek	98.3%	Y	1.6%	Y	0.1%		0.0%	
Scottish	98.2%	Y	1.7%	Y	0.1%	Y	0.0%	
Dutch	98.2%	Y	1.7%	Y	0.1%	Y	0.0%	
Irish	98.1%	Y	1.8%	Y	0.1%	Y	0.0%	
French Canadian	97.9%		2.1%		0.1%		0.0%	
French except Basque	97.9%	Y	1.9%	Y	0.2%		0.0%	
Cuban**	97.7%		2.1%		0.2%		0.0%	
Nation	**97.7%**		**2.1%**		**0.2%**		**0.0%**	
White*	97.4%	Y	2.4%	Y	0.2%		0.0%	
European	97.0%	Y	2.7%	Y	0.3%	Y	0.0%	
Mexican**	96.9%	Y	2.9%	Y	0.2%		0.0%	
Dominican**	94.4%	Y	5.1%	Y	0.5%	Y	0.0%	
Portuguese	94.4%	Y	4.6%	Y	1.0%	Y	0.1%	Y
Asian Indian*	93.9%	Y	5.4%	Y	0.6%	Y	0.2%	Y
Black/African American*	93.5%	Y	5.7%	Y	0.7%	Y	0.1%	Y
Puerto Rican**	93.4%	Y	5.7%	Y	0.7%	Y	0.1%	Y
Vietnamese*	92.8%	Y	6.5%	Y	0.7%	Y	0.1%	Y
Chinese*	89.6%	Y	7.6%	Y	2.4%	Y	0.5%	Y
Korean*	86.3%	Y	11.9%	Y	1.6%	Y	0.2%	Y
Filipino*	81.1%	Y	15.8%	Y	2.7%	Y	0.4%	Y
Japanese*	70.4%	Y	24.9%	Y	4.1%	Y	0.6%	Y
Cherokee*	27.5%	Y	64.3%	Y	7.5%	Y	0.8%	Y

*From Race Question, totals include multiple responses

**From Hispanic Origin Question

Remaining ethnicities from Ancestry Question

"Y" denotes meaningful deviation from National responses (beyond 3 standard deviations)

Source: 2008 American Community Survey (ACS), U.S. Census

Instructions for Applying Statistical Testing to ACS 2007 Data

This document provides some basic instructions for obtaining the ACS standard errors needed to do statistical tests, as well as performing the statistical testing.

Obtaining Standard Errors

Where the standard errors come from, and whether they are readily available or users have to calculate them, depends on where the ACS data is coming from. If the estimate of interest is published on American FactFinder (AFF), then AFF should also be the source of the standard errors. Possible sources for the estimates and standard errors are listed below:

2008 American Community Survey

	<5 yrs		5–17 yrs		Age >64 yrs		Median Age	
Mexican**	12.2%	Y	24.8%	Y	4.4%	Y	25.7	Y
Puerto Rican**	10.2%	Y	22.8%	Y	6.9%	Y	29.0	Y
Dominican**	9.2%	Y	22.5%	Y	6.3%	Y	29.5	Y
Black/African American*	8.5%	Y	21.7%	Y	8.3%	Y	30.6	Y
Asian Indian*	9.0%	Y	16.4%	Y	6.0%	Y	32.4	Y
Korean*	7.5%		17.8%		9.4%	Y	34.1	Y
European	7.9%	Y	20.7%	Y	7.2%	Y	34.1	Y
Filipino*	8.1%	Y	19.0%	Y	9.9%	Y	34.6	Y
Vietnamese*	8.1%	Y	18.8%	Y	7.7%	Y	34.7	Y
Cherokee*	7.5%		19.0%	Y	8.8%	Y	34.8	Y
Italian	7.0%		19.1%	Y	11.2%	Y	35.4	Y
Chinese*	7.5%	Y	16.8%		9.9%	Y	36.1	Y
Portuguese	6.6%		17.1%		11.2%	Y	36.3	Y
Japanese*	7.6%		17.5%		13.1%		36.3	
Greek	6.9%		18.4%		12.9%		36.8	
Nation	**6.9%**		**17.4%**		**12.8%**		**36.9**	
Irish	6.4%	Y	17.4%		12.5%	Y	38.1	Y
American	6.8%		19.0%	Y	15.0%	Y	38.2	Y
White*	6.5%	Y	16.6%	Y	14.3%	Y	38.6	Y
Polish	5.9%	Y	16.6%	Y	12.6%		38.7	Y
German	6.2%	Y	16.8%	Y	13.4%	Y	38.9	Y
Norwegian	6.2%	Y	16.7%	Y	13.5%	Y	39.5	Y
Czech	5.6%	Y	15.6%	Y	14.5%	Y	40.6	Y
French except Basque	5.5%	Y	15.9%	Y	14.9%	Y	41.4	Y
French Canadian	5.7%	Y	14.9%	Y	13.3%		41.4	Y
Cuban**	6.4%		14.6%	Y	19.2%	Y	41.4	Y
Swedish	5.4%	Y	15.4%	Y	15.3%	Y	42.4	Y
Russian	5.5%	Y	15.2%	Y	16.1%	Y	42.4	Y
Hungarian	5.2%	Y	15.0%	Y	16.0%	Y	42.8	Y
Dutch	5.4%	Y	15.2%	Y	16.5%	Y	43.2	Y
Scottish	4.8%	Y	13.6%	Y	16.0%	Y	44.2	Y
Danish	5.3%	Y	15.0%	Y	18.0%	Y	44.7	Y
British	4.9%	Y	12.4%	Y	15.5%	Y	45.1	Y
English	4.6%	Y	14.0%	Y	20.6%	Y	46.9	Y
Scotch-Irish	4.3%	Y	12.0%	Y	24.1%	Y	50.1	Y
	<5 yrs		5–17 yrs		>64 yrs		Median Age	

*From Race Question, totals include multiple responses

**From Hispanic Origin Question

Remaining ethnicities from Ancestry Question

"Y" denotes meaningful deviation from national response (beyond 3 standard deviations)

1. ACS data from published tables on American FactFinder
All ACS estimates from tables on AFF include either
the 90 percent margin of error or 90 percent confidence
bounds. The margin of error is the maximum difference
between the estimate and the upper and lower confidence
bounds. Most tables on AFF containing 2005 or later
ACS data display the margin of error.

Use the margin of error to calculate the standard error
(dropping the "+/−" from the displayed value first) as:

$$\text{Standard Error} = \text{Margin Error} / Z$$

where $Z = 1.65$ for 2005 and earlier years and 1.645 for
2006 and later years.

	2002	2003	2004	2005	2006	2007	2008	Increase since 2002 (avg per year)
Mexican*	23,999,836	25,287,619	25,894,763	26,781,547	28,339,354	29,166,981	30,738,559	3.65%
Vietnamese**	1,859,547		1,267,510	1,418,334	1,475,798	1,508,489	1,431,980	2.87%
Filipino**			2,148,227	2,282,872	2,328,097	2,412,446	2,425,697	2.86%
Cuban*	1,357,744	1,363,769	1,437,828	1,461,574	1,520,276	1,611,478	1,617,010	2.67%
Asian Indian**			2,245,239	2,319,222	2,482,141	2,570,166	2,495,998	2.51%
Puerto Rican*	3,608,309	3,717,941	3,874,322	3,781,317	3,987,947	4,120,205	4,216,533	2.40%
Chinese, except Taiwanese**			2,829,627	2,882,257	3,090,453	3,045,592	3,077,783	2.02%
Ukrainian	880,278	869,799	893,502	963,263	961,113	970,667	998,246	1.97%
Czech	1,411,073	1,426,354	1,462,413	1,555,767	1,637,218	1,625,318	1,593,535	1.91%
Black or African American**	35,824,849	36,186,830	36,597,015	36,844,565	39,151,870	39,663,004	40,211,186	1.82%
Korean**			1,251,092	1,246,240	1,335,075	1,344,171	1,344,267	1.73%
Greek	1,213,807	1,229,023	1,309,766	1,291,381	1,380,258	1,380,043	1,350,600	1.69%
Total Nation	**280,540,330**	**282,909,885**	**285,691,501**	**288,378,137**	**299,398,485**	**301,621,159**	**304,059,728**	**1.29%**
Italian	16,632,885	16,726,217	16,817,286	17,235,187	17,829,184	17,844,191	17,748,513	1.05%
Welsh	1,859,547	1,890,237	1,913,101	1,928,031	1,959,794	1,920,993	1,980,323	1.02%
Polish	9,292,875	9,303,599	9,385,233	9,770,544	10,024,683	9,976,267	9,887,099	1.00%
Irish	34,262,120	33,992,086	34,487,790	34,668,723	35,975,855	36,495,800	36,278,332	0.93%
Russian	3,000,233	2,974,942	3,016,988	3,009,876	3,105,965	3,152,959	3,129,738	0.69%
German	48,276,212	47,842,275	48,202,654	49,178,839	50,764,352	50,753,530	50,271,790	0.66%
Portuguese	1,388,223	1,349,161	1,335,171	1,378,995	1,442,077	1,471,549	1,419,428	0.37%
Scottish	5,712,574	5,811,085	5,752,571	5,858,678	6,006,955	6,019,281	5,827,046	0.33%
Swedish	4,365,979	4,253,810	4,325,823	4,259,792	4,417,115	4,340,436	4,390,058	0.09%
Norwegian	4,641,376	4,494,107	4,585,209	4,601,154	4,669,516	4,655,711	4,643,339	0.01%
Danish	1,464,332	1,435,000	1,477,096	1,434,060	1,516,126	1,449,183	1,458,787	-0.06%
Lithuanian	715,973	719,575	719,280	712,332	722,879	745,888	712,165	-0.09%
Slovak	817,649	811,172	809,066	819,412	838,385	813,968	808,191	-0.20%
Hungarian	1,574,444	1,494,953	1,527,156	1,521,762	1,563,081	1,564,569	1,538,824	-0.39%
Swiss	1,025,408	984,443	1,033,014	1,017,277	1,018,910	1,018,853	997,233	-0.47%
English	28,394,187	28,402,887	28,410,295	27,761,546	28,290,369	28,177,386	27,516,394	-0.53%
French	9,839,776	9,677,776	9,496,451	9,529,969	9,651,364	9,616,496	9,446,760	-0.69%
Dutch	5,202,267	5,059,238	5,087,191	5,079,268	5,187,864	5,070,740	4,928,607	-0.93%
French Canadian	2,205,941	2,187,922	2,233,999	2,265,648	2,240,648	2,184,246	2,079,170	-1.02%
American	19,941,762	19,676,981	20,061,233	20,535,853	20,372,454	19,381,268	17,927,125	-1.87%
Japanese**			832,039	833,761	829,767	803,092	710,063	-4.29%
Scotch-Irish	5,288,552	5,098,850	5,323,888	5,289,309	5,393,554	5,313,956	3,538,444	-8.24%

*From Hispanic Origin Question

**From Race Question, some data not available; "Black or African American" includes all responses; Asian ethnicities include only single responses

Source: American Community Surveys (2002 to 2008) Summary Social Data

If confidence bounds are provided instead (as with most ACS data 2004 and earlier), calculate the margin of error first before calculating the standard error:

$$\text{Margin of Error} = \max \,(\text{upper bound–estimate}, \text{estimate–lower bound})$$

All published ACS estimates use 1.65 (for 2005 and previous years) or 1.645 (for 2006 and later years) to calculate 90 percent margins of error and confidence bounds. Other surveys may use other values.

2. ACS public-use microdata sample (PUMS) tabulations
Using the methods described in the 2007 Accuracy of the PUMS documentation, available at http://www.census.gov/acs/www/Products/PUMS/codelist2007.html users can calculate standard errors for tabulations from the 2007 ACS PUMS files. Users can find accuracy documents for previous year's PUMS with appropriate instructions at http://census.gov/acs/www/Products/PUMS/codelist2007.html.

NOTE: ACS PUMS design factors *should not* be used to calculate standard errors of full ACS sample estimates, such as those on AFF.

Obtaining Standard Errors for Derived Estimates

Once users have obtained standard errors for the basic estimates, there may be situations where users create derived estimates, such as percentages or differences that also require standard errors.

All methods in this section are approximations and users should be cautious in using them. They may be overestimates or underestimates of the estimate's standard error, and may not match direct calculations of standard errors or calculations obtained through other methods.

- Sum or Difference of Estimates

$$SE(A + B + ...) = SE(A - B - ...) = \sqrt{SE(A)^2 + SE(B)^2 + ...}$$

- Proportions and Percents
Here we define a proportion as a ratio where the numerator is a subset of the denominator, for example the proportion of persons 25 and over with a high school diploma or higher.

Let $P = \frac{A}{B}$.

$$SE(P) = \frac{1}{B} \sqrt{SE(A)^2 - P^2 \times SE(B)^2}$$

If the value under the square root sign is negative, then instead use

$$SE(P) = \frac{1}{B} \sqrt{SE(A)^2 + P^2 \times SE(B)^2}$$

If P = 1 then use

$$SE(P) = \frac{SE(A)}{B}$$

If Q = 100% × P (a percent instead of a proportion), then SE(Q) = 100% × SE(P).

- Means and Other Ratios
If the estimate is a ratio but the numerator is not a subset of the denominator, such as persons per household, per capita income, or percent change, then

$$SE\left(\frac{A}{B}\right) = \frac{1}{B} \sqrt{SE(A)^2 + \left(\frac{A}{B}\right)^2 \times SE(B)^2}$$

- Products
For a product of two estimates–for example if users want to estimate a proportion's numerator by multiplying the proportion by its denominator—the standard error can be approximated as

$$SE(A \times B) = \sqrt{A^2 \times [SE(B)]^2 + B^2 \times [SE(A)]^2}$$

Users may combine these procedures for complicated estimates. For example, if the desired estimate is $P = \frac{A+B+C}{D+E}$, then SE(A + B + C) and SE(D + E) can be estimated first, and then those results used to calculate SE(P).

For examples of these formulas, please see the 2007 Accuracy of the Data document at http://census.gov/acs/www/Downloads/ACS/accuracy2007.pdf

Instructions for Statistical Testing

Once standard errors have been obtained, doing the statistical test to determine significance is not difficult. The determination of statistical significance takes into account the difference between the two estimates as well as the standard errors of both estimates. For two estimates, A and B, with standard errors SE(A) and SE(B), let

$$Z = \frac{A - B}{\sqrt{(SE(A))^2 + (SE(B))^2}}$$

If Z < –1.645 or Z > 1.645, then the difference between A and B is significant at the 90 percent confidence level. Otherwise, the difference is not significant. This means that there is less than a 10 percent chance that the difference between these two estimates would be as large or large by random chance alone.

Users may choose to apply a confidence level different from 90 percent to their tests of statistical significance. For example, if Z < –1.96 or Z > 1.96, then the difference between A and B is significant at the 95 percent confidence level.

This method can be used for any types of estimates: counts, percentages, proportions, means, medians, etc. It can be used for comparing across years, or across surveys. If one of the estimates is a fixed value or comes from a source without sampling error (such as the Census 2000 SF1), use zero for the standard error for that estimate in the above equation for Z.

NOTE: Making comparisons between ACS single-year and multiyear estimates is very difficult, but can be done with caution. Instructions for applying statistical testing to ACS Multiyear data will be forthcoming.

This is the method used in determining statistical significance for the ACS Ranking Tables published on AFF. Note that the user's determination of statistical significance may not match the Ranking Table's result for the same pair of estimates, because the significance tests for the Ranking Tables are made using unrounded standard errors. Standard errors obtained from the rounded margins of error or confidence bounds are unlikely to match the unrounded standard error, and so statistical tests may differ.

Using the rule of thumb of overlapping confidence intervals does not constitute a valid significance test and users are discouraged from using that method.

Critical Thinking

1. Explain the difference between methods of data collection used by the U.S. Census.

2. Will regularly updated Census data on ethnic groups derived from the American Community Survey provide a more robust source of timely information?

3. Use the American Fact Finder to create a profile of your state and your community. Are these findings surprising?

From *Building Blocks*, September 15, 2010. Copyright © 2010 by National Council of Urban Education Associations. Reprinted by permission.

Nation's Linguistic Diversity: Population Speaking a Language Other than English at Home Increases by 140 Percent in Past Three Decades

The number of people 5 and older who spoke a language other than English at home has more than doubled in the last three decades and at a pace four times greater than the nation's population growth, according to a new U.S. Census Bureau report analyzing data from the 2007 American Community Survey and over a time period from 1980–2007. In that time frame, the percentage of speakers of non-English languages grew by 140 percent while the nation's overall population grew by 34 percent.

Spanish speakers accounted for the largest numeric increase—nationwide, there were 23.4 million more speakers in 2007 than in 1980 representing a 211 percent increase. The Vietnamese-speaking population accounted for the largest percentage increase of 511 percent (1.0 million speakers) over the same timeframe.

The new report, Language Use in the United States: 2007 identifies the states with the highest concentrations of some of the most commonly spoken non-English languages. The languages, and some of the states with the highest percentage of speakers of these languages, include: Spanish (Texas, California and New Mexico), French (Louisiana and Maine), German (North Dakota and South Dakota), Slavic languages (Illinois, New York, New Jersey and Connecticut), Chinese (California, New York, Hawaii and Massachusetts) and Korean (Hawaii, California and New Jersey).

"The language data that the Census Bureau collects is vital to local agencies in determining potential language needs of school-aged children, for providing voting materials in non-English languages as mandated by the Voting Rights Act, and for researchers to analyze language trends in the U.S.," said U.S. Census Bureau Director Robert M. Groves.

Data on the speakers of non-English languages, as well as their English-speaking ability, routinely are used to help shape legislative, legal and marketing decisions.

Of the 281 million people 5 and older in the United States in 2007, 55.4 million individuals—or 20 percent—reported speaking a language other than English at home. While the Census Bureau codes 381 detailed languages, data tabulations generally are not available for all of those detailed groups. Instead, the Census Bureau collapses them into smaller sets of "language groups." The simplest collapse uses four major groups: Spanish, other Indo-European languages, Asian or Pacific Island languages, and all other languages. Of those people surveyed in this report, 62 percent spoke Spanish, 19 percent spoke other Indo-European languages, 15 percent spoke an Asian or Pacific Island language, and 4 percent spoke some other language.

Among people who spoke a language other than English at home, a majority reported speaking English "very well." The range varied from around 50 percent of the Asian or Pacific Island language speakers to 70 percent of those who spoke some other language.

The report also found:

- After English and Spanish (34.5 million speakers), Chinese (2.5 million speakers) was the language most commonly spoken at home. Five other languages have at least 1 million speakers: Tagalog (1.5 million speakers), French (1.4 million speakers), Vietnamese (1.2 million speakers), German (1.1 million speakers) and Korean (1.1 million speakers).

- The largest group of English-only speakers (78.3 million) were 41 to 64, compared with the 42.3 million speakers 5 to 17, and 72.4 million speakers aged 18 to 40 and 32.6 million speakers 65 and over.

- Among Spanish speakers, nearly as many were native-born as foreign-born—17.0 million versus 17.5 million, respectively. This was not the case for the other three major language groups—all three were sizably more foreign-born. Also, of Spanish speakers, 53 percent reported speaking English "very well."

- Not all languages have grown in use over the years: Italian, Yiddish, German, Polish and Greek were spoken at home by fewer individuals in the United States in 2007 than in 1980.

Also being released today are state by state and national tables, using the 2006–2008 American Community Survey

Table 1 Detailed Languages Spoken at Home and Ability to Speak English for the Population 5 Years and Over for the United States: **Release Date: April, 2010**

	Number of Speakers	Margin of Error[1]	Spoke English less than "Very Well"	Margin of Error[1]
Population 5 years and over	280,564,877	7,708	24,252,429	67,280
Spoke only English at home	225,488,799	83,368	(X)	(X)
Spoke a language other than English at home	55,076,078	81,124	24,252,429	67,280
Spoke a language other than English at home	**55,076,078**	**81,124**	**24,252,429**	**67,280**
SPANISH AND SPANISH CREOLE	**34,183,747**	**52,633**	**16,120,772**	**54,213**
Spanish	34,183,622	52,636	16,120,749	54,210
Ladino	125	98	23	38
OTHER INDO-EUROPEAN LANGUAGES	**10,347,377**	**49,301**	**3,405,878**	**26,398**
French	**1,358,816**	**14,743**	**292,422**	**5,842**
French	1,304,758	14,891	284,809	5,734
Patois	28,475	2,268	4,835	982
Cajun	25,583	1,550	2,778	463
French Creole	**621,135**	**13,313**	**273,888**	**7,401**
Italian	**807,010**	**10,810**	**231,736**	**5,267**
Portuguese	**678,334**	**11,600**	**289,899**	**7,246**
Portuguese	676,963	11,509	289,771	7,251
Papia Mentae	1,371	673	128	109
German	**1,120,670**	**12,812**	**196,957**	**4,113**
German	1,119,963	12,808	196,929	4,111
Luxembourgian	707	237	28	37
Yiddish	**162,511**	**5,616**	**50,957**	**2,997**
Other West Germanic languages	**269,600**	**7,680**	**62,711**	**3,558**
Pennsylvania Dutch	117,547	5,840	38,494	2,884
Dutch	132,191	4,206	22,358	1,715
Afrikaans	18,943	1,653	1,781	384
Frisian	919	324	78	60
Scandinavian languages	**132,956**	**3,989**	**17,474**	**1,384**
Swedish	56,713	2,979	6,842	856
Danish	29,728	2,126	4,025	641
Norwegian	41,197	2,287	5,781	655
Icelandic	5,170	849	798	476
Faroese	148	100	28	47
Greek	**340,028**	**9,204**	**90,360**	**3,633**
Russian	**846,233**	**13,514**	**430,850**	**8,004**
Polish	**632,362**	**12,763**	**274,693**	**6,910**

(continued)

Table 1 Detailed Languages Spoken at Home and Ability to Speak English for the Population 5 Years and Over for the United States: **Release Date: April, 2010** (continued)

	Number of Speakers	Margin of Error[1]	Spoke English less than "Very Well"	Margin of Error[1]
Serbo-Croatian languages	**273,729**	**9,634**	**115,165**	**5,050**
Serbocroatian	152,331	6,705	71,216	3,743
Croatian	57,565	3,663	19,912	1,626
Serbian	63,833	4,113	24,037	2,239
Other Slavic languages	**318,051**	**8,552**	**122,058**	**4,305**
Bielorussian	1,363	436	716	257
Ukrainian	142,711	6,414	68,487	3,641
Czech	55,382	2,336	13,253	1,228
Lusatian	189	133	78	113
Slovak	32,227	2,364	8,666	1,063
Bulgarian	57,016	3,514	21,129	1,659
Macedonian	22,134	2,294	7,715	1,185
Slovene	7,029	988	2,014	549
Armenian	**220,922**	**7,558**	**98,041**	**4,096**
Persian	**359,176**	**9,536**	**137,765**	**4,990**
Hindi	**531,313**	**10,495**	**114,070**	**4,656**
Gujarati	**301,658**	**8,943**	**108,352**	**5,093**
Urdu	**335,213**	**9,621**	**102,364**	**4,602**
Other Indic languages	**619,954**	**14,103**	**238,583**	**7,599**
India n.e.c.[2]	81,125	5,875	29,167	2,688
Bengali	190,090	6,733	79,837	3,695
Panjabi	208,387	7,698	91,416	4,614
Marathi	54,223	2,599	7,610	1,055
Bihari	151	144	115	129
Rajasthani	464	286	103	80
Oriya	4,790	845	1,013	401
Assamese	1,215	449	56	56
Kashmiri	833	368	202	151
Nepali	34,139	2,990	14,857	2,047
Sindhi	6,907	1,034	1,398	423
Pakistan n.e.c.[2]	13,092	2,184	5,560	1,334
Sinhalese	22,278	2,330	6,904	1,200
Romany	2,260	775	345	216
Other Indo-European languages	**417,706**	**10,116**	**157,533**	**5,868**
Jamaican Creole	19,872	3,141	5,870	2,324
Krio	6,900	1,358	1,839	631
Hawaiian Pidgin	108	101	(B)	—
Pidgin	2,527	691	390	268

(continued)

Table 1 Detailed Languages Spoken at Home and Ability to Speak English for the Population 5 Years and Over for the United States: Release Date: April, 2010 (continued)

	Number of Speakers	Margin of Error[1]	Spoke English less than "Very Well"	Margin of Error[1]
Gullah	352	361	18	32
Saramacca	112	112	46	71
Catalonian	1,917	505	292	158
Romanian	146,840	6,050	58,351	3,126
Rhaeto-romanic	39	64	(B)	—
Welsh	2,452	517	262	135
Irish Gaelic	22,279	1,670	3,455	629
Scottic Gaelic	1,445	353	31	33
Albanian	125,220	6,363	57,358	3,605
Lithuanian	42,306	2,545	14,331	1,473
Lettish	16,149	1,622	3,794	687
Pashto	15,788	2,400	5,849	1,044
Kurdish	12,982	2,291	5,564	1,050
Balochi	268	376	18	30
Tadzhik	150	134	65	80
ASIAN AND PACIFIC ISLAND LANGUAGES	**8,267,977**	**30,947**	**4,041,963**	**24,276**
Chinese	**2,455,583**	**20,609**	**1,370,874**	**12,506**
Chinese	1,554,505	16,654	848,358	11,270
Hakka	1,086	386	537	251
Kan, Hsiang	291	342	(B)	—
Cantonese	437,301	10,320	273,042	7,005
Mandarin	381,121	10,132	199,507	6,442
Fuchow	2,671	730	2,282	630
Formosan	76,131	3,306	45,426	2,302
Wu	2,477	557	1,722	460
Japanese	**457,033**	**7,972**	**211,017**	**5,822**
Korean	**1,048,173**	**13,449**	**610,340**	**8,799**
Mon-Khmer, Cambodian	**182,387**	**6,650**	**98,764**	**4,369**
Hmong	**185,401**	**5,616**	**88,556**	**3,655**
Thai	**139,845**	**4,572**	**72,998**	**3,157**
Laotian	**147,865**	**6,238**	**74,772**	**3,481**
Vietnamese	**1,204,454**	**17,809**	**731,555**	**12,113**
Other Asian languages	**644,363**	**11,834**	**192,046**	**5,903**
Kazakh	1,006	513	404	276
Kirghiz	131	135	53	60
Karachay	698	331	248	193
Uighur	3,190	911	2,069	797
Azerabaijani	1,282	458	492	218

(continued)

Table 1 Detailed Languages Spoken at Home and Ability to Speak English for the Population 5 Years and Over for the United States: **Release Date: April, 2010** *(continued)*

	Number of Speakers	Margin of Error[1]	Spoke English less than "Very Well"	Margin of Error[1]
Turkish	107,405	5,588	44,045	3,103
Turkmen	221	261	14	23
Mongolian	8,430	1,528	5,164	1,055
Tungus	326	271	198	219
Dravidian	2,146	708	274	189
Gondi	76	64	(B)	—
Telugu	171,495	5,658	35,703	2,040
Kannada	35,902	2,307	5,229	964
Malayalam	112,378	4,849	35,254	2,399
Tamil	130,731	5,047	22,220	2,150
Munda	2,334	771	587	339
Tibetan	9,764	1,679	6,096	1,364
Burmese	35,281	3,910	22,295	3,121
Karen	3,924	1,182	3,596	1,134
Kachin	178	154	109	127
Miao-yao, Mien	17,421	1,974	7,996	1,140
Paleo-siberian	44	32	(B)	—
Tagalog	**1,444,324**	**16,857**	**455,975**	**9,514**
Other Pacific Island languages	**358,549**	**9,464**	**135,066**	**4,853**
Indonesian	60,657	3,805	28,111	2,145
Achinese	32	53	(B)	—
Balinese	272	159	108	70
Cham	891	479	376	262
Javanese	441	218	268	178
Malagasy	935	404	243	196
Malay	12,440	1,566	4,191	804
Bisayan	23,644	2,185	8,981	1,491
Sebuano	10,027	1,190	3,321	638
Pangasinan	2,144	648	1,088	441
Ilocano	76,896	4,252	40,764	2,825
Bikol	812	347	210	121
Pampangan	5,432	1,226	1,884	564
Micronesian	5,514	1,397	3,035	951
Carolinian	187	236	14	21
Chamorro	17,985	1,664	2,856	573
Gilbertese	173	124	102	100
Kusaiean	1,056	564	526	360
Marshallese	10,739	1,930	5,672	1,329

(continued)

Table 1 Detailed Languages Spoken at Home and Ability to Speak English for the Population 5 Years and Over for the United States: Release Date: April, 2010 (continued)

	Number of Speakers	Margin of Error[1]	Spoke English less than "Very Well"	Margin of Error[1]
Mokilese	448	282	205	196
Mortlockese	40	63	40	63
Palau	4,153	1,175	1,491	590
Ponapean	2,347	720	981	393
Trukese	5,434	1,465	2,728	801
Ulithean	39	71	39	71
Woleai-ulithi	51	62	(B)	—
Yapese	795	392	282	186
Melanesian	973	369	464	304
Polynesian	723	468	163	141
Samoan	57,368	3,813	14,396	1,328
Tongan	26,322	2,865	8,411	1,251
Niuean	17	28	(B)	—
Tokelauan	290	275	193	208
Fijian	3,701	987	1,226	400
Marquesan	605	500	392	412
Rarotongan	124	137	(B)	—
Maori	659	278	115	85
Nukuoro	141	154	(B)	—
Hawaiian	24,042	2,094	2,190	405
ALL OTHER LANGUAGES	**2,276,977**	**29,341**	**683,816**	**12,172**
Navajo	**170,822**	**4,710**	**39,724**	**2,566**
Other Native North American languages	**203,127**	**4,352**	**32,140**	**1,874**
Aleut	1,236	374	235	134
Pacific Gulf Yupik	8	13	(B)	—
Eskimo	2,168	391	552	164
Inupik	5,580	616	1,453	254
St Lawrence Island Yupik	993	256	392	171
Yupik	18,626	927	6,896	606
Algonquian	288	146	57	65
Arapaho	1,087	366	13	22
Atsina	45	35	(B)	—
Blackfoot	1,970	577	217	149
Cheyenne	2,399	567	77	62
Cree	951	392	83	66
Delaware	146	123	37	67
Fox	727	195	161	143
Kickapoo	1,141	293	476	160

(continued)

Table 1 Detailed Languages Spoken at Home and Ability to Speak English for the Population 5 Years and Over for the United States: **Release Date: April, 2010** *(continued)*

	Number of Speakers	Margin of Error[1]	Spoke English less than "Very Well"	Margin of Error[1]
Menomini	946	381	375	248
French Cree	75	71	53	66
Miami	168	275	85	139
Micmac	230	159	25	28
Ojibwa	6,986	867	788	277
Ottawa	312	174	34	43
Passamaquoddy	982	254	60	46
Penobscot	144	98	8	13
Abnaki	86	89	(B)	—
Potawatomi	824	271	82	67
Shawnee	321	203	20	35
Yurok	491	387	8	17
Kutenai	200	124	65	70
Makah	176	96	53	51
Kwakiutl	85	62	21	32
Nootka	10	18	(B)	—
Clallam	146	143	2	5
Coeur D'alene	174	126	(B)	—
Columbia	17	27	(B)	—
Cowlitz	110	179	91	146
Salish	1,233	362	282	178
Okanogan	284	215	31	51
Puget Sound Salish	207	119	99	103
Quinault	128	202	(B)	—
Haida	118	72	23	38
Athapascan	1,627	351	318	148
Ahtena	18	27	(B)	—
Ingalit	127	164	(B)	—
Koyukon	58	53	7	11
Kuchin	1,217	422	302	189
Tanaina	11	24	(B)	—
Chasta Costa	84	101	5	10
Hupa	174	175	(B)	—
Apache	14,012	1,527	495	185
Kiowa	1,274	466	122	72
Tlingit	1,026	277	84	55
Mountain Maidu	319	176	22	38
Northwest Maidu	32	53	32	53
Sierra Miwok	216	261	(B)	—

(continued)

Table 1 Detailed Languages Spoken at Home and Ability to Speak English for the Population 5 Years and Over for the United States: **Release Date: April, 2010** *(continued)*

	Number of Speakers	Margin of Error[1]	Spoke English less than "Very Well"	Margin of Error[1]
Nomlaki	38	49	(B)	—
Wintun	24	26	(B)	—
Foothill North Yokuts	407	204	111	113
Tachi	45	74	26	43
Santiam	50	81	(B)	—
Siuslaw	6	9	(B)	—
Klamath	95	73	26	44
Nez Perce	942	329	114	83
Sahaptian	1,654	589	102	67
Upper Chinook	58	54	6	10
Tsimshian	68	66	(B)	—
Achumawi	68	61	(B)	—
Atsugewi	15	26	(B)	—
Karok	700	373	38	44
Pomo	648	318	96	95
Washo	227	152	22	30
Cocomaricopa	44	49	10	16
Mohave	330	193	21	25
Yuma	172	97	55	59
Diegueno	228	138	139	123
Delta River Yuman	483	191	110	98
Havasupai	90	101	47	79
Walapai	458	197	22	19
Yavapai	139	90	(B)	—
Chumash	39	69	39	69
Tonkawa	29	36	(B)	—
Yuchi	4	10	(B)	—
Crow	3,962	523	261	202
Hidatsa	806	341	36	38
Mandan	104	96	40	57
Dakota	18,804	1,363	1,855	402
Chiwere	60	52	(B)	—
Winnebago	1,340	357	84	67
Kansa	7	10	(B)	—
Omaha	457	192	9	13
Osage	260	153	53	59
Ponca	131	96	9	14
Alabama	165	88	33	39
Choctaw	10,368	1,180	2,430	582

(continued)

Table 1 Detailed Languages Spoken at Home and Ability to Speak English for the Population 5 Years and Over for the United States: **Release Date: April, 2010** *(continued)*

	Number of Speakers	Margin of Error[1]	Spoke English less than "Very Well"	Margin of Error[1]
Mikasuki	188	131	43	63
Koasati	59	53	4	8
Muskogee	5,072	708	995	226
Chetemacha	89	64	19	32
Keres	13,073	1,181	810	234
Iroquois	76	71	(B)	—
Mohawk	1,423	494	166	99
Oneida	527	335	309	295
Onondaga	239	180	7	14
Cayuga	6	12	(B)	—
Seneca	1,353	446	152	97
Tuscarora	179	152	18	27
Cherokee	12,320	1,264	2,012	488
Arikara	103	83	(B)	—
Caddo	51	64	12	21
Pawnee	122	111	20	28
Wichita	242	175	39	49
Comanche	963	341	102	114
Mono	349	362	(B)	—
Paiute	1,638	568	193	104
Northern Paiute	12	21	(B)	—
Chemehuevi	15	27	(B)	—
Ute	1,625	467	85	53
Shoshoni	2,512	435	182	83
Hopi	6,776	1,473	1,274	385
Cahuilla	139	148	(B)	—
Cupeno	11	20	(B)	—
Luiseno	327	203	14	26
Serrano	5	10	(B)	—
Pima	8,190	1,297	1,204	436
Yaqui	425	158	43	40
Tiwa	2,269	604	73	78
Tewa	5,123	864	707	361
Towa	2,192	578	606	225
Zuni	9,432	1,996	1,341	944
Chinook Jargon	644	736	114	119
American Indian	8,888	1,076	1,487	382
Jicarilla	455	155	66	61
Chiricahua	457	313	(B)	—

(continued)

Table 1 Detailed Languages Spoken at Home and Ability to Speak English for the Population 5 Years and Over for the United States: **Release Date: April, 2010** *(continued)*

	Number of Speakers	Margin of Error[1]	Spoke English less than "Very Well"	Margin of Error[1]
Spokane	20	25	8	15
Hungarian	**94,125**	**3,675**	**27,473**	**1,825**
Arabic	**760,505**	**15,845**	**263,704**	**8,573**
Hebrew	**216,615**	**7,104**	**40,291**	**2,704**
African languages	**710,214**	**15,252**	**234,509**	**6,819**
Amharic	146,337	6,535	64,140	3,196
Berber	1,475	550	455	222
Chadic	5,091	1,254	1,533	673
Cushite	90,434	5,808	50,577	3,806
Sudanic	8,966	1,835	5,728	1,391
Nilotic	4,964	1,399	1,577	507
Nilo-hamitic	525	357	223	180
Nubian	129	124	34	56
Saharan	19	30	(B)	—
Khoisan	19	32	(B)	—
Swahili	72,404	4,763	15,897	1,793
Bantu	42,098	3,028	11,507	1,977
Mande	27,657	3,314	11,719	1,747
Fulani	22,469	2,407	10,544	1,569
Gur	849	494	225	242
Kru, Ibo, Yoruba	267,174	9,400	54,983	3,218
Efik	5,497	1,091	613	239
Mbum	340	394	127	149
African	13,767	1,970	4,627	1,076
Other and unspecified languages	**121,569**	**6,870**	**45,975**	**3,512**
Finnish	25,806	1,589	4,782	618
Estonian	5,938	734	1,484	348
Lapp	23	31	5	8
Other Uralic languages	31	51	31	51
Caucasian	6,870	1,607	3,294	897
Basque	1,649	473	527	216
Syriac	61,272	5,133	25,099	2,476
Aztecan	1,327	485	1,035	389
Sonoran	63	62	(B)	—
Misumalpan	127	201	127	201
Mayan languages	6,832	1,277	5,257	1,084
Tarascan	470	395	414	381
Mapuche	214	289	36	60
Oto-Manguen	2,596	947	2,147	878

(continued)

Table 1 Detailed Languages Spoken at Home and Ability to Speak English for the Population 5 Years and Over for the United States: **Release Date: April, 2010** (continued)

	Number of Speakers	Margin of Error[1]	Spoke English less than "Very Well"	Margin of Error[1]
Quechua	935	420	437	241
Aymara	63	76	20	32
Arawakian	1,960	641	614	331
Chibchan	48	58	24	40
Tupi-guarani	456	306	248	163
Uncodable Entries	4,889	621	394	153

[1] Data are based on a sample and are subject to sampling variability. The degree of uncertainty for an estimate arising from sampling variability is represented through the use of a margin of error. The value shown here is the 90 percent margin of error. The margin of error can be interpreted roughly as providing a 90 percent probability that the interval defined by the estimate minus the margin of error and the estimate plus the margin of error (the lower and upper confidence bounds) contains the true value. In addition to sampling variability, the ACS estimates are subject to nonsampling error (for a discussion of nonsampling variability, see Accuracy of the Data). The effect of nonsampling error is not represented in these tables.

[2] N.E.C. stands for not elsewhere classified. These are languages where respondents indicated they spoke either INDIAN or PAKISTAN. For Indian, it cannot be determined if the respondent spoke a native American language or spoke a language from India. For Pakistan, respondents wrote in Pakistan but it cannot be determined which one of the languages spoken in Pakistan is actually being spoken. To distinguish these languages, n.e.c. is used to indicate they are not classified in any other language code.

An '(B)' entry in the estimate column indicates that either no sample observations or too few sample observations were available to compute an

An '(X)' entry in any column indicates that the question does not apply.

An '—' entry in the margin of error column indicates that either no sample observations or too few sample observations were available to compute a standard error and thus the margin of error. A statistical test is not appropriate.

Source: U.S. Census Bureau, 2006–2008 American Community Survey

multiyear data, that list every language reported by at least one person in the sample period.

The tables detail the 303 languages other than English spoken at home. Those languages include:

- 134 Native American categories;
- 19 African language categories;
- 8 Chinese language categories;
- 22 Other Asian language categories;
- 39 Pacific Island language categories;
- 12 Indic language categories.

The tables provide estimates of many languages that have not been published since the 2000 Census, including: Albanian, Amharic, Bengali, Cushite, Kru, Panjabi, Pennsylvania Dutch, Romanian, Serbocroatian, Tamil, Telugu and Ukrainian. A list of the tables can be found here: http://census.gov/population/www/socdemo/language/detailed-lang-tables.xls.

As with all surveys, statistics from sample surveys are subject to sampling and nonsampling error. All comparisons made in the reports have been tested and found to be statistically significant at the 90 percent confidence level, unless otherwise noted. Please consult the data tables for specific margins of error.

The American Community Survey is an ongoing survey of approximately 3 million addresses every year and provides one of the most complete pictures of our population available.

While the 2010 Census will produce a count of the nation's population and basic demographics, the American Community Survey provides statistics on more than 40 topics, such as income, educational attainment, housing, family structure and more. All survey responses are strictly confidential and protected by law.

public-news-alert mailing list
public-news-alert@lists.census.gov
http://lists.census.gov/mailman/listinfo/public-news-alert

Critical Thinking

1. Does the number of languages used in America surprise you?

2. Is having such linguistic capacity and resources an asset for international relations, especially commerce? Should we develop more fluency and literacy in more languages as an educational policy?

3. Is linguistic diversity divisive and does such pluralism challenge the bonds of union required for a country and its political order?

Editor's note—News releases, reports and data tables are available on the Census Bureau's home page. Go to http://census.gov and click on "Releases."

A Profile of Today's Italian Americans

*A Report Based on the Year 2000 Census
Compiled by the Sons of Italy*

Report Highlights

I. Ethnicity

- Over 15.7 million people in the United States identify themselves as Italian Americans. They constitute nearly six percent (6%) of the U.S. population.
- Italian Americans are the nation's fourth largest European ancestry group after the Germans, Irish and English.

German	43,000,000	15%
Irish	30,600,000	11%
English	24,500,000	9%
Italian	15,700,000	6%

- Despite being in the U.S. for more than 120 years, Italian Americans still strongly identify with their Italian roots.

    The number of people who identified themselves as Italian American in the Year 2000 Census increased by 1,000,000 people or seven percent (7%) compared to the 1990 census.
- Italian Americans are the only European group whose population has increased since the 1990 census.

    In fact, the number of Americans claiming German, Irish, English and Polish descent decreased nearly 19 percent collectively–dropping from 128 million in 1990 to 108 million.
- Italian is the fourth European language most spoken in U.S. homes.

II. Demographic Information

Median Age:	34 years old
Marital Status:	married
Family Size:	one child
Median Income:	$61,300/year (in 1999) [National Median Income: $50,000/year]
Education:	High School Graduates: 29% [National Percentage: 28.5%]
	College Graduates: 18.5% [National Percentage: 15.5%]
Advanced Degrees:	Master's Degree: 7% [National Percentage: 6%]
	Professional Degree: 2% [National Percentage: 2%]
	Doctorate Degree: 0.85% [National Percentage: 0.95%]
Occupation:	White Collar workers: 66% [National Percentage: 64%]
	Blue Collar workers: 34% [National Percentage: 36%]

III. Geographic Information

A. The Ten States with the Most Italian Americans

New York	2,700,000
New Jersey	1,500,000
California	1,450,000
Pennsylvania	1,400,000
Florida	1,001,000
Massachusetts	860,000
Illinois	745,000
Ohio	676,000
Connecticut	634,000
Michigan	451,000

B. States with 15% or More Italian Americans or More than One Million Italian Americans

State	# of Italian Americans	% of Population
California	1,450,000	4%
Connecticut	630,000	19%
Florida	1,004,000	6%
New Jersey	1,500,000	18%
New York	2,700,000	14%
Pennsylvania	1,420,000	12%
Rhode Island	200,000	19%

C. The Ten Metro Areas with Most Italian Americans

Metro Area	# Italian Americans	# Total Population
New York	3,400,000	21,200,000
Philadelphia	886,000	6,189,000
Boston	801,000	5,800,000
Chicago	637,000	9,158,000
Los Angeles	568,000	16,373,000
San Francisco	423,000	7,039,000
Washington/ Baltimore	378,000	7,600,000
Pittsburgh	358,000	2,359,000
Detroit	321,000	5,456,000
Cleveland	278,000	2,946,000

D. The Ten Cities with the Most Italian Americans

City	# of Italian Americans	# Total Population
New York	692,800	8,008,300
Philadelphia	140,000	1,517,600
Chicago	101,900	2,896,000
Los Angeles	95,300	3,695,000
Phoenix	58,600	1,321,000
San Diego	55,800	1,223,400
Boston	49,000	589,100
San Jose, CA	43,200	893,900
Pittsburgh, PA	40,000	335,000
San Francisco	39,200	776,800

Demographic Chart
United States Census Analysis
U.S. Italian American Demographics vs. Total Population Demographics*
Figures Rounded to the nearest 100

	Italian American Population	Total U.S. Population
Total Population	15,723,000	281,422,000
Male	49.5% (7,789,000)	48% (137,916,000)
Female	50.5% (7,935,000)	52% (143,506,000)
Population 17 and under	14% (2,240,000)	13% (37,007,000)
Median Age	33.8	35.4
Male	33.1	34.1
Female	34.6	36.6
Marital Status (Population 15 and over)		
Male: Never Married	32% (1,916,000)	30% (32,381,000)
Female: Never Married	27% (1,665,000)	24% (27,532,000)
Male: Now Married	57% (3,375,000)	59% (62,692,000)
Female: Now Married	54% (3,296,000)	55% (62,309,000)
Male: Divorced	8% (468,000)	8.5% (9,255,000)
Female: Divorced	10% (623,000)	11% (12,305,000)
Family		
Number of Families	3,948,000	72,262,000
Average Family size	3.08	3.14
Median Income In 1999 Living Environment	$61,297	$50,046
Urban	88% (13,809,000)	79% (222,358,000)
Rural	12% (1,914,000)	21% (59,064,000)
Place of Birth		
U.S. Native	96% (15,119,000)	89% (250,314,000)
Foreign Born	4% (604,000)	11% (31,108,000)
Foreign Born: % from Europe	76% (459,000)	16% (4,916,000)
Naturalized Citizen	2.5% (409,000)	4.5% (12,543,000)
Not a Citizen	1.2% (195,000)	6.5% (18,565,000)
Education (Population 25 and Over)	9,853,000	182,212,000
High School Graduate	29% (2,893,000)	28.5% (52,169,000)
Bachelor's Degree	18.5% (1,843,000)	15.5% (28,318,000)
Master's Degree	7% (691,000)	6% (10,771,000)
Professional School Degree	2% (229,000)	2% (3,620,000)
Doctorate Degree	0.85% (84,000)	0.95% (1,754,000)
Occupation (Employed 16 years and older)		
Total In Workforce	49% (7,692,000) /(15,700,000)	46% (129,722,000) /(281,422,000)
White Collar Occupations	66% (5,081,000) /(7,692,000)	64% (82,472,000) /(129,722,000)
Blue Collar Occupations (Includes farmers, police officers & fire fighters)	34% (2,611,000) /(7,692,000)	36% (7,205,000) /(129,722,000)

Italian American Population
of the U.S. All 50 States and the District
of Columbia*

State	# of Italian Americans	Of State
Alabama	56,220	1.3%
Alaska	17,944	2.9%
Arizona	**224,795**	**4.4%**
Arkansas	34,674	1.3%
California	**1,450,884**	**4.3%**
Colorado	**201,787**	**4.7%**
Connecticut	**634,364**	**18.6%**
Delaware	**72,677**	**9.3%**
District of Columbia	12,587	2.2%
Florida	**1,003,977**	**6.3%**
Georgia	**163,218**	**2.0%**
Hawaii	22,094	1.8%
Idaho	34,553	2.7%
Illinois	**744,274**	**6.0%**
Indiana	**141,486**	**2.3%**
Iowa	49,449	1.7%
Kansas	50,729	1.9%
Kentucky	62,383	1.5%
Louisiana	**195,561**	**4.4%**
Maine	58,866	4.6%
Maryland	**267,573**	**5.1%**
Massachusetts	**860,079**	**13.5%**
Michigan	**450,952**	**4.5%**
Minnesota	**111,270**	**2.3%**
Mississippi	40,401	1.4%
Missouri	**176,209**	**3.1%**
Montana	28,031	3.1%
Nebraska	42,979	2.5%
Nevada	**132,515**	**6.6%**
New Hampshire	**105,610**	**8.5%**
New Jersey	**1,503,637**	**17.9%**
New Mexico	43,218	2.4%
New York	**2,737,146**	**14.4%**
North Carolina	**181,982**	**2.3%**
North Dakota	5,328	0.8%
Ohio	**675,749**	**6.0%**
Oklahoma	49,970	1.4%
Oregon	**111,462**	**3.3%**
Pennsylvania	**1,418,465**	**11.6%**
Rhode Island	**199,077**	**19.0%**
South Carolina	81,377	2.0%
South Dakota	7,541	1.0%
Tennessee	94,402	1.7%
Texas	**363,354**	**1.7%**
Utah	57,512	2.6%
Vermont	**38,835**	**6.4%**
Virginia	**257,129**	**3.6%**
Washington State	**191,442**	**3.2%**
West Virginia	69,935	3.9%
Wisconsin	**172,567**	**3.2%**
Wyoming	15,286	3.1%

*Listed in alphabetical order. States in bold have percentages of Italian
Americans five percent or above or more than 100,000 Italian Americans.

State-By-State Percentages of Italian Americans*
All States and the District of Columbia

State	# of Italian Americans	% of Population
Rhode Island	199,077	19.0%
Connecticut	634,364	18.6%
New Jersey	1,503,637	17.9%
New York	2,737,146	14.4%
Massachusetts	860,079	13.5%
Pennsylvania	1,418,465	11.6%
Delaware	72,677	9.3%
New Hampshire	105,610	8.5%
Nevada	132,515	6.6%
Vermont	38,835	6.4%
Florida	1,003,977	6.3%
Ohio	675,749	6.0%
Illinois	744,274	6.0%
Maryland	267,573	5.1%
Colorado	201,787	4.7%
Maine	58,866	4.6%
Michigan	450,952	4.5%
Louisiana	195,561	4.4%
Arizona	224,795	4.4%
California	1,450,884	4.3%
West Virginia	69,935	3.9%
Virginia	257,129	3.6%
Oregon	111,462	3.3%
Wisconsin	172,567	3.2%
Washington State	191,442	3.2%
Montana	28,031	3.1%
Wyoming	15,286	3.1%
Missouri	176,209	3.1%
Alaska	17,944	2.9%
Idaho	34,553	2.7%
Utah	57,512	2.6%
Nebraska	42,979	2.5%
New Mexico	43,218	2.4%
North Carolina	181,982	2.3%
Indiana	141,486	2.3%
Minnesota	111,270	2.3%
District of Columbia	12,587	2.2%
Georgia	163,218	2.0%
South Carolina	81,377	2.0%
Kansas	50,729	1.9%
Hawaii	22,094	1.8%
Iowa	49,449	1.7%
Tennessee	94,402	1.7%
Texas	363,354	1.7%
Kentucky	62,383	1.5%

State	# of Italian Americans	% of Population
Oklahoma	49,970	1.4%
Mississippi	40,401	1.4%
Alabama	56,220	1.3%
Arkansas	34,674	1.3%
South Dakota	7,541	1.0%
North Dakota	5,328	0.8%

*Listed in order of Percentage of the Population.

The 50 U.S. Metropolitan Areas with the Most Italian Americans

Rank	Area	Italian Population	Total Population
1	New York—Northern NJ—Long Island	3,394,397	21,199,865
2	Philadelphia—Wilmington, DE—Atlantic City	886,102	6,188,463
3	Boston—Worcester—Lawrence, MA	801,020	5,819,101
4	Chicago—Gary, IN—Kenosha, IL	646,399	9,157,540
5	Los Angeles—Riverside—Orange County, CA	568,153	16,373,645
6	San Francisco—Oakland—San Jose, CA	422,969	7,039,362
7	Washington, DC—Baltimore, MD	377,893	7,608,070
8	Pittsburgh, PA	358,317	2,358,695
9	Detroit—Ann Arbor—Flint, MI	321,443	5,456,428
10	Cleveland—Akron, OH	277,628	2,945,831
11	Miami—Fort Lauderdale, FL	206,119	3,876,380
12	Providence—Fall River—Warwick, RI	200,626	1,188,613
13	Tampa—St. Petersburg—Clearwater, FL	199,457	2,395,997
14	Hartford, CT	191,676	1,183,110
15	Buffalo—Niagara Falls, NY	190,038	1,170,111
16	Rochester, NY	183,815	1,098,201
17	Phoenix—Mesa, AZ	158,959	3,251,876
18	Albany—Schenectady—Troy, NY	148,073	875,583
19	San Diego, CA	133,304	2,813,833
20	Seattle—Tacoma—Bremerton, WA	127,106	3,554,760
21	Denver—Boulder—Greeley, CO	123,553	2,581,506
22	St. Louis, MO	117,754	2,603,607
23	Syracuse, NY	115,057	732,117
24	New Orleans, LA	109,710	1,337,726
25	Atlanta, GA	109,023	4,112,198
26	Scranton—Wilkes-Barre—Hazelton, PA	107,307	624,776
27	West Palm Beach—Boca Raton, FL	106,774	1,131,184
28	Dallas—Fort Worth, TX	106,287	5,221,801
29	Houston—Galveston—Brazoria, TX	105,645	4,669,571
30	Las Vegas, NV	102,708	1,563,282
31	Orlando, FL	99,033	1,644,561
32	Sacramento—Yolo, CA	96,515	1,796,857
33	Youngstown—Warren, OH	86,968	594,746
34	Minneapolis—St. Paul, MN	81,803	2,968,806
35	Columbus, OH	77,307	1,540,157
36	Portland—Salem, OR	76,540	2,265,223
37	Milwaukee—Racine, WI	75,977	1,689,572
38	Cincinnati—Hamilton, OH	75,698	1,979,202
39	Allentown—Bethlehem—Easton, PA	69,671	637,958
40	Norfolk—Virginia Beach—Newport News, VA	62,854	1,569,541
41	Springfield, MA	61,640	591,960
42	Utica—Rome, NY	59,015	299,896
43	Kansas City, MO—KS	57,191	1,776,062
44	Jacksonville, FL	44,953	1,100,491
45	New London—Norwich, CT	44,279	293,566
46	Daytona Beach, FL	42,719	493,175
47	Sarasota—Bradenton, FL	41,407	589,959
48	Raleigh—Durham—Chapel Hill, NC	41,033	1,187,941
49	Charlotte—Gastonia—Rock Hill, NC—SC	40,998	1,499,293
50	Harrisburg—Lebanon—Carlisle, PA	39,258	629,401

The 50 U.S. Cities with the Most Italian Americans*

Rank	Area	Italian Population	Total Population
1	New York city, NY	692,739	8,008,278
2	Philadelphia City, PA	140,139	1,517,550
3	Chicago City, IL	101,903	2,895,964
4	Los Angeles City, CA	95,263	3,694,834
5	Phoenix City, AZ	58,578	1,320,994
6	San Diego City, CA	55,764	1,223,341
7	Boston City, MA	49,017	589,141
8	San Jose City, CA	43,165	893,889
9	Pittsburgh City, PA	39,632	334,563
10	San Francisco City, CA	39,144	776,733
11	Yonkers City, NY	36,907	196,086
12	Columbus city, OH	35,236	711,644
13	Buffalo City, NY	34,379	292,648
14	Las Vegas City, NV	32,124	478,868
15	Houston City, TX	31,899	1,954,848
16	Cranston City, RI	27,359	79,269
17	Toms River, NJ	27,250	86,452
18	Jacksonville city, FL	25,385	735,503
19	Waterbury City, CT	24,476	107,271
20	Providence City, RI	23,960	173,618
21	Virginia Beach City, VA	23,949	425,257
22	Metairie, Louisiana	23,259	145,852
23	Rochester City, NY	22,077	219,766
24	Cleveland City, OH	22,053	478,393
25	Seattle City, WA	21,754	563,375
26	San Antonio City, TX	21,697	1,144,554
27	Syracuse City, NY	20,778	147,326
28	Worcester City, MA	19,950	172,648
29	Stamford City, CT	19,873	117,083
30	Portland City, OR	19,810	529,025
31	Tucson City, AZ	19,636	486,591
32	Warwick City, RI	19,549	85,808
33	Denver City, CO	19,333	554,636
34	Omaha City, NE	18,716	390,112
35	Baltimore City, MD	18,492	651,154
36	Levittown, NY	18,020	53,063
37	Mesa City, AZ	17,724	397,215
38	Charlotte City, NC	17,676	542,131
39	Revere City, MA	17,662	47,283
40	Milwaukee City, WI	17,499	596,956
41	Indianapolis City, IN	17,442	782,414
42	Medford City, MA	17,390	55,765
43	Scottsdale City, AZ	17,283	202,744
44	Tampa City, FL	17,096	303,512
45	St. Petersburg City, FL	16,736	247,793
46	Albuquerque City, NM	16,721	448,627
47	Coral Springs City, FL	16,709	117,482
48	Colorado Springs City, CO	16,692	360,798
49	Sterling Heights City, MI	16,556	124,471
50	Norwalk City, CT	16,397	82,951

*Based on Year 2000 U.S. Census.

The Order Sons of Italy in America

- The **Order Sons of Italy in America (OSIA)** is the largest and oldest national organization of Italian American men and women in the United States.

- Founded in 1905, OSIA now has 600,000 members and supporters and a network of more than 700 chapters coast to coast.

- Originally established as a mutual aid society for the early Italian immigrants, today OSIA is the leading service and advocacy Italian American organization.

- OSIA promotes the study of Italian language and culture in American schools and universities; conducts research on Italian American traditions, culture, history and heritage; and encourages closer cultural relations between Italy and the United States.

- The **Sons of Italy Foundation (SIF)** is a private, grant-making philanthropic institution established by OSIA in 1959. To date, the **SIF has given more than $83 million** to scholarships, medical research, cultural preservation, disaster relief and other projects.

- The **Commission for Social Justice (CSJ)** is the anti-defamation arm of OSIA. The CSJ is committed to fighting racism, prejudice, and the stereotyping of all races, religions and cultures.

- OSIA's national headquarters is in Washington, D.C. near Capitol Hill.

Bibliography

For extensive bibliographies on Italian American history, literature and culture, visit OSIA's Web site at www.osia .org see "Italian American Culture and History—Research and Reports" or the American Italian Historical Association at www.mobilito.com/aiha.

Italians In America: A Celebration **Gay Talese, editor.**

An illustrated history of Italian Americans that begins with the 15th century explorers, and traces the Italians in America from the American Revolution to the present day.

Available through the ORDER SONS OF ITALY at a discount. For details, call: 202/547-2900 or see www.osia.org at "Market Place"

Blood of My Blood **by Richard Gambino. New York: Anchor Books, 1975.**

Landmark study on the Italian America experience.

The Children of Columbus **by Erik Amfitheatrof. Boston: Little Brown, 1973.**

Perhaps the most intelligently written study on what Italian immigrants found in "la Merica."

The Italian American Experience: An Encyclopedia **LaGumina, Cavaioli, Primeggia and Varacalli, eds. New York: Garland Press, 1999.**

Excellent reference book on Italian American history, literature, culture and issues.

The Italian American Reader **Bill Tonelli, editor; William Morrow & Co.**

The first hardcover, mainstream press anthology of Italian American writing, this collection of 68 fiction and non-fiction pieces presents three generations of Italian American writers.

WOP! A Documentary History of Anti-Italian Discrimination **by Salvatore J. LaGumina. Toronto: Guernica, 1999.**

Documents the prejudice and discrimination the early Italian immigrants faced through citing newspaper articles, speeches and political cartoons of the late 19th and early 20th centuries.

Critical Thinking

1. Is the Italian language generally offered in high schools? In universities?

2. Italian Americans constitute nearly ____% of the U.S. population. Has this varied much over the last 100 years?

3. Does the clustering of Italian Americans in settlements that are considerably higher than their percentage of the country's population a troubling or a beneficial social fact? Why?

Polonia in Numbers

How Many of Us Are out There?

Official census numbers show almost a million increase in the population of Poles in the United States in only 5 years. That's a 9% increase. Poles make up, on estimate, 3.1% of the population of the United States.

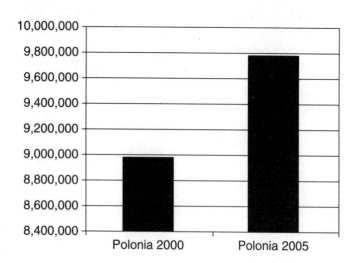

Most Polish Metropolitan Areas in 2000

Chicago	831,774
Detroit	479,659
Philadelphia	288,440
New York	268,228
Buffalo—Niagara Falls, NY	209,303
Pittsburgh, PA	209,032
Milwaukee—Waukesha, WI	190,076
Cleveland-Lorain-Elyria, OH	186,571
Minneapolis-St. Paul, MN-WI	148,876
Los Angeles	122,680
Boston	120,245
Newark	120,193
Bergen-Passaic, NJ	95,403
St. Louis, MO	67,084
Houston	59,254
Omaha, NE	32,132
Jersey City, NJ	27,673

Top 13 Polish States

78% of all Poles live in the 13 states with the highest Polish populations.

State	2000 Census	2005 ACS	Rate of Change
New York	986,106	997,987	+1%
Illinois	932,996	995,445	+7%
Michigan	854,844	919,007	+8%
Pennsylvania	824,146	885,218	+7%
New Jersey	576,473	572,918	−1%
Wisconsin	497,726	533,787	+7%
California	491,325	530,733	+8%
Florida	**429,691**	**523,162**	**+22%**
Ohio	433,016	474,569	+10%
Massachusetts	323,210	325,663	+1%
Connecticut	284,272	303,047	+7%
Minnesota	240,405	265,706	+11%
Texas	228,309	261,511	+15%

As shown by the above table, only one of the 13 states noticed a decline in the Polish population, and that decrease was quite insignificant—only one percent. All the other states noticed an increase in the population of the Poles, with ten states getting 7% and above.

We Are Educated

National statistics show that 80% of the total population (over 25 years old) of the United States are High School graduates. 88% of Poles are High School graduates. National statistics also show that 24% of the total population of America holds a Bachelor's degree or higher. 33% of Poles hold Bachelor's degree or higher.

We Are Houseowners

National statistics demonstrate that 73% of Poles are house-owners, while 27% rent their housing unit. Only 66% of all the people in America own their house, and 34% rents. Therefore, 7% more Poles own their house than an average American.

We Are Doing Quite Well

Only 6% of Poles live below the poverty level, that is a half of the national average. Median income of a Polish family exceeds the average one by $11,589 (Polish—$61,635 compared to the Average—$50,046). Median value of a Polish housing unit is $137,300, which exceeds the national average by $17,700.

Poles in Michigan

Michigan, too, experienced a significant increase in the Polish population. The number of Poles rose from 854,815 to 919,007. That's an 8% jump. Poles make up, on estimate, 7% of the Michigan population.

Michigan Poles are also more educated than an average Michigander. 87% of Poles over 25 years old are High School graduates and 24% hold a Bachelor's degree or higher. The state average is, respectively, 83% and 22%.

Michigan Polish population also is more likely to own a house than an average person. 81% of Poles are house own-ers, while 19% rent. On average, only 74% of the people own their home.

Only 6% of the Poles are currently below the poverty level. That's 4% less than a state average. Median income of Polish families also exceeds the average one by $7,565 (Polish—$61,022, Average—$53,457).

Also, a median value of the Polish housing unit exceeds the average one by $11,200.

Tri-County Polish Population

In terms of the Tri-County Poles, we see similar trends as state and nationwide. In Wayne County more Poles are house owners than the average (82% to 67%). Also, more people are High School graduates and hold higher educa-tion diplomas (83% and 18% to, respectively, 77% and 17%). Only 5% of the Poles live below the poverty level, compared to the average of 16%.

Also, Polish median family income is much greater than average—$61,500 compared to $48,805. The average value of the Polish home is also much greater than average and it amounts to $118,100 compared to $99,400.

In Macomb County more Poles are house owners than the average (84% to 79%). Also, more people are High School graduates (86% as compared to 83%). The number of

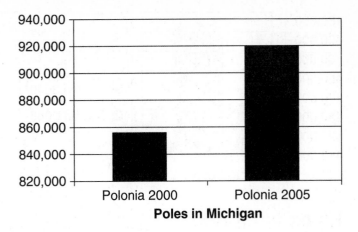

Poles in Michigan

highly educated people is the same—17%. Only 4% of the Poles live below the poverty level, compared to the average of 6%.

Polish median family income is greater than average—$65,341 compared to $62,816. The average value of the Polish home is slightly smaller than average though—$137,800 compared to $139,200.

In Oakland County more Poles are house owners than the average (81% to 75%). Also, more people are High School graduates and hold higher education diplomas (93% and 41% to, respectively, 89% and 38%).

Only 4% of the Poles live below the poverty level, compared to the average of 5%. Also, Polish median family income is much greater than average—$83,401 compared to $75,540.

The average value of the Polish home is also much greater than average—$189,300 compared to $181,200.

Poles in Ohio

The number of people of Polish ancestry in Ohio increased from 433,016 in the year 2000 to 474,569 in 2005. That's a 10% increase. Poles make up, on estimate, 4% of the Ohio population.

The Ohio Poles exhibit the same patterns as the rest of the Polonia nationwide. 76% of the Poles are house owners, compared to 69% of the statistical Ohioan. Poles are also more educated, with 89% high school graduation rate and 27% completing higher education, compared to 83% average high school graduation rate and 21% of the population completing an institution of higher learning (the numbers apply to people 25 years old and above). In terms of poverty, only 6% of Poles in Ohio live below the poverty level, which is 4% lower than the state average of 10%.

Also, Polish median family income exceeds the aver-age one by almost $8,000 (compare $58,301 to $50,037). The average value of the Polish home also exceeds the average one by over $10,000 (compare $115,900 to $103,700).

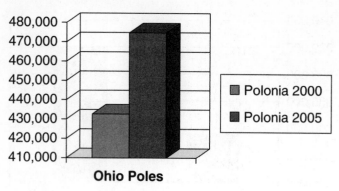

Ohio Poles

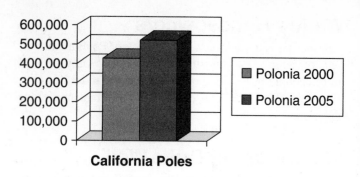

California Poles

Poles in Florida

The Polish population of Florida increased from 429,691 in 2000 to 523,162 in 2005. That's almost 100,000 more Polish people (22%) in only a period of 5 years. Poles make up, on estimate, 3% of the Florida population.

The Florida Poles exhibit the same characteristics as Poles nationwide. More Poles are house owners than average Florida residents (78% compared to 70%). Poles are also better educated, with 88% holding High School diplomas, and 28% holding Bachelor's degree or higher.

The state average is 80% high school graduates and 22% Bachelor degree holders. In terms of median family income, the Florida Poles beat the statistical Floridian by 17%! (Compare $53,270 to $45,625). Considering poverty, only 6% of the Polish-Americans in Florida live below the poverty level, compared to 12% state statistic. Also, the average value of a Polish house exceeds the average value of a housing unit by $13,600 (compare $119,100 to $105,500).

Poles in California

The Poles make up roughly 1.4% of the total California population. Their number increased from 491,325 in 2000 to 530,733 in 2005. That is an 8% increase. The Polish population of California displays the same patterns as the Polonia throughout the country.

Poles are more likely to be house owners than the average Californian (compare 64% to 60%). Poles are also much more educated—94% of Poles finished High School and 44% holds a Bachelor's degree or higher. Only 76% of the California population are High School graduates, and only 27% hold a Bachelor's degree or higher (the numbers apply to the population 25 years old and above).

In terms of poverty, only 6% of Poles live below the poverty level, compared to 14% of the average Californians! Poles also make much more money—average family income for Poles is $75,502, while the statistical California family earns $53,025. The median value of the Polish home is also significantly higher than the average Californian—compare $270,900 to $211,500.

Poles in Georgia

The Poles of Georgia make up 1% of their state's population. In Georgia, as elsewhere, there has been a growth of the Polish population between the 2000 Census and the 2005 American Community Survey. The population rose from 82,765 to 103,061. That's a 25% increase!

It is not surprising that the Polish population of Georgia exhibits the same trends as the Poles in California, Michigan, and other states. 71% of the Poles own their house, compared to 67% of the average Georgians. Poles are also much better educated, with 95% holding High School diplomas and 46% holding Bachelor's degrees or higher. In the total Georgia population, only 76% of the people graduated from High School and only 24% hold a Bachelor's degree or higher (the total population refers to people 25 years of age and older). Also, only 5% of the Poles live below the poverty level, compared to 13% of the total population. Georgia Poles also make more money than the average Georgians—compare $73,135 median Polish family income to the average $49,280. The median value of the Polish home ($158,400) also exceeds that of the average Georgia home ($111,200).

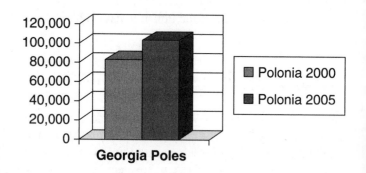

Georgia Poles

Poles in Missouri

The Polish population in Missouri increased by 20% between the 2000 U.S. Census and the 2005 American Community Survey. Poles make up 2% of the population of the state.

Just like the Poles in other corners of the United States, Missouri Polish population is "above the average." 74%

Characteristics	Polish Population of St. Louis	Total Population of St. Louis
Percentage of the population owning their home	57	47
Percentage of the population 25 years old and over who graduated from High School	83	71
Percentage of the population 25 years old and over who hold a Bachelor's degree or higher	36	19
Percentage of the population living below the poverty level	12	24
Median family income	$49,551	$32,585
Median value of the home	$78,200	$63,900

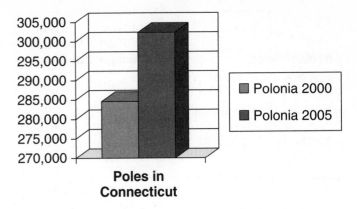

Poles in Connecticut

of the Poles are house owners, compared to 70% of the total population. In terms of education, 90% of the Poles 25 years old and above graduated from High School and 33% hold a Bachelor's degree or higher (compared to 81% High School and 22% Bachelor's degree in the total population).

Poles also tend not to live below the poverty level, since only 6% of the Polish population experiences such hardships, compared to 11% of the total population. In material terms, Poles also exhibit "above the average" trends. Median family income of the Polish family exceeds the average one by over $10,000 (Polish—$57,515; Missouri Average—$46,044). Also, the median value of the Polish home exceeds the average one by over $22,000 ($112,000 vs. $89,900).

The Independent City of St. Louis shows the same patterns. Poles make up 2% of the population of the city, but the increase of the population between 2000 and 2005 was minimal—the Polish population rose by 5 people (the total population of the city, on the contrary, decreased by 15,000 people).

Poles in Connecticut

Poles make up 9% of the population of the state of Connecticut. The Polish population increased by 7% in five years, growing from the number of 284,272 in year 2000 to 303,047 in year 2005.

Not surprisingly, the Poles of Connecticut are not worse from their friends in other states. 75% of the Polish population are house owners, compared to 67% state average. 87% of Poles above the age of 25 are High School graduates

and 31% hold a Bachelor's degree or higher. In the general population 25 years old and over, 84% are High School graduates and 31% hold a Bachelor's degree. The percentage of Poles in poverty is half of the state average (4% compared to 8%). Polish median family income exceeds the average state one by $2,000 (compare Polish $68,553 to State—$65,521). However, the average median value of the Polish home is lower than the state average by almost $10,000 (compare Polish—$156,700 to State—166,900).

Poles in Illinois

Poles make up 8% of the population of Illinois. The Polish population increased from 932,996 to 995,445 in just five years. That's a 7% increase.

As a historic place of Polish significance, the Illinois Polonia is not disappointing. The average house ownership in the state—67% is exceeded by Poles by 9% (76% of Poles are house owners). Illinois Poles are also better educated, with 86% holding a High School diploma (compared to 81% state average) and 28% holding a Bachelor's degree or higher (with 26% state average). Only 4% of Poles live below the poverty level, compared to 10% state average.

Economically speaking, Poles also exceed the average by all means. Median family income of a Polish family is $66,001 compared to $55,545 state average. Average median value of a Polish home also exceeded the state average (compare $165,000 to $130,800).

The Windy City has always been associated with the Poles. And the Polish population of the city follows the same patters than Poles everywhere else in the United States.

The population of Polonia decreased in size over the last five years (from 210,421 to 184,621), just like the entire population of the city did. However, the Poles still make up almost 7% of the city's population.

Increase of the population between 2000 and 2005 was minimal—the Polish population rose by 5 people (the total population of the city, on the contrary, decreased by 15,000 people).

Characteristics	Polish Population of Chicago	Total Population of Chicago
Percentage of the population owning their home	60	43
Percentage of the population 25 years old and over who graduated from High School	77	72
Percentage of the population 25 years old and over who hold a Bachelor's degree or higher	26	25
Percentage of the population living below the poverty level	8	19
Median family income	$54,154	$42,724
Median value of the home	$152,700	$132,400

Source: Census 2000 and 2005 American Community Survey.

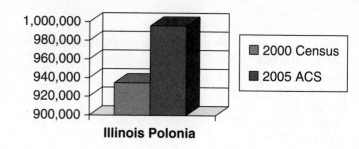

Illinois Polonia

Critical Thinking

1. What are the sources and causes of the increase in Polish Americans in America?

2. Which socioeconomic indicator in this article reveal the most about this ethnic group? How so?

3. Can Polish Americans influence electoral outcomes in the states profiled in this article?

From *The American Institute of Polish Culture,* 2006/2007. Copyright © 2007 by Piast Institute. Reprinted by permission.

Irish-American Heritage Month (March) and Saint Patrick's Day (March 17): 2010

O riginally a religious holiday to honor St. Patrick, who introduced Christianity to Ireland in the fifth century, St. Patrick's Day has evolved into a celebration for all things Irish. The world's first St. Patrick's Day parade occurred on March 17, 1762, in New York City, featuring Irish soldiers serving in the English military. This parade became an annual event, with President Truman attending in 1948. Congress proclaimed March as Irish-American Heritage Month in 1995, and the President issues a proclamation each year.

Population Distribution

36.3 million
Number of U.S. residents who claimed Irish ancestry in 2008. This number was more than eight times the population of Ireland itself (4.4 million). Irish was the nation's second most frequently reported ancestry, trailing only German.[1]

135,000
Number of Irish-born U.S. residents in 2008. Those from Ireland are much older (a median of 56 years old) and have a higher median household income ($70,591) than U.S. residents as a whole (37 years and $52,029, respectively).[2]

24%
Percent of Massachusetts residents who were of Irish ancestry in 2008. This compares with a rate of 12 percent for the nation as a whole.[3]

Irish-Americans Today
32%
Percentage of people of Irish ancestry, 25 or older, who had a bachelor's degree or more education. In addition, 92 percent of Irish-Americans in this age group had at least a high school diploma. For the nation as a whole, the corresponding rates were 28 percent and 85 percent.[4]

$59,290
Median income for households headed by an Irish-American, higher than the $52,029 for all households. In addition, 9 percent of people of Irish ancestry were in poverty, lower than the rate of 13 percent for all Americans.[5]

39%
Percentage of employed civilian Irish-Americans 16 or older who worked in management, professional and related occupations. Additionally, 27 percent worked in sales and office occupations; 15 percent in service occupations; 10 percent in production, transportation and material moving occupations; and 8 percent in construction, extraction, maintenance and repair occupations.[6]

71%
Percentage of householders of Irish ancestry who owned the home in which they live, with the remainder renting. For the nation as a whole, the homeownership rate was 67 percent.[7]

Places to Spend the Day
4
Number of places in the United States named Shamrock, the floral emblem of Ireland. Mount Gay-Shamrock, W.Va., and Shamrock, Texas, were the most populous, with 2,623 and 1,807 residents, respectively. Shamrock Lakes, Ind., had 153 residents and Shamrock, Okla., 123. (Statistic for Mount Gay-Shamrock is from Census 2000; the other statistics are 2008 estimates.)[8]

9
Number of places in the United States that share the name of Ireland's capital, Dublin. Since Census 2000, Dublin, Calif., has surpassed Dublin, Ohio, as the most populous of these places (44,297 compared with 38,536, respectively, as of July 1, 2008).

If you're still not into the spirit of St. Paddy's Day, then you might consider paying a visit to Emerald Isle, N.C., with 3,641 residents. Other appropriate places in which to spend the day: the township of Irishtown, Ill., several places or townships named "Clover" (in South Carolina, Illinois, Minnesota and Pennsylvania) and the township of Cloverleaf, Minn.[9]

The Celebration
40.7 billion and 2.5 billion
U.S. beef and cabbage production, respectively, in pounds, in 2008. Corned beef and cabbage is a traditional St. Patrick's Day dish. The corned beef that celebrants dine on may very well have originated in Texas, which produced 6.5 billion pounds

worth of beef. The largest producers of cabbage are New York, which produced 584 million pounds and California, which produced 528 million pounds.[10]

$35 million

Value of potted florist chrysanthemum sales at wholesale in 2008 for operations with $100,000 or more sales. Lime green chrysanthemums are often requested for St. Patrick's Day celebrations.[11]

Following is a list of observances typically covered by the Census Bureau's Facts for Features series:

    Black African-American History Month (February)
    Super Bowl
    Valentine's Day (Feb. 14)
    Women's History Month (March)
    Irish-American Heritage Month (March)/
      St. Patrick's Day (March 17)
    American Indian/Alaska Native Heritage Month (November)
    Asian/Pacific American Heritage Month (May)
    Older Americans Month (May)
    Cinco de Mayo (May 5)
    Thanksgiving Day
    Mother's Day
    Labor Day
    Grandparents Day
    Hispanic Heritage Month (Sept. 15–Oct. 15)
    Unmarried and Single Americans Week (Sept. 19–25)
    Halloween (Oct. 31)
    Veterans Day (Nov. 11)
    The Holiday Season (December)
    Hurricane Season Begins (June 1)
    Father's Day
    The Fourth of July (July 4)
    Anniversary of Americans with Disabilities Act (July 26)
    Back to School (August)

Notes

1. Sources: 2008 American Community Survey www.census.gov/acs/www/Products/ and Ireland Central Statistics Office www

.cso.ie/releasespublications/documents/population/current/popmig.pdf

2. Source: 2008 American Community Survey www.census.gov/acs/www/Products/

3. Source: 2008 American Community Survey www.census.gov/acs/www/Products/

4. Source: 2008 American Community Survey www.census.gov/acs/www/Products/

5. Source: 2008 American Community Survey www.census.gov/acs/www/Products/

6. Source: 2008 American Community Survey www.census.gov/acs/www/Products/

7. Source: 2008 American Community Survey www.census.gov/acs/www/Products/

8. Sources: American FactFinder and population estimates www.census.gov/popest/cities/SUB-EST2008-4.html

9. Sources: American FactFinder and population estimates www.census.gov/popest/cities/SUB-EST2008-4.html.

10. Source: USDA National Agricultural Statistics Service http://usda.mannlib.cornell.edu/MannUsda/viewDocumentInfo.do?documentID=1101 and http://usda.mannlib.cornell.edu/MannUsda/viewDocumentInfo.do?documentID=1183

11. Source: USDA National Agricultural Statistics Service http://usda.mannlib.cornell.edu/MannUsda/viewDocumentInfo.do?documentID=1072

Critical Thinking

1. What do these data tell us about Irish Americans?
2. Which indicators are surprising? Why?
3. How is St. Patrick's Day celebrated in your area or region?

Editor's note—The preceding data were collected from a variety of sources and may be subject to sampling variability and other sources of error. Facts for Features are customarily released about two months before an observance in order to accommodate magazine production timelines. Questions or comments should be directed to the Census Bureau's Public Information Office: telephone: 301-763-3030; fax: 301-763-3762; or e-mail: pio@census.gov.

From U.S. Census Bureau, February 22, 2010.

Still Unmelted after All These Years[1]

JOHN DAVID KROMKOWSKI

Are Polish Americans or Italian Americans or African Americans uniformly distributed through the United States? No; in fact, America is stunningly "unmelted". Just look. MAPS 1-4 Distribution by State of Polish, Italian, Irish, and "American".

A bowl of raw meat and uncooked potatoes, celery, carrots and onions is not per se appetizing. But even in a well simmered and tasty soup or stew, you can tell by looking that there are carrots, potatoes, celery, onions and meat. So let's not despair. Let's investigate.

The Ancestry Question on the US Census has produced a stunning array of information about how Americans self-describe themselves. The self-describing aspect of the US Census, especially The Ancestry Question is an highly important feature of data collection in a pluralistic democracy. Unlike the Race Question on the US Census which was constitutionally and historically imposed and rooted in pseudo-scientific and political assumptions of exclusion, the Ancestry Question emerged from a more current understanding[2] of ethnicity and its organic character and growth through the self-determined iterations rooted in the person, family, household and neighborhoods that constitute the American experience of immigration, urbanization and the attendant cultural pluralism of democratization and freedom fostered by a wide range of forces that accompanied American political development especially for the past seven decades. These social economic, political, and personal dynamics make the demography of ethnicity in America seem messy. Indeed, the ostensible messiness of immigration, the articulation of ancestry and identity rooted in ethnicity may well explain the slow evolutionary process and the significant impediments to collection of demographic information. Uniform data would be achieved by replacing the variety of Race and Ethnic Origin Questions associated with Hispanic, Asian, Indigenous Peoples with a single Ancestry question and the tabulation of the multiple responses that are clearly evident in America. Nonetheless, now that Ancestry data has been collected for the last three Censuses and the computer driven computational revolution is firmly in place, demographic analysis can employ standard protocols and verifiable methods that enable a fresh look at the data and thus establish connections, patterns and places and further discussion, interpretations and a scientific understanding of American pluralism.

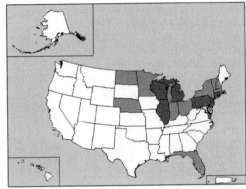

Legend

Data Classes
Percent
- ☐ 0.0–2.5
- ▨ 2.7–5.2
- ■ 6.7–9.3

TM-PCT037. Percent of Persons of Polish Ancestry: 2000.
Universe: Total population.
Data Set: Census 2000 Summary File 3 (SF 3)—Sample Data
United States by State.

Source: U.S. Census Bureau, Census 2000 Summary File 3, Matrices P1, and PCT18.

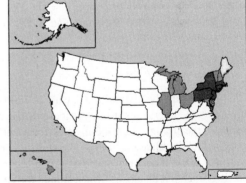

Legend

Data Classes
Percent
- ☐ 0.2–3.9
- ▨ 4.3–9.3
- ■ 11.6–19.0

TM-PCT034. Percent of Persons of Italian Ancestry: 2000.
Universe: Total population.
Data Set: Census 2000 Summary File 3 (SF 3)—Sample Data
United States by State.

Source: U.S. Census Bureau, Census 2000 Summary File 3, Matrices P1, and PCT18.

This article investigates one such method: State Similarity Scores. A Similarity Score investigates the "distance" between States. Consider three cities: Baltimore, MD; Washington, DC and Chicago, IL. Baltimore is about a 40 mile drive from Washington. The driving distance between Washington and

Legend

Data Classes
Percent
- ☐ 0.1–7.9
- ▨ 9.3–13.5
- ▰ 14.8–22.5

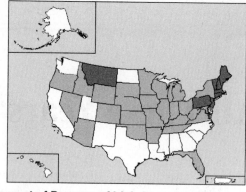

TM-PCT033. Percent of Persons of Irish Ancestry: 2000.
Universe: Total population.
Data Set: Census 2000 Summary File 3(SF 3)—Sample Data
United States by State.

Source: U.S. Census Bureau, Census 2000 Summary File 3, Matrices P1, and PCT18.

Legend

Data Classes
Percent
- ☐ 1.4–6.8
- ▨ 7.5–12.0
- ▰ 13.5–20.9

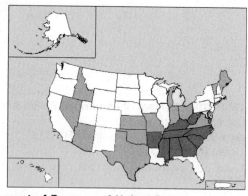

TM-PCT047. Percent of Persons of United States or American Ancestry: 2000.
Universe: Total population.
Date Set: Census 2000 Summary File 3 (SF 3)—Sample Data
United States by State.

Source: U.S. Census Bureau, Census 2000 Summary File 3,
Matrices P1, and PCT18.

Chicago is roughly 710 miles. Chicago is 720 miles from Baltimore on the interstates. Knowing these distances, we can conceive of the triangle that these cities form and how they are geographically related.

In the two dimensional space of a map, a computer can now easily crunch out distances from a simple formula derived from Phythagoras.

$$\text{Distance}^2 = a^2 + b^2 \text{ or}$$
$$\text{Distance} = \sqrt{(a^2 + b^2)}$$

For example, using latitude and longitude to get the distance between Chicago and Baltimore, we find the difference between Chicago's latitude and Baltimore's latitude and the difference between Chicago's longitude and Baltimore's longitude.

$$a = \text{Lat}_{\text{Chicago}} - \text{Lat}_{\text{Baltimore}} \text{ and } b = \text{Long}_{\text{Chicago}} - \text{Long}_{\text{Baltimore}}$$

So, $\text{Distance} = \sqrt{\left(\text{Lat}_{\text{Chicago}} - \text{Lat}_{\text{Baltimore}}\right)^2 + \left(\text{Long}_{\text{Chicago}} - \text{Long}_{\text{Baltimore}}\right)^2}$

In three dimensions, we'd add c^2, to handle perhaps altitude for Google Earth. The theorem isn't limited to our spatial definition of distance. It can apply to any orthogonal dimensions: space, time, movie tastes, colors, temperatures, and even ancestry responses. There is no limit to the number of variables. The focus, however, of this research is race, ethnicity and ancestry data form the US Census 2000. Appropriately, this type of investigation is also known as Nearest Neighbor Analysis. To find out how closely related any two states in terms of ethnicity, our equation would look like this:

$$\text{Distance} = \sqrt{\left(\text{Ancestry1}_{\text{State 1}} - \text{Ancestry1}_{\text{State 2}}\right)^2 + \left(\text{Ancestry2}_{\text{State 1}} - \text{Ancestry2}_{\text{State 2}}\right)^2 + \cdots + \left(\text{Ancestry N}_{\text{State 1}} - \text{Ancestry N}_{\text{State 2}}\right)^2}$$

For this paper I used 56 of the largest ethnicities[3] as orthogonal dimensions: Asian Indian, Asian Multiple Response, American Indian, "American", Arab, Austrian, Black or African American, Belgian, British, Canadian, Chinese, Cuban, Czech, Czechoslovakian, Danish, Dutch, English, Finnish, French excluding Basque, Filipino, French Canadian, German, Greek, Guamanian and/or Chamorrian, Jamaican, Japanese, Korean, Hawaiian, Hispanic or Latino Other, Hungarian, Irish, Lithuanian, Mexican, Native Not Specified, Norwegian, "Others", Other Asian, Other Pacific Islander, Puerto Rican, Polish, Portuguese, Russian, Samoan, Scandinavian, "Scotch Irish", Scottish, Slovak, Slovene, "Some Other Race", Sub Saharan African, Swedish, Ukrainian, Vietnamese, Welsh, and West Indian.[4]

For any two states, we can calculate a measure of similarity. A measure of 0, would mean that the two states are identical, i.e. they have exactly the same percentage of Polish American, Italian Americans, Irish Americans, African Americans, etc. The largest "distance" between two states was between DC and North Dakota at 91.429. The closest "distance" between two states was between Tennessee and Arkansas 3.720. Table 1 shows each state's "nearest cultural neighbors" and the "distance" metric.

If we look at only the closest connection for each of state, some distinct networks or groupings emerge. The largest of these clusters happens to correspond roughly to "The South".

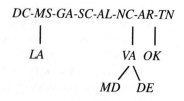

Table 1 Nearest Neighbors along 56 dimensions of Ethnicity/Ancest

First Closest			Second Closest		Third Closest	
AL	SC	5.947	GA	7.213	NC	7.639
AK	WA	12.354	OK	12.893	CO	15.157
AZ	NV	9.405	TX	16.69	CO	17.233
AR	TN	3.720	NC	7.809	VA	8.382
CA	TX	10.344	AZ	19.1	NM	21.128
CO	WA	9.759	OR	9.958	KS	12.213
CT	MA	11.011	RI	14.181	NJ	14.499
DC	MS	33.68	LA	37.691	GA	40.758
DE	VA	10.625	MI	12.782	NJ	12.936
FL	NY	10.115	VA	10.430	NJ	11.253
GA	SC	4.179	AL	7.213	MS	9.648
HI	CA	47.499	NM	49.38	TX	51.121
ID	OR	7.619	WY	9.058	WA	10.961
IL	NJ	13.474	MI	13.955	DE	14.214
IN	MO	5.327	OH	6.3	KS	7.847
IA	NE	8.916	MT	13.289	WI	13.514
KS	IN	7.847	MO	8.337	OR	8.670
KY	WV	6.661	TN	13.896	IN	14.001
LA	MS	12.163	SC	13.077	GA	13.124
ME	VT	4.781	NH	7.475	RI	19.544
MD	VA	12.451	SC	12.606	GA	13.117
MA	RI	7.942	CT	11.011	NH	16.286
MI	OH	10.340	MO	10.977	PA	11.927
MN	SD	11.895	WI	13.981	IA	15.716
MS	GA	9.648	SC	9.947	LA	12.163
MO	OH	4.801	IN	5.327	KS	8.337
MT	WY	9.427	IA	13.289	OR	14.668
NE	IA	8.916	WI	11.648	WY	15.914
NV	AZ	9.405	CO	13.675	IL	14.786
NH	VT	4.607	ME	7.475	MA	16.286
NJ	NY	6.026	FL	11.253	DE	12.936
NM	CA	21.128	TX	23.53	AZ	27.923
NY	NJ	6.026	FL	10.115	DE	14.651
NC	VA	5.9	AL	7.639	AR	7.809
ND	SD	17.030	MN	17.407	WI	24.532
OH	MO	4.801	IN	6.3	PA	6.692
OK	AR	12.557	AK	12.893	FL	14.080
OR	WA	4.784	ID	7.619	KS	8.670
PA	OH	6.692	MO	10.27	IN	10.718
RI	MA	7.942	CT	14.181	NH	16.638
SC	GA	4.179	AL	5.947	NC	9.094
SD	MN	11.895	WI	14.146	IA	14.527
TN	AR	3.720	NC	9.043	VA	9.934
TX	CA	10.344	AZ	16.69	NV	18.018
UT	ID	14.655	OR	20.362	WA	21.495
VT	NH	4.607	ME	4.781	MA	17.455
VA	NC	5.9	AR	8.382	TN	9.934
WA	OR	4.784	CO	9.759	KS	10.921
WV	KY	6.661	IN	14.056	MO	17.644
WI	NE	11.648	IA	13.514	MN	13.981
WY	OR	8.960	ID	9.058	MT	9.427

Other networks also emerged, when considering only the first closest connection:

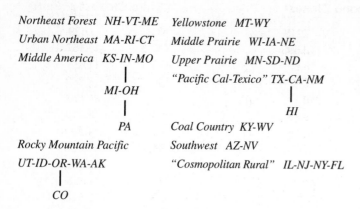

Northeast Forest NH-VT-ME	*Yellowstone* MT-WY
Urban Northeast MA-RI-CT	*Middle Prairie* WI-IA-NE
Middle America KS-IN-MO	*Upper Prairie* MN-SD-ND
MI-OH	*"Pacific Cal-Texico"* TX-CA-NM
PA	HI
	Coal Country KY-WV
Rocky Mountain Pacific	*Southwest* AZ-NV
UT-ID-OR-WA-AK	*"Cosmopolitan Rural"* IL-NJ-NY-FL
CO	

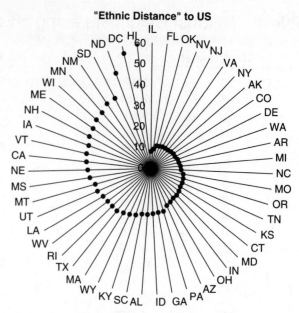

Figure 1 "Ethnic Distance" to US.

We can also connect all of the States with the minimum possible distance among states, i.e a "minimum spanning tree", as follows:

Finally, we can also measure the distance of each State to the United States as a whole. Illinois and Florida are very similar to the entire US, while North Dakota, DC and Hawaii are furthest in "distance" from the US in our 56 dimensional ethnic space. See Figure 1.

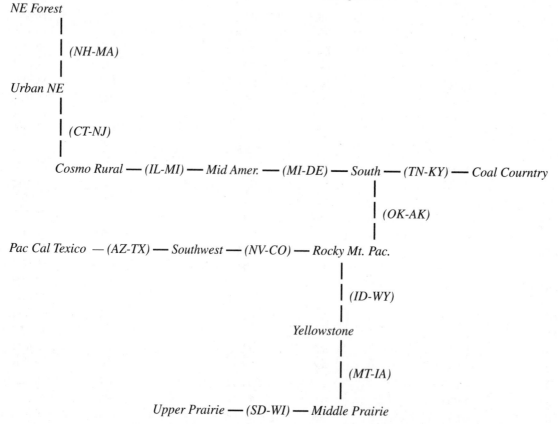

Notes

1. With acknowledgments to Michael Novak, The Rise of the Unmeltable Ethnics (1972) and Paul Simon's 1975 album and song.

2. Although, in some ways the Ancestry Question is arguably back to the future. See *Saint Francis College v. al-Khazraji*, 481 U.S. 604 (1987). A unanimous Court held that that persons of Arabian ancestry were protected from racial discrimination under Section 1981. The history of the definitions of "race", presented by the Court, is well worth reading because it shows how prior to the 20th century "race" and "ancestry" were synonymous concepts. After outlining the history and usage of the term "race", Justice White and the Court rejected the claim that "a distinctive physiognomy" is essential to qualify for 1981 protection and concluded: "We have little trouble in concluding that Congress intended to protect from discrimination identifiable classes of persons who are subjected to intentional discrimination solely because of their **ancestry or ethnic characteristics.**" William J. Brennan, Jr., in a separate concurrence, added that "Pernicious distinctions among individuals based solely on their **ancestry** are antithetical to the doctrine of equality upon which this nation is founded." (Emphasis supplied).

3. Some of these categories also come from the Race and Hispanic origin questions of the Census. Even though the Ancestry Question captures ethnic responses like Japanese, Korean, Cuban, Mexican and Black or African American, the Census Bureau sanitizes its Ancestry data, so that these responses are only readily available from the Race and Hispanic origin questions.

4. Older analysis of ethnic disimilarity differs from this method because it grouped ancestry responses into larger but far fewer categories such as "Old Stock", "Eastern and Southern European", "Asian", etc. Calculating similarity in 56 dimensional space was simply not possibly with hand calculations employed by previous researchers.

Critical Thinking

1. Were you surprised by the lack of uniform distribution of ethnic groups in America?

2. What is State Similarity Score?

3. Write a narrative that explains the "minimum spanning tree" or the other clustering of closest connections discerned from the Nearest Neighbor Analysis?

UNIT 4

Indigenous Ethnic Groups

Unit Selections

22.   **Who Is a Native American?,** Peter Ortiz,
23.   **Tribal Philanthropy Thrives,** Daniel Gibson
24.   **American Indian and Alaska Native Heritage Month: November 2008,** U.S. Department of Commerce, Economics and Statistics Administration, U.S. Census Bureau,

Learning Objectives

- How should commitments to the self-determination of people be ensured and enforced?

- What value conflicts, if any, are beyond compromise?

- How does gaming affect the work ethic?

- What are the most compelling issues that face indigenous ethnic communities? Economy? Culture?

- What social, economic, and political conditions will affect the next indigenous ethnic generation?

- Should the claims of ethnic groups in defense of culture, territory, and unique institutions be honored and protected by law and public policy? Is sovereignty an issue?

- Because of the strides of the current Native American community, will the next generation enter the middle class, mainstream of America? Should that be a goal?

- Does improving economically and in terms other quality of life indicators mean the denial of traditional cultural values and practices?

Student Website
www.mhhe.com/cls

Internet Reference

American Indian Science and Engineering Society (AISES)
ww.aises.org

The contemporary issues of Native Americans as well as the descendants of all conquered indigenous peoples add their weight to the claims for cultural justice, equal protection, and due process in our hemisphere, but in fact this is a worldwide phenomenon. The United Nations provided a media forum for attention to indigenous populations and NGOs committed to human rights address global economic interests regarding the protection of human and physical ecologies. In the United States, relationships between indigenous peoples were marginalized and isolated. Their cultures were articulated in folkloric and touristic ways when interaction with mainstream America occurred. Such traditional relations were challenged during The Civil Rights Era. Moreover, the celebration of the Bicentennial of the American Revolution in 1976 and the re-organization of Native Americans in ways that claimed their empowerment over the dominance of the Bureau of Indian Affairs and their victories in the Courts and in legislative authority produced a new threshold from which the renegotiation of relationships could begin. With new cultural confidence and economic capacity most notably in the gaming industry, the descendants of native peoples entered a new epoch of American pluralism. While some may argue that the reclamation and revival of tradition and power are unique social and political events a wider view suggests that native populations are but another manifestation of ethnicity and ethnic group's articulation of its power and the pursuit of its agenda within the contexts of the American legal and economic order. Acute popular consciousness of indigenous peoples was heightened when attempts of cultural entrepreneurs to celebrate the 500th anniversary of Christopher Columbus's voyage of discovery encountered strong resistance from advocates of Native Americans. The exploration of roots and new remedies for the conquest that turned many into a permanent underclass has awakened indigenous people, and a code of international conduct in protection of cultural rights has entered international law.

The following articles represent a cross section of the current experience of indigenous ethnic groups, their forced accommodation of a high-tech world, the environmental and cultural effects of rapid change, and the challenges to a renewal of their identifying traditions. The indigenous ethnic populations remember and invite us to recall their struggles, to find ways of shaping and sharing the new sense of pluralism offered within the American experience, and the spiritual sources of ethnic identity that people encounter as the legitimacy of ancient practices widens.

© TongRo Image Stock / Alamy

Indigenous ethnic communities have encountered a complex array of historical, social, cultural, and economic forces. As a result, in the late twentieth century, the traditions of indigenous ethnic groups have been renegotiated by yet another generation. The North and South American economies and pluralistic cultures, as well as those of other continents, are a challenging stage for their quest for self-sufficiency as well as their aspirations for the preservation of a unique cultural legacy. Current indigenous ethnic leaders challenge past perceptions. They find it increasingly difficult to strike a balance between traditional values and new demands. Native Americans have increasingly interfaced with the American legal system at the state level on issues of land use and gaming, which represent part of this current redefinition. Finally, however, they are challenging themselves to be themselves, and examples of indigenous self-help reveal insights into how personal leadership and service to the community weave the social fabric of civil society. Novel approaches toward the peaceful reconciliation of conflict should be explored more thoroughly. Ethnicity is built upon the truth and strength of a tradition. Senses of family and community, and an unwillingness to give up claims have led to standoffs with many forces within America. From this perspective, this unit details ways in which an ethnic group retrieves its rights and heritage to preserve an ancient culture from amnesia and extinction.

Who Is a Native American?

PETER ORTIZ

George Armstrong Custer predicted Native Americans soon would be extinct before he ordered his soldiers to kill them at the Battle of Little Bighorn in 1876. Just as Custer discovered in his fatal encounter with Lakota and Cheyenne warriors, the native tribes proved resilient in surviving impossible odds.

More than 4 million U.S. citizens in 2003 identified as Native Americans, either alone or in combination with another race. This is a little more than 1 percent of the total 294 million people living in the United States, far fewer than the 10 to 25 million believed to be living in North America when European settlers arrived about 500 years ago. Those settlers spread fatal diseases, imposed genocide, forced assimilation, stole land, broke treaties, destroyed cultures and committed other crimes that ravaged indigenous societies.

Centuries of dehumanization resulted in the educational, economic and health disparities evidenced by Native Americans today. But refusal to succumb also nurtured a strong will embodied by many Native Americans who now comprise more than 560 federally recognized tribes and nations spread across 34 states and 140 more tribes applying for federal recognition.

That strong will has empowered Native-American entrepreneurs and those in the corporate world to thrive in a society where mainstream values sometimes run counter to their traditional beliefs. Yet Jackie Gant's frustration is clear when she speaks of how many people only envision slot machines and blackjack tables when they think of Native Americans as an economic force.

Gant, national executive director of the Native American Business Alliance, met Bush administration officials in the White House in September to let them know of the 10,000 Native-American-owned businesses listed in her database. Her organization's mission is to create networking opportunities and promote Native-American businesses as suppliers to corporate America and government agencies. Her group has the support of corporate sponsors including United Parcel Service, Ford Motor Co., General Motors, DaimlerChrysler, Toyota, The Coca-Cola Co., General Mills, Target and The Walt Disney Co. At the meeting, she tried to convey the strength of a people who saved the first white settlers from starvation and influenced the founding fathers in shaping the Constitution. Gant is a member of the Oneida Nation of the Thames, Canada, and Munsee-Delaware Nation.

"As I stood, I felt the weight of Indian country on my shoulders and I knew the words I spoke needed to be heard," Gant says.

Gant and other Native Americans have made great strides in dispelling myths and bringing attention to their issues, but the widespread ignorance of their history still pervades the highest levels of leadership, up to and including the president himself. President Bush displayed a lack of knowledge on the most crucial issue facing Native Americans—sovereignty—when he was asked in August what tribal sovereignty in the 21st century meant to him.

"You are a . . . you have been given sovereignty, and you are viewed as a sovereign entity," Bush told journalists of color gathered in Washington, D.C.

Bush's response rang hollow and was reminiscent of the countless false promises many white men have made to Native Americans over centuries. Sovereignty speaks to the right of Native Americans to control their own land where they are free to shape their economic and spiritual destiny and maintain their traditions and culture. The lack of substance and depth in Bush's answer typified the harmful perceptions, attitudes and actions that have persisted for centuries among white leaders.

Those who say that the wrongs of the past are history and that it is time to move forward frustrate Native Americans, for it is the ignorance of history that defines their present situation and continues to threaten their future. Forgetting and ignoring the past is not an option, but Native Americans live in a white man's world. Their challenge lies in enlightening non-Natives about their history, traditions, cultures and rights as distinct governments, while creating a prosperous future on their own terms.

Entrepreneurial Spirit

Entrepreneurs, such as Margaret Rodriguez, demonstrate the strong desire of Native Americans to succeed. A member of the Salt River Pima-Maricopa Indian community in Arizona, Rodriguez started her company, Au Authum Kí, 12 years ago when bankers refused to lend her money. Her company generated $24 million in revenue for 2003. Au Authum Kí translates into "the people's home."

Rodriguez's projects have ranged from a $1.9-million contract for rebuilding a high-tech structure to house a weather squadron at a Tucson Air Force Base to having her workers camp within the Grand Canyon, where they installed portable classrooms on the Havasupai reservation. She also started a charity last year that builds homes for members of her tribal community who can't afford them.

Table 1 Top 10 Native-American States by Population

California	683,922
Oklahoma	394,831
Arizona	327,547
Texas	239,907
New Mexico	202,529
New York	186,024
Washington	164,642
North Carolina	139,223
Florida	134,036
Michigan	123,322

Source: U.S. Census Bureau.

The entrepreneurial spirit isn't unique to Rodriguez as the economic muscle of Native Americans continues to grow, according to the Selig Center for Economic Growth and the U.S. Census Bureau. Americans who identified themselves solely as Native Americans and Alaska Natives numbered 2.4 million and 4.1 million when they identified with one or more races, according to the 2000 census. Most Native Americans, 43 percent, lived in the West, while 11 states comprised 62 percent of the Native-American population.

Despite their small population, Native Americans are expected to see their buying power jump from $47.7 billion in 2004 to $65.6 billion in 2009. Native Americans will account for 0.6 percent of total U.S. buying power in 2009, up from 0.5 percent in 1990, according to the Selig Center.

The 2001 Survey of Minority Owned Business Enterprises by the Census Bureau reported 197,300 Native-American- and Alaska-Native-owned businesses in the United States that employed 298,700 people. From 1992 to 1997, their numbers increased 84 percent, compared with 7 percent for all U.S. businesses.

But even with successes such as Rodriguez, much of the attention remains focused on gaming. Gant, a Harvard University graduate, credits some casinos for pulling tribal members out of poverty when little economic opportunity existed. About 201 of the 562 federally recognized tribes are engaged in gaming, but most are small operations that provide a few jobs to members in dire need of work. Casinos and gaming operations must be located on tribal lands, and federal law dictates that tribes use gaming revenue to fund services, such as education, law enforcement, tribal courts, health care, social services and infrastructure improvements.

Native Americans must live in a white man's world. Their challenge lies in enlightening non-Natives about their history, traditions, cultures and sovereign rights, while creating a prosperous future on their own terms.

Casinos also have helped spur new small businesses. But the reality is that most Native Americans don't benefit from casinos. About 60 percent live outside of reservations, with the rest living on tribal lands or bordering rural areas. A report by the National Congress of American Indians shows Native Americans ranking last or near last on nearly all social, health, education and economic barometers. Their poverty rate from 2001 to 2003 was 23 percent, similar to that for African Americans and Latinos, while the poverty rate for whites and Asian Americans was about 10 percent. About one-third of the Native-American population on reservations live in poverty. From 2001 to 2003, Latinos, at 32.8 percent, were the only group to surpass Native Americans, 23.8 percent, for those without health coverage.

Native Americans also continue to struggle because of the federal government's early attempts to educate them with a total disregard for their culture. Children were prevented from speaking their language, practicing traditional customs and wearing indigenous dress. Native Americans were not taught the reading, writing and math skills of their white peers and instead were steered toward trades that did not guarantee a secure job because of racial barriers.

About 75 percent of Native Americans 25 years and older earned a high-school degree or more, compared with 84 percent of the U.S. population in 2002. About 14 percent of Native Americans 25 years and older earned at least a bachelor's degree or higher, compared with 27 percent for the overall population.

Maggie Necefer remembers when she was forbidden to speak her language as a student in the 1960s. Necefer's Navajo nation established the first tribal college in 1968 and is now among 34 tribal colleges in the United States. She serves as academic vice president at Dine College, which offers 17 degree programs and includes Navajo language and Navajo studies degrees.

"They paid missionaries to put up these schools and the whole intent was to proselytize, to kill the savage and save the man," Necefer recounts of her border school experience. "Oftentimes, we had missionaries come into the schools and tell us what god to believe in."

Necefer kept her language and culture, thanks to her family, and later completed bachelor's, master's and doctoral programs. She represents a model for students; in her, they can see that a Native American can survive from an imposed educational system and retain their culture.

"It is just taking ownership of our own education and what education should be for our people," Necefer says. "We validate the cultural identity and cultural piece interspersed with Western knowledge to prepare balanced individuals who can live in both worlds."

Corporate America's Gap

Much of corporate America, like society itself, does not understand Native Americans. When corporate America is focused on diversity, rarely are Native Americans mentioned in the same breath as African Americans, Latinos and Asian Americans, Gant says.

"We are able to compete like any other non-Native organizations, provided we are given the opportunity to do so by corporate America," Gant says.

Table 2   Median Income from 2001 to 2003

Asian Americans	$55,089
Whites	$47,957
Native Americans and Alaska Natives	$34,740
Latinos	$33,913
African Americans	$29,987

Source: U.S. Census Bureau.

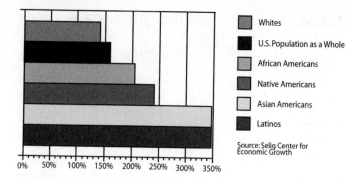

Figure 1   Native-American Buying Power.   Projected rate of increase 1990–2009.

Source: Selig Center for Economic Growth.

Stormy Hicks, 58, heeded the advice from his father when he told the then 8-year-old that he was of the Shawnee Nation, but to keep that a secret between the two. Thomas Hicks took pride in his native heritage, regaling his son with stories of relatives dressed in buck skin and visiting him near his tribe's reservation in West Virginia. But Native Americans in the early 1900s often were denied jobs and faced discrimination.

Hicks is president of ITT Automotive Industries, a company that generates $500 million to $600 million a year in sales and makes fuel and brake lines as well as various plastic parts. For 20 years, he worked at Ford, where he started as a design engineer and ran manufacturing plants in Brazil and Mexico. He retired from Ford as executive director in charge of worldwide logistics and transportation in 1998.

For many years, Hicks kept his Native-American heritage a secret, even when some in corporate America realized the value that people of color brought to their ranks.

"I wasn't embarrassed by it," Hicks says. "In the corporate world, they wanted senior executives who were minorities and I never wanted to give that to the corporations I worked for. I just kept it to myself."

Hicks' wife Elizabeth, who was inducted as a non-native member of his tribe, researched her husband's lineage and urged him to acknowledge his heritage to everyone. He took her advice 10 years ago and regrets not doing it sooner.

"She started to realize there was something missing from my life," Hicks says.

Hicks kept true to his Native-American values even as he remained silent. His struggle speaks to the experiences of many Native Americans who must balance two worlds that have historically clashed from the time European settlers arrived. A legendary chief from Hicks' Shawnee tribe, Tecumseh, echoed the anger of Native Americans when he tried to rally them against white land invasion in the early 1800s.

Hicks did not face the life-and-death choice Tecumseh and many Native Americans grappled with in their fight. But Tecumseh not only called for Native Americans to stand up to white injustice, he also showed compassion by not killing noncombatants. He urged other Native Americans to emulate the same humane treatment. His example survived in future generations.

"I've labored with it throughout my whole career whenever I've had to make big layoffs," Hicks says. "I think as part of Native-American culture, one of our teachings is you always

take care of your people, and I'm not sure corporate America does that all the time."

Hicks' success did not come from conforming to the corporate culture, but rather adopting a Native-American approach. He avoided hiring excess employees and trained them in different skills so they could increase their chances of staying employed if layoffs were necessary. Hicks clashed with his supervisors and figures he could be in a higher position if he just played the corporate game.

"I worked with a very senior guy . . . who told me that sometimes I thought more of the people than the bottom line," Hicks recalls. "My response was the people are the bottom line and if you treat them right, they will produce the bottom line you need."

Hicks urges Native Americans entering or in corporate America to find strength in their traditions. "I would tell them to be true to themselves and to their heritage, that the native way does not have to be subjugated by the corporate way," he says.

Tracy Stanhoff, president of the American Indian National Chamber of Commerce, says corporate America and government contractors need to do better to inform Native-American businesses about opportunities and mentorships. Her organization started two years ago and represents the 12-member chamber of commerce nationwide, she says.

Stanhoff is a member of the Prairie Band Potawatomi Nation out of Kansas. She sees her organization supporting mentoring opportunities that she did not have when she started her advertising and graphics design business in 1988 at age 26.

"There are lots of issues that have to do with a lack of outreach from corporate America and their diversity departments," Stanhoff says. "We need to step up and say, 'Hey, don't forget about us.'"

Business on the Reservation

Lois Taylor and Barbara Poley steered clear of corporate America when they joined a nonprofit group to help jump-start tribal businesses on their Hopi reservation. The Hopi Foundation has helped the Hopi realize their entrepreneurial spirit without having to compromise traditions by leaving the reservation.

"Education for our people should validate the cultural identity and cultural piece interspersed with Western knowledge to prepare balanced individuals who can live in both worlds."

—Maggie Necefer, Dine College

The Hopi reservation occupies 1.5 million acres in northeastern Arizona and many of its residents live in remote areas. The idea for one business, Native Sun, sprung from the objections of many Hopi who did not want a power company's electrical grid crossing over sacred cultural land. Many choose instead to use kerosene lamps and battery-operated lights.

"They did not want to be subservient to a company that would provide them electricity," he adds. "They are staunchly independent."

The Hopi Foundation in 1988 helped start Native Sun, a Hopi-run business that sells solar panels, batteries and equipment. Two years ago, the company became a limited corporation with a majority Hopi board. Hopi living in remote areas are able to harness the sun's energy via solar panels placed on top or near their homes. When banks denied loans to families who could not afford the solar panels, the foundation started a revolving loan fund and maintained "one of the lowest default rates of any institution," Taylor says.

Like many tribes on reservations, the challenges of high unemployment, poor health and inadequate educational opportunities are a daily reality. In some Hopi villages, unemployment can reach as high as 55 percent. Reservations were created by the federal government with the promise of sovereignty and protection. In exchange, Native Americans had to relinquish land as white settlers hungered for more property. The reservations often consisted of the worst land, but today, Hopi and other Native Americans refuse to leave, saying the reservation serves as the spiritual connection to their ancestral roots.

"The Hopi people have a year-long religious calendar . . . and one of the key and important principles was for us to work with micro-enterprises that were compatible with the Hopi lifestyle," Taylor says.

Out of that desire, another business, Gentle Rain Designs, was born. Hopi women already sewing from their homes created the cooperative and now design fleece items ranging from jackets and vests to pillows and purses, all from recycled plastic. The women operate a small shop on the reservation and sell their clothing to boutiques outside the reservation, allowing them to work around their tribal ceremonies.

"If we are going to have survival on our own reservations, we have to build up the capacity and sustainability with businesses we produce on the reservation," Poley says.

Fred DuBray does not dwell on monetary gain when he talks about the growth of the InterTribal Bison Cooperative he directs in South Dakota. DuBray, a member of the Cheyenne River Sioux Tribe, watched the cooperative grow from 1,000 bison in 1990 to 15,000 today with 53 tribes from 18 states participating.

Cultural Competency: Understanding Native Americans in Business Dealings

The great divide between Native-American and corporate culture doesn't mean the two sides can't find common ground to conduct business.

One of Patty Dimitrious missions is helping non-Natives understand proper social and business etiquette when dealing with Native Americans. Dimitriou 35, is a member of the Dine (Navajo) Nation and owner of Alternatives/Alternativos, a multicultural advertising agency in Phoenix, Ariz., specializing in Native American and Latino marketing communications. She offers the following suggestions to clients who do business in "Indian Country."

Making your presence known through direct eye contact or a strong handshake can be interpreted as disrespectful and dominating in Native American circles. Dimitriou advises a more modest tack that does not boast of your presence. It's also a good idea to let your Native-American contact know more about your own family background and personal interests. "It's really important to understand each others' roots and background so that we know how to communicate with each other," Dimitriou says. "By sharing where you and your family are from, you support the Native-American custom of building a sense of relatedness."

Dimitriou decided to pursue a degree in communications after leaving her Navajo Nation, in part to help her better understand how to succeed in a dominant white culture. She since has advised non-Natives who are concerned that they might have offended Native Americans at business encounters.

"Say, for example, a developer goes to meet with a tribal council and he really wants to close the deal, so he is . . . trying to be direct and engaging in the type of behavior white America would say is assertive and knowledgeable," Dimitriou says. "But with his conduct, he is coming across as very combative, aggressive and very disrespectful and he creates the exact opposite outcome he is seeking."

And don't be surprised if you stay long at a tribal council business meeting. Dimitriou has heard of visitors who expected to present at a 5 p.m. meeting and waited until 1 a.m. the next morning. But she encourages clients to appreciate the cultural reasons for longer meetings. "One of the things I think is wonderful about Native-American communication is that everyone is invited to speak freely and express themselves without someone cross-talking them," she says. "The most important things are that everyone is in agreement and that everyone has a chance to share."

—Peter Ortiz

The buffalo provide a healthy food source that could help alleviate some of the serious health problems that afflict many Native Americans.

"The most important aspect . . . is recognition that buffalo is such an important and vital part of Indian culture," DuBray says. "If we can't allow them to exist, we probably can't exist as a people."

White settlers knew of the spiritual bond between the buffalo and Native Americans when they systematically tried to wipe out the animal. Native Americans treated the buffalo and other animals with respect and thanked the animals they slaughtered for providing for their families. That concept was foreign to many whites who only hunted the buffalo for food, profit or to further destroy the Native-American way of life.

A big challenge faced by the cooperative is avoiding the idea of domesticating animals, a concept white settlers brought to the Americas. Native Americans viewed themselves, as well as other living beings, as temporary tenants of land that owned them. DuBray says buffalo need to roam freely, as their ancestors did, and that this is necessary to strengthen the spiritual bond they share with the animal.

"We are working toward restoring them as a wildlife resource, not as a commodity," DuBray says. "For them to provide a healthy source of food, they need a healthy source of food themselves like medicinal plants."

DuBray, 54, acknowledges that individual tribes must make tough decisions about how to use limited land. The Native-American way of raising buffalo requires lots of space that some tribal members may want to use for other economic projects. He has 100 buffalo, while his tribe owns several thousand. But despite the success of the cooperative, suspicion remains of the federal government or real-estate interests wanting to take over the land.

"There are still people out there developing ingenious ways to strip away what is left, so we can't let our guard down," DuBray says. "The only promise the white man kept is the promise to take our land. He took it."

Critical Thinking

1. What myths have you absorbed or heard about Native Americans?

2. What are the impacts of Native Americans on various states?

3. Describe and compare the following aspects of Native American identity: Entrepreneurial Spirit, Corporate America's Gap and Business on the Reservation.

Tribal Philanthropy Thrives

DANIEL GIBSON

A merican Indian tribes all have social values that encourage sharing with those in need. Historically, a deer, tapir or walrus brought in by hunters would be split among tribal members or families. Corn, squash and beans from the fields usually went into a common larder. Work was often divided up into group tasks. The emphasis was on survival of all, common goals and a communal spirit. Today those same values are guiding the gifting of millions of dollars each year from tribes benefiting from gaming income to their surrounding non-Indian communities and to non-gaming tribes. Tribes understand what difficult times are all about, and they are stepping up to the plate in a major fashion to aid and assist those less fortunate.

In 2006 alone, tribal governments nationwide gave more than $150 million to charitable causes, according to the National Indian Gaming Association.

Examples abound across the nation. In California, the **Morongo Band of Mission Indians** near Banning has set up a scholarship program open to all California Native students. In recent years, the tribe has also supported programs of the Special Olympics, the Boy Scouts of America, San Gorgonio Memorial Hospital, the Riverside Sheriffs' Association Relief Fund, the local Little League, the American Cancer Society, Big Brothers/Big Sisters, the YMCA, the AIDS Assistance Program, the American Red Cross and the Juvenile Diabetes Association.

In the Southwest, many tribes are generously providing financial assistance to nearby communities and home states. The **Pascua Yaqui Tribe** near Tucson, Arizona donated more than $1.1 million in 2006 and 2007, including $338,000 to the City of Tucson to purchase land for affordable housing, parks and recreation programs; $150,000 for cultural programs and tourism endeavors in the Town of Guadalupe; and $50,000 to the Tucson School District. "The Pascua Yaqui Tribe is committed to investing in the future of our state," notes former tribal chairwoman Herminia Frias.

In fact, when Arizona voters passed Proposition 202 in 2002, which clarified the legal status of Indian gaming in the state, the legislation called for the gaming tribes to donate substantial revenue to the state. Of these funds, 12 percent goes directly to Arizona cities, towns and counties, while the other 88 percent is divided up among a handful of state departments and programs. Of the latter revenue stream, in 2007 alone Arizona tribes provided more than $46 million to the state's Instructional Improvement Fund for charter schools, $23 million to the Trauma & Emergency Services Fund, $6.5 million for the Arizona Office of Tourism, $6.5 million to the Arizona Game & Fish Department's Wildlife Conservation Fund, $8 million to the Arizona Department of Gaming and $1.8 million to the Arizona Office of Problem Gambling.

The **Soboba Band of Luiseño Indians** in southern California has been a good neighbor to its surrounding towns in Riverside County. In June 2003, the tribe gave $400,000 to the City of Hemet Public Library, but that was just one of its many large contributions in the area in recent years. A room at the tribal hall is filled with plaques of appreciation from local youth sports organizations. The tribe has gifted $60,000 in donations to six local football programs, and some 600 other local kids are benefiting from contributions ranging from $10,000 to $20,000 per year to the local parks and recreation program. The Ramona Outdoor Play, a production incorporating local history held annually in Hemet, is now sponsored by the tribe. When the Vietnam Veterans Memorial Moving Wall visited San Jacinto, it was due to a grant from the tribe. Local chamber of commerce events are sponsored by the tribe, which also provides space and staff for the chamber's annual community fair.

"It comes from a lot of years of local people giving us things," explained vice chairwoman Rosemary Morillo in an article in the Riverside *Press-Enterprise* a few years ago. "People would donate oranges, candy and toys for our kids at Christmas. Now we're able to return that gesture." In the same article, tribal administrator Andrew Masiel stated, "We've always had the desire (to contribute to local community events and charitable causes) but not the resources. But now it's different."

The **Forest County Potawatomi** tribe of Wisconsin is actively helping to fund many programs and projects outside of its reservation. Each year in August, the tribe's Community Foundation selects 20 children's charities from Milwaukee, Waukesha, Washington, Racine and Ozaukee counties to receive at least $50,000 each. This August will mark the 15th anniversary of the program, which has provided more than $7 million to date. The funds are derived from the Potawatomi Bingo Casino on Canal Street in Milwaukee, which hosts special Miracle on Canal bingo games, a two-night dinner and auction, and an annual golf event.

The tribe also is active in funding medical programs. Last December, it donated $45,000 to the Medical College of Wisconsin for research and educational programs focused on diabetes treatment and prevention. It was just the most recent gift in a relationship going back several years. "It's a goal of the tribe to be at the forefront when it comes to eliminating this debilitating disease," says Tom Bolter, the executive director of the tribe's Foundation Enterprise Fund. All told, the tribe has given away tens of millions of dollars since its foundation was established in 1999.

The **Confederated Tribes of the Umatilla Indian Reservation** of Oregon established the Wildhorse Foundation in 2001, which is funded by a set percentage of the Wildhorse Resort and Casino's net income. As the resort's business grows, so do the foundation's annual grants. In 2001, grants totaled $294,000; in 2002, $230,000; in 2003, $470,000; in 2004, $503,000; in 2005, $507,000; in 2006, $589,000; and in 2007, $655,000.

Grants range from $500 to $20,000 and are focused on projects and programs in Umatilla, Union, Morrow and Wallowa counties. For instance, in 2007 the tribe gave a $10,000 grant to provide orthodontic and dental treatment to local children through the nonprofit Advantage Smiles for Kids program; $500 for the Cancer Society Relay for Life; $12,000 for the Pendleton Parks Department for new lifeguard chairs; and $10,000 to the Arts Council of Pendleton for public art exhibitions. Other funds were directed to the City of Ukiah and the City of Echo, the Blue Mountain Nordic Club, Eastern Oregon University, Homestead Youth and Family Services, Oregon Historical Society, St. Andrews Mission and Pilot Rock Fire District.

Perhaps the most generous tribe in the nation is the **Shakopee Mdewakanton Sioux Community** of Prior Lake, Minnesota (see Sept./Oct. 2002 issue). Since the tribe opened its first bingo hall in October 1982, it has given away more than $115 million, and in the fiscal year ending last Sept. 30 it hit an annual high mark of $26 million.

"We need to give back—it's the nature of the Dakota people," explains Bill Rudnicki, the tribal administrator for the past 15 years. So far, the tribe has resisted putting a cap on annual donations. "It's gone up every year," says Rudnicki. "The more you help, the more you see the need out there. It's such a good feeling when we get notes from kids, for example, stating that they wouldn't have had textbooks that year if it weren't for our efforts. It really hits home."

The tribe also donates regularly to the American Red Cross, the American Cancer Society, the American Diabetes Association and the American Heart Association, and recently provided $500,000 over a two-year period to the local hospital. It gives more than $200,000 a year at Christmas to some 44 social service organizations in the Twin Cities to buy toys, clothing, food and other gifts. Contributions can be relatively small but play an important role—such as the $1,000 given to the Emily, Minnesota Police Department to acquire and train a German shepherd drug dog. Or they can be huge. On Oct. 19, 2007, the tribe delivered a check for $10.4 million to the University of Minnesota to fund construction of a new stadium, and has committed $2.5 million for university scholarships.

Despite these major gifts that benefit the general Minnesota populace, "The bulk of what we give is actually to other tribes, to specific programs and projects when we hear of unmet needs," Rudnicki notes. Between 1997 and 1998, the tribe created a formal process for annual donations to other tribes. Last year, 19 tribes were on the receiving end of the Shakopees' generosity.

The Red Lake Band of Chippewa of northern Minnesota—scene of a terrible student shooting in March 2005—is one tribal beneficiary. The Red Lake Boys & Girls Club has also been the recipient of $1 million in Shakopee funding. The Red Lake government wanted to restore its once-famous and lucrative walleye fisheries, and with the help of the Shakopees and the state government, they are now undergoing a strong recovery. "I'm really proud of the tribe's being ahead of the times, in terms of funding 'green' initiatives," says Rudnicki.

In January 2008, the Flandreau Santee Sioux Tribe of South Dakota received a $1 million grant to fund construction of an eldercare center. In February, the Spirit Lake Nation of North Dakota was gifted $1 million to build a new courthouse and undertake other building maintenance and improvement projects. And in March, the Kiowa Tribe of Oklahoma received a $1 million grant to purchase and operate a nearby tourist attraction, Indian City USA.

Soboba Leader Honored

In April, the chairman of the Soboba Band of Luiseño Indians, Robert Salgado, was recognized for his leadership abilities with the presentation of the Wendell Chino Humanitarian Award from the National Indian Gaming Association. Salgado spent nearly two decades guiding his tribe from obscurity to a high-profile position in southern California's political and economic life.

The tribe has an active program of donating funds to local and regional causes (see main story), but Salgado says perhaps his greatest contribution to his tribe and the region was forging a water-rights pact with the Metropolitan Water District of Southern California and the Eastern Municipal Water District, which came after decades of litigation.

He also oversaw the transformation of his reservation from a pocket of poverty to relative affluence, largely due to revenue derived from the Soboba Casino and the Country Club at Soboba Springs. In 2006, the tribe refurbished The Oaks resort, which included construction of a football stadium for the reservation's Noli Indian High School. A semi-professional football team owned by Salgado also uses the facility, revealing another passion of the chairman. Salgado is still widely remembered in the area for his record-setting role on the local high school football team as a kicker, and later roles as a coach for San Jacinto High School and Mt. San Jacinto College.

The tribe is also active in providing loans to tribal governments for economic development and social projects. From 2004 to 2007, $67 million was loaned.

Programs that benefit a wide range of Indian people have also received assistance. For instance, the American Indian College Fund was given $1.8 million over a six-year period. "We've been blessed, and we're grateful for the opportunity to help others," concludes the Shakopee tribal chairman, Stanley Crooks. Details on the tribe's philanthropic program can be found at ccsmdc.org/donations.html.

Critical Thinking

1. What are some philanthropic practices of American Indian tribes?

2. Is this philanthropic predisposition common to all these tribes?

3. Why have there been differences between past philanthropic sharing by the tribes and present practices?

DANIEL GIBSON has been the editor of *Native Peoples* since February 2001. His most recent book is *Pueblos of the Rio Grande: A Visitor's Guide* (Rio Nuevo Publishers).

American Indian and Alaska Native Heritage Month: November 2008

The first American Indian Day was celebrated in May 1916 in New York. Red Fox James, a Blackfeet Indian, rode horseback from state to state, getting endorsements from 24 state governments, to have a day to honor American Indians. In 1990, President George H.W. Bush signed a joint congressional resolution designating November 1990 as "National American Indian Heritage Month." Similar proclamations have been issued every year since 1994. This Facts for Features presents data for American Indians and Alaska Natives, as this is one of the six major race categories.

Note: Unless otherwise specified, the data in the "Population" section refer to the population who reported a race alone or in combination with one or more other races.

Population

4.5 million
As of July 1, 2007, the estimated population of American Indians and Alaska Natives, including those of more than one race. They made up 1.5 percent of the total population.[1]

8.6 million
The projected population of American Indians and Alaska Natives, including those of more than one race, on July 1, 2050. They would comprise 2 percent of the total population.[2]

44,803
Increase in the nation's American Indian and Alaska Native population from July 1, 2006, to July 1, 2007. The population of this group increased by 1 percent during the period.[3]

30.3
Median age of the single-race American Indian and Alaska Native population in 2007, younger than the median of 36.6 for the population as a whole. About 27 percent of American Indians and Alaska Natives were younger than 18, and 8 precent were 65 and older.[4]

689,120
The American Indian and Alaska Native population in California as of July 1, 2007, the highest total of any state. California was followed by Oklahoma (393,500) and Arizona (335,381).

About 8,300 American Indians and Alaska Natives were added to Texas' population between July 1, 2006, and July 1, 2007. That is the largest numeric increase of any state. Georgia (3.4 percent) had the highest rate of increase during the period.[5]

5
Number of states where American Indians and Alaska Natives were the largest race or ethnic minority group in 2006. These states are Alaska, Montana, North Dakota, Oklahoma and South Dakota.[6]

11
Number of states with more than 100,000 American Indian and Alaska Native residents on July 1, 2007. These states were California, Oklahoma, Arizona, Texas, New Mexico, New York, Washington, Florida, North Carolina, Michigan and Alaska. Combined, these states were home to 62 percent of the nation's American Indian and Alaska Native residents.[7]

18%
The proportion of Alaska's population identified as American Indian and Alaska Native as of July 1, 2007, the highest rate for this race group of any state. Alaska was followed by Oklahoma (11 percent) and New Mexico (10 percent).[8]

146,500
The number of American Indians and Alaska Natives in Los Angeles County, Calif., as of July 1, 2007. Los Angeles led all of the nation's counties in the number of people of this racial category.

Maricopa County, Ariz., added about 2,300 people to this group between July 1, 2006, and July 1, 2007, leading the nation's counties in this category.[9]

10
Among counties or equivalents with total populations of 10,000 or more, number that were majority American Indian and Alaska Native, as of July 1, 2007. Shannon, S.D., led the way, with 87 percent of its population being a member of this race group.[10]

Families and Children

537,500
The number of American Indian and Alaska Native families in 2007. Of these:

- 314,900 were married-couple families, including those with children.
- 146,400 were married couples with their own children, under the age of 18.[11]

3.57

Average number of people in an American Indian and Alaska Native family in 2007. This was larger than the national average size for all families (3.2 people).[12]

Housing

56%

The percentage of American Indian and Alaska Native households who own their owned home in 2007.[13]

$116,700

Median value of homes owned by American Indians and Alaska Natives.[14]

Languages

27%

Percentage of American Indians and Alaska Natives 5 and older who spoke a language other than English at home.[15]

Education

76%

The percentage of American Indians and Alaska Natives 25 and older who had at least a high school diploma. Also, 13 percent had at least a bachelor's degree.[16]

61,976

Number of American Indians and Alaska Natives 25 and older who have a graduate or professional degree.[17]

Businesses

$26.9 billion

Receipts for American Indian- and Alaska Native-owned businesses in 2002. These businesses numbered 201,387.

20,380

Number of American Indian- and Alaska Native-owned firms in the Los Angeles-Long Beach-Riverside combined statistical area, making that area number one in the metro category. Among counties, Los Angeles had the highest number of firms (13,061).

38,125

Number of American Indian- and Alaska Native-owned firms in California, which led the states. Oklahoma, Texas, New York and Florida followed.

Nearly 3 in 10

Number of American Indian- and Alaska Native-owned firms that operated in construction and other services (such as personal services, and repair and maintenance).

24,498

Number of American Indian- and Alaska Native-owned firms that had paid employees. These businesses employed 191,270 people.

3,631

Number of American Indian- and Alaska Native-owned firms with receipts of $1 million or more. These firms accounted for nearly 2 percent of the total number of American Indian- and Alaska Native-owned firms and more than 64 percent of their total receipts.

178

Number of American Indian- and Alaska Native-owned firms with 100 or more employees. These firms generated nearly $5.3 billion in gross receipts—24 percent of the total revenue for American Indian- and Alaska Native-owned employer firms.

New York; Los Angeles; and Gallup, N.M.

The three cities with the largest number of American Indian- and Alaska Native-owned firms, with 7,134; 5,767; and 2,642, respectively.[18]

Jobs

25%

The percentage of civilian employed American Indian and Alaska Native people 16 and older who worked in management, professional and related occupations. In addition, 23 percent worked in sales and office occupations and about the same percentage worked in service occupations.[19]

Caregivers

54%

Percentage of American Indians and Alaska Natives 30 and older who lived with grandchildren and were responsible for caring for their care. The corresponding rate for the population as a whole was 40 percent.[20]

Veterans

165,200

The number of American Indian and Alaska Native veterans of the U.S. armed forces.[21]

Income and Poverty

$35,343

The 2007 median income of households where the householder reported being American Indian and Alaska Native and no other race.[22]

25.3%

The 2007 poverty rate of people who reported they were American Indian and Alaska Native and no other race.[23]

Health Insurance

32.1%

The percentage of people who reported they were American Indian and Alaska Native and no other race who lacked health insurance coverage, based on a three-year average (2005-2007).[24]

Notes

1. Source: Population estimates www.census.gov/Press-Release/www/releases/archives/population/011910.html
2. Source: Population projections www.census.gov/Press-Release/www/releases/archives/population/012496.html
3. Source: Population estimates www.census.gov/Press-Release/www/releases/archives/population/011910.html
4. Source: Population estimates www.census.gov/Press-Release/www/releases/archives/population/011910.html
5. Source: Population estimates www.census.gov/Press-Release/www/releases/archives/population/011910.html
6. Source: Population estimates www.census.gov/Press-Release/www/releases/archives/population/011910.html
7. Source: Population estimates www.census.gov/Press-Release/www/releases/archives/population/011910.html
8. Source: Population estimates www.census.gov/Press-Release/www/releases/archives/population/011910.html
9. Source: Population estimates www.census.gov/Press-Release/www/releases/archives/population/012463.html
10. Source: Population estimates www.census.gov/Press-Release/www/releases/archives/population/012463.html
11. Source: 2007 American Community Survey for the American Indian and Alaska Native alone population. http://factfinder.census.gov
12. Source: 2007 American Community Survey for the American Indian and Alaska Native alone population. http://factfinder.census.gov
13. Source: 2007 American Community Survey for the American Indian and Alaska Native alone population. http://factfinder.census.gov
14. Source: 2007 American Community Survey for the American Indian and Alaska Native alone population. http://factfinder.census.gov
15. Source: 2007 American Community Survey for the American Indian and Alaska Native alone population. http://factfinder.census.gov
16. Source: 2007 American Community Survey for the American Indian and Alaska Native alone population. http://factfinder.census.gov
17. Source: 2007 American Community Survey for the American Indian and Alaska Native alone population. http://factfinder.census.gov
18. Source for data in this section: *American Indian- and Alaska Native-Owned Firms: 2002* www.census.gov/Press-Release/www/releases/archives/business_ownership/007013.html
19. Source: 2007 American Community Survey for the American Indian and Alaska Native alone population. http://factfinder.census.gov
20. Source: 2007 American Community Survey for the American Indian and Alaska Native alone population. http://factfinder.census.gov
21. Source: 2007 American Community Survey for the American Indian and Alaska Native alone population. http://factfinder.census.gov
22. Source: Income, Earnings, and Poverty Data from the 2007 American Community Survey www.census.gov/Press-Release/www/releases/archives/income_wealth/010583.html
23. Source: Income, Earnings, and Poverty, Data from 2007 American Community Survey www.census.gov/Press-Release/www/releases/archives/income_wealth/012528.html
24. Source: *Income, Poverty, and Health Insurance Coverage in the United States: 2007,* www.census.gov/Press-Release/www/releases/archives/income_wealth/010583.html

Critical Thinking

1. Can you explain why Alaska is no longer among the twelve U.S. states with the highest populations of American Indians and Alaska Natives?
2. What did Red Fox James do and why is his contribution important?

Editor's note—The preceding data were collected from a variety of sources and may be subject to sampling variability and other sources of error. Facts for Features are customarily released about two months before an observance in order to accommodate magazine production timelines. Questions or comments should be directed to the Census Bureau's Public information Office: telephone: 301-763-3030; fax: 301-763-3762; or e-mail: pio@census.gov.

From U.S. Census Bureau, November 2007.

UNIT 5

African Americans

Unit Selections

25. **Black (African-American) History Month: February 2010** *U.S. Department of Commerce, Economics and Statistics Administration, U.S. Census Bureau*
26. **Transcript of Obama's Speech,** Barack Obama
27. **Redefining Black Women in America,** Krissah Thompson

Learning Objectives

- Characterize relationships between ethnic and racial groups on your campus.

- Is race-based violence increasing? Defend your answer.

- What are the most compelling issues that face African American communities?

- In what respects are desegregation, integration, discrimination, and prejudice woven into the discussion of contemporary issues related to African Americans?

- What role will new African immigrants play in the African American community?

- What social, economic, and political conditions have supported the expansion of an African American middle class?

- What factors explain the persistence of an African American underclass? In what respect is this question related to integration?

- In what respect is attention to education an answer to economic and social integration of African Americans?

- Does the name African Americans augment the development of pluralism? Discuss in terms of Afrocentrism and integration.

- Why does the relationship between blacks and Jews continue to erupt as an important aspect of group relations in America?

Student Website
www.mhhe.com/cls

Internet References

National Association for the Advancement of Colored People (NAACP)
    www.naacp.org
AIDs and Black New Yorkers
    www.villagevoice.com/2000-06-13/news/emergency-call/1

An article by Lerone Bennett, published in *Ebony* more than a decade before the election of President Barack Obama, expressed the thrust of an argument that has defined the discussion within Negro, black, and African American communities. It is that historical moments define a peoples' identity and a series of pivotal, dramatic events inform the identity of African Americans and perhaps all Americans as well. Bennett's case is that tableaux of African American history that has framed the experiences of race and ethnicity: the arrival, the founding of communities and settlements, Nat Turner's War, the multiple moments and venues of emancipation, the Booker T. Washington and W. E. B. DuBois strategic crossroads, migrations, *Brown vs. Board of Education,* Montgomery, Little Rock, and that day in Memphis when time and everything else stopped. The March on Washington and *Brown v. Topeka* prompted Bennett to use the phrase—"The Triumph of the Spirit" is acknowledged in memory and in the personal national holiday devoted to Martin Luther King, Jr. The drama of the American promise of liberty and justice for all, the reality of various pieces of the American Dream that are shattered, and partial moments of harmony today are evoked not in the aspiration toward the common good but in reaction to the fear of a common enemy, and the threatening power of evil continues to oscillate in the public mind of America. America has come a long way since the 1988 New York Times editorial that suggested an appropriate introductory focus for the following collection of articles about an ethnic group that traces its American ancestry to initial participation as "three-fifths" of a person status in the U.S. Constitution to its later exclusion from the freedoms of this polity altogether by the U.S. Supreme Court's Dred Scott decision. The editors of the Times wrote in the article "Negro, Black, and African American" (December 22, 1988): The archaeology is dramatically plain to older adults who, in one lifetime, have already heard preferred usage shift from colored to Negro to black. The four lingual layers provide an abbreviated history of civil rights in this century. The following glimpses of the African American reality, its struggles for freedom, its tradition and community, its achievements, and the stresses of building bridges between worlds reveal a dense set of problems. More importantly, they suggest pieces of authentic identity rather than stereotype. Becoming a healthy ethnic society involves more than the end of ethnic stereotyping. The basis of ethnic identity is sustained by authentic portrayals of positive personal and group identity. The cultivation of ethnicity that does not encourage disdain for and self-hatred among members and groups is an important psychological and social artifice. Progress on issues of race involves examination of a complex of historical, social, cultural, and economic factors. Analysis of this sort requires assessment of the deep racism in the American mentality, that is, the cultural consciousness and the institutions whose images and practices shape social reality. These patterns of change within African American populations compel discussion of the emerging black middle class. The purpose and influence of the historically black university, the reopening of the discussion of slavery and the separate-but-equal issue, and the renewed attention to Afrocentric education are clear evidence of the ambivalence and ambiguity inherent in the challenges of

a multicultural society. Earlier dichotomies—slave/free, black/white, and poor/rich—are still evident, but a variety of group relations based on historical and regional as well as institutional agendas to preserve cultural and racial consciousness have complicated the simple hope for liberty and justice that was shared by many Americans. Many African Americans still face challenges in housing, employment, and education.

Discrimination and prejudice based on skin color are issues rarely broached in mainstream journals of opinion. Ethnic and racial intermarriage and the influence and impact of skin hue within the African American community raise attendant issues of discrimination and consciousness of color. This concern began in eighteenth- and nineteenth-century laws and practices of defining race that shaped the mentalities of color consciousness, prejudice, and racism in America. Other dimensions of the African American experience can be found in this unit's accounts of African American traditions and experiences of self-help and the family. New perspectives on the civil rights era can be gained from reflective accounts of the leaders who influenced the direction of social change that reconfigured race and ethnic relations in America.

As this debate continues, patterns of change within African American populations compel discussion of the emerging black middle class. Earlier dichotomies—slave/free, black/white, poor/rich—are still evident, but a variety of group relations based on historical and regional as well as institutional agendas to preserve cultural and racial consciousness have complicated the simple hope for liberty and justice that was shared by many Americans. Issues of race and class are addressed in this section.

Changing circumstances within the larger American society and the civil rights agenda itself have been affected by success and failure, and once-clear issues and solutions have taken on more complex structural, economic, and philosophical dimensions. The growing gap between blacks and whites in terms of education, financial status, and class and the growing crime and death rates of young black men paint a daunting picture of past policies and of this population's future. To be sure, African Americans have made advances since the civil rights movement of the 1960s. They have made dramatic gains in education, employment, and financial status. Unfortunately, they still are portrayed as being part of an urban underclass when only one-third of their population is actually in this group. While not all African Americans are poor, those who are poor are in desperate situations. Will help come from the African American population that now constitutes part of the middle and upper classes of American society? Scholarly differences of opinion concerning the composition of the urban underclass do not minimize the hardships that many endure. The growth of the underclass, its isolation from society, and society's inability to help it are tremendous obstacles that face our nation. Concrete strategies for improving this situation call upon both the public and the private sectors in areas of education, employment, and training. Suggestions for meeting future needs of this population and pragmatic policy responses also will help the general population.

Black (African-American) History Month: February 2010

To commemorate and celebrate the contributions to our nation made by people of African descent, American historian Carter G. Woodson established Black History Week. The first celebration occurred on Feb. 12, 1926. For many years, the second week of February was set aside for this celebration to coincide with the birthdays of abolitionist/editor Frederick Douglass and Abraham Lincoln. In 1976, as part of the nation's bicentennial, the week was expanded into Black History Month. Each year, U.S. presidents proclaim February as National African-American History Month.

Population

41.1 million

As of July 1, 2008, the estimated population of black residents in the United States, including those of more than one race. They made up 13.5 percent of the total U.S. population. This figure represents an increase of more than a half-million residents from one year earlier.[1]

65.7 million

The projected black population of the United States (including those of more than one race) for July 1, 2050. On that date, according to the projection, blacks would constitute 15 percent of the nation's total population.[2]

18

Number of states with an estimated black population on July 1, 2008, of at least 1 million. New York, with 3.5 million, led the way. The other 17 states on the list were Alabama, California, Florida, Georgia, Illinois, Louisiana, Maryland, Michigan, Mississippi, New Jersey, North Carolina, Ohio, Pennsylvania, South Carolina, Tennessee, Texas and Virginia.[3]

38%

Percentage of Mississippi's population that was black in 2008, highest of any state. Blacks also made up more than a quarter of the population in Louisiana in 2008 (32 percent), Georgia (31 percent), Maryland (30 percent), South Carolina (29 percent) and Alabama (27 percent). They comprise 56 percent of the population in the District of Columbia.[4]

67,000

The increase in Georgia's black population between July 1, 2007, and July 1, 2008, which led all states. Texas (64,000), North Carolina (45,000) and Florida (41,000) also recorded large increases.[5]

24

Number of states or equivalents in which blacks were the largest minority group in 2008. These included Alabama, Arkansas, Delaware, District of Columbia, Georgia, Illinois, Indiana, Kentucky, Louisiana, Maine, Maryland, Michigan, Minnesota, Mississippi, Missouri, New York, North Carolina, Ohio, Pennsylvania, South Carolina, Tennessee, Virginia, West Virginia and Wisconsin. (Note: Minorities are part of a group other than single-race non-Hispanic white.)[6]

1.4 million

The number of blacks in Cook County, Ill., as of July 1, 2008, which led the nation's counties in the number of people of this racial category. Orleans Parish, La., had the largest numerical increase in the black population between July 1, 2007, and July 1, 2008 (16,400).[7]

Among counties with total populations of at least 10,000, Claiborne County, Miss., had the largest percent of population that was black (84.4 percent). Claiborne led 77 majority-black counties or equivalents, all of which were in the South.[8]

30%

The proportion of the black population younger than 18 as of July 1, 2008. At the other end of the spectrum, 8 percent of the black population was 65 and older.[9]

Note: Unless otherwise noted, the estimates in this section refer to the population that was either single-race black or black in combination with one or more other races.

Serving Our Nation

2.3 million

Number of single-race black military veterans in the United States in 2008. More military veterans are black than any other minority group.[10]

Education

83%

Among blacks 25 and older, the proportion who had at least a high school diploma in 2008.[11]

20%

Percentage of blacks 25 and older who had a bachelor's degree or higher in 2008.[12]

1.4 million

Among blacks 25 and older, the number who had an advanced degree in 2008 (e.g., master's, doctorate, medical or law). In 1998, 857,000 blacks had this level of education.[13]

2.5 million

Number of black college students in fall 2008. This was roughly double the corresponding number from 15 years earlier.[14]

Voting

About 2.1 million

The increase in the number of black voters between the 2004 and 2008 presidential elections, to 16.1 million. The total number of voters rose by 5.4 million, to 131.1 million.[15]

55%

Turnout rate in the 2008 presidential election for the 18- to 24-year-old citizen black population, an 8 percent increase from 2004. Blacks had the highest turnout rate in this age group.[16]

65%

Turnout rate among black citizens in the 2008 presidential election, up about 5 percentage points from 2004. Looking at voter turnout by race and Hispanic origin, non-Hispanic whites and blacks had the highest turnout levels.[17]

Income, Poverty and Health Insurance

$ 34,218

The annual median income of single-race black households in 2008, a decline of 2.8 percent (in 2008 constant dollars) from 2007.[18]

24.7%

Poverty rate in 2008 for single-race blacks, statistically unchanged from 2007.[19]

19.1%

The percentage of single-race blacks lacking health insurance in 2008, not statistically different from 2007.[20]

Families and Children

63%

Among households with a single-race black householder, the percentage that contained a family. There were 8.5 million black family households.[21]

44%

Among families with single-race black householders, the percentage that were married couples.[22]

1.2 million

Number of single-race black grandparents who lived with their own grandchildren younger than 18. Of this number, 50 percent were also responsible for their care.[23]

Homeownership— the American Dream

46%

Nationally, the percentage of households with a householder who was single-race black who lived in owner-occupied homes.[24]

Jobs

27%

The percentage of single-race blacks 16 and older who worked in management, professional and related occupations.[25]

Businesses

$ 88.6 billion

Revenues for black-owned businesses in 2002. The number of black-owned businesses totaled nearly 1.2 million in 2002. Black-owned firms accounted for 5 percent of all nonfarm businesses in the United States.

129,329

The number of black-owned firms in New York in 2002, which led all states. New York City alone had 98,080 such firms, which led all cities.

10,716

The number of black-owned firms operating in 2002 with receipts of $1 million or more. These firms accounted for 1 percent of the total number of black-owned firms in 2002 and 55 percent of their total receipts, or $49 billion.

969

The number of black-owned firms with 100 or more employees in 2002. Firms of this size accounted for 24 percent of the total revenue for black-owned employer firms in 2002, or $16 billion.[26]

Note: The 2007 Preliminary Estimates of Business Ownership by Gender, Ethnicity, and Race will be available in July 2010 and the more detailed 2007 Black-Owned Businesses report will be published in February 2011.

Following is a list of observances typically covered by the Census Bureau's Facts for Features series:

Black African-American History Month (February)
Super Bowl
Valentine's Day (Feb. 14)
Women's History Month (March)
Irish-American Heritage Month (March)/
 St. Patrick's Day (March 17)
American Indian/Alaska Native Heritage Month
 (November)
Asian/Pacific American Heritage Month (May)
Older Americans Month (May)
Cinco de Mayo (May 5)
Thanksgiving Day
Mother's Day
Labor Day
Grandparents Day
Hispanic Heritage Month (Sept. 15–Oct. 15)
Unmarried and Single Americans Week (Sept. 19–25)
Halloween (Oct. 31)
Veterans Day (Nov. 11)
The Holiday Season (December)
Hurricane Season Begins (June 1)
Father's Day
The Fourth of July (July 4)
Anniversary of Americans with Disabilities Act (July 26)
Back to School (August)

Notes

1. Source: Population estimates www.census.gov/Press-Release/www/releases/archives/population/013733.html

2. Source: Population projections www.census.gov/Press-Release/www/releases/archives/population/012496.html

3. Source: Population estimates www.census.gov/Press-Release/www/releases/archives/population/013734.html

4. Source: Population estimates www.census.gov/Press-Release/www/releases/archives/population/013734.html

5. Source: Population estimates www.census.gov/Press-Release/www/releases/archives/population/013734.html

6. Source: Population estimates www.census.gov/Press-Release/www/releases/archives/population/013734.html

7. Source: Population estimates www.census.gov/Press-Release/www/releases/archives/population/013734.html

8. Source: Population estimates www.census.gov/Press-Release/www/releases/archives/population/013734.html

9. Source: Population estimates www.census.gov/Press-Release/www/releases/archives/population/013733.html

10. Source: 2008 American Community Survey http://factfinder.census.gov

11. Source: Educational Attainment in the United States: 2008 www.census.gov/Press-Release/www/releases/archives/education/013618.html

12. Source: Educational Attainment in the United States: 2008 www.census.gov/Press-Release/www/releases/archives/education/013618.html

13. Source: Educational Attainment in the United States: 2008 www.census.gov/Press-Release/www/releases/archives/education/013618.html

14. Source: School Enrollment-Social and Economic Characteristics of Students: October 2008 www.census.gov/Press-Release/www/releases/archives/education/014354.html

15. Source: Voting and Registration in the Election of 2008 www.census.gov/Press-Release/www/releases/archives/voting/013995.html

16. Source: Voting and Registration in the Election of 2008 www.census.gov/Press-Release/www/releases/archives/voting/013995.html

17. Source: Voting and Registration in the Election of 2008 www.census.gov/Press-Release/www/releases/archives/voting/013995.html

18. Source: Income, Poverty, and Health Insurance Coverage in the United States: 2008 www.census.gov/Press-Release/www/releases/archives/income_wealth/014227.html

19. Source: Income, Poverty, and Health Insurance Coverage in the United States: 2008 www.census.gov/Press-Release/www/releases/archives/income_wealth/014227.html

20. Source: Income, Poverty, and Health Insurance Coverage in the United States: 2008 www.census.gov/Press-Release/www/releases/archives/income_wealth/014227.html

21. Source: 2008 American Community Survey http://factfinder.census.gov

22. Source: 2008 American Community Survey http://factfinder.census.gov

23. Source: 2008 American Community Survey http://factfinder.census.gov

24. Source: 2008 American Community Survey http://factfinder.census.gov

25. Source: 2008 American Community Survey http://factfinder .census.gov

26. Source: Black-Owned Firms: 2002 www.census.gov/prod/ec02/ sb0200csblk.pdf

Critical Thinking

1. How is Black History Month celebrated in your area or region?

2. In your view, which of the social and economic indicators reported are most significant and meaningful?

3. What do you make of problematic data related to families and children and the absence of incarceration rates in this report?

Editor's note—The preceding data were collected from a variety of sources and may be subject to sampling variability and other sources of error. Facts for Features are customarily released about two months before an observance in order to accommodate magazine production timelines. Questions or comments should be directed to the Census Bureau's Public Information Office: telephone: 301-763-3030; fax: 301-763-3762; or e-mail: pio@census.gov.

From *U.S Department of Commerce, Economics, and Statistics Administration*, December 2009.

Transcript of Obama's Speech

The following is a transcript of Sen. Barack Obama's speech, as provided by Obama's campaign.

We the people, in order to form a more perfect union. Two hundred and twenty one years ago, in a hall that still stands across the street, a group of men gathered and, with these simple words, launched America's improbable experiment in democracy.

Farmers and scholars; statesmen and patriots who had traveled across an ocean to escape tyranny and persecution finally made real their declaration of independence at a Philadelphia convention that lasted through the spring of 1787.

The document they produced was eventually signed but ultimately unfinished. It was stained by this nation's original sin of slavery, a question that divided the colonies and brought the convention to a stalemate until the founders chose to allow the slave trade to continue for at least 20 more years, and to leave any final resolution to future generations.

Of course, the answer to the slavery question was already embedded within our Constitution—a Constitution that had at its very core the ideal of equal citizenship under the law; a Constitution that promised its people liberty, and justice, and a union that could be and should be perfected over time.

And yet words on a parchment would not be enough to deliver slaves from bondage, or provide men and women of every color and creed their full rights and obligations as citizens of the United States.

What would be needed were Americans in successive generations who were willing to do their part—through protests and struggle, on the streets and in the courts, through a civil war and civil disobedience and always at great risk—to narrow that gap between the promise of our ideals and the reality of their time.

This was one of the tasks we set forth at the beginning of this campaign—to continue the long march of those who came before us, a march for a more just, more equal, more free, more caring and more prosperous America.

I chose to run for the presidency at this moment in history because I believe deeply that we cannot solve the challenges of our time unless we solve them together—unless we perfect our union by understanding that we may have different stories, but we hold common hopes; that we may not look the same and we may not have come from the same place, but we all want to move in the same direction—towards a better future for our children and our grandchildren.

This belief comes from my unyielding faith in the decency and generosity of the American people. But it also comes from my own American story.

I am the son of a black man from Kenya and a white woman from Kansas. I was raised with the help of a white grandfather who survived a Depression to serve in Patton's Army during World War II and a white grandmother who worked on a bomber assembly line at Fort Leavenworth while he was overseas.

I've gone to some of the best schools in America and lived in one of the world's poorest nations. I am married to a black American who carries within her the blood of slaves and slaveowners—an inheritance we pass on to our two precious daughters.

I have brothers, sisters, nieces, nephews, uncles and cousins, of every race and every hue, scattered across three continents, and for as long as I live, I will never forget that in no other country on Earth is my story even possible.

It's a story that hasn't made me the most conventional candidate. But it is a story that has seared into my genetic makeup the idea that this nation is more than the sum of its parts—that out of many, we are truly one.

Throughout the first year of this campaign, against all predictions to the contrary, we saw how hungry the American people were for this message of unity.

Despite the temptation to view my candidacy through a purely racial lens, we won commanding victories in states with some of the whitest populations in the country. In South Carolina, where the Confederate Flag still flies, we built a powerful coalition of African-Americans and white Americans.

This is not to say that race has not been an issue in the campaign. At various stages in the campaign, some commentators have deemed me either "too black" or "not black enough."

We saw racial tensions bubble to the surface during the week before the South Carolina primary. The press has scoured every exit poll for the latest evidence of racial polarization, not just in terms of white and black, but black and brown as well.

And yet, it has only been in the last couple of weeks that the discussion of race in this campaign has taken a particularly divisive turn.

On one end of the spectrum, we've heard the implication that my candidacy is somehow an exercise in affirmative action, that it's based solely on the desire of wide-eyed liberals to purchase racial reconciliation on the cheap.

On the other end, we've heard my former pastor, Rev. Jeremiah Wright, use incendiary language to express views that have the potential not only to widen the racial divide, but views that denigrate both the greatness and the goodness of our nation—that rightly offend white and black alike.

I have already condemned, in unequivocal terms, the statements of Rev. Wright that have caused such controversy. For some, nagging questions remain.

Did I know him to be an occasionally fierce critic of American domestic and foreign policy? Of course. Did I ever hear him make remarks that could be considered controversial while I sat in church? Yes. Did I strongly disagree with many of his political views? Absolutely—just as I'm sure many of you have heard remarks from your pastors, priests or rabbis with which you strongly disagreed.

But the remarks that have caused this recent firestorm weren't simply controversial. They weren't simply a religious leader's effort to speak out against perceived injustice.

Instead, they expressed a profoundly distorted view of this country—a view that sees white racism as endemic, and that elevates what is wrong with America above all that we know is right with America, a view that sees the conflicts in the Middle East as rooted primarily in the actions of stalwart allies like Israel, instead of emanating from the perverse and hateful ideologies of radical Islam.

As such, Rev. Wright's comments were not only wrong but divisive, divisive at a time when we need unity; racially charged at a time when we need to come together to solve a set of monumental problems—two wars, a terrorist threat, a falling economy, a chronic health care crisis and potentially devastating climate change; problems that are neither black or white or Latino or Asian, but rather problems that confront us all.

Given my background, my politics, and my professed values and ideals, there will no doubt be those for whom my statements of condemnation are not enough. Why associate myself with Rev. Wright in the first place, they may ask? Why not join another church?

And I confess that if all that I knew of Rev. Wright were the snippets of those sermons that have run in an endless loop on the television and YouTube, or if Trinity United Church of Christ conformed to the caricatures being peddled by some commentators, there is no doubt that I would react in much the same way

But the truth is, that isn't all that I know of the man. The man I met more than 20 years ago is a man who helped introduce me to my Christian faith, a man who spoke to me about our obligations to love one another; to care for the sick and lift up the poor.

He is a man who served his country as a U.S. Marine, who has studied and lectured at some of the finest universities and seminaries in the country, and who for over thirty years led a church that serves the community by doing God's work here on Earth—by housing the homeless, ministering to the needy, providing day care services and scholarships and prison ministries, and reaching out to those suffering from HIV/AIDS.

In my first book, "Dreams From My Father," I described the experience of my first service at Trinity.

"People began to shout, to rise from their seats and clap and cry out, a forceful wind carrying the reverend's voice up into the rafters . . . . And in that single note—hope!—I heard something else; at the foot of that cross, inside the thousands of churches across the city, I imagined the stories of ordinary black people merging with the stories of David and Goliath, Moses and Pharaoh, the Christians in the lion's den, Ezekiel's field of dry bones.

"Those stories—of survival, and freedom, and hope—became our story, my story; the blood that had spilled was our blood, the tears our tears; until this black church, on this bright day, seemed once more a vessel carrying the story of a people into future generations and into a larger world.

"Our trials and triumphs became at once unique and universal, black and more than black; in chronicling our journey, the stories and songs gave us a means to reclaim memories that we didn't need to feel shame about . . . memories that all people might study and cherish—and with which we could start to rebuild."

That has been my experience at Trinity. Like other predominantly black churches across the country, Trinity embodies the black community in its entirety—the doctor and the welfare mom, the model student and the former gang-banger.

Like other black churches, Trinity's services are full of raucous laughter and sometimes bawdy humor. They are full of dancing, clapping, screaming and shouting that may seem jarring to the untrained ear.

The church contains in full the kindness and cruelty, the fierce intelligence and the shocking ignorance, the struggles and successes, the love and yes, the bitterness and bias that make up the black experience in America.

And this helps explain, perhaps, my relationship with Rev. Wright. As imperfect as he may be, he has been like family to me. He strengthened my faith, officiated my wedding, and baptized my children.

Not once in my conversations with him have I heard him talk about any ethnic group in derogatory terms, or treat whites with whom he interacted with anything but courtesy and respect. He contains within him the contradictions—the good and the bad—of the community that he has served diligently for so many years.

I can no more disown him than I can disown the black community. I can no more disown him than I can my white grandmother—a woman who helped raise me, a woman who sacrificed again and again for me, a woman who loves me as much as she loves anything in this world, but a woman who once confessed her fear of black men who passed by her on the street, and who on more than one occasion has uttered racial or ethnic stereotypes that made me cringe.

These people are a part of me. And they are a part of America, this country that I love.

Some will see this as an attempt to justify or excuse comments that are simply inexcusable. I can assure you it is not. I suppose the politically safe thing would be to move on from this episode and just hope that it fades into the woodwork.

We can dismiss Rev. Wright as a crank or a demagogue, just as some have dismissed Geraldine Ferraro, in the aftermath of her recent statements, as harboring some deep-seated racial bias.

But race is an issue that I believe this nation cannot afford to ignore right now. We would be making the same mistake that Rev. Wright made in his offending sermons about America—to simplify and stereotype and amplify the negative to the point that it distorts reality.

The fact is that the comments that have been made and the issues that have surfaced over the last few weeks reflect the complexities of race in this country that we've never really worked through—a part of our union that we have yet to perfect.

And if we walk away now, if we simply retreat into our respective corners, we will never be able to come together and solve challenges like health care, or education, or the need to find good jobs for every American.

Understanding this reality requires a reminder of how we arrived at this point. As William Faulkner once wrote, "The past isn't dead and buried. In fact, it isn't even past." We do not need to recite here the history of racial injustice in this country.

But we do need to remind ourselves that so many of the disparities that exist in the African-American community today can be directly traced to inequalities passed on from an earlier generation that suffered under the brutal legacy of slavery and Jim Crow.

Segregated schools were, and are, inferior schools; we still haven't fixed them, fifty years after Brown v. Board of Education, and the inferior education they provided, then and now, helps explain the pervasive achievement gap between today's black and white students.

Legalized discrimination—where blacks were prevented, often through violence, from owning property, or loans were not granted to African-American business owners, or black homeowners could not access FHA mortgages, or blacks were excluded from unions, or the police force, or fire departments—meant that black families could not amass any meaningful wealth to bequeath to future generations.

That history helps explain the wealth and income gap between black and white, and the concentrated pockets of poverty that persists in so many of today's urban and rural communities.

A lack of economic opportunity among black men, and the shame and frustration that came from not being able to provide for one's family, contributed to the erosion of black families—a problem that welfare policies for many years may have worsened.

And the lack of basic services in so many urban black neighborhoods—parks for kids to play in, police walking the beat, regular garbage pick-up and building code enforcement—all helped create a cycle of violence, blight and neglect that continue to haunt us.

This is the reality in which Rev. Wright and other African-Americans of his generation grew up. They came of age in the late fifties and early sixties, a time when segregation was still the law of the land and opportunity was systematically constricted.

What's remarkable is not how many failed in the face of discrimination, but rather how many men and women overcame the odds; how many were able to make a way out of no way for those like me who would come after them.

But for all those who scratched and clawed their way to get a piece of the American Dream, there were many who didn't make it—those who were ultimately defeated, in one way or another, by discrimination.

That legacy of defeat was passed on to future generations—those young men and, increasingly, young women who we see standing on street corners or languishing in our prisons, without hope or prospects for the future. Even for those blacks who did make it, questions of race, and racism, continue to define their worldview in fundamental ways.

For the men and women of Rev. Wright's generation, the memories of humiliation and doubt and fear have not gone away; nor has the anger and the bitterness of those years.

That anger may not get expressed in public, in front of white co-workers or white friends. But it does find voice in the barbershop or around the kitchen table. At times, that anger is exploited by politicians, to gin up votes along racial lines, or to make up for a politician's own failings.

And occasionally it finds voice in the church on Sunday morning, in the pulpit and in the pews. The fact that so many people are surprised to hear that anger in some of Rev. Wright's sermons simply reminds us of the old truism that the most segregated hour in American life occurs on Sunday morning.

That anger is not always productive; indeed, all too often it distracts attention from solving real problems; it keeps us from squarely facing our own complicity in our condition, and prevents the African-American community from forging the alliances it needs to bring about real change.

But the anger is real; it is powerful; and to simply wish it away, to condemn it without understanding its roots, only serves to widen the chasm of misunderstanding that exists between the races.

In fact, a similar anger exists within segments of the white community. Most working- and middle-class white Americans don't feel that they have been particularly privileged by their race.

Their experience is the immigrant experience—as far as they're concerned, no one's handed them anything, they've built it from scratch. They've worked hard all their lives, many times only to see their jobs shipped overseas or their pension dumped after a lifetime of labor.

They are anxious about their futures, and feel their dreams slipping away; in an era of stagnant wages and global competition, opportunity comes to be seen as a zero sum game, in which your dreams come at my expense.

So when they are told to bus their children to a school across town; when they hear that an African-American is getting an advantage in landing a good job or a spot in a good college because of an injustice that they themselves never committed; when they're told that their fears about crime in urban neighborhoods are somehow prejudiced, resentment builds over time.

Like the anger within the black community, these resentments aren't always expressed in polite company. But they have helped shape the political landscape for at least a generation.

Anger over welfare and affirmative action helped forge the Reagan Coalition. Politicians routinely exploited fears of crime for their own electoral ends. Talk show hosts and conservative commentators built entire careers unmasking bogus claims of racism while dismissing legitimate discussions of racial injustice and inequality as mere political correctness or reverse racism.

Just as black anger often proved counterproductive, so have these white resentments distracted attention from the real culprits of the middle-class squeeze—a corporate culture rife with inside dealing, questionable accounting practices and short-term greed; a Washington dominated by lobbyists and special interests; economic policies that favor the few over the many.

And yet, to wish away the resentments of white Americans, to label them as misguided or even racist, without recognizing they are grounded in legitimate concerns—this too widens the racial divide, and blocks the path to understanding.

This is where we are right now. It's a racial stalemate we've been stuck in for years. Contrary to the claims of some of my critics, black and white, I have never been so naive as to believe that we can get beyond our racial divisions in a single election cycle, or with a single candidacy—particularly a candidacy as imperfect as my own.

But I have asserted a firm conviction—a conviction rooted in my faith in God and my faith in the American people—that working together we can move beyond some of our old racial wounds, and that in fact we have no choice if we are to continue on the path of a more perfect union.

For the African-American community, that path means embracing the burdens of our past without becoming victims of our past. It means continuing to insist on a full measure of justice in every aspect of American life.

But it also means binding our particular grievances—for better health care, and better schools, and better jobs—to the larger aspirations of all Americans, the white woman struggling to break the glass ceiling, the white man whose been laid off, the immigrant trying to feed his family.

And it means taking full responsibility for own lives—by demanding more from our fathers, and spending more time with our children, and reading to them, and teaching them that while they may face challenges and discrimination in their own lives, they must never succumb to despair or cynicism; they must always believe that they can write their own destiny.

Ironically, this quintessentially American—and yes, conservative—notion of self-help found frequent expression in Rev. Wright's sermons. But what my former pastor too often failed to understand is that embarking on a program of self-help also requires a belief that society can change.

The profound mistake of Rev. Wright's sermons is not that he spoke about racism in our society. It's that he spoke as if our society was static; as if no progress has been made; as if this country—a country that has made it possible for one of his own members to run for the highest office in the land and build a coalition of white and black, Latino and Asian, rich and poor, young and old—is still irrevocably bound to a tragic past.

But what we know—what we have seen—is that America can change. That is the true genius of this nation. What we have already achieved gives us hope—the audacity to hope—for what we can and must achieve tomorrow.

In the white community, the path to a more perfect union means acknowledging that what ails the African-American community does not just exist in the minds of black people; that the legacy of discrimination—and current incidents of discrimination, while less overt than in the past—are real and must be addressed.

Not just with words, but with deeds—by investing in our schools and our communities; by enforcing our civil rights laws and ensuring fairness in our criminal justice system; by providing this generation with ladders of opportunity that were unavailable for previous generations.

It requires all Americans to realize that your dreams do not have to come at the expense of my dreams; that investing in the health, welfare and education of black and brown and white children will ultimately help all of America prosper.

In the end, then, what is called for is nothing more, and nothing less, than what all the world's great religions demand—that we do unto others as we would have them do unto us. Let us be our brother's keeper, Scripture tells us. Let us be our sister's keeper. Let us find that common stake we all have in one another, and let our politics reflect that spirit as well.

For we have a choice in this country. We can accept a politics that breeds division, and conflict, and cynicism. We can tackle race only as spectacle—as we did in the O.J. trial—or in the wake of tragedy, as we did in the aftermath of Katrina—or as fodder for the nightly news.

We can play Rev. Wright's sermons on every channel, every day and talk about them from now until the election, and make the only question in this campaign whether or not the American people think that I somehow believe or sympathize with his most offensive words.

We can pounce on some gaffe by a Hillary supporter as evidence that she's playing the race card, or we can speculate on whether white men will all flock to John McCain in the general election regardless of his policies.

We can do that.

But if we do, I can tell you that in the next election, we'll be talking about some other distraction. And then another one. And then another one. And nothing will change.

That is one option. Or, at this moment, in this election, we can come together and say, "Not this time." This time we want to talk about the crumbling schools that are stealing the future of black children and white children and Asian children and Hispanic children and Native American children.

This time we want to reject the cynicism that tells us that these kids can't learn; that those kids who don't look like us are somebody else's problem. The children of America are not those kids, they are our kids, and we will not let them fall behind in a 21st Century economy. Not this time.

This time we want to talk about how the lines in the emergency room are filled with whites and blacks and Hispanics who do not have health care, who don't have the power on their own to overcome the special interests in Washington, but who can take them on if we do it together.

This time we want to talk about the shuttered mills that once provided a decent life for men and women of every race, and the homes for sale that once belonged to Americans from every religion, every region, every walk of life.

This time we want to talk about the fact that the real problem is not that someone who doesn't look like you might take your job; it's that the corporation you work for will ship it overseas for nothing more than a profit.

This time we want to talk about the men and women of every color and creed who serve together, and fight together, and bleed together under the same proud flag.

We want to talk about how to bring them home from a war that never should've been authorized and never should've been waged, and we want to talk about how we'll show our patriotism by caring for them, and their families, and giving them the benefits they have earned.

I would not be running for president if I didn't believe with all my heart that this is what the vast majority of Americans want for this country. This union may never be perfect, but generation after generation has shown that it can always be perfected.

And today, whenever I find myself feeling doubtful or cynical about this possibility, what gives me the most hope is the next generation—the young people whose attitudes and beliefs and openness to change have already made history in this election.

There is one story in particular that I'd like to leave you with today—a story I told when I had the great honor of speaking on Dr. King's birthday at his home church, Ebenezer Baptist, in Atlanta.

There is a young, 23-year-old white woman named Ashley Baia who organized for our campaign in Florence, South Carolina. She had been working to organize a mostly African-American community since the beginning of this campaign, and one day she was at a roundtable discussion where everyone went around telling their story and why they were there.

And Ashley said that when she was 9 years old, her mother got cancer. And because she had to miss days of work, she was let go and lost her health care. They had to file for bankruptcy, and that's when Ashley decided that she had to do something to help her mom.

She knew that food was one of their most expensive costs, and so Ashley convinced her mother that what she really liked and really wanted to eat more than anything else was mustard and relish sandwiches. Because that was the cheapest way to eat.

She did this for a year until her mom got better, and she told everyone at the roundtable that the reason she joined our campaign was so that she could help the millions of other children in the country who want and need to help their parents, too.

Now Ashley might have made a different choice. Perhaps somebody told her along the way that the source of her mother's problems were blacks who were on welfare and too lazy to work, or Hispanics who were coming into the country illegally. But she didn't. She sought out allies in her fight against injustice.

Anyway, Ashley finishes her story and then goes around the room and asks everyone else why they're supporting the campaign. They all have different stories and reasons. Many bring up a specific issue. And finally they come to this elderly black man who's been sitting there quietly the entire time.

And Ashley asks him why he's there. And he does not bring up a specific issue. He does not say health care or the economy. He does not say education or the war. He does not say that he was there because of Barack Obama. He simply says to everyone in the room, "I am here because of Ashley."

"I'm here because of Ashley." By itself, that single moment of recognition between that young white girl and that old black man is not enough. It is not enough to give health care to the sick, or jobs to the jobless, or education to our children.

But it is where we start. It is where our union grows stronger. And as so many generations have come to realize over the course of the two-hundred and twenty one years since a band of patriots signed that document in Philadelphia, that is where the perfection begins.

Critical Thinking

1. What are the major themes of this speech?

2. In what respects has the conversation about race in America changed over the past two years?

3. In your opinion, what are the most memorial sentences of this speech? Why?

Public Domain, March 18, 2008.

Redefining Black Women in America

BET's Debra Lee wants to move beyond demeaning stereotypes.

KRISSAH THOMPSON

Bonnie McDaniel refused to let her now 24-year-old daughter watch Black Entertainment Television growing up.

She hated the oversexed, booty-shaking music videos. She thought the programming objectified black women. She would bad-mouth the network with her girlfriends.

This week, the author and entrepreneur joined 130 other successful black women—influential in politics, entertainment and nonprofits—at the Mandarin Oriental Hotel to talk about portrayals of black women in the media, the problems facing black girls in urban schools, the state of the black family and other weighty issues.

The sponsor of this gathering of African American alpha women: BET.

"I've been invited to many events by BET, but this is the first one I have attended," McDaniel, who lives in Fairfax, said to the cable network's chief executive Debra Lee at one of the event's workshops. "I didn't like a lot of the messages and images that were coming out. But we have the power to change that."

Lee listened and nodded.

The two-day summit—a first for BET—was her idea. Lee said it came to her after the BET Awards last year, which included a controversial performance by hip-hop artists Lil Wayne and Drake, who brought underage girls onto the stage to dance while they rapped "I wish I could [expletive] every girl in the world."

The network has long come under fire for its music videos that critics say perpetuate racial stereotypes of African Americans and demean women. In 2008, a group called "Enough Is Enough" protested outside of Lee's home for more than five months.

"I just still feel like, as much as we've tried, it's still a heavily male dominated music genre," Lee said, describing her feeling after the 2009 awards show.

She said her thoughts turned from the show to the scene in Washington, where Lee has mingled with first lady Michelle Obama, presidential senior adviser Valerie Jarrett, domestic policy chief Melody Barnes and other African American women at the center of power. Then, Lee said, she took out her Rolodex of successful black women and phoned Essence's

Beauty and Cover Director Mikki Taylor, political commentator Donna Brazile, journalist and author Gwen Ifill, actresses Tatyana Ali and Tasha Smith, and others.

"We are at the start of a new decade and a new opportunity. Our president and first family are shining examples that anything is possible," Lee said. "It's such an exciting time, [and] I said [to myself] how can we get powerful black women together and discuss issues that are important to us?"

The result, "Leading Women Defined," looks like a historically black sorority meeting on steroids. Women with important jobs in Hollywood, in New York and in the White House led portions of the conversation, including starlet Raven-Symone and children's rights advocate Marian Wright Edelman.

The event, which along with panels and luncheon speakers included a mentoring trip to Dunbar High School and a Chrisette Michele concert, was not open to the public but free to the invitees. Lee said she wants it to become an ongoing network of successful black women who come together to create positive change—by "starting a black Emily's List or adopting a school, whatever we decide."

She and her team handpicked every participant—and some women, such as McDaniel, were politely critical of the network. Others, including Tricia Rose, a professor at Brown University and author of "The Hip Hop Wars," have been harshly critical.

The network's most vociferous detractors, such as lawyer and blogger Gina McCauley, found the entire thing ironic, and called it a PR stunt. "What are they leading? Black girls to a life of objectification?" asked McCauley, who was not at the event.

Lee seemed prepared for the flak.

The network turns 30 this year, and Lee said the women's conference is part of its ongoing movement into a new phase. Several times, BET staffers referred to the network as "the new BET," though they made no apologies for its controversial past. A historical video highlighted the now-defunct "Video Soul" and "Teen Summit" programs, but not "BET Uncut," a raunchier late-night show that drew complaints.

"We've been really concerned with trying to show different facets of black life," Lee said. "I think black women really want to see themselves as professionals, as mothers, as daughters. We want the whole spectrum of our womanhood to be reflected."

Lee pointed to the launch of its newest channel Centric, which targets African Americans 25- to 54-years-old, and the hiring of filmmaker Loretha Jones (producer of "The Fighting Temptations" and "The Five Heartbeats") as president of BET's original programming 18 months ago, along with the creation of a new brand strategy last year based around themes such as family, creativity and social activism. The network has since debuted several programs—including a talk show hosted by comedienne and actress Mo'Nique; "The Family Crews," about a black nuclear family pursuing their dreams; and "Sunday Best," a gospel music competition hosted by Kirk Franklin. Popular broadcast journalist Ed Gordon also agreed this week to return to the network, bolstering its tiny news division.

"I love my job, but my job is more difficult in certain ways than I would have imagined," Jones told the women gathered for the conference. "I have to choose stories and make decisions from a really balanced perspective, because we have so little representations of ourselves. We cannot get away with things that other people can get away with."

The sessions that engendered some of the most passionate discussions were about representations of black women, who have long grappled with the psychological repercussions of not fitting American mainstream ideals of beauty. It's an old conversation that feels like it is shifting, some of the women said.

A survey conducted by Essence and Procter & Gamble, which was an event co-sponsor, found that 80 percent of black women respondents were concerned about the way they are portrayed in mainstream media. But more than 90 percent said Obama's role as first lady would have a positive effect on images of black women.

Jarrett, who stopped by to greet the women and stump for the administration's health-care plan, said they see the opportunity inside the White House.

She told the story of a letter she received from an 11-year-old black girl who wrote after reading about Jarrett in Essence. "Maybe I can grow up and be like you," the girl said. Jarrett

wrote back and invited her to the White House. "It's those little gestures that we want to encourage," Jarrett said, before hurrying back to meet with the president.

But along with the admiration and pretty, glossy magazine covers of the first lady, there have come blogs with demeaning depictions of her, noted Harriette Cole, acting editor-in-chief of Ebony magazine and a panelist. Late last year, an image of the first lady with monkey features appeared at the top of search results when "Michelle Obama" was typed into Google Images.

"People don't want to believe that the Obamas exist, even though they do," Cole said. "That means that they don't want to believe that *we* exist."

Rose, the Brown University hip-hop scholar, said she doesn't sense that the consciousness about the Obamas' images has translated to critical thinking about wider representations of African Americans. As for BET, she is cautiously optimistic about the changes she's seen, but noted that Lee offered no blanket promises to ban programming that stereotypes African Americans or demeans women.

"This kind of thing is glacial," Rose said. "It's only so quickly that you can make changes and survive. I think there's still quite a way to go. If you're going to show shaking behinds to 12-year-old boys, you're going to get a pretty good market share, but what is going to interrupt that profit motive? We have to hold [BET] accountable along with all the other networks."

McDaniel agreed. At the end of the conference, she said she believed Lee does intend to make changes at the network, but just in case she planned to "become an annoyance to her."

"I'm going to remind her of what she told us."

Critical Thinking

1. Does this conference address most of the issues of concern related to gender and race?
2. In what respects are education and income as well as gender and race the topic of this discussion?

From *The Washington Post*, March 13, 2010. Copyright © 2010 by Washington Post Writers Group. Reprinted by permission via PARS International Corp.

UNIT 6

Hispanic/Latino/a Americans

Unit Selections

28. **Who's Hispanic?,** Jeffrey Passel and Paul Taylor
29. **Race and Hispanic Origin of the Foreign-Born Population in the United States: 2007,** *American Community Survey Reports,* January 2010
30. **Latino Agricultural Workers and Their Young Families: Advancing Theoretical and Empirically Based Conceptualizations,** Sandra Barrueco, and Robert O'Brien

Learning Objectives

- What does the debate about the use of the words Hispanic and Latino/a suggest about the cultural agenda of minority groups?

- Does television programming, film, and entertainment adequately address our understanding of pluralism within the Hispanic and Latino cultures?

- When do ethnic and racial issues foster understanding? Does the charge of racialism within the Hispanic/Latino community expose the limits of solidarity? How about the existence of color consciousness that is present in the population?

- Does the historical anti-immigrant position of African Americans explain this matter, or does such an argument simply fuel allegations of discrimination?

- What are the strengths and weaknesses of strong bonds within ethnic communities? What role does ethnic media play in the formation and continuity of community? Can ethnic media cross over to wider audiences?

- In what respects is Hispanic/Latino American culture becoming part of mainstream American culture? What can be expected for relationships between Hispanic ancestry populations and the newest immigrants from Spanish-speaking countries?

- Are Portuguese-speaking groups Hispanic?

- On December 10, 1996, the Mexican government passed a law to allow dual citizenship to persons living in the U.S. What does this policy portend for the relationship between Mexico and the United States? Should statehood for northern Mexico become an option? At present, is this law of citizenship a threat to or an opportunity for ethnic group relations?

- Hispanic voters are concentrated in California, Texas, Florida, and New York. How significant or crucial to electoral success are these states for presidential elections? Explain.

Student Website

www.mhhe.com/cls

Internet References

Latino American Network Information Center (LANIC)
   http://lanic.utexas.edu
National Council of La Raza (NCLR)
   www.nclr.org

The following collection of materials on Hispanic/Latino Americans is a composite of findings about ethnicities. The clustering of these ethnicities and nationalities, as well as their relationship to the Spanish language, seems to be sufficient evidence of the commonalities that constitute the shared expression of this complex of past and contemporary politics. Yet the use of the terms Hispanic and Latino that differentiate them from Anglo-American foundations and their social expression as they search for a cultural and political terrain are but the surface of the process of intergroup dynamics in the United States.

A comprehensive survey of Hispanic/Latino Americans, sponsored by the Pew Hispanic Center and the Henry J. Kaiser Family Foundation, confirmed what many observers of race and ethnic relations have long noted: Rather than being an ethnic population, Hispanic/Latino Americans are an artifact of the U.S. Census. In reality, this U.S. Census category or data cluster comprises significantly diverse groups. With differences arising from experiences in different countries of origin, the cultural and political perspectives suggest that this fastest growing population in various locations and distinct communities with varied agendas is certainly not homogenous and monolithic. The survey found that respondents representative of immigrants and descendants of immigrants from Mexico, Puerto Rico, Cuba, and other Central and South American countries fully appreciated that learning English was essential to success in the United States. Moreover, 60 percent of this population usually and predominantly speaks English. Such fine-grain analysis of ethnic and racial populations tends to reveal the malleability of identity and the problem of census data and categorization—1980 census.

The articles in this unit propose angles of vision that enable us to view the process of accommodation and change that is articulated in political practice, scholarship, advocacy, and art. The issues presented provocatively shift traditional perspectives from the Eastern and Midwestern mindset toward the Western and Southwestern immigration to the United States. The Immigration Act of 1965 induced a process not unlike the period of large-scale eastern and southern European immigration between 1880 and 1924. This immigration includes scores of various ethnic groups, and cultural/geographic descriptions are not the clearest form of ethnic identity. Hispanic/Latino Americans are not a single ethnic group. The designation of various ethnic population, whose ancestry is derived from Spanish-speaking countries, by the words Latino and Hispanic is a relatively recent phenomenon in the United States.

The term Hispanic was used in the 1970s and Latino was added to the U.S. Census in 1990. The cultural, economic, and political differences and similarities among various Hispanic/Latino communities, as well as the wide dispersal of these communities, suggest the need for care in generalization about Latino and Hispanic American populations. Does geographic location in the United States significantly influence personal and group issues? The realities of these groups—whether they are

© Charles Smith/CORBIS

political refugees, migrant workers, descendants of residents settled prior to territorial incorporation into the United States, long-settled immigrants, recent arrivals, or the children and grandchildren of immigrants—present interesting and varied patterns of enclave community, assimilation, and acculturation, as well as isolation and marginalization. Hispanic/Latino American linkages to Central and South American countries and Spain, the future of their emerging political power, and their contributions to cultural and economic change within the United States are interesting facets of the Hispanic/Latino American experience.

The Hispanic/Latino experience is a composite of groups seeking unity while interacting with the larger arena of ethnic groups that constitute American society. Convergent issues that bridge differences, as well as those that support ideological and strategic differences, bode a future of both cooperation and conflict. What issues bind Hispanic or Latino groups together? What values cause cleavages among these populations? What does bilingualism mean? Is bilingualism a freedom-of-speech issue? Is bilingualism a concern of non-Spanish-speaking persons in the United States? What are the implications of establishing an official public language policy?

Competition and conflict over mobility into mainstream leadership positions are aspects of American society that may be exacerbated by the misuse of ethnic indicators. Nonetheless, indicators of social cohesion and traditional family bonds are apparently non-competitive and non-conflictive dimensions of robust ethnic experiences. Thus, fears that Hispanic/Latino Americans may not relish competitive pressures are assuaged by the capacities of family and community to temper the cost of any such failure. This complex dynamic of personal and group interaction is a fascinating and fruitful topic for a society seeking competitiveness and stronger community bonds. Cast in this fashion, the American dilemma takes on a new and compelling relevance.

Who's Hispanic?

JEFFREY PASSEL AND PAUL TAYLOR, PEW HISPANIC CENTER

I s Sonia Sotomayor the first Hispanic ever nominated to the U.S. Supreme Court? Or does that distinction belong to the late Justice Benjamin Cardozo, who served on the court from 1932-1938 and whose ancestors may or may not have come from Portugal?

Unscrambling Cardozo's family tree is best left to historians and genealogists.[1] Here we take a stab at a more daunting question. Just who is a Hispanic?

If you turn to the U.S. government for answers, you quickly discover that it has two different approaches to this definitional question. Both are products of a 1976 act of Congress and the administrative regulations that flow from it.

One approach defines a Hispanic or Latino as a member of an ethnic group that traces its roots to 20 Spanish-speaking nations from Latin America and Spain itself (but not Portugal or Portuguese-speaking Brazil).

The other approach is much simpler. Who's Hispanic? Anyone who says they are. And nobody who says they aren't.

The U.S. Census Bureau uses this second approach. By its way of counting, there were 46,943,613 Hispanics in the United States as of July 1, 2008, comprising 15.4% of the total national population.

But behind the impressive precision of this official Census number lies a long history of changing labels, shifting categories and revised question wording—all of which reflect evolving cultural norms about what it means to be Hispanic.

Here's a quick primer on how the Census Bureau approach works.

Q: I immigrated to Phoenix from Mexico. Am I Hispanic?

A: You are if you say so.

Q: My parents moved to New York from Puerto Rico. Am I Hispanic?

A: You are if you say so.

Q: My grandparents were born in Spain but I grew up in California. Am I Hispanic?

A: You are if you say so.

Q: I was born in Maryland and married an immigrant from El Salvador. Am I Hispanic?

A: You are if you say so.

Q: My mom is from Chile and my dad is from Iowa. I was born in Des Moines. Am I Hispanic?

A: You are if you say so.

Q: I was born in Argentina but grew up in Texas. I don't consider myself Hispanic. Does the Census count me as an Hispanic?

A: Not if you say you aren't.

Q: Okay, I get the point. But isn't there something in U.S. law that defines Hispanicity?

A: Yes. In 1976, the U.S. Congress passed the only law in this country's history that mandated the collection and analysis of data for a specific ethnic group: "Americans of Spanish origin or descent." The language of that legislation described this group as "Americans who identify themselves as being of Spanish-speaking background and trace their origin or descent from Mexico, Puerto Rico, Cuba, Central and South America and other Spanish-speaking countries." Standards for collecting data on Hispanics were developed by the Office of Management and Budget (OMB) in 1977 and revised in 1997. Using these standards, schools, public health facilities and other government entities and agencies keep track of how many Hispanics they serve (which was a primary goal of the 1976 law).

However, the Census Bureau does *not* apply this definition in counting Hispanics. Rather, it relies entirely on self-reporting and lets each person identify as Hispanic or not. The 2000 Census form asked the "Hispanic" question this way:

Is This Person Spanish/Hispanic/Latino?

*Mark (X) the "No" box if **not** Spanish/Hispanic/Latino.*
- _____ **No,** not Spanish/Hispanic/ Latino
- _____ Yes, Mexican, Mexican Am., Chicano
- _____ Yes, Puerto Rican
- _____ Yes, Cuban
- _____ Yes, other Spanish/Hispanic/Latino - *Print group - - >* _____

That question wording will be tweaked slightly in the 2010 Census, but the basic approach will be the same: People will be counted as Spanish/Hispanic/Latino if—and only if—that's what they say they are. These self-reports are not subject to any independent checks, corroborations or corrections. Theoretically, someone who is Chinese could identify himself as Hispanic and that's how he would be counted.

Q. But the Census also asks people about their race and their ancestry. How do these responses come into play when determining if someone is Hispanic?

A. They don't. In the eyes of the Census Bureau, Hispanics can be of any race, any ancestry, any country of origin. The result is that there are varying patterns relating to where people come from and how they choose to identify themselves on the Census. For example, some 99% of all immigrants from Mexico call themselves Hispanic. But just 87% of immigrants from Venezuela adopt this label, as do 86% of immigrants from Argentina, 70% of immigrants from Spain, and only 67% from Panama. As for race, 54% of all Hispanics in the U.S. self-identify as white, 1.5% self-identify as black, 40% do not identify with any race and 3.8% identify as being two or more races.[2]

Q. What about Brazilians, Portuguese, and Filipinos? Are they Hispanic?

A. They are in the eyes of the Census if they say they are, even though these countries do not fit the official OMB definition of "Hispanic" because they are not Spanish speaking. For the most part, people who trace their ancestry to these countries do not self-identify as Hispanic when they fill out their Census forms. Only about 4% of immigrants from Brazil do so, as do just 1% of immigrants from Portugal or the Philippines.[3] These patterns reflect a growing recognition and acceptance of the official definition of Hispanics. In the 1980 Census, about one in six Brazilian immigrants and one in eight Portuguese and Filipino immigrants identified as Hispanic. Similar shares did so in the 1990 Census, but by 2000, the shares identifying as Hispanic dropped to levels close to those seen today.

Q. How do Hispanics themselves feel about the labels "Hispanic" and "Latino"?

A. The labels are not universally embraced by the community that has been labeled. A 2006 survey by the Pew Hispanic Center found that 48% of Latino adults generally describe themselves by their country of origin first; 26% generally use the terms Latino or Hispanic first; and 24% generally call themselves American on first reference. As for a preference between "Hispanic" and "Latino", a 2008 Center survey found that 36% of respondents prefer the term "Hispanic," 21% prefer the term "Latino" and the rest have no preference.

Q. What about Puerto Ricans? Where do they fit in?

A. Puerto Ricans are U.S. citizens by birth—whether they were born in New York (like Judge Sotomayor) or in the Commonwealth of Puerto Rico (like her parents). According to the Census, some 97% of all persons born in Puerto Rico and living in the mainland United States consider themselves Hispanics. Overall, Puerto Ricans are the second largest group of Hispanics in the 50 states and District of Columbia—they make up 9% of the mainland Hispanic population, well behind the Mexican-origin share of 64%, but ahead of the 3.5% share of Cubans. In 2007, the 4.1 million persons of Puerto Rican origin living in the mainland United States exceeded Puerto Rico's population of 3.9 million.

Q. So, bottom line: Is Judge Sotomayor the first Hispanic to be nominated to the U.S. Supreme Court, or not?

A. By the OMB's definition, yes - Cardozo's Portuguese roots (assuming he in fact had them) don't make him Hispanic. But by the Census Bureau approach, not necessarily - for it would depend on how Cardozo would have chosen to identify himself. However, there's an important historical footnote to consider. The terms "Hispanic" and "Latino" hadn't yet been coined for official data when Cardozo was alive. In the 1930 Census, the only effort to enumerate Hispanics appeared as part of the race question, which had a category for "Mexican." That scheme gave way to several other approaches before the current method took hold in 1980. In short, Cardozo would have had no "Hispanic" box to check — and thus no official way of identifying himself as Hispanic. So, by the ever shifting laws of the land, Sotomayor would indeed appear to be the first Hispanic nominated to the high court. Case closed!

Notes

1. Justice Benjamin Cardozo was a Sephardic Jew whose ancestors immigrated to the American colonies from England. According to one biographer, the family fled from Portugal to Holland in the 17th Century after having been forcibly converted to Christianity. Although not widely disputed, there does not seem to be definitive proof that the family was from Portugal. Originally settled by Celts, Portugal became an independent kingdom in the 12th

Century but was ruled by the King of Spain from 1580 until 1640, when the Portuguese Restoration War reestablished its independence.

2. From American FactFinder, 2007 American Community Survey, table B03002. The race figures are for "race alone."

3. Source: Pew Hispanic Center tabulations from American Community Survey, 2007, Integrated Public Use Samples

Critical Thinking

1. What differentiates an ethnic category from the name of an ethnic group?

2. Has the US Census explanation clarified the meaning of the word Hispanic?

3. What is the difference between Hispanic and Latino/a?

Race and Hispanic Origin of the Foreign-Born Population in the United States: 2007

American Community Survey Reports

ELIZABETH M. GRIECO

Introduction

This report describes the race and Hispanic-origin composition of the foreign-born population in the United States in 2007 and compares it to that of the total and native-born populations.[1] It shows that the foreign born have a pattern of race and Hispanic origin reporting that is markedly different from the native population.

New waves of immigrants began arriving in the United States following amendments to the Immigration Act in 1965 that abolished the national origins quota system, resulting in a shift away from traditional source countries to a greater diversity in the origins of the foreign born. Unlike during the great migration of the late 1800s and early 1900s when the majority of immigrants to the United States came from countries in

Europe, most of the immigrants who arrived after 1970 were from countries in Latin America and Asia. This change is clearly reflected in the foreign-born population through time. In 1960, 75 percent of the foreign-born population were born in Europe. In 1980, 39 percent were born in Europe, while 52 percent were born in Latin America or Asia.[2] By 2007, 80 percent of the foreign-born population were born in either Latin America or Asia (Figure 1).

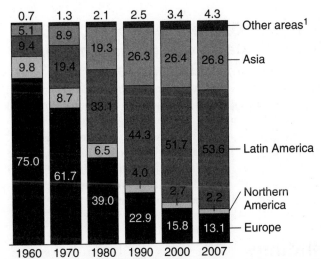

Figure 1 Percent Distribution of Foreign-Born Population by Region of Birth: 1960 to 2007 (Data based on sample. For information on confidentiality protection, sampling error, nonsampling error, and definitions, see www.census.gov/acs/www/)

Other areas include Africa and Oceania.

Source: U.S. Census Bureau, Census of Population, 1960 to 2000, and 2007 American Community Survey.

Defining Nativity: Who Is Foreign Born?

Nativity refers to whether a person is native or foreign born. The native-born population includes anyone who was a U.S. citizen or U.S. national at birth. Respondents who were born in the United States, Puerto Rico, a U.S. Island Area (U.S. Virgin Islands, Guam, American Samoa, or the Commonwealth of the Northern Mariana Islands), or abroad of a U.S. citizen parent or parents, are defined as native. The foreign-born population includes anyone who was not a U.S. citizen or U.S. national at birth. Respondents who are not U.S. citizens as well as those who have become U.S. citizens through naturalization are considered foreign born.

Over the last 40 years, immigration from Latin American and Asia has been the major force changing the racial and ethnic composition of the American population. The influx of newcomers from these regions has resulted in rapid growth in the number of Hispanics and Asians in recent decades. For the three groups with the oldest historical roots in the United States—non-Hispanic Whites, non-Hispanic Blacks, and American Indian and Alaska Natives—natural increase, not immigration, has been the main source of growth since 1970. The shift in immigrant source countries, combined with modest differences in natural increase among the different race and Hispanic-origin groups, has resulted in increased racial and ethnic diversity, which is reflected in the decreasing proportion of non-Hispanic Whites through time.[3] The proportion of the total population that was White, not Hispanic was 83 percent in 1970 and 76 percent in 1990. By 2007, 66 percent of the total population was White, not Hispanic.[4]

The foreign born, through their own diverse origins, will continue to contribute to the racial and ethnic diversity of the United States. How they translate their own backgrounds and report their adopted identities have important implications for the nation's racial and ethnic composition. This report discusses the race and Hispanic origin of the foreign born, first separately as distinct concepts, then combined to highlight the unique racial and ethnic patterns reported by this population. Race by the largest countries of birth and detailed Hispanic origin by nativity are also discussed. The proportion of foreign born in each race group and detailed Hispanic origin is also shown. Unless otherwise stated, the information presented in this report is based on data collected by the U.S. Census Bureau in the 2007 American Community Survey (ACS).[5]

People in Each Race Group Can Be Either Hispanic or Not Hispanic, and Hispanics May Be Any Race

Race and Hispanic origin are treated as separate concepts in the federal statistical system. The ACS asks both a race and Hispanic-origin question. The question on race asks respondents to report the race or races they consider themselves to be. The question on Hispanic origin asks respondents if they are Spanish, Hispanic, or Latino. Both questions are based on self-identification. See Appendixes A and B for additional information about race and Hispanic origin in the ACS.

Findings
Nearly Half of All Foreign Born in the United States Are Hispanic

In 2007, the total population of the United States was 301.6 million, which included 38.1 million foreign born, representing 12.6 percent of the total population.

Approximately 15 percent of the total population reported a Hispanic origin. However, 10 percent of the native-born population were Hispanic compared with 48 percent of the

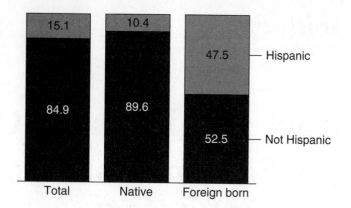

Figure 2 Percent Distribution of Population by Hispanic Origin and Nativity: 2007 (Data based on sample. For information on confidentiality protection, sampling error, nonsampling error, and definitions, see www.census.gov/acs/www/)

Source: U.S. Census Bureau, 2007 American Community Survey.

foreign-born population (Figure 2).[6] Foreign-born Hispanics composed 6 percent of the total population.

The Pattern of Races Reported By the Foreign Born Is Notably Different from That of Natives.

While the majority of both the native and foreign-born populations reported only one race, the distribution of races reported differed (Table 1). The foreign born were more likely than the native born to report Asian and Some Other Race, but were less likely to report White, Black, and Two or More Races.[7] Most natives were White (78 percent), followed by Black (13 percent). By comparison, most of the foreign born were White (46 percent), Asian (23 percent), and Some Other Race (21 percent). The native born were more likely to report more than one race than the foreign born. Approximately 2.3 percent of the native born and 1.3 percent of the foreign born reported two or more races.

The Majority of Both Native and Foreign-Born Hispanics Are Either White or Some Other Race, But Native Hispanics Are More Likely to Report More Than One Race

Among native-born Hispanics, 54 percent were White and 38 percent were Some Other Race. Among foreign-born Hispanics, 54 percent were White while 43 percent were Some Other Race.[8] Native Hispanics were more likely to report Two or More Races (5.4 percent) than foreign-born Hispanics (1.5 percent).

Most of the non-Hispanic foreign born reported their race as either Asian (44 percent) or White (39 percent). By comparison, the majority of non-Hispanic natives were White (81 percent). Overall, both the non-Hispanic native and foreign-born populations were more likely to report Black than the Hispanic native and foreign-born populations.

Table 1 Population by Nativity, Race, and Hispanic Origin: 2007
(Numbers in thousands. Data based on sample. For information on confidentiality protection, sampling error, nonsampling error, and definitions, see www.census.gov/acs/www/)

Hispanic origin and race	Total		Native		Foreign born	
	Number	Percent	Number	Percent	Number	Percent
Total	301,621	100.0	263,561	100.0	38,060	100.0
One race	295,112	97.8	257,542	97.7	37,570	98.7
White	223,005	73.9	205,594	78.0	17,412	45.7
Black or African American	37,335	12.4	34,362	13.0	2,972	7.8
American Indian and Alaska Native	2,365	0.8	2,238	0.8	127	0.3
Asian	13,233	4.4	4,325	1.6	8,908	23.4
Native Hawaiian and Other Pacific Islander	435	0.1	329	0.1	106	0.3
Some Other Race	18,739	6.2	10,694	4.1	8,045	21.1
Two or More Races	6,509	2.2	6,020	2.3	489	1.3
Not Hispanic	**256,194**	**100.0**	**236,201**	**100.0**	**19,993**	**100.0**
One race	251,424	98.1	231,652	98.1	19,772	98.9
White	198,553	77.5	190,838	80.8	7,715	38.6
Black or African American	36,657	14.3	33,872	14.3	2,785	13.9
American Indian and Alaska Native	2,019	0.8	1,996	0.8	23	0.1
Asian	13,077	5.1	4,210	1.8	8,867	44.4
Native Hawaiian and Other Pacific Islander	402	0.2	306	0.1	96	0.5
Some Other Race	715	0.3	429	0.2	286	1.4
Two or More Races	4,769	1.9	4,549	1.9	221	1.1
Hispanic	**45,427**	**100.0**	**27,361**	**100.0**	**18,067**	**100.0**
One race	43,688	96.2	25,890	94.6	17,798	98.5
White	24,452	53.8	14,755	53.9	9,697	53.7
Black or African American	677	1.5	490	1.8	187	1.0
American Indian and Alaska Native	346	0.8	242	0.9	104	0.6
Asian	156	0.3	115	0.4	41	0.2
Native Hawaiian and Other Pacific Islander	33	0.1	23	0.1	10	0.1
Some Other Race	18,024	39.7	10,264	37.5	7,759	42.9
Two or More Races	1,740	3.8	1,471	5.4	269	1.5

Source: U.S. Census Bureau, 2007 American Community Survey.

The Majority of Foreign Born Are White, Asian, Or Some Other Race, but the Pattern of Race Reporting Varies by Country-of-Birth Groups

About 9 out of 10 of the foreign born were White, Asian, or Some Other Race, but this pattern varies by different country-of-birth groups (Table 2). For example, most of the foreign born from Mexico and El Salvador reported either White or Some Other Race. Among the foreign born from Mexico, 53 percent were White and 45 percent were Some Other Race, while among the foreign born from El Salvador, 45 percent were White and over half (52 percent) were Some Other Race. By comparison,

87 percent of the foreign born from Cuba were White, with 9 percent Some Other Race. Among the foreign born from the Dominican Republic, 25 percent were White and 62 percent Some Other Race, with 8 percent Black and 4 percent Two or More Races.

Most of the Hispanics in the United States are of Mexican Origin, Regardless of Nativity

Of the 45.4 million Hispanics in the United States, 64 percent were of Mexican origin (Table 3). Mexican represented the largest Hispanic origin for both the native and foreign-born populations (both approximately 64 percent).

Table 2 Foreign-Born Population by Race for Countries with 750,000 or More Foreign Born: 2007 (Numbers in thousands. Data based on sample. For information on confidentiality protection, sampling error, nonsampling error, and definitions, see www.census.gov/acs/www/)

Country of Birth	Total	One race							Two or More Races
		Total	White	Black or African American	American Indian and Alaska Native	Asian	Native Hawaiian and Other Pacific Islander	Some Other Race	
NUMBER									
Total	38,060	37,570	17,412	2,972	127	8,908	106	8,045	489
Mexico	11,739	11,625	6,233	28	78	17	1	5,267	114
China[1]	1,930	1,921	22	2	–	1,896	1	1	9
Philippines	1,701	1,671	21	3	1	1,641	3	2	30
India	1,502	1,480	22	3	3	1,417	1	35	22
El Salvador	1,104	1,084	496	6	4	2	–	575	20
Vietnam	1,101	1,094	6	1	–	1,086	1	–	7
Korea[2]	1,043	1,031	10	3	–	1,018	1	–	11
Cuba	983	968	851	25	–	1	–	91	15
Canada	830	823	754	18	7	34	1	10	8
Dominican Republic	756	727	191	63	2	3	–	468	29
PERCENT									
Total	100.0	98.7	45.7	7.8	0.3	23.4	0.3	21.1	1.3
Mexico	100.0	99.0	53.1	0.2	0.7	0.1	–	44.9	1.0
China[1]	100.0	99.5	1.1	0.1	–	98.2	–	0.1	0.5
Philippines	100.0	98.2	1.3	0.2	–	96.5	0.2	0.1	1.8
India	100.0	98.6	1.4	0.2	0.2	94.4	–	2.4	1.4
El Salvador	100.0	98.2	44.9	0.6	0.4	0.2	–	52.1	1.8
Vietnam	100.0	99.4	0.5	0.1	–	98.6	0.1	–	0.6
Korea[2]	100.0	98.9	1.0	0.3	–	97.6	0.1	–	1.1
Cuba	100.0	98.4	86.6	2.5	–	0.1	–	9.2	1.6
Canada	100.0	99.1	90.8	2.1	0.8	4.1	0.1	1.2	0.9
Dominican Republic	100.0	96.2	25.3	8.3	0.3	0.4	–	61.9	3.8

Dash (-) represents zero or rounds to zero.

[1] Includes respondents who reported their county of birth as China, Hong Kong, Taiwan, or Paracel Islands.

[2] Includes respondents who reported their county of birth as Korea, South Korea, or North Korea.

Source: U.S. Census Bureau, 2007 American Community Survey.

However, differences in the distribution of Hispanic origin by type are revealed when the population is divided by nativity. For example, among the native-born Hispanic population, 15 percent were Puerto Rican, compared with less than 1 percent of the foreign-born Hispanic population. There are more native-born Puerto Rican Hispanics than foreign-born Puerto Rican Hispanics in part because individuals born in Puerto Rico are classified as natives of the United States. By comparison, foreign-born Hispanics were more likely than their native-born counterparts to report their origin as Cuban, Salvadoran, Dominican, Guatemalan, Colombian, Ecuadorian, Honduran, and Peruvian.

Over Two-Thirds of All Respondents Reporting Asian Are Foreign Born

While 13 percent of the total population of the United States was foreign born in 2007, the proportion of the Asian race group that was foreign born was higher than the national average (Figure 3). Of the 13.2 million people in the Asian population, 67 percent were foreign born. Two other race groups also had a higher proportion of foreign born than the total population. Forty-three percent of the 18.7 million people in the Some Other Race population were foreign born, as were 24 percent of the 435,000 people

Table 3 Hispanic Population by Nativity and Type: 2007 (Numbers in thousands. Data based on sample. For information on confidentiality protection, sampling error, nonsampling error, and definitions, see www.census.gov/acs/www/)

Hispanic type	Total		Native		Foreign born	
	Number	Percent	Number	Percent	Number	Percent
Total	**45,427**	**100.0**	**27,361**	**100.0**	**18,067**	**100.0**
Caribbean	6,940	15.3	5,181	18.9	1,758	9.7
Cuban	1,611	3.5	628	2.3	983	5.4
Dominican	1,208	2.7	482	1.8	726	4.0
Puerto Rican	4,120	9.1	4,071	14.9	49	0.3
Central American	32,706	72.0	18,713	68.4	13,993	77.5
Costa Rican	118	0.3	47	0.2	70	0.4
Guatemalan	872	1.9	265	1.0	607	3.4
Honduran	533	1.2	153	0.6	380	2.1
Mexican	29,167	64.2	17,538	64.1	11,629	64.4
Nicaraguan	302	0.7	100	0.4	202	1.1
Panamanian	135	0.3	65	0.2	69	0.4
Salvadoran	1,474	3.2	506	1.9	968	5.4
Other Central American	106	0.2	39	0.1	67	0.4
South American	2,499	5.5	761	2.8	1,738	9.6
Argentinean	194	0.4	60	0.2	134	0.7
Bolivian	83	0.2	29	0.1	54	0.3
Chilean	107	0.2	37	0.1	69	0.4
Colombian	799	1.8	243	0.9	555	3.1
Ecuadorian	533	1.2	172	0.6	361	2.0
Peruvian	462	1.0	125	0.5	336	1.9
Uruguayan	50	0.1	13	–	38	0.2
Venezuelan	178	0.4	49	0.2	129	0.7
Other South American	93	0.2	33	0.1	60	0.3
All other Hispanic[1]	3,283	7.2	2,705	9.9	577	3.2

Dash (-) represents zero or rounds to zero.

[1]Other Hispanic includes all other general Hispanic origin responses such as "Hispanic," "Spanish," or "Latino."

Source: U.S. Census Bureau, 2007 American Community Survey.

in the Native Hawaiian and Other Pacific Islander population. By comparison, of the 2.4 million people who were American Indian and Alaska Native, only 5.4 percent were foreign born.

Over Half of All Foreign-Born Blacks Came from Countries in the Caribbean, and Over One-Third from Countries in Africa

Of the 37.3 million Blacks in the United States, 3 million were foreign born, representing 8 percent of the total Black population. Of the foreign-born Black population, 54 percent were born in countries in the Caribbean, including Jamaica (19 percent), Haiti (17 percent), and Trinidad and Tobago (6 percent). An additional 34 percent were born in countries in Africa, including Nigeria (6 percent), Ethiopia (4 percent), and Ghana (3 percent).

Approximately 5 percent were born in countries in South America, including Guyana (4 percent), and 4 percent in countries in Central America.[9,10] Countries from the remaining regions of the world—Europe, Asia, Northern America, and Oceania—when combined represented about 3 percent of the Black foreign born.

Most of the Foreign Born Who Are American Indian and Alaska Native or Some Other Race Are from Central America

Of the 127,000 foreign born in the American Indian and Alaska Native population, 77 percent were born in countries in Central America (Figure 4). Most were born in Mexico. While the foreign born from Mexico represented 31 percent of the total foreign-born population, they also represented 62 percent of

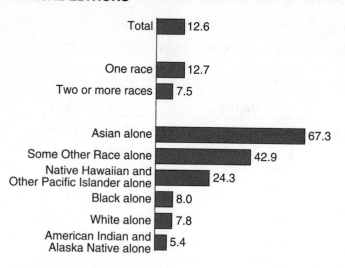

Figure 3. **Percent Foreign Born by Race: 2007** (Data based on sample. For information on confidentiality protection, sampling error, nonsampling error, and definitions, see www .census.gov/acs/www/)

Source: U.S. Census Bureau, 2007 American Community Survey.

Figure 4 **Percent Distribution of the Foreign-Born American Indian and Alaska Native Alone Population by World Region and Country of Birth: 2007** (Data based on sample. For information on confidentiality protection, sampling error, nonsampling error, and definitions, see www.census.gov/ acs/www/)

Source: U.S. Census Bureau, 2007 American Community Survey.

the foreign born who were American Indian and Alaska Native. The additional Central American countries included Guatemala (8.7 percent), El Salvador (3.3 percent), Honduras (2.1 percent), and the remaining Central American countries (1.1 percent).[11] The foreign born from Canada represented 5.4 percent of all foreign born who reported American Indian and Alaska Native.

Of the 8 million foreign born in the Some Other Race population, 81 percent were born in countries in Central America (Figure 5). The foreign born from Mexico represented 65 percent, followed by El Salvador (7.2 percent), Guatemala (4.5 percent), Honduras (2.2 percent), and the remaining Central American countries (1.9 percent). The foreign born from the Dominican Republic composed 5.8 percent of all foreign born who were Some Other Race.

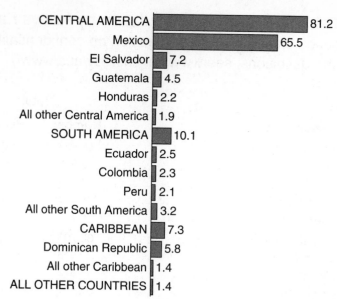

Figure 5 **Percent Distribution of the Foreign-Born Some Other Race Alone Population by World Region and Country of Birth: 2007** (Data based on sample. For information on confidentiality protection, sampling error, nonsampling error, and definitions, see www.census.gov/acs/www/)

Source: U.S. Census Bureau, 2007 American Community Survey.

Overall, about 40 Percent of All Hispanics Are Foreign Born, but This Proportion Varies Considerably among Specific Hispanic-Origin Groups

About 13 percent of the total population was foreign born. However, the proportion foreign born varies considerably when the population is divided by Hispanic origin and type. While 40 percent of all Hispanics were foreign born, the foreign born composed only about 8 percent of the non-Hispanic population (Figure 6).

The proportion foreign born among the Hispanic population was heavily influenced by the size and composition of the Mexican-origin population. Of the 45.4 million Hispanics, 64 percent were of Mexican origin. Of the 29.2 million Mexican Hispanics, 40 percent were foreign born.

The remaining Central American origins, when combined, represented about 8 percent of the Hispanic population.[12] Although they represent a smaller proportion of all Hispanics, these origin groups have a substantially higher proportion of foreign born than Mexican Hispanics. Overall, 67 percent of the remaining Central American origins were foreign born, ranging from 51 percent for Hispanics of Panamanian origin to 71 percent for Hispanics of Honduran origin. Approximately 6 percent of all Hispanics had South American origins.[13] About 70 percent of all Hispanics with South American origins were foreign born, the highest being Uruguayan (75 percent), Peruvian (73 percent), and Venezuelan (73 percent).[14]

Only one-fourth of Hispanics with a Caribbean origin were foreign born.[15] This proportion reflects the size and

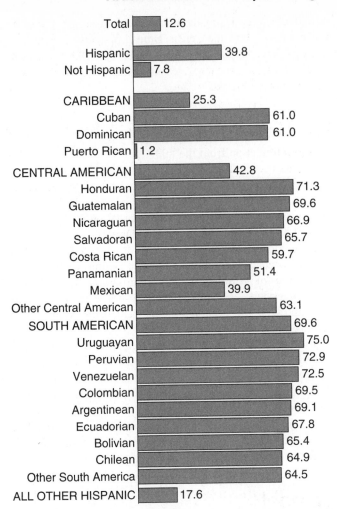

Total	12.6
Hispanic	39.8
Not Hispanic	7.8
CARIBBEAN	25.3
Cuban	61.0
Dominican	61.0
Puerto Rican	1.2
CENTRAL AMERICAN	42.8
Honduran	71.3
Guatemalan	69.6
Nicaraguan	66.9
Salvadoran	65.7
Costa Rican	59.7
Panamanian	51.4
Mexican	39.9
Other Central American	63.1
SOUTH AMERICAN	69.6
Uruguayan	75.0
Peruvian	72.9
Venezuelan	72.5
Colombian	69.5
Argentinean	69.1
Ecuadorian	67.8
Bolivian	65.4
Chilean	64.9
Other South America	64.5
ALL OTHER HISPANIC	17.6

Figure 6   Percent Foreign Born by Hispanic Origin and Type: 2007   (Data based on sample. For information on confidentiality protection, sampling error, nonsampling error, and definitions, see www.census.gov/acs/www/)

Source: U.S. Census Bureau, 2007 American Community Survey.

composition of Hispanics of Puerto Rican origin. Puerto Rican Hispanics composed 59 percent of all Caribbean Hispanics, but less than 2 percent were foreign born. By comparison, 60 percent of Dominican and 61 percent of Cuban Hispanics were foreign born.[16]

Conclusion

In 2007, there were 38.1 million foreign born in the United States, representing about 1 in 8 residents. Most foreign born were White (46 percent), Asian (23 percent), or Some Other Race (21 percent). Relatively few foreign born were Two or More Races. This pattern of race reporting was considerably different from the native born, most of whom reported their race as White (78 percent) or Black (13 percent). The race group with the highest proportion of foreign born was Asian (67 percent), followed by Some Other Race (43 percent), and Native Hawaiian and Other Pacific Islander (24 percent).

Approximately 80 percent of the foreign-born population were born in Latin America or Asia. Race reporting varies

among country-of-birth groups, sometimes greatly. For example, the foreign born from Mexico, which represented the largest foreign-born group, reported either White (53 percent) or Some Other Race (45 percent). By comparison, 87 percent of the foreign born from Cuba reported White, while the majority of the foreign born from Vietnam (99 percent), China (98 percent), Korea (98 percent), the Philippines (97 percent), and India (94 percent) reported Asian.

Just over 18 million, or 47 percent of the foreign-born population, were of Hispanic origin. Most Hispanic foreign born were White (54 percent) or Some Other Race (43 percent). Over three-fourths of all Hispanic foreign born were of Central American origin, of whom 83 percent were Mexican. Of the 45.4 million Hispanics in the United States, 40 percent were foreign born. The proportion of foreign born varies among the detailed Hispanic groups. For example, among Hispanics of Mexican origin, 40 percent were foreign born; of Cuban origin, 61 percent; and of Salvadoran origin, 66 percent.

This report reviewed the race and Hispanic origin of the foreign-born population in 2007. As was demonstrated, the foreign born have a pattern of race and Hispanic origin reporting that is very different from the native born. This difference reflects the shift in immigrant source countries over the last 40 years, from predominantly European countries to countries in Latin America and Asia. As both race and Hispanic origin are based on self-identification, this difference may also reflect how the foreign born interpret the concepts of race and ethnicity within the context of the American cultural landscape. It is likely that, in the future, the origins of immigrants may continue to shift and, when combined with changing views of the meaning of race and Hispanic origin, the foreign born will continue to contribute to the racial and ethnic diversity of the United States.

Source of the Data and Accuracy of the Estimates
The American Community Survey

Many of the findings presented in this report were based on the American Community Survey (ACS) data collected in 2007. These data were based on the population living in either households or group quarters (which include correctional facilities, nursing homes, college dormitories, group homes, and overnight shelters) that were included in the ACS sample. The U.S. Census Bureau is both the sponsor and the collector of the American Community Survey.

The 2007 ACS is based on a sample of just under 3 million housing unit addresses and a separate sample of just under 200 thousand people living in group quarters. ACS figures are estimates based on this sample and approximate the actual figures that would have been obtained by interviewing the entire household and group quarters populations using the same methodology. The estimates from the 2007 ACS sample may also differ from estimates based on other survey samples of housing units and group quarters and the people living within those housing units and group quarters.

The Decennial Census

Other findings presented in this report that were not derived from the 2007 ACS were collected from previously published findings based on data from each decennial census conducted by the Census Bureau since 1900. Because the structure of the decennial census has changed over time, some of the data were based on complete censuses (100 percent of the population, from 1900 to 1930) and some were based on sample populations of various sizes (ranging from 5 percent to 20 percent, from 1940 to 2000). In general, the decennial censuses collected data from the population living in households as well as those living in group quarters such as those described above. For more information about the source and accuracy details of the decennial censuses, refer to Working Paper No. 81, "Historical Census Statistics on the Foreign-Born Population of the United States: 1850 to 2000," available at www.census.gov/population/www/documentation/twps0081.html.

Sampling and Nonsampling Error

Sampling error occurs when the characteristics of a sample are measured instead of those of the entire population (as from a census). Note that sample-based estimates will vary depending on the particular sample selected from the population, but all attempt to approximate the actual figures. Measures of the magnitude of sampling error reflect the variation in the estimates over all possible samples that could have been selected from the population using the same sampling, data collection, and processing methods.

Estimates of the magnitude of sampling errors are provided in the form of margins of error for all key ACS estimates included in this report. The Census Bureau recommends that data users incorporate this information into their analyses, as sampling error in survey estimates could impact the conclusions drawn from the results. All comparative statements in this report have undergone statistical testing, and comparisons are significant at the 90 percent confidence level unless noted otherwise. This means the 90 percent confidence interval for the difference between the estimates being compared does not include zero.

In addition to sampling error, non-sampling errors may be introduced during any phase of data collection or processing. For example, operations such as editing, reviewing, or keying data from questionnaires may introduce error into the estimates. The primary source of nonsampling error and the processes instituted to control error in the 2007 ACS are described in further detail in the 2007 ACS Accuracy of the Data document (see Web link below).

Title 13, U.S. Code, Section 9, prohibits the Census Bureau from publishing results from which the identity of an individual survey respondent could be determined. For more information on how the Census Bureau protects the confidentiality of data, see the 2007 ACS Accuracy of the Data document, available at www.census.gov/acs/www/Downloads/ACS/accuracy2007.pdf.

For More Information

Further information from the 2007 ACS is available from the American FactFinder on the Census Bureau's Web site, at http://factfinder.census.gov/home/saff/main.html?_lang=en.

A copy of the 2007 ACS questionnaire is available at www.census.gov/acs/www/Downloads/SQuest07.pdf.

Definitions of specific terminology used in this report and in the ACS questionnaire are available at www.census.gov/acs/www/Downloads/2007/usedata/Subject_Definitions.pdf.

Measures of ACS quality—including sample size and number of interviews, response and nonresponse rates, coverage rates, and item allocation rates—are available at www.census.gov/acs/www/UseData/sse/.

Additional information about the foreign-born population is available on the Census Bureau's Web site at www.census.gov/population/www/socdemo/foreign/index.html. For more information about the Hispanic population, visit www.census.gov/population/www/socdemo/hispanic/hispanic.html. For more information about the race-alone populations or Two or More Races population, visit www.census.gov/population/www/socdemo/race/race.html.

Contact

For additional information on these topics, please call 1-866-758-1060 (toll free) or visit www.census.gov.

Suggested Citation

Grieco, Elizabeth M. 2009. *Race and Hispanic Origin of the Foreign-Born Population in the United States: 2007,* American Community Survey Reports, ACS-11, U.S. Census Bureau, Washington, DC.

User Comments

The Census Bureau welcomes the comments and advice of users of our data and reports. Please send comments and suggestions to:
Chief, Population Division
U.S. Census Bureau Washington, DC 20233-8800

Appendixes

Appendix A
Race and Hispanic Origin in the American Community Survey

The American Community Survey (ACS) adheres to federal standards for collecting and presenting data on race and Hispanic origin as established by the Office of Management and Budget (OMB) in 1997. For further information, see *Revisions to the Standards for the Classification of Federal Data on Race and Ethnicity* at www.whitehouse.gov/omb/fedreg/1997standards.html.

The OMB requires federal agencies to use a minimum of five race categories: White; Black or African American; American Indian or Alaska Native; Asian; and Native Hawaiian or Other Pacific Islander. For respondents unable to identify with any of these five race categories, the OMB approved a sixth category—"Some Other Race"—on the ACS questionnaire.

The 2007 ACS question on race includes 15 separate response categories and three areas where respondents can write in a more specific race group. The response categories and write-in answers can be combined to create the five minimum OMB race categories plus Some Other Race. In addition to White, Black or African American, American Indian or Alaska Native, and Some Other Race, seven of the 15 response categories are Asian and four are Native Hawaiian and Other Pacific Islander. The Asian response categories include Asian Indian, Chinese, Filipino, Japanese, Korean, Vietnamese, and Other Asian. The Native Hawaiian and Other Pacific Islander response categories include Native Hawaiian, Guamanian or Chamorro, Samoan, and Other Pacific Islander.

People who responded to the question on race by indicating only one race are referred to as the race *alone* population, or the group that reported *only one* race category. Six categories make up this population: White alone; Black or African American alone; American Indian and Alaska Native alone; Asian alone; Native Hawaiian and Other Pacific Islander alone; and Some Other Race alone. Individuals who chose more than one of the six race categories are referred to as the *Two or More Races* population, or as the group that reported *more than one* race. The six race alone categories and the Two or More Races category sum to the total population.

The OMB defines Hispanic or Latino as "a person of Cuban, Mexican, Puerto Rican, South or Central American, or other Spanish culture or origin regardless of race." In data collection and presentation, federal agencies are required to use a minimum of two ethnicities: "Hispanic or Latino" and "Not Hispanic or Latino." The 2007 ACS question on Hispanic origin includes five separate response categories and one area where respondents can write in a specific Hispanic origin group. The Hispanic origin response categories include: No, not Spanish/Hispanic/Latino; Yes, Mexican, Mexican Am., Chicano; Yes, Puerto Rican; Yes, Cuban; and Yes, other Spanish/Hispanic/Latino. The response categories and write-in answers can be combined to create the two minimum OMB Hispanic origin ethnicities.

For additional information on race and Hispanic origin in the American Community Survey, see *American Community Survey/Puerto Rico Community Survey 2007 Subject Definitions* at www.census.gov/acs/www/Downloads/2007/usedata/Subject_Definitions.pdf.

Appendix B
Definition of Race Categories in the American Community Survey

White—A person having origins in any of the original peoples of Europe, the Middle East, or North Africa. It includes people who indicate their race as "White" or report entries such as Irish, German, Italian, Lebanese, Near Easterner, Arab, or Polish.

Black or African American—A person having origins in any of the Black racial groups of Africa. It includes people who indicate their race as "Black or African American" or provide written entries such as African American, Afro-American, Kenyan, Nigerian, or Haitian.

American Indian and Alaska Native—A person having origins in any of the original peoples of North and South America (including Central America) and who maintain tribal affiliation or community attachment. It includes people who indicate their race as "American Indian or Alaska Native"; who provide either the name of an Indian tribe, such as Iroquois or Sioux, or report entries such as Canadian Indian or Spanish American

Indian; or who provide written responses such as Aleut, Yupik, Athabascan, Tlingit-Haida, or Alaska Indian.

Asian—A person having origins in any of the original peoples of the Far East, Southeast Asia, or the Indian subcontinent. It includes people who indicate their race as "Asian Indian," "Chinese," "Filipino," "Japanese," "Korean," and "Vietnamese," or provide written responses such as Hmong, Pakistani, Thai, or Cambodian.

Native Hawaiian and Other Pacific Islander—A person having origins in any of the original peoples of Hawaii, Guam, Samoa, or other Pacific Islands. It includes people who indicate their race as "Native Hawaiian," "Guamanian or Chamorro," "Samoan," and "Other Pacific Islander," or provide written responses such as Fijian, Tongan, or Marshallese.

Some Other Race—Includes all other responses not included in the "White," "Black or African American," "American Indian or Alaska Native," "Asian," and "Native Hawaiian or

Appendix Table 1   Margin of Error for the Population by Nativity, Race, and Hispanic Origin: 2007 (Numbers in thousands. Data based on sample and are subject to sampling variability. A margin of error is a measure of an estimate's variability. The larger the margin of error in relation to the size of the estimate, the less reliable the estimate. When added to and subtracted from the estimate, the margin of error forms the 90 percent confidence interval. For information on confidentiality protection, sampling error, nonsampling error, and definitions, see www.census.gov/acs/www/)

Hispanic origin and race	Total		Native		Foreign Born	
	Number	Percent	Number	Percent	Number	Percent
Total	(X)	(X)	119	(X)	119	(X)
One race	65	–	123	–	117	–
White	105	–	98	–	93	0.2
Black or African American	47	–	63	–	43	0.1
American Indian and Alaska Native	26	–	23	–	9	–
Asian	30	–	30	–	36	0.1
Native Hawaiian and Other Pacific Islander	11	–	10	–	8	–
Some Other Race	115	–	80	–	75	0.2
Two or More Races	65	–	57	–	16	–
Not Hispanic	9	(X)	80	(X)	80	(X)
One race	53	–	95	–	78	0.1
White	20	–	61	–	57	0.2
Black or African American	44	–	60	–	41	0.2
American Indian and Alaska Native	17	–	17	–	3	–
Asian	28	–	29	–	36	0.2
Native Hawaiian and Other Pacific Islander	9	–	9	–	8	–
Some Other Race	23	–	17	–	13	0.1
Two or More Races	51	–	49	–	11	0.1
Hispanic	9	(X)	80	(X)	81	(X)
One race	39	0.1	77	0.1	81	0.1
White	105	0.2	80	0.3	78	0.4
Black or African American	21	–	18	0.1	10	0.1
American Indian and Alaska Native	17	–	13	–	8	–
Asian	9	–	7	–	4	–
Native Hawaiian and Other Pacific Islander	5	–	4	–	3	–
Some Other Race	116	0.3	80	0.3	75	0.4
Two or More Races	38	0.1	33	0.1	12	0.1

(X) Not applicable.

Dash (-) represents zero or rounds to zero.

Source: U.S. Census Bureau, 2007 American Community Survey.

Appendix Table 2 — Margin of Error for the Foreign-Born Population by Race for Countries with 750,000 or More Foreign Born: 2007

(Numbers in thousands. Data based on sample and are subject to sampling variability. A margin of error is a measure of an estimate's variability. The larger the margin of error in relation to the size of the estimate, the less reliable the estimate. When added to and subtracted from the estimate, the margin of error forms the 90-percent confidence interval. For information on confidentiality protection, sampling error, nonsampling error, and definitions, see www.census.gov/acs/www/)

Country of Birth	Total	One race							Two or More Races
		Total	White	Black or African American	American Indian and Alaska Native	Asian	Native Hawaiian and Other Pacific Islander	Some Other Race	
NUMBER									
Total...............	119	117	93	43	9	36	8	75	16
Mexico	86	88	69	4	7	3	1	65	8
China[1]...............	31	31	3	1	–	31	1	1	2
Philippines	28	28	3	1	–	28	1	1	3
India	25	25	4	1	1	25	1	5	3
El Salvador	27	27	18	2	1	1	–	19	3
Vietnam	27	27	2	1	–	26	1	–	1
Korea[2]..............	26	26	2	2	–	26	–	–	2
Cuba	24	23	22	4	–	1	–	8	3
Canada	17	17	15	3	1	4	1	2	1
Dominican Republic	21	21	10	6	1	1	–	18	4
PERCENT									
Total...............	(X)	–	0.2	0.1	–	0.1	–	0.2	–
Mexico	(X)	0.1	0.4	–	0.1	–	–	0.4	0.1
China[1]...............	(X)	0.1	0.2	0.1	–	0.2	–	–	0.1
Philippines	(X)	0.2	0.2	0.1	–	0.3	0.1	–	0.2
India	(X)	0.2	0.3	0.1	0.1	0.5	–	0.3	0.2
El Salvador	(X)	0.3	1.2	0.2	0.1	0.1	–	1.2	0.3
Vietnam	(X)	0.1	0.2	0.1	–	0.2	0.1	–	0.1
Korea[2]..............	(X)	0.2	0.2	0.2	–	0.3	–	–	0.2
Cuba	(X)	0.3	0.9	0.4	–	0.1	–	0.8	0.3
Canada	(X)	0.2	0.6	0.4	0.2	0.4	0.1	0.3	0.2
Dominican Republic	(X)	0.6	1.2	0.8	0.1	0.2	–	1.4	0.6

X Not applicable.
Dash (-) represents zero or rounds to zero.

[1] Includes respondents who reported their county of birth as China, Hong Kong, Taiwan, or Paracel Islands.
[2] Includes respondents who reported their county of birth as Korea, South Korea, or North Korea.

Source: U.S. Census Bureau, 2007 American Community Survey.

Appendix Table 3   Margin of Error for the Hispanic Population by Nativity and Type: 2007 (Numbers in thousands. Data based on sample and are subject to sampling variability. A margin of error is a measure of an estimate's variability. The larger the margin of error in relation to the size of the estimate, the less reliable the estimate. When added to and subtracted from the estimate, the margin of error forms the 90 percent confidence interval. For information on confidentiality protection, sampling error, nonsampling error, and definitions, see www.census.gov/acs/www/)

Hispanic type	Total		Native		Foreign Born	
	Number	Percent	Number	Percent	Number	Percent
Total	9	(X)	80	(X)	81	(X)
Caribbean	58	0.1	49	0.2	29	0.2
Cuban	33	0.1	20	0.1	24	0.1
Dominican	34	0.1	19	0.1	22	0.1
Puerto Rican	46	0.1	46	0.2	4	–
Central American	73	0.2	75	0.2	85	0.2
Costa Rican	10	–	6	–	7	–
Guatemalan	29	0.1	12	–	23	0.1
Honduran	23	0.1	9	–	18	0.1
Mexican	81	0.2	78	0.2	84	0.3
Nicaraguan	17	–	7	–	12	0.1
Panamanian	9	–	5	–	6	–
Salvadoran	39	0.1	18	0.1	27	0.1
Other Central American	9	–	5	–	6	–
South American	42	0.1	21	0.1	31	0.2
Argentinean	11	–	5	–	9	–
Bolivian	9	–	4	–	7	–
Chilean	9	–	5	–	7	–
Colombian	25	0.1	11	–	21	0.1
Ecuadorian	23	0.1	11	–	16	0.1
Peruvian	21	–	8	–	17	0.1
Uruguayan	7	–	3	–	5	–
Venezuelan	12	–	5	–	9	–
Other South American	10	–	5	–	7	–
All other Hispanic[1]	42	0.1	39	0.1	19	0.1

X Not applicable.
Dash (-) represents zero or rounds to zero.

[1] Other Hispanic includes all other general Hispanic origin responses such as "Hispanic," "Spanish," or "Latino."
Source: U.S. Census Bureau, 2007 American Community Survey.

Other Pacific Islander" race categories. Respondents providing write-in entries such as multiracial, mixed, interracial, or a Hispanic/ Latino group (for example, Mexican, Puerto Rican, or Cuban) in the "Some Other Race" write-in space are included in this category.

Two or More Races—People may have chosen to provide two or more races either by checking two or more race response check boxes, by providing multiple write-in responses, or by some combination of check boxes and write-in responses.

Notes

1. The terms native and native born are used interchangeably in this report.

2. Gibson, Campbell and Kay Jung. 2006. "Historical Census Statistics on the Foreign-Born Population of the United States: 1850 to 2000." U.S. Census Bureau: Population Division Working Paper, Number 81. Available on the U.S. Census Bureau's Web site at www.census.gov/population/www/techpap.html.

3. Perez, Anthony Daniel and Charles Hirschman. 2009. "The Changing Racial and Ethnic Composition of the U.S. Population: Emerging American Identities." *Population and Development Review,* 35:1-51.

4. According to the American Community Survey, in 2007 the proportion of the total population that was White alone, not Hispanic was 66 percent while the proportion that was White alone or in combination with one or more other race groups, not Hispanic was 67 percent.

5. This report includes data for the 50 states and the District of Columbia.

6. The estimates in this report are based on responses from a sample of the population. As with all surveys, estimates may vary from the actual values because of sampling variation or other factors. All comparative statements have undergone statistical testing and are significant at the 90 percent confidence level unless otherwise noted. The margins of error for key estimates are provided in Appendix Tables 1, 2, and 3.

7. The terms White, Black or African American, American Indian and Alaska Native, Asian, Native Hawaiian and Other Pacific Islander, and Some Other Race are used here to refer to people who reported one race only. The term Two or More Races is used to refer to people who reported more than one race.

The use of six single-race populations and one multiple-race population in this report does not imply that this is the preferred method of presenting or analyzing data. The Census Bureau uses a variety of approaches.

8. The estimates of the proportion of native and foreign-born Hispanics who were White are not statistically different.

9. South America includes the countries of Argentina, Bolivia, Brazil, Chile, Colombia, Ecuador, Falkland Islands, French Guiana, Guyana, Paraguay, Peru, Uruguay, and Venezuela. Central America includes the countries of Belize, Costa Rica, El Salvador, Guatemala, Honduras, Mexico, Nicaragua, and Panama.

10. The estimates for Trinidad and Tobago and Nigeria are not statistically different. The estimates for Ghana and Guyana are not statistically different.

11. The estimates for El Salvador and Honduras are not statistically different. The estimates for Honduras and the remaining Central American countries are not statistically different.

12. Central American Hispanics include people with origins in the Spanish-speaking countries of Central America, including Costa Rica, El Salvador, Guatemala, Honduras, Mexico, Nicaragua, and Panama.

13. South American Hispanics include people with origins in the Spanish-speaking countries of South America, including Argentina, Bolivia, Chile, Colombia, Ecuador, Paraguay, Peru, Uruguay, and Venezuela.

14. The estimates for Uruguayan, Peruvian, and Venezuelan are not statistically different.

15. Caribbean Hispanics include people with origins in the Spanish-speaking countries of the Caribbean, including Cuba, Puerto Rico, and the Dominican Republic.

16. The estimates for Dominican and Cuban Hispanics are not statistically different.

Critical Thinking

1. From among the data in this report what immigration patterns and what relationship can you discern about immigrants and the rest of America?

2. What do these socioeconomics indicators forecast?

3. Is this report a source of hope or fear? What?

Latino Agricultural Workers and their Young Families: Advancing Theoretical and Empirically Based Conceptualizations

SANDRA BARRUECO, PHD AND ROBERT O'BRIEN, PHD

The widely—circulated image of a frightened preschooler clinging to her mother during the heart of the recent immigration raids has led to increased awareness of the agricultural worker community in the United States. Developing a deeper understanding of the plight and strengths of this largely Mexican immigrant community has also become a priority for early childhood intervention programs, which are increasingly available in rural areas (Barnett, Epstein, Friedman, Sansanelli, & Hustedt, 2009; Barnett & Yarosz, 2007). As both researchers and service providers prepare to engage more with agricultural worker families, a thorough description and multidisciplinary review of findings from the fields of psychology, health, education, and services is needed. This paper synthesizes and discusses these findings within a comprehensive, theoretical framework, with the goal of further understanding the key characteristics that should be considered when collaborating with this community[1]. Research and practice implications are presented at the end of this paper to further dialogue along these multiple avenues. Indeed, aspects of this work have been presented to the government to assist in the creation of a nationally representative study of Migrant and Seasonal Head Start (MSHS), a federally—funded comprehensive early childhood intervention program tailored to young agricultural worker families (O'Brien, Barrueco, López, & D'Elio, in press).

Theoretical Framework and Developmental Pathway

The lives of agricultural worker families are comprised of a complex constellation of physical, psychological, sociological, political, and even meteorological facets. The role of each facet, and their interaction among one another, may be conceptualized from the perspective of the theoretical gestalt and more detailed conceptual pathway presented in Figures 1 and 2.

These models are adapted from the cultural conceptualizations of human development by Bronfenbrenner (1979) and Super & Harkness (1999), as well as frameworks utilized in other studies of young children (e.g., ACF, 2006; NCES, 2002; West et al., 2007).

The contextual model presented in Figure 1 focuses on children, which reflects both the concentration of early interventions services on agricultural children's developmental and school readiness outcomes, as well as the central role that children (and dedication to one's children) play in the lives of Latino agricultural worker families (e.g., Gloria & Segura-Herrera, 2004; Parra-Cardona, Bulock, Imig, Villarruel, & Gold, 2006). A particularly apt feature of this model is the placement of MSHS, directly affecting children's development while concurrently influencing family and home experiences through its services to parents, families, and the community. The broader institutional contexts influence each of the layers within the model: formal State and Federal policies—as well as more informal community contexts—impact the families, children, and early childhood programs, such as MSHS. These larger institutional influences can strongly affect families and programs simultaneously; an example is the current focus on the status and role of immigrants in the United States. Touching upon all of these is the larger context of values, beliefs, and practices from both the United States and the home country of the agricultural worker family, such as cultural variations in parents' approaches to child rearing. Finally, an overarching force in the systems of this child contextual model are the less predictable impacts of time and weather that play a central role in the daily functioning of families and programs for agricultural workers. In all, family practices, program participation, communities, policies, culture, time, weather, and even children's own individual characteristics come together to influence development in a dynamic, interrelated fashion.

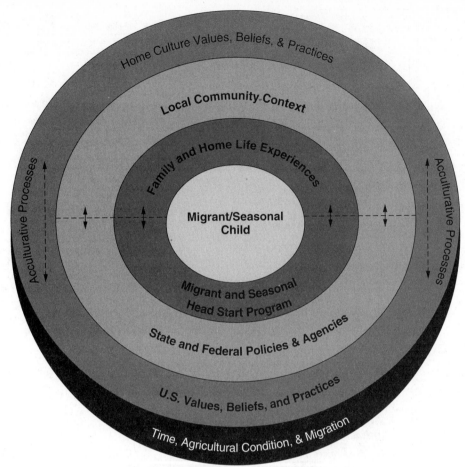

Figure 1 Developmental Contexts of Children within Agricultural Worker Families Participating in MSHS.

The conceptual pathway presented in Figure 2 provides a more detailed analysis of the familial, programmatic, and sociocultural influences implicated in the development of young children of agricultural worker families. Providing a strong influence on this pathway was Super and Harkness' (1999) developmental niche, which identifies three concurrent and culturally-relevant facts to the familial experience.[2] Due to space considerations, this paper focuses primarily on elucidating these family influences, along with the community, cultural, and meterological factors at play in the development of young children within agricultural worker families. Individuals interested in reading more about classroom-based practices and other intervention approaches for this community are referred to O'Brien, Barrueco, López, & D'Elio (in press).

Understanding Agricultural Workers and their Young Children
Regions of Origin, Language and Education

Significant percentages of agricultural workers originate from Mexico (94%, with 2% from Central America and 1% from other countries). Given the strong Latin American presence among agricultural workers, it may not be surprising that the overwhelming majority of agricultural workers participating in MSHS primarily speak Spanish (86%; ACF, 2007). However, Mexico is also comprised of communities with indigenous heritages and languages, particularly in the southern region. In recent decades, the proportion of agricultural workers from Veracruz, Guerrero, Oaxaca, Mòrelos, Chiapas, and Puebla doubled from 9% in 1993–1994 to 19% in 2001–2002 (U.S. Department of Labor, 2005). A greater diversity of non-Spanish languages are spoken in these areas, including 2 types of Huasteco, 5 types of Mazateco, 14 types of Nahuatl (Aztec), 9 types of Otomi, and 4 types of Popoluca, among many others (Gordon, 2005). Creole, Mixteco, and Kanjobal are specifically among the most prevalent non-Spanish/non-English languages within the general agricultural community (U.S. Department of Labor, 2005). Given such changes, attention needs to be placed on the particular region that Mexican agricultural workers may be emigrating from *and* the languages they speak.

Yet, regardless of the specific language or languages spoken by farm worker families, literacy rates appear to be limited. 85% of migrant agricultural workers are estimated to struggle to gain information from printed materials in any language (U.S. Department of Labor, 2000). Average educational levels among farm worker parents participating in the MSHS program fall in the 7th to 8th grade range, reflecting Mexican educational policies where citizens pay for their own schooling after the

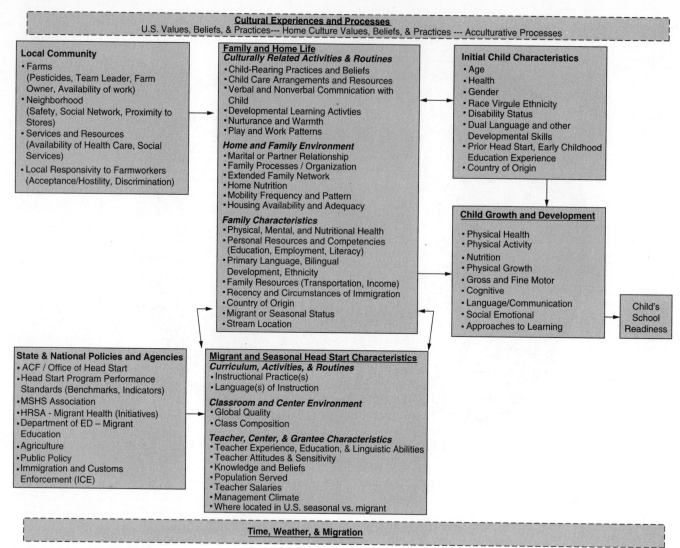

Figure 2 Contextual Pathway

6th grade (ACF, 1999a). Such limited years of formal education and literacy skills certainly influence the development of their young children; importantly, the provision of quality early childhood interventions also can play a vital role in language and literacy facility (e.g., Ezell, Gonzales, and Randolph, 2000).

Mobility within the United States

There has been a tradition in migrant agricultural research, and perhaps within the migrant community itself, to discuss the patterns of North-South annual migrations in terms of three overarching paths: the West Coast, Midwest and East Coast 'streams' (Figure 3) (MSHS TAC-12/National Collaboration Office/AED, 2007). However, the simplicity of this organization currently appears to be a matter of convenience and not accuracy, as family migratory patterns now cross from one stream to another. In addition, families may or may not follow the same pattern from year to year, making the job of anticipating movement and enrollment even more difficult for local programs serving this community. Two national studies (ACF, 1999a; 1999b) explored the reasons why migrant agricultural

workers choose one migrational stream over another, while occasionally engaging in interstream migration. These studies identified agricultural and cultural factors, as well as practical factors (i.e., availability of subsidized health care, child care, legal, and MSHS services), as influences on the choice of migration patterns. Meteorological occurrences may play a particularly strong role in any given year. Shifting weather patterns influence the timing of crop development (e.g., planting, maintenance, and harvesting), while hurricanes, fires and other catastrophes decimate crops (and farm worker's livelihoods) in entire regions.

Concomitant with 'stream' participation, migrant families served by MSHS programs typically engage in four *types* of migration. In the first type, families travel to one or two locations during the annual harvest period and return to their "home-base" after the harvest.[3] In the second type, families travel from farm to farm for an extended period of time, sometimes covering more than one annual harvest, before returning home. For some families, this means moving to various areas of the country before returning to an area that they consider

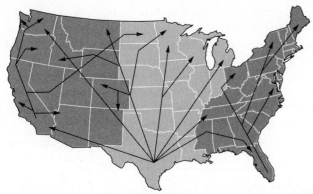

Figure 3   Current Diversity of Agricultural Workers' Migratory Patterns, Overlapping the Traditional 'Streams': Western, Midwestern, and East Coast (MSHS TAC-12/National Collaboration Office/AED, 2007)

more of a "home base." In a third type of migration, families continually move without returning to a consistent home base. Finally, other families move within a relatively small area, traveling from farm to farm, such as nut and grape farmers in the Central Valley in California. Many of these families with a narrower migration zone reside permanently in one area while one member of the family, usually the father (or an adult male), travels relatively short distances for agricultural work (Klayman & Hubbell-McKey, 2000).

Farming and Living Conditions

The circumstances and poverty of agricultural workers often necessitates that both parents work, and some families may not have extended family to assist them due to immigration and continued mobility. Thus, agricultural children may be brought to the fields and other workplaces from infancy, experiencing unhealthy and dangerous conditions including high heat and toxin exposures (e.g., Frank, McKnight, Kirkhorn, & Gunderson, 2004; Koch, 1988). Once in the field, there can be a tendency for children to assist their parents with the field work as soon as they are able (e.g., Bey, 2003). Since both parents in agricultural farm worker families often work long hours and most days of the week, such strenuous and unhealthy activities have serious implications for children's development. Over past decades, the presence of children in the fields greatly decreased as federal agencies worked to target this problem through regulatory approaches as well as the provision of MSHS itself (ACF, 1999).

While the direct exposure of migrant children to negative farming conditions may have attenuated, some researchers remain concerned about indirect effects of living in an agricultural community. For example, pesticides deposited near homes on farms can seep into homes through the water supply, plumbing, house tiles, and other methods (McCauley, Beltran, Phillips, Lasarev, & Sticker, 2001). Parents may carry the pesticides home on clothing and shoes, which can adversely affect young children. Rohlman et al. (2005) identified slower response speed and higher latency rates on fine motor tasks among preschoolers living in agricultural areas, which is consistent with the effects of organophosphate pesticides. In addition, the housing

conditions of young migrant children and their families are often poor, leading to exposure to high levels of heat, pest infestation, lead, and plumbing difficulties (e.g., Slesinger, 1992).

Health and Mental Health

As may be expected, poorer health among agricultural farmworkers and their children have been evidenced. Illness, fatigue, and pain are experienced by many agricultural workers from working long hours in difficult conditions. Further, specific health difficulties include poor nutrition, eye and skin damage from exposure to the sun, musculoskeletal problems, pesticide poisoning, and parasitic infections (e.g., Bechtel, 1998; CDC, 2006; Kandel, 1998; Thompson, 2003). Given that few agricultural positions allow for paid sick leave or worker's compensation, many parents may not attend to health issues in order to keep working. For example, only 42% of agricultural parents participating in MSHS report receiving medical or dental care and 51% report receiving prental care (ACF, 2004). Lack of insurance and paucity of rural medical services are major obstacles. Further, few resources can be brought to bear on physical health maintenance (e.g., regular check-ups, proper nutrition, disease prevention, stress reduction), given that their family household incomes fall in the median range of $12,500 to $14,999, which is well below poverty level (ACF, 2004). As such, agricultural workers may have high morbidity and mortality, with life expectancies that are much shorter than typical U.S. life expectancies (e.g., Kloosterman, Skiffington, Sanchez, & Kiron, 2003; Slesinger, 1992).

Unfortunately, higher mortality rates are also evidenced among migrant children (Slesinger, Christenson, & Cautley, 1986). Although recent relevant data is sparse, studies across the last three decades consistently identify deficits in nutrition, timely immunizations, infection control, and dental health (Koch, 1988; Weathers, Minkovitz, Ocampo, & Diener-West, 2003). For example, nearly a third of migrant children had a Vitamin A deficiency, as well as deficiencies in Vitamin C, Calcium, and Riboflavin; these deficiencies in turn can contribute to infection rates (Chase et al., 1971; Thomas, 1996). While no single cause of these health issues is determinable, it appears that the combination of a higher likelihood of pesticide exposure, along with inadequate nutrition, poor access to medical treatment, poor housing conditions, and extreme poverty contribute to the poorer health of children of agricultural workers. Further, a "lack of an independent means of transportation, lack of knowledge of where to go for needed care, and very high caretaker pressure to work contribute[d] to unmet medical need among migrant children" (Weathers, Minkovitz, O'Campo, & Diener-West, 2004, p. 281). Fortunately, comprehensive early childhood programs aim to address this need, with positive effects evidenced in improved growth rates among Mexican-American migrant children (Dewey, Chavez, Gauthier, Jones, & Ramirez., 1993).

Local Community

Agricultural workers and their families do not exist in isolation. As reflected in Figure 1, they are embedded within, and influenced by the communities in which they live. For example, contributing factors to their health are the availability and prox- imity of medical care (both traditional and non-traditional), pharmacies, and other health and human resources in the large expanses of rural land where they live. Further, agricultural workers' general well-being and mental health are influenced by the attitudes and behaviors of the local community towards them, including the farm owners and team leaders themselves (Hovey & Magaña, 2000; Hovey, Magaña, & Booker, 2001; Hovey & Magaña, 2002a; 2002b). Even discrimination evi- denced at the broader community context is a salient feature in the lives of agricultural workers (Dalla & Christensen, 2005; Parra-Cardona et al., 2006; Ruiz, 2002; Wirth & Dollar, 2004). Finally, the children themselves are not immune from negative community experiences. In an exploratory study by Martin, Gordon, & Kupersmidt (1995), 52% of children from agricul- tural worker families had experienced some form of violence, either as witnesses (46%) or as victims (19%). Such violence exposure exceeds national estimates and approximates those of poverty-stricken, high-crime urban areas (Richters & Martinez, 1993).

Cultural Experiences and Processes

Surrounding many of the aforementioned influences are cul- tural experiences and processes. The acculturative process is not necessarily a simple linear process; the immigrant fam- ily does not always move from being more "ethnic" to more "American" (Chun, Organista, & Marín, 2003). Rather, bi-dimensional models (such as those conceptualized by Berry [1980; 1997] and others) have stronger empirical support.[4] These models of the acculturative process posit that there are two separate influences: 1) the values, beliefs, practices, and language(s) of the home country, and 2) the values, beliefs, practices, and language(s) of the United States. As such, indi- viduals may become *bicultural* by retaining strong ethnic prac- tices and beliefs as they develop American ones. Alternative outcomes may be *assimilation* (low ethnic, high American), *unacculturation* (high ethnic, low American), or *marginaliza- tion* (low ethnic, low American). Notably, bicultural individu- als exhibit more positive outcomes in health and mental health than others, particularly among Latinos (for more on accultura- tion, see Chun, Organista, & Marín, 2003, and Marín, Organi- sta, & Chun, 2005).

Stress and Strengths within Agricultural Farm Worker Families

The cumulative effects of acculturation, hard labor, medical conditions, and unstable employment and housing can take a toll on agricultural workers. Documented rates of depressive symptoms of migrant agricultural workers range from 20% to 57%, and anxiety is also heightened (Alderate, Vega, Kolody, & Aguilar-Gaxiola, 1999; Hovey & Magaña, 2000; Hovey, Magaña, & Booker, 2001; Hovey & Magaña, 2002a; 2002b). The recent increase in immigration raids and suspicion of all immigrants (whether legal or not) have led to documented strain among both parents and children in agricultural commu- nities (e.g., Capps, Casteñeda, Chaudry, & Santos, 2007).

Yet, in the face of such challenges, the agricultural worker community possesses multiple sources of strength. For exam- ple, a qualitative study by Parra-Cardona and colleagues (2006) found that being family-focused was a strong contributor to parents' report of their resiliency. Children are a "source of inspiration when facing adversity and extreme hardship" (372). Like many Latino immigrant parents, agricultural workers are wholeheartedly dedicated to their children's educational suc- cess and linguistic proficiency in English and Spanish (e.g., Gloria & Segura-Herrera, 2004). Further, pride in "*trabajando duro*" (working hard) and a belief that such work improves their children's lives contribute to making meaning of adversity and supporting stronger life satisfaction (Parra-Cardona et al., 2006; Walsh, 2003). Finally, maintaining strong relationships with family and friends can improve farm worker's resiliency and even relate to their children's own socioemotional func- tioning, as independently rated by MSHS teachers (De Leon, Siantz, & Smith, 1993).

Research and Practice Recommendations

The agricultural worker community plays a critical role in the health and development of all Americans; it is through their arduous labor that a bountiful array of fruits and vegetables is made available each year. Further, agricultural workers con- tribute to a $100 billion agricultural industry for rather meager wages (U.S. Environmental Protection Agency, 2009). While agricultural workers are grateful for and invested in their liveli- hood, it comes with significant risks to themselves and their young children. Given these considerations, the following rec- ommendations are provided.

Research

- There is scarce information on the development of young children in agricultural worker families, particularly within the areas of language, numeracy and socioemotional functioning. Much of the health and safety information (an area that should not be overlooked) is also becoming outdated. Given the greater investments in early childhood programs by states and others, this dearth creates a barrier to creating, validating, and providing appropriate and effective interventions for this population.
- Greater proportions of farm workers are of indigenous heritage yet relatively little is understood about individuals stemming from these southern Mexican communities. For example, what are their approaches to child-rearing, community engagement, and verbal and non-verbal communication styles? Even the most basic information is limited, such as the percentage of children and parents who are bilingual (Spanish/ English; indigenous language/English) or even trilingual (indigenous language/Spanish/English). Such information would improve the development of appropriate early childhood interventions, including staffing, trainings, and materials.

Practice

- Innovative methods in providing interventions and services for agricultural worker families are required. One approach is to match the flexibility of the workers' schedules and mobility by providing services at the times and locations they need them. Some MSHS programs open and close centers as farm workers move through an area, while others provide teachers and staff that follow them through the migratory patterns. Such approaches may be fruitful within the health, mental health, and educational arenas. Recent technological advances could also provide another avenue for service or intervention provision. Pay-as-you-go cellular phones and computers at public libraries and schools could provide mechanisms for maintaining connections with service providers and teachers while families are migrating to the most distant rural areas.

- Finally, the process of gaining *la confianza* (trust) of the agricultural community can not be overlooked. Given the past and present experiences of this population, *confianza* can be slow to develop. It often entails frequent and respectful interactions, though this process can be quickened if introductions are made by trusted individuals within or outside the community. Regardless of approach, it is necessary to understand that *confianza* is built on at least three levels: the broader agricultural worker community, the family, and the individual. Addressing and discussing all three in both everyday discussions and when planning intervention and research efforts demonstrates cultural competency and lays the foundation for successful engagement. Therefore, the aspiring practitioner, researcher, or teacher must approach and acknowledge all three in order to successfully understand, collaborate with, and contribute to this important community in the American tapestry.

Notes

1. Occasionally, relatively dated studies are included in this chapter when no better information could be found and the findings contributed to a greater understanding of agricultural children and families.

2. These components are called "Customs of Child Care and Child Rearing," "Physical and Social Settings of Daily Life," and "Psychology of the Caretakers," respectively, in Super and Harkness (1997) original writings. Titles are adapted to better reflect the terminology of the early childhood field.

3. The term "home base" is often used to describe the families' identification of an area to which they almost always return; these are often located in warmer locations for winter housing, although this is not always the case.

4. Research in the past decade has even begun to support a multidimensional process capturing more nuanced patterns and variations in underlying cultural processes, such as the separation of linguistic and cultural practices (e.g., Berry, 2003; Sue, 2003).

References

Alderete, E., Vega, W.A., Kolody, B., & Aguilar-Gaxiola, S. (1999). Depressive symptomatology: Prevalence and psychosocial risk factors among Mexican migrant farmworkers in California. *Journal of Community Psychology, 27,* 457–471.

Administration on Children and Families (1999a). *A Descriptive Study of Children and Families Served by Head Start Migrant Programs.* Washington, D.C.: U.S. Department of Health and Human Services.

Administration on Children and Families (1999b). *Descriptive study of migrant and seasonal farmworker families.* Washington, D.C.: U.S. Department of Health and Human Services.

Administration for Children and Families (ACF), (2004). Executive Summary: Migrant and Seasonal Head Start Research Design Development Project 2002–2004. Washington, DC: U.S. Department of Health and Humand Services.

Administration for Children and Families (ACF), (2006). Head Start Family and Child Experiences Survey (FACES), 2006 Cohort: Supporting Statement for Request for OMB Approval of Data Collection Instruments. Washington, DC: U.S. Department of Health and Human Services.

Administration for Children and Families (ACF), (2007). Head Start Program Fact Sheet: Fiscal Year 2007. Washington, DC: U.S. Department of Health and Human Services.

Barnett, W.S., Epstein, D.J., Friedman,, A.H., Sansanelli, R.A., & Hustedt,, J.T. (2009). *The State of Preschool 2009: State Preschool Yearbook.* Rutgers, NJ: The National Institute for Early Education Research.

Barnett, W.S., & Yarosz, D.J. (2007). *Who Goes to Preschool and Why Does it Matter?* Rutgers, NJ: The National Institute for Early Education Research.

Berry, J. W. (1980). Acculturation as a variety of adaptation. In A. M. Padilla (Ed.), *Acculturation: Theory, models and some new findings* (pp. 9–25). Boulder, CO: Westview.

Berry, J. W. (1997). Immigration, acculturation, and adaptation. *Applied Psychology: An International Review, 46* (1), 5–34.

Bechtel, G.A. (1998). Parasitic infections among migrant farm families. *Journal of Community Health Nursing, 15,* 1–7.

Bey, M. (2003). The Mexican child: From work with the family to paid employment. *Childhood: A Global Journal of Child Research, 10,* 287–299.

Bronfenbrenner, U. (1979). *The Ecology of Human Development: Experiments by Nature and Design.* Cambridge: MA: Harvard University Press.

Capps, R., Casteñeda, R.M., Chaudry, A. & Santos, R. (2007). *Paying the Price: The Impact of Immigration Raids on America's Children.* Washington, DC: Urban Institute.

Centers for Disease Control and Prevention. (2006). Worker illness related to ground application of pesticide-Kern County, California, 2005. *Morbidity and Mortality Weekly Report, 55,* 486–488.

Chase, H. P., Kumar, V., Dodds, J. M., Sauberlich, H.E., Hunter, R.M., Burton, R.S., & Spalding, V. (1971). Nutritional status of preschool Mexican American migrant farm children. *American Journal of Diseases of Children, 122,* 316–324.

Chun, K.M., Organista, P.B. & Marin, G. (2003). *Acculturation: Advances in theory, measurement, and applied research.* Washington, DC: American Psychological Association.

Dalla, R. L., & Christensen, A. (2005). Latino immigrants describe residence in rural Midwestern meatpacking communities:

A longitudinal assessment of social and economic change. *Hispanic Journal of Behavioral Sciences, 27,* 23–42.

De Leon Siantz, M. L. & Smith, M. S. (1993). Parental factors correlated with developmental outcome in the Migrant Head Start child. *Early Childhood Research Quarterly, 9,* 481–504.

Dewey, K. G., Chavez, M. N., Gauthier, C. L., Jones, L. B., & Ramirez, R. E. (1983). Anthropometry of Mexican-American migrant children in northern California. *American Journal of Clinical Nutrition, 37,* 828–833.

Ezell, H. K., Gonzales, M. D., & Randolph, E. (2000). Emergent literacy skills of migrant Mexican-American preschoolers. *Communication Disorders Quarterly, 21,* 147–153.

Frank, A.L., McKnight, R., Kirkhorn, S.R. & Gunderson, P. (2004). Issues of agricultural safety and health. *Annual Review of Public Health, 25,* 225–245.

Gloria, A. M., & Segura-Herrera, T. A. (2004). !!!Somos! Latinas and Latinos in the United States. In D. R. Atkinson (Ed.), *Counseling American Minorities* (6th ed., pp. 279–299). Boston: McGraw Hill.

Gordon, R. G. (Ed.). (2005). *Ethnologue: Languages of the World* (15th ed.). Dallas, TX: SIL International.

Hovey, J.D., & Magana, C.G. (2000). Acculturative stress, anxiety, and depression among Mexican farmworkers in the Midwest United States. *Journal of Immigrant Health, 2,* 119–131.

Hovey, J.D., & Magana, C.G. (2002). Exploring the mental health of Mexican migrant farm workers in the Midwest: Psychosocial predictors of psychological distress and suggestions for prevention and treatment. *The Journal of Psychology, 136,* 493–513.

Hovey, J.D., & Magana, C.G. (2002a). Cognitive, affective, and physiological expressions of anxiety symptomatology among Mexican migrant farmworkers: Predictors and generational differences. *Community Mental Health Journal, 38,* 223–237.

Hovey, J.D., & Magana, C.G. (2002b). Psychosocial predictors of anxiety among immigrant Mexican migrant farmworkers: Implications for prevention and treatment. *Cultural Diversity & Ethnic Minority Psychology, 8,* 274–289.

Kandel, W. (2008). *Profile of Hired Farmworkers: A 2008 Update* (Economic Research Report 60). Washington, DC: United States Department of Agriculture.

Klayman, D. & McKey, R.H. (2000). *Descriptive Study of Migrant and Seasonal Farmworker Families.* Department of Health and Human Services: Washington, DC.

Kloosterman, Skiffington, Sanchez, & Kiron, (2003). *Migrant and Seasonal Head Start and Child Care Partnerships: A Report from the Field.* Education Development Center: Newton, MA.

Koch, D. (1988). Migrant day care and the health status of migrant preschoolers: A review of the literature. *Journal of Community Health Nursing, 5,* 221–233.

Marín, G., Organista, P.B., & Chun, K. M. (2005). Accultural research: Current issues and findings. In G. Bernal, J.E., Trimble, A.K., Burlew, & F. T. Leong. (2003). *Handbook of Racial and Ethnic Minority Psychology* (pp. 208–219). Thousand Oaks, CA: Sage Publications.

Martin, S.L., Gordon, T.E., & Kupersmidt, J.B. (1995). Survey of exposure to violence among the children of migrant and seasonal farm workers. *Public Health Reports. 110,* 268–276.

MSHS TAC-12/National Collaboration Office/AED (2007). *Migrant and Seasonal Head Start center locator directory.* Washington, DC: Migrant and Seasonal Head Start Collaboration Office.

McCauley, L.A., Beltran, M., Phillips, J., Lasarev, M., & Sticker, D. (2001). The Oregon Migrant Farmworker Community: An Evolving Model for Participatory Research. *Environmental Health Perspective, 109,* 449–455.

National Center for Education Statistics (2002). *Early Childhood Longitudinal Study, Birth Cohort, 9-month data collection: 2001–02.* Washington, DC: U.S. Department of Education.

National Center for Farmworker Health (NCFH). (2003). Overview of America's farmworkers: Farmworker health. Retrieved from www.ncfh.org/aaf_03.php

O'Brien, R., Barrueco, S., López, M.L., & D'Elio, M.A. (in press). *Design of the National Migrant and Seasonal Head Start Survey.* Washington, DC: Department of Health and Human Services.

Parra-Cardona, J., Bulock, L.A., Imig, D.R., Villarruel, F.A., & Gold, S.J. (2006). "Trabajando duro todos los días": Learning from the life experiences of Mexican-origin migrant families. *Family Relations, 55,* 361–375.

Richters, J.E. & Martinez, P. (1993). The NIMH Community Violence Project: I. Children as victims and witnesses to violence. *Psychiatry, 56,* 7–21.

Rohlman, D. S., Arcury, T. A., Quandt S. A., Lasarev, M., Rothlein, J., Travers, R., Alys Tamulinas, A., Scherer, J., Early, J., Marín, A., Phillips, J., & McCauley, L. (2005). Neurobehavioral performance in preschool children from agricultural and non-agricultural communities in Oregon and North Carolina. *Neuro Toxicology, 26,* 589–598.

Ruiz, P. (2002). Hispanic access to health/mental health services. *Psychiatric Quarterly, 73,* 85–91.

Slesinger, D.P., Christenson, B.A. & Cautley, E. (1986). Health and mortality of migrant farm children, *Social Science & Medicine, 23,* 65–74.

Slesinger, D P. (1992). Health status and needs of migrant farm workers in the United States: a literature review. *Journal of Rural Health, 8,* 227–234.

Super, C.M., & Harkess, S. (1997). The cultural structuring of child development. In J. Berry, P.R & T. S. Dasen, (Eds.), *Handbook of cross-cultural psychology: Basic processes and human development* (2nd ed., vol. 2, pp. 1–39). Boston, MA: Allyn & Bacon.

Super, C. M., & Harkess, S. (1999). The environment as culture in developmental research. In S. L. Friedman & T. D. Wachs (Eds.), *Measuring environment across the life span: Emerging methods and concepts* (pp. 279–326). Washington, DC: American Psychological Association.

Thomas, E.C. (1996). *Bitter Sugar: Migrant Farmworker Nutrition and Access to Service in Minnesota.* St. Paul, MN: The Urban Coalition.

Thompson, B., Coronado, G.D., Grossman, J.E., Puschel, K., Solomon, C.C., Islas, I., Curl, C.L., Shirai, J.H., Kissel, J.C., & Fenske, R.A. (2003). Pesticide take-home pathway among children of agricultural workers: Study design, methods, and baseline findings. *Journal of Occupational and Environmental Medicine, 45,* 42–53.

U.S. Department of Labor. (2000). Findings from the National Agricultural Workers Survey (NAWS) 1997–1998: A demographic and employment profile of United States farmworkers (Research Report No. 9). Washington, DC: U.S. Department of Labor.

U.S. Department of Labor (2005). Findings from the National Agricultural Workers Survey (NAWS) 2001–2002: A

Demographic and Employment Profile of United States Farm Workers (Research Report No. 9). Washington, DC: U.S. Department of Labor.

U.S. Environmental Protection Agency (2009). *Major Crops Grown in the United States.* Retrieved from www.epa.gov/agriculture/ag101/cropmajor.html

Walsh, F. (2003). Family resilience: A framework for clinical practice. *Family Process, 42,* 1–18.

Weathers A, Minkovitz C, O'Campo P, Diener-West M. (2003). Health services use by children of migratory agricultural workers: exploring the role of need for care. *Pediatrics, 111,* 956–963.

Weathers, A., Minkovitz, C., O'Campo, P., & Diener-West, M. (2004). Access to care for children of migratory agricultural workers: Factors associated with unmet need for medical care. *Pediatrics, 113,* 276–282.

West, J. Tarullo, L., Aikens, N., Sparchman, S., Ross, C., & Carlson, B.L. (2007). *FACES 2006: Study Design.* Washington, DC: U.S. Department of Health and Human Services.

Wirth, J. B., & Dollar, S. C. (2004). Concerns of Hispanics and service providers in southwest Missouri. *Great Plains Research, 14,* 253–270.

Acknowledgments—Funding was provided in part by the U.S. Department of Health and Human Services (DHHS), HHSP23320045009XI. The contents do not necessarily represent the positions or policies of the DHHS, and endorsement by the Federal government should not be assumed. Our heart-felt gratitude goes to Wendy DeCourcey, Ph.D. who provided invaluable feedback. We also thank Michael López, Ph.D., Mary Ann D'Elio, and many other colleagues for their suggestions.

Critical Thinking

1. What five aspects of this report are most revealing of the condition of agricultural workers?

2. Can a 'family support' policy for agricultural workers be improved by the states or the national government?

3. Are the private sector and our overall pattern of food production and consumption as well as international commerce dependent of legal and illegal workers? What does this mean for America?

UNIT 7
Asian Americans

Unit Selections

31. **Asian/Pacific American Heritage Month, May 2010,** *U.S. Department of Commerce, American Community Survey, Census Bureau News,* May 2010
32. **To Be Asian in America,** Angela Johnson Meadows

Learning Objectives

- Examine the origin and sources of misinformation about Asian Americans.

- Does public attention to the activities of Asian Americans associated with Islamic countries seem to be increasing?

- The public passions generated during World War II have subsided, and anti-Japanese sentiment is no longer heard. Do you agree or disagree with this statement? Why? Is this phenomenon related to current perceptions of Arab Americans? Can current detainments be analogized to the Japanese internment camps?

Student Website
www.mhhe.com/cls

Internet References

Asian American Studies Center
www.aasc.ucla.edu/default.asp
Asian Americans for Equality
www.aafe.org
Asian-Nation
www.asian-nation.org/index.shtml

The Asian American context discussed in this unit provides perspectives on immigrants' adjustment and their reception in various regimes and cultures. Asian Americans are engaged in the ongoing issue of cultural formation, the recovery of tradition, and the incorporation of new ethnicities from Asian into mainstream cultural entertainment. The political and economic forces that frame relationships at the personal and cultural levels pose dilemmas and attendant choices that define current situations and the artifices used to heighten or diminish Asian ethnicities in America. The variety of religious traditions that Asian immigrants bring to America is another dimension of cultural and moral importance. In what respect are non-Judeo-Christian/Islamic faith traditions issues of consequence? The aftermath of conflict and resulting analysis have riveted attention on the ethnic factor. The details of familial and cultural development within these Asian American communities compose worlds of meaning that are a rich source of material from which both insights and troubling questions of personal and group identity emerge. Pivotal periods of conflict in the drama of the American experience provide an occasion for learning as much about ourselves as about one of the newest clusters of ethnicities—the Asian Americans.

Asian Americans are engaged in the ongoing issue of cultural formation, the recovery of tradition, and the incorporation of new ethnicities from Asian into mainstream cultural entertainment. The political and economic forces that frame relationships at the personal and cultural levels pose dilemmas and attendant choices that define current situations and the artifices used to heighten or diminish Asian ethnicities in America.

The intrinsic complexity of immigration as a social issue is one reason for the lack of comprehensive and long-range planning evidenced by U.S. immigration laws. The extreme diversity in our immigration sources clearly adds to the complexity of this issue. Throughout this nation's history, immigration has been both praised and reviled. Immigrant success stories are mingled with fear that the foreigner will take jobs and that our infrastructure will be strained. The late 1900s is a turning point in U.S. immigration history, not only because it signals the beginning of direct federal controls but also because it reflects new immigrant sources, whose ability to assimilate will be questioned. The first general immigration law was enacted in 1882. In general, it established a 50-cent head tax per immigrant and gave the treasury secretary jurisdiction over immigration matters. The 1882 act also excluded convicts, paupers, and mentally defective aliens. Earlier that year Congress had passed the Chinese Exclusion Act, which based ineligibility for admission to the United States on national origin. The act also prohibited foreign-born Chinese from becoming citizens and placed a 10-year ban on the admission of Chinese workers. In 1890 there were 107,488 Chinese aliens on the American mainland; because of the Exclusion Act that number had dwindled to 61,639 by 1920.

Thousands of Chinese aliens had come to the West Coast as contract laborers to build the railroads in the mid-1850s. By 1880 there were 189,000 Chinese in the United States. Their sheer numbers coupled with the fact that most were unskilled and worked for low wages generated hostility and adverse public opinion. Calls for restrictive measures grew until Congress responded with the 1882 act. However, the issue did not disappear after the act's passage. In the next several decades, Congress would take further restrictive measures against the Chinese. In 1884 in fact, Congress amended the Chinese Exclusion Act. The section dealing with Chinese workers was extended to cover all Chinese, regardless of whether they were Chinese subjects. The immigrant head tax increased to $1.00 in 1884. Thousands of Japanese immigrants arrived in the late 1800s. Initially, Hawaiian sugar plantations were their destination, where they worked as contract labor. Canadians and

© Blend Images/Getty Images

Mexicans also streamed across our land borders in this period to work in factories and fields. Congress amended the 1882 Chinese Exclusion Act again in 1892, as it was about to expire. The 1892 act extended the exclusion provisions for an additional 10 years and required all Chinese workers to obtain a residence certificate within 1 year. In 1893 Congress passed an act that reinforced prior immigration laws. It also required ship owners to collect information about incoming aliens to help identify those who were excludable. Boards of inquiry were established in 1893 to deal with immigration problems, including deportation. Calls for more regulation and restriction of immigrants continued through the turn of the century. Various members of Congress proposed a literacy test again and again as an immigration control to exclude aliens who were unable to read in any language. Legislation to accomplish this was vetoed by presidents Cleveland, Taft, and Wilson. In 1917, a literacy test for incoming aliens was enacted over President Wilson's veto. Between 1901 and 1920, 14,531,197 immigrants entered the United States.

In 1901, an immigrant anarchist assassinated President McKinley. Theodore Roosevelt, who succeeded McKinley, told Congress that U.S. policy should be to systematically exclude and deport anarchists. Two years later, Congress responded by adding anarchists to the growing list of excludable aliens in the first federal law making political ideas and beliefs grounds for deportation. The 1903 immigration act also barred epileptics, insane persons, and professional beggars from entry. In addition, it raised the head tax to $2.00 and re-codified the contract labor law. Congress passed a subsequent statute in 1907, which raised the head tax to $4.00 and earmarked these revenues for use in defraying the costs of enforcing U.S. immigration laws. The 1907 act also created a commission to study immigration, which came to be known as the Dillingham Commission after the senator who chaired it. The commission submitted a 42-volume report in 1911. It concluded that the immigrants who started coming to the United States in the late 1800s adversely affected the American labor movement.

The following articles on Asian Americans invite us to reflect on the fact that the United States is related to Asia in ways that would seem utterly amazing to the worldview of the American founders. The growth of the Asian American population since the immigration reform of 1965, the emergence of Japan and other Asian nations as international financial powers, and the image of Asian American intellectual and financial success have heightened interest in this cluster of ethnic groups.

Asian/Pacific American Heritage Month: May 2010

In 1978, a joint congressional resolution established Asian/Pacific American Heritage Week. The first 10 days of May were chosen to coincide with two important milestones in Asian/Pacific American history: the arrival in the United States of the first Japanese immigrants (May 7, 1843) and contributions of Chinese workers to the building of the transcontinental railroad, completed on May 10, 1869. In 1992, Congress expanded the observance to a month-long celebration. Per a 1997 Office of Management and Budget directive, the Asian or Pacific Islander racial category was separated into two categories: one being Asian and the other Native Hawaiian and Other Pacific Islander. Thus, this Facts for Features contains a section for each.

2010 Census

3

Number of Asian languages 2010 Census questionnaires are available upon request: Chinese, Vietnamese and Korean.[1]

13

Number of Asian languages 2010 Census ads are in: Bengali, Chinese (Mandarin and Cantonese), Hindi, Hmong, Japanese, Khmer, Korean, Laotian, Tagalog, Thai, Urdu and Vietnamese. The Census has gone to great lengths to be true to the ethnicities it is trying to reach. For example, Chinese Americans are depicted in ads for Chinese Americans, rather than generic images of the Asian population.[2]

19

Number of Asian languages 2010 Census Language Assistance Guides are in: Bengali, Burmese, Cebuano, Chinese (Traditional and Simplified), Hindi, Hmong, Ilocano, Japanese, Khmer, Korean, Laotian, Malayalam, Tagalog, Tamil, Telugu, Thai, Urdu and Vietnamese. In addition, they are available in the following Native Hawaiian and Other Pacific Islander languages: Chamorro, Chuukese, Marshallese, Samoan and Tongan.[3]

Asians

15.5 million

The estimated number of U.S. residents in July 2008 who said they were Asian alone or Asian in combination with one or more other races. This group comprised about 5 percent of the total population.[4]

5.1 million

The Asian population in California, the state that had the largest Asian population on July 1, 2008, as well as the largest numerical increase from 2007 to 2008 (105,000). New York

(1.5 million) and Texas (956,000) followed in population. In Hawaii, our nation's only majority-Asian state, Asians made up the highest proportion of the total population (54 percent). Asians were the largest minority group in Hawaii and Vermont.[5]

2.7%

Percentage growth of the Asian population between 2007 and 2008, the highest of any race group during that time period. The increase in the Asian population during the period totaled more than 400,000.[6]

3.62 million

Number of Asians of Chinese descent in the U.S. in 2008. Chinese-Americans were the largest Asian group, followed by Filipinos (3.09 million), Asian Indians (2.73 million), Vietnamese (1.73 million), Koreans (1.61 million) and Japanese (1.30 million). These estimates represented the number of people who were either of a particular Asian group only or were of that group in combination with one or more other Asian groups or races.[7]

Income, Poverty and Health Insurance

$70,069

Median household income for single-race Asians in 2008.[8]

Median household income differed greatly by Asian group. For Asian Indians, for example, the median income in 2008 was $90,528; for Vietnamese-Americans, it was $55,667. (These figures represent the single-race population.)[9]

11.8%

Poverty rate for single-race Asians in 2008, up from 10.2 percent in 2007.[10]

17.6%

Percentage of single-race Asians without health insurance coverage in 2008, not statistically different from 2007.[11]

Education

50%

The percentage of single-race Asians 25 and older who had a bachelor's degree or higher level of education. This compared with 28 percent for all Americans 25 and older.[12]

85%

The percentage of single-race Asians 25 and older who had at least a high school diploma. This compared with 85 percent for all Americans 25 and older.[13]

20%

The percentage of single-race Asians 25 and older who had a graduate (e.g., master's or doctorate) or professional degree. This compared with 10 percent for all Americans 25 and older.[14]

Voting

How many more Asians voted in the 2008 presidential election than in the 2004 election. All in all, 49 percent of Asians turned out to vote in 2008—up about 4 percentage points from 2004. A total of 3.6 million Asians voted.[15]

Businesses

Source for the statements referenced in this section, unless otherwise indicated: Asian-Owned Firms: 2002 www2.census .gov/econ/sbo/02/sb0200csasian.pdf

1.1 million

Number of businesses owned by Asian-Americans in 2002, up 24 percent from 1997. The rate of increase in the number of Asian-owned businesses was about twice that of the national average for all businesses.

More than $326 billion

Receipts of Asian-American-owned businesses in 2002, up 8 percent from 1997. An estimated 319,468 Asian-owned businesses had paid employees, and their receipts totaled more than $291 billion. There were 49,636 Asian-owned firms with receipts of $1 million or more, accounting for 4 percent of the total number of Asian-owned firms and nearly 68 percent of their total receipts.

   In 2002, more than three in 10 Asian-owned firms operated in professional, scientific and technical services, as well as other services, such as personal services, and repair and maintenance.

2.2 million

Number of people employed by Asian-owned businesses. There were 1,866 Asian-owned firms with 100 or more employees, generating nearly $52 billion in gross receipts (18 percent of the total revenue for Asian-owned employer firms).

47%

Percentage of all Asian-owned firms that were either Chinese-owned or Asian Indian-owned.

Nearly 6 in 10

Proportion of all Asian-owned firms in the United States in California, New York, Texas and New Jersey.

112,441

The number of Asian-owned firms in New York City, which led all cities. Los Angeles (47,764), Honolulu (22,348) and San Francisco (19,639) followed.

28%

The proportion of Asian-owned businesses that were home based. This is the lowest proportion among minority respondent groups.[16]

Languages

2.5 million

The number of people 5 and older who spoke Chinese at home in 2008. After Spanish, Chinese was the most widely spoken non-English language in the country. Tagalog, Vietnamese and Korean were each spoken at home by more than 1 million people.[17]

Serving Our Nation

276,079

The number of single-race Asian military veterans. About one in three was 65 and older.[18]

Jobs

48%

The proportion of civilian employed single-race Asians 16 and older who worked in management, professional and related occupations, such as financial managers, engineers, teachers and registered nurses. Additionally, 22 percent worked in sales and office occupations, 16 percent in service occupations and 11 percent in production, transportation and material moving occupations.[19]

The 'Net

73%

Percentage of Asians living in a household with Internet use—the highest rate among race and ethnic groups.[20]

Counties

1.4 million

The number of Asians (self-identified as Asian alone or in combination with one or more other races) in Los Angeles County, Calif., in 2008, which tops the nation's counties.[21]

19,000

Santa Clara County, Calif.'s Asian population increase from 2007 to 2008, the largest in the nation.[22]

58%

Percent of the population of Honolulu County, Hawaii, that was Asian in 2008, which led the country. Honolulu was the only majority-Asian county in the nation.[23]

Age Distribution

35.8

Median age of the single-race Asian population in 2008. The corresponding figure was 36.8 years for the population as a whole.[24]

The Future

40.6 million

The projected number of U.S. residents in 2050 who will identify themselves as Asian or Asian in combination with one or more other races. They would comprise 9 percent of the total population by that year.[25]

162%

The projected percentage increase between 2008 and 2050 in the population of people who identify themselves as Asian or Asian in combination with one or more other races. This compares with a 44 percent increase in the population as a whole over the same period of time.[26]

Native Hawaiians and Other Pacific Islanders

1.1 million

The estimated number of U.S. residents in July 2008 who said they were Native Hawaiian and Other Pacific Islander, either alone or in combination with one or more other races. This group comprised 0.4 percent of the total population.[27]

California had the largest population (282,000) in 2008 of Native Hawaiians and Other Pacific Islanders (either alone or in combination with one or more other races), followed by Hawaii (281,000) and Washington (55,000). California had the largest numerical increase (6,000) of people of this group. In Hawaii, Native Hawaiians and Other Pacific Islanders comprised the largest proportion (22 percent) of the total population.[28]

2.4%

Percentage growth of the Native Hawaiian and Other Pacific Islander population between 2007 and 2008—second to Asians among race groups. The increase in the Native Hawaiian and Other Pacific Islander population during the period totaled about 26,000.[29]

Income, Poverty and Health Insurance

$57,721

The median income of households headed by single-race Native Hawaiians and Other Pacific Islanders.[30]

16.3%

The poverty rate for those who classified themselves as single-race Native Hawaiian and Other Pacific Islander.[31]

18.5%

The three-year average (2006-2008) percentage without health insurance for single-race Native Hawaiians and Other Pacific Islanders.[32]

Education

15%

The percentage of single-race Native Hawaiians and Other Pacific Islanders 25 and older who had at least a bachelor's degree. This compared with 28 percent for the total population.[33]

87%

The percentage of single-race Native Hawaiians and Other Pacific Islanders 25 and older who had at least a high school diploma. This compared with 85 percent for the total population.[34]

5%

The percentage of single-race Native Hawaiians and Other Pacific Islanders 25 and older who had obtained a graduate or professional degree. This compared with 10 percent for the total population of this age.[35]

Businesses

Source for the statements referenced in this section: Native Hawaiian- and Other Pacific Islander-Owned Firms: 2002 www2.census.gov/econ/sbo/02/sb0200csnhpi.pdf

28,948

Number of Native Hawaiian- and Other Pacific Islander-owned businesses in 2002, up 49 percent from 1997. The rate of growth was more than three times the national average. The 3,693 Native Hawaiian- and Other Pacific Islander-owned businesses with paid employees employed more than 29,000 and generated revenues of $3.5 billion.

2,415

Number of Native Hawaiian- and Other Pacific Islander-owned firms in Honolulu.

$4.3 billion

Receipts for Native Hawaiian- and Other Pacific Islander-owned businesses in 2002, up 3 percent from 1997. There were 727 Native Hawaiian- and Other Pacific Islander-owned firms with receipts of $1 million or more. These firms accounted for 3 percent of the total number of Native Hawaiian- and Other Pacific Islander-owned firms and 67 percent of their total receipts.

In 2002, nearly 21,000 Native Hawaiian- and Other Pacific Islander-owned firms operated in health care and social assistance; other services (such as personal services, and repair and maintenance); retail trade; administrative and support and waste management and remediation services; professional, scientific and technical services; and construction.

28

Number of Native Hawaiian- and Other Pacific Islander-owned firms with 100 or more employees. These firms generated $698 million in gross receipts—20 percent of the total revenue for

Native Hawaiian- and Other Pacific Islander-owned employer firms.

53%

Percentage of all Native Hawaiian- and Other Pacific Islander-owned firms in Hawaii and California. These two states accounted for 62 percent of business revenue.

Serving Our Nation

26,810

The number of single-race Native Hawaiian and Other Pacific Islander military veterans. About one in five was 65 and older.[36]

Jobs

24%

The proportion of civilian employed single-race Native Hawaiians and Other Pacific Islanders 16 and older who worked in management, professional and related occupations, such as financial managers, engineers, teachers and registered nurses. About the same percent worked in service occupations. Meanwhile, 28 percent worked in sales and office occupations and 14 percent in production, transportation and material moving occupations.[37]

Counties

179,000

Native Hawaiian and Other Pacific Islander population (alone or in combination with one or more other races) in Honolulu County, Hawaii, in 2008, which led the nation. Among counties, Clark County, Nev. (home of Las Vegas) had the largest numerical increase in this race since July 2007—857. Hawaii County, Hawaii, had the highest percentage of people of this race (30 percent).[38]

Age Distribution

29.8

The median age of the single-race Native Hawaiian and Other Pacific Islander population in 2008. The median age was 36.8 for the population as a whole.[39]

The Future

2.6 million

The projected number of U.S. residents in 2050 who will identify themselves as Native Hawaiian and Other Pacific Islander or Native Hawaiian and Other Pacific Islander in combination with one or more other races. They would comprise 0.6 percent of the total population by that year.[40]

132%

The projected percentage increase between 2008 and 2050 in the population of people who identify themselves as Native Hawaiian and Other Pacific Islander or Native Hawaiian and Other Pacific Islander in combination with one or more other races. This compares with a 44 percent increase in the population as a whole over the same period of time.[41]

Following is a list of observances typically covered by the Census Bureau's *Facts for Features* series:

African-American History Month (February)
Super Bowl
Valentine's Day (Feb. 14)
Women's History Month (March)
Irish-American Heritage Month (March)/St. Patrick's Day (March 17)
Asian/Pacific American Heritage Month (May)
Older Americans Month (May)
Cinco de Mayo (May 5)
Mother's Day
Hurricane Season Begins (June 1)
Father's Day
The Fourth of July (July 4)
Anniversary of Americans With Disabilities Act (July 26)
Back to School (August)
Labor Day
Grandparents Day
Hispanic Heritage Month (Sept. 15-Oct. 15)
Unmarried and Single Americans Week
Halloween (Oct. 31)
American Indian/Alaska Native Heritage Month (November)
Veterans Day (Nov. 11)
Thanksgiving Day
The Holiday Season (December)

Notes

1. Source: 2010 Census Web site http://2010.census .gov/2010census/

2. Source: 2010 Census Web site http://2010.census .gov/2010census/

3. Source: 2010 Census Web site http://2010.census .gov/2010census/

4. Source: Population estimates www.census.gov/newsroom/ releases/archives/population/cb09-75.html

5. Source: Population estimates www.census.gov/newsroom/ releases/archives/population/cb09-76.html

6. Source: Population estimates www.census.gov/newsroom/ releases/archives/population/cb09-75.html

7. Source: 2008 American Community Survey http://factfinder .census.gov

8. Source: 2008 American Community Survey http://factfinder .census.gov

9. Source: 2008 American Community Survey http://factfinder .census.gov

10. Source: Income, Poverty, and Health Insurance Coverage in the United States: 2008 www.census.gov/newsroom/releases/ archives/income_wealth/cb09-141.html

11. Source: Income, Poverty, and Health Insurance Coverage in the United States: 2008 www.census.gov/newsroom/releases/ archives/income_wealth/cb09-141.html

12. Source: 2008 American Community Survey http://factfinder .census.gov

13. Source: 2008 American Community Survey http://factfinder .census.gov

14. Source: 2008 American Community Survey http://factfinder .census.gov

15. Source: Voting and Registration in the Election of November 2008 www.census.gov/newsroom/releases/archives/voting/ cb09-110.html

16. Source: Characteristics of Businesses: 2002 www.census.gov/ newsroom/releases/archives/business_ownership/cb06-148.html

17. Source: 2008 American Community Survey http://factfinder .census.gov

18. Source: 2008 American Community Survey http://factfinder .census.gov

19. Source: 2008 American Community Survey http://factfinder .census.gov

20. Source: Computer and Internet Use in the United States: October 2007 www.census.gov/newsroom/releases/archives/ communication_industries/cb09-84.html

21. Source: Population estimates www.census.gov/newsroom/ releases/archives/population/cb09-76.html

22. Source: Population estimates www.census.gov/newsroom/ releases/archives/population/cb09-76.html

23. Source: Population estimates www.census.gov/newsroom/ releases/archives/population/cb09-76.html

24. Source: Population estimates www.census.gov/popest/national/ asrh/NC-EST2008-asrh.html

25. Source: Population projections www.census.gov/newsroom/ releases/archives/population/cb08-123.html

26. Source: Population projections www.census.gov/newsroom/ releases/archives/population/cb08-123.html

27. Source: Population estimates www.census.gov/newsroom/ releases/archives/population/cb09-75.html

28. Source: Population estimates www.census.gov/newsroom/ releases/archives/population/cb09-76.html

29. Source: Population estimates www.census.gov/newsroom/ releases/archives/population/cb09-75.html

30. Source: 2008 American Community Survey http://factfinder .census.gov

31. Source: 2008 American Community Survey http://factfinder .census.gov

32. Source: Income, Poverty, and Health Insurance Coverage in the United States: 2008 www.census.gov/newsroom/releases/ archives/income_wealth/cb09-141.html

33. Source: 2008 American Community Survey http://factfinder .census.gov

34. Source: 2008 American Community Survey http://factfinde r.census.gov

35. Source: 2008 American Community Survey http://factfinder .census.gov

36. Source: 2008 American Community Survey http://factfinder .census.gov

37. Source: 2008 American Community Survey http://factfinder .census.gov

38. Source: Population estimates www.census.gov/newsroom/ releases/archives/population/cb09-76.html

39. Source: Population estimates www.census.gov/popest/national/ asrh/NC-EST2008-asrh.html

40. Source: Population projections www.census.gov/newsroom/ releases/archives/population/cb08-123.html

41. Source: Population projections www.census.gov/newsroom/ releases/archives/population/cb08-123.html

Critical Thinking

1. When did the acknowledgement and celebration of Asian/ Pacific American Heritage begin?

2. What patterns do these data reveal about various Asian ethnicities?

Editor's note—The preceding data were collected from a variety of sources and may be subject to sampling variability and other sources of error. Facts for Features are customarily released about two months before an observance in order to accommodate magazine production timelines. Questions or comments should be directed to the Census Bureau's Public Information Office: telephone: 301-763-3030; fax: 301-763-3762; or e-mail: PIO@census.gov.

From *U.S. Department of Commerce, American Community Survey,* May 2010. Public Domain.

To Be Asian in America

ANGELA JOHNSON MEADOWS

C. N. Le barely remembers fleeing Vietnam for the United States when he was 5. Sketchy images of riding a cargo ship to Guam, having his documents processed and boarding a plane that would take him to Arkansas are all that remain of the life-altering experience.

But the reason for leaving his war-ravaged homeland is crystal clear. After military pressure from communist North Vietnam caused the South Vietnamese government to collapse in 1975, Le's family was in jeopardy.

"The U.S. government knew that those who worked for the U.S. military were going to be persecuted pretty harshly if they stayed back in Vietnam," says Le, whose parents both were U.S. military workers. "So [the U.S. government] made arrangements for their Vietnamese employees and their families to be evacuated."

Le and his family spent their initial days in the United States at Fort Chaffee, an Arkansas military base that served as a processing center for Vietnamese refugees.

"We had a little playground there that kids would play on, so in a lot of ways my experience was more of a typical kid's experience . . . than a refugee experience," recalls Le, a visiting assistant professor at the University of Massachusetts Amherst.

"Adults who had more of a recognition of what was going on would probably tell you, like my parents have said, it was a pretty traumatic experience for them, having to leave their country, leave everything behind and try to start life in a whole new country," Le says.

Le's status as a refugee is different from that of Chinese, Asian Indians, Japanese and some other Asians who have come to America, yet regardless of country of origin or mode or time of arrival, the majority of these immigrants share a common goal—a better life. For some, that means educational or professional opportunities they were denied in their homelands; for others, it's escaping political turmoil; and for others still, it's sacrificing the comforts of middle-class life to provide better chances for their children. It is the quintessential U.S. immigrant story.

"We spoke Chinese in the home and ate Chinese food in the home. The home life was one thing, but going out into the regular world, you have to fit in; there is a certain amount of biculturalism."

—Lora Fong, Greenbaum, Rowe, Smith & Davis

There are nearly 12 million people of Asian heritage living in the United States. Asian Americans (a term used by *DiversityInc* to describe both immigrant and American-born Asians) represent East Asian nations such as China, Japan and Korea; South Asian countries including India, Pakistan and Nepal; and Southeast Asian nations such as Thailand, Vietnam and Malaysia.

Still only 4.6 percent of the U.S. population, the Asian-American segment is experiencing astronomical growth. Between 2000 and 2050, the population is expected to surge 213 percent, according to the U.S. Census Bureau. The projected general-population growth during the same time? A paltry 49 percent.

But this growth isn't a 21st-century phenomenon. Historians have traced their presence in the land that evolved into the United States of America as far back as 1763, when Filipinos traveling aboard Spanish galleons jumped ship in New Orleans to escape imprisonment and fled into the Louisiana bayou to establish the first recorded Filipino settlement in America. Some argue their history in the United States dates back to the 1400s.

The Chinese were the first group of Asians to arrive in great numbers, appearing in the mid-1800s. The lure? The potential economic prosperity of the 1848 California Gold Rush and job opportunities associated with agriculture and the building of the intercontinental railroad.

Asian Americans were recruited as laborers—mostly men who were enticed by the opportunity to earn money to support their families or indentured servants who were sent to work off the debts of other Asians back home.

"These people were often deceived," says Gary Okihiro, director of the Center for the Study of Ethnicity and Race and a professor of international and public affairs at Columbia University. "Although these [work and payment] conditions were spelled out to them, they were oftentimes unfulfilled."

Many planned to return to their homelands when their contracted work period ended, but were prevented by U.S. immigration laws.

"They locked those that were here in the U.S.," says Okihiro. "Their remittances were crucial for the sustenance of their families back in Asia, so they were oftentimes trapped into remaining in the U.S."

Subsequent Asians came in waves, with the largest population arriving after the 1965 passage of the Immigration and Nationality Act. Immigrants and their offspring from China, the Philippines, India, Vietnam, Korea and Japan now account for the largest Asian populations in the country.

A Brave New World

W.E.B. DuBois once described the African-American experience as one of a double-consciousness, rooted in the need to navigate between one's own culture and that of the mainstream. It is an experience that rings true for Asian immigrants and their descendants as well.

"When they arrive, they begin to realize that they're different," says John Kuo Wei Tchen, the founding director of the A/P/A Studies Program and Institute at New York University. "Identities get challenged and they have to deal with what it means to be American or resident alien."

Some Asian Americans relied on assimilation as a means of blending in with American society and as an attempt to escape anti-Asian sentiments that heightened during World War II. "This question about how much they wanted to or did assimilate is a question of how much they were permitted to assimilate," says Okihiro.

Today, ties to home remain strong for new Asian immigrants; however, many families experience acculturation—the process of assimilating new ideas into an existing cognitive structure—with U.S.-born generations.

"Parents would like to think their children are going to be very embracive and very welcoming of the parents' own culture," says Franklin Ng, a professor in the anthropology department at California State University–Fresno. "Parents may have these kinds of supportive mechanisms, encouraging them to go to a temple, or ethnic church, so their children will become familiar with their ethnic culture . . . [but] the youth are having their own trajectory."

Growing up in a Southern California suburb, Le struggled with his Vietnamese name. By the time he reached high school, racial and ethnic tensions had set in and Le decided to go by the name Sean. "At that age, you just want to fit in and be like everyone else," he says.

But a college course on race and ethnicity changed his thinking. "That's when I became more socially conscious . . . and really began to see that my identity . . . was a source of strength . . . rather than a source of embarrassment. I wanted to go back to my Vietnamese name. The name Sean didn't really fit my identity," says Le, who is also the founder of Asian-Nation .org, an online resource for Asian-American historical, demographic, political and cultural issues.

Today, Le uses his first and middle initials, a way to keep his Vietnamese name—Cuong Nguyen—without having to face the pronunciation problems of non-Asians.

This balancing act isn't limited to language issues. Many struggle with the expectations of both their family and mainstream society.

"We were raised in the family to be in a very consistent way with the traditional Chinese culture," says Lora Fong, a third-generation Chinese American. "We spoke Chinese in the home and ate Chinese food in the home. The home life was one thing, but going out into the regular world, you have to fit in; there is a certain amount of biculturalism."

When Fong's father died in 1984, her Chinese and American worlds collided. She was working at IBM at the time, a company that often assisted employees in making funeral arrangements for loved ones.

"I was a team leader, I was frequently running projects and giving assignments and keeping people on task," says Fong, now an attorney at Greenbaum, Rowe, Smith & Davis in Woodbridge, N.J. Fortunately, Fong had a Chinese-American supervisor who understood that her professional persona was in stark contrast to her status within her traditional Chinese family.

"He knew that I could not take on a role of being in charge [in my family]," Fong recalls. "He just said, 'She's the daughter. She's the youngest. She's not running things. The company does not have a role there, so just back off.' And that was really antithetical to the way the company took on a role in an employee's personal life. That was such a dichotomy."

Striving for Success

Despite viewing America as the proverbial land of opportunity, the path to a better life has not been without roadblocks, particularly for those who arrived prior to 1965. Chinese in the United States were denied citizenship in the late 1800s, while immigration of all Asians, except for Filipinos (whose residence in a U.S. territory gave them the status of nationals), was halted in 1924 through the National Origins Act. It wasn't until the Immigration and Nationality Act of 1965 that Asian Americans were accepted into the country in larger numbers. The gates to the United States were opened, particularly to those with expertise in the medical, science and technology fields, explaining in part the proliferation of Asian Americans in those disciplines today.

In the face of language barriers, cultural adjustments and government and societal oppression, Asian Americans as a whole appear to have done quite well in America. A look at demographic data shows that Asian Americans as a group surpass all other racial and ethnic groups in the country in median household income and education levels. And while many marketers are turned off by the small size and myriad languages of the population, the buying power of Asian Americans is projected to jump 347 percent between 1990 and 2009, compared with a modest 159-percent increase for the overall population.

For aspirational Asian Americans, social mobility is a priority and education often is viewed as the method of achievement. This focus contributes to the group's economic success.

"Researchers suggest that one legacy of Confucianism in many Asian countries (notably China, Korea, Japan and Vietnam) is the notion that human beings are perfectible if they work to improve themselves," write Yu Xie and Kimberly A. Goyette, authors of *Demographic Portrait of Asian Americans*. "Given this cultural heritage, some Asian Americans may be more likely than whites to believe that hard work in school will be rewarded."

"In China, you have a kind of high-stakes testing," adds Tchen, referring to the country's civil-service system. "The emperor constantly recruits the best to come to the capital or to work . . . It's not so odd for higher education to be seen as the modern variation of that practice."

Mia Tuan's mother and father encouraged higher learning.

"Even though my parents knew nothing about the U.S. educational system . . . it was always assumed that I would go to college," says Tuan, an associate professor of sociology at the University of Oregon.

How They Score Class of 2003 SATs

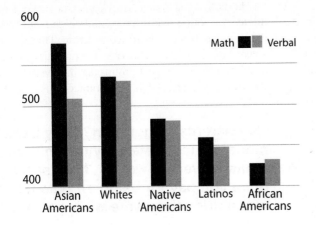

U.S. Asian Population

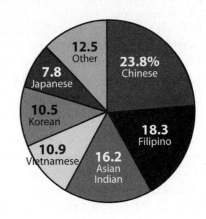

Educational Attainment
People 25 years and older, 2004

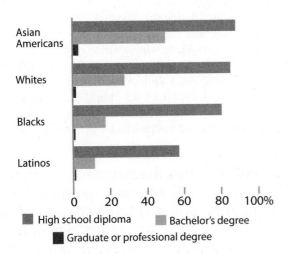

Median Family Incomes
In U.S. Population 25+

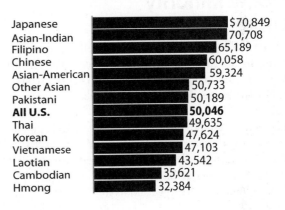

Asian-American Buying Power
Projected rate of increase 1990–2009

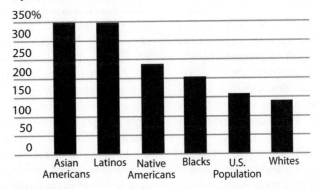

Figure 1 Asian-American Statistics.

Sources: College Board, U.S. Census Bureau, University of Georgia's Selig Center for Economic Growth.

Tuan's mother wanted her daughter to be the next Connie Chung. "Connie opened that door and parents encouraged us to go through that same door," says Tuan.

"I chose to not be the next Connie Chung, but a whole cohort of Asian-American women did hear that call and answered that call . . . When I told them I was going into sociology, they didn't know what the hell that was, but it was a Ph.D., so that counted for something."

But educational attainment isn't a priority for all Asians in America.

"If you come from a rural society where schooling and education was not such a benefit to your ability to raise crops . . . your emphasis on education would be different," says Tchen. "That would be true for Hmong or Southeast Asians . . . They don't necessarily relate to higher education as a way to better themselves."

This is played out in the educational statistics of Asian Americans. For example, in 2000, 76 percent of Asian Indians and 67 percent of Chinese Americans between the ages of 25 and 34 had a college degree or higher, compared with 43 percent of Filipino Americans and 27 percent of Vietnamese Americans.

The Model Minority and Other Myths

While the myths of universal affluence and intelligence among Asian Americans are just that, it hasn't stopped society from pinning them with the "model minority" label. They are seen as smart, wealthy and successful, and on the surface, it appears to be a positive perception.

"My parents' generation? They liked the model minority stereotype," says Tuan. "In their mind, it has served us well . . . They saw it as the price you pay for being an outsider and it was a price they were willing to pay."

But a look behind the stereotype and its implications reveals a troubling story.

"A lot of these [income] statistics can be misleading," says Le. "Family median income is mainly inflated because Asian-American families tend to have more workers . . . They're more likely to live in urban areas where salaries are higher, but the cost of living is also higher."

Per capital income for Asian Americans in the 2000 census measured $20,719, compared with $21,587 for the overall population.

A look at Fortune 500 companies illustrates that an intense focus on education really doesn't guarantee professional success. Despite high education levels, Asian Americans represent less than 1 percent of senior-management ranks or corporate boards.

"Everybody cites the success of Asian Americans, yet if you compared the level of education and position with that of white people, they come below white people," says Okihiro. "Their investment in education does not pay off. There's a glass ceiling for them."

Tuan's father was a diplomat with the Taiwanese government; however, after the U.S. office closed, he found it wasn't easy to translate his skills. He ended up opening a pizza shop.

"They lost a lot of status," says Tuan of her parents, whose migration to the United States erased the prestige of their

advanced degrees. "That put pressure on the next generation to make it worthwhile."

The belief that Asian Americans can succeed on their own dilutes the notion that some could benefit from programs ranging from Medicaid to affirmative action. Thirteen percent of all Asian Americans live in poverty. Twenty-three percent of Asians outside of the six largest groups are impoverished, rivaling the 24 percent of blacks of this economic status.

> **"My parents' generation? They liked the model minority stereotyype. In their mind, it has served us well . . . They saw it as the price you pay for being an outsider and it was a price they were willing to pay."**
>
> —Mia Tuan, University of Oregon

"With this spotlight on the talented tenth, there is neglect of those who may be in the lower tiers," says Ng.

Tuan recalls a meeting with faculty members and graduate students in her department.

"At one point [during the meeting] a graduate student said, 'We take issue with the fact that the department isn't hiring minorities,' " says Tuan, who was one of three recently hired Asian Americans in the department. "I was stunned when the student said that, and I said, 'So, do we not count?' And his answer was basically [that] we didn't, that Asians were this middle category . . . In his mind a minority hire would have been Latino, African American and Native American."

> **"Everybody cites the success of Asian Americans, yet if you compared the level of education and position with that of white people, they come below white people. Their investment in education does not pay off. There's a glass ceiling for them."**
>
> —Gary Okihiro, Columbia University

In addition to not being viewed as a traditional minority, Asian Americans also have an imposed identity as "eternal foreigners." Many American-born Asians have at least one story of being asked about their origins. A reply such as Fresno or Washington, D.C., is often met with the incredulous response of: "No, where are you *really* from?"

Even high-profile American-born Asians can't escape the stereotype. When Tara Lipinski defeated Michelle Kwan in the 1998 Winter Olympics figure-skating competition, MSNBC ran a headline that read: "American beats out Kwan." Kwan, who was born in Torrance, Calif., is just as American as Lipinski.

This misconception has some basis in truth, says Le. Approximately two-thirds of Asian Americans are immigrants. "But the social implications are that when someone is judged to be a foreigner, it is easier for that person to be treated as if they're not a real American . . . It becomes easier to deny them the same rights and privileges that are given to real Americans."

Asian Americans also face the perception that they are all the same. When Ng first settled in Fresno, Calif., he was taunted by a group of teenagers who ordered him to "Remember Pearl Harbor Day," an allusion to Japan's attack on the United States. As a child growing up in a Chicago suburb during the Korean War era, Tchen received the label of "gook," a disparaging term for Southeast Asians. Both Ng and Tchen are Chinese.

> "The experience of being treated as foreigners, exotics, outsiders, hordes, dangerous, those kinds of images that are recycled in American media . . . perpetuate some kind of basis for people of different backgrounds to come together."
>
> —John Kuo Wei Tchen, New York University

But perhaps the most notable misidentification occurred in 1982, when 27-year-old Vincent Chin visited a suburban Detroit strip club to celebrate his impending nuptials. While there, Chin encountered a couple of disgruntled autoworkers, one of whom had recently been laid off. The autoworkers hurled insults at Chin and blamed him for the demise of Detroit's auto industry. After Chin left the club, the two men met up with Chin in front of a fast-food restaurant and beat him with a baseball bat. Chin, who was Chinese—not Japanese, as his attackers had assumed—slipped into a coma and died five days later.

The Asian-American Identity in America

Asian Americans represent nearly 25 countries and speak at least as many languages; however, it is the challenges stemming from stereotypes, misconceptions, discrimination and exclusion that help this disparate group to unite under the umbrella term of "Asian American."

"The experience of being treated as foreigners, exotics, outsiders, hordes, dangerous, those kinds of images that are recycled in American media . . . perpetuate some kind of basis for people of different backgrounds to come together," says Tchen.

"A pan-Asian orientation is useful as sort of an instrument for coalition building for political advancement," adds Ng. "Asian Americans are ignored in the corridors of power, and collectively they can have more impact and can address issues that are more common."

Although Fong identifies first as a Chinese American, she's also concerned about broader Asian-American issues.

"We are all sharing a unique experience in terms of people's pre-conceived notion of who we are and what we should or shouldn't be doing in this society," says Fong, who is a past president of the Asian Pacific American Lawyers Association of New Jersey.

In addition to fighting shared struggles, Asian Americans have been able to collectively celebrate the accomplishments of Asian Americans of various backgrounds. Norman Mineta, U.S. Secretary of Transportation, and Elaine Chao, U.S. Secretary of Labor, are two of the highest-ranking Asian Americans in the Bush administration. Andrea Jung, chairman of the board and CEO of Avon Products, and Indira Nooyi, president and chief financial officer at PepsiCo, are just a few people who have broken what career consultant Jane Hyun describes as the "bamboo ceiling" of corporate America. And the presence of Asian Americans in sports and entertainment continues to flourish.

"When I was growing up . . . there was not exactly a wide range," says Tuan. "But if you were to ask—and I do ask these questions of the students—to name five prominent Asian-American public figures, they can come up with them now . . . I can only see that as being a good thing, because it shifts this notion of what's possible or who or what an Asian American is or what they're capable of. That's very powerful to me."

Critical Thinking

1. What does the concept Model Minority mean?
2. Describe the various ethnic groups that constitute the category Asian American.
3. In what respects do socioeconomic indicators for Asian American differ from other ethnic/racial categories?

From *DiversityInc*, April 2005, pp. 29–47. Copyright © 2005 by DiversityInc Media LLC. Reprinted by permission.

UNIT 8

European and Mediterranean Ethnics

Unit Selections

33. **Migrations to the Thirteen British North American Colonies, 1770–1775: New Estimates,** Aaron Fogelman
34. **Fecund Newcomers or Dying Ethnics? Demographic Approaches to the History of Polish and Italian Immigrants and Their Children, in the United States, 1880–1980,** John Radzilowski
35. **Ethnics No More or Ethnogenesis: From Syrian to Arab American,** Philip Kayak and Kristine Ajrouch
36. **Neither Natural Allies Nor Irreconcilable Foes: Alliance Building Efforts between African Americans and Immigrants,** Yusuf Sarfati and Cheryl McLaughlin

Learning Objectives

- What lessons can be learned from the experiences of eastern and southern Europeans?

- Discuss the ways ethnic groups are portrayed in film and video. What are the limits of ethnic comedy?

- Are you surprised by the variety, diversity, and intensity of opinions and positions on public policy found within and among various ethnic populations?

- A new era of ethnic data collection began with the 1980 Census. A considerable shift toward self-identification began, which allowed persons to claim specific and/or multiple categories. Does the earlier scheme of designating groups have any scientific or political merit? Does personal identification trump all other considerations? How does ethnicity of an earlier era suggest the tension between worlds of meaning discussed in this section?

- When the U.S. Commission on Civil Rights held hearings on issues related to eastern and southern European ethnic groups in the United States, leaders of these groups objected to the names Euro-Ethnic and Euro-American. They preferred specific ethnicities such as Polish American and Italian American. Can you explain why this was so?

- Does "Whiteness" provide a cultural legacy comparable to and ethnic heritage and culture? If so, what texts are central to this culture and meaning tradition?

- Comment on the idea that the legacy of multiple ancestral origins an ethnic identities of European Americans derived from an earlier era of immigration reveals a lack of relevancy and the marginality of these ethnic populations to the central ethnic issues of our time.

- Who decides that your ethnicity is meaningless? How can they do this?

- What is a central ethnic issue? By what criteria do we decide the importance and preferential protection of one ethnic group vis-à-vis another group?

- What lessons can be learned from the experiences of eastern and southern Europeans?

Student Website
www.mhhe.com/cls

Internet References

Africa News Online
www.africanews.com

Cultural Survival
www.culturalsurvival.org

The North-South Institute
www.nsi-ins.ca

Order Sons of Italy in America
www.osia.org

The National Italian American Foundation
www.niaf.org

The Chicago Jewish News Online
www.chicagojewishnews.org

Polish American Congress
www.pac1944.org/

Polish American Journal
www.polamjournal.com

Mediterranean and eastern European immigrants entered an industrializing economy that required their labor, much like plantation production in an earlier period required the indentured servant and the slave. But they also met a cultural and political climate of potent challenges and denials of their integrity, religious traditions, and existence. Personal interpretative reflections on the relevance of ethnicity to one's self-concept and the search for clearer expressions and more representative indexes of group identity are included in this unit.

Ethnic identity and recent concerns of ethnic groups include language preservation, fair hearings for homeland interests, enclave neighborhoods, inclusion in ethnic studies, and their articulation of historical American expressions of fairness, justice, and equity, as well as the collection of accurate data among all ethnic groups in America. These values are thoroughly patterned into their world view and their appropriation of the expansive promise of the American icon—the Statue of Liberty.

Ethnicity in America for these immigrants became a complex of identifications and loyalties that included sentimental attachment to home village, region, or nation; a certain religious affiliation; and the notion of being part of a distinct religious culture. But immigration and their ethnicity in America included loyalty to America and an identification with a particular city, district, or neighborhood in which they settled, membership in the local ethnic community and its institutional expressions, and often a sense of belonging to a certain class or distinct occupation. Thus ethnicity was essentially a local identity. The relative saliency of its components and each of these elements of ethnic and religious identity changed under the impact of events and with the passing generations.

The U.S. Census in 1980 and 1990 began the systematic collection of ethnic data. Census data on ethnicity is derived from self-identification. This method captures the respondent's sense of personal and group identity. Prior to 1980, the paucity of quantified information on ethnic variety was a profound impediment to the analysis of the ethnic composition of America and to the electoral participation of ethnic voters and ethnic organizations. Appreciating the variety of ethnicities that constitute the American population begins with dispelling the conventional categories and counts. Readers may be interested in exploring the concept of social distance and group affinity in relation to information provided in these articles and as tools for testing and discovering patterns of race and ethnic interest in various issues.

Moynihan and Glazer in Beyond the Melting Pot (1964), the report of the Kerner Commission, and findings of the National Center for Urban Ethnic Affairs confirmed that ethnicity was a salient factor. The descendants of Mediterranean and eastern European immigrants, even into the fourth generation, were just barely moving toward the middle class, absent in the professions, and rarely admitted to prestigious universities or colleges. More specifically, Italian and Polish people, like blacks and Hispanics/Latinos, were found to be excluded from the executive suites and boardrooms of America's largest corporations, publicly regulated utilities, and philanthropies.

Ethnicity is often associated with immigrants and with importation of culture, language, stories, and foods from foreign

© gulfimages / Alamy

shores. Appalachian, Western, and other regional ethnicities are evidence of multigenerational ethnic cultural development within the American reality. The persistent, ongoing process of cultural formation and personal identity are expressed locally in unique and intriguing folkways, dialects, languages, myths, festivals, food displays, and other enduring monuments and visible signs of the past and of the public dimension of cultural consciousness that constitutes ethnicity.

The emergence of interest in retracing the pathways of these immigrant groups and assessing their participation in intergroup relations in America are topics of many scholarly disciplines. The inclusion of the following articles is but a peek behind the curtain of this neglected dimension of race and ethnic relations in America. Apropos of the selection of articles and our attempt to understand current attention to this persistent cluster of ethnic Americans (the descendants of Mediterranean and eastern European groups, which have been ignored and neglected, mislabeled white-ethnics and/or Euro-ethnics) is Noel Ignatiev's provocative book "How the Irish Became White." Irish immigrants, though not a Mediterranean or an eastern European American ethnic group, had a similar experience in America of being different from and perceived as racially apart from the American regime, owing to their conquered status in the British Empire. Irish American freedom and participation in American life was the prototype of the American Dream. After all, it was this American promise that resonated in their hearts and minds in 1965 when a coalition of Mediterranean and eastern European Americans was accomplished in the national government. This group also supported some of the 1965 Voting Rights Act that ensured fair elections for the disenfranchised in the South. This legislative coalition accomplished, through deliberative democracy-instituted fundamental change that significantly altered the terms of race and ethnic relations.

The massive migration of peoples during the past four decades, which has included significantly large Mediterranean and eastern European populations, has re-engaged the immigrant factor in American politics and the ethnic factor among all Americans. Should ethnic populations be denied their distinctiveness through absorption into the mass of modernity, can their distinctiveness accompany them into mainstream modern Americans?

Migrations to the Thirteen British North American Colonies, 1700–1775: New Estimates

AARON FOGLEMAN

Mainstream historians have finally begun to study the long-neglected, yet extremely important topic of eighteenth-century immigration. Bailyn and DeWolfe's study, *Voyagers to the West,* and other monographs and articles on this subject appeared with increasing frequency during the 1980s.[1] Accurate statistics for immigration during the eighteenth century as a whole are lacking, however, and this gap has forced historians to rely on approximations that are sometimes sketchy and do not reveal much about the varied and complex nature of immigration during that century.

Although it is difficult to compile immigration statistics for the eighteenth century, it is still possible to update the work of previous historians, and for many reasons it is important to do so. With better information on immigration available, historians can compare the relative effects of immigration and natural increase in causing the phenomenal population growth of the colonies in the eighteenth century and of the United States during the early national period. Also, if one simply wants to know approximately how many people of each ethnic or racial group arrived and helped to shape early American society, a single reference with this information would be valuable. In this article, I review some recent estimates of eighteenth-century immigration, showing their accomplishments and problems, and then present an alternative method which corroborates some earlier estimates and provides more information for reference purposes than was heretofore available.

It is impossible to establish definitively the volume of eighteenth-century immigration to America. The only records kept over a long period of time for any ethnic group are the ship lists maintained in Philadelphia for German-speaking passengers arriving from 1727 to 1808.[2] Still, there is enough demographic and other data available for eighteenth-century America to allow historians cautiously to estimate the levels of immigration (and other demographic measures)–not crude, "ballpark" guesses, but

cautious estimates which can illuminate a great deal about life in early America. Historians will continually correct and hopefully improve these estimates as the rework old data, discover new data, and develop new mettrods. But what we have now is suggestive.

Whereas in the past historians relied on rough guesses of the levels of eighteenth-century immigration, they have recently begun to use sophisticated residual methods that may be more accurate. Twenty-five years ago, Potter estimated that 350,000 whites immigrated from 1700 to 1790—an estimate which was, in his own words, "little more than a shot in the dark." About 10 years later, Henretta concluded that "nearly 400,000" whites arrived between 1700 and 1775. Higham suggested that about 450,000 came in the eighteenth century, over half of whom were Irish. More recently, Fogel and several of his colleagues used a simulation model of generational progression and an estimated set of mortality, net reproduction, and gross reproduction rates to measure net migration as a residual, concluding that 822,000 more whites arrived in the colony-states from 1607 to 1790 than migrated out of this region. For the period 1700 to 1790 their figure was 663,000 whites. Yet in 1981, Galenson used a different residual method, in which he took into account the high mortality of immigrants shortly after their arrival, as they adjusted to the new disease environment, concluded that a net migration of 435,694 whites and 220,839 blacks took place between 1650 and 1780, and that 346,099 whites and 196,411 blacks arrived from 1700 to 1780, a figure close to Potter's.[3]

Still more recently, Gemery has provided the best summation of all these estimates, as well as many older ones, and pointed out some problems with their sources and methodologies. Given the scarcity of appropriate statistics for the eighteenth century, it is not surprising that the range for net migration calculated by the previously mentioned historians is fairly substantial—from 350,000 to 663,000 for 1700 to 1790. Realizing that estimates of early mortality and fertility rates were tenuous at best, Gemery opted to present a set of plausible immigration estimates from 1700 to 1820, rather than making a single estimate. Using a scale of annual rates of natural increase based on various estimates by historians measuring fertility and mortality, along with his own estimates for mortality during the overseas passage and the period of adjustment by migrants thereafter, Gemery concludes that the "New England pattern" was the most favorable for demographic growth and all other regions were moving in that direction during the eighteenth century. He calculates net migration as a residual, with the results being a plausible range of 765,000 to 1,300,000 white immigrants for the period 1700 to 1820 and a more precise one of 278,400 to 485,300 for the period 1700 to 1780. Allowing for the fact that this estimate does not cover the decade 1780 to 1790, his range runs only somewhat below that established by previous estimates. Gemery understands the difficulties in measuring and generalizing from mortality and fertility rates in early America. He concludes his article with a call for more research—more precise demographic data—so that the range of migration estimates can be narrowed.[4]

This note suggests an alternative method for measuring eighteenth-century migration—one that avoids the impasse created by relying too heavily on fertility and mortality rates, which are difficult to establish for the colonial period. My method is also somewhat simpler, yet corroborates the results of residual methods, especially Gemery's, while yielding more detailed information. The method relies on three sources of information for estimating the volume and timing of eighteenth-century immigration, all of which yield strong estimates for some ethnic groups and time periods, and somewhat weaker estimates for others. The first source is the work of ethnic-group historians who have produced plausible estimates of immigration for their respective groups. The second source (most important for the British and Irish immigration) is the more qualitative aspects of the ethnic-group historians' work on the timing, flow, and general conditions of the various migrations. The last source is an improved surname analysis of the first federal census in 1790, which, when used in conjunction with the above two sources, allows one to infer what the levels of migration may have been in previous decades, producing what Gemery calls "quasi-numbers."

The first source produces the strongest estimates. Ethnic-group historians have used information on ship departures and arrivals, as well as samples of how many immigrants could be carried by different kinds of ships, to arrive at reasonable estimates of total immigration of Germans, northern and southern Irish, Scots, African slaves, and others. Grouping the best of these estimates by decade and ethnic group into an estimate of overall immigration in the eighteenth century conveys a clear sense of how immigration varied over time and between ethnic groups, something other estimates have not done.

In the past, relying heavily on the estimates of ethnic-group historians would have been a risky enterprise.

However, the recent trend among historians has been to lower the estimates of their perhaps more filiopietistic predecessors. Since Dunaway's calculation of at least 250,000 Scots–Irish immigrants in the eighteenth century, Leyburn estimated 200,000 from 1717 to 1775. Still later, Dickson found approximately 109,000 to 129,000 for the years 1718 to 1775. And very recently, Wokeck has found even Dickson's estimates to be too high. For Germans, older estimates of 200,000 to North America before 1800 by both Mönckmeier, along with 225,000 to 250,000 before 1770 by Clarence Ver Steeg, have been revised downward by Fenske (125,000 for the entire century) and Wokeck (about 100,000 in the years 1683 to 1776). Butler has drastically revised the immigration estimates for French Huguenots by Higonnet from 14,000 to about 1,500 (or at most 2,000)—all before 1700. On the other hand, Bailyn and DeWolfe conclude that 100,000 to 150,000 Scots–Irish came before 1760 and over 55,000 Protestant Irish arrived from 1760 to 1775. Furthermore, they raise Graham's estimate for Scots from less than 25,000 for 1763–1775 to approximately 40,000 for 1760–1775. And Doyle has recently emphasized that there was a large southern Irish immigration into the colonies, which Dickson may have overlooked. Extreme accuracy will never be possible, given the nature of eighteenth-century statistics, but given such recent work, we can make significantly better estimates of the volume of immigration of some ethnic groups than was previously possible.[5]

The second source of information for this method, the discussions by the ethnic-group historians of the more qualitative aspects of migration, helps give one a sense of when peaks and valleys in immigration occurred, even when no actual data on volume are available. Population pressure, famine, unemployment, rack-renting (the doubling or tripling of rents after the expiration of long-term leases in order to accelerate the removal of tenants from the land), and active recruitment by colonials were major causes of the British and Irish emigration to the colonies. Extended discussions of these developments throughout the eighteenth century give a rough indication of how the total estimated immigration for each group should be distributed over the decades.

The third source of information, Purvis' recent surname analysis of the 1790 federal census, serves as a check and a supplement to estimates of immigration of each ethnic group by indicating, to some extent, the plausible proportions of the total immigration one could expect from various groups. Purvis calculated the percentage distribution of each white ethnic group (immigrants and their descendants) in the total population of 1790. His work contains some problems, but represents a marked improvement over Hansen and Barker, and the McDonalds, who did not include non-British ethnic groups.[6]

The method allows one to make use of the expertise of those who best understand the history of immigration. Using conservative estimates for each group tends to correct any bias toward inflation of numbers for filiopietistic or other reasons. This method essentially represents a trade-off:

instead of the residual methods using decennial population figures from *Historical Statistics* and the sketchy fertility and mortality data compiled by other historians, my method relies on an improved surname analysis of the 1790 Census as a check for the increasing expertise of ethnic-group historians who, in turn, rely on actual data regarding immigrants—ship and passenger lists. The results are presented in Tables 1, 2, and 3.

The quality of the estimates varies by time and ethnic group, but the tables as a whole are useful. The "most accurate" estimates are based on solid information produced by the ethnic-group historians. The "less accurate" estimates should be used with care, but the sum totals for these ethnic groups, especially Africans, Germans, northern and southern Irish, and to some extent the Scots, and Welsh, are plausible and the distribution by decade probably reflects a small margin of error in most cases. It is only the "least accurate"

estimates that are dubious, and for this reason they should be used with the greatest care, if at all.

In spite of the problem with filling in the gaps which ethnic-group historians have not yet thoroughly covered, this method as a whole produces enlightening results for most ethnic groups during most of the period in question. The sum total of 585,800 immigrants—278,400 blacks and 307,400 whites—is consistent with Gemery's findings (from 278,400 to 485,300 whites). Indeed, the two methods, one using fertility and mortality data calculating immigration as a residual, and the other relying on actual estimates of immigration by the ethnic-group historians, tend to provide a check for each other. Yet the second method provides much more reference information, listing immigration by decade and ethnic group instead of merely the sum total.

Further study of individual ethnic groups will surely require that adjustments be made to these tables, but they

Table 1 Estimated Decennial Immigration by Ethnic Group into the 13 Colonies, 1700–1775

Decade	Africans	Germans	Northern Irish	Southern Irish	Scots	English	Welsh	Other	Total
1700–09	9,000	(100)	(600)	(800)	(200)	<400>	<300>	<100>	(11,500)
1710–19	10,800	(3,700)	(1,200)	(1,700)	(500)	<1,300>	<900>	<200>	(20,300)
1720–29	9,900	(2,300)	(2,100)	(3,000)	(800)	<2,200>	<1,500>	<200>	(22,000)
1730–39	40,500	13,000	4,400	7,400	(2,000)	<4,900>	<3,200>	<800>	(76,200)
1740–49	58,500	16,600	9,200	9,100	(3,100)	<7,500>	<4,900>	<1,100>	(110,000)
1750–59	49,600	29,100	14,200	8,100	(3,700)	<8,800>	<5,800>	<1,200>	(120,500)
1760–69	82,300	14,500	21,200	8,500	10,000	<11,900>	<7,800>	<1,600>	157,800
1770–75	17,800	5,200	13,200	3,900	15,000	7,100	<4,600>	<700>	67,500
Total	278,400	84,500	66,100	42,500	35,300	<44,100>	<29,000>	<5,900>	(585,800)

Note. Figures were rounded to the nearest 100 immigrants. Estimates are divided into three categories: most accurate-no demarcation, less accurate—(), and least accurate-< >.

Sources: See Appendix.

Table 2 Estimated Proportional Distribution of Ethnic-Group Immigrants in the 13 Colonies by Decade, 1700–1775

Decade	Africans	Germans	Northern Irish	Southern Irish	Scots	English	Welsh	Other	Total
1700–09	.03	(.00)	(.01)	(.02)	(.01)	<.01>	<.01>	<.02>	(.02)
1710–19	.04	(.04)	(.02)	(.04)	(.01)	<.03>	<.03>	<.03>	(.03)
1720–29	.04	(.03)	(.03)	(.07)	(.02)	<.05>	<.05>	<.03>	(.04)
1730–39	.14	.15	.07	.17	(.06)	<.11>	<.11>	<.14>	(.13)
1740–49	.21	.20	.14	.22	(.09)	<.17>	<.17>	<.19>	(.19)
1750–59	.18	.35	.21	.19	(.11)	<.20>	<.20>	<.20>	(.20)
1760–69	.30	.17	.32	.20	.28	(.27)	<.27>	<.27>	.27
1770–75	.06	.06	.20	.09	.42	.16	<.16>	<.12>	.12
Total	1.00	1.00	1.00	1.00	1.00	1.00	1.00	1.00	1.00

Note. The estimates are divided into three categories: most accurate-no demarcation, less accurate-( ), and least accurate—< >. Slight adjustments were made to account for rounding errors.

Source: From Table 1.

Table 3 Estimated Proportional Distribution of Immigration per Decade in the 13 Colonies by Ethnic Group, 1700–1775

	1700–09	1710–19	1720–29	1730–39	1740–49	1750–59	1760–69	1770–75	TOTAL 1700–75
Africans	.78	.53	.45	.53	.53	.41	.52	.26	.48
Germans	(.01)	(.18)	(.10)	.17	.15	.24	.09	.08	.14
Northern Irish	(.05)	(.06)	(.09)	.06	.08	.12	.14	.20	.11
Southern Irish	(.07)	(.08)	(.14)	.10	.08	.07	.05	.06	.07
Scots	(.02)	(.03)	(.04)	(.03)	(.03)	(.03)	.06	.22	(.06)
English	<.03>	<.06>	<.10>	<.06>	<.07>	<.07>	(.08)	.10	<.08>
Welsh	<.03>	<.05>	<.07>	<.04>	<.05>	<.05>	<.05>	<.07>	<.05>
Other	<.01>	<.01>	<.01>	<.01>	<.01>	<.01>	<.01>	<.01>	<.01>
Total	1.00	1.00	1.00	1.00	1.00	1.00	1.00	1.00	1.00

Note. The estimates are divided into three categories: most accurate-no demarcation, less accurate-( ), and least accurate-< >. Slight adjustments were made to account for rounding errors.

Source: From Table 1.

do reflect in a simpler and more usable way the approximate magnitude of colonial immigration in the eighteenth century. I do not mean to evoke the old, filiopietistic practice of inflating numbers (I have used conservative estimates for each ethnic group), but it is ironic that the work of ethnic-group historians, once looked upon with disdain by many, may have provided the beginning of a methodology which yields important and usable results that corroborate the work of more sophisticated techniques.

Appendix
Africans

If immigrants are people who voluntarily leave their homeland to find a better life elsewhere, then African slaves are not immigrants. But in strictly demographic terms, immigrants are people who came from somewhere else, as opposed to being a product of the natural increase in the indigenous population. In this sense everyone who came from elsewhere was an immigrant, including slaves, transported convicts, and so forth. I have included Africans in these tables of immigration by "ethnic" group because they contributed to early American demographic growth in the same ways as the other groups in the tables. The Africans actually came from a variety of different ethnic backgrounds, but taken together, their numbers more than triple those of the largest European group, the Germans. (On the importance of ethnicity among African slaves in the American colonies see, for example, Ira Berlin, "Time, Space, and the Evolution of Afro-American Society," *American Historical Review*, LXXXV [1980], 44–78.)

Since the appearance of Philip D. Curtin, *The Atlantic Slave Trade, A Census* (Madison, 1969), a bitter debate has arisen on the volume of the Atlantic slave trade and Curtin's figures are no longer acceptable without qualification. (For a good summary of the debate see David Henige, "Measuring the Immeasurable: The Atlantic Slave Trade, West African Population and the Pyrrhonian Critic," *Journal of*

African History, XXVII [1986], 295–313.) I have used Curtin's figures for North America (137) as modified by Paul E. Lovejoy in "The Volume of the Atlantic Slave Trade: A Synthesis," *Journal of African History,* XXIII (1982), 487.

Germans

I have used my own method to calculate the volume and distribution of colonial German immigration. The large majority of Germans came through the port of Philadelphia, for which there are good records (passenger lists), especially for the period after 1726. The greatest difficulty occurs when one tries to measure the volume and distribution for other ports. To do this, I divided the ethnic-German population of 1790 into two geographical groups—one settled overwhelmingly by immigrants through the port of Philadelphia, the other settled by immigrants through all other ports. Next, a ratio of immigrants to 1790 population was calculated for the first, or Philadelphia, group which was then extended to the second group to estimate the number of immigrants necessary to produce the known 1790 population for that group.

Using Purvis' surname analysis of the ethnic-German population in 1790 ("European Ancestry," 98), the following two geographical groups were created. The German population of some states had to be divided because its roots were in the immigration through Philadelphia and other ports:

To measure the immigration through Philadelphia I used a variety of sources. For the early period (1700–1726), these included the text from Strassburger and Hinke, *Pennsylvania German Pioneers;* Julius F. Sachse, *The German Pietists of Provincial Pennsylvania* (Philadelphia, 1895), 1–10; Martin G. Brumbaugh, *A History of the German Baptist Brethren in Europe and America* (Morris, Ill., 1899), 54–70. Also, I estimated that approximately 500 Germans, who were part of the large migration to New York beginning in 1709, eventually moved to Pennsylvania and contributed to the growth of the population in Group 1—see Walter A. Knittle, *Early Eighteenth Century Palatine Emigration* (Philadelphia,

Group 1

State	1790 White Population	% German	Total Germans
Tennessee	31,913	6.6	2,106
Kentucky	61,913	4.9	2,996
New Jersey	169,954	6.5	11,047
Pennsylvania	424,049	38.0	161,139
Delaware	46,310	2.6	1,204
2/3 Maryland	139,099	12.7	17,666
2/3 Virginia	294,745	4.5	13,264
7/8 North Carolina	252,179	5.1	12,861
Total	1,420,162	15.7	222,283

Group 2

State	1790 White Population	% German	Total Germans
Maine	96,002	1.2	1,152
New Hampshire	141,097	0.1	141
Vermont	85,268	0.2	171
Massachusetts	373,324	0.3	1,120
Rhode Island	64,470	0.1	64
Connecticut	232,374	0.4	929
New York	314,142	9.1	28,587
1/3 Maryland	69,550	12.7	8,833
1/3 Virginia	147,372	4.5	6,632
South Carolina	140,178	5.5	7,710
1/8 North Carolina	36,025	5.1	1,837
Georgia	52,886	3.5	1,851
Total	1,752,688	3.4	59,027

1937); Henry Z. Jones, *The Palatine Families of New York* (Universal City, Calif., 1985).

For the period 1727–1775, I used the passenger lists in Strassburger and Hinke, which are not entirely comprehensive, but do represent the best collection of immigrant lists for any ethnic group in the eighteenth century. They include all male passengers 16 years and older well enough to disembark at Philadelphia and sign an oath of allegiance to the king. Further, many of the more than 300 ship lists for this period also contain lists of women and children, or list a total number of passengers and/or "freights" (children were counted as half freights or not at all). This allows one to calculate the ratio of total passengers to adult males, a figure that changed over the decades. After controlling for these changes, the difference between "passengers" and "freights," and adding the Moravian immigrants, who settled in Pennsylvania but immigrated primarily through New York (see John W. Jordan, "Moravian Immigration to Pennsylvania, 1734–1765," *Pennsylvania Magazine of History and Biography*, III [1909], 228–248; *idem*, "Moravian Immigration to America, 1734–1800," unpub. ms. [Historical Society of Pennsylvania, Philadelphia, n.d.]), a fairly complete picture of German immigration through Philadelphia for the years 1700–1775 can be compiled.

Records for other ports are incomplete, although historians and genealogists constantly make new discoveries.

I have reproduced data from several sources here to give an idea of the distribution through other ports which produced the ethnic-German population for Group 2 in 1790. These sources include Knittle, *Early Eighteenth Century Palatine Emigration;* Jones, *Palatine Families in New York;* Daniel I. Rupp, *Thirty Thousand Names of German, Swiss, Dutch, French, and Other Immigrants in Pennsylvania from 1727 to 1776* (Philadelphia, 1875); newspaper and other accounts located in the research files of the Museum of Early Southern Decorative Arts in Winston-Salem, N.C.; Jane Revill, (ed.), *A Compilation of the Original Lists of Protestant Immigrants to South Carolina, 1763–1773* (Columbia, 1939).

	Group 1		Group 2	
	N	%	N	%
1700–09	0	0	50	0
1710–19	1,000	2	2,548	41
1720–29	2,161	3	0	0
1730–39	12,477	19	138	2
1740–49	14,201	21	594	9
1750–59	24,971	37	1,033	16
1760–69	7,712	12	1,690	27
1770–75	4,211	6	242	4
Total:	66,733	100%	6,295	100%

The following is the estimated distribution by decade for all known immigrants by port of entry (Group 1—Philadelphia, Group 2—other ports). Group 1 is fairly complete, but Group 2 is incomplete:

	GROUP 1	GROUP 2	
1700–75 immigration:	$\dfrac{66{,}700}{222{,}300}$ =	$\dfrac{\times}{59{,}000}$	$\times \approx 17{,}700$
1790 population:			

Because the data in Group 2 is so incomplete, I have extended the ratio of immigrants-to-1790 population for Group 1 to Group 2, for whom the 1790 population is known. The following results were achieved:

Total immigration through 1770–75: 66,700 + 17,700 = 84,400. (All figures were rounded to the nearest 100 persons.)

About 17,700 Germans (21 percent of the total) immigrated through ports other than Philadelphia, and 84,400 immigrated through all ports of the 13 colonies during the period 1700–1775. (The final estimate in Table 1 was adjusted to account for rounding errors.)

The validity of this calculation rests on two assumptions (in addition to the assumption that Purvis' surname analysis is reasonably accurate). The first is that the fertility/mortality experience, or rate of natural increase, was the same for both groups. The second is that the time pattern of arrival was the same for both groups, or that the differences were such that the net effect was the same.

To deal with the first assumption, the work of Gemery must be addressed ("European Immigration to North America"). He found that the widest discrepancies in the rate of natural increase during the colonial period occurred between northern and southern colonies in the seventeenth century. By the eighteenth century the fertility/mortality experience for whites in all regions was becoming similar. This, along with the fact that both Group 1 and Group 2 contain inhabitants from northern and southern colonies, tends to make this assumption reasonable, although there is some error introduced in the final estimates because of it.

The second assumption is more difficult to make, since the above table clearly shows a discrepancy in the distribution of known immigrants in the two groups. There are many factors which could have contributed to the same number of immigrants from 1700 to 1775 producing differing numbers of inhabitants in 1790. These include when they arrived, their age, and to what degree they came as families (early or late in the reproductive period), or single individuals. Group 2 contains more earlier immigrants, which means they had time to produce more descendants by 1790 than their counterparts in Group 1. On the other hand, there were also more immigrants in Group 2 in the 1760s and 1770s (relative to the middle decades of the century) than were in Group 1, which means that more of Group 2 had relatively less time

to reproduce by 1790 than was true for Group 1. These two characteristics tend to cancel one another out, at least to a degree. There is no doubt some error was introduced by assuming equal growth rates and timing of immigration for both groups, but the reasons outlined above and the fact that a large majority clearly emigrated to Philadelphia tends to indicate that the margin of error in the final estimates of Tables 1–3 is small.

Lastly, German immigration from 1775 to 1790 did have some effect on the population of 1790, but it was very slight. During the war years, 1775–1783, German immigration ceased almost completely, except for some 3,000 "Hessian" deserters (see Rodney Atwood, *The Hessians: Mercenaries from Hessen-Kassel in the American Revolution* [Cambridge, 1980], 254). Immigration into Philadelphia resumed in 1785, and by 1790 only 1,467 persons had arrived (calculated from Strassburger and Hinke, III. 3–44).

The final estimate in Table 1—84,500—is lower than Wokeck's generally accepted figure of 100,000 German-speaking persons immigrating through all ports before 1776 (see "German Immigration to Colonial America," 12). I distributed the final total, including the "unknown" immigrant figure arrived at by the above calculation, according to that of the known immigrants listed above. Some adjustments were made for the early decades, however, because there are fairly complete records for the large emigration from 1709 to 1714 to New York and North Carolina (represented in Group 2). Therefore few "unknown" immigrants in Group 2 were added to the period before 1720.

Northern and Southern Irish

Estimates of the volume of northern Irish, which includes primarily people of Scottish descent ("Scots–Irish"), but also native Irish from the northern counties, have fluctuated wildly through the years. Dunaway estimated 250,000 Scots-Irish arrived in the eighteenth century (*The Scotch–Irish of Colonial Pennsylvania*, 41) and Maldwyn A. Jones calculated the same number for the entire colonial period ("Scotch–Irish," in Thernstrom, *Harvard Encyclopedia of American Ethnic Groups*, 896). Further, Leyburn concluded that 200,000 Scots-Irish immigrants arrived from 1717 to 1775 (*The Scotch-Irish*, 180–181). Until recently, Dickson was the only historian to present some quantitative evidence justifying his calculations, and to show how the flow of immigration varied over time. He concluded that 109,000 to 129,000 Ulster Irish immigrated into the colonies from 1718 to 1775.

On the other hand, the immigration of Catholic, "southern," or non-Ulster Irish was largely ignored until the work of Audrey Lockhart, *Some Aspects of Emigration from Ireland to the North American Colonies between 1660 and 1775* (New York, 1976) and David N. Doyle, *Ireland, Irishmen and Revolutionary America, 1760–1820* (Dublin, 1981) appeared. Although Lockhart does not attempt to estimate the numbers of immigrants arriving, she does present important evidence on the volume of immigrant-carrying ships, which, when used with other evidence, allows one to make an estimate of the total number of immigrants arriving and to show how this migration varied over time. Doyle's work has helped alert historians to this large immigration. He also showed with qualitative evidence how southern Irish emigration varied over the decades, paralleling to a large degree Ulster Irish emigration.

But Doyle has overestimated the numbers of this emigrant group. He states that about 90,000 southern Catholic Irish came before 1776 (almost all in the eighteenth century), up to 30,000 native (that is, Catholic) Ulster Irish, and 10,000 southern Anglo-Irish (Protestant), even though there were only 156,000 to 166,000 inhabitants in the United States in 1790 who descended from all these groups. He attributes their slow natural growth rate to the large number of single men emigrating, who had to marry non-Irish women in America (51–76, especially 61 and 70–71). They did marry and have children, however, and even if all "Irish" found by surname analysis in the 1790 census were not really "100 percent" Irish (due to marriage migration), the number of immigrants from which they descended must have been much lower than Doyle indicates.

My estimates of 66,100 northern and 42,500 southern Irish in Table 1 are based upon Lockhart, Dickson, and the very recent work of Wokeck, who has found passenger lists for the Delaware ports which allowed her to calculate approximate passenger-per-ship ratios for both northern and southern Irish and extend them to the number of ships arriving from 1729 to 1774. See "Irish Immigration to the Delaware Valley." Wokeck calculated 17,296 southern Irish and 35,399 northern Irish arriving in the Delaware ports from 1729 to 1774. I have grouped them by decade as follows:

Decade	Southern	Northern	Total
1729	723	296	1,019
1730–39	3,328	2,510	5,838
1740–49	4,106	5,225	9,331
1750–59	3,639	8,099	11,738
1760–69	3,811	12,067	15,878
1770–74	1,689	7,202	8,891
Total	17,296	35,399	52,695

According to Lockhart's tables, 45 percent of all the immigrant-carrying ships went to the Delaware ports during this same time period (calculated from Appendix C, 175–208). From Dickson's tables (Appendix E, 282–287) one can calculate that 57 percent of immigrant-carrying ships from northern Ireland went to Delaware Valley ports, although this data only reflects the situation in the years 1750 to 1775. If one extends Dickson's figure to the entire period 1729–1774, the following calculations can be made for total Irish immigration into all ports of the 13 colonies in the years 1729–1774:

Southern Irish				Total
1729	723	+ .45	=	1,607
1730–39	3,328	+ .45	=	7,396
1740–49	4,106	+ .45	=	9,124
1750–59	3,639	+ .45	=	8,087
1760–69	3,811	+ .45	=	8,469
1770–74	1,689	+ .45	=	3,753
Total	17,296	+ .45	=	38,436

Northern Irish				Total
1729	296	+ .57	=	519
1730–39	2,510	+ .57	=	4,404
1740–49	5,225	+ .57	=	9,167
1750–59	8,099	+ .57	=	14,209
1760–69	12,067	+ .57	=	21,170
1770–74	7,202	+ .57	=	12,635
Total	35,399	+ .57	=	62,104

To estimate immigration for the remaining years, 1700–1728 and 1775, the following steps were taken. According to Lockhart's tables, 13 percent of all immigrant-carrying ships from southern Ireland from 1700 to 1775 arrived in the first three decades of the eighteenth century—2 percent from 1700 to 1709, 4 percent from 1710 to 1719, and 7 percent from 1720 to 1729. Thus 87 percent arrived in the years 1730–1775. Subtracting the 1,903 that Wokeck found for 1729, and extending her passenger-per-ship ratio for 1770–1774 to the nine ships Lockhart found arriving in the colonies in 1775, one can calculate total southern Irish immigration from 1700 to 1775 as follows:

$$38,436 \quad -1,903 + 180 = .87x$$
$$x = 42,199 \text{ immigrants}$$

This total number is distributed as follows for 1700–1729:

$$1700\text{–}09 \ .02 \times 42,199 = 844$$
$$1710\text{–}09 \ .04 \times 42,199 = 1,688$$
$$1720\text{–}09 \ .07 \times 42,199 = 2,954$$

In Table 1, I inflated the figure for the 1720s to 3,500 because of the higher passenger-per-ship ratio prevalent for that decade in the few instances in Lockhart's tables where this information was given.

Since Dickson's tables do not include the number of ships arriving before 1750, and since Wokeck has shown that Dickson's method consistently overestimated the number of immigrants per ship, the only option remaining for calculating northern Irish immigration from 1700 to 1728 is to make use of the proportion of southern Irish to total Irish for the period closest to 1700–1728. From 1729 to 1739 southern Irish immigration equaled 58 percent of the total. Thus one can calculate:

	Southern			Total				Northern
1700–09	844	+	.58	=	1,455	1,455	− 844 =	611
1710–19	1,688	+	.58	=	2,910	2,910	− 1,688 =	1,222
1720–29	2,954	+	.58	=	5,093	5,093	− 2,954 =	2,139

All these calculations can be summarized as follows:

Total Irish Immigration Through All Ports, 1700–1775

Decade	Southern	Northern	Total
1700–09	844	611	1,455
1710–19	1,688	1,222	2,910
1720–29	2,954	2,139	5,093
1730–39	7,396	4,404	11,800
1740–49	9,124	9,167	18,291
1750–59	8,087	14,209	22,296
1760–69	8,469	21,170	29,639
1770–75	3,933	13,185	17,118
Total	42,495	66,107	108,602

In Table 1 all figures were rounded to the nearest 100 immigrants. Purvis found 16.3 percent (c. 520,000 persons) of the white population in 1790 to be of Scots–Irish and Irish descent, or northern and southern Irish (see "European Ancestry," 98). The ratio of immigrants 1700–1775 to the total population in 1790 was thus .21 (108,600 + 520,000), a factor which will be used to help calculate immigration for other ethnic groups with less quantitative evidence available than the Irish.

Scots

It is difficult to get a sense of the overall number of Scottish immigrants in eighteenth-century America. Graham estimates that emigration to America was "sporadic" from 1707 to 1763. From 1763 to 1775 less than 25,000 departed. Emigration was truly massive only in the years 1768–1775, when 20,245 left Scotland for America, see *Colonists from Scotland,* 185–189. Graham's figures, however, are probably too low. Using the same ratio of immigrants to 1790 population as existed for the northern and southern Irish (.21), combined with Purvis' finding that 5.3 percent (or c. 168,000) of the white population in 1790 was of Scottish descent ("European Ancestry," 98) allows an estimate of 35,300 Scottish immigrants from 1700 to 1775.

The lack of good data for pre-1760 immigration prohibits the labeling of these estimates as "most accurate."

Nevertheless, because of the similarities between the Scottish and Irish emigration experience to America—both began in the early eighteenth century, and were caused by population pressure, rack-renting, and agricultural dislocations which occurred in both places at about the same time—I have opted to distribute the total immigration for the period 1700–1760 in the same manner as the Irish (both northern and southern combined). It is only in the late 1760s and 1770s that Scottish emigration to the North American colonies noticeably differs from the Irish. The Irish emigration was larger in real numbers, but the Scottish emigration became relatively more intense (compared to the earlier Scottish migrations) as Graham has shown. For these reasons I have labeled the pre-1760 estimates as "less accurate" and the post-1760 estimates, based on Graham's work, as "most accurate."

English

Estimates of English immigrants are even scarcer than those for Scottish. Furthermore, the English are the only ethnic group for which significant immigration occurred in both the seventeenth and eighteenth centuries, which makes it impossible to use Purvis' surname analysis of the 1790 census to assist in calculating eighteenth-century immigration. E. Anthony Wrigley and Roger S. Schofield, *Population History of England, 1541–1871: A Reconstruction* (Cambridge, Mass., 1981) found net migration in England from 1701 to 1775 to be 423,162 (calculated from Table 7.11, 219), but the only period for which there are statistics available for arrivals in the thirteen colonies is the 1770s. Here Bailyn and DeWolfe found about 4,500 English emigrants bound for America during the years 1773–1776 in the Register maintained in London, as opposed to 3,600 Scottish emigrants (*Voyagers to the West,* 92). In the absence of any other data, I have made the assumption that the ratio of English to Scottish emigrants in the 1770s extended back to 1700, which would mean about 44,100 English immigrants arrived in the colonies during the period in question. This is not to say that the emigration history of Scotland and England are exactly parallel and there is little reason to accept this figure as being very accurate, but it does compare well with Richard S. Dunn's estimate of 25,000 English servants arriving in the colonies during these years, see "Servants and Slaves: The Recruitment and Employment of Labor," in Jack P. Greene and J.R. Pole (eds.), *Colonial British America: Essays in the New History of the Early Modern Era* (Baltimore, 1984), 159. Similar to the Scottish and Irish emigrants, the English, too, were plagued by population pressure and agricultural dislocations that coincided with these developments elsewhere in the realm. Thus I have distributed the total figure throughout the decades in the same manner as the southern and northern Irish. My figures for English immigrants are no doubt the weakest in Table 1 and for this reason I have labeled them "least accurate."

Welsh

There is little literature on Welsh immigration in eighteenth-century America and quantitative estimates are virtually nonexistent. Rowland Berthoff found the first "sizable" Welsh immigration to have taken place in the years 1680–1720, when a few hundred arrived in Pennsylvania. But he does not discuss any other Welsh immigration before the nineteenth century. See "Welsh," in Thernstrom, *Harvard Encyclopedia,* 1011–1012. Yet Arthur H. Dodd did find Welsh settlements in Maryland (1703), North Carolina (1733), South Carolina (1737 and 1780), and Virginia (1740 and 1762), although he made no estimate of their numbers. See *The Character of Early Welsh Emigration to the United States* (Cardiff, 1953), 2. In contrast to the English, most Welsh emigration to the colonies appears to have taken place in the eighteenth century, making it possible to use Purvis' work in this calculation. My estimate of 29,000 Welsh immigrants is based upon his estimate of 4.3 percent of the white population being of Welsh descent in 1790 (Purvis, 98), or about 138,000 people, and the same ratio of immigrants to 1790 population used for the Irish (.21). The 29,000 figure is distributed over the decades in the same manner as the Irish. The advantage of being able to use Purvis' work is offset, however, by the lack of discussion in the literature of the causes, conditions, and timing of the Welsh emigration in the eighteenth century, which has led me to label all these estimates "least accurate."

Others

Purvis ("European Ancestry," 98) gives the following percentages for white ethnic distribution in 1790: Dutch 3.1, French 2.1, and Swedish 0.3. Most of these groups arrived before 1700, but there were occasional immigrations of these and other groups during the eighteenth century. For example, over 200 French-speaking passengers arrived in Charleston from 1763 to 1773 (calculated from Revill, *Protestant Immigrants to South Carolina,* [Columbia, 1939], 18, 112, 127). I have placed "other" immigration at a minimal 1 percent of the total per decade to cover this and other such scattered examples during this period and labeled them "least accurate."

Notes

1. See Bernard Bailyn, with the assistance of Barbara DeWolfe, *Voyagers to the West: A Passage in the Peopling of America on the Eve of the Revolution* (New York, 1986). This book, along with Bailyn's companion volume, *The Peopling of British North America: An Introduction* (New York, 1986), provide important bibliographic material on the subject.

2. The most comprehensive and best-edited publication of these lists is Ralph B. Strassburger and William J. Hinke (eds.), *Pennsylvania German Pioneers. A Publication of the Original Lists of Arrivals in the Port of Philadelphia from 1727–1808,* (Norristown, Pa., 1934), 3 v. They list all males sixteen years and older (and some women and children) well enough to disembark upon arrival and sign oaths of loyalty to the British king. Because the large majority of Germans landed in Philadelphia after 1726, these lists are the starting point for any estimation of German immigration into all ports during the colonial period.

3. See James Potter, "The Growth of Population in America, 1700–1860," in David V. Glass and D.E.C. Eversley (eds.), *Population in History: Essays in Historical Demography* (London, 1965), 645; James A. Henretta, *The Evolution of American Society, 1700–1815: An Interdisciplinary Analysis* (Lexington, Mass., 1973), 11; John Higham, *Send These to Me. Immigrants in Urban America* (Baltimore, 1984; rev. ed.), 18; Robert W. Fogel et al., "The Economics of Mortality in North America, 1650–1910: A Description of a Research Project," *Historical Methods,* XI (1978), 100; David W. Galenson, *White Servitude in Colonial America: An Economic Analysis* (Cambridge, 1981), 212–218.

4. Henry A. Gemery, "European Immigration to North America, 1700–1820: Numbers and Quasi-Numbers," *Perspectives in American History,* I (1984), 318, 320.

5. Wayland F. Dunaway, *The Scotch-Irish of Colonial Pennsylvania* (Chapel Hill, 1944), 41; James G. Leyburn, *The Scotch-Irish: A Social History* (Chapel Hill, 1962), 180–181; R.J. Dickson, *Ulster Emigration to Colonial America, 1718–1775* (London, 1966), 20–64; Marianne Wokeck, "Irish Immigration to the Delaware Valley before the American Revolution," forthcoming in David B. Quinn (ed.), *Ireland and America, 1500–1800;* Wilhelm Mönckmeier, *Die deutsche überseeische Auswanderung. Ein Beitrag zur deutschen Wanderungsgeschichte* (Jena, 1912), 13; Clarence Ver Steeg, *The Formative Years, 1607–1763* (New York, 1964), 167; Hans Fenske, "International Migration: Germany in the Eighteenth Century," *Central European History,* (1980), 344; Marianne Wokeck, "German Immigration to Colonial America: Prototype of a Transatlantic Mass Migration," in Frank Trommler and Joseph McVeigh (eds.), *America and the Germans: An Assessment of a Three-Hundred-Year History* (Philadelphia, 1985), I, 12; Jon Butler, *The Huguenots in America: A Refugee People in New World Society* (Cambridge, Mass., 1983), 49; Patrice L. R. Higonnet, "French," in Stephan Thernstrom, Ann Orlov, and Oscar Handlin (eds.), *Harvard Encyclopedia of American Ethnic Groups* (Cambridge, Mass., 1980), 381; Bailyn and DeWolfe, *Voyagers to the West,* 25–26; Ian C.C. Graham, *Colonists from Scotland: Emigration to North America, 1707–1783* (Ithaca, 1956), 185–189; David N. Doyle, *Ireland, Irishmen and Revolutionary America, 1760–1820* (Dublin, 1981), 51–76.

6. The oft-quoted figures from U.S. Bureau of the Census, *Historical Statistics of the United States, Colonial Times to 1970, Bicentennial Edition, Part 2* (Washington, D.C., 1975), Series Z 20–23, 1168 originate from a study conducted primarily by Howard F. Barker and Marcus L. Hansen, "Report of the Committee on Linguistic and National Stocks in the Population of the United States," American Historical Association, *Annual Report for the Year 1931,* (Washington, D.C., 1932), I, 107–441. Forrest McDonald and Ellen Shapiro McDonald recently revised these estimates, "The Ethnic Origins of the American People, 1790," *William and Mary Quarterly,* XXXVII (1980), 179–199. See Thomas L. Purvis, "The European Ancestry of the United States Population, 1790," *William and Mary Quarterly,* XLI (1984), 98. A

symposium in that volume contains an enlightening discussion between Purvis, Donald H. Akensen, and the McDonalds on the problems and merits of the various estimates available for the 1790 population.

Purvis improves upon previous work by more carefully analyzing distinctive surnames known to be borne by a certain percentage of a European group and then calculating an arithmetical coefficient sufficiently accurate to allow computation of the proportion of people belonging to that nationality within the United States in 1790. The number of individuals with the same surnames, multiplied by the appropriate numerical constant, equals the approximate size of the group in the United States. The problem with this method is that the surnames from the base population with which Purvis initially worked was not always representative of the actual immigrant population. For immigrants from the European continent he found sufficient passenger lists and other information which adequately reflect the actual population of immigrants. For British and Irish immigrants, however, the dearth of seventeenth- and eighteenth-century passenger lists and censuses forced Purvis to rely on nineteenth-century

surname lists from Britain and Ireland, rather than surname lists from the actual immigrant population. Another problem with Purvis' method is that he was unable to distinguish between Scots–Irish and Scottish surnames, which forced him to assume that the number of Scots–Irish was twice the number of Scots in 1790.

Critical Thinking

1. What ethnic groups constituted the first immigrants to America?

2. Prior to reading this article, did you have any inkling of ethnic diversity in colonial America? Why?

3. Does this account of ethnic diversity change your image of the founding era?

AARON FOGLEMAN is Assistant Professor of History at the University of South Alabama.

The author thanks John Shy, Kenneth Lockridge, and Rosalind Remer for their helpful comments on this article.

Fecund Newcomers or Dying Ethnics? Demographic Approaches to the History of Polish and Italian Immigrants and Their Children in the United States, 1880–1980

JOHN RADZILOWSKI

Introduction

The massive wave of immigration to the United States from east-central and southern Europe between 1880 and 1924 remains one of the most significant migration events in American history. The size of this migration was well understood even by contemporaries. However, interest in immigrant demography after the initial act of immigration has been infrequent, if not wholly lacking. This has limited our understanding of the communities formed out of this migration and their impact on U.S. history.

This is particularly unfortunate as the large-scale immigration from east-central and southern Europe created very special demographic conditions that not only have shaped the nature of the communities created by this migration but also have played a major role in forming contemporary and later scholarly perspectives on those communities. Immigrants from east-central and southern Europe arrived in the United States largely as young laborers, either unmarried or recently married. Unlike immigration from Ireland or Germany, immigration from east-central and southern Europe occurred very intensively within a fairly short period of time. As a result, these immigrants had large numbers of children within the span of a few decades after arriving in the New World. This immigrant "baby boom," which peaked roughly in the years 1915–25, has been largely overlooked by scholars and yet represents an important explanatory tool for understanding the impact of this period of immigration on subsequent U.S. history.

Efforts to understand what were once called "new immigrants" generally have emphasized cultural explanations, traditionally revolving around the question of the degree to which immigrants and their children "assimilated" into American culture and society or retained their ethnicity.[1] Most recently, this line of inquiry has tended to focus on the degree to which European immigrants and their children were considered (or considered themselves) "white."[2]

Views of immigrants at the time of their arrival tended to see the massive wave of newcomers as a threat to the American way of life.

A wide variety of books and articles raised alarms that the new immigrants were "out-breeding" old-stock Americans and those with preferred ethnic pedigrees in northern and western Europe. In the writing of the time, views of the newcomers had distinct racial, biological, and sexual overtones. Edna Ferber, in her novel *American Beauty* (1931), contrasted the crude sexual energy of Polish immigrant men with the weakness of the New England Yankees: "These men were very male, too. . . . You saw the sinews rippling beneath the cheap stuff of their sweaty shirts. Far, far too heady a draught for the digestion of this timorous New England remnant of a dying people. For the remaining native men were stringly of withers, lean shanked, of vinegar blood, and hard wrung."[3]

In the decades following World War II, this image of vigorous, young (though racially threatening) immigrants was forgotten, replaced with the image of ethnic communities that were assimilating and/or dying out. They were viewed as communities in which only the old retained significant traces of ethnicity. This was a view countered in the late 1960s and 1970s by proponents of the "new ethnicity."[4]

These two contrasting opinions, however, are themselves the result of observers viewing two different sides of a peculiar demographic artifact: the massive though forgotten baby boom among southern and east-central European immigrants in the early decades of the twentieth century. To consider this baby boom and its implications for the study of immigration, scholars could, for example, track the birthrates of four of the largest European immigrant groups, two from western Europe (Irish and Germans) and two from east-central and southern Europe (Poles and Italians), comparing them to the rates for other groups.

The Forgotten Baby Boom

In 1960, the U.S. census analyzed the age of the so-called foreign-stock population—that is, immigrants and their U.S.-born children. The survey showed that children of immigrants were significantly older on average than the population as a whole.[5] Figure 1 illustrates that the median age of the U.S. population was 29.5 years, whereas the median

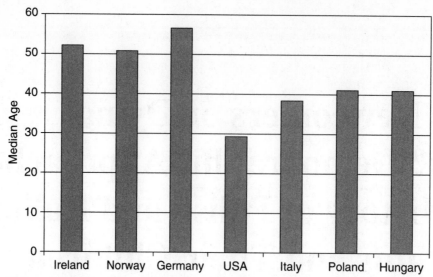

Figure 1 Median Age of Select Foreign Stock Groups versus U.S. Median Age, 1960.

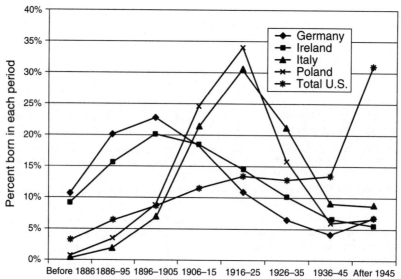

Figure 2 Decades of Birth of Children of Immigrants versus Overall U.S., 1960.

age of the children of immigrants was significantly higher. There was also a disparity between immigrant groups from western and northern Europe and those from east-central and southern Europe. Italians and Poles had median ages of 38.6 and 41.3 respectively, while the median age of second-generation Germans was 56.6 and 52.2 for Irish.

This comparatively old population among eastern and southern European Americans in 1960 was the result of a very high number of births in the period between 1906 and 1935. Figure 2 tracks the number of people born in each decade who were alive in 1960 among the four groups in comparison with the overall U.S. populations. The most notable feature is the dramatic spike in births among Italians and Poles in this 30-year period. Of all Polish Americans alive in 1960, more than one-third were born between 1916 and 1925. One-quarter were born between 1906 and 1915. Among Italians, 30 percent were born in the period 1916–25 and 21 percent in the decade before and the decade after this peak, respectively. Interestingly, a similar though less dramatic peak among Germans and Irish can be observed in the period 1886–1905.

The peak in births among Polish and Italian immigrants coincides closely with the peak years of immigration to the United States where the dominant stream of newcomers was from east-central and southern Europe. Arrivals to the United States increased sharply after 1900 and continued at high levels until the start of World War I in 1914. The peak year of immigration was 1907, when about 1.3 million immigrants arrived on America's shores.[6] Thus, within a decade of their arrival in the United States, immigrants from east-central and southern Europe began to have very large families.

It might be argued that the 1960 census analysis is unfairly skewed against the children of the earlier wave of immigrants, since the average life expectancy of a person born in 1900 was less than 50 years.[7] However, we can also turn to other bodies of evidence to confirm the size and nature of this baby boom.

One such approach is to examine birthrates among particular immigrant groups. The high number of children being born to immigrant women was of particular concern to a variety of groups after 1900, including social reformers, advocates of immigration restrictions, and the growing eugenics movement.[8] In 1909, the Dillingham Commission of the U.S Congress was charged with investigating immigration with an eye toward restriction and devoted one of its volumes of research to immigrant birthrates. Titling its volume *The Fecundity of Immigrant Women,* the commission's researchers used childbirth statistics from the 1900 census for immigrant women in Rhode Island, Ohio, and Minnesota.[9]

Table 1 compares the major groups under consideration. The figures indicate that Italian and, especially, Polish women were having large families already by 1900 in comparison to women who were born in the United States of native-born parents. Although rural women overall had more children, among Polish women in rural Minnesota, almost three-quarters reported bearing more than five children. Figures for Italian women are much more in line with their Irish and German counterparts, although Italian women generally had more children per year of marriage than either Irish or German women. This resulted in communities where half the population was below the age of 16.[10] By 1910, the number of children of Polish immigrants exceeded the number of actual immigrants.[11] Table 1 indicates that the nativist fear of immigrant birthrates had some factual basis and was not simply the result of feverish race prejudice.

The figures from 1900, however, represent only the start of significant immigration from east-central and southern Europe. Further evidence of the baby boom among immigrants from these regions can be found by sampling particular ethnic communities. To further illustrate how the immigrant baby boom played out on the local level, Table 2 provides examples of baptism and school enrollment from parish jubilee books of east-central and southern European communities.[12]

For all east-central and southern European parishes for which statistics were readily available, baptisms peaked within the same period identified by the census as the peak period of births. In the case of Holy Trinity parish in Utica, New York, a Polish Roman Catholic parish, baptisms peaked in 1910 at about 450. This peak occurred two years after the parish's peak year for marriages, 1908.[13] As might be expected for most of the parishes surveyed, school enrollments peaked slightly later. In the 1930s, both baptisms and school enrollments drop off, as might be predicted from Figure 2.

The Baby Boom and the Shape of Immigrant Communities

Births among Poles and Italians in the United States increased dramatically in the two decades after 1905. In the sample taken by the census in 1960 births among Poles increased more than 2.75 times from the decade 1896–1905 to the decade 1906–15 and more than 3.1 times among Italians. The Polish baby boom occurred slightly earlier than the Italian boom, but the Italian was slightly more sustained.

Equally significant as the rise in births in the period 1906–25 is the sharp decline thereafter (see Figure 3). Although the number of U.S. births declined slightly among nearly all groups in the 1930s and early 1940s, the drop-off among east-central and southern Europeans was nearly as dramatic as the previous baby boom had been. The generation of immigrants that had created the baby boom in the period 1906–25 began to pass out of the prime childbearing years by the 1930s.

The peculiar demography of these communities was the result of mass emigration from east-central and southern Europe that affected mainly people of childbearing age—mostly the young—and that occurred within a relatively compact period of time and was halted artificially by the immigration restrictions of 1924. (German or Irish immigration, by contrast, was more consistent over the course of period from the 1840s to the 1920s but without the dramatic peaks seen among groups such as Poles and Italians.) This demography

shaped southern and east-central ethnic communities in the United States in important ways.

The large number of young people in these communities created a well-defined second generation whose collective experiences were quite distinct from those of their immigrant parents. There was little overlap between the generations, contrary to what would have been the case had immigration occurred more gradually over a longer period of time. Unlike their parents, who came from relatively diverse regional and local backgrounds, this large cohort of the children of the immigrants came of age in an American context. This second generation has often been overlooked by scholars of these communities.[14] At the same time, it has been recognized that ethnic culture and the markers of that culture underwent profound change, in response both to the changing American context of the 1920s and 1930s and to the changing internal dynamics of the ethnic groups' own communities. Among those internal dynamics, scholars must now consider the impact of demography.

One of the most obvious responses to the large number of young people in their own communities was the development of a vast array of ethnic youth organizations and activities beginning in the 1920s. These ranged from scholarship programs to baseball leagues to summer camps to folk dance and scouting groups. Ethnic fraternal organizations led the way, devoting pages of their newspapers to youth concerns, creating insurance policies for the children of immigrants, and directly sponsoring youth activities.[15] To one extent or another, the leadership of each immigrant community affected by the baby boom recognized some form of "youth problem"—namely, large numbers of young people whose connections to the ancestral culture (or its diaspora mutation) were often tenuous and whose loyalty to the new community organizations created in their parents' generation was up for grabs.

One result of too many ethnic youth concentrated in relatively new immigrant neighborhoods without strong community structures was a spike in crime and gang activity. As the children of immigrants entered the ages when criminal and deviant activity reaches its peak, many observers—both internal and external—felt that the immigrant communities were spiraling out of control.[16] By the 1920s, there were nearly 150 Polish street gangs in the city of Chicago, the largest number of any ethnic group. The next most numerous gangs in Chicago were Italian (48), Irish (75), and African American (63).[17] In Detroit and Chicago, Polish youth were the largest single group of inmates in the juvenile justice system.[18]

Ethnic street gangs were based in neighborhoods and made up of boys between the ages of 8 and perhaps 20. Some of the gangs identified by University of Chicago researchers were merely groups of boys who hung around with each other, played sports, and sometimes engaged in petty mischief or theft.[19] Others had a more dangerous nature. One University of Chicago field researcher reported that

> A very noticeable development in the summer months have been [sic] the universality of boys' gangs in the segregated residential areas [i.e., ethnic neighborhoods]. Every community where there are any considerable number of children living in somewhat congested community has the boys' gangs developed [sic]. These appear to flourish most often during evening hours. These gangs are often found on the street at relatively late hours. Their danger to individuals [sic] and to communities is very apparent.[20]

Crime remained a significant problem in urban immigrant communities from the 1910s through the early 1930s. By the late 1930s, a large proportion of the children of the immigrant baby boom began to age out of the high crime years (ages 13–17).

Table 1   Childbearing among Married Native White and First-Generation Immigrant Women, Rhode Island, Ohio, and Minnesota, 1900

Rhode Island

	Percentage bearing no children	Percentage bearing +5 children	Average number of children	Average years married per child borne
Native white of native parentage	17.5	9.2	2.0	5.6
Irish	7.6	42.1	3.7	2.9
German	9.5	24.9	3.0	3.5
Italian	5.1	40.8	3.8	2.8

Cleveland, Ohio

	Percentage bearing no children	Percentage bearing +5 children	Average number of children	Average years married per child borne
Native while of native parentage	15.2	6.3	1.6	5.2
Irish	8.6	40.9	3.5	2.8
German	4.7	36.7	3.5	2.9
Italian	4.9	33.9	3.4	2.6
Polish	2.3	60.5	4.4	2.2

48 Rural Counties, Ohio

	Percentage bearing no children	Percentage bearing +5 children	Average number of children	Average years married per child borne
Native white of native parentage	5.7	16.8	3.4	4.1
Irish	5.0	37.4	4.6	3.1
German	3.8	36.5	4.7	3.0
Italian	4.5	31.4	4.5	3.0
Polish	2.7	49.6	5.6	2.5

Minneapolis, Minnesota

	Percentage bearing no children	Percentage bearing +5 children	Average number of children	Average years married per child borne
Native white of native parentage	12.7	5.9	2.4	5.7
Irish	7.3	35.7	4.1	3.1
German	5.4	24.0	4.0	3.5
Polish	9.7	54.8	5.4	2.6

21 Rural Counties, Minnesota

	Percentage bearing no children	Percentage bearing +5 children	Average number of children	Average years married per child borne
Native white of native parentage	5.1	14.9	3.4	4.2
Irish	7.2	39.2	4.9	2.9
German	1.8	50.5	5.2	2.7
Polish	1.7	73.9	6.7	2.1

Source: U.S. Immigration Commission, *Fecundity of Immigrant Women,* 61st Cong., 3rd sess. (Washington, DC, 1909). The category of women bearing no children was for women under age 45 married 10–19 years. For an explanation of the methodology, see the introduction to this volume of the Commission's reports.

Table 2 Baptisms and School Enrollments in Selected East European Immigrant Church Parishes, 1900–40

Baptism

Name	Ethnicity	Location	Founded	1900	1905	1910	1915	1920	1925	1930	1935	1940	Peak Year	Peak Amt
St. Joseph	Slovenian	Joliet, IL	1891	149	194	181	199	150	151	86	68	80	1915	199
St. Mary	Polish	Green Bay, WI	1898	21	66	62	71	64	52	45	24	42	1911	68
St. Joseph*	Polish	Norwich, CT	1904	n/a	95	159	201	197	106	67	59	41	1917	260
St. Ladislaus	Polish	Chicago, IL	1914	n/a	n/a	n/a	16	36	57	54	45	40	1927	79
St. Wenceslaus	Polish	Chicago, IL	1912	n/a	n/a	n/a	112	144	134	118	65	84	1926	140
St. Florian	Polish	Hamtramck, MI	1908	n/a	n/a	74	871	1119	476	294	249	360	1917	1492
St. Stanislaus Kostka	Polish	Brooklyn, NY	1896	367	629	690	736	352	267	186	165	204	1908	917
Holy Cross	Polish	Minneapolis, MN	1886	109	186	280	429	146	140	73	64	105	1914	438

School Enrollment

Name	Ethnicity	Location	Founded	1900	1905	1910	1915	1920	1925	1930	1935	1940	Peak Year	Peak Amt
St. Joseph	Slovenian	Joliet, IL	1896	199	218	480	641	692	802	831	659	513	1929	873
St. Laurence	Polish	Philadelphia, PA	1882	303	369	365	496	640	932	822	510	342	1928	957
St. Stanislaus B & M	Polish	New York, NY	1908	n/a	n/a	375	584	900	955	868	589	378	1922	1000
Most Holy Rosary	Italian	Perth Amboy, NJ	1925	n/a	n/a	n/a	n/a	n/a	152	n/a	219	205	1934	229
St. Florian	Polish	Hamtramck, MI	1911	n/a	n/a	n/a	876	2546	2553	2415	1677	1234	1924	2853
Holy Trinity	Polish	Utica, NY	1899	n/a	220	420	759	1022	1368	1083	645	517	1924	1393

*Counts births rather than baptisms

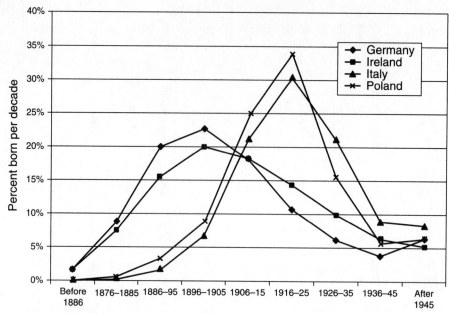

Figure 3 **Decades of Birth of Children of Immigrants from Germany, Ireland, Italy, and Poland, 1960.**

The 1940s and Beyond

When the United States entered World War II in December 1941, the high number of births among east-central and southern European immigrants in the early and mid-1920s meant that their children fell into the age cohorts most likely to see military service (men between the ages of 18 and 26). The result was extremely high rates of service among east-central and southern Europeans. A survey taken in the spring of 1944 among Polish–American parishes revealed that in a few communities, an astonishing 40 percent of all parish members were in service.[21] Although similar contemporary surveys do not exist for other east-central and southern European groups, there is little reason to doubt that similar high rates of service were found among those groups as well.

The 1980 U.S. census provides an excellent benchmark date for examining veteran status among various groups, since it was the first census to include the ancestry self-identification question with the largest possible number of living World War II veterans. Table 3 demonstrates that among Poles and Italians, World War II veterans made up half or more of all veterans within those groups. World War II veterans also made up a larger percent of the overall community among these two groups than in the other selected groups—nearly 10 percent in the case of Polish Americans. A similar survey conducted on Ukrainian–American veterans in the 2000 census suggests that this profile is shared by the many smaller east-central and southern European groups and not confined to Poles and Italians.[22] Although the Census Bureau does not report data from Jewish Americans—the majority of whom had roots in the same period of mass immigration—there is no reason to suggest that the Jewish pattern of military service in World War II would vary substantially from other east-central and southern European ethnic groups.

The large generation of the children of the east-central and southern European immigrants who arrived before 1924 had a powerful common experience during the war years. The war affected their families and communities in critical ways that deserve further research. This was especially true of those born in the years after 1920, who were the most likely to experience military service. Those born prior to 1921 were more likely to experience the war through the service of younger relatives and by work in war-related industries. These young people had important, formative experiences away from family, church, and community that emphasized a common American identity rather than a purely ethnic one and further inculcated them with a strong sense of patriotism. Beyond this, however, it is difficult to assess more fully the war's impact on the life courses of this large cohort of white ethnics without further research.[23]

Little in-depth research has been conducted on postwar east-central and southern European ethnic communities.[24] The demographic profile of these groups suggests the need for additional research that transcends both the dominant paradigm of "whiteness" and the old assimilation versus retention dichotomy. The demography and age structure of an ethnic group matters, and thus east-central and southern Europeans cannot be understood as simply conforming to a paradigm that sees all white ethnics as the same or similar. In what ways did demography affect how east-central and southern Europeans in post-World War II America perceived their own evolving ethnic and racial identity, the position of their communities on a changing urban landscape, and their interaction with larger economic and political forces, including the in-migration of new (and by then younger) racial and ethnic minorities?

Conclusions

Demography provides a framework in which to understand the cultural, economic, and social developments surrounding communities created from the massive migration from east-central and southern Europe to the United States prior to the 1924 change in immigration laws. Their processes of cultural change and organizational restructuring were directly affected by their unique demographic patterns. Those patterns differed sharply from older immigrant communities and from the American mainstream. The initial immigrant generation created institutions and cultural markers that were adapted to the American milieu. As the massive baby boom in these communities came of age, however, it forced a reordering of cultural norms and

Table 3   World War II Veterans in Selected Groups, 1980[1]

	Veterans as a Percent of All Males Age 161	WWII and WWII/Korean Veterans	WWII Vets as a Percent of Total Population	WWII Vets as a Percent of All Veterans
Overall U.S.	34.2	11,092,169	4.8	40.5
African American	25.6	669,760	2.5	32.3
German American	37.3	1,126,599	6.2	39.3
Irish American	40.5	746,302	7.2	43.5
Italian American	37.4	574,758	8.3	50.7
Polish American	41.6	368,541	9.7	52.6

[1]*1980 Census of the Population* Vol. 1, *Characteristics of the Population, Chapter C: General Social and Economic Characteristics.* Part 1, *United States Summary* (Washington, DC, 1983), tables 85, 179. This table combines the categories of World War II veterans and veterans who served in both World War II and Korea, which the census tabulated separately.

institutional priorities. Our understanding of this process remains limited. How did the "baby boom" of second-generation ethnics, which came of age during the 1920s and 1930s and had formative experiences during the war years, force them to imagine their ethnic and racial identity anew in an American context that was itself undergoing rapid change?

The demography of the "new immigrants" should also force us to consider how scholars of immigration have traditionally conceptualized immigrant communities. The notion of immigrant generations as clear and distinct cohorts was originally developed with so-called new immigration clearly in mind. Yet, this immigration wave occurred within a relatively short time period compared to the older immigration from western and northern Europe and, perhaps, the more recent wave of immigration from Latin America and Asia. As we have seen, this brief but intense wave of newcomers created unique demographic characteristics that do not transfer readily as a model to earlier immigrants and constitute conditions that may never be repeated in U.S. history. In this respect, the 1924 restriction on immigration from east-central and southern Europe had especially profound effects on European ethnic communities from those areas, creating conditions that were quite unlike those of other groups before or since.

Moreover, the unique demographic profile has influenced both the historiography and the popular perceptions of this immigrant wave in ways that scholars and other observers have largely failed to recognize. In light of the forgotten baby boom among southern and east-central European immigrants, the observations of concerned nativists early in the twentieth century, as well as the views of proponents of various scholarly approaches, from the original assimilation theory to the "new ethnicity" to the "whiteness" paradigm, call to mind the story of the wise men and the elephant in which the blindfolded sages each touch a different part of the elephant and come to quite different conclusions about its nature.

Notes

1. See, for example, Oscar Handlin, *The Uprooted: The Epic Story of the Great Migrations that Made the American People* (Boston, 1951); Rudolph J. Vecoli, "*Contadini* in Chicago: A Critique of *The Uprooted,*" *Journal of American History* 51, no. 3 (December 1964): 404–17.

2. See, for example, Noel Ignatiev, *How the Irish Became White* (New York, 1996); David Roediger, *Working toward Whiteness: How America's Immigrants Become White: The Strange Journey from Ellis Island to the Suburbs* (New York, 2005).

3. Edna Ferber, *American Beauty,* 69, quoted in Stanislaus A. Blejwas, "Puritans and Poles: The New England Literary Image of the Polish Peasant Immigrant," *Polish American Studies* 42, no. 2 (Autumn 1985): 46–88. There is a body of recent research related to early-twentieth-century perceptions of immigrants. See, for example, Matthew Frye Jacobson, *Barbarian Virtues: The United States Encounters Foreign People at Home and Abroad* (New York, 2000); John Radzilowski, "Views of Polish Peasants in Europe and the United States, 1890s–1930s," *Polish Review* 47, no. 4 (2002): 393–406.

4. See Dirk Hoerder, "Cultural Retention of Acculturation: The Current Debate on Multiculturalism in Historical Perspective," in *Ethnicity Culture City Polish Americans in the U.S.A.: Cultural Aspects of Urban Life, 1870–1950, in Comparative Perspective,* ed. T. Gladsky et al. (Warsaw, 1998), 29–49.

5. U.S. Bureau of the Census, "Age of the Foreign Stock by Country of Origin: 1960," *1960 Census of the Population: Supplementary Reports,* PC(S1)-47, July 28, 1965 (hereafter "Age of the Foreign Stock"). I have found no effort to analyze the results of this report in light of the literature on immigration, though the census has available some statistical reports on the history of the foreign-born population. See Campbell J. Gibson and Emily Lennon, "Historical Census Statistics on the Foreign-born Population of the United States: 1850–1990," http://census.gov/population/www/documentation/twps0029/twps0029.html.

6. Philip Taylor, *Distant Magnet: European Immigration to the USA* (New York, 1971), 103. See also Roger Daniels, *Coming to America: A History of Immigration and Ethnicity in American Life* (New York, 1990), 188–89.

7. See National Center for Health Statistics, *Health, United States, 2004* (Hyattsville, MD, 2004), Table 27, http://cdc.gov/nchs/data/hus/hus04trend.pdf#027.

8. On the latter, see Edwin Black, *War against the Weak: Eugenics and America's Campaign to Create a Master Race* (New York, 2003).

9. The number of Poles in Rhode Island and the number of Italians in Minnesota were not large enough in 1900 to be calculated separately and are thus not included.

10. John Radzilowski, "Hidden Cosmos: The Life Worlds of Polish Immigrants in Two Minnesota Communities, 1875–1925," (PhD diss., Arizona State University, 1999), 152–55, 194,

200–01; idem, *Out on the Wind: Poles and Danes in Lincoln County, Minnesota, 1880–1905* (Marshall, MN, 1992), 53.

11. U.S. Bureau of the Census, *Thirteenth Census of the United States, taken in the Year 1910*. Vol. 1: *Population: General Report and Analysis* (Washington, DC, 1913), 968–69.

12. Parish histories only rarely provide this type of statistic. The histories chosen for Table 2 were chosen by looking though all such histories in the collection of the Immigration History Research Center at the University of Minnesota. Thanks are extended to the staff for allowing me to browse the stacks. Works used are *Most Holy Rosary Parish, Perth Amboy, N.J., Golden Anniversary, 1908–1925* (Perth Amboy, NJ, 1958); *St. Stanislaus Kostka, Brooklyn, Greenpoint, New York* (New York, 1972); *Golden Anniversary, St. Ladislaus Parish, 1914–1964* (Chicago, 1964); *St. Wenceslaus Parish, Golden Jubilee, 1912–1962* (Chicago, 1962); Louis L. Makulec, *Church of St. Stanislaus Bishop and Martyr on East Seventh Street in New York City, 1874–1954* (New York, 1954); Rev. Constantine Klukowski, *History of St. Mary of the Angels Catholic Church, Green Bay, Wisconsin, 1898–1954* (Pulaski, WI, 1956); Fr. Boleslaw Kumor, *Dzieje Parafii Polskiej Rzymsko-Katolickiej św. Józefa w Norwich, Conn., 1904–1979* (Norwich, CT, 1980); *Pamiętnik Diamentowego Jubileuszu Parafji św. Wawrzyńca w Philadelphia, Pennsylvania, 1882–1957* (Philadelphia, 1957); *History of St. Joseph's Parish, Joliet, Illinois, 1891–1941* (Joliet, IL, 1941); *Church of the Holy Cross, Minneapolis, Minnesota, 1886–1986* (Minneapolis, 1986); *Holy Trinity Church, Utica, New York, Diamond Jubilee, 1896–1971* (Utica, NY, 1971).

13. *Holy Trinity Church, Utica, New York, Diamond Jubilee, 1896–1971*, 37, 42.

14. See Thaddeus C. Radzilowski, "The Second Generation: The Unknown Polonia," *Polish American Studies* 43, no. 1 (Spring 1986): 5–12.

15. See, for example, John Radzilowski, *The Eagle and the Cross: A History of the Polish Roman Catholic Union of America, 1873–2000* (New York, 2003), 176–90; June Granatir Alexander, *Ethnic Pride, American Patriotism: Slovaks and Other New Immigrants in the Interwar Era* (Philadelphia, 2004); Myron B. Kuropas, *Ukrainian-American Citadel: The First One Hundred Years of the Ukrainian National Association* (Boulder, CO, 1996), 296 passim.

16. See John Radzilowski, "Crime, Delinquency, Deviance, and Reform in Polish Chicago, 1890s–1940s," Fiedorczyk Endowed Lecture in Polish and Polish-American Studies, Central Connecticut State University, New Britain, April 25, 2001; idem, "Conflict between Poles and Jews in Chicago, 1900–1919," *Polin: Studies in Polish Jewry* 19 (2007): 117–33.

17. Frederick M. Thrasher, *The Gang: A Study of 1,313 Gangs in Chicago*, 2d ed. (Chicago, 1936), 191–93.

18. Radzilowski, "Crime, Delinquency, Deviance, and Reform in Polish Chicago."

19. On the more benign form of the Polish youth gang, see Burton W. Taylor, "Our Club Juniors: A Study of a Boy Gang in South Chicago," Ernest Watson Burgess Papers, Joseph Regenstein Library Special Collections, University of Chicago, box 179, folder 7. See also James R. Barrett and David R. Roediger, "The Irish and the 'Americanization' of the 'New Immigrants' in the Streets and Churches of the Urban United States, 1900–1930," *Journal of American Ethnic History* 24, no. 4 (Summer 2005): 3–33.

20. Paul Cressy, "Report on Summer Work with the Juvenile Protective Association of Chicago, 1925," Burgess Papers, box 129, folder 5, 3.

21. John Radzilowski, "American Polonia in World War II: Toward a Social History," *Polish American Studies* 58, no. 1 (Spring 2001): 63–80. The survey resides in the archives of the Polish Museum of America in Chicago. Extant results of the survey are found in the accompanying article: Stanley Schmidt and Sally Smyrski, "Data on Polish-American Participation in World War II," *Polish American Studies* 58, no. 1 (Spring 2001): 81–96. Unfortunately, similar contemporary data are not known to exist on other groups mentioned in this study.

22. Oleh Wolowyna, "Ukrainian Veterans in the United States: Census Data Profile," *Ukrainian Weekly,* Jan. 11, 2004, http://www.ukrweekly.com/Archive/2004/020406.shtml.

23. A few studies of selected groups have been conducted on this matter that might provide models but do not speak to the unique experiences of second-generation east-central and southern European Americans. See, for example, Glen H. Elder Jr., Aimée R. Dechter, and Hiromi Taniguchi, "World War II Mobilization in Men's Worklives: Continuity or Disruption for the Middle Class?" CDE Working Paper 99–20, Center for Demography and Ecology, University of Wisconsin-Madison, 1999, http://ssc.wisc.edu/cde/cdewp/99–20.pdf; John Modell, Marc Goulden, and Sigurdur Magnusson, "World War II in the Lives of Black Americans: Some Findings and Interpretations," *Journal of American History* 76 (1989): 830–48.

24. One more recent work is rather impressionistic but valuable, though it largely overlooked ethnicity: Robert Bruno, *Steelworker Alley: How Class Works in Youngstown* (Ithaca, NY, 1999). Cf. my review of this work, at http://h-net.org/reviews/showrev.cgi?path=288131081625556. One important study of postwar Polish Americans in Detroit is Paul Wrobel, *Our Way: Family, Parish, and Neighborhood in a Polish-American Community* (Notre Dame, IN, 1979).

Critical Thinking

1. Does demography shaped the course of ethnic group development?

2. In what respects are these factors still in play for Italian Americans and Polish Americans?

3. Explain the importance of this historical research and its relationship to other types of historical accounts of ethnicity.

From *Journal of American Ethnic History,* vol. 27, no. 1, Fall 2007, pp. 60–75. Copyright © 2007 by University of Illinois Press. Reprinted by permission.

Ethnics No More or Ethnogenesis: From Syrian to Arab American

Ethnic group formation and dissolution have long been of interest to sociologists. The process has not been easily described and, when done, often details the former event as it pertains to larger European ethnic groups. What is missing is information on the life course (including their demise) of smaller, non-European ethnic groups and their potential re-emergence through panethnic affiliations. In this regard, our aim is twofold: to trace the decline of a small ethnic group (Syrian-Americans) and to assess its possible rebirth as part of the emerging "Arab-American" community. To do this, we will focus on the intersection of the social, institutional, and cultural life of Syrian and other, newer Arab communities within pre- and post-9/11 American society.

This report is based on the growing literature on Arab-Americans and the live experience of the authors. Philip Kayal, a second and third generation Syrian American, addresses the rapid assimilation (hence demise) of the Christian Syrian American community, and Kristine Ajrouch, a third generation Muslim Lebanese American and second generation Iranian American, who argues for ethnic continuity through ethnogenesis, the formation and/or rebirth of ethnic consciousness and community, albeit in a different form.

A culture-based definition of ethnicity involves ties to family, food, national origin, language, and religion. The United States historically sought to minimize the practice and influence of such factors as immigrants who entered the country were encouraged to immediately shed their cultural ways in favor of a purely American identity. The factors that define what it is to be "American" in a cultural sense are perhaps best understood as the act of leaving behind any clue that links a person to their ancestral origins, except perhaps in the area of religion which has historically remained important to Americans. Yet, religious expression and practice is often transformed to reflect the cultural demands of living in the United States. Kayal concentrates on the religious institutions of the Syrian Christian community to illustrate its assimilation. Born and eventually raised in a Melkite, Greek-Catholic parish in Brooklyn, New York, Kayal was educated in the parochial schools of that city, up to and including his doctoral studies at Fordham University where he rediscovered his Melkite/Syrian origins. For Kayal's parent's generation, a parochial school education would ensure his general acceptance into the broader Catholic society that surrounded them. From their vantage point, they believed that religion (Catholicism in particular) was the legitimate venue for expressing an acceptable American identity. Kayal's minority status as a Melkite within the emerging American Roman Catholic Church and the liberating theology of Vatican Council II influenced and shaped his sociological perspective on ethno-religions and American pluralism.[1]

Anglo-Conformity

A classic immigrant experience detailing acculturation pressures often involves the experience of a name change. For instance, Ajrouch's maternal grandfather left what was known as Syria (present day south Lebanon) in the early 1900s for the United States and upon entry had his name changed (though it is not absolutely clear from family stories if it was he or the immigrant officials who changed it) from Habhab to Eastman. The story he always told informed us that he was a *man* from the *East,* and so he changed his name to reflect that origin, hence the family name of "Eastman." Even immigrants who entered between the 1960s and 1980s often faced pressure to modify at the least, their first name. For instance, Mohammed became Mike, Ibrahim became Abe, and Hussein or Hassan became Sam. With family and given names modified, distance from the original culture and transition to an American culture begins.[2]

Ajrouch's maternal grandfather was one of the few Muslims who left his homeland for the West in the early 1900s. Most migrants from Syria to the United States were Christians, and thus as a Muslim he represented a pioneer of sorts. He settled in Detroit, Michigan. Today the metro-Detroit area is home to the largest and most visible concentration of Arab Americans in the United States. He went back to his homeland in 1925 and married, bringing his young bride of 15 years of age to a country that she thought had streets paved with gold. Though she was young when she left her homeland (her name also changed upon arrival. Identified by the name Adeebe when interacting with co-ethnics, the rest of the United States knew her as Ida) she was ambitious and courageous. In 1965, with the passage of the family reunification act, and 40 years after she arrived in the United States, she proceeded to send for her siblings, bringing to the United States two sisters and two brothers in the early 1970s. She was a legendary cook, making her own bread, rolled grape leaves *(wad'aiesh), kibbee,* and stuffed cabbage *(malfouf).* She remained bilingual throughout her life, though she spoke primarily English in her home. And she identified strongly with being Muslim, particularly with being Shi'a from the south. Her expression of that religion, however, took on an American flavor. Her religion was personal and private, not a public identity. She valued the American way of being judged as an individual, not as an member of a group. During the 40 years between her arrival and the monumental changes that happened in the world, including the Great Depression, World War II, and the creation of Lebanon as a sovereign state separate from Syria, she became a U.S. citizen, proud to be American, but also proud of her newly discovered Lebanese origins. The Syrian identity was never discussed, except when she would bring out her original papers, which identified her as Syrian. That detail was brushed away as insignificant.

Everything changed when waves of immigration from Lebanon after the civil war broke out in the mid 1970s and the 1982 invasion of Israel brought a higher proportion of Muslims to the United States Such immigrants were leaving Lebanon because of political strife and all-out war. They arrived with a strong national and religious identity, and entered a United States publicly committed to diversity, or at the least, recognizing it as a fact of life. The Civil Rights movement, worldwide challenges to empire building, along with increased immigration from non-European countries during the same era contributed to a re-awakening of ethnicity in the United States.

Up until the 1960s, the Christian Arabs in America were essentially from the cities of Greater Syria. "Arabs" have always been here, perhaps even coming with Columbus. Larger numbers migrated when the Ottomans began drafting them into the military at the turn of the last century. Being traders and entrepreneurial, Syrians came in ever-increasing numbers until 1924 when the Quota act limited them to 100 entrees a year. Americans eventually came to know these "Turks" as Syrians, though they themselves had to first adopt that identity. They arrived as Melkite Catholics, Maronite Catholics, or Syrian Orthodox communicants from Damascus, Aleppo, Beirut, Homs, Zahleh, Jezzeine, etc. The Syrians had Turkish passports, spoke Arabic, but had limited collective loyalties not extending much beyond family, village, and religious tradition. In time, after World War II, they became Syrians and eventually many became Lebanese, whether they were geographically "real" Lebanese or not. They never referred to themselves as Turks or Arabs, though in Arabic they would query whether or not a person was "Arab."[3] While the Syrians wanted to fit in to become Americans and succumbed quickly to acculturation pressures, they also wanted to maintain their cultural heritage. They did so by joining their ethnicity with their rites and religions, creating in effect, ethno-religions. They could disguise their ethnicity under a religious umbrella and thus appear as just another religion in the land of religious pluralism and toleration. This transformation and its consequences began the decline in being known as Syrians.

From Syrians to Lebanese

It always puzzled the Syrians that so many of them were willing to be known as Lebanese and to actively take on that identity. These Lebanese ate Syrian bread (pita), published the *Syrian World,* and went to the "Syrian Church" (Melkite, Maronite, or Orthodox). In 1930, the community published *The Syrian American Directory Almanac,* listing several hundred often "interconnected" Syrian businesses. After a concerted effort by the influential Mokarzel family who owned the Al-Hoda Press, a nascent Lebanese American identity began emerging in earnest by the Second World War when the Maronite Patriarch secured a firman from the Ottomans designating Lebanon as a special province.[4] By 1943, with French support, Lebanon became its own legal entity separate from that of Syria.

Unlike their predominantly Muslim Syrian neighbors, the Lebanese began to see themselves as "westerners," steadfast Catholics always loyal to Rome, and, quite remarkably, as Phoenicians rather than Arabs. They pride themselves on being French-speakers, now one of that nation's official languages. Their French "protectors" effectively taught them that Arabs were Muslims, thus, increasing the appeal of a Lebanese identity to Syrian Christians. The once singular Syrian American community thus became known as the Syrian–Lebanese community. An unholy alliance, these two populations continued to share institutional space, whether religious, entrepreneurial, or social, up until the Lebanese Civil War (1975–1990) and the occupation of that country by Syria until 2005. None of these developments were particularly problematic to the Syrians except that the Lebanese among them were being pulled into a Phalangist framework that had an anti-Arab, anti-Muslim, and anti-Syrian ideology that created conflicts with the Syrians and now with other newly established American Arab populations. For the most part, however, life on the "Arab street" in American cities continued as usual until relatively recently. Now they are, for all practical purposes, two distinct ethnic groups with the Lebanese still insisting on their unique identity and putting their Maronite Church at the center of its cultural continuity, making that rite its own ethno-religion. The Syrians as such began falling under the radar. If anything, when Americans, especially New Yorkers, think of Syrians, they think of "Syrian Jews," a parallel ethno-religion existing beside the church supported Syrian–Lebanese community. Up until the early 1970s, to be a Melkite, Maronite, or Syrian (Antiochian) Orthodox, meant *ipso facto* to be supportive of the ethnic community.

While most of the Lebanese in this country up to the 1980s were Maronite Catholics, many were also Melkites and Orthodox. Some Syrians, mostly Aleppians, were Maronites, but the majority were Eastern Orthodox and Melkites (aka Greek-Catholics). Maronite Aleppians were not disabused of their identity or affiliation until the two countries became separate entities and Maronite and Lebanese became interchangeable identities in this country. They are hardly existent anymore as a recognizable group. To be sure, not all Melkite Americans are Syrians. Many are Lebanese and today others are Palestinian and Jordanian. Being Byzantine, Melkites are part of an international religious community or rite (Ukrainians, Ruthenians, etc.), and the Maronites are not. The former can more easily become an American tradition within Roman Catholicism, but the latter desires to remain an ethno-religion. Ideological issues regarding loyalties, origins, and identities would continually vex community integration up until the present, especially when Muslims from Syria and Lebanon began arriving in ever, increasing numbers after 1965. Whether the earlier wave of American Syrians and Lebanese see these recent immigrants as fellow ethnics or primarily as Muslims is the question at hand.

A Christian Syrian–Lebanese community that shared space, a common culture, and vaguely defined political and social goals began to really splinter by the end of the twentieth century. Before then, there was a vibrant Syrian American press (dominated by the Lebanese), a Syrian literary "Pen" League, national, and regional Syrian–Lebanese Federations, and local and national charitable organizations, whether they worked for educational purposes or for improving public relations. **ALSAC,** the fund raising arm of St. Jude's Research Hospital was known originally as Associated Lebanese–Syrian American Charities (ALSAC), but morphed into Aiding Leukemia Stricken American Children. Created and organized by famed Lebanese entertainer Danny Thomas, its internal operations were controlled by the Syrian–Lebanese though the charity itself did not receive all that much funding from Syrian–Lebanese communities.

Identity and Community Support

To become a Syrian or Lebanese American, the immigrants first had to distinguish themselves from Turks and Armenians with whom they were clumped. Then they had to transcend their provincial hometown origins and religious affiliations, something they neither were eager to do nor successful at. They initially worked together on joint projects like their naturalization and race issues, wherein they were deemed not eligible for citizenship since they were defined as nonwhites coming from Asia. Together and over time (1910–1920) they won the right to be citizens. Though they protested the establishment of the state of Israel, they never really became an integrated, institutionally complete ethnic group intent on becoming an interest group. Despite their notable cultural heritage and their own economic success here, they shunned the spotlight, preferring to assimilate, speak English in public, and, fearing rebuke, not bring attention to themselves.

Their status further deteriorated after Israel's establishment and the powerful rise of the Jewish American community into American consciousness and politics. The events of 9/11 only made it harder to be identified in a positive way as Syrians. Now Arabs in general (and Syria in particular) have become state enemies. The Syrians (especially the Christians), learning their history from the French, were NEVER comfortable being identified as Arabs though their own religious leaders or Patriarchs consistently remind them of their Arab cultural identity. As Americans, many Syrians also began to view Arabs and Muslims as embarrassments and enemies.[5]

Even though the long-term Syrian community in Brooklyn is very well known, there is not one store, restaurant, or business which declares itself Syrian, the Damascus Bakery not withstanding. All are identified as Middle Eastern or Lebanese. In Paterson, New Jersey, which at one time was almost entirely made of Syrians from Aleppo (some Lebanese and non-Aleppians belong to the Orthodox church there and others to the Syrian-Armenian-rite Catholic Church), for the most

part, ethnic stores and shops do much the same thing. The same is true in Boston and Central Falls, Rhode Island. Known for decades especially in the Northeast as "Syrian bread," pita has become the popular name. *Khobiz* (its appellation in Arabic) should have replaced Syrian bread. No one knows where "pita" came from though the owner of the Damascus bakery once announced with great pride at a meeting of the Syrian Young Men's Association in Brooklyn that "he invented the term." For acceptance by Americans (and broader appeal and sales), Syrian cuisine had to be hidden.[6]

Though both the Syrians and Lebanese sent more money home for "reconstruction" after the First World War than any other American ethnic group, the Lebanese were tied to their country for religious reasons (i.e., it was the Maronites who pushed for a separate, sovereign Lebanon state) and the Syrians were not. As Catholic Christians, the Maronites also had western leanings and formed powerful political organizations to sustain this relationship. To survive the Turks, they had to become passive resistors (hiding identities, community data, income, etc. from the Ottoman tax collectors), but when the move came for Arab independence, it began in Lebanese intellectual circles (both Christian and Muslim) via the Lebanese printing press. The Syrians benefited, but the Lebanese dominated the movement and were acknowledged for doing so. Their ascendancy was assured. Hence today, the more than two dozen national American "Syrian" political leaders would now be identified as "Lebanese" as would countless Hollywood actors whether true of them or not. Up until the Lebanese Civil War and then Lebanon/Hizbollah's conflict with Israel in 2006, there was a certain cache in being known as Lebanese (progressive, western, and Christian).

In the fall of 2001, the Museum of the City of New York sponsored "A Community of Many Worlds: Arab Americans in New York City." Its opening was delayed because of the horrific destruction of the World Trade Center. Though New York had been the première Arab American city before Detroit/Dearborn took over in the 1970s, the show's curators could barely collect any funds from the Syrian–Lebanese in Brooklyn. All in all, no more than five families donated any substantial amounts. The new and growing Arab Muslim population of New York was equally as reticent to donate. They simply could not transcend their more localized identities (sect, hometown, nation, etc). Yet they arrived in hordes to see their history in New York and to celebrate their culture, making it one of the most successful shows in the museum's history. Unlike an ethnic parade, it was a quiet affair held by and in a city agency. The Syrian and Lebanese Christians came to recall their history. The Muslims, on the other hand, came to celebrate their growing presence. That they all gathered in one place at one time was an accomplishment. But it was not a political or viable community statement.

Jump ahead six years to the funding of "the Arab–American Experience" a proposed ethnic film effort for PBS and the situation is no better. More money and donators were found, but hardly $50K has so far been raised from "the community." The establishment of the Arab American National Museum in Detroit has faired better. Partially funded by Gulf countries, it also drew support from the newer Arab ethnic groups that populate the Midwest. Internalized Arab-phobia is a serious illness and is the root explanation for this lackadaisical support.[7] Until very recently, projects designed to destigmatize the growing Arab–American community were generally undervalued by the community itself. Not a surprising situation, given the historical and confusing ambivalence about being Arab.

Starting in the spring of 2007, plans for the dual language Khalil Gibran International Academy (named after the famed Lebanese American Christian poet) in Brooklyn became public knowledge. Headed by Debbi Almontaer, an educator and fellow curator of the New York Arab Community exhibit, the project almost immediately met with resistance by suddenly concerned New Yorkers. The argument was that it was a radical Islamist school supporting the "intifada." The school was planned for Downtown Brooklyn, the original, immigrant base of the largest Syrian–Lebanese community in the country. Not one Syrian–Lebanese came publicly to the defense of the school, though this community tried for decades to sustain Arabic language classes.

De-Stabilizing the "community"

Several internal social forces conspired to weaken the Syrian–Lebanese community either as a singular entity or separately. Even if regional affiliations carried over from the Old World could be overcome (and they were eventually), there were sectarian differences which became accentuated when the Catholic Syrians and Lebanese began using the Latin Catholic school systems. This brought them into a western framework, albeit Irish one, almost immediately and cut them off from their Syrian Orthodox compatriots. The Irish were obsessed with four things: Americanization and the de-ethnicization of immigrants, creating a singular American Catholic identity for all Catholic ethnics, forbidding out-marriages to non-Catholics and latinizing their Eastern Rite communicants for the sake of integration and uniformity. The Lebanese Maronites were historically liturgically latinized and proud of it, actually calling themselves "the Irish of the East." The Melkites had to de-Byzantinize themselves in order for the Irish to accept them as Catholics. For whatever reason, the Irish could simply not understand the Byzantine rite wherein people blessed themselves "backward" (from right to left), owed allegiance to both Pope and Patriarch, had icons instead of statues in their churches, stood during liturgy and use the vernacular languages like Arabic and Greek, and, most importantly, had a married clergy.

Rome put an end to this swiftly and to make sure the Byzantines and Maronites would not re-emerge as autonomous entities anytime in the near future, forbade them their own hierarchies until the 1960s, long after the damage was done. Even here Rome supervised the appointment of their Exarchs and Eparchs (Bishops) rather than the Eastern Patriarchates themselves. This formal division of the community into Catholics and Orthodox was not the "Syrian" tradition. Informally, the Syrian Christians often socialized together. Their own churches collectively sponsored HUGE social events called *Mahrajans* where thousands of people gathered for long holiday weekends to mix, meet, and celebrate their culture among themselves. In the *Blad*

(old country), when intermarriages took place between rites and/or religions, the couple married in the male's tradition. In this country, as long the marriage took place in a Syrian church, everyone was happy. The Irish or Roman Catholics had nothing positive to say about these religious or ritual "intermarriages."

Over time, from the 1950s to the 1970s, the Catholic Syrians became more western in their thinking because they attended Irish Catholic schools, learned western theology, and began to massively out-marry. Eventually though, as they organized themselves into a separate dioceses under their own Bishop, the Melkites began to re-Byzantinize themselves . . . almost to a fault.[8] Year by year and parish by parish, churches returned to their liturgical traditions, while replacing Arabic with English, and the move was on to become an American Eastern rite or Melkite Catholics devoid of ethnicity. This may have been a great idea on paper, but those that actually affiliated with these churches did so because of their ethnic identities and histories, albeit altered and refined by the time the third and fourth generation arrived. As Melkites evolved into an American Byzantine Catholic tradition, they began attracting a non-Arab clergy and "American" communicants to their ranks which further pushed the churches into purely religious organizations rather than Syrian churches. Congregants were English speaking and many disaffected American Catholics saw the Melkite tradition as an alternative way of being Catholic. These churches, the bastion of ethnicity, were no longer only Syrian. The Maronites likewise began rediscovering their unique heritage, but they were more interested in maintaining an "ethnic identity" as an ethno-religion than reaching out to either the larger American population or other Arab–American communities.

What had happened is that the Byzantine Melkites were going "universal."[9] They already constituted an international rite and were now determined to be American Eastern rite Catholics in communion with Rome. But they did so at the same time they were becoming "Greek" or Byzantine Catholics to the extreme. From Latinized Easterners to super Byzantines speaking English. If the third generation was going to return to the "religion of their grandparents," they returned to something that was less Arab but so Byzantine as to create cultural dissonance. A patriarchal language, liturgical structure, and theology from the court of Byzantium are not easily understood in a secular, efficient, and modern urban society. The Maronites had it a bit easier because historically they identify with the west and their descendents here could depend on the Lebanese affiliation for reinforcement of ethnicity. The Syrian Orthodox, being in an Eastern Orthodox frame of reference, have begun building relations with Greeks and Russians, etc.

Caught in between two cultures, the Melkites have the most difficulty. Older Syrian Melkite Catholics who remained affiliated wanted their church to be an ethno-religion wherein their ethnicity could be fused with an acceptable religious identity, much like the Orthodox Greeks do. Their children seem not to care about this integration and want to be Americans either as Melkite or Latin Catholics. If they choose the former they did so as cultural pluralists. If they become Latins, they would be anglo-conformists and not Syrian identified at all. Over time, more and more Syrian Catholics chose the latter.

What is left, therefore, in the ethnic group at large, is an attenuated Arab culture focusing on food and family retained ethnic traditions ambiguously sustained by its religious traditions. Culturally, however, as fate would have it, even the food has become commercialized and no longer controlled by the ethnic group. A cultural identifier is thus weakened. Americans in any major metropolis are familiar with *Mishwie* or *Shish Kabob* (popular Armenian name), *hummus, babaganouch, tabouli, batlaweh (Baklavah), lebaneh*, etc., and now even *Kibbeh*, often times in unrecognizable forms. So it is in America. . . . as the food goes, so does the ethnic group.

This situation is exacerbated by the demographics. The 2000 Census lists 1,202,871 Americans who identify as Arabs. Arab–American scholars note the real number is closer to 3,000,000. Writers still claim that the largest segment of the Arab–American population are Christians. That would mean over 1,500,000 people. Yet in terms of identification with Syrian Christian institutions, Syrian Christians are now and perhaps never were a large population cohort. At best, they number 200,000 recognized adherents over three and now four generations. The active Lebanese Christian community is larger (perhaps 500,000), but like the Syrians, dispersed, suburbanized, intermarried, and assimilated.[10] Even where there was some population density, these communities never dominated any particular zip code. In a matter of one generation, the Syrians of lower Manhattan (the original Syrian community on Washington Street where ironically the World Trade Center buildings collapsed) moved to downtown Brooklyn, then Park Slope, and finally Bay Ridge. A generation later their offspring have relocated to Staten Island and now are all over the Northeast. Their ethnically exclusive summer residences in Tannersville, New York, and the Pocono Mountains in Pennsylvania and Asbury Park, and Point Pleasant in New Jersey have ceased to exist as such. Cool mountains are no competition for air-conditioners and Disney world vacations.

External social forces also play a role in ethnic group dissolution. Whether political, economic, social, or culture, it is very difficult for an ethnic group to maintain boundaries, group consciousness, and solidarity if the dominant culture is hostile and the ethnic group so acculturated that being an ethnic and American are hard to distinguish. Nothing weakens or destroys ethnicity more than economic success and/or assimilation. Philip Hitti (1924), the famed Princeton historian wrote "that the Syrians arrived in the Middle Class." They came with middle class values, such as commitment to hard work and thrift. Moreover, they wanted to be Americans. It was the immigrant Syrians who became millionaires by the Second World War, not their children. These immigrants also became English speakers quickly. If their private social life remained ethnic, their own Americanization over time, made it unlikely their children would continue these traditions, except in the symbolic areas of food maintenance, some folk dancing, and kinship loyalty.[11] Arabic language usage lasted through the second generation with smatterings of quaint Arabic expressions surviving into the third. The children became educated, entered every profession, and operated as Americans of Syrian or Lebanese ancestry, but not as Syrian Americans committed to institutional

continuity and maintenance. As Americans, the issue of endogamous marriages became impossible, if not undesirable. Unlike Syrian Jews who literally forbade out-marriages and who lived in tight ethnic enclaves that restricted contact even with Ashkenazi Jews, the Syrian Christians neither had the will or demographic capacity of doing the same. The church sponsored *Mahrajans* and national ethnic (Syrian–Lebanese) conventions, for all practical purposes, have ceased to exist and the parishes are left with smaller *Hafli's* or dances where American music dominates, save for interludes of Arabic music and dance. The participants enthusiastically dance the *Debke* out of context. It is symbolic ethnicity at its best.

It is hard to maintain ethnicity in the age of MTV wherein mass media in general celebrates American consumerism, individualism, social change, fast food, mobility, and living in the moment. With the passing of the immigrant generation by 2000, few adults are around to pass on history and tradition. Those that are long-lived have become Americanized themselves.[12] Few were interested in learning their ancestral history, except the intellectual classes, and they did that from books and history classes rather than from the direct narratives of their parents or grandparents.

If intermarriage is the test of assimilation, the Syrians were well on the way to full integration from the 1940s onward. Articles in the *Syrian World* dealing with the "marriage crisis" among Syrians constantly appeared. The issue was the upward mobility of the males who married up and out as well as the demographic problem of sex ratios. Christian Syrian women, often well educated, frequently married educated Syrian American men in quasi-arranged marriages. Freedom of choice existed, nonetheless, but the dispersion of the community into suburbia made it impossible, if not unnecessary, to maintain this objective. Hardly an in-group marriage among the third generation offspring of the Syrian elites (those who built the clothing empires in NYC and elsewhere) has occurred in the last 30 years.

At the same time that this integration of the American Syrian population was going on, immigration spurred by the changes in immigration law in 1965 brought thousands of Egyptians (Coptic and Muslim), Palestinians and Jordanians (Christian and Muslims alike), and Iraqis (Chaldeans and Muslims) into the United States. Since 1967, over 750,000 "Arabs" have entered the country from a multitude of Arab countries. They could not have been more different from the Syrian–Lebanese who were already here. Many were professionals and academicians who were fiercely loyal to their Arab roots and not willing to either assimilate quickly or be identified as terrorists. The professionals among them formed the Association of Arab–American University Graduates (AAUG). One could hope they would revive the dwindling and weakening Arab communities already here. They did generally, but often in parallel organizations that bypassed the churches. Downtown shopping districts in Paterson, Boston, Dearborn, Detroit, and Brooklyn have been re-Arabized, and are flourishing, but so too have some very middle class areas like Bay Ridge and Brooklyn. Instead of reviving interests in Arab culture/history among the Syrian–Lebanese living there, it made them hostile.[13] Smart shopping areas in Bay Ridge became overwhelmed with Palestinian and Egyptians wearing Muslim clothing to the dismay of Syrians who, by this point, were thinking like Americans with regards to Muslims and terrorism.

Institutionally, when these recent Christian immigrants found a local church of their rite and denomination, they were both welcomed and rejected. In some cases, they were fresh blood that replaced the displaced suburban Syrians and in others they burdened these institutions with ethnic concerns. Deciding the language of the liturgy would be a case in point. American Syrians wanted English, yet Palestinian Melkites wanted Arabic in the services. Nonattending Syrian communicants donate thousands a month to church maintenance for family and historical reasons, and the newer immigrants use the facilities, but contribute little to their maintenance. The question becomes institutional survival . . . what group should the hierarchy "cater" to? In many cities, the urban Syrian and Lebanese Christian churches moved to the suburbs in an effort to follow their congregants. The development and maintenance of ethnic identity among Muslims from the same region involves additional factors.

The Next Wave of Immigrants

Though a very small number of Muslims left what was known as Greater Syria in the early twentieth century, the major wave of immigration for the Muslim Syrian–Lebanese emerged with the passage of the Immigration and Nationality Act Amendments of 1965. The most remarkable characteristics of this act are that immigrants were no longer distinguished by their race or historical link to the United States. Admission occurred on a first-come, first-serve basis. With this act, the leading principle was family connection and reunification: "eighty percent of the numerically limited visas were for close relatives of American citizens or residents" (Mills, 1994:16). This shift in principle allowed the parents, spouses, and children of any adult American citizen to enter the country without the enforcement of numerical restrictions. In addition, brothers and sisters were placed high on the quota list, thus accelerating the process of change in immigrant composition. This second wave of Lebanese emigration left their home countries due to political disputes and all-out warfare. Whereas the first wave, both Christian and Muslim, embraced American mores, the second wave waited much longer before settling in. Orfalea (1988) states that these first and second wave immigrants attended the same churches and mosques yet did not socialize with one another much. All that changed, however, beginning with the Israeli–Arab war in 1967, followed by ones in 1972 and then 1982.

Political unrest and the rise of Islamic fundamentalism in the Middle East coupled with anti-Islamic sentiments in the United States has led to a more intense practice of Islam, making it much more important than it had been with previous generations (Aswad, 1992, 1997). One example of how such events influenced identity among the Muslims who emigrated from south Lebanon involves the Iranian Revolution and hostage crisis in 1979. This event drew a spotlight on Islam and the Middle East, but perhaps more significantly for Muslims living in the United States influenced drastic changes by promoting conservative interpretation and practices that permeated religious institutions. The Islamic Center of America, founded in Detroit, Michigan during 1950s by a group of first and second generation Muslim Lebanese had developed as a mosque center for descendants of immigrants to provide education about Islam, as well as serve as a social hall for weddings and community gatherings. It essentially operated as an ethnic hall. Parties and weddings often included music; families sat together during the Sunday services. In the early 1980s, however, all this changed. Inspired by the Islamic Revolution in Iran, a picture of Ayatollah Khomeini appeared in the foyer, and suddenly women could not enter unless they covered their head. Men and women were strongly encouraged to sit on opposite sides of the room. The U.S. born resisted, but a new immigrant generation dominated the operations of the center, and prevailed. Continued influx of Muslim immigrants throughout the 1980s and 1990s also contributed to the increased importance of Islam to Muslims in America. For instance, Muslims in America often perceive a decline in moral standards, "a significant change in American values and a serious lowering of ethical standards, since the hippie/sexual/feminist revolution(s)" (Haddad and Smith, 1996, p. 21). Thus, Islam becomes a refuge because it dictates a way life that can guarantee protection of themselves and their family from the perceived social ills that plague American society. While remarkably more severe than the culture conflict experienced by the first wave of Syrians, this generational/ethnic conflicts also occurs in all Syrian American Christian traditions.

Although the various immigrant waves from Syria and Lebanon have in common the Arabic language, music, art/literature, and a basic cultural understanding regarding Arab customs, religion can be a powerful basis for group belonging. As indicated, an example is the Maronites of Lebanon. This religious sect draws upon its historical experiences to root their primary identity. Abu-Laban states that ". . . for specific Arab-speaking groups, notably the Maronites of Lebanon, religion provides, at the social psychological level, the primary basis for group consciousness. Members of this religious group define their ethnicity not in terms of their Arabic language and heritage, but rather in terms of Maronite (Christian) historical and territorial roots" (Abu-Laban, 1980:22). Religion, in fact, is the primary affiliation upon which ethnic relations exist in Lebanon (Salibi, 1988). Religion is a key aspect of Arab culture and becomes an "important social boundary, across which marriage is difficult." (Aswad, 1997:213).

Religion is of central importance to ethnic identity. Those who are Muslim, however, utilize Islam to carve out an identity in non-Muslim countries. Sossie Andezian (1986) writes how Islam helps the Muslim immigrant to define him- or herself by opposition to the non-Muslim. The interaction of the immigrant and host society, along with the struggle within the community to maintain its members' identity, sparks the revival of religious customs and beliefs, which in the country of origin are reserved for the more "religious" believers. Religious practices enable Arab immigrants to maintain social norms that might otherwise disappear outside of their native country.

If the ethno-religions of the Syrian community, either separately or together, at first functioned to preserve a truncated Arab culture, they also worked against the establishment of a broader Arab–American community and identity. They were the major structural limitations on broader and newer ethnic loyalties. Not until the first two generations passed from the scene could the organizational talent and wealth of members of these religions and rites be put to broader use. The Syrian churches simply siphoned off energy, leadership, money, and skills to localized projects. Each tradition held on to their elites as if their existence depended on them. At any given moment, some individuals may have transcended these primal loyalties, but organizationally, and until now, the churches did not and would not participate in any secular or political movements that would bring them into contact with the "Arab others." Overtime, education, assimilation, and changes in the socio-political environment altered these loyalties and boundaries.

Prejudice and Discrimination

The Syrians were responsible for securing a white identity for Middle Eastern immigrants in the early 1900s (Gaultieri, 2001). The denial of U.S. citizenship at the turn of the century forced the Syrian–Lebanese to embrace the racial hierarchy as they actively lobbied to be "white" as opposed to the "other" (black or Mongol). Yet, prejudiced attitudes and discrimination experiences remained as they do among the first generation for most immigrant groups. There is, however, a distinct difference in the encounters of prejudice and discrimination experienced pre- and post 9/11.

Prejudiced attitudes and discriminating actions before 9/11 were without question an issue with which to contend. Above and beyond the immigrant status issue, the Syrian–Lebanese were targets of negative attitudes in part because of events that occurred in the Middle East. An overall negative American attitude existed, conveyed, and supported through mass media imagery. The portrayals of the culture that represents Arab-speaking countries conveyed a barbaric, backward, and primitive people. The Disney film *Aladdin* invited attention from the American Arab Anti-Discrimination Committee, who succeeded in having the lyrics to the opening song removed ("where they cut off your hand if they don't like your face"), but only after the film had been released. Ron Stockton's (1994) systematic analysis of cartoons documents the ways in which negative stereotypes of "Arabs" exist in mass media and political cartoons. In fact, Stockton suggests that the effects of such caricatures involve a high cost to domestic populations of Arab ancestry. Dehumanizing images potentially influence identity development in harmful ways among those who trace their ancestry to an Arab-speaking nation. Nabeel Abraham (1994), in the same edited volume, chronicles violent acts against those of Arab ancestry in the United States, and presents such atrocities as openly tolerated by mainstream American society. Such incidents operate to produce various paths of ethnic identity development. The effect may result in a move to distance one from the Arab-speaking Middle East, or conversely to seek out others with similar origins as a means to cope with the negativity.

Among immigrants and their children from Lebanon, individual experiences are also evident. In a study Ajrouch carried out during 1995 regarding ethnic identity among children of Lebanese Muslim immigrants, participants relayed their perceptions and experiences of being of Arab ancestry and growing up in the United States (see Ajrouch 2000 and 2004 for details of this study). It was the boys in the group who narrated stories of discrimination. The difficulties experienced emerged as a consensus. One told stories about how he went so far as to deny his heritage and pass himself off as Italian. In general, they discuss the challenge of having to answer for the actions of one or two "bad apples," a situation that many placed in the "cultural other" category must do from time to time. Consider the following scenario, told by Henry, a 15-year-old boy:

> I walk home sometimes, and people, they drive around in cars you know, skinheads. One time, they went too far. One time; I had a rock, because I knew they were going to yell something, I had a rock in my hand. They drove by, I knew it, they yelled, same exact thing always. And I threw the rock—(What do they yell to you?) Hey, you, F- you A-rab, something like that. And sometimes they go over the line. Camel back, something like that. And then I threw the rock at the car, and I hit the back of the window. And it broke.

The above narrative speaks to the potentially violent encounters young men face, and illustrates the nature of discriminatory experiences. It was primarily boys who told stories of facing prejudice or discrimination based on their heritage. Henry's narrative also hints at the racialized aspect of the experience as he describes the perpetrators as "skinheads," a term that signifies individuals who adhere to white supremacy ideas. Moreover, the above story illuminates ways in which Lebanese may come to adopt an "Arab" identity above and beyond a national origin identity. Identified by others as such, it may be easier to simply embrace that identity than to reject it.

Post 9/11 Influences

After 9/11, the American media had succeeded in creating one integrated perception: Arab-Muslim-Terrorist. In some combination, the terms are used interchangeably. Regardless of generation, ethnic background, social class, or religious affiliation, one identity implied the others. What to do?[14] Whatever vestige of Syrian pride in Arab origins existed would be undermined by the misuse and mispronunciations of Arab names on TV, their accented depictions, their swarthiness, and subversiveness. ***REEL BAD ARABS*** by Jack Shaheen (2001) provides thousands of examples of this stereotype throughout American movie and TV history. How do the Americanized Syrian and Lebanese compensate for this biased cultural hegemony that their children are exposed to in school textbooks, movies, and television? Not only can't they, but they don't seem to bother, the Arab Anti-Defamation Committee not withstanding.

That having been said, not all the news is bad. Just like the period after the 1967 "war" which stirred the nascent interests of Arab Americans to organize, there remain remnant populations of Syrians and Lebanese who now support the Arab cause, but not necessarily their own ethnic groups, save for the Lebanese American Phalangists who after the occupation of Lebanon by Syria have become fiercely defensive about the rights and freedom of that country. A small segment to be sure, but very articulate and media savvy. They dissociate from Arabness, their own historical roots, and the larger Arab American population in general. These nationalists have created wedges between the Lebanese and other Arab American populations including the Syrians to whom they owe their origins. Tensions also exist within some Melkite parishes wherein the pastors are Lebanese and the congregants Syrians. The pastors act like everyone in the community is Lebanese or want to be and that Syria and Syrian American concerns are secondary. Something similar is beginning to occur in Detroit where Iraqi Christian Chaldeans have settled. Some leaders there refute the claim that they are Arabs. But their American born children and now the third and fourth generation Syrians and Lebanese are on the scene and are more able to see the "bigger picture" politically. Not necessarily interested in religious survival or even ethnic group continuity, they have become supportive of broader ethno-political issues regarding American foreign policy.

Likewise, newer immigrants whether Christian or Muslim, Syrian, Lebanese, Egyptian, Palestinian, or Jordanian, do not enter with this historical baggage. They place their national and cultural loyalties first and do not think in the traditional sectarian categories of the American Syrians and Lebanese. They are articulate spokespeople for Arab causes and interests and have established parallel American Arab organizations that also attract informed American Syrian–Lebanese.[15]

The post 9/11 world has directed attention to those of Arab ancestry in a stigmatizing way, particularly those who identify as Muslims. It should be noted, however, that it may not be only Lebanese Muslims who are negatively affected. As Ajrouch was carrying out a study on aging, health, and social relations (see Ajrouch, 2005 for details), she interviewed a 68-year-old Lebanese Christian man in his home, and in the middle of the interview he paused, looked directly at Ajrouch and stated his frustration with media coverage and portrayals of Arab and Muslim culture. Those horrific events serve to make the religion and culture both more prominent in the everyday language of Americans, but simultaneously more negative. Events following 9/11 including the War on Terror, the emergence of Homeland Security, the Patriot Act, as well as more micro transformations such as heightened security at airports have altered the lives of Middle Eastern Americans in many ways. Such tendencies resemble the experiences of Italians, Germans, and Japanese during World War II. For instance, when the United States was at war with Italy, Child (1943) warned that second generation Italians were at risk of rejecting American identity and values if they encountered pervasive anti-Italian sentiment from the American government and public. Because Muslims and those of Arab ancestry feel less welcomed by the dominant culture, it may be that they exhibit a stronger affinity with a panethnic group status, i.e., Arab.

U.S. Foreign Policy

There are often forces, seemingly opposed, which operate at the same time in a given community. If Syrian ethnic group solidarity was being weakened, it was also being transformed by other social forces into something broader. What did not occur for the immigrants, deriving an ethnic identity based on language heritage, occurred among the third and fourth generation. Educated

Syrian and Lebanese both began calling themselves Arabs and identifying with the larger and growing Arab American community, spurred on by the political problems of the Middle East which impacted on their lives here. They were not doing this for social or cultural reasons but for economic and political ones and they did so as concerned Americans. Because of growing hostility and discrimination, this generation of Syrians and Lebanese Americans did so for self-protection. After the 6 Day War (1967), knowledgeable Syrians willingly became Arabs because of the injustices that ensued. Palestinian rights became everyone's issues and the biases of the American press made becoming Arab a necessity. Since Syrians were perceived as Arabs and, therefore terrorist (if not Muslims), they had to become Arabs to defend themselves.[16]

The Syrian and Arab–American response was not unusual and mirrored the strategies of other minorities. Claim the category of discrimination (Arab) and redefine it. And they did it as Americans committed to cultural pluralism. The position of Arab American organizations is that it is not good public policy to be so biased in favor of Israel. How else to defend the civil rights and liberties of the community . . . all segments of which were under scrutiny, if not attack, then to go public with accurate information and historical data? If anything heightened interest in Arab–American civil rights, it is the still unsolved murder of Alex Odeh, president of the Arab American Anti-Discrimination Committee, in 1985, presumably at the hands of the Jewish Defense League. Indeed, the founders and leaders of the contemporary, national Arab organizations were almost all professional Syrian and Lebanese, third generation Americans, including: The Arab–American Institute, Zogby International (pollster organization), and the Arab American anti-Discrimination Committee. Membership of the newly formed and broad based Network of Arab American Professionals is substantially third and fourth generation Syrian and Lebanese and Palestinian.[17]

If the objectives were civil rights and raising consciousness about Arab/Palestinian concerns, another motivation was simply economics. It is bad for the American economy to be anti-Arab. This growing market and economy needs to be cultivated and Arab Americans are acutely aware of this. The recent Dubai–American ports incident is a case in point, but other issues of trade, armaments, and cultural exchanges are also on the table. For example, a generation of future Arab leaders is no longer educated in this country. This is the main focus of the new magazine, **Arab American Business** which featured an entrepreneurial Syrian American on the cover. Under the leadership of Darrel Issa, the five Arab American members of Congress have tried to hammer this point home.

Nothing creates or unites a community or population more than a common enemy and today that enemy is a) the recent, if not continuous, bombing of Lebanon by Israel, b) the mass media depiction of Arabs as Islamofascists, c) the profiling of Arab Americans by American counter-terrorism agencies, d) the American bias in favor of Israel, e) the plight of the Iraqi and Palestinian people, and f) the characterization of Syria as an enemy state. Combined together and with the need to protect civil rights, the stage is set for the genesis of a new Arab–American community.

Ethnogenesis and Pan Ethnic Identity

Arab ethnicity encompasses a broad spectrum of peoples, religions, and nationalities. It is an identity which includes an array of characteristics that often times conflict with one another. Nevertheless, an emerging literature addresses the major components of Arab ethnicity as well as the diversity one finds within Arab ethnic groups (Ajrouch & Jamal, 2007; McCarus, 1994; Naber & Jamal, 2007; Suleiman, 1999). Mary C. Sengstock (1982) explored the formation of ethnic identity among Chaldeans in America. She found that the most pressing issue among Chaldeans, who are Christian and originate from Iraq, is the identity question: Are they Arabs or Chaldeans? She observed that those who immigrated earlier, had a higher economic status and lived in the suburbs of Detroit tend to identify themselves as Chaldean. Those who are more recent immigrants, had a comparatively lower economic status and live in the city of Detroit, more often identified themselves as Arab. Beyond wave of immigration, national origin, and religion, it appears that socio-historical periods and events weigh heavily on ethnic identity formations. The impact of socio-historical events influences members of a group differentially depending on their age. For younger Arab–American cohorts in particular, an event such as 9/11 may influence the likelihood of feeling marginalized, and hence a higher propensity to not identify with the dominant society. The consequential effect may contribute to an ethnic identity that incurs minority status elements among younger age groups. On the other hand, despite the fact that the 9/11 bombers were essentially Saudis, a country aligned with the United States, the biased framing of the event (implicating all Arabs) by the American mass media establishment may lead to a higher likelihood of feeling embarrassed at being Arab. This may in turn prompt younger generations to distance themselves from such an identity, leading to the demise of an Arab ethnic identity.

In the United States, pan-ethnic labels serve two almost contradictory roles depending on the "institutions" that promote the label. On the one hand, the pan-ethnic label may provide a means for categorizing the "other," as subordinate to and different from the dominant "white" mainstream, especially when the dominant mainstream designates such pan-ethnic classifications. Immigrant and ethnic groups may find themselves in the awkward situation of having to denounce a pan-ethnic label if it is seen as denying them "American" privilege. On the other hand, it may indicate a form of "mainstream assimilation." If the pan-ethnic identity is itself a symbolic identity (Waters, 1990), one that emerges at the discretion of the 'ethnic' individual, then the identity may signify a resource that supports assimilation. The acceptance or rejection of an Arab American pan-ethnic label, and the degree to which it is salient, may reveal deeper insight into the ways that individuals and groups assimilate. For instance, it is quite possible to identify strongly with aspects of the immigrant culture as well as that of the dominant host society simultaneously. More centrally, it may indicate the extent to which the Arab American pan-ethnic identity signifies potential and acceptable incorporation into dominant society while still reinforcing both community consciousness and institutional integration. This, in turn, allows the ethnic group (or minority) to bargain from a position of strength relying on its resources to defend its interests, ensuring equality as opposed to oppression and subjugation. A pan-ethnic identity will potentially position the new ethnic group to occupy a more respectable place in our pluralistic society. The emergence of an Arab American community provides a mechanism by which to bargain from a position of strength with the dominant society to achieve political, economic, and social goals.

What remains to be seen is whether or not cultural ethnicity and political issues can cement ties among various Arab American groups that are long lasting institutionally. It is quite possible that each group—religious or national origin—will continue to have their own agendas, yet still be able to join forces over shared interests: the wars in Lebanon, the rights of Palestinians, biased foreign aid agreements, etc. Or they may balkanize and split apart into separate constituencies based on religion and/or nationality. Americans, despite the promotion of multiculturalism, really only accept and support in the long run religious pluralism, not ethnic continuity. Arab styled ethno-religions will solve this dilemma in the short run, but generational changes in time will recreate the institutional conflicts that faced the Syrian Christians and that are again emerging among them. That the leaders of all the Christian Arabs are situated in the Middle East and that these communities are bi-local should keep them tied to Arab networks and socio-political issues. This should make cooperation with American Arab Muslims more likely and successful.

Endnotes

1. This is the general thesis of Will Herberg in **Protestant, Catholic, Jew** and formed the basis of Kayal's Ph.D. dissertation on the role of religion in the assimilation process. Eventually this dissertation evolved into the first book on Syrian Lebanese Americans since Hitti's 1924 book on Syrians in America.

2. A remarkably similar story is told by Ed Aryain in **From Syria to Seminole.** Ed was originally called Mohammed and hailed from Henna, 18 miles from Damascus. His biography is both a travelogue and history lesson depicting the plight and success of Syrian peddlers throughout the Midwest.

3. The term "Arab" is a cultural not racial or ethnic identifier. In Syria, the term is usually reserved for Bedouins, not city dwellers. It would not be in the consciousness of urbane Syrian Christian immigrants to identify themselves as Arabs since no one thought in those terms, especially the Christians who under the Ottomans were organized by religious tradition or rite. The arrangement was called the "millet" system of government.

4. Nothing is more telling about this bifurcated identity than the poem or message of the great "Lebanese–American" K. Gibran "To Young Americans of Syrian Origin," wherein he admonishes American Syrians to stand tall in the United States because of their heritage. He clearly saw himself as Syrian, not Lebanese, and as an "American." He writes "I am a descendent of the people that built Damascus, and Biblus, and Tyre, and Sidon, and Antioch, and now I am here to build with you, and with a will." It is to be proud of being an American, but it is also to be proud that your fathers and mothers came from a land upon which 'God laid His Gracious hand and raised His messengers. "Young Americans of Syrian origin, I believe in you." From The Syrian World 5 (10): 24–25 (June, 1931).

5. This perspective is more likely on the East and West coasts where Syrian and Lebanese Christians predominate. When attempting to raise funds for either the NYC Museum show or the Arab American film documentary referred to shortly in the text, many Arab Christians angrily refused to donate because the word Arab was in the title of the project. This may not be the case in Detroit which has a very large and diversified Arab population that is institutionally strong and politically influential.

6. In 1979, the New York Daily News ran a story by Suzanne Hamlin on Syrian bread before it became Pita. Entitled "A Bakery Grows in Brooklyn," the author acknowledges that even though the name "Syrian bread" was used throughout the Eastern Seaboard and elsewhere, most Americans now know it as Pita. The question is why did the name Syrian have to be downplayed so much for the American public's acceptance? It was simply more appealing and economically feasible to hide its origins.

7. While there are complex historical reasons why this dissociation with Arabness would occur, suffice it to say that it is nothing new. Perhaps starting with the Crusades, such Western feelings about Arabs have waxed and waned during the various European colonization attempts of the Middle East. American perceptions are no different in their variance. At the time of the Presbyterian missionary movement in the mid 1800s, Syria and Palestine were both admired as the cradle of Christianity, but the missionaries also chose to ignore the local Christians, seeing them as backward and superstitious. Since the Muslims refused to let them proselytize among them, they turned to the Christians and converted many of them to Protestantism. Anti–Arab feelings increased here after the establishment of Israel and Arab Americans became subject to a constant barrage of anti-Arab propaganda that the community could not defend itself against. The events of 9/11 only confounded the problem.

8. This revitalization was years in the making and began during Vatican Council II under the leadership of famed Melkite Patriach Maximus V Sayegh. In this country, the Melkite renaissance was spurred by Archimandrite Joseph Raya, pastor of St. John Chrysostom parish in Atlanta, Georgia, and the Melkite Laymen's Association. This association with the help and support from American born Melkite priests wanted an independent Byzantine rite that would be authentically Eastern, though in a western society. See Kayal (1975 for more details.

9. As reported in a joint message of the Melkite Bishops of English Speaking Eparchies to their American constitutents: "The precious Melkite patrimony has come from the land of our forefathers;" yet this patrimony is universal and not bound to a specific culture or ethnic group. The success in all the English-speaking eparchies of attracting new members of various ethnic groups and religious traditions gives witness to the universality of the Melkite Church. Our Church must act, not like a foreigner in a strange land, but as a rightful member of the nation in which it lives. See Sophia: the Journal of the Melkite Greek Catholic Eparchy of Newton, Vol 18, # 1, Fal, 2007, 4.

10. After approximately 150 years of residency, it is virtually impossible to estimate the number of Syrians in this country. Many were originally classified as from Turkey in Asia and others entered from South America via Mexico. Dispersal of the community and intermarriage over four generations makes classification even more difficult. The author's own brother married out as did all three of his children, yet they all identify with their Melkite church in Brooklyn, though living outside the city. Our numbers are derived from the total of registrants in all three Christian archdioceses in the United States at the present

time. The official Catholic Directory lists only 26,000 registered Melkites in the United States and approximately 75,000 Maronties in two Dioceses. Everyone I spoke to agrees that these numbers are too low. The Maronite Chancery suggested that there may be 1,000,000 Maronites all over the United States and the descendents of just the Brooklyn Melkite Community would easily number 26,000. The Antiochian Archdiocese officially registers 65,000 communicants, but other sources list the number at 350,000. It would seem impossible for an Eparchy encompassing the entire United States to maintain itself with such small numbers. Fortunately for all three traditions, immigration has given birth to dozens of mission churches that will increase their numbers substantially. Melkites would have to rely on conversions to sustain themselves, thus weakening the church's ties to ethnicity and ethnic communities.

11. If name changing and clothing are the first things to go in the acculturation process, religion is generally considered the last. In between is food, music, and dance. In an attempt to preserve the culinary traditions of the community, Kayal and his cousin Virginia Gerbino published *A Taste of Syria* in 2003. It was the first such book since Helen Corey's, *The Art of Syrian Cookery,* the cover of which indicated that it was a "culinary trip to the land of Syria AND Lebanon." It was published in 1962 by Doubleday. Apparently, the Lebanese were still Syrians at that time.

12. Sociological theory emphasizes generational assimilation. In reality, immigrants themselves Americanize over time. First generation Syrian Americans who are over 85 years old are hardly ghettoized at this point. While bilingual, many only speak English now and are quite in tune with American cultural norms. The traditional Syrian "Sittau" has become an American-type grandmother.

13. Paterson, New Jersey is a case in point. It was the original home base for a large and prosperous Syrian Christian community in New Jersey. Three churches were built in the South Paterson neighborhood that housed the immigrants, but all three have relocated within 2 miles of each other in suburban Clifton and Little Falls. But downtown has remained Arab. Since 1970, thousands of Palestinians and Syrian Lebanese Muslims have repopulated the district, opening dozens of restaurants and dry goods stores. The original Christian bakeries and merchants have learned to accommodate them even though these newer groups have opened up their own businesses to accommodate their regional clientele. The Christians are ambivalent to say the least. They use the bakeries (Christian owned), but rarely go to the more than dozen Muslim owned restaurants even if owned by Syrians preferring a suburban Syrian restaurant in Little Falls that is Christian owned. When speaking to the Melkite pastor about "eating out in Paterson," he directed me to what he called "our" restaurants. None were Muslim.

14. The Arab–New York Museum show was scheduled to open early in the fall of 2001. The World Trade Center bombings particularly stunned the planners. What to do? Open on schedule or postpone the event indefinitely till emotions calmed down. After several deliberations with the very sympathetic Museum staff and the realization that "we are Americans, not terrorists and we had nothing to do with this attack," the show's opening was moved to March, 2002.

15. This is not to say that Arab American sectarianism is no longer present. It simply recedes and re-emerges in response to international issues playing out in the Middle East. It is also generationally based. As indicated, the establishment of pan-national Arab American organization did in fact occur, but the

Lebanese Civil War and the invasion of Iraq and subsequent sectarian attacks between and among Muslims and Christians has created some resentment here as well.

16. Stigmatization often leads to group dissolution and disengagement unless the victims claim the category and redefine it positively. The language of analysis regarding Arabs has always been controlled by the west as famed philosopher and political commentator Edward Said (1979) has taught us. Like Blacks and gays (especially during AIDS) responded to discrimination by joining forces and enfolding upon themselves, so have American Arabs.

17. As reported in Vol. 8, Issue 2: p. 8 of *Arab American Business,* "the group is comprised of about 5000 young professionals. . . ." They are your doctors, your lawyers, your engineers. . . . they are part of the fabric of American society; they're an integral to the nation's landscape. . . . the negative stereotypes of the Arab "bad guy" without a counter image have prompted this groundswell of activism by members of the community." NAAP was founded nine months before 9/11. "The terror attacks fueled the growth of the organization."

Selected References

Abraham, N. 1994. Anti-Arab racism and violence in the United States. In E. McCarus (ed.) *The Development of Arab-American Identity* (pp. 155–214). Ann Arbor: University of Michigan Press.

Abraham, Sameer Y and Nabeel Abraham. 1983. *Arabs in the New World: Studies on Arab-American Communities.* Detroit: Wayne State Press.

Abraham, Nabeel and Andrew Shryock. 2000. *Arab Detroit: From Margins to Mainstream.* Detroit: Wayne State University.

Abu-Laban, Baha. 1980. *An Olive Branch on the Family Tree.* Canadian Government: McClelland and Stewart Ltd.

Ajrouch, Kristine J. (2000) "Place, Age, and Culture: Community living and ethnic identity among Lebanese American adolescents" *Small Group Research,* 31, 4, 447–469.

Ajrouch, K. J. (2004) Gender, Race, and Symbolic Boundaries: Contested spaces of identity among Arab-American adolescents. *Sociological Perspectives, 47,* 371–391.

Ajrouch, K. J. (2005). Arab-American immigrant elders' views about social support. *Ageing & Society, 25* (5) 655–673.

Ajrouch, K. J. & Jamal, A. (2007) Assimilating to a white identity: The case of Arab Americans. *International Migration Review,* 41(4), 860–879.

Andezian, Sossie. 1986. "Women's Roles in Organizing Symbolic Life: Algerian female immigrants in France." In Rita James Simon and Caroline B. Brettell (Eds.), *International Migration: The female experience.* New Jersey: Rowman & Allanheld. pp. 254–65.

Aswad, Barbara. 1974. *Arabic-Speaking Communities in American Cities.* New York: Center for Migration Studies.

Aswad, Barbara. C. 1992. The Lebanese Muslim community in Dearborn, Michigan. In *The Lebanese in the World: A century of emigration* edited by A. Hourani and N. Shehadi (pp. 167–187). London: The Centre for Lebanese Studies in association with I.B. Tauris & Co Ltd.

Aswad, Barbara C. 1997. "Arab American Families." In Mary Kay DeGenova (Ed.) *Families in Cultural Context.* Mayfield, California: Mayfield Publishing Company.

Benson, Kathleen and Philip M. Kayal. 2002. *A Community of Many Worlds: Arab-Americans in New York City.* New York: The Museum of the City of New York/Syracuse University Press.

Child, I.L. 1943. *Italian or American? The Second Generation in Conflict.* New Haven, CT: Yale University Press.

Gaultieri, S. 2001. "Becoming 'White': Race, Religion and the Foundations of Syrian/Lebanese Ethnicity in the United States." *Journal of American Ethnic History* 20(4):29–58.

Haddad Y. Y. and J. I. Smith. 1996. Islamic values among American Muslims. In *Family and Gender among American Muslims* edited by B. C. Aswad and B. Bilge (pp. 19–40). Philadelphia: Temple University Press.

Hitti, Philip. 1924. *The Syrians in America.* New York: George Doran.

Jamal, A. & Naber, N. (2007) *From Invisible Citizens to Visible Subjects: Arab Americans and Race Before and After 9–11.* Syracuse University Press.

Kayal, Philip, editor. 1995. The *Coming of the Arabic Speaking People to the United States* (Adele Younis). New York. Center for Migration Studies.

Kayal, Philip and Joseph Kayal. 1975. *The Syrian-Lebanese in America: A Study in Religion and Assimilation.* Boston: C. K. Hall and Co.

McCarus. Ernest. 1994. *The Development of Arab-American Identity.* Ann Arbor: University of Michigan Press.

Naff, Alixa. 1985. *Becoming American; The Early Arab Immigrant Experience.* Carbondale, Ill: South Illinois University Press.

Orfalea, G., 1988. *Before the Flames: A Quest for the History of Arab Americans* Austin: University of Texas Press.

Orfalea, Gregory. 2006. *The Arab Americans: A History.* Northampton: Olive Branch Press.

Pate, J'Nell. 2006. *From Syria to Seminole.* Lubbock, Texas: Texas Tech University Press.

Salibi, Kamal. 1988. *A House of Many Mansions.* University of California Press.

Said, Edward. 1978. *Orientalism.* New York: Vintage Books.

Sengstock, Mary. C. 1982. *Chaldean Americans: Changing Conceptions of Ethnic-Identity.* New York: Center for Migration Studies.

Shaheen, Jack. 2001. *Reel Bad Arabs: How Hollywood Vilifies a People.* Olive Branch Press: Northampton.

Sherman, William C., Paul Whitney, John Guerrero. *Prairie Peddlers: The Syrian-Lebanese in North Dakato.* Bismark: University of North Dakota Press.

Stockton, R. 1994. Ethnic archetypes and the Arab image. In E. McCarus (ed.) *The Development of Arab-American Identity.* (pp. 119–154) Ann Arbor: University of Michigan Press.

Suleiman, Michael, 2006. *Arab-American Experience in the United States and Canada: A Classified, Annotated Bibliography.* Ann Arbor: Pierian Press.

Suleiman. Michael, editor. 1999. *Arabs in America: Building a New Future.* Philadelphia: Temple University Press.

Waters, Mary C 1990. *Ethnic options: Choosing identities in America.* Berkeley, CA: University of California Press.

Critical Thinking

1. What does ethnogensis mean?
2. What is the central thrust of this historical account?
3. Does the name of an ethnic group really matter?

From *National Center for Urban Ethnic Affairs,* Occasional Papers, June 2010, pp. 1–34. Copyright © 2010 by National Center for Urban Ethnic Affairs. Reprinted by permission.

Neither Natural Allies Nor Irreconcilable Foes

Alliance Building Efforts between African Americans and Immigrants

ANDREW GRANT-THOMAS, YUSUF SARFATI, AND CHERYL STAATS

African American – immigrant relations have been under increased scrutiny by a range of stakeholders, including researchers, community organizers, policy makers, and philanthropic leaders. From gang violence to political representation, from labor concerns to negative stereotypes, black Americans and immigrants face a variety of challenges. In some communities, in certain arenas, each group regards the other as a rival. A pervasive media storyline that underscores instances of conflict while all but ignoring signs of cooperation only exacerbates the difficulties. Nevertheless, opportunities to unite are present, and some community organizers are working actively, and successfully, to form strong alliances between the groups. In this article, we briefly outline some of the key challenges, opportunities, and strategies that define these alliances.

Numerous barriers confront those who try to forge constructive relationships between African American and immigrant communities. Structural challenges include the socioeconomic marginalization that marks many African American and immigrant communities and often leads members of each group to live in close proximity to each other, sometimes provoking tensions over the allocation of limited resources. Whether at the federal, state, or local government level, or at the community level, most immigrants receive little help with integrating socially, economically, or politically into their new communities. Conversely, the members of receiving communities typically receive little help anticipating or accommodating the community changes that often accompany the new arrivals, creating fertile ground for inter-group friction. These strains are compounded by the unfavorable perceptions that African Americans and immigrants too often harbor about each other, the existence of an anti-immigrant wedge movement, and the prevalence of a conflict narrative in the mainstream media that encourages a zero-sum mentality among both groups.

These and other significant challenges notwithstanding, opportunities to unite and to achieve important relationship-building and policy successes exist. A great many African Americans and immigrants share the need for education reform in low-opportunity neighborhoods, for better workplace safety measures and wage reforms, for an end to racial profiling practices, and so on. Many progressives regard the two communities as core constituents within any viable, broad-based movement for expanded social justice in the United States. Current alliance-building efforts may yet prove to be the seedbed for such a movement.

From our conversations with dozens of organizers representing a wide range of social justice organizations and alliances, we identified a set of approaches based on alternative logics around which African American-immigrant alliances are formed: *intercultural relationship-building, issue-based organizing,* and *workplace-based organizing.* These three do not exhaust the range of alliance-building efforts in the field; nor are they mutually exclusive.

Community organizers who espouse an intercultural relationship-building approach aspire to build strong multicultural communities. For them, establishing healthy relationships among people of color is an important value in itself. Insofar as relationship-building reshapes identities and interests, it is also seen as a prerequisite for effective issue campaigns. These organizers suggest that interpersonal trust between the communities needs to be established first, and can be done only by addressing commonly held misconceptions through the deliberate re-education of each community. Without the trust born of solid relationships, racial and xenophobic tensions invariably emerge, and partnership development becomes episodic at best. Re-education measures can range from preparing simple cultural exchange events to engaging in specialized curriculums and trainings.

While acknowledging the importance of relationship building, issue-based organizers argue that the best way to build solidarity across lines of race, ethnicity, and nativity is through appeals to shared "bread and butter" interests. Trust develops most surely as a byproduct of common struggle, preferably one that yields tangible successes. In contrast, these organizers claim that inter-group relationship challenges, as such, provide uncertain motivation for partnerships, especially among poor and working-class people likely to have more pressing concerns. "Issue-first" alliances are typically formed between organizations, rather than within particular organizations.

Finally, in some sectors of the economy, especially in low-paying jobs, African Americans and immigrants work side by side, making workplaces the frontlines of negotiations and *de facto* solidarity between the groups. These sectors include construction work, the hotel industry, restaurants, and the meat-packing industry. Some workplaces are home to initiatives that operate in the absence of formal coalitions. Unlike initiatives shaped by the first two approaches, these initiatives mobilize constituents not around their identities as "African Americans," "immigrants," or people of color, but around their common identity as workers. In other words, the goal of the organization is not to support immigrant or African American issues, as such, but to promote worker issues. The goal is presented in a color-blind manner, and the organizers try to emphasize the salience of associational rather than communal identities.

No matter which strategy or combination of strategies community organizers use, ongoing efforts and existing opportunities for further collaboration offer grounds for hope about the future of African American – immigrant alliance building work. Creating alliances that endure and prosper is a challenging task, but the potential benefits make such efforts worthwhile. Cooperation between African Americans and immigrants in the United States is crucially important for creating an inclusive pluralistic democracy in which people of different races and cultures thrive by recognizing both their differences and similarities and working for common goals.

Critical Thinking

1. What are the reasons for friction between African Americans and immigrants?

2. What can be done to alleviate misunderstandings between African Americans and recent immigrants?

From *Kirwan Institute Update*, Spring 2008. Copyright © 2008 by Kirwan Institute for the Study of Race and Ethnicity. Reprinted by permission.

UNIT 9

Horizons in Pluralism

Unit Selections

37. **Bigots I Have Loved,** Mark Phillips
38. **From Every End of This Earth,** Steven V. Roberts

Learning Objectives

- Is ethnic group conflict the cause of political violence, or do manipulative, politically ambitious persons arouse ethnic suspicions to divide and conquer opponents?

- What signs have you seen of an increase in racist, anti-Semitic, anti-Muslim and anti-Arab, anti-immigrant, and anti-minority group acts that recent studies apparently confirm?

- What sources of information about Islam shape your understanding of this creed? Can one expect that Islam will be influenced by the American experience of assimilation and acculturation in ways that parallel the transformations of Judaism and Catholicism in America?

- What sources of information about the relationship between religion and science and between religions and culture shape our understanding of these approaches to the question on unity and diversity of the human condition?

- The intersection of scientific claims and culture has entered a new phase in the era of genetic mapping. What implications and imperatives does this debate have for race and ethnic relations? For public policy? For the allocation of medical resources and research agendas?

- Explain how dialogue among conflicting parties about dilemmas that are essential to technological and economic change can enable us to share and shape the burden of social change?

Student Website

www.mhhe.com/cls

Internet References

CNN Election Headquarters
http://edition.cnn.com/ELECTION/2010/results/main.results

President-Elect Obama's Website
http://change.gov

The words race, religion, and ethnicity have been used to describe a wide and sometimes ill-defined and contradictory set of experiences and identities. The apparent confusion arises because race and ethnicity are contextual—more a social process than a primordial and fixed given of biology and origin. Their meanings change in each place with time and circumstances for each group. The discussion of race, religion, and ethnicity that is included in the selections found in this unit indicates methodological approaches and interpretive categories that frame the current ferment in this field at the practical and theoretic levels. However, one finding is beyond doubt. Patterns of intersection of religion, race, and ethnicity are definitely specific to the locations and regimes within which they are embedded. Moreover, even the claims and efficacy of scientific knowledge and applications appear to be influenced by their historically and most significantly by the privileging of certain ways and languages of knowing within respective power-fields established and maintained by regimes. In certain respects, race and ethnicity are both indigenous and transplanted social inventions that have become rooted in the social experience and fostered by regime development. Articles in this section invite us to pursue the search for fresh insight into and consciousness of the social and symbolic formation of cultures. The debate regarding the relationship of various ways of knowing invites us to search for understanding and particular skills, competencies, and rules for dialogue among religious, ethnic, and political traditions. Support of civilization and peaceful means of resolving differences are clearly imperative. While the situation of these issues is worldwide, understanding and action in this arena is nearly always local and specific. The American Constitution initiated and institutionalized the divisive tradition of exclusionary race relations. For generations, slaves and their descendants were not considered, nor legally warranted rights, as persons. American legal and political entities supported a race-conscious culture that sustained its economy. This fundamental pattern continues even as a more complex web of cultures and economic development changed the social composition of the population. Aided by an open immigration policy that sought the benefits of large-scale population growth, industrialization, and urbanization, America began to transform itself. The transformation yielded American ethnicities and a new free-associational form of religiosity— a traditional alien to the dominant Protestant churches. When Catholicism and Judaism become socially effective and entered the power field new claims were woven into the deep structures of a changing cultural and social fabric.

The theory and practice of developing a new political culture and an inclusive constitutional tradition drew its energy and inspiration from a wellspring of hope articulated in American aspiration to—liberty and justice for all—manifested in the Declaration of Independence. In the United States, after nearly a century of social and regime construction and reconstruction, our understanding of pluralism, at best, yields the following findings: Ethnicity is one of the modern identities developed by the largely peasant migrants who poured into the United States during the last two centuries. Religion and ethnicity are interwoven in complex, but discernible ways. Christians and Jews constitute

© Photograph by Jan Smith.

the overwhelming majority of the American immigrant populations. Since 1965, Islamic immigrants have joined a rather small number of earlier Muslim communities. Such generic designations of these three Abrahamic faiths seem clear. The facts of significant theological and institutional differences within each of these religious traditions are frequently diminished, blurred, and even conflated. Integrating social processes generated a socially and politically dominant rhetoric that would define the evolution of America from a Protestant country to one that accepted the combined label of Protestant–Catholic–Jewish by the mid-1950s. By the mid-1960s, another set of public symbols would challenge America's self-definition when Patrick Moynihan and Nathan Glazer's study, Beyond the Melting Pot, invited a closer analysis of persistent diversity that was personally and politically relevant. The emergence of the ethnic and religious factors within scholarly discourse is not unrelated to the emergence of immigrants and children of immigrants into academia. Their engagement in the social production of knowledge, the widening of horizons and interpretations of reality, and the attendant paradigm shift mark an important moment of political development. For most immigrants, their ethnicity became a cultural modality that emerged as they became Americans and their religious faith and institutions were influenced by the new dynamics of American development. This new notion of peoplehood replaced loyalty to village or region as the reference point around which they organized their sense of life, located the place of their family in the moral and physical universe, and shaped their community. The enormity of the educational effort that is required as we attempt to move beyond the ethnocentrism and racism that bred hatred and destructive relationships between persons and communities is revealed in a number of ways. Philosophic and theological reflection on the foundations of anthropological and epistemological issues associated with explaining human variety and the characteristics of human consciousness is important in this time of national and world crisis. It is precisely at this intersection of social philosophy and science and its grappling with evil uses of power that the crucial breakthroughs in understanding are likely to appear.

The historic role that voluntary groups have played in the reduction of bias and bigotry also needs to be acknowledged and revitalized. Voluntary associations can take part in a host of state and local initiatives to improve intergroup relations. Schools and parents can help children understand commonalities and differences among ethnic traditions and groups. The experiences of families and a formal pedagogy rooted in accurate and locally relevant resources are essential building blocks for understanding diversity. Group relations are manifested on campuses, in neighborhoods, in the workplace, in access to and competition for public services, and in the marketplaces. In many situations, relationships are driven by general prejudice and specific exclusionary acts and omissions ranging from hateful speech, to physical violence, to profiling and neglectful ignorance. Concrete strategies for improving this situation call upon both the public and the private sectors in areas of relief, institution building, education, employment, and training. The emergence of new findings and scholarly contentions in genetics and its applications to medicine are intersecting race, ethnicity, and religion. The outcome of this great debate may establish new horizons for which our understanding of the human condition in an era of science and human rights may enable us to perceive the wonders of pluralism with deepened insight and respect for

its awesome complexity and profound unity. The history of immigration and ethnic group diversity is embedded in the history of America from its earliest times, as noted in the previous units the process of the peopling of this continent. More recent social historical facts have often been ignored or forgotten in contemporary debates about our tradition of being an immigrant-receiving continent.

From the 1850s to the 1870s, immigrants from Britain and northern Europe settled in America. To these European and perhaps to some Asian immigrants in the American West, America represented freedom to enter the economic struggle without constraints of state- and status-bound societies whose limits could not be overcome except through emigration. Yet this historical pathway to liberty, justice, and opportunity came to be perceived as a "tarnished door" when the deep impulses of exclusion and exclusivity came to the fore. The victims were aliens who, ironically, achieved the American promise but were denied the reward of acceptance and incorporation into the very culture they helped to fashion. The following articles describe the immigrant experience and raise once again the issues that every large-scale multiethnic regime must address: How can unity and diversity be channeled into political, economic, and cultural well being? What are the legitimate limits and strengths of ethnic groups in the expression of policy regarding countries toward which some affinity may be attributed?

Bigots I Have Loved

Mark Phillips

Promising that his all-white team alone was worthy of the scoreboard, his looming shrine, he thundered over the grunts and snarls of the boys scrimmaging on each end of the dry field. His players called him Boomer. The varsity was preparing to play a team with a black halfback, and I knew he had designated one of his runners to play the sacrificial role of the talented enemy halfback. From where I practiced with the junior varsity, I felt his booms: "Get the spook. Get that spook."

None of us boys walked off the field in protest of the metaphorical lynching. I admit this with difficulty, but we loved the racist coach, who is now honored on the wall of fame in the football stadium at my old high school. He was the only one of my high school teachers to contact me after my father died during my freshman year of college. He drove to my home, sat with my family at the kitchen table and shared gently his sympathy.

Perhaps it's insensitive of me to bring up my late coach in this way after so many years. When you've loved as many bigots as I have, knowing how to remember them can be as hard as that dusty, cracked ground upon which I felt the words "get that spook." And perhaps Faulkner was mistaken and the past really is past—bigotry little more than a rusty whip handle unearthed at the site of a Mississippi plantation. I've heard that our current president is irrefutable evidence that bigotry in the United States is now a group of feeble old men peering watery-eyed through holes in tattered white sheets; that fear of racism is as irrational as fear of ghosts.

Perhaps I should let bygones be bygones.

A Slur for a Slur

On my way home from work on election day, I stopped for a beer. The Irish bartender glanced at my Obama shirt and told a joke to the guy on the stool next to me. "Did you hear that Obama is ahead?"

"No. Is he?"

"Yes—but that will change when the white people get off work and vote."

I asked the same guy, "Do you know if they serve seven-course Irish dinners here?"

"Whaddya mean?"

"You know, a six-pack and a potato."

My wife is mostly Irish and I'm partly, but my retort by slur was inexcusable, and, anyhow, you could say that my spirit of reconciliation was found wanting. I knew that stupid hate might sputter like old grease on the grill as soon as my plug for Obama was noticed in that establishment where a patron can scribble whatever he desires on a dollar bill before the bartender tacks it to the wall above the bottles of whiskey. Where the father of our nation gushes, "I like Boobies!"

Since election day, I've bought beer at the business where I heard the racist joke, and it wouldn't be impolite of you to ask why. In my neck of the woods, that bar is one of the few with Guinness on tap, and I am a weak man, but the answer is also that some of my fellow Americans drink elbow to elbow there and—for me—climbing up on one of those stools can be like going home again.

The first bigoted joke I heard as a child was told by a friend who had heard it from his father. In my backyard, my innocent friend asked, "What did God say when he made the second n———?" I still hear the birdy, quavering voice of my friend—who walked to church with me on Sunday mornings—as he finishes the joke by assuming the Word of God. In the punch line, God does not remind us that He created all people in His image or demand an end to lynching and holocausts and laughter at hatred. Instead—on the green grass of my childhood—He says, "Oops, burnt another one."

Although I've made myself forget, surely I laughed. I was already fluent in the tongues of bigotry, though I never used the word dago in the presence of my best friend, who was Italian.

Fear and Loathing

After he led us in prayer, thanking Our Father for supper, my own father made occasional ethnic slurs while telling us about his day at the power plant or commenting on some news he'd heard on the radio while driving home to our working-class New York town, where eventually Timothy McVeigh would grow up. Usually the slurs were spoken as if he were reporting the weather, but he was not so casual when race riots erupted in nearby Buffalo. He feared that the violence would spread to Pendleton, home to merely a few black families.

We once ventured into the inner city to cheer the Buffalo Bills, the blue-collar defending champs of the upstart American Football League. My father parked the car on the small, yellowed yard of a house on mostly boarded-up Jefferson Avenue, paid the owner a two-dollar fee, and marched us to the game among an influx watched—predatorily, I imagined—by blacks sitting on front steps and porches, whole families bemused at the sight of so many whites staring straight ahead with silly terror in their eyes as they hurried up the avenue of false promises.

Ticket scalpers and hot dog vendors hawked at busy intersections, and when we reached crumbling War Memorial Stadium—or the Old Rockpile, as it was called in western New York—my father said, for the second time that afternoon, "We'll be lucky if our car isn't stripped when we get back."

Somehow my father and the rest of us whites worrying toward the stadium had come to the backward conclusion that blacks had a history of harming whites. Dad and I had given little thought to what it felt like for the two blacks who attended my school or the few who labored at the power plant, but now we feared being in the minority. Inside the decaying but thick walls of the stadium, things would be made right again: the coaches and quarterbacks and security guards would be white like most of the fans.

Even a boy could sense that football was the way America worked: a hierarchy of owner and directors and coaches and stars right on down to the wounded, grunting and anonymous offensive linemen on whose wide shoulder pads every touchdown rested. Yet our nation had two working classes: one inside and one outside the walls.

Anti-Catholic

When he emigrated from the North of Ireland to the United States, my paternal great-grandfather carried the heirloom of anti-Catholic bigotry. Three generations of Phillipses lived in an Irish neighborhood of South Buffalo, and on their way home from public school my father and uncles and other Protestant boys often fought Catholic boys who were on their way home from parochial school.

My grandfather referred to Catholics as cat-lickers, though he married one who agreed to give up her faith. Before I met the woman I would marry, who has kept her faith, I suspected that Catholics had tails and horns—a fear she has mostly dispelled.

Until my grandfather took a new job in the power plant he had helped build, all of the Phillips men were disposable iron workers. In three separate accidents, my great-grandfather and two of his sons died on construction jobs. My grandfather broke two ribs and bruised a lung in another.

My father inhaled welding fumes all day in a plant so polluted with coal dust and fly ash that if he wore a white shirt, no matter how long he had scrubbed his skin after work, the cloth would gray as he perspired. My maternal grandfather broke a leg on a road construction job; two other kin survived crushing injuries on logging jobs; another lost several fingers in a machine shop. Nearly every iron worker in the family had a damaged back before he reached retirement age, and they were among the lucky ones. When their bodies were broken or lifeless, industry purchased new bodies. Helplessly, my father knew this. On a sidewalk in a nearby town we once passed a stranger in a grandiose suit, glittering watch, gleaming shoes; my father spit on the concrete and muttered, "You son of a bitch."

My father, his killed grandfather, and two killed uncles did put food on the table while they lived. They could have been limited to starvation wages or sent to the endless unemployment line; and weren't they forever reminded? Aren't we all? On some level they must have sensed that the privileged had twisted the word black into a definition for those who are perceived as lower class in America—and that their own skin pigment was no guarantee that they would be perceived as white.

In his book *How the Irish Became White,* historian Noel Ignatiev could be referring to my kin when he notes of his depiction of oppressed eighteenth and nineteenth century Irish-Americans, "I hope I have shown that they were as radical in spirit as anyone in their circumstances might be, but that their radical impulses were betrayed by their decision to sign aboard the hunt for the white whale," which, he adds, "in the end did not fetch them much in our Nantucket market."

During the hike to the Old Rockpile, Dad bought us lunch at a hamburger stand. On the sidewalk, he counted his change and realized that the black cashier had accidentally handed him a 20-dollar bill rather than a five; he got back in line, corrected the mistake, and explained to me, "They would have taken it out of her pay." It was a warm autumn day, and as usual he was wearing a dark shirt that hid the coal dust, the blackness flushing from his pores as he perspired.

Still White

I never heard my mother use the racial epithets that were second nature to other adults in my family and neighborhood. I like to think she was too bright to be bigoted. She had graduated first in her high school class but didn't attend college, as she explained it to me when I was a teenager, "because back then college was just for rich girls who wanted to find richer husbands."

She grew up with American Indians. Her father's small, swampy farm edged within a half mile of the Tonawanda Indian Reservation, where, until he died in his 80s, one of her uncles lived with an Indian woman in a cabin with no toilet. My mother's younger sister married a man from the reservation, and although my grandparents loved their half-Indian grandchildren, their complaints about "lazy Indians" were sometimes slung at their gainfully employed son-in-law, and they were sure that "them Indians must have took it" whenever a possession disappeared from the farm. Until my grandfather landed a job on a state road crew when he was in his 40s, they were poor, but my grandparents could always visit the reservation to witness destitute poverty, to be assured that though they couldn't afford to buy more than three pairs of underwear for each of their daughters, they were still white.

I was spending a weekend on the farm when the brother of my grandmother's closest friend killed himself on the reservation. Charlie Moses lived with his sister, who telephoned my grandmother minutes after the rifle blast. Over the phone, my grandmother asked Arlene, "Was he drunk?" I begged them to take me along, but my grandparents ordered me to stay behind as they hurried out to their old American Motors sedan.

Early the next morning they returned to the reservation to clean Arlene's parlor, and I went fishing in the muddy creek that shaped the sinuous east and north boundaries of the farm. I returned to the yard hours later dragging a stringer of gasping and flopping bullheads and rock bass, tormented by a cloud of mosquitoes, and encountered my grandmother kneeling on the grass with her hands plunged in a pail of soapy, pink water. I asked what she was doing, and she replied, "Trying to get brains off these curtains." She held up a curtain and said, "Who ever would have thought Charlie Moses had so much brains?"

Civil Rights

We danced to James Brown and Aretha Franklin, and perhaps the sensual celebration awakened us to the images and calls of truth arisen. By then it was 1970 and some of us paid attention when our American history teacher taught about slavery, the KKK and racial segregation, and he asked, "How come you don't see anyone except whites in this class?"

Some of us were appalled by the old news footage of police assaulting peaceful civil-rights protesters with truncheons, torrents of water, snarling dogs, and Southern law, and were stirred by the brave, truthful poetry of Reverend King, though by then he had been assassinated by a white supremacist.

When the school board banned Eldridge Cleaver's *Soul on Ice* from the library, a small group of us protested, not because we admired the author's murderous, misogynistic rage but because we possessed some vague understanding that his eloquence was an incantation of Emerson's self-reliance come home to roost. We argued that the school was supposed to be educating us, and Cleaver was an American reality.

Of course, none of us walked off the football field: other players might have been granted our positions.

Family Debates

Lincoln and Douglas we weren't, but my father and I had a series of debates about racial issues. At first we disagreed about the banning of *Soul on Ice,* but as in all serious discussions involving race in America, we soon found it necessary to abolish boundaries and time—to visit George Wallace as well as Eldridge Cleaver, South Boston as well as Birmingham, and Africa as well as Harlem.

He never argued overtly that blacks were genetically inferior, but my father was opposed to court-ordered integration of schools and affirmative action and believed that blacks had accumulated more rights and opportunities than had whites. I was 17. My mother, who knew her socially defined and confined place, listened in silence to our debates, which began during supper and lasted for hours.

My father thought about our disagreements while at work and I at school, and each of us charged into the new evening armed with arguments we believed to be fresh and potent. My father actually asked a black worker at the power plant what he thought about the Black Panthers and reported triumphantly, "He told me they're all crazy."

We debated for three or four evenings in a row and then, weary from arguments that seemed to be going nowhere except into a recycling bin, gave it a rest. We mostly avoided each other until he came to me after two days of quiet and said, "You know, all that black and white stuff we talked about, some of it you were right. You still got a lot to learn in life, but some of it you were right."

I nodded and looked away, embarrassed and proud like a son who has realized that for once his father has not let him win at basketball, that he has actually beaten his flawed hero. Which only goes to show that my father was right about one thing: even though I never again heard him utter a racial epithet, I still had a lot to learn about hate and love.

Hiding

He was slowly dying. Men seldom develop cancer of the prostate until at least age 50, but some studies have reported that welders have an earlier and higher incidence. He had been diagnosed with prostate cancer at age 40, and because it had already spread into his bones where it was inoperable, a surgeon had removed my father's testicles to deprive the tumors of some of their hormonal fuel.

He continued to limp into the power plant to support his family. On the days when he was in too much pain to work despite the drugs, his fellow welders did his jobs and hid him in a storage room so the big bosses wouldn't know to fire him. He eventually found it impossible to climb the stairs to the second-floor time clock and took an early retirement, which lasted several months.

He still was unable to wear a white shirt.

Critical Thinking

1. What is bigotry?

2. What is the generational factor in this account of ethnic and racial understandings?

3. Is life review of attitudes and behavior related to self understanding and race and ethnic relations a source and foundation for the discovery of identity in a pluralistic society?

From Every End of This Earth

Steven V. Roberts

Introduction

As I listened to Barack Obama's inaugural address, I heard him say, "We are a nation of Christians and Muslims, Jews and Hindus, and nonbelievers. We are shaped by every language and culture, drawn from every end of this earth." I knew then that I had a title for this book. I liked the lilt of his language, but more than that, I shared his sense of what makes America great. This country's genius flows from its diversity. "We know," said the new president, "that our patchwork heritage is a strength, not a weakness." Or as Eddie Kamara Stanley of Sierra Leone puts it, "It's the nation of nations, you can see every nation in America." But diversity only describes color, not character; ethnicity, not ingenuity. Over many generations, the immigrants who chose to come here, and were strong enough to complete the journey, were among the most ambitious, the most determined, the most resilient adventurers the Old World had to offer. "The greatness of our nation . . . must be earned," said the new president, and building that greatness has never been "for the fainthearted." Rather, he added, "it has been the risk-takers, the doers, the makers of things" who have led the way. "For us they packed up their few worldly possessions and traveled across oceans in search of a new life." The "fainthearted" stayed behind.

This book is about the doers, the risk-takers, the makers of things that Obama describes. The president knows them well because his own father was an immigrant from Kenya, and his stepfather was from Indonesia. I know them well, too. All four of my grandparents came from the "Pale of Settlement," areas on the western edge of the Russian empire where Jews were allowed to live in the nineteenth century. They were born between 1881 and 1892, and while they all described themselves as Russian, borders have shifted so often since then that their hometowns today are in three different countries: Poland, Belarus, and Lithuania. Both of my grandfathers were carpenters, "makers of things," who settled in Bayonne, New Jersey. One lived with us, in a house he had built himself, while my other grandparents were three blocks away. I thought that everybody grew up that way, and indeed, most of my friends did. Our grandparents all had accents and our babysitters all were related. If our families weren't Russian or Polish, they were Irish or Italian, with an occasional Czech or Ukrainian or Slovak thrown in. I grew up thinking WASPs were a tiny minority group.

Most of our relatives had fled a life of poverty or persecution in the Old Country and would not talk about the past; they wanted to leave all that behind and become American. But I was lucky. My Grandpa Abe used to tell me tales of his youth in Bialystok, a town

that achieved a fleeting notoriety when Mel Brooks used the name "Max Bialystok" for the main character in his play *The Producers.* In fact Abe, like many immigrants, moved more than once, and spent his teenage years as a Zionist pioneer in Palestine, working on the first roads ever built in what is now Tel Aviv. He arrived in America on April 7, 1914, aboard a ship called the *George Washington,* which sailed from Bremen, a port on the North Sea. The manifest spells both of his names wrong ("Awram Rogowski" instead of "Avram Rogowsky") and persistent mistakes like that have hampered the search for my family's records. On her birth certificate, my mother is listed as "Dora Schaenbein," while in fact her name was Dorothy Schanbam. At her ninetieth birthday party I took note of that discrepancy and joked that perhaps we were celebrating the wrong woman.

This background left me with a lifelong interest in ethnicity and immigration. My previous book, *My Fathers' Houses,* chronicled my family's arrival in the New World and the lives we made here. This book is really an update, the stories of thirteen families who are living the journey today that Grandpa Abe and my other ancestors made almost one hundred years ago. In a sense I have been working on this volume for my entire writing life. As a teenager, I had an after-school job on the *Bayonne Times,* the local daily, and one of my first assignments was to write about an émigré artist who was decorating the walls of the Police Athletic League building, a dilapidated old place where I played basketball. When I eventually became a reporter on the city staff of the *New York Times* in 1965, I convinced the editors to let me do a series about the ethnic neighborhoods of New York. One favorite was Arthur Avenue, an old Italian section near the Bronx Zoo, and I remember coming back from that assignment with some great anecdotes, and a box of delicious cannolis from a local bakery. On weekends my wife and I occasionally roamed the Lower East Side, the district where many Eastern European Jews first settled in America. One favorite destination was Katz's deli on Houston Street, started by Russian immigrants in 1888 and famous for its slogan, "Send a salami to your boy in the army!"

My next assignment for the *Times* took us to Los Angeles in 1969, and while most reporters from eastern news outlets focused on the glamorous side of California, I was always more interested in the Armenians of Glendale than in the actresses of Hollywood. I wrote about farm towns like Kerman, where the Portuguese–American home was the center of social life. Or villages like Solvang, which still celebrates its Danish heritage. And I profiled old mining camps—including one actually named Chinese Camp—where you could still sense the spirit of the immigrant laborers who built those historic settlements. I spent a lot of time in the Central Valley writing about Cesar Chavez and the United Farm Workers union, and I remember him describing how the grape growers were still defined by powerful ethnic loyalties. In fact, Chavez (a Mexican–American himself) told me he had to conduct three separate negotiations with the Armenian, Italian, and Yugoslav farmers. One man who could occasionally bridge those rivalries was Tony Coelho, a Portuguese–American congressman who once invited me to a lunch he held regularly at a Basque restaurant in his hometown of Fresno. For one meal, at least, the warring tribes of the valley would sit side by side at long family-style tables, but Coelho's peacemaking had limits. When he tried to join the Hispanic caucus on Capitol Hill by invoking his Iberian heritage he was flatly rejected.

When I moved to Europe for the *Times* in 1974 and settled in Athens, I got to write about immigration from a different perspective. Many Greeks were deeply anti-American, because they thought Washington had sided with Turkey in their endless dispute over Cyprus. But their animosity was tempered by the fact that they all had cousins in Queens or Chicago. I often said that if you waded into a protest demonstration in front of the American embassy and announced that you were awarding six scholarships to Michigan State, the protesters would immediately drop their signs and sign their names. On one reporting trip to southern Greece I interviewed Stavroula and Paraskevas Kourtsounis, whose three children had all moved to Long Island. Their home village of Skoura was dying; all the young people had left. But like many immigrants, they still regularly sent back cash from America. One villager described the place as "an old-age home with green dollars," and the stores in Sparta, the biggest town near Skoura, took dollars as readily as drachmas. Remittances were a sturdy pillar of the Greek economy and in every village it was common to see a black-clad *yaya,* or grandmother, return from the post office, furtively open an envelope, and slip a wad of greenbacks into her clothing. The American embassy told me that nineteen thousand recipients of Social Security payments had retired to Greece, which was a whole lot cheaper than Greenwich or Greenpoint. So many transplants had settled around Sparta that when their monthly checks arrived in the mail, the banks sent mobile vans to the surrounding villages to cash them. When I tracked down the Kourtsounis sons, Pete and Sam, to include them in this book, they graciously told me they had displayed my article about their parents on the wall of their diner for many years. Then Pete said a bit uncomfortably, "I'm surprised to hear from you. I thought you'd be . . . gone by now." I assured him that I'd been a *very* young man when I interviewed his parents.

I returned to America in 1977, just in time to cover the decision of many ethnic voters to abandon the Democrats and join the Republicans. These were my people. In Bayonne, hardly anybody had a last name with fewer than three syllables or that ended in a consonant (okay, so a few Ryans and Robertses were the exception). I had bowled at the Knights of Columbus hall and played on teams sponsored by the Elks Club and the VFW. And since many of my *Times* colleagues didn't know a kielbasa from a cauliflower, I became the paper's expert on these "Reagan Democrats." My assignment took me to Pittsburgh, where private delivery services, run out of storefronts on Butler Avenue, sent packages directly to relatives back in Poland; and to Charlestown, an Irish neighborhood of Boston once represented in Congress by Jack Kennedy, where voters told me that his brother Ted was too liberal to be

president. And I was in Milwaukee's Serb Hall (which still has a Friday-night fish fry) in the fall of 1980 when an overflow crowd went nuts for Ronald Reagan—and convinced me he would be the next president.

After Reagan won, I covered Congress for the next six years and learned how new ethnic groups were starting to rival the old Italian and Irish political machines. My brother Glenn worked for Norm Mineta, the son of Japanese immigrants and the first Asian–American to sit in Congress. (The adjoining district was represented by Leon Panetta, an Italian, and a lot of people got them confused. Mineta was frequently invited to address Italian organizations and was even named, as I recall, to at least one Italian hall of fame.) Norm had two constituencies: his voters back in San Jose, California, and Asians from all over the country who saw him as their hero and advocate. He worked this vein well, mining the Asian groups for campaign cash, but there was a problem. All of them—Chinese, Filipinos, Vietnamese, Koreans—were fiercely proud of their national cuisine and insisted on providing the food for the fund raisers. I realized that many ethnic congressmen served two constituencies, and to illustrate the point, I wrote a story about lawmakers of Lebanese ancestry. The list included both senators from South Dakota, Jim Abdnor and James Abourezk, and Representative Mary Rose Oakar of Ohio, the first Arab-American women to serve in Congress. But the most interesting case was George Mitchell, a senator from Maine. Orphaned at a young age, he was adopted by a Lebanese Christian family and learned some basic Arabic serving Mass in the town of Waterville. That linguistic ability should serve him well as President Obama's peace envoy to the Middle East.'

In 1997 I started teaching a course in feature writing at George Washington University, and I encouraged my students to write about their families. I wanted them engaged and energized by their material, and as I still tell them, your grandmother never says "no comment." What I didn't expect were the powerful and poignant stories they produced. They taught me that the immigrant experience is as vibrant today as it was when Avram Rogowsky set sail from Bremen in the spring of 1914. No one example, or even a half dozen, can capture the entirety of that experience, but I hope this book resembles the mosaics I used to see in the ruins of ancient Greece. Separtely, these thirteen families reflect fragments of line and color; fitted together, they complete a whole picture. In a few cases I've changed their names to protect their privacy, but in every other way these stories are as true as I can tell them.

Over the last hundred years, one diamension of the immigrant experience as never changed: it is one of the most challenging journeys any human being ever makes. The words of the Indian poet Rabindranath Tagore remain wise: "You can't cross the sea merely by standing and staring at the water." Bao and Tuyen Pham tried many times to escape from Vietnam, and once, drifting aimlessly on the open ocean, Tuyen thought she would have to slit her wrists and feed her blood to her children to keep them alive. When the Phams finally washed up on the shore of Thailand, Tuyen was pregnant with a daughter, who was then born in a refugee camp in the Philippines. They named her Thai Phi in honor of the two countries that gave them sanctuary before they moved to Pennsylvania. Eddie Stanley fled the African nation of Sierra Leone one step ahead of a rebel army that decapitated his father and seized his sister as a sex slave. His wife and two children spent more than two years in primitive refugee camps before he was able to bring them to America. Jose and Beti Reyes both entered this country illegally by sneaking across the border with Mexico. Both were arrested, thrown in jail, and deported to their native El Salvador. Both returned, evaded capture for years, and eventually became citizens. Immigration is not for the "fainthearted."

Some journeys, of course, were not so dramatic or dangerous. Asis Banerjie got on a plane in New Delhi and flew to Cleveland for graduate study at Case Western Reserve University. Pablo Romero traveled by bus from Mexico to California, where he picked lettuce under a program that legally imported farmworkers. But every immigrant faces the pain of dislocation, of missing home, of living in two worlds and never feeling completely comfortable in either one. Marie Aziz, a political refugee from Afghanistan, quotes these lines by the thirteenth-century poet Rumi, to describe her feelings toward her homeland:

> *Listen to the song of the reed,*
> *How it wails with the pain of separation:*
> *"Ever since I was taken from my reed bed*
> *My woeful song has caused men and women to weep.*
> *I seek out those whose hearts are torn by separation*
> *For only they understand the pain of this longing."*

Rumi's words are as true today as they were 800 years ago. Every immigrant is like a reed plucked from its bed. "That's why they say East and West never meet," says Tuyen Pham. "We stand in the middle. Sometimes, when I stay here, I feel homesick, but when I go back I don't feel I can stand to live there. I think Bao and I are the sacrifice generation. We don't belong to Vietnam, we belong to America, but inside there is something that is not really American." Ulla Kirschbaum Morris Carter says simply, "I have no roots" in America. "Here, I don't have anybody with whom I share a past. There's nobody who knows anything about me." Those who do share her past are back in Germany, where she was born, or in Cairo or Beirut or Athens, the cities where she lived most of her adult life. But they're not in the hills of northern California where she lives now. Malak Kemal came from Burma 25 years ago but still warns her three daughters to be careful. "My mother has this immigrant mentality—always be nice, don't say anything bad, because they can always send us back," says her youngest child, Deeba, who resides in Minnesota. "And I always say, 'You know, Mom, there's freedom of speech in America.' But she would say, 'No, no, we're immigrants.' "

For the "sacrifice generation," one goal keeps them going: making a better life for their children. And in many cases they have. Sarah and Nicholas Stern left Ukraine with $120 apiece; now they own an apartment overlooking Central Park and a condo in Florida. One son runs the family investment company; the other just graduated from law school. Haaroon Kemal never learned much English or made much money after he arrived from Burma, but his three daughters all finished college and two are now earning graduate degrees. Jose Reyes was an illiterate farm boy from El Salvador who opened a successful restaurant in Washington; his daughter, Ana, earned a degree in marketing and took over as the manager. Pablo Romero dropped out of school in rural Mexico at age 11; his daughter Kaija-Leena went to Harvard.

But being a child of immigrants can be a complicated way to grow up. Generation Next is often pulled between the past and the future, between celebrating their own tradition and creating their own identity. For years, Haaroon Kemal dreamed of escaping the tyranny of Burma and enjoying the freedom he would find in America. But once he got here, that very freedom became a threat—to the purity of his religion, the virtue of his daughters, the authority he commanded in the family. As a result he swaddled his girls in "bubble wrap" and banned them from talking to "anything that looked like a man." Indira Banerjie, who came to America as a teenager, dropped out of school and ended her hopes of becoming a doctor to enter an arranged marriage with her husband, Asis, a fellow Brahmin from the Indian state of West Bengal. Today she sends her two daughters mixed signals: Don't do what I did, get your degrees, become independent women. And by the way, marry a Brahmin from West Bengal. The bad news for Indira: her daughter Piyali has four tattoos. The good news: one depicts the sacred Hindu symbol Om. This constant search for a new identity is so common in the Indian community that there's a label for it: "ABCD," or "American-Born Confused *Desi*." (*Desi* is slang for a South Asian immigrant.)

Sometimes children from the same family take very different paths. Ana Reyes manages the family restaurant but her two brothers want to be rock stars. Tom and Maggie Chan's son Herbert went to college in northern California and joined the family business, importing fireworks from China; he lives downstairs from his parents and within walking distance of his grandmother in San Francisco's Chinatown. Arthur, Herb's younger brother, came east for college and redefined his "Chineseness" by identifying with all people of color and joining a Hispanic dance troupe. "That was all new to my parents, being Asian as part of a general minority, empathizing with the experience of black Americans or Latinos or other marginalized populations," he says. "It wasn't just about being Chinese." Today Arthur lives in New York and wants to be a filmmaker. These paths are not straight and these lives are not predictable. Haaroon Kemal did not want his daughters to live in the dorms at the University of California at Irvine because they would be tempted by too many outside influences. He was right in a way, but the influences they encountered in college made them more Eastern, not Western, more conservative, not liberal. All three became devout Muslims and adopted headscarves, a garment their own mother seldom wears.

All immigrants, of any era, are part of the "sacrifice generation." All understand Rumi's description of them as "those whose hearts are torn by separation." And all have children who must make their own way in the New World. It happened in my family and our name tells the tale. Grandpa Abe dropped the "sky" from Rogowsky at some point and I was born "Rogow," the same name my cousins on that side still have. As a young man my father had occasionally used the name Atlas to obscure his Jewish origins, and he changed our name to Roberts when I was two. My father always worried about his place in America, but I never have. That gave me the freedom to embrace my heritage, not evade it. The first time my parents ever attended a seder, a Jewish ritual celebrating Passover, it was at my house (and my Catholic wife cooked the dinner). In my heart I'm a Rogow, even a Rogowsky, not a Roberts. But I understand my father's impulse to blend into American culture. If Odysseus had landed in Troy, New York, instead of Troy, Turkey, he might have changed his name to Oates or O'Dwyer. Or perhaps Dr Sseus.

In other ways, however, the modern immigrant experience is very different from Grandpa Abe's day, starting with the countries that send people to America. Growing up, I never met families like the ones in this book—from Rwanda and Burma, El Salvador and Sierra Leone. But my hometown has changed dramatically. Bayonne's roster of churches now includes the Arabic Assembly of

God and El Ultimo Llamado, First Filipino Baptist and True Light Korean United Methodist. Our Lady of Assumption, once the center of the Italian community, now offers masses and pastoral counseling in Spanish. Arabic signs have sprouted in some neighborhoods. The recent winner of an essay contest about the Holocaust, sponsored by local Jewish organizations, is a Muslim from Pakistan who wears a headscarf. Many of the stores on Broadway once owned by Jews are now run by Indians. Today the people of Bayonne, like the rest of America, truly come "from every end of this earth," not just Krakow or Calabria or Killarney.

After Abe left Russia he was out of touch with his sister for 50 years. Mail was blocked, travel was impossible, phone calls were a fantasy. In the mid-1960s, he learned from a distant relative that he had a sister alive in Moscow, and they met once before he died. Today most immigrants are in constant contact with relatives back home. Asis Banerjie's mother still lives in the remote Bengali village where he grew up without electricity or indoor plumbing, but he talks to her frequently by cell phone. Eddie Stanley's mother, back in Sierra Leone, doesn't always recognize his voice on the phone, but when he sings her a song from his childhood, she knows who it is. Pablo Romero's daughters have spent summer vacations with his family in Mexico. Alice Ingabire-Schaut returned to Rwanda and videotaped the whole visit. I know of a Brazilian woman, in this country illegally, who got married in New Jersey. Since her family could not obtain visas to attend the wedding, her sister-in-law took digital photos and sent them during the ceremony to the bride's relatives, clustered around a laptop in Brazil. Kushi Gavrieli celebrated his son's bar mitzvah in his home village in Israel's Negev Desert (complete with musicians in Kurdish dress; most of the villagers originally immigrated to Israel from the Kurdish region of Iran). Pete Kourtsounis actually built a house in his home village in Grace and vacations there every summer, but he's too Americanized now to lapse back into his old life. So he imported most of the building materials from Home Depot, and he can no longer tolerate the Greek custom of late nights, heavy dinners, and skimpy breakfasts. When he's back, he hangs out with other *xeni,* or foreigners, not the locals. And a bunch of them have convinced a café owner to put omelets on the menu, so the *xeni* can enjoy a proper American breakfast.

The flow of information across borders is matched by a flow of capital. In Bayonne there might have been an Italian family that imported cheese or olive oil from the Old Country, but today many immigrants have established strong business and professional ties with their homelands. Marie Aziz returned to Afghanistan for the first time in 24 years, as head of an agricultural aid program financed by the American government. Asis and Indira Banerjie actually moved back to India for 14 years after he got his doctorate in America. Today they live in Ohio, but Asis owns factories making high-tech plastics in both countries and does business throughout Asia. Tom Chan's family fled China in terror after the communist revolution, but now he practically commutes from San Francisco to Liuyang, the center of China's fireworks industry. He's there so often the staff of the Grand Sun City Resort hotel saves him the same room, number 1211.

Many immigrants regularly send money to relatives back home and private remittances are by far the most important aid program in the world. Eddie Stanley can only afford a hundred dollars every few months, but to his mother in Sierra Leone, even that sum is "a very big thing." Alice Ingabire-Schaut works two jobs, selling shoes and cleaning churches, to support her mother and two

sisters back in Rwanda. But many others expect her help as well and sometimes the demands can be overwhelming. "Most people, from any third world country, believe that once you reach America, it's a safe heaven. An answer to everything," she says. "Some of those, who know I'm married to a white American, think I have all the potential to help them. They think I am rich and I have it all. They don't know that I have to work twice as hard to maintain my life and my marriage and also care for my family needs in Africa." This reaction back home—"They think I am rich"—is a common problem that can create enormous frustrations. Haaroon Kemal's daughter Ameera says her father suffered from a "pavement-of-gold imagination" back in Burma. "There was a gap between his expectations and what life became," adds her sister Deeba, and he was never able to help the rest of his family immigrate to America. "He still holds on to a lot of feelings of anger," says his daughter Khalida. But for those who have prospered in their new country, directing donations to charities back home can be a source of great pride and satisfaction. Jose Reyes eagerly displayed a blown-up copy of a check for $1,860, the amount he helped raise for a library back in El Salvador. Munr Kazmir, a wealthy doctor in New Jersey, has financed a school in Pakistan, based on a Western model, that is designed to counteract the influence of fundamentalist Islam.

This is a book of stories. It's not about policies or politics. But it comes out at a time when immigration is a hot topic and many dimensions of the problem are being debated in Washington and across the globe. For example:

- President George W. Bush tried and failed to enact legislation that would provide a path to citizenship for the 12 million undocumented workers now living in America. Republicans decided that fanning anti-immigrant feelings would energize their base and drive them to the polls, and many GOP candidates in 2008 ran strongly against "amnesty" for illegals. But Obama, the son of an immigrant, believes strongly in reform and in March 2009 he told a town hall meeting in California that "the American people . . . appreciate and believe in immigration." These newcomers, he said, "have become our neighbors. They've been our friends. They may have children who have become U.S. citizens." But he also warned that undocumented workers who have "broken the law" would not get a "free ride." They would have to pay fines, learn English, and "go to the back of the line" behind other applicants who have played by the rules. But "over a period of time," he said, illegal immigrants should have the chance to "earn [their] citizenship."
- Obama did deal with legal immigrants on a critical issue just days after taking office. He signed legislation reversing a policy of the Bush administration that forced newcomers to wait five years before receiving benefits under a program called S-CHIP, which provides health insurance for poor children. Access by immigrants—legal and illegal—to social services and aid programs will continue to be a major source of controversy.
- Early in 2009, the U.S. military began a new recruitment program: skilled immigrants living here under temporary visas could join the army and attain citizenship in as little as six months. Both sides will gain something. The military desperately needs recruits with medical and language skills, and that is what these immigrants possess. Nurses who

speak Pashto. Doctors fluent in Farsi. To say nothing of translators and intelligence officers who know Arabic—and look Arabic. Uncle Sam needs you! As Lieutenant General Benjamin C. Freakley, the army's top recruitment officer, told the *New York Times,* "The American Army finds itself in a lot of different countries where cultural awareness is crucial. There will be some very talented folks in this group." Talented folks who want to become American citizens but find their way blocked under current rules. Many who are here under work or student visas face years of delay before they can stabilize their status—if ever. Joining the army now enables them to cut through that red tape. Once the model is established it could be extended to other forms of public service. Perhaps a nurse from the Philippines could trade three years of service in a rural area for a quicker path to citizenship. Or a Spanish-speaking math teacher from Honduras could make a similar deal by working in the South Bronx.

- Under a program called H-1B visas, highly skilled and educated immigrants can get work permits if employers prove that comparable Americans are not available. The program has been very popular, but only 65,000 visas are available every year and they are swiftly snapped up by high-tech companies eager to tap this pool of innovation and entrepreneurship. Efforts to raise the cap to 150,000 visas have failed in recent years, blocked by pressure groups claiming that American workers are being displaced by foreigners. In the large stimulus bill signed by Obama in February 2009, financial companies receiving federal funds were actually restricted in their ability to hire holders of H-1B visas. *New York Times* columnist Tom Friedman called this amendment "S-T-U-P-I-D." Every study shows that immigrants make enormous contributions to economic growth and job creation. In a report for the Small Business Administration, University of California economist Robert W. Fairlie found that immigrants were 30 percent "more likely to start a business than are nonimmigrants." Analyzing statistics from the 2000 census, Fairlie found that newcomers represented 16.7 percent of all business owners and generated $67 billions in yearly income. Economists from Harvard and the University of Michigan reported a fascinating trend: when the number of H-1B visas goes up, applications for patents follow the same curve; when visas dwindle, so do patents. Vivek Wadhwa, an executive in residence at Duke University, argues that "more than half of Silicon Valley startups were founded by immigrants over the last decade." Shrinking the number of H-1B visas or restricting their use would be extremely damaging to the U.S. economy, he wrote in *BusinessWeek:* "We will scare away the world's best and brightest who have always flocked to our shores. But the next Silicon Valley won't be located in the U.S. It will likely be in Hyderabad or Shanghai." Not every newcomer will create Google or Intel. But without immigrant men, lawns would not get trimmed and buildings would not get built. And without the women, every hospital and nursing home in this country would collapse overnight. I know this firsthand. My mother's caretakers are all from the same Caribbean island and we refer to them as "Team Jamaica." My mother-in-law's aides are "Team Philippines."

These vital debates will continue. But they are background music for the great human drama of immigration. Every day, families "pack up their few worldly possessions and travel across oceans in search of a new life." Every day, parents join the "sacrifice generation" and place their hopes in their children. Every night, they nurse the "pain of separation," the feelings of longing and loneliness that come from leaving home. These immigrants are like the sun and the rain to America; they replenish our soil and our spirit. We are a better, brighter nation because they come and join us, every day, from every end of this earth.

Afterword

Immigrants have played a central role in the American experience since our earliest days. With the exception of a few purebred Native Americans, every single family in this country today can trace its origins to somewhere else. My wife Cokie's direct ancestor, William Claiborne, was born in the English country of Kent in 1600 and came to Virginia 21 years later as a land surveyor. He became a wealthy planter and trader, led an expedition up the Chesapeake Bay from Jamestown in 1631, and established an outpost on an island he named after his birthplace. Kent Island is the oldest white settlement in Maryland, the state I've called home for 32 years, and I have a grandson named Claiborne who was born 370 years after his forebear landed in America. After my own family arrived from Russia in the early twentieth century, they lived in a world populated almost entirely by fellow immigrants. I have the census forms from 1920, showing where my mother's parents and grandparents were living in Bayonne, New Jersey, barely a year after mom was born. There are a hundred residents listed on the two sheets. About half were born abroad; but when asked where their parents were from, exactly one said America. Most listed Russia, with a sprinkling of Italy, Ireland, Poland, France, Galicia, and Austria. Cokie and I are two ordinary Americans, children of immigrant families, the Claibornes of England and the Rogowskys of Russia. They just happened to make the journey almost 300 years apart.

Newcomers have always contributed heavily to the economic prosperity of America. Some, like William Claiborne, were well connected gentry who traded with their home country. Others, like my people, possessed some skills and education and created small businesses. My great-grandfather owned a dairy farm; one grandfather ran an amusement park, the other built the house I grew up in. Many immigrants were common laborers whose muscle power fueled the rise of an industrial state: Chinese coolies built the western railroads; Irish and German workers dug the Erie Canal in upstate New York; Italian miners quarried slate in eastern Pennsylvania and built the town of Roseto, named for their home village. Of the 146 workers who died in New York's infamous Triangle Shirtwaist Fire of 1911, most were young female immigrants from Italy and Eastern Europe. Today many newcomers still work with their hands, from the Vietnamese harvesting shrimp in Louisiana to the Latinos plucking poultry in North Carolina.

The rise of Hitler in the 1930s, however, sent a new sort of immigrant to these shores: highly educated intellectuals who profoundly influenced the nation's scientific and cultural life. Albert Einstein born in Germany and raised in Switzerland, is probably the best known. But the United States could not have developed a nuclear weapon without Enrico Fermi from Italy and Niels Bohr from Denmark. Hungary's John von Neumann created the modern computer at Princeton's Institute for Advanced Study, and his countryman Michael Curtiz directed the film *Casablanca* in Hollywood. (My son-in-law's grandfather, Franz Frank, escaped the Nazis and spent his career teaching at the University of Texas.) Their legacy lives on in Jerry Yang, a native of Taiwan who co-founded Yahoo!, and George Soros (Gyorgy Schwartz), the Hungarian-born financier and philanthropist. In 2007, two of the three winners of the Nobel Prize for Medicine were foreign-born scientists working in the United States: Mario Capecchi from Italy and Oliver Smithies from the United Kingdom. In 2008, three of the four highest-paid corporate executives were immigrants: Sanjay Jha of Motorola (India); Ray Irani of Occidental Petroleum (Lebanon), and Vikram Pandit of Citigroup (India).

American orchestras have often been led by immigrants, from Zubin Mehta (India) to Georg Solti (Hungary) and Daniel Barenboim (Argentina). Some of our finest buildings have been designed by I. M. Pei (China), Eero Saarinen (Finland), and Frank Gehry, born Ephraim Owen Goldberg in Toronto. Foreign-born writers and filmmakers have enriched the country's cultural life, often by using the immigrant experience as their subject. Junot Diaz, from the Dominican Republic, won the Pulitzer Prize in 2008 for his novel *The Brief Wondrous Life of Oscar Wao,* which is largely set in the Dominican community of Paterson, New Jersey. Jhumpa Lahiri, born in London of Indian parents, has written extensively about Bengali families transplanted to America. Her novel *The Namesake* was made into a movie by the Indian–American director Mira Nair. The story was adapted for the screen by Nair's longtime collaborator, Sooni Taraporevala, whose roots are in India's Parsi Zoroastrian community. The women met as undergraduates at Harvard. American athletics, like the arts, would be much poorer without immigrants. Canadians have long dominated the National Hockey League but today's top scorer, Alexander Ovechkin, is Russian. Pro basketball's brightest stars include Dirk Nowitzki (Germany), Tony Parker (France), Manu Ginobili (Argentina), and Yao Ming (China). My favorite baseball team, the Yankees, features pitchers Chien-Ming Wang (Taiwan) and Mariano Rivera (Panama), second baseman Robinson Cano (Dominican Republic), and outfielder Hideki Matsui (Japan).

And yet, throughout American history, immigrants have been demonized for despoiling or diluting the country's ethnic heritage. In 1753, Ben Franklin called the Germans flocking to Pennsylvania "generally the most stupid sort of their own nation" and warned; "They will soon outnumber us, [and we] will not, in my opinion, be able to preserve our language, and even our government will become precarious." In the mid-nineteenth century, the Irish were widely derided as an ignorant, criminal class. Signs sprouted up announcing, "No Irish Need Apply," and an editorial in the *Chicago Post* said, "Scratch a convict or a pauper and the chances are you tickle the skin of an Irish Catholic." The Know-Nothing Party prospered on an anti-immigrant platform, winning 25 percent of the presidential vote in 1856. Dark-skinned Italians were often considered nonwhite and subject to racial prejudice. In 1891, 11 Italians suspected of killing an Irish police chief were lynched in New Orleans. Cries of "hang the dagos" rumbled through the mob and one newspaper reported: "The little jail was crowded with Sicilians, whose low, receding foreheads, dark skin, repulsive countenances and slovenly attire proclaimed their brutal nature." In the 1920s, the trial and execution of anarchists Nicola Sacco and Bartolomeo Vanzetti, and the rise of Mafia dons like

Al Capone, fueled anti-Italian feelings. During World War II, the internment of more than one hundred thousand Japanese–Americans on the West Coast reflected a shameful spasm of racial intolerance. More than half of those interned were American citizens and my friend Norm Mineta, the first Japanese–American congressman, remembers being evacuated in his Cub Scout uniform. I've seldom encountered overt anti-Semitism but I knew certain clubs at Harvard in the 1960s were closed to me. I once dated a girl from a fancy town in Connecticut who took me to a dance at her country club and whispered, "You might be the first Jew who's ever been in here." I live near a neighborhood that was traditionally hostile to Jews and Catholics. But that changed long ago and my friend Bill Safire, the former *New York Times* columnist, lives in the area and hosts an annual party to break the Yom Kippur fast.

This fear of foreigners lurks just below the surface of American life and 9/11 ignited a wave of retaliation against Muslims. In Columbus, Ohio, a mosque was vandalized, and worshippers found water pouring through the ceiling and copies of the Koran ripped and scattered. In Renton, Washington, Karnail Singh, a Sikh from India who wears a turban (and is not a Muslim), was beaten in the lobby of a motel he owns by a man yelling, "Go back to Allah!" A former student of mine, a dark-skinned woman with an Arabic name, says she is stopped for special scrutiny every time she passes through an airport. That stigma was stoked during the 2008 campaign by an underground rumor that Barack Obama was really a Muslim. The falsehood surfaced when a woman named Gayle Quinnell told John McCain at a rally in Minnesota, "I don't trust Obama. I have read about him. He's an Arab." To his credit McCain protested, "No. Nope. No, ma'am. No, ma'am." But then he added, "He's a decent family man," as if no "Arab" could deserve that description. Even after his election, the Pew Research Center reported that only 48 percent of Americans could correctly identify the president as a Christian and 11 percent still thought he was a Muslim.

Latinos and Asians, the two fastest-growing immigrant groups, incite similar antiforeign phobias. One particularly outspoken fulminator, TV commentator Lou Dobbs, said on CNN that it was "crazy stuff" for President Obama to speak before the U.S. Hispanic Chamber of Commerce. That organization, he ranted, favored "Mexico's export of drugs and illegal aliens to the United States." On St. Patrick's Day he made fun of all "ethnic holidays" and said, in a mocking voice, that perhaps there should be an Asian holiday dedicated to "St. Jing-Tao Wow." Some Republicans have mimicked Dobbs and decided that fanning anti-immigrant fears would energize their conservative base, but others, like Bush adviser Karl Rove, call this attitude "suicidal" for their party. McCain won white men in 2008 by 57 to 41 percent, but they only accounted for 36 percent of the electorate. Obama won 2 out of 3 Latinos, and 3 out of 5 Asians, and those groups will continue to grow in both size and influence. "We're fundamentally staring down a demographic shift that we've never seen before in America," says Jon Huntsman Jr., the former Republican governor of Utah.

The 13 families in this book mirror that shift and make a simple point. The anti-immigrant voices that echo through this country's, history, from Ben Franklin to Lou Dobbs, have always been wrong and are wrong today. Barack Obama is absolutely right when he says, "our patchwork heritage is a strength not a weakness." I see this every day at George Washington University, where I meet talented students from immigrant origins who fill my classes and my heart: Reena Ninan from India and Katicia

Kiss from Hungary, Claritza Jimenez from the Dominican Republic and Malak Hamwi, from Syria, Monica Tavarez from Portugal and Lucy Kafanov from Russia, Charles Vundla from South Africa and Jennifer Tchinnosian from Argentina, Rabitha Aziz from Bangladesh and Sophia Aziz, the daughter of an Egyptian father and Afghan mother who met in Pakistan. When I listen to the voices in this book, and hear the stories of my students, I think of my own grandparents. They had the courage and character to come to a new land, and make a better life for themselves and their grandson. I hope, as you got to know these families, that you thought of your own ancestors, "the risk-takers, the doers, the makers of things." And I hope you will thank them for the gift they have given you and your children.

Critical Thinking

1. In what respects does this material intersect with the policy debate about immigration reform?

2. Does the personal experience of this author help us to understand his view of diversity?

From *From Every End of This Earth*, pp. ix–xiii, xvi–xxiv, 315–320. Copyright © by HarperCollins Publishers. Reprinted by permission.

UNIT 10

International Aspects of Ethnic Relations

Unit Selections

39. **The Ultimate Crime: Katyn and the Invention of Genocide,** John Connelly
40. **Never Underestimate the Power of Ethnicity in Iraq,** Amy Chua and Jed Rubenfeld
41. **Burqa Is Banned in France,** David Gauthier-Villars and Charles Forelle

Learning Objectives

- International events frequently affect the United States. Discuss the ways that such events can affect ethnic populations.

- Explain how the relationship of ethnic Americans to changes and challenges in the world arena provides strength or liability to American interests. Does conflict between ethnic interests and national interests present real or imaginary fears about our activities in international affairs? Explain.

- Explain how increased immigration, technological advances, and a more competitive world market can affect the relationships between ethnic groups.

- Is the American military becoming a society unto itself? Has the end of the military draft isolated military society from the American mainstream? Is national service a duty of citizenship?

- Should the claims of ethnic groups in the United States in defense of culture, territory, and unique institutions be honored and protected by law and public policy?

Student Website
www.mhhe.com/cls

Internet References

Yale University Guide to American Ethnic Studies
www.library.yale.edu/rsc/ethnic/internet.html
American Indian Ritual Object Repatriation Foundation
www.repatriationfoundation.org
Center for Research in Ethnic Relations
www.warwick.ac.uk/fac/soc/CRER_RC
The International Center for Migration, Ethnicity, and Citizenship
www.newschool.edu/icmec

The ethnic factor and international challenges can be seen each day as the winds of political change in the Middle East, and Eastern and Central Europe reveal the saliency of ethnicity and the varied textures of group relations. In America, the ongoing affinity of ethnic populations to the nations of their origin is expressed in subtle as well as obvious ways. Other articles in this collection explain the transmission of ethnic tradition in music and suggest linkages between religion and ethnicity. The story of the interaction of ethnicity and religion is curiously exposed in the etymology of the Greek word @i[ethnikos] (i.e., the rural, Gentile, or pagan people of the ancient Mediterranean world). Though such philological roots no longer drive our principal understanding of ethnicity, the experience of social affinity and cultural affiliation elaborated in the following articles about ethnics deepens our awareness and understanding of ethnicity—a changing yet persistent aspect of human identity and social cohesiveness. As Eric Voegelin noted "the self interpretation of a society does not wait for the social scientist. Societies in historical existence are not merely facts and events and external locations; they are 'little worlds of meaning, *cosmions*, illuminated with meaning from within by human beings who continuously create and bear it as the mode and condition of their self-realization . . . relations between its members and groups of members, as well as its existence as a whole, transparent for the mystery of human existence. . . . members of a society experience it more than as an accident or a convenience; they experience it as of their human essence."

The process of better understanding the multiethnic character of America and the world involves the coordinated efforts of formal and informal education, which are influenced by public and private institutions and the community-based voluntary associations that are the building blocks of society. This collection of articles addresses resistance to the challenges that are embedded in passionately held and politically potent traditions of ethnic opposition. The persistence of confusion, uncertainty, insensitivity, and violence toward and among ethnic groups is sobering and stunning fact. The need for strategies for dealing with the tension and reality of bias are obvious to the reader of this unit. Hatred and prejudice are frequently based on conscious manipulation of powerful images that profoundly shape personal and group identity. Exploring other societies is often a way of gaining fresh perspective on the American reality; differences and commonalities of the situations described in this unit are worth pondering.

Examination, for example, of the legacy of the civil rights laws crafted during the 1960s and the process of shaping a society grounded in exclusionary habits and institutions involves assessment on many levels—the social, the political, the ideological, and the economic. Even on the most basic level of public perception, most agree that progress has been made toward a society of equality and social justice, with increased hopes for decreased segregation in schools and neighborhoods. Yet disparities of these views among ethnic and racial groups indicate that uniformity and a shared sense of the past and present are not generally common. Attempting to overcome such gulfs

© Royalty-Free/CORBIS

of misunderstanding before they lead to more serious forms of conflict is among the great challenges of the present.

Since the breakup of the Soviet empire, ethnicity has reoriented the international arena. New national claims as well as the revival of ancient antagonisms are fragmenting Europe. War, the systematic expression of conflict, and its aftermath are also occasions for the use and misuse of ethnically charged political rhetoric. The presence of a politically relevant past and the invocation of religious warrants for group conflict have indicated the need for new approaches to peacekeeping and educational strategies for meeting and transcending group differences.

Whether these moments are crises of growth or decline will be measured by a host of indicators. Which of these indicators are the most salient is, of course, another question, whose answer depends on our selective invocation of historical materials and ethnic symbols as guides for contemporary analysis.

Ethnic relations have erupted into warfare in Africa, where conflicts have shattered emerging states and thus challenged the hopeful myth of postcolonial renewal as well as the racial/ethnic myth of black solidarity. But Africa's emerging countries are not alone. The Middle East, Central Europe, Canada, Ireland and the Northern Counties, and the Balkans have been venues of destructive conflict. Other simmering cauldrons—not melting pots—illustrate the stakes and consequences of unresolved conflict and distrust concerning land, religion, culture, leadership, and economic production and distribution. The materials in this unit reveal the struggle for rewards and recognitions that fuel human passions, ambitions, and the will to dominate and to govern the affairs and destinies of various peoples that cohabit contiguous regions. Thus, the dramas of regional ethnic struggle and the growth of worldwide ethnic challenges to the constitution of human order itself are increasingly marked by episodes of blatant bigotry and intolerance. Fanaticism and zealotry impose themselves on the stage of history, which is rushing toward a new millennium. The threshold of hope that it promises for those who can recover and embrace the mystery of diversity waits to define the human condition in the twenty-first century.

The Ultimate Crime

Katyn and the Invention of Genocide

JOHN CONNELLY

Recent months have seen remarkable events and developments in the legacy of Katyn, the village in the woods of western Russia where, in April 1940, Stalin's secret police shot some twenty-two thousand Polish military officers. Those killings have bedeviled relations between the two countries ever since.

Most of the officers killed at Katyn were not career military but reservists who, in their everyday lives, worked as lawyers, doctors, writers, or businessmen. Poles, who look back on a history full of invasions from east and west, have seen the Katyn executions as yet one more attempt to rob Poland of the intellectual and cultural elites crucial to self-government. Russians, for their part—and especially during the Soviet era—have routinely denied responsibility for the massacre, blaming the Nazis. Moreover, they wonder why—from the catastrophe of a war that consumed tens of millions of lives, including 6 million citizens of Poland—Poles insist on keeping the memory of Katyn alive. Why not focus instead on the hundreds of thousands of Red Army soldiers who died liberating Poland from Nazi rule in the endgame of World War II?

Since assuming power in 1999, Vladimir Putin has grounded his regime's legitimacy in Russian achievements of the past, above all in the victory over Nazi Germany. He has argued that his countrymen cannot be blamed for Katyn because the killings did not reflect their will; in 2005, Russian prosecutors concluded an investigation of the executions with the assertion that they constituted a legal act at the time of their commission and could not be construed as genocide. Authorities sealed the Katyn archives to independent researchers, and the case seemed closed. Poles expecting a Russian apology were disappointed.

Thus it was a genuine surprise when Putin decided to host a seventieth anniversary commemoration at Katyn this past April, and invited Polish Prime Minister Donald Tusk to attend. Describing the Katyn executions as "atrocities of a totalitarian regime," Putin knelt alongside Tusk before a memorial cross at the mass graves. To the amazement of onlookers, each man blessed himself—the onetime Solidarity activist and the former KGB officer crossing themselves side by side. Political analysts have attributed the gesture, and Putin's new tone, to Russia's desire for better relations with a prosperous Poland, a country with gas resources waiting to be exploited, and also a

gateway to Western Europe, where Russia hopes to gain credits to modernize its energy industries. The Russian edition of *Newsweek* obtained documents showing that Putin ordered a 180-degree shift toward Poland months before the Katyn commemoration, after learning from his ambassador in Warsaw that Polish grumbling over Katyn would frustrate closer ties to the European Union.

Then the story of reconciliation took an unexpected and tragic turn. Four days after Tusk returned to Poland, Polish President Lech Kaczyński, who was famous for anti-Russian diatribes and had not been invited to the event hosted by Putin, embarked on his own Katyn commemoration. Traveling in the same Soviet-made jet that had carried Tusk, he took along a large delegation that included top state officials, historians, military commanders, and representatives of every political party. The plane crashed in thick fog just short of the airport at Smolensk, killing everyone on board.

Putin and Tusk rushed from their respective capital cities to this newest site of Polish tragedy, and as Tusk arose from a quiet prayer, Putin embraced him, helping him to his feet while once again making a sign of the cross. These images, shown repeatedly on Polish television, left a deep impression. So too did the solicitude shown in the days that followed by thousands of Russians, who spontaneously placed flowers and candles at the Polish embassy in Moscow. Russian President Dmitry Medvedev announced a national day of mourning. And Russia's leaders permitted Andrzej Wajda's film *Katyn* to be shown on state television in prime time.

The 2007 film by the acclaimed Polish director had been kept out of movie theaters in Russia; suppressing such perspectives was one of the ways both Soviet and post-Soviet Russian governments propagated the fable of Nazi culpability for Katyn. In Wajda's account, viewers learn that the execution of 20,000 soldiers was only one blow against Poland aimed by Germany and the Soviet Union. Andrzej, the young officer who is the film's protagonist, has a father-in-law who teaches at Jagiellonian University in Krakow. On November 6, 1939, he loyally responds to a summons to attend a lecture by a Nazi official. But instead of a lecture, the professors arrive to find themselves placed under arrest, loaded onto waiting trucks, and hauled off to the concentration camp at Sachsenhausen. Meanwhile, other members of Andrzej's family, stuck in eastern Poland, are arrested by the Soviet secret police and sent to join the 300,000 Polish political leaders, businessmen, and teachers shipped off to exile in the Soviet far east, where many died of hunger and disease. Later, friends of the family take part in the Warsaw Uprising of 1944, where some 200,000 died when the city rose against the Nazi occupiers, as the Red Army waited across the river, providing no assistance. Depicting these baleful events, Wajda gives human dimension to the nature and consequences of the Hitler–Stalin Pact—and in the process implicates both the Nazis and the Soviets in the long-term project of wiping out the Polish nation.

Given the Putin government's unwillingness to ask tough questions about Russian history, showing this film was perhaps the most impressive of all the gestures registered in these days of sudden thaw. For the time being, we cannot know what conclusions Russians drew from Wajda's extraordinary drama, but it must have been bitter medicine. Disagreement has long surrounded the question of whether Katyn can be described as genocide. The definitions adopted by the UN in 1948 would seem to suggest that it qualifies. The Convention described as genocidal "acts committed with intent to destroy, in whole or in part, a national, ethnical, racial, or religious group," among them "killing members of the group." Arguably, Wajda's film depicts Nazis and Soviets as partners in genocide. Thanks in part to Putin's unexpected overture, the idea was at least, and at last, on the table.

Last year, as Poles prepared to commemorate the seventieth anniversary of the 1939 Nazi–Soviet nonaggression pact by which Hitler and Stalin secretly agreed to divide and rule Poland, some in Poland, mostly on the right, insisted on calling the Katyn murders "genocide," while others, mostly on the left, argued that the Soviets had not intended to destroy Poles as a national or ethnic group. In their view, Stalin killed the Polish officers in order to eliminate political enemies, the same way he killed millions of Soviet citizens. In the end, a compromise statement issued by the Polish parliament condemned the mass executions at Katyn as a crime with "characteristics of genocide."

The man who coined the word "genocide," a Polish–Jewish lawyer named Raphael Lemkin (1900-59), believed that violence against civilians attained a new character in World War II. The desire to eradicate a nation was not in itself new. The Tsarist regime, after all, had cooperated with Bismarck's Germany in denying Poles the schools, libraries, newspapers, economic associations, religious institutions, and leaders through which they might live a national life. The hope was that Poles would gradually assimilate, becoming Russians and Germans.

What made the acts of Nazi Germany and Soviet Russia revolutionary, on the other hand, was the willingness to erase nations by destroying the "essential foundations of the life of national groups," as Lemkin wrote in 1943, "with the aim of annihilating the groups themselves."

The same year, Lemkin (who was wounded while fighting against the German invasion and eventually made his way to the United States, where he became a law professor) produced a draft law for the Polish government-in-exile using the word *ludobójstwo*—literally, the killing of a people—to describe Nazi crimes in Poland. This word, Anglicized by Lemkin in the neologism "genocide," was subsequently defined as a crime by the UN Convention on the Prevention and Punishment of the Crime of Genocide, with "nation" understood in the broad sense of a homeland population, meaning a group with common ethnic, cultural, religious, or racial characteristics. The Convention was signed on December 9, 1948, and the UN Declaration of Universal Human Rights the following day.

The word and concept are used more and more often. In 2001, the International Criminal Tribunal for the former Yugoslavia judged the mass killing of Bosnian Muslim prisoners of war in 1995 an act of genocide because the killers "targeted for extinction the 40,000 Bosnian Muslims living in Srebrenica, a group which was emblematic of the Bosnian Muslims in general." The murderers had "deliberately and methodically killed [the prisoners] solely on the basis of their identity." The same can be said of the Polish soldiers at Katyn. Yes, they were killed as political enemies; but they were enemies because they were Poles. In Soviet eyes, ethnic Poles—regardless of political or social background—constituted an implacable threat to Soviet power. That explains why Stalin took the unique step in 1938 of liquidating the Polish Communist Party, first killing its leaders, then disbanding the party. A nation slated for disappearance did not need its own organizations, even if they were Communist. If the Nazis had not turned on the Soviets with their attack of June 1941, that is how things would have stayed.

Why is recognizing an event as genocidal so important? One reason is that unlike other war crimes, genocide is not subject to a statute of limitations. If Katyn was genocide, some of its perpetrators might still be brought to justice, and restitution might be claimed by families of the victims. Beyond these material considerations, genocide as the ultimate crime has a rare claim on a people's self-understanding, whether they are the victims or the perpetrators. Polish insistence that the world know about Katyn grew with each year that Communist governments insisted the Nazis were guilty. Other groups around the world have clamored for recognition as victims of genocide: Chinese and Koreans incensed that the Japanese have done little to recognize the atrocities of Nanking or rape camps, or Native Americans and African Americans who fear their own national tragedies will end up forever buried in the deep past. And what about Cambodians? Is killing millions of one's own people an act of genocide?

In all these cases, groups fear their victimhood will be passed over and ultimately forgotten if it is not stamped with the label of this ultimate crime. Conversely, perpetrators hope to keep their nation from acquiring an indelible moral stain. Why does Turkey refuse to acknowledge the indisputable fact of genocide carried out by a Turkish state almost a century ago? Recognition could potentially involve massive reparations. But there's also the awkward fact that Turkish governments have lied about the event for 90 years, which makes speaking the truth difficult now. Most important, genocide is thought to be radically at odds with Turkish national character. Prime Minster Recep Tayyip Erdoğan insisted last year that "it is not possible for those who belong to the Muslim faith to carry out genocide." Even President Barack Obama, who during his candidacy said that "America deserves a leader who speaks truthfully about the Armenian genocide," chose on this year's Armenian Remembrance Day to refer to the murders as "massacres," "inhumanity," and "Meds Yeghern" (Armenian for "the Crime")—but conspicuously *not* as genocide.

Seen against this background, the willingness of the Russian regime to confront Katyn has been extraordinary. A few days after the crash at Smolensk, President Medvedev astounded Poles by admitting—and not merely to them, but to the Russian people—that "Polish officers were shot by the will of the leaders of the USSR, among them Joseph Stalin." In the weeks that followed, Medvedev placed online facsimiles of the 1940 documents, bearing Stalin's signature, that ordered the Katyn murders. The Web site crashed repeatedly from the deluge of traffic. Finally, the Russian president turned 67 boxes of documents on the crime over to Polish authorities. Soon Russian anti-Stalinists took their cue. War veterans began collecting signatures opposing the display of images of Stalin during May 9 celebrations of the end of World War II, while young socialists demanded the removal from all public places of the name Mikhail Kalinin—chair of the Supreme Soviet in 1940, who approved the Katyn executions. On May 11, Russian members of the EU-Russia Parliamentary Cooperation Committee of the European Parliament approved a resolution proclaiming that "Katyn was a war crime bearing traits of genocide"—precisely the understanding of the Polish parliament.

The new approach goes against Prime Minister Putin's long-standing political strategy of crafting a cleaned-up version of Russia's past. As leader during the "Great Fatherland War" (World War II), Stalin has remained central to that heritage—and even now, Putin has not personally denounced the Soviet leader. Perhaps he embraces the sentiments of the Soviet-era dissident Mikhail Gefter, who said in 1988 that every time Russians try to deal with their past they discover Stalin in themselves. They fear that in the end, attempts to master this past will lead to the edge of an abyss, discrediting any justification for their imperial state. Because they cannot rationally account for the limitless crimes of Stalin's regime, they try to "tame" him. In any case, Putin's pro-Russian campaign, supported by the Russian Orthodox hierarchy, has yielded results over the years: in a recent vote in which over 5 million Russians took part, Stalin—an ethnic Georgian—placed as the third most popular figure in Russia's past, ahead of Pushkin, Lenin, and Dostoyevsky.

But with the release of the Katyn documents bearing Stalin's signature, and with repeated references by both Medvedev and Putin to the "totalitarian" regime and its crime, attitudes may have begun to change. Russian authorities forbade the carrying of Stalin posters on May 9—though in some provincial towns, far from the international press, the generalissimus still smiled upon parades of veterans. Central authorities closed the Lenin Mausoleum for the duration of the festivities and, for the first time, invited active-duty troops from the United States, France, Great Britain, and Poland to take part. Closing a door to Stalin means opening one to the West.

How will Russians deal with the deep and abiding contradictions of their modern history? The dismantling of the Stalin myth, which began with Krushchev, continues apace, with some historians today arguing, for example, that World War II would not have occurred without Stalin's enabling Hitler's aggression, or that Russia could have modernized without starving millions of peasants. Yet completely removing Stalin from Russia's achievements will never be possible. Stalin enabled Russia to victory, and his "modernization" prepared Russia for war. Nikita Mikhalkov, who directed the Oscar-winning drama *Burnt by the Sun* about a Bolshevik general purged by the Soviet leader, recently explained to Reuters the deep split in Russians' view of Stalin. "For the veterans, he is a saint," Mikhalov said; "for those and their relatives who were in gulags, he is evil, a tyrant." He went further, adding a warning: "If you don't control this and balance the two sides out, an unimaginable metamorphosis could happen."

Such a predicament may indeed be unimaginable for Americans, who have neither suffered like the Russians nor worshiped a leader as fervently as the Russians did Stalin. Imagine our reactions to news that Abraham Lincoln not only liberated but also murdered millions of slaves; not only saved the Union but provoked an unnecessary war. What to do with the idea that great good might be inseparable from great evil? The occasional heretic who claims Hitler did something good lets us imagine how disoriented Russians might feel if they try to "balance the two sides out." When the German historian Gotz Aly brought evidence several years ago showing that Hitler had created the modern German welfare state, many Germans assumed he must be condemning welfare as such.

Russia faces historical trials more complex than those that challenged Germany in the 1950s. Perhaps we are witnessing a stage where blame is placed largely on the leader, with the people portrayed as having behaved decently. With his personal guilt for crimes becoming established beyond doubt, questions will emerge about Stalin's support within Russian society. In the German case, penetrating questions were initially asked by outsiders like the young American William Sheridan Allen, who in the late 1950s hit upon the revolutionary idea of asking Germans what precisely they had done to bring Hitler to power. The *Nazi Seizure of Power,* his study of the nondescript town of Nordheim, tells college students to this day how ordinary Germans helped bring Hitler to power. (Significantly, the German publishers titled the book's translation Das haben wir nicht gewollt, or "That Is Not What We Wanted.")

For the moment we don't know what Russians did and did not want as far as Stalinism was concerned. Western authors have been probing these shadows of Russian social history, but most Russians are not eager to disturb the past. Changing minds will not be easy. In the Katyn commemoration, Putin said that "for decades, attempts have been made to cover up the truth about the Katyn executions with cynical lies"—but he went on to add that "suggesting that the Russian people are to blame for that is the same kind of lie and fabrication." And while Medvedev has talked of Stalin's "mass crimes against the people," he has done so in language that makes the dictator appear to have acted alone: "what was done to his own people cannot be forgiven." Genocide implies a dimension of violence impossible to pin simply on one leader. Yet in Germany, almost half a century went by before detailed studies of everyday life and of everyday perpetrators appeared—in part because of the impact of scenes from the 1979 U.S. TV miniseries *Holocaust*.

The effects of films are unpredictable. Wajda's *Katyn* challenged Russian viewers with a new vision of their past. Nikita Mikhalkov, meanwhile, has just released a sequel to *Burnt by the Sun* covering the war years—a film that attempts to fill the yawning post-Stalinist identity gap with a concoction that includes religious faith. The film's title, *Predstoyanie*, means standing before God to be tested or to pray, and the war it presents is full of miraculous coincidences, Orthodox Christian symbolism, and Red Army soldiers dying with prayers on their lips, which was, as Mikhalov has said, of "biblical dimensions." Veterans have disparaged the film as untruthful because in fact soldiers were unbelievers. But if Mikhalkov turns atheists into believers, he does so to give their grandchildren something to hold onto amid the collapse of anti-Western Great Russian patriotism.

As for Russian moviegoers, they voted with their feet in a resounding *nyet,* and went en masse to see *Iron Man 2* instead. Perhaps this is a hopeful sign. After all, far from suggesting a challenging metamorphosis, Mikhalkov's sequel repeats a tired plot line of heroic victory over Nazi barbarism. And because the state funded a propagandistic ad campaign for it, and Mikhalkov is now the director of the Cinematographer's Union, people saw the film not as art but as the ideologically correct work of a state bureaucrat. (Tellingly, the premiere took place inside the Kremlin.)

What better harbinger of an evolving open society than a dusted-off ideology that will not sell? Russians can no longer be ordered to attend films and festivals, and gestures like offering flowers or genuflecting or making the sign of the cross have an effect only when they seem spontaneous. Perhaps the lesson of this year's events at Katyn is that the circumstances in which people say and do what was previously unthinkable are no longer ordered from above. Ksenia Larina, a critic at the independent radio station Echo Moskwy, said that the crash of Kaczyński's plane "changed the course of history," providing an extended moment in which state-run television stations, previously resistant to criticism, suddenly "dropped their plaster masks, revealing human traits." It turned out, Larina continued, that "showing compassion and saying human words before the camera were not so difficult. All the more so if one knows that one risks no danger by doing so."

Critical Thinking

1. Has the importance of the Katyn Forest Massacre been discussed in any of your modern history courses?

2. Can countries that use ethnic identity as a primary bond of union among citizens flourish in an age of globalization?

3. What is genocide? Does the United Nations treaty on human rights and cultural rights outlaw genocide?

Never Underestimate the Power of Ethnicity in Iraq

AMY CHUA AND JED RUBENFELD

Sick to death of "identity politics" at home, Americans ironically find themselves dealing with a tinderbox of ethnic division in Iraq. We may be the least well-equipped nation in the world to manage the kinds of group hatreds that threaten Iraqi society today. Because of our beliefs in the "melting pot" and the United States' own relatively successful—though halting and incomplete—history of assimilation, Americans don't always understand the significance of ethnicity, both at home and especially abroad. In Iraq, our obliviousness to the realities of group hatred was on display from the first days of the occupation, when U.S. officials appointed former members of the almost-exclusively-Sunni Baath Party to the highest government and police positions, apparently unaware that these appointments would provoke the fury of Iraq's Shiites, Kurds and others, who make up more than 80 percent of the population. The outraged reactions forced the Americans to rescind the appointments.

British colonial governments, by contrast, were fastidiously conscious of ethnic divisions. But their policies are a dangerous model. When it was the British Empire's turn to deal with nation-building and ethnicity, the British engaged in divide-and-conquer policies, not only protecting but favoring minorities, and simultaneously aggravating ethnic resentments. As a result, when the British decamped, time bombs often exploded, from Africa to India to Southeast Asia.

The U.S. government's ethnic policy for Iraq has essentially been to have no policy. The Bush administration's overriding goal is the transfer of power by the end of next June from the U.S.-led coalition to a new Iraqi government selected, in theory, through some kind of democratic process. The administration seems strangely confident that Iraq's ethnic, religious and tribal divisions will dissipate in the face of rapid democratization and market-generated wealth. In President Bush's words, "freedom and democracy will always and everywhere have greater appeal than the slogans of hatred."

Unfortunately, recent history suggests just the opposite. Rapid democratization has been attempted in many poor, ethnically divided societies in the last two decades, and the results are sobering. Democratic elections in the former Yugoslavia produced landslide victories for the hate-mongering Franjo Tudjman in Croatia and the genocidal Slobodan Milosevic in Serbia. In Rwanda in the early 1990s, democratization fomented ethnic extremism, yielding the majority-supported Hutu Power movement and the ensuing ethnic slaughter of Tutsis. In Indonesia in 1998, sudden democratization after the fall of Suharto's 30-year dictatorship produced a wave of anti-Chinese demagoguery and confiscations, leading to the devastating flight of more than $40 billion in Chinese-controlled capital.

It is impossible to predict who would win free and fair elections in Iraq, but given the demographic and economic conditions, it is extremely unlikely that such elections in the near future would produce a secular, pro-American outcome.

Iraq's ethnic and religious dynamics involve conflicts that cut across and among Kurds, Turkmens, Shiites, Christians and Sunnis; many horrendous massacres; wholesale confiscations; and deep feelings of hatred and the need for revenge. Iraq's Shiites represent a 60 percent majority, which has suffered cruel oppression at the hands of the Sunni minority. While Iraq's Shiites are far from homogeneous, liberation has already fueled religious demagoguery among vying Islamic clerics and unleashed powerful fundamentalist movements throughout the country. Needless to say, these extremist movements are intensely anti-American, anti-secular, anti-women's rights and illiberal. Meanwhile, Iraq's 20 percent Kurdish minority in the north, mistrustful of Arab rule, represents another source of profound instability. Finally, as many have pointed out, Iraq's oil could prove a curse, leading to massive corruption and a destructive battle between groups to capture the nation's oil, its main source of wealth.

None of this is democracy's fault. The blame for Iraq's current group hatreds rests largely with the fascistic regime of Saddam Hussein, which systematically terrorized and murdered Shiites and Kurds. In addition, Hussein's sadistic secularism spurred the growing fundamentalism among Iraq's Shiites.

Blaming Saddam, however, does not alter the facts. Given the conditions today in Iraq—conditions created by colonialism, autocracy and brutality, not to mention the historical schism between Shiite and Sunni Muslims—hasty national elections could very well produce renewed ethnic radicalism and violence; an illiberal, Islamist regime in which women are murdered by their relatives for the crime of being raped (already happening in Shiite Baghdad); and an anti-American government determined to oust U.S. firms from Iraq's oil fields. Any of these results would create, at best, an awkward moment for the Bush administration.

Combined, they could be catastrophic for American interests, for the Middle East and for Iraq.

Perhaps for these reasons the Bush administration is trying to create a "democratic" government by June without popular elections.

What is to be done? Retreating from democracy is not an option. Unfortunately, few good models exist to guide U.S. ethnic policy in Iraq. The British strategy might have been to pit Shiites against Sunnis, and perhaps Kurds against both. But if we want an Iraq not divided and conquered, but united and self-governing, the way forward will be considerably harder.

The polar opposite of no ethnic policy would be a plan for explicit ethnic and religious power-sharing. For example, a new Iraqi constitution could contain a Dayton-style formula guaranteeing Sunnis and Kurds major government posts. Such a plan might have salutary short-term effects, but enshrining ethnicity and religious division in the constitution would be a perilous strategy. It could harden group identity at the cost of national unity. The one thing potentially worse than rushing to national Iraqi elections might be rushing to such elections while clumsily manipulating combustible ethnic dynamics that few in the United States even understand.

All this suggests a very different alternative: Put the brakes on national democracy, and focus much more energy and resources on local democracy. To date, astonishingly, there have been virtually no city or town elections anywhere in Iraq. Apparently, U.S. policy calls for implementing national self-government first and worrying about local self-government later. The order of priority should be exactly the opposite.

Democracy at the national level will essentially pit the Shiite majority against the hated Sunni minority and autonomy-seeking Kurds in a battle for control over the country's destiny and oil wealth. By contrast, many Iraqi towns and cities are relatively less divided along ethnic and religious lines, and the electoral stakes there would be much lower. In elections for city councils and other municipal positions, the competing candidates and parties would have much less incentive to define themselves along sectarian lines or to engage in ethnic demagoguery.

To sow the seeds of democracy, better to think locally.

Local democracy is the best instruction for national democracy. British and American democracy started locally, not nationally. The message of the U.S.-led coalition to Iraqis should be: We are turning over governance to you, right now, in every one of your neighborhoods, towns and cities. Although oil and certain other national policy matters would be taken off the table—they could not possibly be decided at the town level—local self-government would still represent an enormous transfer of sovereignty. Most

of the Iraqi reconstruction effort will be local: providing water; restoring electricity; building and staffing schools; fostering commerce; establishing town courts; and of course policing. Billions of dollars will be spent on these things over the coming years; crucial policy decisions will be made about priorities, jobs for women, and the distribution of goods and services.

To its credit, after the war, the U.S. military created district and town councils to assist in local governance all over Iraq. Coalition officials refer to these councils as "inclusive" and "democratically selected," but there is a big difference between selected and elected. In fact, the councils appear to have been selected by U.S. military authorities. As one U.S. official candidly acknowledged, "In terms of actual elections, we are not focused on that in our assistance at this point." An October poll indicated that half of all Iraqis did not even know the councils existed.

To be sure, some Iraqi towns might elect fundamentalist clerics as their lawmakers. The coalition must not try to suppress such results. Let Iraqis see their decisions respected. Let them see some towns where fundamentalism reigns and some where it does not. The hopes of a democratic Middle East may depend on it.

Local self-government will not be easy to achieve. Ethnically diverse cities such as Baghdad and Kirkuk could present special challenges. But local governance is a far more realistic goal than trying in the next six months to establish national, democratic government. Instead of premature national elections, the coalition should pursue an interim Iraqi constitution establishing the framework for immediate local self-government. During the ensuing period, coalition authorities would have the job of ensuring fair elections, a free press and freedom of movement (so that Iraqis can also "vote with their feet"). Because they would also retain control over Iraq's oil for an additional year or so, coalition forces must credibly demonstrate that they are keeping the country's oil wealth in trust for the Iraqi people. National elections would be postponed until Iraqis agreed on a permanent constitution, a process that would profit enormously from actual experience with local democracy.

Before she was assassinated, Iraqi Governing Council member Akila Hashimi warned against top-down efforts to remake her country. "Culture creates laws, not the other way around," she said. If democracy is to flourish in Iraq—and elsewhere in the Middle East—it must spread from the bottom up.

Critical Thinking

1. Is ethnic conflict and religious sectarianism woven into a deepened source of intergroup tension?
2. Under what conditions could military forces of another country overcome the desire for self-governing and the passion and prejudice against invaders?

AMY CHUA is a professor at Yale Law School and author of *"World on Fire: How Exporting Free Market Democracy Breeds Ethnic Hatred and Global Instability"* (Anchor Books). **JED RUBENFELD** is also a professor at Yale Law School and a U.S. observer at the Council of Europe.

Burqa Is Banned in France

DAVID GAUTHIER-VILLARS AND CHARLES FORELLE

Paris—France risked the wrath of the Islamic world on Tuesday by banning burqas and other full-body robes worn by some Muslim women, in a long-debated move that shows the depth of concern over the rise of Muslim culture in Europe.

The vote—passed primarily by the center-right party of President Nicolas Sarkozy, with most opposition Socialist Party lawmakers abstaining—came as a number of European countries are trying to figure out how to reconcile the values of modern Europe with more assertive expressions of Islamic faith.

Switzerland, for example, banned the construction of minarets after a referendum last year. Belgium and Spain are discussing measures to outlaw similar full-body cloaks. In Sweden, long known as one of Europe's most tolerant societies, an anti-immigration party that has called for Swedish Muslims to integrate more is expected to win its first Parliamentary seat in this weekend's elections.

In the United States tensions are running similarly high over plans to build an Islamic community center near the site of the World Trade Center destroyed by Muslim terrorists on September 11, 2001, and over a Florida pastor's threat to burn qurans in commemoration of the date last week.

France is facing criticism of its tolerance on other fronts: On Tuesday the European Union's justice commissioner excoriated the Sarkozy administration for its campaign to deport Gypsies, also known as Roma, calling it a "disgrace" and saying the bloc would begin legal proceedings against the French government.

The legislation adopted Tuesday by the Senate, the upper house of the French Parliament, forbids people from concealing their faces in public. It makes no reference to Islam, and includes exceptions for people who need to cover up for work reasons, such as riot police and surgeons.

But it follows a year-long campaign by Mr. Sarkozy's ruling party against the burqa and niqab, head-to-toe robes worn by a small number of France's Muslim women. The burqa is "a sign of enslavement and debasement," Mr. Sarkozy said last year.

The bill is scheduled to come into force after six months. It has already passed the lower house, the National Assembly. At the Parliament's request, the law will be reviewed by France's Constitutional Council before it takes effect. The Council, which reviews the constitutionality of laws after they are passed by Parliament but before they are put into force, has

rejected several bills in recent years. It can censor all or part of the law deemed to contradict the nation's bylaws.

The ban would apply to everyone in France, including visitors. Offenders face a maximum fine of €150 (about $190) and could be asked to attend courses on what the government calls "republican values." Individuals who encourage others to ignore the ban would face tougher penalties: up to one year in prison and a maximum fine of €30,000.

Republican values also include freedom of religion, which makes it problematic to outlaw niqabs and burqas. Before Mr Sarkozy's government submitted the bill to lawmakers, France's highest administrative court, the Conseil d'État, or State Council, which advises the government on proposed laws, said an outright ban on burqas might not be compatible with the country's "international commitments on human rights."

Most women wearing the niqab in France are French nationals—often born to North African parents—who can be seen in suburban areas near Paris, Lyon and Lille. They say the full-body robe is a tool to concentrate on their religious faith and that the planned ban would infringe on their freedom. Some Muslim women say they would get friends to do shopping and run errands for them rather than go out in public with their faces uncovered.

Several Muslim lobby groups had urged the French Parliament not to outlaw the burqa, saying the bill amounted to a populist ploy aimed at stigmatizing France's six million Muslims—Europe's largest Muslim community—and distracting public opinion from other issues, such as high unemployment and sluggish economic growth.

"The government and parliament are trying to put a veil on social and economic problems," said Mohammed Beyakhles, a member of human-rights group United Against Islamophobia.

Last year, Al Qaeda in the Islamic Maghreb, a radical North-African Islamic group affiliated with al Qaeda, threatened to retaliate against France if the country banned the burqa, according to messages posted on Islamic websites. In July, AQIM killed a Frenchman it held hostage in Mali, saying it aimed to retaliate against France's failed attempt at freeing its national.

The Eiffel Tower and the area around it were evacuated Tuesday around 9 p.m. after an anonymous caller phoned in a bomb threat, Paris police said. Police found nothing suspicious, and the area was reopened to tourists later in the evening, according to French media reports. The Saint-Michel subway station near Notre Dame Cathedral—another tourist hub—was also been briefly evacuated.

Both threats were taken seriously, police officials said, because they came a few days after the anniversary of the September 11, 2001, attacks in the United States and minutes after the vote of the burqa bill by the Senate.

Head-to-toe garments such as the niqab, thought to be worn by just 2,000 women in France, are seen by French critics as an affront to France's democratic values. Some politicians have said that active citizenship requires face-to-face communication. Others say full-body robes are a means of forcing women to be submissive. France previously banned headscarves, yarmulkes and other visible religious symbols from being worn in public schools, in the name of separation of state and religion.

Critical Thinking

1. Does a country generally have the rightful capacity to govern types of clothing?

2. Does a burqa present a security threat?

3. Could wearing a mask in America be fairly compared to this matter?

From *The Wall Street Journal*, September 15, 2010. Copyright © 2010 by Dow Jones & Company, Inc. Reprinted by permission via Rightslink.

Test-Your-Knowledge Form

We encourage you to photocopy and use this page as a tool to assess how the articles in *Annual Editions* expand on the information in your textbook. By reflecting on the articles you will gain enhanced text information. You can also access this useful form on a product's book support website at www.mhhe.com/cls

NAME: DATE:

_____

TITLE AND NUMBER OF ARTICLE:

_____

BRIEFLY STATE THE MAIN IDEA OF THIS ARTICLE:

_____

LIST THREE IMPORTANT FACTS THAT THE AUTHOR USES TO SUPPORT THE MAIN IDEA:

_____

WHAT INFORMATION OR IDEAS DISCUSSED IN THIS ARTICLE ARE ALSO DISCUSSED IN YOUR TEXTBOOK OR OTHER READINGS THAT YOU HAVE DONE? LIST THE TEXTBOOK CHAPTERS AND PAGE NUMBERS:

_____

LIST ANY EXAMPLES OF BIAS OR FAULTY REASONING THAT YOU FOUND IN THE ARTICLE:

_____

LIST ANY NEW TERMS/CONCEPTS THAT WERE DISCUSSED IN THE ARTICLE, AND WRITE A SHORT DEFINITION:

We Want Your Advice

ANNUAL EDITIONS revisions depend on two major opinion sources: one is our Advisory Board, listed in the front of this volume, which works with us in scanning the thousands of articles published in the public press each year; the other is you—the person actually using the book. Please help us and the users of the next edition by completing the prepaid article rating form on this page and returning it to us. Thank you for your help!

ANNUAL EDITIONS: Race and Ethnic Relations 11/12

ARTICLE RATING FORM

Here is an opportunity for you to have direct input into the next revision of this volume.
We would like you to rate each of the articles listed below, using the following scale:

1. **Excellent: should definitely be retained**
2. **Above average: should probably be retained**
3. **Below average: should probably be deleted**
4. **Poor: should definitely be deleted**

Your ratings will play a vital part in the next revision.
Please mail this prepaid form to us as soon as possible.
Thanks for your help!

RATING	ARTICLE
	1. Chicago and the Irish
	2. Cajun Country Still Sizzles: But, Podna, You'd Better Partake in the Traditions Soon
	3. Farmer Fills Hala Niche While Feeding His Soul
	4. In Brooklyn, an Evolving Ethnicity
	5. In Armenian Enclave, Turkish Deal Arouses Suspicion: Ethnic Leaders in Glendale, Calif., See Detente Announcement as a Ploy on Day Commemorating 1915 Killings
	6. The Hotel Africa
	7. Racial Restrictions in the Law of Citizenship
	8. *Dred Scott v. Sandford*
	9. "There's No One as Irish as Barack O'Bama": The Policy and Politics of American Multiracialism
	10. *Brown et al. v. Board of Education of Topeka et al.*
	11. 'Bakke' Set a New Path to Diversity for Colleges
	12. *Shaare Tefila Congregation v. Cobb* and *Saint Francis College v. Al-Khazraji*
	13. Historical Discrimination in the Immigration Laws
	14. The Diversity Visa Lottery—A Cycle of Unintended Consequences in United States Immigration Policy
	15. Ancestry 2000: Census 2000 Brief
	16. The American Community Survey: The New Dimensions of Race and Ethnicity in America
	17. Nation's Linguistic Diversity: Population Speaking a Language Other than English at Home Increases by 140 Percent in Past Three Decades
	18. A Profile of Today's Italian Americans: A Report Based on the Year 2000 Census Compiled by the Sons of Italy
	19. Polonia in Numbers: How Many of Us Are out There?
	20. Irish-American Heritage Month (March) and Saint Patrick's Day (March 17): 2010

RATING	ARTICLE
	21. Still Unmelted after All These Years
	22. Who Is a Native American?
	23. Tribal Philanthropy Thrives
	24. American Indian and Alaska Native Heritage Month: November 2008
	25. Black (African–American) History Month: February 2010
	26. Transcript of Obama's Speech
	27. Redefining Black Women in America
	28. Who's Hispanic?
	29. Race and Hispanic Origin of the Foreign-Born Population in the United States: 2007
	30. Latino Agricultural Workers and Their Young Families: Advancing Theoretical and Empirically Based Conceptualizations
	31. Asian/Pacific American Heritage Month: May 2010
	32. To Be Asian in America
	33. Migrations to the Thirteen British North American Colonies, 1770–1775: New Estimates
	34. Fecund Newcomers or Dying Ethnics? Demographic Approaches to the History of Polish and Italian Immigrants and Their Children in the United States, 1880–1980
	35. Ethnics No More or Ethnogenesis: From Syrian to Arab American
	36. Neither Natural Allies Nor Irreconcilable Foes: Alliance Building Efforts between African Americans and Immigrants
	37. Bigots I Have Loved
	38. From Every End of This Earth
	39. The Ultimate Crime: Katyn and the Invention of Genocide
	40. Never Underestimate the Power of Ethnicity in Iraq
	41. Burqa Is Banned in France

BUSINESS REPLY MAIL
FIRST CLASS MAIL PERMIT NO. 551 DUBUQUE IA

POSTAGE WILL BE PAID BY ADDRESSEE

McGraw-Hill Contemporary Learning Series
501 BELL STREET
DUBUQUE, IA 52001

ABOUT YOU

Name   Date
_____

Are you a teacher? ☐ A student? ☐
Your school's name
_____

Department
_____

Address   City   State   Zip
_____

School telephone #
_____

YOUR COMMENTS ARE IMPORTANT TO US!

Please fill in the following information:
For which course did you use this book?
_____

Did you use a text with this ANNUAL EDITION? ☐ yes ☐ no
What was the title of the text?
_____

What are your general reactions to the Annual Editions concept?
_____

Have you read any pertinent articles recently that you think should be included in the next edition? Explain.
_____

Are there any articles that you feel should be replaced in the next edition? Why?
_____

Are there any World Wide Websites that you feel should be included in the next edition? Please annotate.
_____

May we contact you for editorial input? ☐ yes ☐ no
May we quote your comments? ☐ yes ☐ no

NOTES

NOTES

NOTES

NOTES

NOTES

NOTES

NOTES